D1616861

LEGAL TRADITIONS
AND SYSTEMS

LEGAL TRADITIONS AND SYSTEMS

AN INTERNATIONAL HANDBOOK

EDITED BY

Alan N. Katz

GREENWOOD PRESS

NEW YORK · WESTPORT, CONNECTICUT · LONDON

Library of Congress Cataloging-in-Publication Data

Main entry under title:

Legal traditions and systems.

Bibliography: p.
Includes index.
1. Comparative law.   I. Katz, Alan N.
K583.L44   1986   340′.2   85–27158
ISBN 0–313–23830–8 (lib. bdg. : alk. paper)

Library of Congress Catalog Card Number: 85–27158
ISBN: 0–313–23830–8

First published in 1986

Greenwood Press, Inc.
88 Post Road West, Westport, Connecticut 06881

Printed in the United States of America

The paper used in this book complies with the
Permanent Paper Standard issued by the National
Information Standards Organization (Z39.48–1984).

10 9 8 7 6 5 4 3 2 1

To the memory of my parents,
Nathan David Katz and Beatrice Beverly Katz

CONTENTS

TABLES

ACKNOWLEDGMENTS

As editor of this volume, I take full responsibility for any errors or omissions contained herein. A venture of this sort obviously depends upon the good wishes and offices of a large number of people. I am most indebted to the fourteen other contributors to this volume. They all labored under both time and style restrictions with patience and good humor. This book could not have been completed without the assistance of a number of people at Greenwood Press. My thanks go to Marilyn Brownstein for aiding in the initial formulation of this volume, Marie Smith for innumerable helpful suggestions, and to Cynthia Harris and Michelle Scott whose patience and good humor played no small part in seeing this project to its completion. There are also many people at Fairfield University who have added much to this endeavor: Dorothy Sokol Macchio, now a resident of the fair state of North Carolina but during the initial stages of this project, a graduate assistant at the university, who did much of the preliminary, vital, bibliographical research for this project; the staff of the university's Nyselius Library, especially Susan Dunn and Nancy Haag, who have been so gracious and helpful in obtaining research materials for this project; Edward Dew, my colleague in the politics department, who made a number of helpful suggestions; Lee Mihalik, who, among her many other duties, typed the vast bulk of this volume. This book owes much to her generosity and skill; and the Fairfield University Faculty Research Committee, which provided me with a summer research grant to complete the work on this project. Finally, I would like to thank my wife, Lucy, and our children, Laura and Douglas, for their patience, understanding, and support.

LEGAL TRADITIONS
AND SYSTEMS

INTRODUCTION

Alan N. Katz

It is a curious phenomenon that a number of societies have attempted to minimize the role played by members of the legal profession, giving support to Bernard Schwartz's assertion that "the attempt to administer justice without lawyers is a characteristic of both utopias and revolutions."[1] Thomas More, for example, barred them from his *Utopia*.[2] Similarly, in the years after the landing of the *Mayflower*, lawyers were assigned almost no role in America's early political system.[3] More recently, one of the characteristics of the People's Republic of China has been the miniscule role allotted to lawyers in solving that nation's problems.

Despite the attempt to minimize the role played by lawyers in colonial America, members of that profession played a significant role in the politics of the new Republic, for twenty-seven of the fifty-six signers of the Declaration of Independence, seventeen of the first twenty-six United States Senators, and twenty-five of the initial members of the House of Representatives were lawyers.[4] A scanning of the literature regarding contemporary China (especially since the period of the "four modernizations") indicates a similar growth in the importance of both codified law and western-trained lawyers.[5] Thus, despite the hopes of both utopians and revolutionaries, lawyers have ultimately been asked to aid ordinary citizens in dealing with the problems posed by increasingly complex societies.[6] As such, lawyers have become powerful figures in many of the nations of the world.

While many acknowledge a dominant role for the legal profession in modern society, there is much less consensus regarding the role(s) that the law and legal system can play. One reason for this is the difficulty encountered in defining a clear link between the law, the legal system and its personnel, and the general culture found in modern society. This volume is based on the premise that there is a linkage between these concepts and that it is probably best seen in J. H. Merryman and D. S. Clark's definition of "legal tradition":

A legal tradition, as the term implies, is not a set of rules of law about contracts, corporations and crimes, although such rules will almost always be in some sense a reflection of the tradition. Rather, *it is a set of deeply rooted, historically conditioned attitudes about the nature of the law, about the role of law in the society and the polity, about the proper organization and operation of a legal system, and about the way the law is or should be made, applied, studied, perfected, and taught. The legal tradition relates the legal system to the culture of which it is a particular expression. It puts the legal system into cultural perspective.* (my emphasis)[7]

Therefore, in order to study the legal system of most of the nations of the world, this volume will, during the next eighteen chapters, focus upon four of the major ingredients found in the above definition.

The first goal of this volume is to analyze the historical development of the legal systems of the nations studied. This will first involve discovering the sources of the law in each.[8] In addition, an assessment will be made of how the legal pattern in a particular nation (or group of nations) fits into the common law, civil law, "mixed," Scandinavian, and socialist families as well as a number of variations found in some of the Third World nations today (which have been influenced by their colonial legacies as well as their own customary and/or religious law).[9]

Our second goal is to describe one aspect of Merryman and Clark's definition— the organization of legal systems—in the nations to be studied. This volume will attempt to assess the connection between the organization of a nation's legal system, its historical development, family of law, as well as form ("federal" versus "unitary") of government.

A third goal of this volume is to evaluate another component of the legal tradition, the personnel of the law, in each of the nations to be studied. Once again, this is thought to be linked to the historical development of a nation and its legal system. Dias and Paul, for example, have contended that lawyers have played a very significant role in the historical development of first world (Western) nations during the past few centuries—lawyers have articulated the major ideas related to political and social change, developed political structures to accommodate such change, and later transformed the law to the changing political, social, and economic needs of society. They conclude that "the idealized model of an independent legal profession—as a learned group, as trustees of an autonomous legal system—has been derived from this historical experience."[10] On the other hand, they contend that lawyers in the Third World states, because of their very different historical experiences, have played a far different role: "they tend to play brokerage roles—helping to produce an orderly transfer of power, from colonial officials to new national leaders, over political institutions which had been developed by essentially authoritarian and devolutionary political processes."[11]

In addition to the general historical development of the legal profession and its present role(s), this volume will focus on three other issues related to the personnel of the law. The first two of these are the recruitment and training of those entering the profession. Nonet and Carlin contend that these two issues are related:

By controlling access to the profession and the future training of lawyers, legal education has an important bearing on the character of the profession and the orientations of the law. Whether the law becomes the property of a privileged class or of the whole polity depends to some extent upon criteria of access to the profession.[12]

The final issue tied to the personnel of the law relates to mobility within the legal profession, especially as it affects judicial selection and promotion. Schmidhauser indicates the importance of this:

Judicial selection has been considered the first great problem that arises in any judicial system. Solutions to this problem and to the closely related subject of judicial tenure have varied in accordance with the prevailing theoretical conceptions of the nature of justice and political considerations reflecting the distribution of power in the society.[13]

The final goal of this volume is to assess the public's perception of the legal system and its personnel and the role played by the courts in the legal systems studied. In many ways the task of evaluating the public's perceptions of the legal system will be a difficult one because, outside of the first world nations, there is little empirical data on attitudes toward the legal system and its personnel.

Fortunately, other indicators exist for measuring these attitudes. The first among these is the status afforded members of the legal profession. For example, the high prestige of members of the legal profession in England is but one indication of the generally positive view that the average Englishman has toward his/her legal system. A second indicator is the likelihood that the decisions of the legal system are viewed as authoritative by the populace in a particular nation. For example, one measure of the esteem afforded the American Supreme Court is the compliance with its decisions (both by members of the political system and the population at large) despite the fact that the Court has little power to force such compliance. A third measure of the public's views of the legal system is its willingness to utilize the system to solve problems. This is, of course, tied to the historical development of the legal system and its personnel. Japan, for example, has had a tradition of both distrust of legal practitioners and a desire to solve societal problems harmoniously rather than through the adversarial processes afforded by the legal system. Citizens in Japan today are, therefore, quite likely to try to solve their problems through conciliation and mediation rather than through their modern (and highly efficient) legal system. It has already been noted that Americans made great use of lawyers as far back as their colonial period. This pattern has continued and accelerated to the point that Americans today are often described as among the most litigious people in the world. While this description is often used pejoratively, it does indicate a great willingness of Americans to utilize their legal system. A final measure of the public's views of the legal system are the role(s) that it is allowed to play within the larger political system. Hitchner notes five judicial functions common to most societies: (1) establishment of the facts; (2) finding and interpretation of the law; (3) enforcement of authority and remedies; (4) administrative responsibilities; and (5) judicial lawmaking.[14] The extent to which legal systems are allowed to perform these functions will provide us with another measure of status afforded the system and its members.

A second issue related to the roles of the courts involves the concept of judicial independence. This concept often has two meanings: (1) structural independence—the independence of the courts and their personnel from interference by political leaders in the selection, assignment, and promotion of members of the judiciary as well as the remuneration of members of the legal system; and (2) decisional independence—interference (or threats of interference) with decisions of the courts that may run counter to the interests of the government. This volume will, therefore, attempt to evaluate the strength of judicial independence in the nations studied by carefully assessing the personnel policies regarding members of the legal profession as well as discovering any examples of interference in the decisions of the courts.

The final issue related to the role of the courts involves the most controversial aspect of judicial lawmaking, judicial review, that "process whereby a judicial body determines the constitutionality of an activity undertaken by a country's legislature and chief executive."[15] Judicial review was probably first discussed by Plato and is now performed in approximately sixty of the nations of the world.[16] This role is probably most aggressively performed by the American Supreme Court, which often plays an "active" role, "balancing" the power of the president and Congress. Edward Corwin has, in fact, described judicial review as "America's way of hedging its bet."[17] While Theodore Becker has maintained that there is often a very close correlation between the existence of judicial review and judicial independence, it is possible to have an independent judiciary and flourishing democracy without the existence of judicial review.[18] England provides us with the best example of this for the English judiciary plays a less active role in the political process. This is primarily because the length and pattern of historical development in England has created a political system where the extent of trust is such that the British Parliament is not checked and can do everything "except transform a man into a woman and a woman into a man."[19] This volume will then finally attempt to discover whether judicial review exists in the nations to be studied and whether such a function is performed by "regular general-jurisdiction" courts (as in the United States, India, Australia and Japan) or in courts specially designated to perform this function (as in Italy, Germany, and Austria).[20]

L. M. Hager has written that "law and legal institutions are themselves empty bottles. Their worth to society depends upon the quality of the wine poured into them.''[21] The hope is that this volume, in assessing the historical development and organization of the legal system, the personnel of the law, and the public perceptions and the role of the courts might not only well describe the bottles that house the law and legal institutions in the nations to be studied, but the quality of the wine poured into them as well.

NOTES

1. B. McGinty, "Lawyers in Early America," *Early American Life*, February 1982, p. 52.
2. Ibid.
3. Ibid.
4. Ibid.
5. See, for example, F. Butterfield, *China: Alive in the Bitter Sea* (New York: Bantam Books, 1982).
6. McGinty, "Lawyers in Early America," p. 56, comments on this:

Despite the efforts of most of the colonies to suppress lawyers, the people demonstrated an irrepressible appetite for their services. A man who spends every day on the farm, guiding a plow through rock-choked fields, has little time for legal study. A merchant who stands from dawn to dusk behind the counter of a busy store is unlikely to find the time (or the inclination) to peruse Cooke's *Commentaries on Littleton*. A man charged with a serious crime—particularly one for which death is the penalty—will not willingly entrust his fate to a judge who, as often as not, is untrained in the law and has no lawyers to guide him toward a reasonably predictable decision.

7. J. H. Merryman and D. S. Clark, *Comparative Law: Western European and Latin American Legal Systems* (Indianapolis: Bobbs Merrill Co., 1978), p. 3.
8. D. G. Hitchner and C. Levine, *Comparative Government and Politics: An Introductory Essay in Political Science* (New York: Harper & Row, 1968), p. 157, note four major sources of the law: moral and ethical principles, custom, judicial rulings, and legislation.
9. "Mixed" refers to those systems that utilize elements of both the common law and civil law. Among those mixed systems are British Guiana, Cameroon, Sri Lanka, the Philippines, Quebec, Rhodesia, and Scotland. See E. S. Easterly III, "Global Patterns of Legal Systems: Notes Toward a New Geojurisprudence," *The Geographical Review* 67 (April 1977), p. 216.
10. C. J. Dias and J.C.N. Paul, "Observations on Lawyers in Development and Underdevelopment," in C. J. Dias et al., eds., *Lawyers in the Third World: Comparative and Developmental Perspectives* (Uppsala: Scandinavian Institute of African Studies, 1981, p. 339.
11. Ibid., p. 343.
12. P. Nonet and J. E. Carlin, "The Legal Profession," in *International Encyclopedia of the Social Sciences* 9 (1968), p. 68.
13. J. R. Schmidhauser, "Judicial Recruitment," in *International Encyclopedia of the Social Sciences* 8 (1968), pp. 322–323.
14. Hitchner and Levine, *Comparative Government and Politics*, p. 73–176.
15. J. Tannenhaus, "Judicial Review," in *International Encyclopedia of the Social Sciences* 8, (1968), p. 303.

16. See T. L. Becker, *Comparative Judicial Politics: The Political Functioning of the Courts* (Chicago: Rand McNally, 1970), pp. 205–6, for a discussion of the role of judicial review in ancient Greece.

17. H. Abraham, *The Judicial Process: An Introductory Analysis of the Courts of the United States, England and France* (New York: Oxford University Press, 1975), p. 279.

18. Becker, *Comparative Judicial Politics*, pp. 211–14.

19. Abraham, *The Judicial Process*, p. 279.

20. Becker, *Comparative Judicial Politics*, p. 206.

21. L. M. Hager, "The Role of Lawyers in Developing Countries," *American Bar Association Journal* 58 (January 1972), p. 37.

BIBLIOGRAPHY

Abraham, H. *The Judicial Process: An Introductory Analysis of the Courts of the United States, England and France*. New York: Oxford University Press, 1975.

Becker, T. L. *Comparative Judicial Politics: The Political Functioning of the Courts*. Chicago: Rand McNally, 1970.

Cappelletti, M. *Judicial Review in the Contemporary World*. Indianapolis, Ind. Bobbs-Merrill Co., 1971.

Cappelletti, M., and W. Cohen. *Comparative Constitutional Law: Cases and Materials*. Indianapolis, Ind. Bobbs-Merrill Co., 1979.

David, R., and J.E.C. Brierly. *Major Legal Systems in the World Today: An Introduction to the Comparative Study of Law*. 2d. ed. New York: Free Press, 1978.

Dias, C.J., R. Luckham, D.O. Lynch, and J.C.N. Paul, eds. *Lawyers in the Third World: Comparative and Developmental Perspectives*, Uppsala: Scandinavian Institute of African Studies, 1981.

Ehrmann, H. W. *Comparative Legal Cultures*. New York: Prentice-Hall, 1976.

Goutal, J. L. "Characteristics of Judicial Style in France, Britain, and the U.S.A." *American Journal of Comparative Law* 24, no. 1 (Winter 1971), pp. 43–72.

Harris, R. "Judicial Review: Vagaries and Varieties." *Journal of Politics* 38, no. 3 (August 1976), pp. 173–208.

Kommers, D. P. "Comparative Judicial Review and Constitutional Politics—A Review." *World Politics* 27, no. 2 (January 1975), pp. 282–97.

McWinney, E. *Judicial Review*. Toronto: University of Toronto Press, 1969.

Merryman, J. H., and D. S. Clark. *Comparative Law: Western European and Latin American Legal Systems*. Indianapolis, Ind.: Bobbs-Merrill Co., 1978.

Nonet, P., and J. E. Carlin. "The Legal Profession." In D. Sills, ed., *International Encyclopedia of the Social Sciences*, vol. 9 (New York: MacMillan Co. and The Free Press, 1968). Pp. 66–72.

Peltason, J. "Judicial Process: An Introduction." in D. Sills, ed., *International Encyclopedia of the Social Sciences*, vol. 9 (New York: MacMillan Co, and The Free Press, 1968). Pp. 283–91.

Rheinstein, M. "Legal Systems: Comparative Law and Legal Systems." In D. Sills, ed., *International Encyclopedia of the Social Sciences*, vol. 9 (New York: MacMillan Co. and The Free Press, 1968). Pp. 204–10.

Rueschemeyer, D. "The Legal Profession in Comparative Perspective," *Sociological Inquiry*, 47, nos. 3–4 (1977), pp. 97–122.

Shapiro, M. *Courts: A Comparative and Political Analysis*. Chicago: University of Chicago Press, 1981.

1

AFRICA

Harvey M. Feinberg

The evolution of the legal systems in Africa has been very different from developments in the European world. This is primarily because the intervention of colonialism in the late nineteenth century brought with it the sudden imposition of a foreign legal system on the people of each colony. The European colonial powers introduced their own legal systems based on the legal philosophy, laws, and court organizations of the home countries. These systems were imposed on the peoples of each colony in supplementing their own existing legal frameworks.

When the colonies became independent, mainly in the late 1950s and early 1960s, the legal framework established by the former colonial power was retained. However, government leaders also had to contend with the traditional rules and legal institutions of the multiple ethnic groups who lived within the boundaries of a particular new nation. Since that time, government leaders have attempted to blend the two systems, modern and traditional, or to subordinate the traditional systems to the national legal system, or to modify that system inherited from the colonial period in a manner more consonant with local conditions.

There are forty-six independent countries on the continent of Africa. However, the discussion in this chapter will be limited to those countries between the Sahara Desert and the Zambezi River. The Republic of South Africa and the previously white-dominated Zimbabwe have been excluded as well as the Portuguese speaking countries of Angola, Mozambique, and Guinea Bissau.

The foci of this chapter are the Anglophone and the Francophone countries south of the Sahara. The Anglophone countries, Gambia, Ghana, Kenya, Malawi, Nigeria, Sierra Leone, Tanzania, Uganda, and Zambia, use a legal system based upon the English common law tradition. The Francophone countries, Benin, Burkina Faso (formerly Upper Volta), Cameroon, Central African Republic, Chad, Congo (Brazzaville), Gabon, Guinea, Ivory Coast, Mali, Niger, Senegal, Togo (all former French colonies), and Zaire (a former Belgian colony), inherited a system based on the civil law tradition dominant on the European continent. The reader should be cautioned, however, that with such a large number of countries involved, generalization is difficult, especially since scholarly resources are uneven in depth and quality.

THE DEVELOPMENT OF THE LEGAL SYSTEMS

Imperialism and colonialism arrived in Africa mainly during the last two decades of the nineteenth century. The main colonial powers were France and England. The French introduced a legal system based on codes, using the Napoleonic Codes as a foundation. This means that the law predominantly came from statutes organized within the various codes. However, a civil lawyer must take cognizance of the decisions developed around the articles of the code. While these, in theory, do not make law, court decisions, together with academic debate of the cases are still important for understanding many parts of the code. Nevertheless, precedent plays a lesser role in the decisions of judges, and less room existed for judicial interpretation than within the English common law tradition.

The legal situation in English colonies was more complex. The foundation in particular colonies was English common law and statutory law as of a particular date (for example, July 24, 1874, for Ghana and January 1, 1900, for Nigeria). Criminal and penal codes in English colonies had varying origins: English common law was the most important source; Indian colonial law was also important to the development of colonial law; codes from Australia and the West Indies were also introduced into some colonies.[1]

Customary law (except for the harsher elements, such as trial by ordeal, torture, and unusual punishments, those practices deemed to be "repugnant to civilized practice") continue to prevail as a parallel legal system in most of the colonies during the twentieth century. Customary law courts, whether existing prior to the colonial period or created by the colonial government, were most often the courts of first instance, particularly for cases concerning land, inheritance, marital matters, or disputes among members of the society. The colonial governments' courts handled most criminal matters (using European law as the guide) and heard appeals from the customary courts. In addition, a very substantial amount of legislation enacted by the colonial government affected rural Africans and might supersede the laws inherited from the metropole. In the field of land law in many English colonies, for example, local statutes "wholly or substantially restricted the general application of English legal notions."[2]

In ordinary criminal and civil cases, impartiality and the normal rule of law generally seem to have prevailed in the European colonial courts. Thus, where there were issues involving Africans in which the government had no stake, judges or administrators (such as district commissioners) sought to reach judgments based on the available evidence, to try, in the African manner, to "settle the dispute." Ghanaians, for example, regularly brought disputes over traditional leadership positions and land to the colonial courts, undoubtedly because of the perceived impartiality on the part of the English colonial judge. In criminal matters, the Europeans believed that violations of the law had to be punished in the European manner.

On the other hand, colonial subjects could question the impartiality of the courts in those cases in which colonial officials suspected a threat, real or perceived, to their power. This might include not only overt rebellion or rioting, but also writings or speeches that might incite others to discontent or antigovernment activities. Here the courts were anxious to assert the authority of the colonial government. Actions threatening the colonial system, especially before about 1950, would elicit the harshest judicial response. Rights and fundamental freedoms, such as freedom of the press, freedom of speech, or freedom of assembly, might not be extended to colonial subjects. In England, for example, the prosecution was required to prove intent in order to convict a defendant of violating the law against sedition. Colonial subjects could be found guilty without such proof. Scotton notes that freedom of the press was limited as well. He attributes this limitation to the fact that the colonial courts gave precedence to locally passed ordinances "tightly controlling free expression" rather than considering common law interpretations.[3]

Thus, the availability of colonial courts, their jurisdiction, and the degree to which Africans utilized these courts in civil matters or were threatened with criminal prosecution varied from colony to colony. The presence or absence of large numbers of white settlers could also affect the administration of a colonial legal system. Consequently, the image of the courts also varied, depending, in part, on the challenges faced by a particular colonial government and the official response.

Colonialism, in most African states, ended during the late 1950s and early 1960s, as the colonial powers slowly granted independence. In 1957, Ghana became the first black African nation to achieve its independence. The period between the end of World War II and independence was a time of transition, when African leaders shared power with European colonial officials and when Africans and Europeans worked jointly to create a framework for modern governments. During this time, colonial officials and African leaders in many of the colonies followed similar steps to achieve independence. Constitutions were written, elections were held on the basis of universal suffrage, and parliaments created. Africans were appointed or elected to executive and administrative positions and slowly assumed increased responsibility for governing the colony. The final step was the achievement of independence.

Independence constitutions incorporated the principle of separation of powers among the branches of government. This principle, in theory, recognizes the independence of the judiciary. Many but not all of the constitutions included provisions for the protection of fundamental rights: freedom of speech, religion, and the press, and guarantees relating to due process of the law. The foundation of the legal systems continued to be the inherited ideas, statutes, and practices from the former colonial power. This inheritance was substantial. In addition, the courts were organized on a hierarchical basis similar to the court structure of the colonial government.

In most countries during the initial stages of independence, the judges were expatriates, Europeans or Asians; Africans slowly entered the ranks of the judiciary. The number of African members of the bar varied widely, depending on the colony's educational system and the opportunities for Africans to obtain access to higher education. Ghana and Nigeria, for example, had hundreds of lawyers, whereas the East African countries of Kenya and Tanzania had only a handful of African lawyers when they became independent. For those countries with lawyers, most, if not all, had been trained abroad, usually in London or Paris. In Anglophone countries, most of the lawyers were barristers rather than solicitors because the period of training was shorter and few in their own countries cared about the distinction. In addition, at independence few African countries had law schools, law faculties, or law departments in their universities.

The former colonies became independent under modern constitutions that established democratic frameworks for government. The parliamentary model predominated, whereby the prime minister and his cabinet came from the Parliament and were, therefore, dependent on maintaining a parliamentary majority. Before discussing the legal systems as presently constituted, a review of the political trends in black Africa since the early 1960s would be useful.

The first major trend was the revision of independence constitutions. Such revisions often created strong presidential systems of government, abandoning the Westminster model, which had given primacy to the legislative branch. At the same time, most of the Anglophone countries severed their last Commonwealth ties to England by creating republics. This meant that the English queen would no longer be recognized as the head of state and that the Privy Council would not act as the ultimate court of appeal. With this constitutional underpinning, many presidents increased their political power, so that a pattern of executive dominance and authoritarianism developed. This trend toward authoritarianism was strengthened by the establishment in many countries of only one legal political party. The enshrinement of one-party government occurred at a time when political parties in many African countries declined in strength and importance (Tanzania is an important exception). Since parliaments then only included members from the single party, the executive was in a position to pass any laws he saw fit with limited, if any, opposition. In addition, an African leader could alter the country's constitution with little difficulty since his party commanded the necessary votes in the Parliament to overcome entrenched clauses. Finally, the press was rarely allowed to be independent.

Since no opposition to the party in power was allowed and electoral competition was usually eliminated, peaceful political change was next to impossible. An important trend, then, became the unconstitutional overthrow of civilian governments by the military (or the military and the police working together). Coups d'etat frequently led to the suspension of constitutions, the abolition of political parties, and the suspension of legislative assemblies. No less than thirty-seven successful coups have occurred in twenty black African countries since the early 1960s, and other governments have seen attempts made but thwarted to oust civilian leaders. In 1986, more than half of the black African countries are under military rule.

The new military governments took on executive and legislative powers and ruled by decree. Most courts continued to function and most laws continued in force, unless explicitly repealed by decree. Since a constitution was no longer in force, constitutional issues were rarely raised, and it became an open question whether the courts could challenge the validity of decrees. In several countries, including Chad, Ghana, and Niger, the Supreme Court was abolished or suspended. Often, separate, special tribunals were established to try political cases or corruption cases. In short, the military allowed the courts limited, if any, independence, and trials that were "political" were subject to interference. Protection of fundamental rights, in theory, did not exist under military governments.

THE ORGANIZATION OF THE COURT SYSTEMS

Court systems in Africa are organized on a number of different levels. At the top is a final court of appeal, usually called a "Supreme Court." Below this is a second level of appeals court, which may also have limited original jurisdiction. In addition, there is the level of initial courts that have original jurisdiction for civil and criminal cases. These courts conduct trials and may hear cases concerned with customary law issues, especially if this is the lowest level of courts. Some countries may also have justice of the peace courts, customary law courts, and Islamic courts if a sizable proportion of the population are of the Islamic faith. Special courts may also exist.

In Zambia, there is a Supreme Court, a High Court, magistrates' courts (divided into four classes), and local courts. The Supreme Court includes a chief justice, a deputy chief justice, and two associate justices. This is an appellate court and the highest court in Zambia. The High Court is mainly an appellate court but also has original jurisdiction in selected cases. In addition to the chief justice of Zambia, eight justices are members of this bench, although all nine are not required (or expected) to hear a case. Magistrates' courts are divided according to the type of case that can be heard in a particular class of magistrates' court (based on the length of prison term or the size of fine that can be imposed). Magistrates may be lawyers but more likely are individuals who have been trained at the National Institute of Public Administration and do not have a law degree. There are at least thirty-one magistrates' courts in Zambia. At the lowest level, the local courts administer customary law and are manned by individuals who have "a substantial working knowledge of customary law."[4]

Kenya follows a similar pattern. However, the Supreme Court, the Kenya Court of Appeal, only came into existence in 1977 after the demise of the East African Community and the dissolution of the Court of Appeal of East Africa.

The Kenya Court of Appeal includes a chief justice and four associate justices. There are only two types of magistrates' courts, resident magistrates' and senior resident magistrates' courts. The magistrates in these courts must be lawyers. The district magistrates' courts are divided into three classes. In addition, the Kenya judicial system includes Qadi courts and a number of special courts: industrial, juvenile, landlord and tenant, and rent. The lower courts can hear cases in which the choice of law for marriage, divorce, and succession disputes includes statutory law, customary law, Hindu law or Islamic law.

The Zambian and Kenyan patterns tend to be similar to the other Anglophone countries. However, one must consider that the federal nature of Nigeria adds another layer of courts to the system and that the several coups d'etat in Ghana have led to some changes there, most notably the creation, abolition, and then reestablishment of a Supreme Court.

Francophone countries usually have more courts. In addition, the Supreme Court is divided into specialized branches. Another difference is that the constitutional branch of the Supreme Court considers constitutional issues at the request of the president of the country or the leader of the National Assembly. Judicial review of legislation is advisory, occurring at the time when the National Assembly has passed a law but before the law has taken effect. Thus, the opinion of the Court is sought *before* a law is promulgated. Also, within the court systems of Francophone countries are special courts to try cases of treason or other high political crimes involving a president or key political officials.

The court structure in the Ivory Coast is as follows: The Supreme Court includes four branches: a Constitutional Chamber, a Chamber of Accounts, a Judicial Chamber with civil and criminal divisions, and an Administrative Chamber. Salacuse sums up the functions of the Supreme Court when he writes that this Court "settles conflicts concerning the Assembly's legislative competence, advises the government on proposed legislation, and is the court of last resort in the judicial system."[5] More specifically, the Constitutional Chamber advises the government on the "constitutionality of projected bills, decrees and regulations" at the request of the president or the head of the National Assembly. This court also plays a role in monitoring elections and the qualifications of candidates for the National Assembly. The Accounts Chamber "monitors the State treasury and the accounts of secondary public authorities. It also controls public finances, public enterprises of commercial or industrial character, and the State and mixed economy enterprises. It oversees utilization of government subsidies to various institutions."[6] The Judicial Chamber is the "cassation court for final decisions rendered by lower courts. It also promulgates court rules, approves transfers of cases from one court to another, withdrawals of sworn testimony, requests for trials, and handles other procedural matters."[7] This is the final court of appeal from decisions by the lower civil and criminal courts. Finally, the Administrative Chamber acts as a court of appeal for decisions involving a government agency. It also considers cases charging abuse of power and hears appeals "of decisions rendered against administrative authorities."[8]

There are twelve judges associated with the Supreme Court, a chief justice, three deputy chief justices, and nine associate judges.

The courts of assize try criminal cases, using juries made up of citizens over the age of twenty-five. There are at least twenty-six courts of first instance that have original jurisdiction over civil and criminal matters. In addition, the Ivory Coast has a labor court, which is concerned with contractual disputes between labor and management. This court includes a judge and four assessors, two representing management and two employees. Finally, there are two special courts, the Court of State Security and the High Court of Justice. The former court tries crimes against the security of the state and is made up of seven judges who serve for five year terms and are chosen for their "political, administrative or legal ability."[9] The latter court, whose members are chosen by the National Assembly, judges those accused of treason and high government officials charged with major crimes associated with their official positions.

This pattern is similar for many of the other Francophone countries. The chief difference, however, is that a number of countries, such as Senegal, also have justice of the peace courts, which handle cases arising from petty offenses and from customary law. In Senegal, the court includes a judge and assessors or qadis for cases involving Muslims. An important exception to the general pattern described above is Cameroon, where, as a result of the merger of the English colony of West Cameroon with the larger French Cameroon, the country has to contend with two different legal inheritances. In more recent years, the federal system has been abolished and a major effort is underway to unify the two legal traditions.

A major reorganization of the court system was undertaken in Guinea in 1973 in an effort to move away from the French inheritance. At the lowest level, there are village and city ward people's courts. In these courts, the chairman of the political party committee in the particular area acts as the president of the court and is joined for one year terms by two persons elected by the party members. These courts only handle civil cases. Secondly, Guinea has district people's courts that have both civil and criminal jurisdiction. The judge in these courts is either a district commander or a magistrate.[10] Another difference in Guinea is that the Supreme Court does not have the power to advise or rule upon the constitutionality of laws. Finally, certain countries have elaborate customary law court systems, such as Gabon and the Congo.

Courts in black Africa are manned by judges or magistrates, who are, on occasion, assisted by lay assessors. Judges are almost always trained lawyers. The older generation of judges was trained in England or France, while the younger generation may have acquired their legal education from the law faculty of the national university. Many Africans from French colonies acquired their legal training at the University of Paris, while the various Inns of Court in London served as the chief training ground for Africans from English colonies. Judges almost always sit on the highest court in the nation as well as on the other important appeals courts. In some countries, such as Ghana, lengthy years of service as a lawyer determines eligibility for various levels of judgeships.[11] Some magistrates may have received legal training and become lawyers, but the vast majority of magistrates are not lawyers and may or may not have had either legal or administrative training. Magistrates usually hear cases in the courts of first instance or at a slightly higher level. Lay assessors are used by a number of African governments such as Tanzania, Senegal, Gabon, Niger, and the Ivory Coast (on the labor courts). Their role is usually advisory, especially if they have been brought into the court because of their expert knowledge of customary law; some governments allow the assessors a vote, others do not.

Most judges are appointed by the president of the country. Constitutional provisions requiring the president to consult with other leaders, the bar association, or special judicial commissions vary. One method incorporated into many constitutions has been the creation of judicial service commissions or high councils of the judiciary (Conseil Supérieur de la Magistrature), in order, in theory, to reduce the influence of politics in the appointment of judges. These commissions ordinarily include as members the chief justice (often as chairman), representatives of the bar association, and officials from the executive branch.[12] The relative balance of the membership ultimately can influence the degree of the independence of a commission. Such commissions exist in Anglophone and Francophone countries, such as Zambia, Kenya, Malawi, Senegal, and Ivory Coast. In certain countries, such as Zambia, the judicial service commission has the additional responsibility of appointing magistrates to their positions on lower courts.

Data on the number of judges who are lawyers by training is very limited, especially for courts other than the Supreme Court. The main conclusion based on data for ten countries is that the number of judges with legal training is very small, usually less than twenty-four per nation.[13] Lower courts, staffed by magistrates, tend to be larger in number in many countries, though this is not true everywhere. Zambia, for example, in 1974, had thirty-one magistrates' courts and thirteen local courts.[14] Chad has four criminal courts and four magistrates' courts but forty-three justices of the peace, while Mali has only two courts of first instance.[15]

Civil cases are heard by judges and magistrates, perhaps with assessors but without juries. Jury trials for criminal cases are available in Ghana, Ivory Coast, and Senegal. They may also be available in a small number of other African countries in criminal cases, but the use of the jury is not the norm in Africa.

To what extent are the courts used by the general population for the settlement of disputes? The limited research that has been completed on African courts suggests that, in general, the average individual does not know very much about the law, his rights, or the procedures for seeking redress of grievances against illegal actions by government officials. Ignorance may relate to a lack of knowledge of the law because most laws are written in a language unique to lawyers—a language that is largely incomprehensible to the ordinary citizen.[16] Another possible barrier to approaching the courts, especially at the lowest level, and utilizing their services in civil disputes might be the language problem. In Narok, Kenya, Sevareid encountered a magistrate who did not speak the language of the people of the district (Masai) and thus required an interpreter. This situation is exacerbated by Kenya government policy, which requires that magistrates rotate among posts periodically but states that they cannot serve in their home districts. In Ghana, proceedings may be in English or a combination of English and one of the main Ghanaian languages, especially if lawyers are present, making it difficult for an illiterate litigant to follow the proceedings properly.[17] Furthermore, the nature of the proceedings and the educated background of the magistrates may create an intimidating atmosphere for most people, especially rural inhabitants. In addition, sheer poverty, the lack of money to pay lawyers, must be emphasized. The conclusion is that in many African countries, the average individual prefers informal methods of dispute settlement following traditional methods rather than the official government courts.[18]

THE PERSONNEL OF THE LAW

There are at least nineteen law schools or law faculties, located in fourteen of the countries lying between the Sahara Desert and the Zambezi River. A number of countries, such as Benin, Gambia, and Burkina Faso (Upper Volta), have no law schools. All of the law schools are relatively new, having been established between 1957 and 1970. Almost all of them admit students directly from secondary school. The course of study is three years at more than half of the schools, four years at the rest, mainly in the Francophone countries. In a few countries, such as Kenya, a year of practical experience is required before a lawyer is allowed to practice independently.

Actual data on African law students are very limited, though it is clear that they do come from a wide variety of backgrounds. Most of the students are men. In an informal survey of 113 students at the University of Ghana Law School, Griffiths found that over one-third of the students' fathers were farmers. Other fathers' occupations included civil servant, teacher, businessman, professional, minister, and artisan, as well as traditional leader. More than one-third of the mothers were traders, one of the main areas of employment for women in West Africa. Eighty-five of 226 parents had no formal education and another sixty-five had less than a secondary school education. Only nineteen parents (eighteen fathers and one mother) had been to a university.[19] The main point to emphasize regarding this data is that merit, as evidenced by intellectual ability and academic achievement, continues to represent the chief criteria for success in secondary school and admission to universities, including law schools today. At the University of Dar es Salaam, the Faculty of Law "tends to have entrants with qualifications considerably higher than the minimum entrance requirements [to the University where there was, in 1976] . . . fairly heavy competition to obtain admission."[20] This should still (in 1986) be true in other countries as well, since competition for entrance into secondary schools is fierce, and the entrance requirements to law school require either the successful completion of the advanced level course of study in Anglophone countries or the baccalaureate from Francophone secondary schools. Law school populations, therefore, include talented students from a wide variety of socioeconomic backgrounds, a situation aided in many countries by a policy of tuition-free education.

Legal Practitioners

Accurate statistics on the number of lawyers in African countries are difficult to obtain and are not consistent. In addition, the available sources do not always inform the reader about whether the data include lawyers working for governments (as well as judges) in addition to those in private practice. It is clear, however, that the number of African lawyers has increased in most countries since independence. For example, the number of lawyers in Ghana has grown from about forty to sixty in 1948 to over 1,200 by 1982. Substantial growth is also apparent in Kenya and Tanzania. On the other hand, certain Francophone countries have a very small number of lawyers. If the data are accurate, by the middle of the 1960s, most of these countries had less than one hundred lawyers each, with some countries having hardly any legally trained personnel.[21]

African lawyers are among the elite within their countries. They are part of that very small group in each country that has acquired higher education, and university education is an almost automatic road to high status and success. Lawyers have the potential to earn high incomes and the choice of opportunities between government employment (with a variety of benefits) and private practice. Some also serve as political appointees at the highest levels of government.

Lawyers tend to be concentrated in the cities, especially the capitals, leaving the rural areas without easy access to legal representation. For example, over 80 percent of Tanzanian lawyers lived in the four major cities in 1981, with 70 percent alone residing in Dar es Salaam. In Ghana 78 percent of the lawyers in private practice and 84 percent of those in the government legal service were concentrated in Accra, the capital, or Kumasi, the second largest city and part of a key region in the country. At the end of 1968, 199 out of 292 Kenyan lawyers were in Nairobi, and another forty-nine resided in Mombasa, the country's chief port.[22] Not only do the rural areas lack a sufficient number of lawyers, but, in many countries, it is difficult to get urban lawyers to take cases in rural courts because of transportation costs, the travel time involved, and scheduling problems.

Various descriptions suggest that private practice is not easy. Ross notes that

the private practitioner in East Africa practices alone; he is a ''legal jack of all trades'' and often master of none. If he does specialize it is usually in criminal law. His office is poorly organized and equipped, lacking an adequate library. Although the profession is fused—the advocate acting as barrister and solicitor—the lawyer spends most of his time doing court work.[23]

The lawyer's task, in certain countries, is made more difficult by the lack of any research facilities, such as a law library. For example, there are no law libraries in Gabon, Gambia, Niger, Congo, Sierra Leone, or Burkina Faso. Collegial interaction is sharply reduced where there is no bar association, as in Chad, Gabon, Niger, Congo, and Burkina Faso. One can only conjecture about the availability of law journals and law reports. The publication of law journals seems to be limited to just a few countries, such as Nigeria, Ghana, Zambia, Kenya, Uganda, and Tanzania. In addition, considering the difficult economic circumstances of many African countries, it is an open question if the necessary foreign exchange is available for the purchase of subscriptions to journals published in Africa or elsewhere. The official publication of judicial decisions within particular countries also seems to be behind schedule.

The African lawyer must maintain flexible office hours, accept the visits of clients to their homes, or meet them in the clients' offices. One successful Tanzanian lawyer emphasizes this point: "clients come even at home. It is part of African upbringing: anywhere, anytime. Some come to me out of respect. So when they even come home I do listen to their problems there. Once you do a case for a person you become relatives."[24]

In addition to criminal law, land and customary law cases occupy an important part of a lawyer's time. Commercial and company law and civil injury cases are the other major areas of work for attorneys in private practice.[25]

Odenyo raises an interesting question about the image of the lawyer in countries where the majority of the people come from rural backgrounds. He suggests that the lawyer has no comparable role in traditional society in the dispute settlement process. Aside from the accused and the complainant, the mediating group is usually composed of elders in the society, who also decide on a judgment designed to settle the dispute in a manner whereby both sides can live with the decision. Thus,

the role of the lawyers in the Kenyan society is to date undifferentiated in the minds of the rural population, which appears to lump the lawyer together with the generalized category of "knowledgeable person" whose advice is sought on a variety of life situations, not necessarily legal. Part of the reason is that, unlike that of a physician, the role lacks a precursor in the Kenyan traditional society.[26]

Government officials may also view lawyers in private practice with suspicion. Some governments, such as that of Tanzania, do not allow attorneys to represent clients in the primary courts; in the 1960s, the Kenyan government, according to Abel, "prohibited lawyers from participating in nationwide programs of land adjudication, consolidation, and registration."[27] Lawyers are sometimes accused of being too interested in enriching themselves, so that, on the one hand, they bring weak cases to trial rather than work for an out-of-court settlement, "without considering the burden of cost" to the client.[28] On the other hand, government leaders complain that lawyers are unwilling to sacrifice for the nation by working for the attorney general or serving in the less well paid but very important position of judge.[29]

In addition, there may be tension between lawyers and the magistrates who man the rural courts. Magistrates do not have the same educational qualifications as the lawyers, often attending institutes of public administration or government training programs rather than universities. One of Odenyo's informants feared that magistrates penalized litigants with lawyers "because this gives the District Magistrate a chance to show the lawyer that despite the lawyer's training, the Magistrate has more power." This problem, Odenyo believes, stems from the differences in the education of the two, as described above, and different perceptions of the role of each. According to Odenyo, "the lawyer tends to see the magistrate as an ignorant individual wielding power he does not actually deserve, whereas the (magistrate) sees the lawyer as a verbally tricky individual out to prevent the guilty from being punished and to enrich himself in the process."[30]

In this examination of the role of African lawyers, two interesting examples, from Tanzania and Ghana, require discussion. At independence, there were hardly any African lawyers in Tanzania, but the number of African members of the bar has increased substantially since that time. This Africanization of the bar has been paralleled by the employment of many of these lawyers by the Tanzanian government. The result has been a sharp reduction in the number of European lawyers in the country. On the other hand, the government has a conscious policy aimed at employing most of the lawyers in Tanzania, thereby eliminating the private practice of law. Actions have been taken that reduce the available work for remaining lawyers in private practice, and questions have been raised in official circles about the relevance of a private bar in a socialist country. Since 1967, Tanzania has nationalized the major corporations, banks, and agricultural estates, thereby reducing several areas of law that traditionally have been financially attractive for private lawyers. In addition, the government established a Tanzania legal corporation in 1970 or 1971. Its original aim was to provide legal services for the various public corporations under government aegis. By 1981, however, the Tanzania Legal Corporation had been authorized to "represent private individuals at a reasonable fee." Corporation lawyers mainly take civil cases, although they are not barred from aiding Tanzanians in criminal cases as well.

As a result of the creation of the Tanzania Legal Corporation, nationalization policies, and concerns about government intentions, there has been a sharp reduction in the number of lawyers involved in private practice. Between 1970 and 1975, the number of lawyers in private practice dropped from one hundred to forty-three. The government, in 1981, employed 75 percent of all the lawyers, about 90 percent of whom are Tanzanians. These lawyers worked for the attorney general, the legal corporation (about 25 percent), the judiciary (30 percent), and other relevant departments, such as foreign affairs, as well as for a few public corporations. Those few private lawyers left seem to be most occupied with criminal cases; just over three-fifths of these lawyers reported that they spend more than 50 percent of their time on criminal cases.[31]

Perhaps the most active group of lawyers could be found in Ghana. The number of lawyers in Ghana grew at a relatively consistent rate of about fifty men and women entering the profession each year between 1959 and 1973. Approximately 9 percent of the Ghana bar is female, of whom 60 percent work for government agencies and the judiciary. Eight out of eighty-nine judges are women.[32] Ghana's lawyers were most active politically in the period from 1966 to 1969, first as members of the Constitutional Commission (1966–1969), which drafted a new constitution, and then in the Constituent Assembly (1969), which modified and then approved that draft. In addition, many lawyers sought election to the Parliament in 1969, and just under 50 percent of the lawyers were elected. Six lawyers and two judges sat on the eighteen-member Constitutional Commission. This group included Chief Justice E. Akufo Addo, who presided as chairman of the commission. Representatives from the Ghana Bar Association presented evidence at the commission's hearings, and at least six prominent attorneys sent memoranda. Of equal importance, two of the three members of the secretariat were also lawyers. Lawyers formed by far the single largest group among the members of the Constituent Assembly (with thirty-six, including three judges, out of 150 members). In addition, according to Luckham and Nkrumah, the lawyers also "did most of the talking. Of the twenty-five most loquacious members, ten were lawyers," who monopolized more than 50 percent of the speaking time. During the electoral campaign, sixty-three lawyers were among the party candidates for the Parliament, constituting 21 percent of the candidates (businessmen and teachers each comprised 16 percent). Of the 140 successful candidates, thirty-three were lawyers, again, the single largest group (twenty-three teachers comprised the second largest group). Finally, lawyers formed the "single largest group in the cabinet" created by Prime Minister K. A. Busia.[33]

During the regime of Colonel (later General) Acheampong, the Ghana Bar Association was among the strongest critics of military rule and the military government's changes in the court system. It became "(after the suppression of the last remnants of a free press) virtually the only body of organized public opinion that was able to voice such criticism in public." In addition, in 1976–1977, the lawyers "played a prominent role" in promoting opposition to the government and organizing a strike of professionals in Ghana during the month of July 1977.[34]

PUBLIC PERCEPTIONS AND THE ROLE OF THE COURTS

Constitutions

After independence, revised constitutions altered the governmental power balance in favor of the executive. Provisions safeguarding fundamental rights may or may not have been amended, but, in practice, the "primacy of the executive" meant that rights and constitutional protections could survive, in most cases, only if the leadership was prepared to honor those ideals.

The 1957 Ghana Constitution did not guarantee fundamental freedoms. Three years later, the writers of the New Republic Constitution only made a "feeble attempt" to protect basic rights, only requiring the president under Article 13, to include in his inaugural oath a "solemn declaration" to protect the fundamental freedoms of all citizens. Such an approach proved to be totally inadequate because, in 1961, the Supreme Court of Ghana held that the oath, in the words of the Court, did "not create legal obligations enforceable by a court of law."[35]

The original Kenya Constitution included a Bill of Rights. Since 1963, however, Parliament has passed various laws that have had the effect of undermining some of these rights. For example, the law requires voluntary associations to register with a government agency in order to function. Denial means that the organization cannot exist legally; however, under the law, there is no right of appeal to the courts from the decision of the appropriate government official. Freedom of association, in short, has lost its constitutional protection. Press freedom is further threatened by Section 52 of the penal code, which "permits a ban on all publications the Minister believes would endanger public order, security, health or morals."[36]

A presidential commission, charged with rewriting the Tanzanian Constitution, considered whether or not to include a bill of rights in the new document. Ultimately, they rejected the suggestion, based on the following reasoning:

A Bill of Right limits in advance of events the measures which Government may take to protect the nation from the threat of subversion and disorder. . . . Constitutional guarantees for the individual will defeat their own purpose if they serve to protect those whose object is to subvert and destroy democracy itself.[37]

The Commission displayed a distrust of the citizenry in general and sought instead to maintain the government's maximum freedom of action.

The chief means by which governments have kept opposition under control has been the use of preventive detention. Most, if not all, African countries have preventive detention laws, which allow the police to detain, without charge or trial, for lengthy periods of time, persons suspected of acting in a manner contrary to the peace, harmony, or safety of the government and the country in general. Usually, the writ of habeas corpus is suspended, and the action of the government cannot be challenged in any court.

Executive power can be exercised in other ways. For example, the president of the Sudan, under a state of emergency declared in April 1984, gave his government the power "to search private homes [without warrants], control transport, and impose . . . censorship." Decrees also banned "strikes, processions, unauthorized public gatherings and demonstrations."[38] Equally ominous are the words and actions reported from Nigeria in the wake of a coup at the very end of 1983. Just after the New Year, the new head of state, General Mohammed Buhari, was quoted on a Lagos radio broadcast as saying that he "would not condone the nonsense of litigation" to prevent him from punishing dishonest government officials. In April 1984, the military government "published a tough new law . . . giving it the power to close newspapers and radio stations and jail journalists. People charged with publishing a false report or any story that puts Government officials in ridicule or disrepute have the burden of proving their innocence. Trial will be by special tribunal . . . and the tribunal's decision will be final." The grounds for closure of newspapers or radio stations (for up to one year) are rather vague—acting in a manner "detrimental to the interest of the federation."[39]

In sum, preambles to constitutions may include "ethical principles" or ideal goals, but either the full documents fall short in the guarantees enshrined within the document, or the government, through legislation and practice, undermines those guarantees that might exist on paper. It is clear, therefore, that the commitment to fundamental freedoms in practice is not as strong as one would anticipate.

Attitudes toward Judicial Independence

The theory of the independence of the judiciary is enshrined in the constitutions of most African countries. To safeguard this independence, various constitutions state that judges cannot be removed from office except for cause, and elaborate procedures have to be followed before a judge can be impeached. The degree to which this theory is honored varies according to particular leaders and the times and may also depend on whether a civilian government or a military government is in power. In addition, men associated with the executive branch have tended to emphasize subordination of the courts and judges to the needs of the political party, the nation (as interpreted by the leaders), or an ideology (such as socialism in Tanzania), rather than to the rule of law.

The president of Mali warned his judges in 1962 that justice was the servant of his government: "the Mali magistrate must not, in the name of an independent judiciary and the separation of powers, lose sight of the fact that he is above all a fighter for the Union Soudanaise; for, with all such fighters, justice—a social institution of the State—is necessarily the servant of the regime which instituted it."[40] A Malawi government white paper further stressed that judicial review is not an approach judges should consider: "the function of a judge is not to question or obstruct the policies of the Executive Government, but to ascertain the purpose of these policies by reference to the laws made by Parliament and fairly and impartially to give effect to those purposes in the courts when required to do so."[41]

Ironically, Kofi Busia, who had barely escaped arrest by the Nkrumah government, retreated from firm support for judicial independence when he had the opportunity in 1969. Commenting on the draft constitution in February of that year, when he believed that he would soon be elected to head a civilian government under the new constitution, he did say that an independent judiciary was necessary; however, he argued that "this idea of sovereignty of the law in practical terms tends to mean the ultimate power tends to be wielded by judges." Busia opposed giving judges such power because they were not elected, and therefore, in his words, not "directly responsible to the people."[42]

Even justices are not consistent advocates for judicial independence. For example, the chief justice of Tanzania is reported to have defended the role of ideology and party policy in affecting court decisions: "since Tanzania believed in ujamaa then, the interest of many people in land cases should over-ride those of some few individuals. The judiciary could not be used as a tool to oppose ujamaa. . . . As citizens and TANU [Tanzania African National Union] members, the courts are duty bound . . . to further ujamaa."[43]

Intellectuals and lawyers may also be divided on the subject. Rude James presented a paper, "Implementing the Arusha Declaration—the Role of the Legal System," to an interdisciplinary seminar sponsored by the Economic Research Bureau at the University of Dar es Salaam. In the preface to the printed paper, James notes that reactions among the seminar participants varied. There was a "consensus on the danger of a society substituting 'expediency' for 'legality'," the main trend in Tanzania since 1967, according to James. However, only a small minority supported the Euro-American concept "that the courts should play the part of a bulwark between the Executive and Party [on the one hand] and the people [on the other hand]."[44] These ideas, even though expressed by a select group of Tanzanians, nevertheless may reflect the attitudes of other educated Africans about the role of the law and the courts in the young nations of Africa.

Judicial Independence in Practice

Before a discussion is presented concerning interference in the judicial system by the executive or the military, a sharp distinction should be made between ordinary civil and criminal cases and cases with political/constitutional implications. Such a distinction is necessary to an understanding of the relationship of the judiciary to the executive in authoritarian political systems. Two important functions of the courts involve dispute settlement and enforcement of the law against "ordinary" crimes. In these instances, there is hardly any evidence of the court system being pressured by civilian or military authoritarian governments.

Then there are the political cases: crimes against the state or the leaders; ill-defined crimes against the people, such as corruption; or "crimes" engendered by efforts of the political opposition to exercise constitutional rights, such as free speech or freedom of assembly. In such cases, the executive branch exploits the legal system for political purposes: to maintain power, extend power, or suppress the opposition. The regular court system may be used by the prosecution. More often, authoritarian leaders have established special tribunals to try such cases. These special courts are extraconstitutional, created to bypass the regular courts and a judiciary sworn to uphold the rule of law. Public trials may or may not be held in these tribunals, the right to counsel is not guaranteed, and the judges may lack legal training. Political interference is apparent from the various examples of an executive ignoring or altering court decisions in political cases if he is displeased with the results. Also, retroactive laws have been passed to overturn a particular decision, and judges not ruling for the government have been dismissed. The judiciary may, in theory, act as protector of rights, but, for political cases, the established courts are usually avoided by government prosecutors who risk failure if they do not discover guilt where none may exist.

Attempts to interfere with the judiciary have taken a variety of forms. James contends that the courts in Tanzania have become subordinate to the government and the dominant political party because of the increasing role of the party in making appointments to the courts of first instance, the large number of judges and magistrates who are members of the party, and the existence of a branch of the party in the High Court. James also reports that "political functionaries" are involved "behind the scene, in the final decisions in cases pending in court."[45]

In one particularly blatant effort at interference with due process and the rights of citizens to seek redress in the courts, in 1969, the second vice-president, R. Kawawa, ordered all courts in Tanzania to stop hearing certain types of land cases, and for those heard, he tried to dictate the decision. However, for technical reasons, the courts were able to ignore Kawawa's order.[46]

Another means of undermining the established courts has been followed in a small number of countries where "people's" courts have been created, staffed by persons from neighborhoods or by leaders and members of the only political party. These have existed for many years in Guinea and were recently established in Ghana in 1982 by the Rawlings government.

Otuteye emphasizes the "subordination" of the Supreme Court to the president of the Ivory Coast and the president of the National Assembly on constitutional issues. Furthermore, he notes that although the Conseil Supérieur de la Magistrature is a constitutional body, it includes representatives from the executive branch, which he believes is a "further breach in the separation of powers." In addition, Otuteye points out that judges are appointed, not as constitutional officers, but under statute law. Thus, Ivory Coast judges "enjoy little constitutional protection," especially since rules concerning the removal of judges are not included in the constitution. Therefore, the appointment, status, and promotion of judges, although regulated by law, depends on the president for implementation, and the opportunity for executive encroachment against the judiciary is great. Otuteye, finally, asks the all-important question: Is the Ivory Coast Constitution (and, by extension, the constitutions of other African states) just paying "lip-service to the [ideas of] separation of powers and the independence of the judiciary?"[47]

Political power seems to affect the leader's vision and judgment. During the early 1960s, K. A. Busia watched the Nkrumah government undermine the courts and the rule of law in Ghana, including various attacks on the structure of the judiciary and against judges as well. Yet, in 1969, under a restored parliamentary system of government, the Busia administration, angered over a court decision, attacked the integrity of the judges involved. This occurred at a time when the prime minister, under the new Constitution, was entrusted with the responsibility to appoint judges to the new Supreme Court in consultation with the Judicial Council. The appointments, when announced, appeared tainted by political considerations and were perceived as an effort to subordinate the judges of the Supreme Court to the will of the executive. The result was that the Judicial Council's independence was discredited and the image of this new, "democratic" government was tarnished early in Busia's administration.[48]

The worst examples of attack on the integrity and independence of the judiciary can be found in Ghana and Uganda. The rule of law "suffered most in Ghana where latterly the Nkrumah regime displayed a neurotic suspicion of the law, lawyers and, above all, judges, who were regarded as innately subversive of the CPP [Convention People's Party]."[49] On the one hand, the government mistakenly received judicial support when the constitutionality of the Preventive Detention Act was challenged in the case Re Akoto. Dankwa and Flinterman believe that the judges feared reprisals and thus construed the applicable constitutional clauses very narrowly because a ruling against the government, "a decision to the effect that all those detained under the [Preventive Detention Act] had been detained illegally would have invited a sharp reaction from the executive."[50]

On the other hand, in 1963, alleged conspirators, charged with plotting to assassinate President Nkrumah, were tried by a *special* court, presided over by Chief Justice Kobina Arku Korsah and two other judges (W. B. van Lare and E. Akufo Addo). The court acquitted three of the major defendants. The Nkrumah government responded in a vindictive manner. Two days after the decision was announced, President Nkrumah dismissed the chief justice. The Parliament, under the control of the Convention People's Party, the only legal political party at the time, nullified the decision by an act of Parliament, and the defendants were tried again by another special court. A jury trial was allowed, but the system for choosing jurors virtually guaranteed the result: conviction. Also, the judge was allowed no discretion in his approach to the evidence or instructions to the jury. The formality of a court trial was adhered to, but respect for the rule of law was trampled upon. Finally, a constitutional amendment gave the president the right to dismiss judges at will.[51] One result was that between 1964 and 1966 no court decision went against the wishes of the Ghana government. In addition, Ghanaian lawyers refused to represent members of the opposition in cases with political overtones.[52] Thus, in Ghana, the independence of the judiciary was submerged to the interests of the state and security of tenure for judges eliminated. It is ironic that at independence the government selected the phrase "Freedom and Justice" as the motto of Ghana.

The principle of judicial independence in Uganda was also challenged in the late 1960s, resulting in a state of tension between the judiciary and the government of President Milton Obote even before the fateful seizure of power by General Amin. In July 1968, a member of the president's staff, Picho Ali, published an article in the periodical, *Transition* (vol. 7, no. 36), asking questions about the concept of judicial independence and suggesting a more ideological commitment on the part of judges to the direction that the government was taking. A number of letters appeared in the next issue of *Transition* (vol. 7, no. 37, October 1968), criticizing the article and its author, including a letter from an opposition member of Parliament, A. K. Mayanja. The Uganda government charged the editor and Mr. Mayanja with sedition.[53] The defendants were found not guilty by the presiding magistrate. The government, however, continued to detain the two men, and *Transition* did not appear again for several years.[54]

While the events that occurred in Ghana and Uganda, especially under General Amin, have received a great amount of publicity, such severe actions are unusual on the African continent. Violence against judicial officials has not been the norm. The threat to judicial independence is (and has been) real and the ability of the executive to manipulate the judicial system and influence the outcome of trials is substantial. However, the consensus among scholars is that strong action against most judges has not been necessary because judges have been cautious, "passive," or, in the words of one critic, "supine in their posture toward laws challenged on constitutional grounds." Seidman futher suggests that the democratic system has failed in Africa "in part from the weaknesses of the courts in protecting fundamental freedoms."[55] James points to the conflict facing judges in Tanzania, who must consider the proclaimed socialist goals of Tanzanian society that are embodied in the Arusha Declaration, on the one hand, and the rule of law, which they are sworn to uphold, on the other.[56] Pfeiffer concludes that, in Kenya, although there exists the foundation "for an active judicial role in the constitutional life of the country, . . . the *inclination* to exercise the authority inherent in its constitutional charter seems to have not been present."[57]

To a degree, this timidity can be blamed on the general political condition of "executive authoritarianism." In addition, the language of certain laws or constitutional provisions may be sufficiently ambiguous so that judges, interpreting narrowly, can justify ruling in favor of government and against individual freedom.[58] Courts, having little public backing, lack a sufficiently strong constituency to support them in a conflict with the executive. Public opinion cannot be mobilized to defend the courts, and the press, usually under government control, can be used by the executive branch to stir the population to hostility. In addition, since the executive and the legislature are always closely aligned, courts can be isolated by and from the other branches of government.[59] Thus, it is almost a truism that the courts in Africa "have little political voice or physical force to employ in their own promotion or defense," and courts of appeal "have been singularly ineffective sentinels to protect the freedoms that purported to underlay African political systems."[60]

Support for the courts from other institutions has not been easily mobilized. The media in most countries is firmly under government control. Press freedom is, consequently, very limited, and the courts are unable to protect the freedom of the press "without in the long run additionally jeopardizing their *own tenuous freedom* from government interference."[61] Lawyers can also be intimidated. Lawyers in Uganda under Amin were so thoroughly cowed by the regime that they did not speak out. The Ghana Bar Association has been most vigorous in its opposition to authoritarianism after the overthrow of Kwame Nkrumah, but it still was unable, by itself, to prevent the political instability that has spawned at least three coups d'etat since 1966. In short, it is a very difficult road for judges (or lawyers) to follow in order to maintain the independence of the judiciary, and great courage is required of judges who are prepared to base their decisions in politically charged cases exclusively on the rule of law.

Military governments are also a fact of life in Africa. Thus, the following questions must be considered: What happens to the courts when the soldiers take over and suspend the constitution? Is there greater respect for the judiciary from military officers leading a country? In short, are the courts safer under military rule?

On one level, the courts exist at the sufferance of military governments that assume both executive and legislative functions at the time of their coups d'etat, and thus, rule by decree. The courts, generally, are unable or forbidden to question or overrule decrees. In some countries, for example Nigeria and Ghana, the courts actually function as a result of the promulgation of decrees concerning the operation of the courts and the law that is still in force.[62] Military governments also used their power to establish special courts to bypass the regular judiciary. The first Rawlings government in 1979 held hasty trials before special military tribunals and condemned several former Ghanaian government officials to death. After Lt. Rawling's second coup d'etat, his government created so-called people's courts, which have disrupted the judicial system. Consequently, almost unlimited power in reference to the courts rests with the military governments. The military in Benin in 1968, "haughtily overrode the Supreme Court's objections that the unilateral decision to disqualify candidates was patently illegal under the newly ratified constitution."[63]

However, these examples are the exceptions. Many times, one of the main reasons given for military takeover is that the civilian government interfered in judicial affairs. Thus, the military might become the protector of an independent judiciary. To my knowledge, no military government has eliminated the court system entirely; rather, the courts are often the part of government least disturbed and, together with the civil service, usually allowed to continue to pursue their particular task. In addition, since there is no longer a constitution to interpret (the chief source of friction between the courts and civilian governments), the opportunity for clashes is reduced, especially when the courts are forbidden to evaluate decrees. The record, therefore, suggests that the judiciary is no worse off under military governments and may, in fact, be more secure under military governments than under civilian authoritarian governments.

CONCLUSION

Why do African executives fear an independent judiciary? Civilian African leaders have declined, with but four recent exceptions, to voluntarily give up political office. As a result, political opposition has not been tolerated and contested elections for the office of the presidency and sometimes for parliamentary seats have not been allowed. Many African leaders have had an almost messianic belief in their abilities to lead their nations. They have a firm conviction that only they can succeed in bringing unity, success, and true nationhood to their countries. Thus, political and legal actions have been taken to protect power and to prevent opposition to government policies. An independent judiciary, evaluating cases strictly on the basis of the evidence, may appear to defend, support, or sanction the actions of opponents of the government attempting to exercise their constitutional rights of free speech, free press, and freedom of assembly. Acceptance of the right of habeas corpus would prevent the government from incarcerating opponents perceived to be a threat to power but who have not broken the law. In short, an independent judiciary, acting as the protector of constitutional rights, might prevent a government from using the legal system to retain power.

Is it reasonable to expect governments in non-Western countries to follow the Western democratic beliefs in the separation of powers and respect for the independence of the judiciary? In short, by what standards should we judge African governments after only about twenty-five years of independence? It is true that African leaders grew up under colonial governments that were authoritarian in nature and that used the judicial system to enforce the power of the colonial regime. It is also true that most of the major African leaders were educated in the democratic countries of France, England, or the United States and have studied and lived, however briefly, under governments where the principle of an independent judiciary is enshrined in the constitutions or practice of those governments. The constitutions of most of the African nations continue to accept that principle and most governments also accept the hierarchy of courts inherited from the former colonial power. No country within the purview of this chapter has adopted the legal system of the Communist countries on the Soviet Union/Eastern European model. Thus, we can evaluate the events of the past twenty-five years on the basis of the functioning of a system of law that is understood in the Western world. The nations of Africa can, for analytical purposes, be held to the same standards that we apply to the legal systems in the Western world. By those standards, African leaders have failed to live up to the ideals of the nationalist movements of the 1950s and to the basic principles and fundamental rights written into their constitutions.

Are the legal systems in African nations effective and respected branches of government? Robert Seidman believes that most Africans do not turn to the legal system ''as a buttress for the Rule of Law [because] . . . they have neither the literacy nor the sophistication required to invoke law as a protector of fundamental rights."[64] Some governments may also be giving greater emphasis to the law enforcement role of the legal system, as might be seen from the Kenya statistics cited earlier. In addition, the press does not help to build up or improve the image of the courts, especially when campaigns of vilification are engineered by the executive against judges or the courts after unpopular decisions are handed down. Also, reporters may not have an adequate knowledge of legal proceedings and legal language to properly report court decisions and thus distort the results of a particular decision.[65] The courts, because of the pressures of the executive or the timidity of the judges, may not be perceived as independent branches of government. Evidence presented herein also suggests that the formal courts are not the chief avenues used for dispute settlement in many countries. Thus, the conclusion at the moment is that the courts have not developed the respect necessary for them to effectively resist the pressures of the government and are not fully recognized for the important potential they have in the society.

A.N.E. Amissah, a former Ghanaian judge, maintains that "until the people develop values to guide their courts, other than that of upholding state power, the constitutional enactment of the separation of powers is bound to remain largely a declaration of intent."[66] Nevertheless, it should be emphasized that even authoritarians make use of courts and wish to be perceived as upholding the law. Luckham emphasizes this point when he writes that "it is precisely because legality is valued, because men and governments would like the authoritative decisions by the courts to favour them—be it by protecting their rights or extending their powers—that the pressures put on the courts are so powerful."[67] Thus, in contemporary Africa the principle of the rule of law prevails; it is implementation of that principle that is imperfect.

NOTES

The author wishes to gratefully thank the following for their contributions to this effort: J.C.N. Paul and Neville Rubin were very helpful in suggesting resources at the beginning of my research; Marion Doro, Jon Macey, James Paul, and Robert Seidman read drafts and contributed very useful recommendations for improvements; the editor, Alan Katz, aided the process in innumerable ways, not the least of which was his amiable and flexible approach to this whole effort. Though ultimate responsibility is mine, this chapter is a better product because of their assistance.

1. R. Young, "Legal Systems Development," in J. Paden and E. Soja, eds., *The African Experience* (Evanston, Ill.: Northwestern University Press, 1970), pp. 486–87; L. Rosen, "Law and Social Change in the New Nations," *Comparative Studies in Society and History* 20, no. 1 (January 1978), p. 5, n. 3.

2. A. N. Allott, "Discussing African Law," in Law Faculty, University of Ife, ed., *Integration of Customary and Modern Legal Systems in Africa* (Ile-Ife: University of Ife Press, 1971), p. 7.

3. J. F. Scotton, "Judicial Independence and Political Expression in East Africa— Two Colonial Legacies," *East Africa Law Journal* 6, no. 1 (March 1970), p. 87.

4. C. B. Rhyne, ed., *Law and Judicial Systems of Nations* (Washington: World Peace Through Law Center, 1978), p. 862.

5. J. W. Salacuse, *An Introduction to Law in French-Speaking Africa, I: Africa South of the Sahara* (Charlottesville, Virginia: Michie Co., 1969), p. 121.

6. Rhyne, *Law and Judicial Systems*, p. 882.

7. Ibid.

8. Ibid.

9. L. Linossler, "Ivory Coast," *International Encyclopedia of Comparative Law*, vol. 1 (Rockville, Md.: Sijthoff & Noordhoff, 1973), pp. I–117–24.

10. Rhyne, *Law and Judicial Systems*, p. 300.

11. In Ghana, length of service as a lawyer determines eligibility for various levels of judgeships: court of appeals judge, fifteen years standing as a member of the bar; High Court judge, ten years; circuit court judge, six years; district court, Grade I Magistrate, three years. J. Daniels, "Ghana," *International Encyclopedia of Comparative Law*, vol. 1 (Rockville, Md.: Sijthoff & Noordhoff, 1978), p. G–35.

12. Members of the Zambia Judicial Service Commission are: the chief justice (chairman), one judge of the High Court, the chairman of the Public Service Commission, and a presidential appointee (either a judge or a former judge). I. Kaplan, ed., *Zambia: A Country Study* (Washington: U.S. Government Printing Office, 1979), p. 136.

13.

Judges of the Highest Court	*Judges of Other Courts*
Cameroon 10	
Ghana at least 7	Court of appeal, at least 5; high court, at least 12
Ivory Coast 13	
Kenya 5	
Nigeria 12–16	Federal court of appeal, 12
Senegal 10	
Sierra Leone 5	Court of Appeal, 8; High Court, 11
Tanzania 5	High Court, 18
Uganda 3	High Court, 9
Zambia 5	High Court, approx. 12

Sources: *Africa South of the Sahara, 1983–1984* (London: Europa Publishing Co., 1983); Linossier, "Ivory Coast," p. I–119; Rhyne, *Law and Judicial Systems*, p. 630; Daily Times, *Nigeria Year Book, 1984* (Lagos: Nigerian Printing and Publishing Co., 1984).

14. *Zambia Law Directory and Calendar* (Lusaka: Gov't Printer, 1974).

15. *Africa South of the Sahara.*

16. R. B. Seidman, "Law, Development, and Legislative Drafting in English-Speaking Africa," *Journal of Modern African Studies* 19, no. 1 (1981), pp. 133–34. Seidman cites the language used in Zambia's Co-operative Societies Ordinance of 1961, which included obscure and useless words, but concerned ordinary farmers in that country.

17. See P. Sevareid, "The Work of Rural Primary Courts in Ghana and Kenya," *African Law Studies* 13 (1976), pp. 145–54. Sevareid notes, in addition, that the magistrate with whom he was talking admitted that the "Masai were reluctant to use his court for

their personal legal disputes." Dankwa and Flinterman suggest that constitutional cases in Ghana are small in number as a result of the following: (1) ignorance of rights and a populace that does not consider turning to a court of law for remedies; (2) fear of retaliation by administrative officials; (3) cost; and (4) legal complexities. E.V.O. Dankwa and C. Flinterman, "Judicial Review in Ghana," *University of Ghana Law Journal* 14, no. 1 (1977), pp. 5, 7. See also W.C. Ekow Daniels, "Individual Liberty and Police Powers to Regulate Public Law and Order," *Review of Ghana Law* 9, no. 3 (December 1977), p. 231, where he refers to a lack of knowledge about methods to ensure constitutional rights.

18. Ross believes that, as of 1973, "the reality of the situation is that the informal methods of dispute settlement . . . are still an important part of the legal structure in East Africa." S. D. Ross, "A Comparative Study of the Legal Profession in East Africa," *Journal of African Law* 17, no. 3 (1973), p. 290; Rwelamira further suggests that changes in the Tanzania Primary Courts "have drawn Africans closer to the formal legal system than they used to be in colonial times." M.R.K. Rwelamira, "The Tanzanian Legal Profession," in C. J. Dias et al., eds., *Lawyers in the Third World: Comparative and Developmental Perspectives* (Uppsala and New York: Scandinavian Institute of African Studies, 1984), p. 212; L. Rosen, "Law and Social Change," p. 10.

19. J. Griffiths, "On Teaching Law in Ghana and Related Matters," *Law Center Bulletin* 21, no. 1 (1974), pp. 12, 13. See also R. Luckham, "Imperialism, Law and Structural Dependence: The Ghana Legal Profession," in C. J. Dias et al., eds., *Lawyers in the Third World*, pp. 110–11.

20. T. Jackson, *Guide to the Legal Profession in East Africa* (London: Sweet and Maxwell, 1970), p. 25.

21. The latest approximate figures for the number of lawyers in various African nations are: Cameroon—100 (1966); Chad—3 (1977); Gabon—13 (1977); Ghana—1,225 (1982); Ivory Coast—100 (1966); Kenya—900 (1982); Malawi—60 (1972); Nigeria—2,000 (1982); Senegal—38 (1972); Sierra Leone—80 in private practice (1977); Tanzania—250 (1976); Upper Volta—4 (1977); Zambia—250 members of bar association (unspecified larger number of lawyers) (1982); See Rhyne, *Law and Judicial Systems*, R. Abel, "The Underdevelopment of Legal Professions: A Review Article on Third World Lawyers," *American Bar Foundation Research Journal* 3 (Summer 1982), pp. 871–93; American Bar Foundation, *International Directory of Bar Associations* (Chicago: American Bar Foundation, 1967, 1973, 1983).

22. Rwelamira, "Tanzanian Legal Profession," pp. 211, 222; R. Luckham, "The Market for Legal Services in Ghana," *Review of Ghana Law* 8, no. 1 (1976), pp. 14–16; Ross, "Legal Profession in East Africa," p. 280, n. 5.

23. Ibid., p. 281.

24. Rwelamira, "Tanzanian Legal Profession," p. 216; also, A. Odenyo, "Statements of Some Findings of the Research on the Legal Profession in Kenya," unpublished paper presented at the International Legal Center, October 25–27, 1976, p. 18. Odenyo states lawyers "do not restrict their work to the office setting but make contacts and dispense legal advice in a variety of settings." See also B. D. Houghton, "Women Lawyers in Ghana," in C. J. Dias et al., eds., *Lawyers in the Third World*.

25. For example, 46 percent of Ghanaian lawyers spend over 40 percent of their time on land and customary law cases. See Luckham, "Imperialism, Law and Structural Dependence: The Ghana Legal Profession," in Dias et al., *Lawyers in the Third World*,

p. 104; also A. Odenyo, "Professionalism and Change: the Emergent Kenyan Lawyer," in C. J. Dias et al., eds., *Lawyers in the Third World*, p. 191.

26. A. Odenyo, "Professionalization Amidst Change: The Case of the Emerging Legal Profession in Kenya," *African Studies Review* 22, no. 3 (1979), p. 37.

27. R. Abel, "The Underdevelopment of Legal Professions," pp. 876–77.

28. Ross, "Legal Profession in East Africa."

29. Odenyo, "Legal Profession in Kenya," p. 37; Luckham, "Imperialism, Law and Structural Dependence," in C.J. Dias et al., eds., *Lawyers in the Third World*, p. 106; Y. P. Ghai, "Law and Lawyers in Kenya and Tanzania: Some Political Economy Considerations," in C.J. Dias et al., eds., *Lawyers in the Third World*, p. 160. A member of the Kenya Parliament, Martin Shikuku, was quoted in *The Daily Nation*, March 29, 1974: "African lawyers should not be in a hurry to get rich, but should make sacrifices to enable the government to Africanise the judiciary which is a vital institution." Quoted in Odenyo, "Professionalism and Change," in C.J. Dias et al., eds., *Lawyers in the Third World*, p. 203.

30. Ibid., p. 191.

31. Rwelamira, "The Tanzanian Legal Profession," pp. 214–15 and table on p. 216; Abel, "The Underdevelopment of Legal Professions."

32. B. D. Houghton, "The Position of Women Lawyers in Ghana," unpublished paper presented to the International Legal Center, October 25, 1976, Table I; B. D. Houghton, "Women Lawyers in Ghana," in Dias et al., eds., *Lawyers in the Third World*, Tables 5, 7.

33. R. Luckham, "The Constitutional Commission"; R. Luckham and S. Nkrumah, "The Constituent Assembly"; and Y. Twumasi, "The 1969 Election," in D. Austin and R. Luckham, eds., *Politicians and Soldiers in Ghana* (London: Cass Publishers, 1975), pp. 81–83, 92, 96, 121, 144–45; and Luckham, "Imperialism, Law and Structural Dependence," in C.J. Dias et al., eds., *Lawyers and the Third World*, p. 96.

34. Luckham, "The Ghana Legal Profession," p. 98; D. Rothchild, "Military Regime Performance: An Appraisal of the Ghana Experience, 1972–1978," *Comparative Politics* 12, no. 4 (July 1980), p. 463.

35. Ekow Daniels, "Individual Liberty," p. 229.

36. Rosen, "Law and Social Change," p. 13.

37. T. G. Verhelst and Z. B. Plater, "Constitutional Guarantees of the Individual," in T.G. Verhelst, ed., *Legal Process and the Individual: African Source Materials* (Addis Ababa: Center for African Legal Development, 1971), p. 21.

38. "Sudan Leader Invokes Sweeping Powers," *New York Times*, May 1, 1984, p. 8.

39. "Nigerian General Delivers Warning"; "Tough Journalism Law is Published by Nigeria"; "Nigerian Military is Seen as Losing Support," *New York Times*, January 3, 1984, p. 5; April 18, 1984, p. 3; May 1, 1984, p. 11.

40. Quoted in M. Alliot, "The Role of Justice in the Application of Law in the Francophone States of Africa," in Law Faculty, University of Ife, ed., *Integration of Customary and Modern Legal Systems in Africa* (Ile-Ife: University of Ife Press, 1971), p. 82.

41. *Malawi White Paper 002*, no. 20, 1965, cited in Rosen, "Law and Social Change," p. 14n.

42. Quoted in Luckham and Nkrumah, "The Constituent Assembly," p. 97.

43. "Put Ujamaa First," *Daily News*, September 26, 1972, quoted in R. W. James,

"Implementing the Arusha Declaration—the Role of the Legal System," *African Review* 3, no. 2 (1973), p. 182.

44. Ibid., p. 179.

45. Ibid., p. 192; also pp. 180, 187, 189, 193–94. James also refers to "continuing and increasing infringement of the State and Party functionaries in the actual decision making process of the courts." However, enigmatically, he writes: "in order to avoid embarrassment, I have avoided details of this phenomenon." P. 192n.

46. Ibid., pp. 187, 189. Because of certain considerations, including legislative inaction, the courts disregarded Kawawa's order, "the attempted embargo on the courts being quietly ignored."

47. S. C. Otuteye, "Constitutional Innovation in French West Africa—the Experience of Guinea and the Ivory Coast," *University of Ghana Law Journal* 10, no. 1 (1973), pp. 24, 26.

48. A.N.E. Amissah, "The Role of the Judiciary in the Governmental Process: Ghana's Experience," *African Law Studies* 13 (1976), p. 18.

49. L.C.B. Gower, *Independent Africa: The Challenge to the Legal Profession* (Cambridge: Harvard University Press, 1967), p. 79.

50. Dankwa and Flinterman, "Judicial Review in Ghana," p. 43.

51. Ibid., p. 43, n. 76; Amissah, "Role of the Judiciary," pp. 14-15; J. S. Bainbridge, *The Study and Teaching of Law in Africa* (South Hackensack, New Jersey: Rothman, 1972), p. 35.

52. Amissah, "Role of the Judiciary," p. 16.

53. *Uganda v. Mayanja, Neogy, and Consolidated Printers, Ltd.*, Criminal Case No. MMV 7995 of 1968.

54. J. F. Scotton, "Judicial Independence and Political Expression in East Africa—Two Colonial Legacies," *East African Law Journal* 6, no. 1 (March 1970), pp. 1, 18. By early 1970, the editor had been released but Mayanja remained in detention.

55. R. B. Seidman, "Judicial Review and Fundamental Freedoms in Anglophonic Independent Africa," *Ohio State Law Journal* 35, no. 4 (1974), pp. 820, 824–25.

56. R. W. James, "Implementing the Arusha Declaration," p. 180.

57. S. B. Pfeiffer, "Notes on the Role of the Judiciary in the Constitutional Systems of East Africa Since Independence," *Case Western Reserve Journal of International Law* 10, no. 1 (Winter 1978), p. 36. Emphasis added.

58. Seidman, "Judicial Review," pp. 827, 840, 849–50.

59. Amissah, "Role of the Judiciary," pp. 18–21.

60. Pfeiffer, "Notes," pp. 52–53; Seidman, "Judicial Review," p. 850.

61. Scotton, "Judicial Independence," p. 19. Emphasis added.

62. T. O. Elias, *The Judicial Process in Commonwealth Africa* (Legon: University of Ghana, 1977), pp. 99ff, 101. In *Awunor-Williams v. Gbedemah*, December 8, 1969, a Ghana court included this statement in its decision: "judicial power was exercised by the Courts during the era of the National Liberation Council on sufferance. . . . No Decree which was passed by the National Liberation Council could have been struck down by the Courts as unconstitutional." See also R. B. Turkson, "The Survival of the Fundamental Human Rights Provisions of the 1969 Constitution," *Review of Ghana Law* 8, no. 3 (December 1976); Dankwa and Flinterman, "Judicial Review In Ghana," p. 30, n.41; 31; and A. Obilade, *The Nigerian Legal System* (London: Sweet and Maxwell, 1978), p. 46.

63. S. Decalo, *Coups and Army Rule in Africa: Studies in Military Style* (New Haven: Yale University Press, 1976), p. 66.

64. Personal Communication, December 7, 1984.

65. A.N.E. Amissah, *The Contribution of the Courts to Government: A West African View* (Oxford: Clarendon Press, 1981), p. 367.

66. Amissah, "Role of the Judiciary," p. 21.

67. R. Luckham, "The Administration of Justice," *Review of Ghana Law* 9, no. 3 (December 1977), pp. 227–28.

BIBLIOGRAPHY

Abel, R. "The Underdevelopment of Legal Professions: A Review Article on Third World Lawyers." *American Bar Foundation Research Journal* 3 (Summer 1982), pp. 871–93.

Africa South of the Sahara. London: Europa Publications Ltd., 1978, 1983.

Aguda, T. K. "The Role of the Judge with Special Reference to Civil Liberties." *East African Law Journal* 10, no. 2 (1974), pp. 147–63.

Alliot, M. "The Role of Justice in the Application of Law in the Francophone States of Africa." In Law Faculty, University of Ife, ed., *Integration of Customary and Modern Legal Systems in Africa.* Ile-Ife: University of Ife Press, 1971. Pp. 74–83.

Allott, A. N. "Discussing African Law." In Law Faculty, University of Ife, ed., *Integration of Customary and Modern Legal Systems in Africa.* Ile-Ife: University of Ife Press, 1971. Pp. 86–91.

———. *Judicial and Legal Systems in Africa*, 2d ed. London: Butterworths, 1970.

American Bar Foundation. *International Directory of Bar Associations.* Chicago: American Bar Foundation, 1967, 1973, 1983.

Amissah, A.N.E. *The Contribution of the Courts to Government: A West African View.* Oxford: Clarendon Press, 1981.

———. "The Role of the Judiciary in the Governmental Process: Ghana's Experience." *African Law Studies* 13 (1976), pp. 4–28.

Bainbridge, J. S. *The Study and Teaching of Law in Africa.* South Hackensack, N.J.: Rothman Publishers, 1972.

Bentsi-Enchill, K., "The Lawyer's Calling in Africa." *Zambia Law Journal* 3–4, nos. 1–2 (1972), pp. 5–15.

Bringer, P. "The Abiding Influence of English and French Criminal Law in One African Country: Some Remarks Regarding the Machinery of Criminal Justice in Cameroon." *Journal of African Law* 25, no. 1 (Spring 1981), pp. 1–13.

Daily Times. *Nigeria Year Book, 1984.* Lagos: Nigerian Printing and Publishing Co., 1984.

Dankwa, E.V.O., and C. Flinterman. "Judicial Review in Ghana." *University of Ghana Law Journal* 14, no. 1 (1977), pp. 1–44.

Decalo, S. *Coups and Army Rule in Africa: Studies in Military Style.* New Haven: Yale University Press, 1976.

Dias, C. J., and J.C.N. Paul. "Lawyers, Legal Professions, Modernization and Development." In C. J. Dias et al., eds., *Lawyers in the Third World: Comparative and Developmental Perspectives.* Uppsala and New York: Scandinavian Institute of African Studies, 1981. Pp. 11–25.

Ekow Daniels, W. C. "Individual Liberty and Police Powers to Regulate Public Law and Order." *Review of Ghana Law* 9, no. 3 (December 1977), pp. 229–53.

Elias, T.O. *The Judicial Process in Commonwealth Africa.* Legon: University of Ghana Press, 1977.

——— . *Law in a Developing Society.* Lagos: University of Lagos Press, 1969.

Ghai, Y.P. "Law and Lawyers in Kenya and Tanzania: Some Political Economy Considerations." In C. J. Dias, R. Luckham, D.O. Lynch, and J.C.N. Paul, eds., *Lawyers in the Third World: Comparative and Developmental Perspectives.* Uppsala and New York: Scandinavian Institute of African Studies, 1981. Pp. 144-76.

——— . "Legal Education in Kenya and Tanzania." In A. Bockel et al., eds., *Legal Education in Africa South of the Sahara.* Brussels: E. Bruylant, 1979. Pp. 261-82.

Gower, L.C.B. *Independent Africa: The Challenge to the Legal Profession.* Cambridge, Mass.: Harvard University Press, 1967.

Griffiths, J. "On Teaching Law in Ghana and Related Matters." *Law Center Bulletin* 21, no. 1 (1974), pp. 4–28.

Gyimah-Boadi, E., and D. Rothchild. "Rawlings, Populism, and the Civil Liberties Tradition in Ghana." *Issue* 12, nos. 3–4 (1982), pp. 64–69.

Harvey, W. B., ed. *Introduction to the Legal System in East Africa.* Kampala: East African Literature Bureau, 1975.

Houghton, B. D. "The Position of Women Lawyers in Ghana." Unpublished paper presented to the International Legal Center, October 25, 1976.

——— . "Women Lawyers in Ghana." In C. J. Dias et al., eds., *Lawyers in the Third World: Comparative and Developmental Perspectives.* Uppsala and New York: Scandinavian Institute of African Studies, 1981. Pp. 123–43.

Hutchison, T. W., et al., eds. *Africa and Law: Developing Legal Systems in African Commonwealth Nations.* Madison: University of Wisconsin Press, 1968.

Jackson, T. *Guide to the Legal Profession in East Africa.* London: Sweet and Maxwell, 1970.

James, R. W. "Implementing the Arusha Declaration—the Role of the Legal System." *African Review* 3, no. 2 (1973), pp. 179–208.

Jearey, J. H. "Trial by Jury and Trial with the Aid of Assessors in the Superior Courts of British African Territories." *Journal of African Law*, Part I, IV, 3 (1960), pp. 133–46; Part II, V, 1 (1961), pp. 36–47; Part 3, V, 2 (1961), pp. 82–98.

Kaunda, K. "The Functions of the Lawyer in Zambia Today." *Zambia Law Journal* 3–4, nos. 1–2 (1971–1972), pp. 1–4.

Keuning, J. "Some Remarks on Law and Courts in Africa." In Law Faculty, University of Ife, ed., *Integration of Customary and Modern Legal Systems in Africa.* Ile-Ife: University of Ife Press, 1971. Pp. 58–71.

Kludze, A.K.P. "The Jury and the Burden of Proof." *University of Ghana Law Journal* 14, no. 1 (1977), pp. 55–80.

Levasseur, A. A. *The Civil Code of the Ivory Coast.* Charlottesville, Va.: Michie Co., 1976.

Luckham, R. "The Administration of Justice." *Review of Ghana Law* 9, no. 3 (December 1977), pp. 190–228.

——— . "The Constitutional Commission." In D. Austin and R. Luckham, eds., *Politicians and Soldiers in Ghana.* London: Cass Publishers, 1975. Pp. 62–88.

——— . "Imperialism, Law and Structural Dependence: The Ghana Legal Profession."

In C. J. Dias, R. Luckham, D. O. Lynch, and J.C.N. Paul, eds., *Lawyers in the Third World: Comparative and Developmental Perspectives*. Uppsala and New York: Scandinavian Institute of African Studies, 1981. Pp. 90–122.

———— . "The Market for Legal Services in Ghana." *Review of Ghana Law* 8, no. 1 (1976), pp. 7–27.

Luckham R., and S. Nkrumah. "The Constituent Assembly." In D. Austin and R. Luckham, eds., *Politicians and Soldiers in Ghana*. London: Cass Publishers, 1975. Pp. 89–125.

Mundt, R. J. "The Internalization of Law in a Developing Country: The Ivory Coast's Civil Code." *African Law Studies* 12 (1975), pp. 60–101.

Obilade, A. *The Nigerian Legal System*. London: Sweet and Maxwell, 1979.

Odenyo, A. "Professionalization Amidst Change: The Case of the Emerging Legal Profession in Kenya." *African Studies Review* 22, no. 3 (1979), pp. 33–44.

———— . "Professionalism and Change: the Emergent Kenyan Lawyer." In C. J. Dias, R. Luckham, D. O. Lynch, and J.C.N. Paul, eds., *Lawyers in the Third World: Comparative and Developmental Perspectives*. Uppsala and New York: Scandinavian Institute of African Studies, 1981. Pp. 177–203.

———— . "Statements of Some Findings of the Research on the Legal Profession in Kenya." Unpublished paper presented at the International Legal Center, October 25–27, 1976.

Ollennu, N. M. "The Influence of English Law on West Africa." *Journal of African Law* 5, no. 1 (1961), pp. 21–35.

Otuteye, S. C. "Constitutional Innovation in French West Africa—the Experience of Guinea and the Ivory Coast." *University of Ghana Law Journal* 10, 1 (1973), pp. 16–35.

Pfeiffer, S. B. "Notes on the Role of the Judiciary in the Constitutional Systems of East Africa since Independence." *Case Western Reserve Journal of International Law* 10, no. 1 (Winter 1978), pp. 11–53.

Rhyne, C. S., ed. *Law and Judicial Systems of Nations*. Washington: World Peace Through Law Center, 1978.

Rosen, L. "Law and Social Change in the New Nations." *Comparative Studies in Society and History* 20, no. 1 (January 1978), pp. 3–28.

Ross, S. D. "A Comparative Study of the Legal Profession in East Africa." *Journal of African Law* 17, no. 3 (1973), pp. 279–97.

Rothchild, D. "Military Regime Performance: An Appraisal of the Ghana Experience, 1972–1978." *Comparative Politics* 12, no. 4 (July 1980), pp. 459–79.

Rwelamira, M.R.K. "The Tanzanian Legal Profession." In C. J. Dias, R. Luckham, D.O. Lynch, and J.C.N. Paul, eds. *Lawyers in the Third World: Comparative and Developmental Perspectives*. Uppsala and New York: Scandinavian Institute of African Studies, 1981. Pp. 204–25.

Salacuse, J. W. *An Introduction to Law in French-Speaking Africa, I: Africa South of the Sahara*. Charlottesville, Virginia: Michie Co., 1969.

Scotton, J. F. "Judicial Independence and Political Expression in East Africa—Two Colonial Legacies." *East African Law Journal* 6, no. 1 (March 1970), pp. 1–19.

Seidman, R. B. "Judicial Review and Fundamental Freedoms in Anglophonic Independent Africa." *Ohio State Law Journal* 35, no. 4 (1974), pp. 820–50.

———— . "The Reception of English Law in Colonial Africa Revisited." *Eastern Africa Law Review* 2, no. 1 (April 1969), pp. 47–85.

————— . "Law, Development, and Legislative Drafting in English-Speaking Africa." *Journal of Modern African Studies* 19, no. 1 (1981), pp. 133–61.

————— . *Research in African Law and the Processes of Change.* Los Angeles: African Studies Center, University of California, 1967.

Sevareid, P. "The Work of Rural Primary Courts in Ghana and Kenya." *African Law Studies* 13 (1976), pp. 145–54.

Turkson, R. B. "The Survival of the Fundamental Human Rights Provisions of the 1969 Constitution." *Review of Ghana Law* 8, no. 3 (December 1976), pp. 223–31.

Verhelst, T. G. "The Judiciary in Africa." In T. G. Verhelst, ed., *Legal Process and the Individual: African Source Material.* Addis Ababa: Centre for African Legal Development, 1971. Pp. 123–51.

————— , and Z. B. Plater. "Constitutional Guarantees of the Individual." In T. G. Verhelst, ed., *Legal Process and the Individual: African Source Materials.* Addis Ababa: Centre for African Legal Development, 1971. Pp. 9–69.

World Legal Directory. Washington: World Peace Through Law Center, 1974.

2

BENELUX NATIONS

Albert L. Gastman and Scott B. MacDonald

THE DEVELOPMENT OF THE LEGAL SYSTEM

The three Benelux nations of Belgium, the Netherlands, and Luxembourg were formerly known as "the Low Countries." They are linked by a shared historical beginning and, consequently, have many similar social, political, and economic institutions and practices. This is particularly true in law.

In the fifteenth century, the dukes of Burgundy had gained control over most of the principalities that constitute the present Benelux nations. They both reorganized existing political institutions and introduced new ones aimed at consolidating their power in these principalities (or provinces). The heritage of some different concepts and practices of Germanic law gave each of the legal systems of the different provinces a distinctive character. However, because Roman law norms and procedures were influential throughout the area, there was a certain amount of unity to the corpus juris of the Burgundian realm. Furthermore, through Roman legal procedure, the concept developed that the state was responsible for the administration of justice and the enforcement of the rule of law. As a result, courts dependent on nobles and the church were restricted or eliminated.

Duke Charles the Bold ruled the Low Countries from 1467 to 1477. He introduced a central law court called the Parliament or Great Council of Malines, which curtailed some of the powers of the provincial courts. When Charles died in battle against the Swiss, his daughter and heiress Mary was confronted with the discontent that this centralization of the court system and other acts of increasing the ducal power had brought about in the country. Duchess Mary had not only to nullify virtually all the centralization measures her father had taken but to also give the right to both the federal parliament and the local parliaments to meet on their own initiative. This increase in parliamentary power to the detriment of executive power was short-lived. Through Mary's marriage to the Habsburg heir Maximilian, the fate of the Netherlands was closely bound up with that of Austria. In 1504, Joanna, the wife of Mary's son Philip, inherited the Spanish crown and the personal power of the ducal rulers of the Low Countries increased tremendously. The States General could only passively resist this by providing financial resistance to their demands. The central law court, the Great Council of Malines was reinstituted in 1504. The trend of centralization was also renewed in other areas. Nevertheless, when Charles, the son of Philip and Joanna, inherited these different lands in 1515 and 1516, this did not mean that Austria, Spain, and the Netherlands were integrated into one state. They remained separate entities, ruled according to their local customs. Neither were the internal political and legal structures affected by the fact that, in 1519, he was elected German emperor as Charles V.

The Privy Council of the duke started to encroach on the jurisdiction of the Great Council of Malines in the latter years of the reign of Charles. The turmoil brought to the country by the reformation movement caused Charles and, after 1555, his son Philip II, to push for ever more centralization in all political and religious fields. This provoked the revolt of 1566, which was followed by a long and arduous civil war in 1568. In 1581 Philip gave up his rights in the seven northern states. This led to the development of the Republic of the United Provinces of the Netherlands. The other Burgundian lands, comprising the present nations of Belgium and Luxembourg, remained loyal to Philip II who also remained the King of Spain.

The Reformation had undermined the universality of the civil law tradition in Europe. "Sovereignty," a new concept of independence, came into being at this time. For the individual state, this meant ever-increasing internal centralization. Externally, its effect was that transnational institutions became weaker. Rulers tried to bring greater unity to their countries' judicial systems through attempts at codification of the law. Internationally, this had the effect of causing each nation to have distinctly different national legal bodies. This did, however, not mean that these countries obtained well-ordered law codes. In the United Provinces, the writings of jurists like Hugo Grotius gave the Roman-Dutch law a semblance of being an organized system, but as long as each one of the seven provinces jealously defended its own legal institutions these attempts were only partially successful.[1] However, the right of appeal for certain cases from a provincial court to the "Hof van Holland" gave the latter a degree of the standing of a superior court, and brought some unity to the law of the Republic. The Southern Netherlands were ruled by the Spanish branch of the Habsburgs until early in the eighteenth century (thereafter by the Austrian branch). The latter tried to codify the law in their lands, but this proved to be a difficult assignment as local opposition remained strong. The other European monarchs had also found it hard to bring uniformity to their legal systems. The first nation to be truly successful was revolutionary France, where private and criminal law were codified in the first decade of the nineteenth century.

The French Revolution of 1789 spilled over into the Low Countries. The Southern Netherlands were lost by the Habsburgs, and revolutionary leaders took over with the support of the French army. In the Northern United Provinces, the old republican institutions were abolished and the Prince of Orange, who ruled as Stadtholder under the auspices of the sovereign States General, had to flee the country. A new nation was proclaimed, calling itself the Batavian Republic, but it had a very short existence. By 1810, all the lands that now form the Benelux had been annexed by France, and the French legal codes became their law. These codes survived Napoleon's defeat in 1813 and the retreat of the French. They remained the law of the new kingdom of the Netherlands, which comprised the territories of the former Dutch Republic and the Austrian Southern Netherlands.

King William I was inaugurated as king of the reunited Low Countries and made grand duke of adjacent Luxembourg. The constitution of the new kingdom, adopted August 8, 1815, made it into a unitary state. Nothing of the federal structure of the old United Provinces remained. The king, as the executive, was given much authority; nevertheless, one of the basic tenets of the constitution was separation of powers, which meant that the judicial branch was to be given autonomy, even though the constitutional articles stated that justice was done in the name of the king. Religious and language issues caused Catholics and French-speaking citizens in the Southern Netherlands to oppose the rule of the Protestant and Dutch-speaking north. Thus, when a new wave of revolution swept across Europe in 1830, the Southern Netherlands rebelled against King William and declared their independence, naming the new nation Belgium. It became a monarchy with Leopold I of Saxe-Coburg as its first ruler. The following year the new nation's constitution was promulgated which, according to Frank Huggett, an authority on modern Belgium, might well have been written in collaboration by John Locke, Montesquieu, John Adams, and Benjamin Franklin.[2] It guaranteed freedom of association, education, the press, and worship, while safeguards were established to maintain the independence of the judicial system.

Independent Luxembourg kept its tie with the Netherlands for the latter's king remained its grand duke. Constitutional changes in 1841, however, removed all ties that could give a semblance of Dutch tutelage and gave the duchy the clear status of an independent nation. As the laws of succession in the Netherlands and Luxembourg differed, the fact that the countries had the same ruler ended upon the death of King-Grand Duke William III in 1890. In the Netherlands, his daughter succeeded as Queen Wilhelmina; in Luxembourg, a distant cousin, Adolphe of Nassau-Weilburg, became grand duke. As its two larger sister nations, Luxembourg became a constitutional monarchy in which the principles of separation of powers and of ministerial responsibility are fully honored.

All three nations have remained civil law countries as the Napoleonic civil code and other French codes have survived in each. The reason for this was that they were derived from Roman law principles that fit in with the rules and practices of the prerevolutionary law of these lands. In addition, the simplicity and elegance of their form commended them to the authorities of the new governments. ''More important they preserved the chief social conquests of the

Revolution, such as civil equality, religious toleration, equality of inheritance'' and abolition of feudalism and privilege.[3]

In the Netherlands proper a more indigenous civil code, but still based on the principles of the Napoleonic one, was adopted in 1838. In 1947, preparation for a complete revision of the code was started which, among other things, was to make the commercial law code into a part of the civil code. Parts of the new code are at present in force, but it is doubtful if all the changes projected in 1947 will be made. In Belgium and Luxembourg, the French codes also remained in force after the upheaval of 1830. In later years, some changes were made. Belgium promulgated a new penal code in 1867; and Luxembourg, in 1879, which was almost a copy of the Belgium one.[4]

After the upheaval of World War II (which included invasion and occupation by Nazi Germany), the Benelux countries, very much aware of their vulnerability on the international stage, gave their full support to the United Nations and the North Atlantic Treaty Organization. Belgium, Luxembourg, and the Netherlands moved to the creation of a single economic union with the creation of the Benelux on September 5, 1944. Founded in principle on the not overly successful Belgium-Luxembourg Economic Union of 1922, the three countries agreed to create a customs union, abolish tariffs for trade among themselves, and create a single external tariff for trade with others.[5] Benelux unity was further advanced with the February 3, 1958, signing of the treaty instituting the Benelux Economic Union. While Benelux economic integration has proceeded at a slow pace, it has been, in many aspects, a defensive measure taken to offset French politicking in the European Community (EC) and as a fallback in case the EC would fail to work.

In 1950, France, West Germany, Italy, Belgium, Luxembourg, and the Netherlands agreed to join together into what was known as the European Coal and Steel Community (the ECSC). In addition to two executive bodies, a high authority and a council of ministries, a parliamentary assembly and a court of justice were created. The latter was given only cases concerning disputes on coal and steel matters. When, in 1957, the European Economic Community (EEC) and the European Atomic Energy Community, generally referred to as ''Euratom,'' were established, the parliamentary assembly and the Court of Justice were made common to all three communities (ECSC, EEC, and Euratom).

The existence of this European court in Luxembourg has significantly affected the structure of each of the national law systems of the EC members. The treaties establishing the EC communities are now the foundations of fundamental law of Europe, at least in the economic field. Each country has to see to it that its law codes are in conformity with the law of the treaties as it is interpreted by the European court. The importance of this new legal system of Western Europe was underscored by the comment in 1977 of Lord Mackenzie Stuart, judge of the Court of Justice of the European Community, who said: ''it seems to me that the impact of Community law on daily life is increasingly evident.''[6] Mackenzie backed his statement by noting that in the 1963 case of *van Gend en Loos v. Nederlandse Administratie der Belastingen* it was announced by the Court of Justice: "the Community constitutes a new legal order . . . for the benefit of which the states have limited their sovereign rights."[7] In addition, this court in Luxembourg together with the EEC headquarters in Brussels and the parliamentary assembly in Strasbourg have created a new attractive field of employment for lawyers in the Benelux nations.

The EEC impact on the legal system has been the greatest in Luxembourg because of the existence of a large resident foreign population connected to the European Economic Community and the large number of expatriate banks enjoying the benefits of liberal investment regulations. Michel Verwilghen, the noted expert on Luxembourg's judicial system, has shown in his work on the duchy's legal structure how the EEC rules have influenced the decisions of this country's courts.[8] The law here, probably more so than in that of its Benelux counterparts, has felt the effect of supranational rule-making bodies. The Benelux nations are charter members of the Council of Europe, founded in 1947. The council's European Convention on Human Rights gives them internationally binding commitments. This treaty makes it possible for a citizen of one of these three nations to lodge a complaint against his own state for violation of his individual rights as guaranteed by this treaty to the European Commission, which can bring the case to the court of the council at Strasbourg. Of interest also is that decrees made by UN-affiliated bodies are accepted at times as being legally valid in Benelux courts. Thus, in May 1985, the UN group, Council for Namibia, decided to go to court in the Netherlands to sue a multinational company in large part owned by the Dutch government. The suit charges the company with processing uranium mined in Namibia, which is forbidden by a decree of the council. The fact that the Dutch government recognizes the authority of the council and its rules makes this possible, even though the Dutch court, after preliminary hearings, will probably decide against accepting the suit.[9]

THE ORGANIZATION OF THE COURT SYSTEMS

The organization of the Benelux judiciary is derived from the French model. There are courts of first instance, courts of appeal, and the court of cassation. In the Netherlands, as in the two other Benelux nations, the court system is organized along hierarchical lines with the High Court, or the Court of Cassation or Hoge Raad de Nederlandens, at the summit. Supervising the administration of justice by all the courts in the land, this High Court has twenty-two judges and seven solicitors-general.[10] As the Supreme Court, it is the trial court for leading officials and the highest court of appeals for decisions by lower tribunals. It judges only on the basis of the law, not the facts of the case, which are already determined by the lower courts. Furthermore, if the Court of Cassation disagrees with the decision of a lower court, it has the authority to send the case back down for a new hearing. Finally, it is allowed to let a decision stand, while declaring that, in the future, the decision shall be considered to have been reversed, a situation according to Weil, that "is quite unlike cases under adjudication and not merely represent a declaration for the future."[11]

Directly below the Court of Cassation are the five courts of appeal (Gerechtshoven). As of 1980, there were ninety-three judges working on appeals from the nineteen district courts (Arrondissementsrechtsbanken), which have 207 judges.[12] As a rule, the latter usually are presided over by three judges, although, in some cases, one judge is sufficient. The district courts have certain functions as courts of appeals for the cantonal courts (Kantongerechten), which are the lowest courts, having jurisdiction over all civil cases involving less than 5,000 guilders, tenancy claims, and disputes concerning rents, employment contracts, and time payments. Criminal cases, usually of a minor nature, are also dealt with by the sixty-two cantonal courts. Depending on the size of the canton, a court may only have one judge (though in the larger urban areas there are as many as nine). In 1980, these courts had 102 judges.[13] All judges are appointed by the sovereign for life, which means until the retirement age of seventy is reached. They can only be removed by a decision of the High Court for having committed a crime or a misfeasance. The judges of the High Court are appointed from a list prepared by the second chamber of the States General.

In terms of the number of civil cases dealt with by the Dutch courts, the chief burden has consistently fallen on the two lowest courts, much as it does in any other nation. In 1979, for example, the Dutch courts heard 341,022 civil cases, 193,057 in the cantonal courts, 142,512 in the district courts, 5,309 in the courts of appeal, and 144 in the High Court.[14]

In Belgium, the Supreme Court is also the Court of Cassation (Cour de Cassation), modelled after the French court of the same name. Below that are the courts of appeal (Cour d'Appel); courts of Assize (Cour d'Assise); tribunals of the first instance (Tribunals de Premiere Instance); and the two lowest courts, the police court (Tribunals de Police) and the justice of the peace (Justice de Paix). The lowest courts are presided over by a justice of the peace and have authority to deal with minor criminal offenses, where the maximum penalty is seven days' imprisonment, and minor civil suits such as landlord and tenant disputes. As of 1980, there were 188 justices of the peace.[15] Appeals from the justice of the peace and police courts are heard in one of the twenty-six tribunals of first instance. Presided over by three judges, these courts also deal with more serious criminal cases where the maximum penalty is up to five years' imprisonment. The majority of civil cases go through these courts and appeals are sent on to one of the five courts of appeal. Presiding over each of the courts of appeal are five judges making decisions based on a point of law (questions of fact have already been clarified by the lower courts). These courts reflect the linguistic complexities of the Belgium nation-state, as the language of the court in Ghent is Dutch, in Liege, French, and Brussels, bilingual. From here, appeals go to the Court of Cassation.

Before discussing the Court of Cassation, one remaining court needs to be briefly discussed. The courts of assize hear criminal cases in which the permissible sentence ranges from five years' imprisonment to the death penalty. This is the only court with a jury, which makes the Belgian judicial system different from both its Dutch and Luxembourg counterparts. A majority vote decides whether or not a party is guilty, and if a disagreement arises between the jury and judges, the latter may adopt a minority position, hence acquitting the individual on trial. From here, appeals go to the Court of Cassation, which is divided into a civil and a criminal section. Seven judges make up each section, deciding only on the question of law. As the highest court in the land, it is also responsible for deciding jurisdiction in cases of conflict between civil and administrative courts.[16]

Luxembourg's judicial system is, in many aspects, similar to that found in Belgium and, to a lesser extent, the system in the Netherlands. At the lowest level are the justices of the peace (Justices de Paix), which are located in each judicial canton and are presided over by a judge and two deputy judges. The only exception to this is in the district of Esch-sur-Alzette, where there are two judges and two deputies. As in Belgium, this court has original jurisdiction over minor criminal offenses that are committed in its district and in the case of police matters, when the offenders may be imprisoned up to seven days or fined. The Justice de Paix also has jurisdiction over certain civil and commercial matters. Appeals from the lowest courts go to the district tribunals (Tribunals d'Arrondissement). Luxembourg is divided into two judicial districts (Luxembourg and Diekirch). The tribunal of Diekirch has four judges and ten deputy judges, while the Luxembourg Tribunal is somewhat larger, consisting of thirteen judges and ten deputy judges. These courts have both original and appellate jurisdiction in most civil matters. Directly above the district tribunals is the Superior Court of Justice with sixteen members, appointed for life by the grand duke as advised by the Superior Court itself. This court nominates judges for the lower courts, whose members can only be removed by action of the Superior Court.[17] The Superior Court of Justice also sits as a Court of Cassation (and a court of appeal) with judges who have appellate jurisdiction over the decisions rendered by the court of appeal, the assize court, the military court, the district tribunals, and in the past, the court of war crimes. As in the other Benelux countries, the Court of Cassation has jurisdiction only on law, ultra vires actions, and procedure violations. Finally, the Court of Cassation has jurisdiction over the transfer of a case from one court to another and in actions filed against members of the court system.

In Luxembourg, the assize court sits on the first Monday of each month. It has six judges, half from the Superior Court and half from the district tribunals, and has original jurisdiction over all crimes. The assize court has no jury system. The judges themselves decide whether or not an offender is guilty much in the same manner as in the Dutch system. Further, a guilty verdict must be unanimous or a not guilty verdict must be returned.

THE PERSONNEL OF THE LAW

The Legal Practitioners

The Benelux legal profession is well respected. It benefits from a cultural attitude and tradition that supports "rule of law." Being a member of the bench or of the office of the public prosecutor is prestigious. This is also true for attorneys belonging to well-established law offices. The latter are valued and well remunerated by the largely privately owned (despite socialist governments) industrial sector. In addition, these countries play an important role in the international market economy that creates much activity in the contractual field for the legal profession.[18] A law career, therefore, is attractive to many students, and the law schools in the Benelux never lack candidates. The study of law can be pursued in the eight major universities in the Netherlands and the nine in Belgium. In all three countries, students graduated from government-approved secondary schools can apply to law school. To obtain a law degree takes about three or four years. In Luxembourg, there is a university center where a number of law courses are given, but to obtain a law degree a student has to go abroad. The curriculum of the Benelux law schools tends to be more theoretical than those in the common law nations. The case method has, however, become a more popular means of instruction in recent years.[19]

In the past, law students came largely from the middle class because a university education was expensive. Nowadays, however, primarily because of the efforts of progressive ministers and liberal and socialist parliamentarians, there are many more possibilities for obtaining financial aid, and there has been a great increase in students from indigent households at the universities. The rise in enrollment has caused some faculties to institute admission quotas. In the Netherlands, where quotas have not been set, the large number of graduates (between 1,400 and 1,900 in each year from 1975 to 1985) has found it difficult to find employment. The profession has not been overwhelmed by this large number of graduates, however, because many of them have opted to go into business and government service. In addition, new employment opportunities for law graduates have been created by the great amount of social legislation passed over the past few decades.

The number of attorneys admitted to practice in the Netherlands was 3,726 in 1980 (an increase from 2,150 in 1970).[20] One has to both intern at a law office under the supervision of an experienced lawyer (called a "patroon") for three years and be accepted by the Society of Lawyers before beginning practice in the Netherlands.[21] The society is an institution that maintains the standards of the profession and sees that the professional and moral reputation of its members are not tainted by scandal or corruption. Once established, the new attorney may then become a "procureur."[22]

There were 6,096 lawyers in Belgium in 1980.[23] As in the Netherlands, one may not practice unless fulfilling a three year apprenticeship period and becoming a member of the bar. There is a separate bar association for each judicial district. There are, in addition, approximately 1,200 notaries in Belgium. These individuals authenticate and record legal documents and, most importantly, have a monopoly over the preparation of documents for the transference of land or the administration of the estates of deceased individuals.[24]

There are approximately 200 lawyers presently practicing in Luxembourg. They may be divided into three categories: (a) *Avocats-avoues*, who may plead and solicit before all jurisdictions; (b) *avocats-stagiaries*, who may defend in criminal cases but may not solicit civil law cases unless assisted by an *avocat-avoue*; and (c) *agrees*, who may give legal advice and represent individuals before peace courts and arbitration tribunals.[25]

Judges

There is little overlapping between the bar and the bench in the Netherlands. Most law school graduates become either lawyers or judges and remain as such throughout their professional careers. Dutch judges are appointed for life (they serve until 70) by the national government. Judges normally begin in the lower courts and work their way to the higher courts through a series of promotions. The independence of judges is maintained in that they may not be forced to accept a transfer from one bench to another and there are few presumed links between the judiciary and politics. Weil writes that ''this system generates considerable public respect for the judges and the legal system.''[26]

Belgium does have some overlapping between the bar and the bench. The candidate first becomes a *stagiere* (intern) with a law firm. Once this internship stage is passed, a lawyer has to be listed on the roster to become a candidate for a judge's chair. For the lower courts in Belgium, appointments are made by the ministerial cabinet. For the upper levels of the bench, the courts themselves are involved in the nomination process so as not to let the appointment be a political affair. Belgian judges are appointed for life and cannot be transferred without their consent.

Judges in Luxembourg are appointed for life by the grand duke (most are nominated by the Superior Court of Justice). Judges may be promoted within the court system. They may not be forced to move from one court to another without their consent or be removed except by judicial decision.

PUBLIC PERCEPTIONS AND THE ROLE OF THE COURTS

Gordon Weil has written about the administration of justice in Belgium and the Netherlands:

the law is regarded as a function of the state quite separate from the hurly-burly of everyday politics. This approach engenders a considerable public respect for a legal system viewed as an impartial arbiter between individuals and the state. However, it removes from the governing mechanism an element of control and review that other nations, such as the United States, have found a vital part of their decision-making apparatus.[27]

Having largely adopted French codes based on Roman law, the Benelux countries are said to be in the civil law tradition. The fundamental difference between the Anglo-American judicial system based on common law and that based on civil law is that, in the former, the traditional idea was to formulate laws only when social conditions made them necessary while in the latter, the idea was that there must be a codified framework of law in which any law needed by the community could be found. One of the important factors in these differences is that in the common law tradition the judge at times feels that he must not only apply the law but also interpret and, to a degree, even create the law. The civil law judge, on the other hand, feels that his only duty is to strictly apply the law as laid down in the codes and enactments of the legislature. The instigators of the French Revolution and those in sympathy with them in the Low Countries desired to break the power of the old judicial aristocracy because they felt that the rulings of these judges were always in favor of the old privileged classes. The lawmakers of the new revolutionary constitutions wanted to make certain that only the elected representatives of the people created law. The legislators would make laws that they believed would protect the individual from the power of the executive—laws based on the concepts of equality. In the common law tradition the judge has often been seen as the protector of the individual against the state or "the Leviathan." In the civil law tradition, however, the role was reserved for the elected members of the legislature. The concept of judicial review is thus alien to the civil law tradition—only the legislature can decide on the constitutionality of the law. Judges, therefore, were often seen not as protectors but as functionaries whose duty it was to strictly apply the just laws based on reason. Members of the judiciary are, therefore, well respected, but have far less of an aura of being guardians of justice than do their peers in the common law countries.

The French system of administrative law and its court system have also served as a model for the Benelux nations. When public national law issues infringe on the rights of the individual, he must bring his case to the Council of State, or Raad van State, or, as it is called in French-speaking Belgium, le Conseil d'Etat. This institution's court system and law procedures have, in recent decades, been radically modernized, especially in the Netherlands. The individual is now better protected against the illegal action of the state. In cases of bureaucratic abuse of power, the individual citizen can turn to the Council of State, which, as an administrative tribunal, can negate rulings and practices of government institutions as being contrary to the accepted principles of law. Thus, even if the "King" can do no wrong, his servants can. The Council of State, therefore, keeps government officials very aware of the fact that they are liable for their actions, and that they cannot hide behind sovereign immunity.[28] Disputes concerning administrative law must, in certain cases, first be brought before local tribunals. In the Netherlands they are the Colleges van Gedeputeerde Staten (Boards of Commissioned States), which are instituted by the legislatures of the provinces. Appeals from these go to the Council of State.

It should be emphasized, however, that in neither the Netherlands nor in Luxembourg is the Council of State a judicial body. In the Netherlands it is part of the executive branch and its members are appointed by the queen. Appeals of administrative orders are sent to the council, which then sends its decisions to the minister of justice. The minister does not have to abide by the council's decisions but, in most cases, accepts its advice. The council also receives proposals from the cabinet before they are sent to the Parliament and has the power to recommend measures to the Crown. In Luxembourg, members of the council are appointed by the grand duke, upon the advice of the cabinet, legislature, and members of the council. Its powers are similar to that found in the Netherlands. It acts as a high administrative court, is consulted on all administrative decrees, and must be consulted by the cabinet before a bill is sent to the legislature (again, its opinion is not binding). It can play the role of the second legislative chamber (Luxembourg has a unicameral legislature) and thus temporarily veto a bill, and, in a judicial role, decides disputes between the cabinet and the auditing court.[29]

The Council of State in Belgium was created in 1946. Its members are appointed by the king, and the body has both an advisory and administrative function. The former power is similar to that found in the Netherlands and Luxembourg in that it may register advisory opinions on proposed legislation. Those decisions are, however, not binding. The council is the highest administrative court in Belgium. As such, it

may review decisions, acts and regulations of the administrative authorities and state agencies of the executive branch of government . . . reviews the purpose and intention of the statute and assesses the exercise of administrative discretion in light of that review. . . . The Council of State may find that a legal power has been improperly used if legal powers were being exercised for a purpose other than those for which the authority was originally conferred. Thus, royal decrees and ministerial decrees may be declared null and void. The Council of State may not, however, nullify statutes enacted by Parliament or the state assemblies.[30]

It is clear that there is far more reluctance to utilize the courts to solve political-legal problems in the Benelux nations than in the common law nations. In the United States, for example, there is a well-established tradition for political action groups to use the judicial system to obtain their objectives. This is not so in the Benelux. In cases where the constitutionality is at issue, the court is not the appropriate forum. Neither is the judiciary system as easily or successfully used in cases of damages or injury as in the United States for either groups or individuals. One reason is the absence of a jury (except in criminal cases in Belgium), which makes it harder to obtain large financial settlements. Also, most judges, who are all appointed for life, are far less easily swayed by their emotions or some nonlegal consideration than an American jury may be. Furthermore, judges are traditionally very strict in their assessment of damages, and for nonmaterial damages there is no compensation. The rules imposed by each nation's association of lawyers (and sometimes the law itself) keep a lawyer from demanding a percentage of the compensation to be paid in a successful suit. A standard fee is all he or she can expect. Lawyers are, therefore, far less apt to suggest to a prospective client to begin a damage or injury suit.

In legal practices concerning criminal justice, there are also marked differences between civil and common law systems. In the Benelux nations, there is no recourse to a grand jury for indictment, and arraignment does not depend so much on an accuser's testimony as on the findings of an investigating magistrate. The judge instructed to do the investigation advises the authorities if there should be criminal proceedings. To fulfill his function correctly, the judge should be totally independent and keep his distance from the prosecution. At times, it has been said, the contrary happens in civil law systems with dire results for the accused. However, in those civil law countries where the rule to maintain the independence of the investigating judge is strictly observed, it is argued that this inquisitional method better protects the rights of the accused than the adversary method of the common law nations. The major object of the judicial systems, it is felt in the Benelux nations, is not to punish and take vengeance on the criminal but to protect society.[31] This attitude is certainly in conformity with the original concepts of the Napoleonic codifiers.

An issue that is much debated today in the Benelux nations is the manner in which the courts relate to the deprived. To place the accent on social injustices and less on individual rights and duties has been a marked tendency in many Western societies but especially in the civil law ones in the decades since World War II. Understandably, this has influenced the thinking of both lawyers and judges in the Benelux nations. Courts throughout the region (but especially in the Netherlands) have begun to take into consideration the social mores of radical and antiestablishment groups. The belief that many of the problems the individual members of these groups had were the result of the insensitivity of those who were in authority led many judges to be lenient with radical or antiestablishment defendants. For example, trafficking in illegal drugs in Amsterdam is an offense that by law can be severely punished. In actuality, however, many judges give light or suspended sentences in such cases and none to those who use the drugs. To the outside observer it might seem that the law has changed, but, in fact, the letter of the law has remained the same.

At times, these judges have been accused by spokesmen of conservative groups of being influenced by dangerous radical concepts. These court decisions, it is said, are creating an atmosphere of unlawfulness. However, attitudes toward the law are not static. They change with the changes in social mores and outlooks. At present, it would seem that the pendulum is swinging the other way in the Benelux countries, for the public is demanding a stricter observation of the law and the judiciary is beginning to comply. As much as it is the task of the Benelux legal profession to maintain the law that guarantees the social order, it is also its duty to provide new rules to meet the conditions with which the technology of the post industrial world confronts society. That the members of the profession in these nations are aware of this is obvious. Their actions in the legal and judicial fields demonstrate that they understand the challenge of the future.

NOTES

1. H. Grotius, *Inleidinge Tot de Hollandsche Rechts-Geleerdheid* (1631; reprint, Leiden: Universitaire/Pers Leiden, 1952). See the notes attached to this 1952 edition of Hugo Grotius's work, pp. 350–99. R. B. Schlesinger, *Comparative Law* (New York: The Foundation Press, 1980), p. 239.

2. F. E. Huggett, *Modern Belgium* (New York: Frederick A. Praeger, 1969), p. 110.

3. Schlesinger, *Comparative Law*, pp. 634–35, and C.J.H. Hayes, *A Political History of Modern Europe*, vol. 1 (New York: Macmillan, 1957), p. 654.

4. E. H. Kossmann, *The Low Countries, 1780–1940* (Oxford: Clarendon Press, 1978), pp. 190–95, and A. Watson, *The Making of the Civil Law* (Cambridge: Harvard University Press, 1981), pp. 121–22.

5. It was for this union that the acronym "Benelux" was created.

6. Lord M. Stuart, *The European Communities and the Rule of Law* (London: Stevens and Sons, 1977), p. 1.

7. Ibid., p. 2.

8. M. Verwilghen, *Regimes Matrimoniaux, Successions et liberalites, droit international prive et Droit Compare*, vol. 2 (Neuchatel, Switzerland: Les Editions de la Baconstere, 1979), p. 82.

9. G. Weil, *The Benelux Nations: The Politics of Small Country Democracies* (New York: Rinehart and Winston, Inc., 1970), p. 213, and "U.N's Namibia Council Plans Suit on Mining," *New York Times*, May 26, 1985, p. 6.

10. Netherlands Central Bureau of Statistics, *Statistical Yearbook of the Netherlands 1981* (The Hague: Staatsuitgeverij, 1982), p. 359.

11. Weil, *The Benelux Nations*, pp. 187–88.

12. *Statistical Yearbook of the Netherlands*, p. 389.

13. Ibid., p. 389.

14. Ibid.

15. Institut National de Statistique, *Annuaire Statistique de la Beligue, Tome 100, 1980* (Brussels: Ministere de Affaires Economiques, 1980), p. 216.

16. Weil, *The Benelux Nations*, pp. 194–95.

17. G. Smith, "Grand Duchy of Luxemburg," in G. E. Delury, ed., *World Encyclopedia of Political Systems and Parties* (New York: Facts on File, 1983), p. 640. See also the Luxembourg Constitution, Articles 90 and 91.

18. D. Rueschemeyer, *Lawyers and Their Societies* (Cambridge, Mass.: Harvard University Press, 1973), pp. 5, 8. Schlesinger, *Comparative Law*, pp. 543–47.

19. H. P. Tseng, *The Law Schools of the World* (Buffalo: William S. Hein & Co., 1977), pp. 72–75, 252, 266–68.

20. *Statistical Yearbook of the Netherlands*, p. 359.

21. C. S. Rhyne, *Law and Judicial Systems of Nations* (Washington, D.C.: The World Peace Through Law Center, 1978), p. 512.

22. M. L. Snijders, *Het Spel van Staat* (Amsterdam: Scheltema & Hokema, 1960), p. 201.

23. *Annuaire Statistique de la Beligue*, p. 216.

24. M. C. Taeymans, "The Legal System of Belgium," in K. R. Redden, ed., *Modern Legal Systems Cyclopedia*, vol. 3 (Buffalo: William S. Hein Co., 1984), p. 59.

25. Rhyne, *Law and Judicial Systems of Nations*, p. 440.

26. Weil, *The Benelux Nations*, p. 190.

27. Ibid., p. 184.

28. L. Hurwitz, *The State as Defendant* (Westport, Conn.: Greenwood Press, 1981), p. 58.

29. See Weil, *The Benelux Nations*, pp. 132–33, 141, 190, 202–3, 208, for a discussion of the Council of State in the Netherlands and Luxembourg.

30. Taeymans, "The Legal System of Belgium," p. 46.

31. H. W. Ehrmann, *Comparative Legal Cultures* (Englewood Cliffs, N.J.: Prentice Hall, 1976), pp. 87–89.

BIBLIOGRAPHY

Crabb, J. H. *The Constitution of Belgium and the Belgian Civil Code.* Littleton, Colo.: Fred B. Rothman & Co., 1982.

Ehrmann, H. W. *Comparative Legal Cultures.* Englewood Cliffs, N.J.: Prentice-Hall, 1976.

Huggett, F. E. *Modern Belgium.* New York: Frederick A. Praeger, 1969.

Kossmann, E. H. *The Low Countries, 1780–1940.* Oxford: Clarendon Press, 1978.

Motley, J. *The Rise of the Dutch Republic*, vol. 1. New York: Harpers and Brothers, 1900.

Reuschemeyer, D. *Lawyers and Their Societies.* Cambridge, Mass.: Harvard University Press, 1973.

Rhyne, C. S. *Law and the Judicial System of Nations.* Washington, D.C.: The World Peace Through Law Center, 1978.

Smet, L. de, H. Keeris, and W. Vlassenbroeck. *Belgie en Luxemburg.* Roermond, The Netherlands: J. J. Romen and Zonen, 1971.

Smith, G. "Grand Duchy of Luxemburg." In G. Delury, *World Encyclopedia of Political Systems and Parties.* New York: Facts on File, 1983.

Stuart, Lord M. *The European Communities and the Rule of Law.* London: Stevens and Sons, 1977.

Taeymans, M. C. "The Legal System of Belgium." In K. R. Redden, ed., *Modern Legal Systems Cyclopedia*, vol. 3. Buffalo: William S. Hein Co., 1984.

Tseng, H. P. *The Law Schools of the World.* Buffalo: William S. Hein Co., 1977.

Weil, G. *The Benelux Nations: The Politics of Small-Country Democracies.* New York: Rinehart and Winston, Inc., 1970.

Wildeboer, I. H. "Education and Training of Lawyers—The Netherlands." *International Legal Practitioner* (May 1979), pp. 21–23.

3

CANADA, AUSTRALIA, AND NEW ZEALAND

Alan N. Katz

The British Empire has been replaced in the latter decades of the twentieth century by a voluntary association of independent states, the Commonwealth of Nations. While a large number of states are presently full members in the Commonwealth, three of these, Canada, Australia, and New Zealand will be the focus of this chapter.[1]

The British monarch is the head of the Commonwealth, though her powers are merely symbolic. The nations within the Commonwealth consult with each other every two years at the heads of government meetings. These meetings articulate future Commonwealth policy while keeping in mind that the members of the Commonwealth are in free association with each other. The administrative arm of the Commonwealth is the Secretariat, headed by a secretary-general. The Secretariat is responsible for preparing position papers for the governments of the organization and has maintained links with other organizations, both international and regional.

The constitutional structures in Canada, Australia, and New Zealand have much in common. First, while they were initially imposed from above, through the actions of the Parliament in London, the ultimate form of the constitutions were profoundly affected by the actions of local leaders in each of these nations. Second, while the constitutions played a critical role in the development of these nations, there are a variety of other sources of the law in each of them. Finally, the constitutions in each only provided the basic organizational structures for the governments,

the minimum framework necessary for the conduct of government within the country. In particular, the written portions of the constitution do not contain anything corresponding to the elaborate bills of rights or other systems of fundamental limitations on legislative power that have characterized constitutional drafting in Continental Europe especially since World War I.[2]

THE DEVELOPMENT OF THE LEGAL SYSTEMS

It is likely that the Italian navigator John Cabot's discovery of Newfoundland in the 1490s was the first European contact in Canada. The following centuries saw further explorations by the Spanish, Portuguese, French (Jacques Cartier sailed up the St. Lawrence and took possession of the area for France in 1534, and Samuel de Champlain established colonies in Nova Scotia and Quebec at the beginning of the seventeenth century), and British.

A private company, the Company of New France, was given a charter to develop the fur trade. Its efforts were unsuccessful, however, and the charter was revoked and New France was made a colony of the French. The British explorations in many of the same areas ultimately resulted in conflict between the two nations. Each struggle resulted in a British victory, a treaty of peace that ceded new lands to the British, and a period of peace, then followed by the beginning of the cycle again. Thus, the Treaty of Utrecht (1713) ceded much of North America to the British, the Treaty of Paris (1763) ceded it all of New France (with the exception of two small islands off the coast of Newfoundland), and the Treaty of Versailles (1783) made much of present-day Canada part of British North America.

Canada was first given elected representative bodies as a result of the Constitutional Act of 1791. Demands for more self-government, however, resulted in each of the colonies within Canada being given representatives within the legislature in 1840. A federal union called the Dominion of Canada was established as a result of the British North America Act in 1867. This act both became a main source of Canadian constitutional law and led to the union of Upper and Lower Canada with Nova Scotia and New Brunswick.

Canada has one of the most unusual legal systems in the world in that both the civil law (in Quebec) and the common law (in the other nine provinces) predominate today. The Province of Quebec is governed by codes (the first codification in Quebec was established in 1866) based upon the Napoleonic Codes. The remainder of Canada is governed by the common law system (though there are some variances from province to province).

Given these two traditions, it is not surprising to find many sources of the law of Canada.[3] The first and most important of these are the statutes produced by the Canadian Parliament and the ten provincial legislatures. In addition, there is a wide variety of subordinate legislation (ordinances, bylaws, orders in council, regulations, etc.), enacted by individuals or bodies granted such power by the legislative chamber. A second source of Canadian law is the case law, or common law set down by judges over the past six hundred years (the concept of parliamentary sovereignty allows the Canadian Parliament to override principles set out in the common law). A third source is royal prerogative, which generally must be exercised by the advice and consent of the executive branch. Custom and convention are a fourth source of the law. The writings of distinguished legal scholars sometimes serve as a fifth source of the law. Finally, there are a number of constitutional sources of the law. Two of the most important of these are the 1982 Canada Act and the 1867 British North America Act.

While the "discovery" of Australia is generally associated with James Cook's sighting of the continent in 1770, there were previous explorations by the Dutch and the English in the seventeenth century. With the loss of their American colonies and the overcrowding of their own prisons, the British decided, in the latter part of the eighteenth century, to export some of their felons to Australia. That this was against the law of the time seemed to trouble the British little, and banishment to Australia became a common alternative to execution (this practice was ultimately halted in the next century). The nineteenth century saw widespread migration to Australia (nearly a quarter of a million immigrants came to Australia and New Zealand from 1825 to 1851) as a way of both alleviating the shortage of labor in Australia and the dearth of employment opportunities in the United Kingdom.[4] The discovery of gold gave further impetus to this movement, and the population, doubling in a decade, exceeded one million by 1861.[5] The impact of these immigrants was enormous:

These migrants left a permanent stamp on Australian society. They confirmed the British proportion in the population so completely that British institutions, education, way of life, dress, speech and outlook on life were to survive in the Australian Colonies and in the sister settlements in New Zealand long after they had almost been obliterated in the Provinces of Canada.[6]

A series of law courts (magistrates, criminal, civil jurisdiction, court martial, and vice-admiralty) were established by the end of the eighteenth century. However, the military-style government of Australia was riddled with incompetence and corruption. This led to a rebellion in 1808 and a series of reforms to alleviate the situation. These resulted in the establishment of new courts, the replacement of the military government by a mixed civilian-military legislative council, and the establishment of civilian jury trials to replace military juries.[7]

Four of Australia's six states were formed by 1859, and the movement for federalism ultimately resulted in the creation of the Commonwealth of Australia in 1901. The 1931 Statute of Westminster gave further self-government to Australia by stating that the British Parliament could only pass legislation affecting Australia with the consent of the Australian Parliament (though the Australian states are, theoretically, still subject to the British Parliament).

Australia's 1901 Constitution was both the means by which the states formed the federation as well as a vehicle for describing the powers of the government. By most criteria, it can be considered to have done its job successfully:

After seven decades the Constitution remains intact, and if the absence of violence, the development of economic pluralism, freedom from coups d'etat and the preservation of political competition are the criteria of successful constitutionalism, Australia can rightly claim success. Like most successful written constitutions in the Western world, Australia's has provided the guidelines for protecting and developing an ideology that could be called

54 Alan N. Katz

a middle-class, property-owning conservatism. It has established a governmental framework that makes strong government and radical social change difficult; it fragments power, and its institutions have become an effective brake upon radical action; it is a "hasten slowly" document.[8]

While state constitutions, English statutes, and constitutional conventions have served as other sources of Australian law, its 1901 Constitution is unquestionably the major source of the law today.

The Maoris, a people from Polynesia, traveled to New Zealand between the tenth and thirteenth centuries. These seminomadic people depended primarily upon hunting and fishing and numbered nearly a quarter of a million by the time of the western incursions into New Zealand in the late eighteenth century. James Cook took possession of the land for the British in 1769 (though Abel Tasman had sighted the coast of New Zealand over a century earlier). The British did not take possession of the country (and immigrants did not begin to arrive) until 1840. While the Maoris had ceded their rights to Great Britain, the influx of immigrants (like Australia, aided by the discovery of gold) ultimately led to conflict. This was caused by disagreements over the sale of land and ultimately resulted in the deployment of over 20,000 troops against the Maoris. No formal peace treaty was ever signed but the peace was created by legislative acts that allowed the Maoris to more easily sell their land to the new immigrants (who reached 500,000 by the 1880s).[9] As one might expect, the outcome of this new policy was harmful to the Maoris "since the Maoris were unable to resist the temptation to live by selling rather than cultivating their land. They were converted into a virtually landless proletariat, forced to live from intermittent unskilled labour for the Government and European settlers."[10] Later legislation granted the status and privileges of British subjects to the Maoris (though they have attempted to resist assimilation by maintaining their own political and religious organizations).

The New Zealand Constitution Act of 1852 created six provinces and mandated elections for the legislatures and executives of each. A unitary system was created in 1876 with the abolition of the provinces, and New Zealand was granted dominion status in 1907 (though many decades passed before it established any significant diplomatic ties with nations other than England). New Zealand was granted "formal" independence in 1947, when it adopted the Statute of Westminster Adoption Act and the New Zealand Constitutional Amendment (Request and Consent) Act, which put into force the 1931 Statute of Westminster Act of the United Kingdom Parliament granting independence to the former colonies and dominions who had remained loyal to Great Britain during World War I.[11]

New Zealand does not have a single written constitutional document or a bill of rights. Instead, there are a number of constitutional sources. Among these are the common law, statutes of both the New Zealand and United Kingdom Parliaments, and subordinate legislation. The English common law continues to play a major role in New Zealand today for ''the policy of the courts has been to preserve uniformity with the common law in England. This is partly for reasons of convenience and partly because of the assumption prevailing in New Zealand that there is a single common law, the law of England, and that there are not separate, though similar, common laws in different countries.''[12] When New Zealand adopted the Statute of Westminster in 1947 it meant that its Parliament had the sole authority to legislate for the country. This has meant that there is no place for judicial review of parliamentary acts in New Zealand. At the same time, English statutes continue to play an active role in New Zealand:

The quartet of quasi statutes, the Magna Carta of Edward I (1279), the Petition of Right (1627), the Bill of Rights (1688) and the Act of Settlement (1700), being in the nature of solemn compacts between the Sovereign and the people, are all deeply seated in New Zealand constitutional principle. It is, for example, unthinkable that parliament should legislate in a manner inconsistent with Chapter 29 of the Magna Carta.[13]

THE ORGANIZATION OF THE COURT SYSTEMS

Canada has courts both at the federal and provincial level. The systems are integrated, however, in that cases may be appealed from the provincial level to the Supreme Court of Canada. More importantly, ''federal and provincial courts are not necessarily given separate mandates as to the laws that they administer. For instance, although criminal law is made by the Parliament of Canada, it is administered mainly in provincial courts.''[14]

At the apex of the system is the Supreme Court of Canada (appeals had previously been taken to the Judicial Committee of the Privy Council in London but this practice was abolished for criminal cases in 1933 and civil cases in 1949). The Court is composed of one chief justice (who also serves as the chief justice of Canada) and eight puisne justices. The Court hears appeals of serious criminal cases from the provincial supreme courts and the Federal Court. There is no longer any financial limitation on civil cases heard by the Court, though the decision to hear a case is left to the Court itself.

The Federal Court of Canada was established in 1971 to replace the Exchequer Court. The court is staffed by one chief justice and fourteen federally appointed judges serving in trial and appellate divisions. It ''deals with matters generally outside the territorial jurisdiction of any single Province, as well as in certain specialized areas of federal law such as taxation, customs and administrative law. It has exclusive jurisdiction in some areas, such as patent law, while it shares jurisdiction in areas such as admiralty.''[15] The appellate division hears appeals from the trial division as well as from federal boards and commissions.

Each province has a Supreme (or Superior) Court. These courts have both trial and appellate divisions and hear the more serious criminal and civil matters as well as appeals from the lower provincial courts. Each of the provinces (with the exception of Quebec) also has county or district courts. These are intermediate civil and criminal courts. They hear less serious cases as well as appeals from the inferior provincial courts. Each province also has a number of inferior courts. These include juvenile courts, a family court, a small claims court, and magistrates' courts. The latter hear approximately 90 percent of the cases in Canada and are courts of original jurisdiction in the criminal area. Their jurisdiction is limited to cases involving a maximum of a $500 fine or six months imprisonment.[16] There are, finally, a variety of special courts. These include surrogate courts, a court martial appeal board, a tax review board, and the Canadian Transport Commission.

Australia has a somewhat complex court system. There is a separate court system for each state and territory as well as a federal court system to handle issues where the national legislature has jurisdiction. Finally, the High Court of Australia has jurisdiction over the decisions of all these courts. The High Court of Australia consists of a chief justice and six other justices. It sits in Canberra and hears appeals from the other federal and state courts. The basis for the High Court is found in Chapter Three of the Constitution, which derives much of its ideas regarding the courts from the American Constitution. While there are some differences from the American practice (for example, the Australian state courts have federal jurisdiction), the Court was granted the power to review the constitutionality of parliamentary legislation, as in the United States. The Court is also a court of original jurisdiction in a number of areas (for example, questions involving representatives of other nations or treaties between Australia and other nations).[17] Prior to 1975, appeals from the High Court could be taken to the Judicial Committee of the Privy Council in London. The only appeals that may now go to that body are from the state supreme courts.[18]

There are two other federal courts, the federal court and the family court. The former has original jurisdiction in bankruptcy, taxation, patent, and trademark cases (usually before a single judge) and hears appeals from its original jurisdiction (before a full court), territorial supreme courts, single judges (but not full courts) of state supreme courts, and quasi-judicial agencies and tribunals. The family court deals with questions of marriage, divorce, and the annulment of marriages. The decisions of this court may be appealed to the High Court (though the High Court is not required to hear the appeal).

While there is a wide variety of courts within the six states of Australia, most have similar court structures. There are eight supreme courts in Australia—one for each state and territory. These courts hear appeals from the intermediate state courts and possess jurisdiction in all those areas except where limited by statute. Most of the states possess intermediate courts (usually called "district courts," "county courts," or "courts of general session"). These courts hear appeals from the lower state courts and adjudicate more serious criminal and civil cases than those heard in the lower courts. The decisions of these courts may be appealed to the State Supreme Court. At the bottom of the state court system are the inferior courts. Less serious criminal and civil cases are heard here by a magistrate or justice of the peace (juries are utilized in criminal actions in both the intermediate and superior courts). Inferior courts also conduct investigations into violent deaths and preliminary hearings of individuals charged with more serious charges and decide whether prosecution should commence.

New Zealand has a unitary system and a rather simple court system. At the apex of the system is the Court of Appeal. It is composed of a chief justice and five other permanently appointed judges and normally sits in Wellington. It usually sits with three judges, though more may sit in important cases. This court has only appellate jurisdiction, hearing cases from the High Court and inferior courts. The decisions of this court are final, except where cases may be appealed to the Judicial Committee of the Privy Council (while it may hear appeals in civil cases, few appeals are actually brought before it).

The High Court is composed of a chief justice and twenty-six other judges. Cases are generally heard by a single judge or, in criminal matters and civil matters exceeding $3,000 (and where the parties agree), before a judge and jury. The court is a "superior court of original jurisdiction" and grants probate to wills and handles areas previously under the purview of the Courts of Admiralty.[19] A separate administrative division was created in 1968. This consists of not more than six judges and hears appeals from administrative tribunals.

The district courts are courts of original jurisdiction. Minor criminal cases may be heard by a justice of the peace (more serious criminal cases may be heard by a single judge or with a jury). The jurisdiction of the courts in the civil area is limited to those cases not involving claims of more than $12,000. Family courts constitute a division of the district courts and have jurisdiction over most family matters. Special district court judges, known as family court judges, preside over these courts. There is also a children and young persons court, which hears charges against young people under the age of seventeen. There are, finally, a number of administrative tribunals and a Maori Land Court and Maori Appellate Court to adjudicate questions relating to the lands of the Maori people.

THE PERSONNEL OF THE LAW

There are over 35,000 lawyers in Canada today. While the Canadian legal system generally follows that found in the United Kingdom, Canada has a fused legal profession rather than separate barrister and solicitor branches. Canada does, however, retain the institution of the King's Counsel or Queen's Counsel (depending upon the sex of the British monarch at the time of conferral). This is now a largely honorary title given by the government to senior and well-respected lawyers, professors, and, on occasion, politicians.[20]

There are twenty-one law schools and approximately 8,000 students studying law in Canada today.[21] The study of law is a three year, full-time, graduate-level experience. The legal profession is governed by a bar society in each province. The societies set admissions procedures for the profession, establish fee scales, and administer professional discipline. There is, in addition, a Canadian Bar Association that many lawyers join. Admission to the provincial bar requires the passing of an examination established by the bar society and the serving of a one-year apprenticeship period, called "articling." While lawyers may serve in a variety of capacities—politics, business, teaching, and the judiciary—more than 90 percent of the Canadian law students (as opposed to 50 percent in the United States) go into the practice of law after graduation from law school.[22]

There are over five hundred judges serving on the various Canadian courts.[23] Most Canadian judges are appointed from the bar (though there have been a number of academics appointed recently) by the federal government—usually by the minister of justice. Judges are often promoted from one bench to another. While it is widely thought that political activities help one to gain appointment, there is little evidence of this in Canada today. Residence also seems to have little to do with one's chances of gaining appointment (though traditionally three justices of the Supreme Court have come from Quebec, three from Ontario, two from the Western Provinces and one from the Atlantic Provinces).[24] Canadian judges, therefore, seem to be most like their brethren elsewhere: middle-aged (most are appointed in their late forties and early fifties), well-trained in the law, experienced members of the bar (federally appointed judges must have ten years' experience before the bar), not politically active, and ambitious:

These qualifications aside, all newly appointed judges are persons trained and experienced in the law prior to appointment. And all lawyers, prior to engaging in the practice of the law and prior to formal training in the law, are, for the most part, ambitious young persons anxious to engage in a successful career.[25]

While there are some variances from state to state, Australia has largely maintained a divided legal profession, with the barristers maintaining wide audiences before courts, advising the solicitor, not engaging in specialization, and not able to accept work directly from a client, and the solicitor more limited in court appearances, the receiver of legal advice, but able to both specialize and deal directly with the client. There are over 16,000 legal practitioners in Australia today—over 14,000 solicitors and nearly 2,000 barristers.[26]

There are thirteen law schools (or schools offering courses in law) in Australia today.[27] Law schools were initially staffed by practicing lawyers. That has changed, and today most Australian law schools are staffed by full-time academic lawyers. There were nearly 8,000 law students in Australia in the late 1970s—a dramatic increase from the fewer than 3,000 attending school in 1963.[28]

Most Australian states have law societies and bar associations to establish admissions requirements and norms of professional conduct for solicitors and barristers. The Supreme Court of each state determines admissions requirements for that area. Those requirements are usually good character and the necessary educational background. The latter usually includes graduation from a law program and a period of apprenticeship with a senior solicitor or barrister.

Australian judges tend to be appointed from among the senior members of the bar. They are generally appointed for good behavior, and most retire at age 70. Most Australian judges could be described as constituting an elite. This is certainly true of those appointed to the High Court. These individuals tend to be middle-aged (the average appointment age is fifty-three), male (no female has been appointed to this bench), upper-middle class, Protestant, graduates of a high status high school and university, well-respected lawyers (likely selected as Queen's Counsel), politically experienced, and with prior judicial experience.[29]

Approximately 4,200 lawyers are in private practice in New Zealand. The vast majority of these are solicitors. The functions of the solicitors and barristers (including the approximately 30 Queen's Counsels) are essentially the same as found in other nations with links to the United Kingdom though individuals may practice in both capacities.[30] The Law Practitioners Act of 1955 mandates the requirements for admissions to both parts of the profession. They are, generally, the attainment of twenty-one years of age, proof of good character, and the passing of a certifying examination. The act also notes prescribed length of service as either a solicitor or barrister in order to switch to the other branch of the profession.

Four (Auckland, Wellington, Christchurch, and Dunedin) of New Zealand's universities offer programs in the law. The study of law is a four-year under-graduate program. Each student begins by enrolling in a one-year course in the Faculty of Arts and Sciences and then takes a law intermediate examination. Those students who pass the exam then begin the three-year, full-time study in the law and receive a Bachelor of Laws (LL.B.). The course of study is controlled by the Council of Legal Education, which is made up of the deans of the law schools, two judges of the High Court, and four individuals appointed by the law society. The number of students yearly graduating from the four law schools is approximately 450.[31]

Judges of the New Zealand Court of Appeal are appointed from among the most senior and able members of the High Court by the governor-general. The judges of the Court of Appeal simultaneously sit on the High Court but have seniority over all members of the High Court (except for the chief justice and acting chief justice). The judges of the High Court and the district courts are appointed by the governor-general, upon the advice of the attorney-general, from among the most senior lawyers appearing before the bench. Experience and aptitude, rather than political party ties, tend to be the most important factors in the appointment decisions.

PUBLIC PERCEPTIONS AND THE ROLE OF THE COURTS

Canadians today are much more aware of the law and lawyers than in past decades. They are now much more likely to regard themselves as consumers of legal services and are, as such, sometimes critical of what they may feel to be the excessive costs for those services.[32] On the other hand, much has been written about the sanctity of an independent judiciary. In order to ensure that independence, a number of restrictions have been placed upon the lives of judges. They may not, for example, take part in the electoral process by working for a candidate or voting, hold membership in a law society, nor continue in the private practice of law.[33] Some positions restrict where judges may live. Judges are also immune from civil liability so that they may have total freedom of expression.[34] Professor W. R. Lederman concludes the following about the independence of the Canadian judiciary:

A judge is not a civil servant, rather he is a primary autonomous officer of the state in the judicial realm, just as cabinet ministers and members of parliament are the primary official persons in the executive and legislative realms respectively. No minister of the Crown, federal or provincial, has any power to instruct a judge how to decide any one of the cases that comes before him. If a parliamentary body does not like the judicial interpretation of one of its statutes in a particular case, then it can amend the statute, use different words, and hope that this will cause a different judicial interpretation when next the statute is before a court. But that is all a parliamentary body can do or should attempt to do under the constitution. As for ministers of the Crown, when the government is an interested party in litigation or prosecution before the courts, then the minister can instruct counsel to appear and argue in court for the result the executive government would prefer, but that is all a minister can do or should do under the constitution. The judge remains autonomous, both as to his determination of fact and his interpretations of the applicable law.[35]

The Constitution of 1982 gives the Canadian Supreme Court the right to hear constitutional cases. Such cases may come to the Court through ordinary litigation, as a result of a taxpayer's suit, or when the Court is asked to give an advisory opinion on constitutional law by the federal government or one of the provincial governments.[36] Despite this power, Canadian judges tend to be judicially conservative. They see themselves as interpreters of the law and not lawmakers. One judicial scholar has written: "The Canadian Supreme Court has chosen to play a circumscribed role within the legislative judicial system and this study points to the limited policy-making function of the Supreme Court with regard to legislative enactments. This can be seen particularly clearly in contrast to its common law neighbor to the south."[37]

Canada has an ombudsman in nine of its ten provinces (there is no ombudsman at the federal level). In addition, there are a number of specialized ombudsmen to investigate the administration of prisons, transportation, and so forth.

There are generally positive perceptions of the legal system and legal practitioners in Australia. For example, a 1962 study of Sydney residents ranked solicitors second (after doctors) in status among eighteen professions.[38] Similarly, a study a decade later found little cynicism regarding lawyers (for example, nearly 52 percent disagreed with the statement "As soon as you get in the hands of the legal profession you are bound to lose in some way," while only 29 percent agreed with that statement).[39] Sixty-five percent found the law to be "fair to everyone in the community" (an additional 15 percent were not sure of their feelings on this question).[40] Only 27 percent saw the legal system as "too corrupt for my liking," and nearly 84 percent felt that they had never been treated unfairly by the courts.[41]

Australia also has a very clear tradition of judicial independence for both executive and legislative authorities:

Judicial independence and integrity are secured in part by convention and in part by the security of tenure that judges enjoy. The chief justice and the six other justices of the High Court are appointed for life and are removable only by the governor-general on an address from both houses of the Federal Parliament requesting dismissal for reasons of proved misbehavior or incapacity.[42]

The Australian High Court has a similar power of "judicial review" as that found in the American Supreme Court (despite the fact that it is not explicity mentioned in the Constitution).[43] Australia also utilizes an ombudsman in all of its states (except Tasmania) and at the federal level. The powers of the ombudsmen are great: "He acts directly on a complaint from the public or of his own motion, and he has wide-ranging powers of inquiry into 'matters of administration' although he may not inquire into ministerial but merely into departmental, action. One specific area where he has been very useful is his power to investigate administrative delay."[44]

New Zealand also has a well-established tradition of judicial independence. Judges are appointed to hold office for good behavior. In addition, the fixing of the number of high court judges and the provision that their salary may not be reduced during their term on the bench is a further protection of the concept of judicial independence.[45] New Zealand also utilizes the institution of the ombudsman. The ombudsman has the power to investigate government acts and make recommendations to the appropriate minister. If no action is taken, he/she may then make a recommendation to the prime minister and/or to the national legislature.[46] The High Court of New Zealand does not, however, have the power of judicial review for, in New Zealand "laws will be proclaimed by the courts whose jurisdiction extends to the interpretation but not to the striking down at statutes."[47]

NOTES

1. The following are full members of the Commonwealth: Australia, Canada, New Zealand, India, Sri Lanka, Bangladesh, Singapore, Malaysia, Mauritius, Jamaica, Trinidad and Tobago, Guyana, Barbados, the Bahamas, Grenada, Dominica, St. Lucia, Antigua and Barbuda, Tonga, Western Samoa, Fiji, Solomon Islands, Kiribati, Vanuatu, Papua-New Guinea, Malta, Cyprus, the Seychelles, Ghana, Nigeria, Sierra Leone, Tanzania, Uganda, Kenya, Malawi, Zambia, the Gambia, Botswana, Lesotho, Swaziland, Zimbabwe, and the United Kingdom.

While the influence of Great Britain was also great in South Africa, events in that country continue to cause one to question the existence of the rule of law in that country. As a result, the legal system of South Africa will not be included in this chapter.

2. E. McWhinney, *Judicial Review*, 4th ed. (Toronto: University of Toronto Press, 1969), p. 4.

3. See G. L. Gall, *The Canadian Legal System*, 2d ed. (Toronto, Carswell Legal Publications, 1983), chap. 3, for an excellent discussion of the sources of Canadian law.

4. M. Clark, "An Historical Outline," in C. Osborne, ed., *Australia, New Zealand and the South Pacific: A Handbook* (Sydney: Anthony Blond, 1970), p. 10.

5. Ibid., p. 11.

6. Ibid., p. 10.

7. L. G. McLennan and P. J. Norman, "The Legal System of Australia," in K. R. Redden, ed., *Modern Legal Systems Cyclopedia*, vol. 2 (Buffalo, N.Y.: William S. Hein & Co., 1984), pp. 17–18.

8. G. S. Reid, "The Federal Constitution," in C. Osborne, ed., *Australia, New Zealand and the South Pacific: A Handbook* (Sydney: Anthony Blond, 1970), p. 18.

9. B. D. Gray, "The Legal System of New Zealand," in K. R. Redden, ed., *Modern Legal Systems Cyclopedia*, vol. 3 (Buffalo, N.Y.: William S. Hein & Co., 1984), p. 437.

10. M.P.K. Sorenson, "An Historical Outline," in C. Osborne, ed., *Australia, New Zealand and the South Pacific: A Handbook* (Sydney: Anthony Blond, 1970), p. 344.

11. Gray, "The Legal System of New Zealand," p. 441.

12. Department of Statistics, *1984 New Zealand Official Yearbook* (Wellington: P. D. Hasselberg, Government Printer, 1984), p. 287.

13. Gray, "The Legal System of New Zealand," p. 442.

14. *The Legal System of Canada*, Reference Series No. 55 (Ottawa: Publications Section, Department of External Affairs, 1984), p. 3.

15. M. Kinnear, "The Legal System of Canada," in K.R. Redden, ed., *Modern Legal Systems Cyclopedia*, vol. 1 (Buffalo, N.Y.: William S. Hein & Co., 1984), p. 42.

16. C. S. Rhyne, *Law and Judicial Systems of Nations*, 3d ed. (Washington, D.C.: The World Peace Through Law Center, 1978), p. 115.

17. McLennan and Norman, "The Legal System of Australia," p. 34.

18. Ibid., p. 35.

19. Gray, "The Legal System of New Zealand," pp. 453–54.

20. Kinnear, "The Legal System of Canada," p. 33.

21. Ibid., pp. 27–28.

22. Ibid., p. 28.

23. E. Ratushny, "Judicial Appointments: The Lane Legacy," in A. M. Linden, ed., *The Canadian Judiciary* (Toronto: Osgood Hall Law School, York University, 1976), p. 32.

24. Kinnear, "The Legal System of Canada," p. 41.

25. Gall, *The Canadian Legal System*, p. 207.

26. McLennan and Norman, "The Legal System of Australia," p. 49.

27. Ibid., p. 42.

28. See J. Disney et al., *Lawyers* (Sydney: The Law Book Company Ltd., 1977), p. 86, and Rhyne, *Law and Judicial Systems*, p. 39.

29. E. Neumann, *The High Court of Australia: A Collective Portrait*, 2d ed., Occasional Monograph No. 6 (Department of Government and Public Administration, University of Sydney, 1973), pp. 44, 104, 105–6.

30. Gray, "The Legal System of New Zealand," pp. 458–459.

31. Ibid., pp. 462–63.

32. Gall, *The Canadian Legal System*, pp. 315, 318.

33. Ibid., p. 202.

34. Kinnear, "The Legal System of Canada," p. 43.

35. W. R. Lederman, "The Independence of the Judiciary," in A. M. Linden, ed., *The Canadian Judiciary* (Toronto: Osgood Hall Law School, York University, 1976), p. 7.

36. Kinnear, "The Legal System of Canada," p. 41.

37. S. G. Mezey, "Civil Law and Common Law Traditions: Judicial Review and Legislative Supremacy in West Germany and Canada," *International and Comparative Law Quarterly* 32 (July 1983), p. 690.

38. Disney, *Lawyers*, pp. 180–81.

39. R. Tomasic, *Lawyers and the Community* (Sydney: The Law Foundation of New South Wales, 1978), p. 230.

40. Ibid., p. 187.

41. Ibid., pp. 192, 317.

42. D. Whitaker et al., *Area Handbook for Australia* (Washington, D.C.: U.S. Government Printing Office, 1973), p. 185.

43. See McWhinney, *Judicial Review*, and L. Zines, *The High Court and the Constitution* (Sydney: Butterworths, 1981), for a full discussion of this power of the High Court.

44. McLennan and Norman, "The Legal System of Australia," p. 40.

45. Department of Statistics, *1984 New Zealand Official Yearbook*, p. 288.

46. Gray, "The Legal System of New Zealand," pp. 455–456.

47. Ibid., p. 450.

BIBLIOGRAPHY

Cheffins, R. I., and R. N. Tucker. *The Constitutional Process in Canada*. Toronto: McGraw-Hill Company of Canada Ltd., 1976.

Cowen, Z., and L. Zines. *Federal Jurisdiction in Australia*. Melbourne: Oxford University Press, 1978.

Crawford, R. M. *Australia*. London: Hutchinson University Library, 1970.

Department of Statistics. *1984 New Zealand Official Yearbook*. Wellington: P. D. Hasselberg, Government Printer, 1984.

Disney, J., J. Basten, P. Redmond, and S. Ross. *Lawyers*. Sydney: The Law Book Company Ltd., 1977.

Forbes, J.R.S. *The Divided Legal Profession in Australia: History, Rationalization and Rationale*. Sydney: The Law Book Company Ltd., 1979.

Gall, G. L. *The Canadian Legal System*. 2d ed. Toronto: Carswell Legal Publications, 1983.

Gilbert, G. "The Legal System of the British Commonwealth." In K. R. Redden, ed., *Modern Legal Systems Cyclopedia*, vol. 3. Buffalo, N.Y.: William S. Hein & Co., 1984. Pp. 557–71.

Gray, B. D. "The Legal System of New Zealand." In K. R. Redden, ed., *Modern Legal Systems Cyclopedia*, vol. 3. Buffalo, N.Y.: William S. Hein & Co., 1984. Pp. 431–66.

Hogg, P. W. *Constitutional Law in Canada*. Toronto: Carswell Company Ltd., 1977.

Kinnear, M. "The Legal System of Canada." In K. R. Redden, ed., *Modern Legal Systems Cyclopedia*, vol. 1. Buffalo, N.Y.: William S. Hein & Co., 1984. Pp. 9–59.

Laskin, B. *The British Tradition in Canadian Law*. London: Stevens & Sons, 1969.

Lederman, W. R. "Notes: Canadian Legal Education in the Second Half of the Twentieth Century." *University of Toronto Law Journal* 21 (1971), pp. 141–61.

Levine, S. *The New Zealand Political System: Politics in a Small Society*. Sydney: George Allen & Unwin, 1979.

Linden, A. M., ed. *The Canadian Judiciary*. Toronto: Osgood Hall Law School, York University, 1976.

Mallory, J. M. *The Structure of Canadian Government*. Toronto: Gage Publishing Co., 1984.

McLennan, L. G., and P. J. Norman, "The Legal System of Australia." In K. R. Redden, ed., *Modern Legal Systems Cyclopedia*, vol. 2. Buffalo, N.Y.: William S. Hein & Co., 1984. Pp. 9–70.

Mezey, S. G. "Civil Law and Common Law Traditions: Judicial Review and Legislative Supremacy in West Germany and Canada." *International and Comparative Law Quarterly* 32 (July 1983), pp. 689–707.

Neumann, E. *The High Court of Australia: A Collective Portrait*. 2d ed. Occasional Monograph No. 6. Department of Government and Public Administration, University of Sydney, 1973.

Osborne, C., ed. *Australia, New Zealand, and the South Pacific: A Handbook*. Sydney: Anthony Blond, 1970.

Rhyne, C. S. *Law and Judicial Systems of Nations*. 3d ed. Washington, D.C.: The World Peace Through Law Center, 1978.

Russell, P., R. Décary, W. Lederman, N. Lyon, and D. Saberman. *The Court and the Constitution*. Kingston, Ontario: Queen's University, Institute of Intergovernmental Relations, 1982.

Sawer, G. *Australian Federalism in the Courts*. Melbourne: Melbourne University Press, 1967.

Smith, J. "The Origins of Judicial Review in Canada." *Canadian Journal of Political Science* 16, no. 1 (March 1983), pp. 115–34.

Tomasic, R. *Lawyers and the Community*. Sydney: The Law Foundation of New South Wales, 1978.

Weiler, P. *In the Last Resort: A Critical Study of the Supreme Court of Canada*. Toronto: Carswell/Methuen, 1974.

Whitaker, D., P. Just, J. E. MacDonald, K. W. Martindale, R. Shinn, and N. Vreeland. *Area Handbook for Australia*. Washington, D.C.: U.S. Government Printing Office, 1973.

Wynes, W. A. *Legislative, Executive and Judicial Powers in Australia*. 5th ed. Sydney: The Law Book Company Ltd., 1976.

Zines, L. *The High Court and the Constitution*. Sydney: Butterworths, 1981.

4

EASTERN EUROPE

Paul J. Best

Communist states contain about one-third of the world's population, administer about a third of the world's land surface, and control about 25 percent of the world economy. Depending on how one assesses the situation in Afghanistan and Kampuchea, there are fifteen or seventeen countries ruled by Communist parties. An additional five countries, Mozambique, Ethiopia, Angola, Zimbabwe, and the People's Democratic Republic of South Yemen, are ruled by political parties professing a Marxist-Leninist orientation, and they are recognized as "vanguard" parties by Moscow. All Communist or vanguard party-ruled countries, whether pro-Soviet or independent, claim to be following the principles laid down by the fathers of contemporary communism: Karl Marx, Friedrich Engels, and Vladimir Ilyich Ulyanov (Lenin).

THE DEVELOPMENT OF THE LEGAL SYSTEMS

The Philosophical Foundations of Communist Legal Systems

Marx and Engels and their followers teach that human history develops through five epochs. The first epoch, "Primitive Communalism," the earliest period of human existence, was without political organization. People lived at a bare subsistence level. When economic conditions changed because of the introduction of metal tools so that people were able to produce a bit more than the minimal requirements for existence, it became possible for one person to exploit another and the institution of slavery was introduced. This new "Slave Epoch" created the need for the institutionalization of the control of a few (the slaveowners) over the many; this institution and its legal system is called "the state." Next came a shift from ownership of human bodies to ownership of land (the "Feudal Epoch") and the subsequent modification of the legal system to feudal conditions. Beginning in Europe in the eighteenth century, human society has been undergoing a new change—now the emphasis is on the ownership of the means of production (the productive machinery). This new stage is called the "Capitalist Epoch." In slavery, feudalism, and capitalism the state is used as a tool by the ruling class to oppress the workers: armies, police, religion, jails, and the law courts are part of this oppressive mechanism. Thus, the legal system at certain given stages in history is simply a tool used by the slaveowners, feudal landlords, or capitalist entrepreneurs to maintain themselves in power. The specific laws used to carry out the will of the exploiting class depends on the specific state:

If the state and the public law are determined by economic relations, so, too, of course is private law, which indeed in essence only sanctions the existing economic relations between individuals which are normal in the given circumstances. The form in which this happens can, however, vary considerably. It is possible, as happened in England, in harmony with the whole national development, to retain in the main the forms of the old feudal laws [common law] while giving them a bourgeois [capitalist] content. . . . After a great bourgeois revolution, it is also possible for such a classic law code of bourgeois society as the French *Code Civil* to be worked out upon the basis of . . . Roman Law. . . . Bourgeois legal rules merely express the economic . . . conditions of society in legal form.[1]

Marx and Engels thus saw law as a dependent variable: "It must not be forgotten that law has just as little an independent history as religion" and serves the masters of a given epoch of human development.[2] The form may stay the same as human history develops, but the substance will be modified to fit the new economic conditions of capitalism. So, for example, the Romano-Germanic legal system, which had its origin in the slave stage and which was used in feudal times, was adapted to capitalist conditions by the French. Although Marx and Engels saw the nineteenth-century legal apparatus as a mechanism designed to keep the oppressed masses in their place, they believed this situation would not be permanent because, in the fifth epoch of human development, "Socialism-Communism," the pattern of a minority oppressing the majority would be broken. In this stage, the masses would come to power and destroy the old system. This destruction would include the whole state apparatus including, of course, the legal system. It was not at all clear what would take the old state's place, but Marx and Engels were little concerned with this since their major effort was aimed at analyzing capitalism and predicting its collapse. The first major application of Marxist thought in a concrete situation occurred in Russia.

The Formation of the First Marxian-Socialist Legal System

Vladimir Ilyich Ulyanov (Lenin) was born in Simbirsk (now Ulyanovsk), Russia, in 1870. In 1891, while under police restrictions due to radical activities, Lenin, having studied in absentia, was allowed to take the examinations of the law department of the University of St. Petersburg. He passed, received a first-class diploma, and began work the following year as a lawyer. Despite his studies and position, Lenin condemned the then current Imperial Russian legal system. "The state," he said, and all its apparatus "is the product and manifestation of the irreconcilability of class antagonisms. The state arises when, where, and to the extent that class antagonism objectively cannot be reconciled."[3] This state had to be "smashed," "abolished," and replaced firstly by a "Dictatorship of the Proletariat" and later by a socialist state that would "wither away" as society approached full-scale communism.[4] The new Soviet state that began in November 1917 with the overthrow of the provisional government was not expected to be equipped with a legal system; rather, the armed masses would begin administering the new society based on revolutionary necessity.[5] During the chaotic first years of the Soviet regime, the Communists ran a revolution while fighting a civil war and foreign intervention. They paid little attention to the matter of a formal legal system, and, while many decrees were issued by the new government, Soviet law did not start to be codified until 1921. Lenin withdrew from political life in 1922 due to ill health and died in 1924. During the struggle for power that followed Lenin's demise, legal experimentation took place, but it was left to Joseph Vissarionovich Djugashvili (Stalin) to put the Soviet legal system into its final form. Stalin taught that a dialectical paradox took place in the development of the Soviet state, for it needed to become the strongest state the world had ever known before it could "wither away" as communism was approached. Therefore, a complete legal structure was required.

In 1936, under provisions of the new Stalinist constitution of the Union of Soviet Socialist Republics, the Dictatorship of the Proletariat appeared to end because the Soviet Union was now declared to be a "State of All the People." Nevertheless, the power of the state has remained at the highest level, and Soviet leaders have declared it foolish to believe that the Soviet people could let their guard down while major capitalist powers still existed. Only after all countries had started down the path to socialism could the state start to decline. Since the date when the whole world will adopt socialism cannot be precisely known, the Soviet state must remain vigilant and powerful. The first principle of Soviet law, therefore, is the protection of the Revolution and its gains. This principle supersedes all formal law and allows for state actions that might, in other circumstances, be considered illegal. It should be noted, parenthetically, that Engels did not think revolution could be exported. "The victorious proletariat can force no blessings of any kind upon any foreign nation without undermining its own victory by so doing."[6] This, however, has not prevented the USSR from imposing its experience on other countries in Europe and Asia. In any case, the Soviet legal system has gone through three stages. The first was that of the "Dictatorship of the Proletariat—where formal law was deemphasized and the needs of the Revolution were paramount. Individuals, except the leaders (and not even many of them during the purges), had no particular value, and whole categories of purported enemies-of-the-people were liquidated with little formal proceedings. The Soviet attitude was that "law is a political measure, it is politics" and any action was justified if it supported the Revolution.[7] Since "the legal system would soon fall into disuse . . . it was hardly necessary to adhere strictly to rules set in formal documents expected soon to be pushed aside as irrelevant to the communist society of the Bolsheviks' dreams.''[8] Nevertheless, this stage saw the enactment of legal codes that institutionalized Soviet power.

The second stage, called the "Building of Socialism," began in 1928 with Stalin's industrialization and forced collectivization program. During this period, it was claimed that a "State of All the People" was being constructed and corresponding changes in the law were made, signaling the end of the Dictatorship of the Proletariat. Actually, of course, the 1930s was the time of the Great Terror and extralegal mass repression on an extraordinary scale.

In 1961 Nikita Khrushchev declared that the bases of socialism had been constructed and that the Soviet Union was entering the third stage, that of the "Construction of the Foundations of Communism."[9] Since Khrushchev's fall in 1964, this present period is referred to as that of "Developed Socialism." It is said that in Developed Socialism the legal system becomes more important, although the protection of revolutionary gains by whatever means necessary is still recognized.

Soviet jurists have proposed that "Socialist Legality," which seems to be similar to Western "due process of law," be the basic legal concept of Developed Socialism. "Soviet legal science regards socialist legality as the precise observance and execution of the Soviet Constitution and the laws and subordinate enactments based on it by all state organs, mass organizations, persons in office and citizens.''[10]

The Soviets contend that their legal system constitutes a new type not previously seen. This view has been accepted by some in the West. John N. Hazard, for example, the dean of American legal experts on Communist systems, agrees that the Soviet system is a new type. Other commentators, however, see the Soviet legal system as a Romanist one that favors the state and its Communist ruling elite over the individual.

Whatever the case, the Soviet legal system is at the present time a very extensive one, as large as or larger in scope than any in the contemporary world. It is this system that dominates in the six Soviet bloc countries in Eastern Europe and which has strongly influenced Yugoslavia, Albania, and other Communist states.

The Formation of the East European Legal System

Political Eastern Europe, that area of central Europe between the USSR (geographic East Europe) and political Western Europe, contains eight countries ruled by Communist parties. The Communist parties in East Europe all came to power in the 1944–1948 period as a direct result of World War II. In six cases, "fraternal assistance" by the Soviet Union assured the seizure of power. In Yugoslavia and Albania, indigenous guerrilla movements brought the Communist parties to power. This made for resistance to Soviet control. In the 1944–1948 period, Moscow was supreme in East Europe, and the Soviet paradigm was uncritically used in establishing Communist regimes. This model was based on theories of Marx and Engels and Leninist and Stalinist practice. The establishment of a Communist regime meant the transplantation of Soviet usage in all things, including the legal system. Only one country (Yugoslavia) started to diverge during Stalin's lifetime, and that occurred only after Tito was expelled from the Soviet bloc in 1948. The Soviet Union's attempted rapproachement with Tito in 1956 frightened Albania, which was fearful of being swallowed by Yugoslavia, into defection in that year.[11] Other attempts to diverge too greatly from the Soviet model have been successfully repressed (German Democratic Republic—1953; Poland—1956, 1970, 1976, 1981; Czechoslovakia—1968; Hungary—1956). Even Tito, who apparently thought he would succeed Stalin as the leader of the Communist bloc, introduced a system more Soviet than the one in the Soviet Union and only changed course after the connection with the USSR was cut by the Soviets themselves.[12]

We may ask, then, is there a common core in the Communist legal systems of Eastern Europe? Professor John Hazard in his book *Communists and Their Law* concludes that, "There are universals found in all . . . of the Marxian socialist states which provide reason to conclude that the legal systems of those states, in spite of a wealth of differences and a vocabulary and even a 'grammar' inspired by the Romanist systems, constitute a distinctive legal family."[13] Thus, Hazard feels that the Marxian-Socialist legal system is on a par with the Anglo-American system, the Continental European system, and those derived from holy writ. He cites the "Declaration of the Twelve Communist Parties in Power" of 1957 for the basic principles of socialism: (1) leadership of the Marxist-Leninist party; (2) state ownership of the basic means of production; (3) gradual socialist reconstruction of agriculture; (4) planned economy; (5) socialist revolution in ideology and culture; (6) friendship among nationalities; (7) defense against external and internal enemies; and (8) proletarian internationalism.[14]

Legal systems based on these principles have enough in common to be considered a group. Despite Hazard's labors, not everyone agrees that the Communists have created a new legal system.[15] Whether or not there is a Marxian-socialist legal system and whether or not it encompasses all Communist countries is not a problem that can be solved here. We will concentrate on the six East European states that are bound to the USSR by political ties (through the Communist party), economic ties (through the Council of Mutual Economic Assistance), and military ties (through the Warsaw Pact). Yugoslavia and Albania will also be included in the discussion, since they have been heavily influenced in their development by the Soviet Union and the other East European countries and since their legal systems are substantially compatible with the rest of Eastern Europe.

No country in Eastern Europe can claim to have a continuous legal history although some populations have existed as national groups for over 1,000 years. Bulgaria, while an empire in medieval times, was long under Turkish domination

(1340–1876); Yugoslavia exists as a united country only since 1918; Albania has been independent only since 1912; Hungary has existed since AD 950 but with a long period of Austrian Habsburg domination; Romania had a gap of 1,000 years of historical silence between the Daco-Roman times and 1450; Czechoslovakia has been a complete unit only since 1918; Germany has been known since Roman times, but the present East Germany is a very recent creation of the Soviet Union; Poland came on the historic stage in AD 966, but was partitioned from 1772 to 1918. The nineteenth and twentieth centuries, then, are the places to look for the development of modern legal systems in Eastern Europe.

Poland

Poland entered the twentieth century as a land divided among three occupying powers. Eastern and central Poland was in the Russian Empire as the Polish Kingdom and the "Vistula Lands"; south and southeast Poland was the Austrian province of Galicia; while west and northwest Poland was part of the Prussian provinces called Pomerania, Silesia, and the Grand Duchy of Poznan. A Polish state returned to the map of Europe in November 1918, and in the following twenty years a full-scale legal apparatus was created. The major problem Poland had was unifying and codifying its law, which had Prussian, Austrian, and Russian sources, plus the Napoleon Code (with Russian amendments), and, in two small areas (Spisz and Orawa), Hungarian law. The codification program was nearly completed by the beginning of World War II.[16] A complete underground state existed in Poland during World War II, which included law courts and the execution of justice, and a government-in-exile functioned in London. The Soviets decided to form a "friendly" government when the Red Army occupied the country, and a Communist regime was imposed. This new republic was based on "popular-democratic" (Soviet) principles, and "The Soviet army gave decisive assistance in the consolidation of power by the popular democratic camp, led by the Polish Workers' Party [Communist party]."[17]

The interwar system, including civil, criminal, administrative, and labor law, was continued, but those parts of the law considered favorable to the former ruling class were disregarded. The legal structure of the new Polish People's Republic was established in the 1947–1952 period, when all resistance to Communist rule in Poland was crushed. During this period a "Sejm Ustawodawczy" (Constitutional Parliament) was elected in rigged voting on January 17, 1947, and, dominated by Communists and their allies, passed all the laws necessary to give legal foundation to Communist rule. Finally, the Constitution was put into effect on July 22, 1952.[18]

Czechoslovakia

In the interwar period, Czechoslovakia had to amalgamate a country that, in the west, had been under Austrian law (with the exception of Hlucinsko—Upper

Silesia) and in the east under Hungarian law. During the nearly twenty years of peace, laws were passed for the whole country, but Austrian or Hungarian law remained in effect in their specific areas unless specific changes took place. As a result of World War II, most of the Subcarpathian region was lost to the USSR. In the 1948–1968 period, the country was treated as a single unit, and there was an uncritical application of ''the pattern of Soviet law not only in substance but also in form.''[19] Since 1968, Czechoslovakia has been a federal state of two units, the Czech lands (Bohemia and Moravia) and Slovakia. Czechoslovakia followed a different pattern of communization, since it was an Allied power in World War II and its government-in-exile had cooperated with the USSR by transferring the eastern-most province of Subcarpathian Ruthenia to the USSR and by accommodating the Soviet foreign policy. Despite government attempts to placate and appease the USSR, the indigeneous Czechoslovakia Communist party pressed for more and more power within the postwar regime until the non-Communists were forced out of political office and the Communists seized complete power. After a thorough-going purge of all non-Communist elements from the state and legal apparatus in 1948, a Communist constitution was enacted by a legislature dominated by the Communist party.[20]

German Democratic Republic (GDR)

If the establishment of people's regimes in Poland and Czechoslovakia had at least some basis in existing states, the establishment of the GDR was totally artificial. The Soviet occupation zone of Germany under Soviet military admin-istration was transformed into a Soviet-type state through a series of decrees issued by the Soviet Military Administration (SMAD). At the same time, political activity was directed toward the establishment of the hegemony of the German Communist party. The main left-wing non-Communist party, the Social Dem-ocratic party, was put out of action by a forced merger with the Communist party to form the Socialist Unity party (Sozialistische Einheitspartei), the current name for the ruling Communist party. On October 7, 1949, the foundation of the German Democratic Republic was established by the voting of a constitution by the provisional Volkskammer (People's Chamber) legislature.[21] Since the GDR had been established essentially to reflect Soviet interests in the heart of Europe, it also follows the Soviet example in state structure. The Ministry of Justice of the GDR was de-Nazified, and 80 percent of the 2,500 judges, and state-employed lawyers were deprived of their positions, and a new civil admin-istration was established. Law faculties were purged, Soviet-type legal training was established, and by 1949 the GDR reflected the USSR's pattern of government.[22]

Hungary

Hungary represents a different case than Poland, Czechoslovakia, or the GDR in that the Soviets established a provisional coalition government of non-Fascists and Communists on Hungarian territory overrun by the Soviet Army in December 1944. The Communists, with the Soviet occupation army's help, over the next three years squeezed the non-Communists out of power so that, in June 1948, the last independent party was absorbed by the Hungarian Communist party to form the Hungarian Workers' party. On August 20, 1949, a Constitution of the Hungarian People's Republic was declared, which had the usual Soviet trappings.

Romania

On August 23, 1944, Romania switched sides in World War II, turning from an alliance with Nazi Germany to support of the Allied powers. In contributing twelve divisions to the front, Romania was stripped of its armed forces and the country was occupied by the Red Army. By March 1945 a "puppet" regime was in place, opposition to the regime was destroyed, and the legal system was "adjusted" to serve revolutionary legality.[23]

Bulgaria

Bulgaria suffered no less than did Romania despite the fact that, although a formal ally of Nazi Germany, it had never declared war on the USSR or engaged in hostilities against her. The about-face of Romania in 1944 suddenly placed Bulgaria in the position of having Soviet forces drawing near to its frontier. The Soviets declared war on Bulgaria on September 5 and crossed the Danube on September 8. On September 9 a pro-Communist government was installed, and all the Soviets had to do was establish garrisons and maintain order while, over the next two years, all opposition to communization was liquidated.

Yugoslavia and Albania

Yugoslavia and Albania are two variants of the same type. In both cases indigenous Communist forces obtained power. The actual seizure of power, while influenced by the proximity of the Soviet army, was not caused by it. In Yugoslavia, pro-Communist partisans led by Josip Broz Tito managed to suppress their opponents while fighting the Germans. The 1945–1948 period represents an attempt to uncritically apply Soviet experience to local conditions.[24] However, the Yugoslavs refused to allow direct Soviet control in their country, either in recruiting agents for the USSR or for the establishment of joint Soviet-Yugoslav economic ventures. In a major miscalculation, Stalin thought that by formally expelling Yugoslavia from the ranks of the Cominform (Communist Information Bureau) he could either cause Tito to be overthrown or to repent of his sins. The Yugoslavs were temporarily thrown off balance, but they soon recovered equilibrium and began to build their own "national" non-Soviet Communist state. The Yugoslavs began to criticize the Soviet system, focusing on its over-centralization and bureaucratization.[25] After 1950, this critique caused a number of major changes that have altered Yugoslavia substantially. Yugoslavia has decentralized, moved toward workers' self-management in industry and a federalized Communist party, and made the federal structure of the state a political reality—rather than a facade, as in the USSR.[26] These changes, along with nonalignment in foreign policy, have taken Yugoslavia along a separate path that has continued even after the death of Tito in 1980. In regard to the legal system, Yugoslavia retains a system similar to the other states of East Europe but is unaffected by heavy pressure that the Soviets bring to bear from time to time on the six Soviet bloc countries to modify laws in favor of Soviet practice.

Albania represents a peculiar quirk among Communist states. Like Yugoslavia, power was seized by a domestic Communist movement when the Germans withdrew. Albania has gone through several phases during the past forty years. From 1945 to 1948, the Albanians cooperated closely with the Yugoslav Communists, and the Yugoslavs did to Albania those very things that the Soviets did in the countries they occupied but which the Yugoslavs would not allow the Soviets to do in Yugoslavia. The split between Yugoslavia and the USSR allowed Albania to shake itself loose of Yugoslavian control and to gravitate toward the distant Soviet Union. When Nikita Khrushchev tried to court Tito to rejoin the Communist camp, the Albanian Stalin, Enver Hoxha, saw his position threatened, so he moved Albania under the wing of China. When Mao Zedong passed from the scene, Albania turned inward, declaring itself to be the only true Communist state in the world. One may characterize Albania as having suffered through forty years of xenophobic and paranoic one-man dictatorship. All opponents, real or imagined, have been liquidated, including the close collaborator of Hoxda, Prime Minister Mehmet Shehu, who is said to have committed suicide in 1981. Recent reports indicated that a slight opening to the outside is being made, and this trend is expected to continue.[27] Albania today shares many common features of the East European legal system but refuses to adopt the latest Soviet innovations.

THE ORGANIZATION OF THE LEGAL SYSTEMS

The court systems in Eastern Europe, like the laws they administer, generally parallel the Soviet model. Poland, the GDR, Hungary, Romania, Bulgaria, and Albania are unitary states and thus fairly uncomplicated in administrative structure. Their court systems resemble those of the fifteen constituent republics of the USSR. Yugoslavia and Czechoslovakia, however, are federal states and thus are more complex in their administration of justice. Czechoslovakia is the simpler of the two since it is a federated state of only two republics. Yugoslavia is quite complex and comes closer to the USSR national government in its make-up. Yugoslavia has five constituent republics (Slovenia, Croatia, Serbia, Montenegro, and Mecedonia) plus two autonomous regions (Kosovo and Vojvodina) attached to the Serbian republic.

The six unitary states of East Europe generally follow a three-layered pattern in court structure. At the top is the Supreme Court. The powers of this Court include final appeals jurisdiction in all areas, original jurisdiction in a few matters (usually high treason and international law problems), and supervision of lower court activities. East European supreme courts have no right to review the law, that is, to decide whether laws are constitutional or not, for the legislative body is supreme, and executive and judicial activities are subordinate to it. This, however, is not peculiar to East Europe; it is the norm of most parliamentary systems.

The Supreme Courts do not consist of a single chamber with a few justices but are rather large bodies, frequently having up to one hundred judges. Further, the Supreme Courts are divided into four or five chambers that adjudicate the various types of cases that come before the Court. The Albanian Supreme Court, for example, has four chambers; Czechoslovakia, five chambers (military, civil and family, criminal chambers plus a plenary chamber and a presidium chamber); Hungary, five (criminal, civil, military, labor, and economic); and Poland, four (civil, criminal, labor, and social insurance).[28]

Below the Supreme Court in the six unitary states are the provincial courts. Yugoslavia and Czechoslovakia have an intermediary layer of courts. Czechoslovakia has the Supreme Court of the Federation in Prague, then a supreme court for the Czechlands and a supreme court for Slovakia—below these two intermediary courts are the provincial courts.[29] In Yugoslavia, there is a Federal Supreme Court in Belgrade and below it are supreme courts of the individual republics before one reaches the provincial courts.[30] Included in the provincial level are courts of the largest cities (e.g., East Berlin, Warsaw, Bucharest, Sofia) and, of course, of the provinces themselves (e.g., 15 in GDR, 52 in Poland, 40 in Romania, 28 in Bulgaria). These courts are "elected" by and are subordinate to provincial legislatures. At the lowest level is the district court. Districts include rural counties, towns, and wards of the largest cities.

All the East European states also have a separate military court structure that is subject to the supreme court of each country. There are also state arbitration commissions that handle domestic and foreign quarrels about goods and services. Finally, outside the regular court structure, at the level of the work place, are totally lay "comrades courts." These amateur groups are used to encourage work discipline, comradely relationships, and the proper attitude toward domestic life and to suppress absenteeism, alcoholism, and hooliganism. These citizens' courts have been allowed to impose small fines, disciplinary measures, and reprimands. The success of this use of peer-group pressure cannot be easily assessed.[31]

All the East European countries use a special mechanism called the procuracy to supervise the state and judicial apparatus. This scheme is derived from a Prussian idea that was later taken over by the Imperial Russian state. The Bolsheviks did away with the procuracy but later revived it as one of many mechanisms to ensure Communist party control within the state, and the Soviet procuracy was transplanted into East Europe at the end of World War II. The procuracy is a separate bureaucracy that functions at all levels of government for supervision and control. It is headed by a procurator general who is charged with the duty to see that socialist legality is observed, that state property and civil rights are protected, criminals are prosecuted, and that socialist social systems are preserved. The procurator general is elected by the national legislature in the same way that supreme court justices are chosen. However, provincial and district procurators are appointed from above and are independent of local legislative bodies.[32] Because the procurator general is (1) always a high-level communist party functionary; (2) is "elected" by a legislature controlled by the Communist party; and (3) he and the apparatus appointed by him function independently of local legislatures and the Ministry of Justice on a nationwide scale, the procuracy can be seen as simply another "system of multiple and counter checking, . . . for factfinding and control, with ultimate responsibility neither to the . . . [legislature] nor to the Government but to the highest organs of the Party itself."[33]

The ministries of justice in each of the East European states maintain the legal system by supervising and controlling the judges and the courts (the judges are civil servants on the ministries' payroll). These ministries oversee the carrying out of laws and provide penal facilities. Several of the East European states have state notary bureaus under the justice ministry, which function like the French model; that is, the notarial bureaus are places where oaths can be taken, property transferred, documents signed, deeds and wills drawn up and witnessed, and other similar paperwork can be accomplished.

THE PERSONNEL OF THE LAW

Legal Practitioners

Legal training in East Europe is the province of the university, for independent law institutes never developed as in the USSR. The only exception is that advanced legal study may be done in one of the specialized sections of the academy of sciences, where a doctor of laws degree may be earned.

Legal training is not taken at the post-graduate but rather at the undergraduate level. Students enter the university after ten to twelve years of primary and secondary education. Admission to university departments of law is based on completion of secondary education (usually a college preparatory type), passing a specific written entrance examination for that department of the university, an oral examination, and recommendation by the secondary school. In addition, it does not hurt if the Communist youth organization and/or a Communist party member also recommends admission.

Admission quotas are part of the state plan and are decided upon by the Ministry of Higher Education and the Ministry of Justice, which determine the number of positions to be made available in the law departments, based on an estimate of the number of new legal trainees that the state will require at the time when a particular class graduates. Legal studies take four to five years if one studies full-time and five to six years for evening and correspondence courses. Besides the study of the law of the specific country, languages are also taught along with Marxist philosophy, history of the Communist party, dialectical and historical materialism, and political economy.

Candidates for legal training in Albania may apply to the University of Tirana, and Bulgarian candidates also have only one school (University of Sofia), but in Czechoslovakia there are four university law departments; the GDR has four; Hungary has three; and Poland has nine law departments plus two specialized canon law schools run by the Roman Catholic church at the Catholic Theological Academy in Warsaw and the Catholic University of Lublin. Romania has three universities with law departments. In one of these, Cluj-Napoca, law is taught not only in Romanian but also German and Hungarian (Romania, although a unitary state, recognizes the existence of two "co-inhabiting nationalities").[34] Yugoslavia maintains twelve law departments in the universities of its various divisions in which law is taught in the local language.[35]

Graduates of law faculties may have a number of possibilities of employment available to them, but they are not absolutely free to choose. In Communist states it is a matter of policy that those who have attended publicly-supported schools must work in an assigned position in their area of training for a three to five year period. Theoretically, at least, the state plan has foreseen where the needs lie and has allocated resources to train people to fill these needs. In practice, however, the planning system is not so efficient, and there are many ways around the requirement to accept assigned work. The clever student or one with good connections will get what he or she wants while the not-so-clever or not-so-well-connected ones will get disagreeable assignments.

Despite its abhorrence of lawyers because they are seen as willing tools and lackeys of the oppressive legal systems of slavery, feudalism, and capitalism, the Marxian socialist system is a great consumer of legal talent. Law graduates are placed in the following areas in each nation: (1) the state court systems—as judges and clerks; (2) public administration—as legal consultants to state enterprises and commercial institutions (various state banks and the state-owned domestic and foreign insurance companies); (3) civil service—in consultant positions in the state governmental apparatus; (4) Ministry of Justice—in administrative offices and supervisory commissions, the Notarial Bureau and arbitration commissions; (5) Ministry of Internal Affairs—in the regular (civil) police; (6) Ministry or Office (Committee) of State Security—in the secret police; (7) Ministry of Defense—as legal advisors and functionaries in the military courts; (8) procurator's office—as supervisors of state apparatus; (9) Ministry of Foreign Affairs—in the diplomatic service; (10) the Communist party—as advisors with the Communist party apparatus; (11) the Communist Youth League—even though the usual upper-age for membership in the youth leagues is twenty-five, special exceptions up to forty-five and beyond can be made for valuable administrators; (12) cooperative activities—as advisors to collective farms, crafts cooperatives, and public organizations; and (13) lawyers' cooperatives—lawyers are not able to set up a completely private practice. They must join a cooperative that more or less tightly controls its members, depending on the practice of a given country.

In regard to the latter option, each of the East European states has a bar association, but each state has different rules as to who may or must belong. The general pattern is that lawyers in the public sector do not belong while those in the lawyers' cooperatives must belong in order to practice.[36]

Judges

Justices of the Superior Court are officially elected to office by the national legislatures (usually for a five-year term). In theory the people's representatives in the legislatures elect the judges in a democratic fashion. Practically speaking, however, the judges are appointed by the ruling Communist party's Central Committee Secretariat in a process called Nomenklatura. This means that the Communist party has the right to recruit and nominate people to key governmental positions. After selections are made, nominees' names are presented to the rubber-stamp legislature for approval. The "election" of the nominees is a foregone conclusion, since only one candidate for a position is presented, the legislature is dominated by Communist party members, and no preconfirmation hearings are held. It is unheard of that a nominee is not confirmed, and it is inconceivable that a Supreme Court nomination be rejected as sometimes occurs in the United States. Judges are almost always members of the Communist party, but, in a few rare cases, highly competent, trusted, non-party members may be found in office.

Judges of the provincial courts are selected in the same manner as those of the upper courts, but the provincial party apparatus, with some supervision from the central authorities, makes the selection. District court judges are elected either in the general elections or by the district legislature. In either case, the selection of nominees is still within the domain of the Communist party. When the "election" takes place, there is only one candidate, who is either a Communist party member or a trusted non-party person. Rarely is anyone ever not elected, although one author mentions that some judges, who somehow ran afoul of the regime, were not reelected and this was chalked up to the "democratic process."[37] At the lowest level, a rather large percentage of judges are women— up to 40 percent in some countries.

Judges in Eastern Europe, today, besides being acceptable to the Communist party, are selected on the basis of legal training. They usually have completed four to five years of study, have undergone an apprenticeship, and have passed an appropriate state examination.[38] In the past, judges were selected more for their political reliability than any attainments in education, whether general education or legal. The chief criterion was working-class origins and a "revolutionary mentality."[39]

Assessors

Another feature of the East European court systems is the use of so-called lay assessors whenever a case is first heard (lay assessors are rarely used in appeals procedures). Even though the judge is "elected," this is not considered sufficient. In order to bring the courts "closer to the people," two lay people sit together with the judge to adjudicate a case. These lay assessors vote along with the judge in order to reach a verdict. Theoretically (though this rarely occurs), the two lay assessors can out-vote the professional judge, since only a majority vote is needed. The assessors are generally chosen for a two-year period to be part of a bank of people available to sit for up to two weeks a year. Assessors are selected to serve by work collectives (that is, names are sent in by work units within a district).

PUBLIC PERCEPTIONS AND THE ROLE OF THE COURTS

There are several patterns of public reaction to the legal system in Eastern Europe. In those countries where the Marxian socialist system was imposed by outside force (Poland, GDR, Hungary, Romania, Bulgaria), the regimes have never achieved full legitimacy. In the Czechoslovakian case, where there was strong support for the seizure of power, though not necessarily majoritarian, this support has dissipated over the years, and the 1968 Warsaw Pact invasion dissolved it entirely. That the Soviet Union has had to use force or threat of force a number of times (the imposition of martial law in Poland in 1981 is the last such case) shows how much these regimes ultimately must depend on coercion to maintain control.

The current lack of a firm domestic base in the six Soviet-bloc states plus the memory of the excesses committed during the Dictatorship of the Proletariat period—now euphemistically referred to as the "errors of the cult of the individual"—create a difficult situation for the ruling Communist parties. The existence of overwhelming Soviet power and the rivalries between the East European states leave the common citizen with no hope of relief. Acceptance of the status quo appears to be the only way to survive.

The court system is not seen by the public as a means of protection against government and party abuse. The courts cannot oppose party policy but rather are considered as assistants in performing tasks designated by the party: "All three branches of government—legislative, executive, judicial—must be considered to be members of the same team under the guidance of the Communist party."[40] Any tendency toward judicial autonomy has been diverted back to strong party leadership and control in those countries where there was any chance of the party losing its grip.[41]

It may be asked, then, whether justice can be obtained in East Europe. Certainly the day of summary procedure for political offenses is in the past, although the Communist party can easily call up this reserve in case it feels threatened (e.g., internment in Poland in the martial law period, 1981–1983).[42] In non-punitive, nonpolitical cases, justice can be found. It seems unlikely that a squabble over an automobile accident, for example, would have any political overtones (except, of course, if a high party member were involved), and a reasonable solution could be reached.

However, in those cases where political offenses are alleged, an entirely different set of rules applies. These cases are especially sensitive and whatever independence a judge might have had in nonpolitical cases is gone. Nevertheless, demands for an independent court system have cropped up in Poland, the GDR, Czechoslovakia, Romania, and Yugoslavia.[43] In addition, attempts to resist regime oppression have taken the term of "legalism." For example, the Chapter 77 document circulated in Czechoslovakia appealed to Czechoslovak law and the fact that it had signed the "International Convention on Economic, Social and Cultural Rights." Other East European states had also signed these agreements, thus making them, in a sense, part of domestic law. These regimes have thus accepted some sort of norms and values as having universal validity.[44] The party, however, strongly resists legalism since "as far as the party is concerned . . . the law [must] be administered in a revolutionary or a 'class spirit', of which the party is the sole legitimate interpreter."[45]

Those lawyers who wish to oppose the party in political cases and truly attempt to defend their clients frequently find themselves in trouble. They are often accused of "slandering the authorities and the political system." In Poland, for example, this has taken the form of a continuous struggle between certain members of some of the advocate's collectives and the state apparatus.[46]

Developed Socialism and the Future of the East European Legal System

Soviet-bloc states currently claim to have entered the period of "developed socialism" (Yugoslavia and Albania do not worry about this piece of terminology), a phase of development further down the path to full-scale communism. During this period "under the leadership of the communist party . . . an important step is taken towards laying the material-technical foundation of Communism" toward the victory of world socialism.[47] "Socialist humanism" will develop to allow freedoms not found during the Dictatorship of the Proletariat and the Building of the Foundations of Socialism. Economic planning will become more precise and "the growth of the guiding role of the Communist party will be united with a further development of socialist democracy, the increasing role of social organizations and production units in this higher stage of the building of socialism."[48] There is also to be increasing cooperation among the Communist states.

The USSR also uses several mechanisms to maintain control of the Soviet-bloc states: (1) the Warsaw Pact, a military organization headed by a Soviet general with headquarters in Moscow. The use of armed forces directly by the

Soviet Union alone (East Germany–1953, Hungary–1956) or in concert (Czech-oslovakia–1968) or the threat of their use has kept the bloc states in line. Soviet troops are stationed today in Poland, GDR, Czechoslovakia, Hungary, and Bulgaria; (2) the various economies, which are bound to the USSR's by means of the Council of Mutual Economic Assistance, a not-too-successful response to the European Economic Community; (3) regular party consultation and Moscow's controls in ideology and strategic and tactical policy;[49] (4) East European Soviet-bloc Communist states are further constrained by law. The so-called Brezhnev Doctrine limits sovereignty in that "each Socialist state has a duty to depend not only on its own independence and sovereignty and its own gains of socialism but also the sovereignty and gains of socialism in all other Socialist states."[50]

"Socialist International Law," in the Soviet bloc at least, states that there is a right and duty to intervene to preserve communism and that this act is legal if one sees "laws and norms of law [as] subordinated to the laws of social development. . . . The class approach . . . cannot be discarded in the name of legalistic considerations."[51] Only Romania within the Soviet bloc has dissented from the Soviet view on the right to intervene while Yugoslavia and Albania flatly reject the concept.[52] What then does one have today in Eastern Europe? "The Western doctrine of the rule of law, that justice should be administered independently of political considerations and that all citizens should be equal before the law, is rejected in the Eastern European states."[53]

Some commentators write, however, that administration of law is becoming depoliticized in that ideological considerations are less used in criminal matters and squabbles between citizens. In this area, the courts function quite similarly to those of the Romanist European continental legal system.[54] In general, in conflicts between state and personal interests, clearly the state has the advantage in those areas that are considered political.

In the end, though, any real or apparent resistance to the Communist party control is ruthlessly put down outside the letter of the law. When social scientists look at the legal system in Eastern Europe, they see a reflection of the society which produced it. They see a Romanist-type legal system remolded to fit Communist party needs. Legalities take a backseat to power: "The conclusion cannot be avoided that if there is any principle that Communists hold sacred and which they will defend at all costs, it is the Communist party's monopoly rule."[55]

NOTES

1. F. Engels, "Ludwig Feurbach and the End of Classical German Philosophy," in *Karl Marx and Frederick Engels: Selected Works* (New York: International Publishers, 1968), p. 627.

2. K. Marx, "The German Ideology," in R. C. Tucker, ed., *The Marx-Engels Reader*, 2d ed. (New York: W. W. Norton & Co., Inc., 1978), p. 188.

3. V. I. Lenin, *The State and Revolution* (Moscow: Foreign Languages Publishing House, n.d.), p. 12.

4. Ibid., pp. 25–35.

5. Ibid., pp. 78, 79.

6. Tucker, *The Marx-Engels Reader*, p. 677.

7. J. Hazard et al., *The Soviet Legal System* (Dobbs Ferry, N.Y.: Oceana Publications, Inc., 1969), p. 5.

8. Ibid., p. 6.

9. See *The Road to Communism: Documents of the 22nd Congress of the Communist Party of the Soviet Union* (Moscow: Foreign Languages Publishing House, 1961).

10. V. M. Chkhikvadze, ed., *The Soviet State and Law* (Moscow: Progress Publishers, 1969), p. 266.

11. Not without reason, see Milovan Djilas, *Conversations with Stalin* (New York: Harcourt, Brace and World, 1962), p. 143.

12. Ibid., p. 130.

13. J. N. Hazard, *The Communists and Their Law: A Search for the Common Core of the Legal Systems of the Marxian Socialist States* (Chicago: University of Chicago Press, 1969), pp. 527–28.

14. For the full statement of the "Declaration" see D. N. Jacobs, ed., *The New Communist Manifesto and Related Documents* (New York: Harper Torchbooks, 1962), pp. 169–82; quoted in Hazard, *The Communists and Their Law*, pp. 6–7 and summarized by H. J. Berman in his review of Hazard in *The American Political Science Review* 66, no. 1 (March 1972), pp. 240–41.

15. See Berman, *American Political Science Review*, p. 240, and H. J. Berman, *Justice in the USSR: An Interpretation of Soviet Law* (Cambridge, Mass.: Harvard University Press, 1963).

16. See chapter on "Unifikacja i Kodyfikacja Prawa" (The unification and codification of law), in J. Bardach, B. Lesnodorski, and M. Pietrzak, *Historia Panstwa i Prawa Polskiego* (The History of the Polish state and law) (Warsaw: Panstwowe Wydawnictwo Naukowe, 1979), pp. 562–65.

17. Ibid., p. 633.

18. A rather interesting book that is quite revealing in regard to the process used to eliminate the opposition is M. Rybicki, ed., *Sejm Ustawodawczy Rzeczypospolitej Polskiej: 1947–1952* (The constitutional parliament of the Polish Republic 1947–1952) (Warsaw: Istytut Panstwa i Prawa, Polska Akademia Nauk, 1977). See my review of this book in *Canadian-American Slavic Studies* 15, no. 4 (1981), pp. 629–30.

19. A. Bohmer et al., *Legal Resources and Bibliography of Czechoslovakia* (New York: Frederick A. Praeger, Inc., 1959), unnumbered introductory pages.

20. Z. Suda, "The Entry of Czechoslovakia into the Communist Party-State System," *The Czechoslovak Socialist Republic* (Baltimore, Md.: The Johns Hopkins Press, 1969), pp. 31–38.

21. H. Heitzer, *GDR: An Historical Outline* (Dresden: Verlag Zeit im Bild, 1981), p. 268.

22. See "Der Beginn des Aufbaus der antifaschistisch-demokratischen Justiz," in *Staats-und Rechtsgeschichte der DDR: Grundriss* (The History of State and Law of the GDR: Outline)(Berlin: Staatsverlag der Deutschen Demokratischen Republik, 1983), pp. 49–52.

23. *Communist Takeover and Occupation of Rumania* (Washington, D.C.: Government Printing Office, 1955), pp. 12–13, 20.

24. M. G. Zaninovich, *The Development of Socialist Yugoslavia* (Baltimore, Md.: The Johns Hopkins Press, 1968), p. 57.

25. Ibid., p. 74.

26. J. C. Fisher, *Yugoslavia—A Multinational State: Regional Difference and Administrative Response* (San Francisco: Chandler Publishing Co., 1966), p. 24.

27. L. Zanga, "Albania's Opening Up," *Radio Free Europe Research*, August 1, 1984; and D. Binder, "Albania Opens Its Door a Crack," *New York Times Magazine*, November 11, 1984. With the death of Hoxha on April 11, 1985, and his replacement by Ramiz Alia the "opening" may become larger more rapidly.

28. C. S. Rhyne, ed., *Law and Judicial Systems of Nations*, 3d rev. ed. (Washington, D.C.: World Peace Through Law Center, 1978), pp. 260, 317; *Poland: A Handbook* (Warsaw: Interpress Publishers, 1974), p. 181.

29. Rhyne, *Law and Judicial Systems of Nations*, p. 175.

30. Ibid., p. 846.

31. R. C. Gripp, *The Political System of Communism* (New York: Dodd, Mead & Co., 1973), p. 120.

32. See, for example, the chart on the legal system of the GDR on p. 193 in *Staats- und Rechtsgeschichte der DDR: Grundriss*.

33. A. J. Groth, *People's Poland: Government and Politics* (San Francisco: Chandler Publishing Co., 1972), p. 45.

34. See *Hungarians and Germans in Romania Today* (Bucharest: Meridiane Publishing House, 1978).

35. See H. P. Tseng, *The Law Schools of the World* (Buffalo, N.Y.: William S. Hein & Co., 1977).

36. See Rhyne, *Law and Judicial Systems of Nations*, for country-by-country requirements.

37. O. Ulc, *The Judge in a Communist State: A View from Within* (Athens, Ohio: Ohio University Press, 1972), p. 13.

38. *100 Questions, 100 Answers: GDR* (Berlin: Panorama DDR, 1974), p. 46.

39. Ulc, *The Judge in a Communist State*, pp. 1–10.

40. J. N. Hazard, *The Soviet System of Government*, 4th rev. ed. (Chicago: University of Chicago Press, 1968), pp. 170–71.

41. O. Ulc, *Politics in Czechoslovakia* (San Francisco: W. H. Freeman and Co., 1974), p. 94.

42. S. Pomorski, and K. Defert, "Universally Accepted Norms and Their Application in National Legal Systems: A Comparative Study of Polish and American Criminal Law and Their Interaction with Modern International Human Rights Legislation," *Denver Law Journal* 57, no. 4 (Fall 1980), p. 486.

43. S. White, J. Gardner, and G. Schopflin, *Communist Political Systems: An Introduction* (New York: St. Martin's Press, 1982), p. 238.

44. Pomorski and Defert, "Universally Accepted Norms," p. 468.

45. White, Gardner, Schopflin, *Communist Political Systems*, p. 239.

46. M. Ziomecki, "The Polish Legal Profession," *Studium Papers* 9, no. 1 (January 1985), pp. 35–38.

47. B. Ponomarev, "XXV CPSU Congress, and Its International Meaning," *The Problems, Theories and Practices of Developed Socialism* (Prague: "Peace and Socialism," International Publisher, 1977), p. 16 (in Russian).

48. A. Koseski, *Rozwiniete Spoleczenstwo Socjalistyczne* (The Developed Socialist Society) (Warsaw: Wydawnictwo Ministerstwa Obrony Narodowy, 1975), p. 213.

49. See appropriate chapters of R. Staar, *Communist Regimes in Eastern Europe*, 4th ed. (Stanford, Calif.: Hoover Institution Press, 1982).

50. Quoted from "Vedecka Konference, 'Aktualni problemy Ceskoslovenske socialisticke vedy a statu a pravu' ve svetle XIV sjezdu KSC ci XXIV sjezdu KSSS," *Pravnik: Teoreticky casopis pro stazku statu a prava* III, no. 1–2 (1972), p. 78 by J.C. Gidynski, "Socialist International Law," *The Polish Review* 19, no. 3–4 (1974), p. 138.

51. S. Kovalev, "Sovereignty and International Obligations of the Socialist Countries," *Pravda*, September 26, 1968, English translation in *The Current Digest of the Soviet Press* 20, no. 39 (1969), p. 10ff, quoted in Gidynski, "Socialist International Law," pp. 140–41.

52. See R. Neagu, *European Security: A Romanian Point of View* (Bucharest: Meridiane Publishing House, 1977), and other official Romanian publications on international affairs.

53. White, Gardner, and Schopflin, *Communist Political Systems*, p. 236.

54. Ibid., p. 237.

55. J. N. Hazard, *Managing Change in the USSR: The Politico-Legal Role of the Soviet Jurist* (New York: Cambridge University Press, 1983), p. 11.

BIBLIOGRAPHY

Berman, H. J. *Justice in the USSR: An Interpretation of Soviet Law*. Cambridge, Mass.: Harvard University Press, 1963.

Bottomore, T. *A Dictionary of Marxist Thought*. Cambridge, Mass.: Harvard University Press, 1983.

Brown, J. F. *Bulgaria Under Communist Rule*. New York: Praeger Publishers, 1970.

David, R., and J. Brierly. *Major Legal Systems of the World Today*. 2d ed. London: Stevens Co., 1978.

Dziewanowski, M. K. *The Communist Party of Poland*. 2d ed. Cambridge, Mass.: Harvard University Press, 1976.

Fischer-Galati, S. *The Socialist Republic of Romania*. Baltimore, Md.: The Johns Hopkins Press, 1969.

Fisher, J. C. *Yugoslavia—A Multinational State: Regional Difference and Administrative Response*. San Francisco: Chandler Publishing Co., 1966.

Franklin, B., ed. *The Essential Stalin: Major Theoretical Writings, 1905–1952*. New York: Anchor Books, 1972.

Gripp, R. C. *The Political System of Communism*. New York: Dodd, Mead & Co., 1973.

Groth, A. J. *People's Poland: Government and Politics*. San Francisco: Chandler Publishing Co., 1972.

Gsovski, V., and K. Grzybowski. *Government, Law and Courts in the Soviet Union and Eastern Europe*. New York: F. A. Praeger Publishers, 1959.

Hazard, J. N. *The Communists and Their Law: A Search for the Common Core of the Legal Systems of the Marxian Socialist States*. Chicago: University of Chicago Press, 1969.

———. *Managing Change in the USSR: The Politico-Legal Role of the Soviet Jurist*. New York: Cambridge University Press, 1983.

Hazard, J. N., I. Shapiro, and P. B. Maggs. *The Soviet Legal System: Contemporary*

Documentation and Historical Commentary. Dobbs Ferry, N.Y.: Oceana Publications, Inc., 1969.

Heidenheimer, A. J. *The Governments of Germany.* 3d ed. New York: Thomas J. Crowell Co., 1971.

Ioffe, O. S., and P. B. Maggs. *Soviet Law in Theory and Practise.* New York: Oceana Publications, 1983.

Kovrig, B. *The Hungarian People's Republic.* Baltimore, Md.: The Johns Hopkins Press, 1970.

Oren, N. *Revolution Administered: Agrarianism and Communism in Bulgaria.* Baltimore, Md.: The Johns Hopkins Press, 1973.

Oteka, A. *The History of the Romanian People.* Bucharest: Scientific Publishing House, 1970.

Pano, N. C. *The People's Republic of Albania.* Baltimore, Md.: The Johns Hopkins Press, 1968.

Rakowska-Harmstone, T., and A. Gyorgy, eds. *Communism in Eastern Europe.* Bloomington, Ind.: University of Indiana Press, 1979.

Rhyne, C. S., ed. *Law and Judicial Systems of Nations.* 3d rev. ed. Washington, D.C.: World Peace Through Law Center, 1978.

Scharf, C. B. *Politics and Change in East Germany: An Evaluation of Socialist Democracy.* Boulder, Colo.: Westview Press, 1984.

Staar, R. F. *Communist Regimes in Eastern Europe.* 4th ed. Stanford, Calif.: Hoover Institution Press, 1982.

———, ed. *Yearbook on International Communist Affairs.* Stanford, Calif.: Hoover Institution Press, published annually.

Suda, Z. *The Czechoslovak Socialist Republic.* Baltimore, Md.: The Johns Hopkins Press, 1969.

Toma, P., and I. Volgyes. *Politics in Hungary.* San Francisco: W. H. Freeman & Co., 1977.

Tseng, H. P. *The Law Schools of the World.* Buffalo, N.Y.: William S. Hein & Co., 1977.

Tucker, R. C., ed. *Lenin Anthology.* New York: Norton & Co., 1975.

———. *The Marx-Engels Reader.* New York: Norton & Co., 1978.

Ulc, O. *Politics in Czechoslovakia.* San Francisco: W. H. Freeman & Co., 1974.

White, S., G. Gardner, and G. Schopflin. *Communist Political Systems: An Introduction.* New York: St. Martin's Press, 1982.

Zaninovich, M. G. *The Development of Socialist Yugoslavia.* Baltimore, Md.: The Johns Hopkins Press, 1968.

5

FEDERAL REPUBLIC OF GERMANY

Alan N. Katz

The laws and legal system of the Federal Republic of Germany, like most nations on the European continent, are closer to the French than the Anglo-American pattern. This similarity is seen in at least three critical areas: (1) the existence of code law rather than case law—the findings of the courts are based upon statutory law rather than on judge-made or common law; (2) the legal process tends to be much more inquisitorial, with the judge playing a very active role in the courtroom (for example, deciding to admit or exclude evidence as well as to question witnesses); and (3) judges are selected by the Ministry of Justice and are civil servants.

Despite the slower and later development of a unified legal system in Germany than many of its neighbors, the Federal Republic of Germany has a complex and efficient legal system. In addition, the German people seem quite willing to utilize the legal system rather than bargaining or informal negotiations to solve many of their problems. As we shall see in the final section of this chapter, this willingness to utilize the system and the relative satisfaction with its workings has played no small role in the stability of the German government since the end of World War II.

THE DEVELOPMENT OF THE LEGAL SYSTEM

Germanic tribes first appeared near the end of the second century B.C. From that time until early in the fifth century, the five German tribes (Frisians, Alemans, Franks, Saxons, and Thurigians) alternated between periods when they attempted to encroach upon the Roman Empire and others when they beat back attempts by the Romans to control them. Through much of this period, the Rhine and Danube rivers constituted a truce line between the Romans and the German tribes. With the end of the Roman Empire, Germanic law replaced Roman law throughout much of central Europe. This law varied from area to area, with some systems of law dominant over large areas while others operated only in a single town. Some of these systems had their own books of law. Among the first of these was a book published by Euric, the leader of the West Goths (another Germanic people who probably originated in Scandinavia and later divided into the Ostrogoths and Visigoths) probably between 470 and 475. Later law books of the West Goths were written by Reckessuinth, Erwig, and Egica, though these were quite similar to already existing Roman codes.

Charles Martel, the leader of the Franks, established the Carolingian dynasty in the eighth century. The Franks soon began an economic and political penetration of lands east of the Rhine. This was a prelude to the later unification developed by Martel's grandson, Charlemagne. This brought much of present-day Germany, France, Austria, Switzerland, the low countries, and northern Italy under one administration—the Holy Roman Empire. This period saw the introduction of lay judges, reforms in procedure, and measures to regulate family relations and property rights, as well as attempts to adapt the ancient law to more modern conditions. Many reforms were introduced by the church in its own interests, but these played a major, positive role in the development of society:

For law, they were what the Empire was for politics. They served to unify society into that harmony of government and morals typified by the union of State and Church, without, however, destroying the autonomy of the various peoples united under the Empire. Thus they did not supplant the preexisting systems of Germanic law, but stood alongside of them, aiding their development, amending them, supplying their defects, and giving a unity of purpose. It was natural that the capitularies should be the most important legal sources in their own day, and that their effects should be recognizable long afterwards in later epochs. They were one of the most civilizing influences of the Middle Ages. Like the constitutions of the Roman emperors, which with slow, incessant labor completed the edifice of Rome's law, they introduced the elements of universality, or moral philosophy, and of Christianity.[1]

During this period relations between individuals were regulated by a principle known as the "personality of the law." Under this principle one's actions were regulated by one's origin and status. This meant that an individual's personal law (usually that of his tribe or nation) took precedence over the law in the territory in which he resided (the territorial principle).

With the fall of the Holy Roman Empire and the consequent absence of a strong central authority, the development of German law slowed dramatically. Not unexpectedly, legal developments mirrored political developments, with a proliferation of special courts and jurisdictions and the absence of a centralized judicial organization. In addition, the German royal court no longer enjoyed a dominating position within the legal hierarchy.

In the later Middle Ages, German law, much like that of its neighbors, was influenced by Roman legal codes reintroduced into the area by Italian jurists. This adoption of Roman law came about easily because there were no common legal institutions in Germany (as, for example, there were in England) which could oppose the influence of Roman law. In addition, the German law at this time was increasingly unsuited to the more complex demands of the time:

> In the accepted view, the judge made his decisions on the basis of traditional legal knowledge, practical wisdom, experience and practicality, and from an intuitive perception of what best answered the objective and concrete facts of the case. But such an irrational method of finding law, unreasoningly based on tradition, seemed increasingly incongrous as the social and economic circumstances of the later Middle Ages became more complex, variegated and developed. There was thus a legal vacuum and Roman law flowed in, not because its rules were substantially better or juster than those of traditional German law but because it offered a whole range of concepts and methods of thinking which enabled lawyers to grasp difficult factual problems, to place them in a rational framework, to see their implications, and to make them the object of reasoned argument.[2]

The enthusiasm by which Roman law was met in German universities led to its spread throughout the land. German scholars played a major role in reinterpreting Roman law and the law that did develop was, in fact, an amalgam of German custom and Roman law.

By the sixteenth century, however, there was increasing unhappiness with Roman law as a means of regulating the daily lives of Germans. There was, however, still no strong central authority to lead in the development of a more unified legal system. As an example of both the general unhappiness with the Roman codes and the centrifugal tendencies of the politics of the times, the eighteenth and nineteenth centuries saw the proliferation of German kingdoms.

The Napoleonic Codes were adopted in many parts of Germany as a result of the French occupation of Germany; at the same time, individual provinces of Germany (such as Saxony in 1863) developed their own codes. It was not until the creation of the German Reich in 1871 that there were significant developments toward a unified code for the entire empire. In short order, the Penal Code was created in 1871, soon followed by the Law on the Constitution of the Courts, the Codes of Criminal and Civil Procedure in 1877, the Civil Code in 1896, and the Commercial Code the following year. Probably the most important of these was the Civil Code, also known as the Burgerliches Gesetzbuch or "BGB." This code was originally composed of some 2,400 paragraphs, each precisely defining the law governing Germans in their daily lives. This new code (and, in fact, all the codes) modernized German law and differed in important ways from the Napoleonic Codes. Stanley Rothman, for example, feels that Prussian nationalism aided the maintenance of traditional Germanic notions in parts of the codes and that German authoritarianism and paternalism resulted in a very different focus to the codes.[3]

Both the Weimar Republic and Third Reich had profound (and essentially negative) influences upon the development of German law. While a modernization and rationalization of the law continued during the Weimar Republic, this period also saw a politicization of the legal system with a number of hostile jurists doing all they could to undermine the Republic. This ultimately led to a general decline in confidence in the judiciary. While the Nazis indicated a desire to replace many German codes because they felt them to have been too much influenced by the Roman codes, they made few changes in the codes themselves. They did, however, continue the politicization of the legal system by removing "suspects" ("non-Aryans" and political dissenters) from the bench and developing special courts to deal with political crimes. Millions of Germans were arrested and imprisoned by such courts, drastically expanding the concept of a "political crime." In addition, a special People's Court, dominated by party members, was created to judge political crimes when the regular courts proved reluctant to do so. The Nazis could so easily trample on the concept of an independent judiciary because they argued that the Fuhrer and the party, not the judiciary, had the ultimate responsibility of interpreting the law of the nation.

The lawlessness of the Nazi period was replaced by the founding of the Federal Republic at the end of World War II. Its constitution, the Basic Law, was adopted on May 23, 1949, and differs from the Bismark Constitution of 1871 and the Weimar Constitution of 1919 in that it provides for clearer constitutional balances (for example, there is no equivalent of Article 48 of the Weimar Constitution, which gave emergency decrees by the president the force of law), greater independence for the various branches of the government (Article 97, for example, guarantees the independence of the German judiciary), as well as greater protection for the personal freedom of the individual (there is, for example, a constitutional guarantee of judicial review when an individual has been injured by the exercise of public authority).

THE ORGANIZATION OF THE GERMAN COURT SYSTEM

Germany has a federal system of government. The Basic Law divides it into ten states (Lander) and West Berlin, each with a good deal of independent power. Each of these units have parliaments that enact legislation. However, the overwhelming percentage of the law involved in litigation in Germany is federal and not state law—a reversal of the pattern found in the United States. More importantly, there is a single nationwide court structure in Germany with all of the courts, with the exception of the courts of last resort, regarded as land courts. The various land governments have the responsibility for appointing the judges and providing financial and administrative support for the two levels of trial courts and the intermediate court of appeals. The federal government has similar responsibilities for the courts of last resort.

There are two levels of ordinary trial courts in the Federal Republic. The lowest are the approximately eight hundred local courts (Amtsgerichte). These courts adjudicate minor criminal and civil matters. In addition, they handle family matters, probate, bankruptcy, as well as aid in the drafting of wills, and serve as a registry of deeds. These courts are located in both small towns and large cities throughout the country. A single judge hears each case in these courts. The total number of judges on the bench of any local court will, however, vary from two or three to more than fifty, depending upon the population of the area. The second level of trial courts are the ninety-three district courts (Landesgerichte). These courts have both original and appellate jurisdiction, serving as courts of original jurisdiction in more serious criminal and civil cases as well as hearing appeals from the local courts. Cases are heard in these courts by panels of three judges.

There are nineteen intermediate appellate courts (Oberlandesgerichte) in the Federal Republic. These courts are organized regionally with at least one such court in each state. Each court has appellate jurisdiction over most of the decisions of the local and district courts in its jurisdiction. In addition, they serve as the court of last resort on questions of purely land law (of which there are few) and civil cases whose monetary amount does not exceed DM 40,000. There are 149 judges serving on these courts (usually in divisions of 4 or 5) with an average of 72 per court. The intermediate appellate courts resemble state supreme courts in the United States. However, because there are more than one court in some states, they cannot be said to be the highest court in the state. In addition, their decisions are far more likely to be reviewed by higher courts than are those of the state supreme courts in the United States.[4]

At the apex of the ordinary court system is the Federal Supreme Court (Bundesgerichtshof, or "BHG") located in Karlsruhe. The Court is composed of 110 judges (usually organized into divisions or senates). It has the power to review decisions of the Intermediate Court of Appeals and, in some cases, directly review decisions of the district courts. The Court also acts as the supreme disciplinary tribunal for most lawyers, Notars (public officers primarily concerned with authenticating legal documents), chartered accountants, tax consultants, and members of the civil service. Because this Court is responsible for most criminal and civil appeals, its workload is enormous—for example, in 1979 it dealt with nearly 4,000 cases.[5]

There are five other sets of courts in the Federal Republic of Germany. All of these (with the exception of the Federal Patent Court) are first organized on the state level with appeals made to one of the Federal Supreme Courts of Special Jurisdiction. The administrative courts are the first of these special courts. They deal with disputes under private law that are not of a constitutional nature. They may involve suits by private individuals against state authorities or actions by civil servants against their employers. The General Administrative Courts (Allgemeine Verwaltungsgerichte) are composed of three judges and two laymen. These courts first review acts of the administration. Their decisions may then be appealed to one of the eleven, three-judge State Supreme Administrative Courts (Oberverwaltungsgerichte) and then to the Federal Administrative Court (Bundesverwaltungsgericht) in Berlin. The labor courts are the second special courts. Labor-related cases are first heard in the local labor courts (Arbeitsgerichte), then appealed to the state labor courts (Landesarbeitsgerichte), and then to the Federal Labor Court (Bundesarbeitsgericht) in Kassel. The social courts are the third special courts. They deal with such matters as compulsory medical insurance, social insurance, and unemployment insurance. Once again, cases originate at the local level (Sozialgerichte), may be appealed to the state level (Landessozialgerichte) and then to the Federal Social Insurance Court (Bundessozialgericht) in Berlin. The tax courts are the fourth special courts. These courts only operate on two levels: cases originate in one of the state courts (Finanzgerichte) and may be appealed to the Federal Tax Court (Bundesfinanzhof) in Munich. The patent courts are the final special courts. The Federal Patent Court (Bundespatentgericht) first hears appeals from the Federal Patent Office in Munich. Its decisions may then be appealed to the Patent Senate of the Federal Supreme Court.

There are, finally, a Federal Constitutional Court, located in Karlsruhe, and a constitutional court in each of the states. These courts have the responsibility for ascertaining whether particular laws are inconsistent with the Basic Law. Both the federal and state governments as well as the Bundestag (if a motion receives a vote of one-third of its members) may have any federal or state law reviewed by the Federal Constitutional Court. The Court may bring impeachment proceedings against the Federal President, actions for the removal of judges, deal with constitutional disputes between the various states as well as between the states and the federal government, and serve as the only body competent to ban specific political parties.

The Federal Constitutional Court is composed of two panels (Senates) with eight judges on each. Each Senate has its own separate jurisdiction and is administratively separate from the other. The first Senate deals with the basic liberties located in Articles 1–20 of the Basic Law, while the second is charged with handling conflicts between the various levels of government as well as election disputes, disagreements involving international law, and questions related to the constitutionality of political parties. Approximately 90 to 95 percent of the Court's caseload in the period from 1951 to 1976 dealt with constitutional complaints.[6]

THE PERSONNEL OF THE LAW

The Legal Practitioners

There are two major types of legal practitioners in the Federal Republic of Germany, the Rechtsanwalt, or independent legal consultant, and the Notar. There are, in addition, a smaller group of legal advisors and lawyers (Prozessagenten and Rechtbeistande) who give legal advice. These are individuals who have not been admitted as Rechtsanwalt but give legal advice and occasionally represent clients in a court of law. These practitioners are limited by the Federal Act to Prevent Unauthorized Legal Consultation and must be admitted by the presiding judge of the district court in the area in which they wish to practice.

Such Rechtsbeistande will be admitted to practice (and will, henceforth, be referred to as Prozessagenten) in the local courts if they prove a need for their service as well as reliability and some legal training.[7]

There were 25,141 attorneys (Rechtsanwalt) in the Federal Republic in 1979.[8] Most German attorneys practice independently, though some may share a practice together. The German law excludes the right of self-representation in criminal proceedings. This produces a virtual monopoly on pleading and representation for attorneys (one notable exception is in the local courts). While the Rechtsanwalt also do the vast majority of legal consultation, they do not have a monopoly in the area.

There were 6,928 Notars in the Federal Republic in 1979.[9] The German Notar is not comparable with the American notary public. He is required to be an attorney and is generally appointed to his position after years in legal practice. The Notar has the same legal qualifications as the Rechtsanwalt and, in some districts, the functions are combined. The Notar frequently assists in drafting legal documents and is required by law to authenticate legal documents such as wills and real estate transactions.

The organized bar in the Federal Republic is composed of two main divisions. The first of these is a mandatory group, the Chamber of Lawyers. They are organized in each of the intermediate courts of appeals districts and are united in a national body called the Bundesrechtsanwaltskammer. The second is a voluntary group, the German Bar Association, which is composed of local groups of lawyers.

Legal education began in Germany in the fourteenth century. However, for many decades the number of students studying law at the universities was as limited as the professional opportunities for lawyers. It was, in fact, not until the nineteenth century that the law faculties began to dramatically increase. Even then, there were only two hundred law professors in the entire nation (this number had grown to nearly four hundred by the late 1960s).[10] Throughout much of its history, German legal education has been characterized by two conflicting tendencies: the view that the law be studied as a pure science and a stress on practical training. Braun and Birk write about this tension: "This dualism of abstract metatheory and practical training dominates in the history of the legal sciences not only until the 19th century but also until now. Also the modern discussion on the necessities of the reform of the legal education is essentially a discussion of the sense and function of a practice or theory-orientated education."[11]

There are common state requirements for the beginning of legal study in the Federal Republic: the passing of a final secondary school examination (the Arbitur) which generally takes place after nine years at a high school ("Gymnasium") or an examination of an equal value. A German university is traditionally divided into five departments or faculties: law, medicine, philosophy, natural sciences, and socioeconomic sciences. Any student passing the Arbitur examination may, therefore, study law, not in a separate law school, but in the law department of any university. There were approximately thirty universities with faculties of law in the Federal Republic in 1983.[12]

German legal education has been characterized by a two-stage process. The first is a minimum of seven semesters of formal university study. During this period students at law faculties in each of the states follow a curriculum that varies little from school to school. At the end of this period students may take the formal governmental examinations that, again, vary little from state to state. The difficulty of the exams can be seen by the fact that only 1 percent of the students in 1980 took their exams after seven semesters while 45 percent needed eleven semesters in order to pass the exams.[13] The individual who passes the exams is now referred to as a "Referendar" and now begins a two-and-one-half-year (two years prior to 1982) period of practical training. During this time the individual has to pass through seven stages of training, the most important of which are at a civil court, criminal court or prosecutor's office, administrative body, and at the bar. During this period the Referendar receives a government salary and is considered a temporary civil servant. At the end of this training the individual takes a second examination, which consists of a number of written parts in addition to an oral section before a panel of four individuals from various sections of the legal profession. The performance level on this part of the examination is far better than on the initial examination. In 1980 nearly 91 percent passed this stage of the exam.[14] Upon passing the second examination, the individual is now known as an "Assessor" and is eligible to enter any branch of the legal profession, including the judiciary.

The background of most law students is decidedly middle class. For example, it has been estimated that 30 to 35 percent of all German lawyers are the children of college graduates and 40 to 45 percent have grown up in the families of civil servants.[15] Dahrendorf points out that working-class children are only more poorly represented in the faculties of medicine than that of law.[16] Lawyers also tend to play a major role in German society. Over half of German civil servants, approximately 50 percent of cabinet ministers and secretaries for ministerial departments, and one-third of the directors of the personnel departments of Germany's largest corporations have, at one time, been attorneys.[17] Dahrendorf, finally, concludes that the study of law plays a vital role in the creation of Germany's elite: "in principle, the law faculties of German universities accomplish for German society what the exclusive Public Schools do for the English, and the grand écoles for the French. In them an elite receives its training."[18]

In addition to employment as a civil servant, private practicing attorney, or in-house counsel for a financial institution or commercial enterprise, the assessor may also serve as a prosecuting attorney, pursue an academic career, or serve as a presiding judge.

Public Prosecutors

There were 3,233 public prosecutors in the Federal Republic in 1979.[19] Prosecutors are civil servants and tend to share the background, attitudes, and social positions of the judiciary rather than those of the practicing bar. In some states it is possible for individuals serving as prosecutors to be transferred to the bench and for judges to be transferred to the prosecutor's office.

Law Professors

The professor in a law faculty has life tenure (usually until between 65 and 68 years of age). Promotion is generally based upon scholarly activity and normally takes the form of movement from one university to a higher and better-paying position at another. A measure of the relative prestige of the university professor (though it has declined somewhat as a reaction to the student revolts in the late 1960s) is seen in the salaries of law professors: usually equivalent to that of a judge presiding over the court of appeal but occasionally as much as that of the president of the highest federal courts of appeal.[20] Most professors are aided by assistants who do much of the teaching and help with their research. The assistants have passed the second examination and are usually working on their doctoral dissertations. They are normally paid the same salary as a beginning judge or a lower court judge, and if they should later decide to serve on the bench, two years of university service may be applied toward life tenure. Full professors may also serve as part-time judges or may decide to later transfer over to the bench on a full-time basis. Most professors enjoy the university life as well as the significant impact that they may have on Germany's law. The professor is free to publish what he wishes, and his research may influence the course of the nation's law. Ruggiero Aldisert, an American circuit court judge, writes about the influence of the German law professor:

This small, elite group of German scholars, the law professors, is to the German tradition what the American trial and appellate judges are to the common law tradition. If in the United States the law is what the judges say it is, I believe it is accurate to say that the law in a civil law jurisdiction is what the scholars say it is.[21]

Judges

There were 16,657 permanent judges in the Federal Republic in 1981.[22] In Germany the term "qualified to be a judge" is applied to all assessors. Upon the passing of the second examination, an individual can choose to embark upon any number of career options, including that of a judge. No additional education is needed nor will any new training be given while on the job. There is a new school for judges (Richter Academie), which offers short courses for those who have been on the bench for some time. This is, however, more like the courses offered by the National Judicial College in the United States than the French pattern, which requires additional training before appointment to the bench.

The key agencies responsible for administering the court system are the federal Ministry of Justice and the ministry in each of the eleven state governments. The ministries are charged with the administration of the court systems, the development of legislation aimed at improving the systems, and the appointment and assignment of judges. The state ministries are also responsible for administering examinations, admitting lawyers to practice, and appointing prosecutors. Judges serving on the local courts, District courts, and Intermediate Courts of Appeals are appointed by the state ministries. All other judges (who constitute a small minority) are appointed by the federal Ministry of Justice.

Those who wish to serve on the bench generally apply directly to the state ministries. Because these positions are highly competitive, only those who have done well on the second state examination stand any chance of being appointed. This is followed by a personal interview and a careful screening of the applicant's personal file. A decision is then made by the minister of justice, based upon the candidate's file, recommendations from the personnel department of the ministry, and the quota for new judges in the state (in some of the smaller states only three or four new appointments are made in a single year). Those fortunate enough to be selected will receive an initial appointment for a number of years (in some states three) after which the individual acquires tenure until the mandatory retirement age.

A judge may apply to fill a vacancy (in the various courts, among the presiding officers of the various divisions, within sections of the prosecutor's office, or within the ministries of justice) by filing an application with the presiding judge of his court. This application then goes to the president of the appellate court and ultimately to the minister of justice. He then chooses from among the candidates for the vacancy. The vast majority of those appointed to the appellate bench have, therefore, served on lower courts. However, it is possible for a staff attorney for the Court of Last Resort or a member of the professional staff of the Ministry of Justice to be appointed to the appellate bench.

The major variation from this pattern occurs in the Federal Constitutional Court. While judges of this court possess the same professional qualifications as other members of the bench, they are elected by the Bundestag and Bundesrat (each selects half of the members) rather than appointed by the minister of justice. Election is to a specific chamber, and one may not transfer to the other chamber. Judges are elected for twelve years (they may not be reelected), but they may not serve beyond the mandatory retirement age of 68. The legislature may not, however, impeach any member of the Court—this may only be done by the federal president, upon a motion of the Court itself.

Because judges of the Federal Constitutional Court are elected by members of the national legislature, the selection process is often a matter of intensive bargaining. The Court's membership has often reflected the balance of power in the legislature, and some seats have been regarded as the ''property'' of one party or the other. Despite the political horse-trading involved in the selection process, the quality of those elected to the Court remains quite high:

The Bundesrat has usually preferred high-level civil servants with excellent records in state administration. The lower house tends to nominate active politicians and judges from other federal courts. But both houses have recently drawn more candidates from their own ranks, that is, state justice ministers and leading members of the judicial selection committee. Membership on the court is regarded as a very prestigious appointment and the quality of candidates is indicative of the status this new institution now has in the political system. Its strong penetration by state governments and parties also sets it apart from the traditional judiciary and makes it a clear "child of the Republic."[23]

German judges come from the same overwhelmingly middle- and upper-middle-class background as other members of the profession. For example, a recent study found that only 6 percent of the judges came from working-class backgrounds, although that class represented 45 percent of the population. The same study found that half of the members of the judiciary come from the top 5 percent of the socioeconomic groups in Germany.[24] Similarly, the bench remains an area of male domination with, in 1973, fewer than 10 percent of Germany's judges being female.[25] A recent study of the career patterns of appellate judges found both extensive judicial experience (for example, 100 percent of those on the Court of Last Resort had previously served on the district court level and 85 percent on the Intermediate Court of Appeals) as well as experience in the prosecutor's office and in the various ministries of justice.[26] Similarly, Kommers found that judges of the Federal Constitutional Court had a wide range of prior experiences—only twelve, for example, had careers exclusively confined to the civil service or the bench, while a significant number had served in the legislature, were law professors, or had long careers in private practice.[27] However, the overall separation of the bar and the bench is seen in the few numbers on the appellate bench who had previous experience as private practitioners.

Studies have also found members of the judiciary to hold moderate-to-conservative political attitudes. For example, a major study conducted in 1971 found that 52.3 percent of the judges sampled saw danger to the regime from the extreme left while only 16.3 percent saw a similar danger from the extreme right. On the other hand, the same study found general support among justices for the regime with almost all of the judges supporting the three major parties and a surprisingly high 40 percent (60 percent among those under the age of 35) indicating a willingness to take part in a demonstration if they were in agreement with its goals.[28]

The German system is also characterized by the use of lay judges in criminal and certain civil cases. Juries were eliminated during the Weimar Republic, and the Federal Republic substituted the lay judge (Schoeffen) as a replacement for the jury. Mixed tribunals exist at both the district court level (one professional judge and two lay judges) and the county court level, where major felonies are tried by three professional judges and six lay judges. The latter are elected by municipal councils, need not have any special training, and serve for a specified period of time. Interestingly, they tend to be drawn from the upper reaches of society. For example, a recent study found only 12 percent of the lay judges to be blue-collar workers, while 21 percent were independent businessmen and professionals, 24 percent white-collar workers, and 25 percent civil servants.[29]

PUBLIC PERCEPTIONS AND THE ROLE OF THE COURTS

There are a variety of ways of measuring the impact of a nation's judicial system upon its polity. Popular views of the courts and their personnel often give one some impression of the judicial system. A second measure is the degree of independence given to the judiciary. A third is the role(s) that the judicial system is allowed to play within the national political system. All three of these types of evidence will be assessed here in order to measure the impact of the judicial system upon the contemporary political system in the Federal Republic of Germany.

It is not surprising, in the wake of World War II, to find negative public attitudes toward the German government in the late 1940s and early 1950s. In fact, nearly fifteen years later, the classic study by Almond and Verba (*The Civil Culture*) found a pragmatic attitude toward politics, coupled with an absence of good will and emotional attachment to the Federal Republic. By the 1970s, however, public attitudes indicated a good deal of support for Bonn's democratic institutions (for example, successive studies in 1955, 1972, and 1978 by the Institut für Demoskopie found 30 percent, 52 percent, and then 71 percent indicating positive feelings toward the Basic Law).[30] Such changes were due to the system's performance in both the economic and political sphere as well as to the socialization of a generation of younger citizens accustomed to living in a stable democratic society. These positive feelings toward the system were also reflected in the public's views toward the legal system and its personnel.

Recent studies have continued to show positive perceptions of the legal system and its personnel. For example, a 1978 Allensbach Institut für Demoskopie poll asked people to name professions that they held in the greatest esteem. The esteem registered for a "lawyer" tied with "ambassador, diplomat" and was only exceeded by "doctor," "clergyman," and "professor," but exceeded "nuclear physicist," "pharmacist," "author," "engineer," "politician," and "independent businessman."[31] A second study by the Allensbach Institut asked, "Generally speaking, can we or can we not have complete confidence in German Justice, that is, the judges and the courts?" The results of these polls, once again, indicate the increased confidence in the legal system and its personnel. The percentage of those who answered "can have complete confidence" increased from 26 percent in November 1964 to 32 percent in January 1975 to 40 percent in November 1978.[32] Finally, a January 1979 study by the Allensbach Institut asked people their opinion of various public institutions and whether they felt those institutions had any impact on political events in Germany. The federal constitution court received good marks in this poll with 42 percent indicating "very good" or "good" personal feelings about it compared to 34 percent with mixed feelings and 13 percent with "poor" or "very poor." Forty-eight percent of the sample felt that the court had a "very strong" or "strong" influence on the government as opposed to the 26 percent who felt the influence was "medium" and the 18 percent who responded "limited" or "very limited."[33]

As one indication of the importance attached to judicial independence, a 1978 study found that an "independent judiciary" was one of the most-often-cited conditions needed for a democracy.[34] The protection afforded the judiciary by the Basic Law is another indication of the significance attached to an independent judiciary. For example, judges are granted tenure until retirement. Article 97 also states that judges are independent, are only subject to the law, and may not be transferred against their will or removed from office except by impeachment. The Basic Law further protects the Federal Constitutional Court by making it administratively independent (as opposed to all other courts, which are dependent upon the appropriate justice ministers). The Court is also given the authority to draw up its own budget and supervise (and fire) all of its employees. Judges of the Court are also made exempt from administrative rules and regulations applicable to judges on all state and federal benches.

While Germany had some experience with "constitutional review" (the resolution of disputes between levels of government or the determination of the validity of constitutional amendments), the concept of "judicial review" did not become significant until after the creation of the Federal Constitutional Court. The Frankfurt Constitution of 1849 had created a federal Supreme Court (Reichsgericht) to deal with constitutional disputes, but the court never functioned and fell to the power of Prussia's authoritarianism. While the Weimar Republic's Staatsgerichtshof could not hear the constitutional complaints of its citizens, it did inherit some of the powers of the Reichsgericht. It was not, however, an independent tribunal, but functioned as a branch of the Supreme Court.

The traditional German view of the separation of powers posited no strong role for the courts. Kommers, for example, writes:

The predominant German teaching during the nineteenth century was that the courts did not have the authority to nullify legislative acts. The legislature was the supreme lawmaker. The supremacy of parliament was supported by the doctrine of sovereignty and the doctrine of separation of powers. The German idea of law . . . constituted a third support. Traditional German teaching holds that statutes are the sole source of law. It follows that judicial decisions may not be regarded as sources of law as in the Anglo-American legal system. The German judge's first and only duty is to enforce the law as it is written.[35]

After a Nazi period that rejected both the principle of a written constitution and limits on governmental power, the Allies insisted upon an independent judiciary and support for the rule of law. Brinkman writes that the new Federal Republic clearly stated, in the Basic Law, that the state "must conform to the principles of republican, democratic and social government based on the rule of law."[36] Brinkman further states about the new role for Germany's judiciary:

Thus, legalism was reintroduced into the German political system with the resulting reliance on authoritative judicial decisions to resolve political disputes rather than a preference for purely political methods. The groundwork was laid for the judicialization of politics so that judges are now regarded as the final arbiters of certain political controversies.[37]

Hase and Reute contend that the court is involved in five types of actions or procedures on a daily basis: (1) "quasi-political" procedures such as the banning of a political party or the removal of fundamental protections from an individual or group of individuals; (2) "quasi-penal" procedures such as the removal of the federal president and federal judges from office; (3) "control of legislation" to decide whether legislation is in accord with the principles enunciated in the Basic Law. These are procedures initiated by one-third of the members of the federal Parliament, state governments, the judiciary, or the federal government; (4) controversies between the various state agencies having to do with their rights and/or duties; and (5) "complaints of unconstitutionality" brought by individual citizens on the grounds that their rights have been violated by actions of the state. This is, by far, the most frequent action before the court.[38]

The Federal Constitutional Court has played a significant role in the politics of the Federal Republic since its inception in 1951. For example, by the mid 1970s it had interpreted about half of the 151 articles in the Basic Law and had found 54 separate federal and 35 state laws to be unconstitutional.[39] It angered the office of the Federal Chancellor when it agreed with state claims that the attempt by Chancellor Adenauer to create a second television network under his control violated the rights of the states to govern their own cultural affairs. It further found a 1974 abortion law to be unconstitutional, upheld the constitutionality of treaties with the Soviet Union and Poland, and, in enunciating a view that the Republic is a "militant democracy," banned the Communist and neo-Nazi political parties in the 1950s. Most recently, the Court, by a six-two vote, upheld the right of Chancellor Kohl to ask the federal president to dissolve the Bundestag on January 7, 1983. This shortly followed Kohl's arranging to lose a vote of confidence (despite his parliamentary majority) on December 17, 1982, and necessitated a new election on March 6, 1983. This election resulted in a victory for Kohl's party.[40]

Given the constitutional power of the Court (for example, Article 93 of the Basic Law states that the Court should settle disputes between states, between the federal government and the state governments, and between federal institutions, as well as resolve questions related to the constitutionality of statutes and administrative actions), it is not surprising that the Court has involved itself in so many controversial cases. However, this is somewhat unexpected, given the lack of tradition of an activist constitutional court in Germany. More importantly, these decisions have been well received by the German population:

It is a remarkable fact that the extensive political role of the Court . . . has become firmly established within so short a time . . . there is little evidence to show that political and administrative authorities resent the constraints placed upon them by the decisions made in Karlsruhe. Indeed it appears that from the point of view of the political actors the

Court has an *Entlastungseffekt* (the provision of relief) which they often welcome. Problems which for various reasons cannot be or have not been resolved by the executive and legislative organs (and that includes the parties, too) may come before the Court, and if that happens, then it can at least indicate what is or might be a definitive answer. Armed with such authoritative guidance, it becomes easier for the representative institutions to overcome the reservations and internal conflicts of interest to which they may be exposed and which inhibit their capacity to act.[41]

These and other actions of the court have, however, produced some criticism, mostly from those who oppose the judicialization of politics. They see judicial review as incompatible with the notion of parliamentary democracy and complain that the court has given too many political rather than legal decisions. Some critics have even suggested changing both the selection process and the jurisdiction of the Court.

When assessing whether the Court has overstepped its constitutional powers, three factors ought to be taken into consideration. First, the Court helped to play an important role in developing a unified constitutional ideology in the Federal Republic. This was especially true during the first two decades of the Republic, when there was less stability and support for the norms of the democratic system. Second, there are significant constitutional and procedural limitations on the Court. Three stand out: (1) it is far more bound by the rule of precedent than other German courts because it cannot easily ignore its own decisions, which bind public officials and have the force of general law; (2) like the U.S. Supreme Court, the Court lacks any right of initiative—its jurisdiction is dependent upon claims being brought to it; and (3) it can annul but usually not redraft legislation and can only decide issues on the basis of constitutionality and not political expediency. Third, the legalism of the German system means that institutions have utilized the Court by placing political questions in legalistic terms, thereby helping to further produce the judicialization of politics. As already noted, many political actors see a major value in having these controversial political problems brought before the Court.

Despite its controversial nature, therefore, it is clear that the Court has played a vital role in the Federal Republic in both creating greater support for the system and legitimizing the concept of judicial review:

judicial review, although not firmly anchored in Germany's constitutional tradition, has gained acceptance in the political system of the Federal Republic. Judicial review has worked in Germany because it has been used almost daily as an instrument in the process of settling constitutional disputes: It has been used by judicial institutions to raise and adjudicate questions of wide import under the Basic Law; by large numbers of Germans who have come increasingly to identify the Constitutional Court with the protection of their constitutional liberties; and by legislative minorities, political parties, and governmental organs as an alternative forum for the resolution of constitutional controversies which do not get settled satisfactorily elsewhere. Indeed, the German experience seems to show that judicial review, once regarded as a unique feature of American constitutionalism, can flourish in constitutional traditions substantially different from the American.[42]

NOTES

1. F. W. Maitland, "Prologue," in F. W. Maitland et al., *A General Survey of Events, Sources, Persons and Movements in Continental Legal History* (New York: Augustus M. Kelley, Publishers, 1968), p. 44.

2. K. Zweigert and H. Kotz, *An Introduction to Comparative Law*, vol. 1 (New York: Elsevier-Holland, 1977), p. 135.

3. S. Rothman, *European Society and Politics* (Indianapolis and New York: Bobbs-Merrill Co., Inc., 1970), p. 629.

4. D. J. Meador, "Appellate Subject Matter Organization: The German Design from an American Perspective," *Hastings International and Comparative Law Review* 5 (1981), p. 37.

5. H. Aldinger, "The Legal System of the Federal Republic of Germany," in K. R. Redden, ed., *Modern Legal Systems Cyclopedia*, vol. 3 (Buffalo: William S. Hein Co., 1984), pp. 129–30.

6. *Federal Republic of Germany: Law and Administration of Justice* (Bonn: Press and Information Office of the Government of the Federal Republic of Germany, 1979).

7. U. Schultz and P. Koessler, "The Practicing Lawyer in the Federal Republic of Germany: A Summary of the Major Rules Governing the Profession of West German Lawyers and Their Effects upon the Manner in which Foreign Lawyers Can Collaborate with West German Colleagues," *International Lawyer* 14 (Summer 1980), pp. 531–32.

8. *Federal Republic of Germany*.

9. Ibid.

10. M. Braun and R. Birk, "Germany, Federal Republic," *Comparative Law Yearbook* 5 (1981), pp. 69–70.

11. Ibid.

12. Among these are universities at Augsburg, Bayreuth, Berlin, Bielefeld, Bochum, Bonn, Bremen, Cologne, Frankfurt, Freiburg, Giessen, Goettinger, Hamburg (2), Hannover, Heidelberg, Kiel, Konstantz, Mainz, Mannheim, Marburg, Muenster, Munich, Osnabruck, Passau, Regensburg, Saarbrucken, Trier, Tuebungen, and Wuerzburg. See D. J. Meador, "German Appellate Judges: Career Patterns and American-English Comparisons," *Judicature* 67, no. 1 (June-July 1983), p. 20.

13. Braun and Birk, "Germany, Federal Republic," p. 74.

14. Ibid., p. 77.

15. D. Rüeschemeyer, *Lawyers and Their Society: A Comparative Study of the Legal Profession in Germany and the United States* (Cambridge, Mass.: Harvard University Press, 1973), p. 96.

16. R. Dahrendorf, *Society and Democracy in Germany* (New York: Doubleday & Co., 1967), p. 238.

17. Ibid., p. 232; Rüeschemeyer, *Lawyers and Their Society*, pp. 35, 71.

18. Dahrendorf, *Society and Democracy in Germany*, p. 236.

19. *Federal Republic of Germany*.

20. W. K. Geck, "The Reform of Legal Education in the Federal Republic of Germany," *The American Journal of Comparative Law* 25, (Winter 1977), p. 106.

21. R. J. Aldisert, "Rambling Through Continental Legal Systems," *University of Pittsburgh Law Review* 43 (Summer 1982), p. 952.

22. Aldinger, "The Legal System of the Federal Republic of Germany," p. 133.

23. D. P. Conradt, *The German Polity* (New York and London: Longman, Inc., 1978), pp. 184–85.

24. T. Rasehorn, "Die dritte Gewalt in der zweiten Republik," *Aus politik und zeitgeschichte*, no. 39 (September 27, 1975), p. 5, cited in D. Conradt, *The German Polity*, p. 179.

25. A. J. Heidenheimer and D. P. Kommers, *The Governments of Germany* (New York: Thomas Y. Crowell, 1975), p. 265.

26. See Meador, "German Appellate Judges," especially pp. 24–25.

27. D. P. Kommers, *Judicial Politics in West Germany: A Study of the Federal Constitutional Court* (Beverly Hills and London: Sage Publications, 1976), pp. 144–49, for a discussion of the background characteristics of appointees to the constitutional court.

28. M. Riegel, "Political Attitudes and Perceptions of the Political System by Judges in West Germany" (paper, World Congress of the International Political Science Association, Montreal, 1973), pp. 2a, 8, 9, 11, cited in Conradt, *The German Polity*, p. 180.

29. G. Casper and H. Zeisel, "Lay Judges in the German Criminal Courts," *Journal of Legal Studies* 1 (January 1972), p. 183.

30. D. P. Conradt, "Political Culture, Legitimacy and Participation," in W. E. Patterson and G. Smith, eds., *The West German Model: Perspectives on a Stable State* (London: Frank Cass & Co., Ltd., 1981), p. 20.

31. Cited in E. Noelle-Neumann, *The Germans: Public Opinion Polls, 1967–80* (Westport, Conn.: Greenwood Press, 1981), p. 321.

32. Ibid., p. 156.

33. Ibid., p. 187.

34. Conradt, "Political Culture, Legitimacy and Participation," p. 24.

35. D. P. Kommers, *Judicial Politics in West Germany*, pp. 35–36.

36. G. Brinkman, "The West German Federal Constitutional Court: Political Control Through Judges," *Public Law* 25 (1981), p. 86.

37. Ibid., p. 85.

38. F. Hase and M. Ruete, "Constitutional Court and Constitutional Ideology in West Germany," *International Journal of the Sociology of Law* 10 (1982), pp. 268–69.

39. Kommers, *Judicial Politics in West Germany*, pp. 207, 215.

40. See R.E.M. Irving and W. E. Patterson, "The Machtwechsel of 1982–83: A Significant Landmark in the Political and Constitutional History of West Germany," *Parliamentary Affairs* 36, no. 4 (Autumn 1983), pp. 417–35.

41. N. Johnson, "The Interdependence of Law and Politics: Judges and the Constitution in West Germany," *West European Politics* 5, no. 3 (July 1982), p. 245.

42. Kommers, *Judicial Politics in West Germany*, p. 299.

BIBLIOGRAPHY

Aldinger, H. "The Legal System of the Federal Republic of Germany." In K. R. Redden, ed., *Modern Legal Systems Cyclopedia*, vol. 3. Buffalo: William S. Hein Co., 1984. Pp. 109–53.

Aldisert, R. J. "Rambling Through Continental Legal Systems." *University of Pittsburgh Law Review Journal* 43 (Summer 1982), pp. 935–93.

Bachof, O. "West German Constitutional Judge Between Law and Politics." *Texas International Law Journal* 11 (1976), pp. 403–19.

102   Alan N. Katz

Blair, P. *Federalism and Judicial Review in West Germany*. Oxford: Clarendon Press, 1984.
———. "Law and Politics in Germany." *Political Studies* 26, no. 3 (September 1978), pp. 348–62.
Blankenburg, E. "Studying the Frequency of Civil Litigation in Germany." *Law and Society Review* 9 (Winter 1975), pp. 307–19.
Braun, M., and R. Birk. "Germany, Federal Republic." *Comparative Law Yearbook* 5 (1981), pp. 69–81.
Brinkman, G. "The West German Federal Constitutional Court: Political Control Through Judges." *Public Law* 25 (1981), pp. 83–104.
Casper, G. "Guardians of the Constitution." *University of Southern California Law Review* 53 (1980), pp. 773–85.
Cohen, E. J. "The German Lawyer-Attorney Experiences With a Unified Profession." *International and Comparative Law Quarterly* 9 (October 1960), pp. 580–99.
Conradt, D. P. *The German Polity*. New York and London: Longman, Inc., 1978.
———. "Political Culture, Legitimacy and Participation." In W. E. Patterson and G. Smith, eds., *The West German Model: Perspectives on a Stable State*. London: Frank Cass & Co., Ltd., 1981. Pp. 18–34.
Dahrendorf, R. *Society and Democracy in Germany*. New York: Doubleday & Co., Inc., 1967.
Edinger, L. J. *Politics in Germany: Attitudes and Processes*. Boston: Little, Brown & Co., 1968.
Federal Republic of Germany: Law and the Administration of Justice. Bonn: Press and Information Office of the Government of the Federal Republic of Germany, 1979.
Feld, W. "The German Administrative Courts." *Tulane Law Review* 26 (1962), pp. 495–506.
Forrester, I. S., and H. Ilgen. *The German Legal System*. South Hackensack, N.J.: Fred B. Rothman & Co., 1972.
Geck, W. K. "The Reform of Legal Education in the Federal Republic of Germany." *The American Journal of Comparative Law* 25 (Winter 1977), pp. 86–119.
Hahn, H. J. "Trends in the Jurisprudence of the German Federal Constitutional Court." *The American Journal of Comparative Law* 16, no. 4 (1968), pp. 570–79.
Hase, F., and M. Reute. "Constitutional Court and Constitutional Ideology in West Germany." *International Journal of the Sociology of Law* 10 (1982), pp. 267–76.
Heidenheimer, A. J., and D. P. Kommers. *The Governments of Germany*. New York: Thomas Y. Crowell, 1975.
Irving, R. E. M., and W. E. Patterson. "The Machtwechsel of 1982–83: A Significant Landmark in the Political and Constitutional History of West Germany." *Parliamentary Affairs* 36, no. 4 (Autumn 1983), pp. 417–35.
Jacobs, D. N., D. P. Conradt, B. G. Peters, and W. Safran. *Comparative Politics: An Introduction to the Politics of the United Kingdom, France, Germany and the Soviet Union*. Chatham, N.J.: Chatham House Publishers, Inc., 1983.
Johnson, N. "The Interdependence of Law and Politics: Judges and the Constitution in West Germany." *West European Politics* 5, no. 3 (July 1982), pp. 236–52.
———. "Law as the Articulation of the State in Western Germany: A German Tradition Seen from a British Perspective." *West European Politics* 1, no. 2 (May 1978), pp. 177–92.

Kohler, R. "The Study and Practice of Law in Germany." *American Bar Association Journal* 54 (October 1968), pp. 992–94.

Kommers, D. P. "The Federal Constitutional Court in the West German Political System." In J. B. Grossman and J. Tannenhaus, eds., *Frontiers of Judicial Research*. New York: John Wiley & Sons, Inc., 1969. Pp. 73–132.

———. *Judicial Politics in West Germany: A Study of the Federal Constitutional Court.* Beverly Hills and London: Sage Publications, 1976.

Lorenz, D. "The Constitutional Supervision of the Administrative Agencies in the Federal Republic of Germany." *Southern California Law Review* 53 (1980), pp. 543–82.

Meador, D. J. "Appellate Subject Matter Organization: The German Design from an American Perspective." *Hastings International and Comparative Law Review* 5 (1981), pp. 27–72.

———. "German Appellate Judges: Career Patterns and American-English Comparisons." *Judicature* 67, no. 1 (June-July 1983), pp. 16–27.

Mezey, S. G. "Civil Law and Common Law Traditions: Judicial Review and Legislative Supremacy in West Germany and Canada." *International and Comparative Law Quarterly* 32 (July 1983), pp. 689–707.

Noelle-Neumann, E. *The Germans: Public Opinion Polls, 1967–80.* Westport, Conn.: Greenwood Press, 1981.

Rhyne, C. "Federal Republic of Germany." In *Law and Judicial Systems of Nations.* Washington, D.C.: The World Peace Through Law Center, 1978.

Rothman, S. *European Society and Politics.* Indianapolis and New York: Bobbs-Merrill Co., Inc., 1970.

Rüeschemeyer, D. *Lawyers and Their Society: A Comparative Study of the Legal Profession in Germany and in the United States.* Cambridge, Mass.: Harvard University Press, 1973.

Rupp, H. G. "The Federal Constitutional Court and the Constitution of the Federal Republic of Germany." *St. Louis University Law Journal* 16 (1972), pp. 359–83.

———. "Judicial Review in the Federal Republic of Germany." *The American Journal of Comparative Law* 9 (1960), pp. 29–47.

Schramm, G. N. "The Recruitment of Judges for the West German Federal Courts." *The American Journal of Comparative Law* 21 (1973), pp. 691–711.

Schultz, U., and P. Koessler. "The Practicing Lawyer in the Federal Republic of Germany: A Summary of the Major Rules Governing the Profession of West German Lawyers and Their Effects upon the Manner in which Foreign Lawyers Can Collaborate with West German Colleagues." *International Lawyer* 14 (Summer 1980), pp. 531–43.

Sontheimer, K. "Intellectuals and Politics in Western Germany." *West European Politics* 1, no. 1 (February 1978), pp. 30–41.

Walpole, N. C., et al. *Area Handbook for Germany.* Washington, D.C.: U. S. Government Printing Office, 1960.

Zweigert, K. and H. Kotz. *An Introduction to Comparative Law*, vol. 1. New York: Elsevier-Holland, 1977.

6

FRANCE

Alan N. Katz

France is often portrayed as the leader of the Romano-Germanic family of legal systems. Reasons offered for the centrality of the French legal system are that France took the lead in codifying its laws, its democratic political system developed early, and its language became the language of the aristocracy in Europe.[1]

The Romano-Germanic legal systems differ from the common law systems in three major ways: (1) The law is not merely the province of judges and practitioners. It is studied by large numbers of people who do not intend to practice law but see it as important to success in a variety of careers. This interest in the law is seen in the large numbers who seek a legal education, the value placed on that education (for example, the vast proportion of France's 15,000 law graduates each year have no difficulty finding employment), and in the fact that legal scholarship is a more important source of the law than in the common law countries. (2) The law is far more concerned with substantive rules than with procedure. The latter is perceived as having more to do with the administration of justice and not as a source of justice itself. (3) The primary source of the law in the Romano-Germanic nations is legislation and not case law. Some of these distinctions have, however, diminished over time. For example, while case law has been very important in the Anglo-American tradition, it has now been superseded by statutes in many areas. In addition, the French now share many of the traditional Anglo-American concerns for procedural fairness, including a commitment to an independent judiciary, a belief in procedural due process, the presumption of the innocence of the accused, the rejection of ex post facto laws, and the belief that no action is punishable except on the basis of the law.

THE DEVELOPMENT OF THE LEGAL SYSTEM

Much of what is present-day France was governed by Roman law until the fall of the Western Roman Empire in 476. The Burgundians, Visigoths, and

Franks set up kingdoms during the succeeding decades until the latter gained dominion over the land in the sixth century. However, the invaders were less developed than their new subjects and never attempted to impose their own laws upon them. Thus, Roman law continued to remain important in France well after the fall of the Empire.

The major source of Roman law until the twelfth century was the *Alarician Breviary* (506). This was a consolidation of Roman scholarly writings and legislation prepared by King Alaric II. The *Breviary* played a major role in the development of French law. However, local customs persisted and contributed to that same development. David writes about this period that "the Roman law actually applied in France during this period deviated from the *Breviary* locally on many points because of special practical needs, the influence of Germanic concepts and, increasingly, as time went on, simple ignorance."[2]

By the ninth century France was divided between the south (or the "Midi") and the north. The Midi was an area south of a line extending from Geneva to La Rochelle and "lived under a single customary law based on Roman law, which, although greatly altered from Roman times was relatively uniform, stable, comprehensive, and ascertainable."[3] While Roman law ultimately dominated over the local coutumes in the south, the reverse was true in the north. In the larger (about two-thirds of the territory), less densely populated and less highly civilized north, the barbarian, rather than Roman law had been dominant at an early age and this largely Germanic law (in the form of nearly 300 local coutumes) became the customary law. France's legal system continued to reflect this north-south division until the time of the revolution.

Various governments attempted to both strengthen the hold of Roman law and extend the influence of written law during the succeeding decades. For example, while Germanic law dominated in the north, Roman law was significant in the field of contracts and references were generally made to it where the coutumes were silent or ambiguous about an issue.[4] In addition, the existence of sixty "grand coutumes" and nearly three hundred local coutumes created a legal diversity that ultimately undermined the authenticity and authority of some of the coutumes. Consequently, in an effort to make the law more certain, Charles VII ordered the Ordinance of Montil-les-Tours in 1454 to reduce the coutumes to written form. David contends that this development placed the French law in an intermediate position between the law governing England and that of the other continental nations because the French monarch, ruling a larger and less unified nation than England, did not attempt to utilize the law or the courts to create a common law. This would be achieved at a later date through codification. On the other hand, the French law was more uniform and coherent than any of the other continental legal systems of the same period.[5]

In the centuries prior to the Revolution, judicial decisions, scholarly writings, and legislation grew as sources of the French law. Beginning in 1254 the opinions of the Parliaments de Paris were collected. The higher French judiciary remained, for many decades, particularly resistant to interference from other branches of government. This both helped France to develop a tradition of an independent judiciary as well as to spare French law the arbitrariness found among some of its continental neighbors. In addition, the work of legal scholars such as Charles Dumoulin (1500–1566) and Robert Joseph Pothier (1699–1772) contributed to what was almost a "common law" of France: "Their works consisted of procedural guides, expositions of customary law, commentaries on judicial decisions, and treatises, all based primarily on observation of court procedure and decisions. The writers' objective was to describe court practice and explain it systematically, and thus to facilitate legal research and the use of the law."[6] Finally, in the decades prior to the Revolution, there were a series of "grand ordonnances" that were preliminary steps to the codification of French law. Among these legislative ordinances were those dealing with civil procedure (1667), criminal procedure (1670), commercial law (1673), maritime law (1681), gifts (1731), wills (1735), and perpetuities (1747).

Modern scholars now see the revolutionary period and the Napoleonic Codes as a transitional period in which feudal rights were abolished and replaced with more modern (and specific) rights.[7] The basic goal of codification was to eliminate the diversity in the law created by the coutumes. The proponents of codification wished, according to Barere, to "realize the dreams of all philosophers, and to make the laws simple, democratic, accessible to all citizens."[8] A first effort in this direction had been made as early as 1454, with the decision to promulgate the Ordinance of Montil-les-Tours. Other efforts toward codification had been attempted in 1560, 1576, and 1614. These had, however, been beaten back by the efforts of the parlements (these were appellate courts in specific geographic areas) of the various provinces. Consequently, by abolishing the parlements, the Revolution removed one of the greatest obstacles to codification. The civil code was contemplated by the convention in 1791 and was ultimately promulgated in March 1804 with the title of *Code civil des Français*. It was the first and most famous of the five Napoleonic Codes. The other four were the Code of Civil Procedure (1806), Code of Commerce (1808), Code of Criminal Procedure (1811), and Penal Code (1811).

The codes primarily consolidated legislation enacted prior to the Revolution. Contrary to popular notion, the codes did not represent a radical departure with the past. The draftsmen of the codes were primarily late-middle-aged lawyers and judges and acted as such:

It was inevitable that they conceive of a code in terms of their own background, experiences and even prejudices. "Written reason" for them was the law they had always known. In contracts and torts, already essentially unified through the work of the French Romanists, practically no innovations can be found. In other fields, they confined themselves to choosing between differing bodies of customary law.[9]

The codes did not achieve all of their purposes: "The codification did not succeed in substituting a fully rational and logical law for France's historical and traditional law. It did not produce the break that had been expected between the solutions of the prerevolutionary system and those of the new system. Nor did it make the law accessible to the masses as had been intended."[10] The codes did, however, leave their mark upon the French legal system: (1) their clarity and simplicity made the law better known to the masses of the French people; (2) their centering upon the concept of universal justice influenced relations between the individual and his government; and (3) their elevation of the importance of the legislature reduced pressure on the judiciary to serve as a source of the law. David and de Vries write, regarding the latter, that

the Civil Code became in the nineteenth century the symbol of the desirability and effectiveness of creating law exclusively through representative assemblies rather than through the courts. . . . The judiciary, under a statutory duty since the Revolution to express reasons for their decisions, found their most satisfactory starting point in the articles of the Codes. . . . Not until the end of the century, when code rules literally applied proved inadequate and even incompatible with social and economic changes in many cases, did the legislative positivist view begin to wane, opening the way to the increasingly dominant role of the courts.[11]

The codes not only had a profound impact at home, but also placed France at the forefront of the world's legal systems. This was especially so during the nineteenth century:

It was an age of nation-making. In Europe it saw the creation, or the remaking of Germany, Italy, Belgium, Roumania, Bulgaria, and Greece; on the American continent it saw the birth of fifteen new nations; while in the East it saw Japan, Siam, Turkey and Egypt opened to the penetration of European ideas. Of these twenty-five nations almost all sought to mark their accession to political maturity, or their adhesion to the European circle, by a general revision and codification of their laws; and in almost every case the model followed was that of the *Code Napoleon*.[12]

The existence of ten constitutions from the period of the Revolution until 1958 gives ample evidence that all of the problems of governing were not solved by the Revolution. Because France has not been blessed with the same consensus regarding constitutional principles as has England, each government has been a reaction to constitutional principles found in its predecessor:

The First Republic was the consequence of a rebellion against the monarch of the *ancient regime*; the Second Republic followed the Revolution of 1848 and the deposition of the July Monarchy; the Third Republic was a reaction to the military failures of Louis Napoleon as well as to the bloody suppression of the Paris Commune; and the Fourth Republic was both a reaction to the Vichy regime and an attempt to restore the democratic *status quo ante bellum*.[13]

The contemporary French Fifth Republic is also somewhat of a reaction to past regimes. In attempting to establish a government that would weaken the power of the legislature, political parties, and interest groups (called ''inter-mediaries'' by Charles de Gaulle), the constitution of the Fifth Republic centered powers in the hands of the executive and greatly diminished the power of the legislature. While the personality of de Gaulle clearly dominates the early years of the Republic, it must be remembered that a strong executive is a recurrent theme in French constitutional theory:

The restoration of a genuine monarchy long ago became unthinkable in France, but the glorification of kings and the association of national greatness with monarchial regimes are still emphasized in schools of republican France.[14]

There have been some significant changes to the legal system during the Fifth Republic. Among these has been the modernization of the court system and improvements in the training of judges and rules of procedure. The most important change, however, dealt with the judicial review function of the courts. France has never had a tradition of judicial review. Neuborne writes about this that

The impossibility of harmonizing substantial judicial review with a rigidly orthodox vision of judges as skilled mechanics operating a syllogism machine blocked the emergence of judicial review of legislative activity in France until the proclamation of the Fifth Republic in 1958. An unbroken tradition dating from Revolutionary France and extending through the Third and Fourth Republics authorized the legislature to act as final arbiter of the meaning of an array of French constitutions as well as the Declaration of the Rights of Man.[15]

However, the Fifth Republic's limitation on the power of the legislature created a need for some form of judicial review. That function has been assumed by a new institution, the Constitutional Council. The role of this body and the place of judicial review in contemporary France will be discussed in the last section of this chapter.

THE ORGANIZATION OF THE FRENCH COURT SYSTEM

France has two separate and distinct court systems, the ordinary or regular courts and the administrative courts. There is a historic reason for this duality. The creation of administrative courts has its basis in the Revolution's fear that the ordinary courts might interfere with the executive or administrative branch of the government. This is seen in a statute of August 1790: ''The judicial functions are and will remain forever separate from administrative functions. The judges will not be allowed, under penalty of forfeiture, to disturb in any manner whatsoever, the activities of the administrative corps, nor to summon before them the administrators, concerning their functions.''[16] The administrative courts were later developed to check on potential administrative abuses while maintaining the existing separation of powers between judicial and administrative functions.

There are two levels to the French administrative court system. The first is the Regional Councils or Administrative Tribunals (Tribunaux Administratifs) found in the twenty-three national regions plus Paris. Each of the councils is staffed by four to six members—one president and three to five conseillers. These individuals tend to be upper-level civil servants, most of whom are recruited from the Ecole Nationale d'Administration. Citizens bring complaints to the councils regarding the actions of administrative agencies. The councils then conduct investigations of the complaints and ultimately make public their decisions. This often takes the form of the annulment of a government action or a determination that the government must pay the citizen damages as compensation for its actions.

The second level in the administrative system is the Council of State (Counseil d'Etat). The Council has original jurisdiction over very important and/or controversial cases as well as appellate jurisdiction (approximately one quarter of the lower councils' decisions are appealed). Only one of the five sections of the Council (the litigation section) deals with administrative law. The remaining sections are involved with giving advisory opinions, supervising the rules of administrative agencies, and drafting legislation for the cabinet. The members of the Council constitute an administrative elite, the vast majority of whom come from the graduates of the Ecole Nationale d'Administration. The litigation section is made up of nine subsections, each consisting of a president and conseillers. The Council handles a multitude of cases yearly, providing inexpensive and equitable access to the public as a check against potential administrative actions. The efficiency of the administrative courts and the willingness of the French government to assume the burdens for its occasionally improper actions has been widely applauded:

Yet not only does the French state accept liability for fault under the droit administratif, but as outlined earlier, for its risk. In other words, if proper administrative action results in an unequal burden on, or a social injustice to, a citizen, the state bears the cost of equalizing the burden—without the need to introduce a bill in the legislature. In effect, the droit administratif is developing in the direction of absolute liability to ensure equitable sharing among all citizens of the burden of government action. This may well be far from an unmixed blessing, but the French administrative court system, with the Counseil d'Etat standing at its apex, has operated so successfully and has proved to be such a bulwark against arbitrary actions by the centralized state that it richly merits the careful attention that has been extended to it increasingly by students and practitioners of government alike.[17]

Reforms during the Fifth Republic have replaced the 359 Courts of First Instance with 172 Courts of Major Instance (Tribunaux de Grand Instance). These are all located in the various departments (the highest administrative subdivision), though the larger divisions may have two or more such courts.

These courts adjudicate important civil cases and occasionally hear appeals from other courts. Each court has an uneven number of judges (usually three), and decisions are reached by a majority vote. Decisions of these courts may be appealed to the Courts of Appeal.

At the bottom of the criminal court hierarchy are the 455 police courts (Tribunaux de Police) and 172 correctional or criminal courts (Tribunaux Correctionnels). The jurisdiction of the police courts is limited to minor offenses—those involving the imposition of small fines or jail sentences of not more than sixty days. The correctional courts, like the Courts of Major Instance, are manned by at least three judges. The jurisdiction of these courts covers more serious criminal cases (heavier fines and up to five years' imprisonment).

The Assize Court (Cour d'Assise) is a court of original jurisdiction for the most serious criminal cases as well as an appellate court hearing appeals from the lower criminal courts. There are ninety-five Assize Courts—one for each department. These courts are usually staffed by members of the Courts of Appeal but may occasionally be served by members from a lower bench. Three judges sit in on appeals. The more serious criminal cases that originate in this court are heard by a panel of three judges and nine citizens. (A guilty verdict requires eight votes.)

There are twenty-seven Courts of Appeal (Cours d'Appel)—one for each of the judicial districts (composed of a few departments). These courts hear appeals from both the lower criminal and civil courts as well as from the various special courts, many of which deal with the area of social legislation. Each of the Courts of Appeal has from three to five judges. Their decisions on points of fact are final. Decisions based on points of law may be appealed to the Supreme Court of Appeal.

At the apex of the court system is the Supreme Court of Appeal (Cour de Cassation). Its jurisdiction on points of law is final in both civil and criminal cases. It is composed of three sections, each one served by a president and fifteen judges. Criminal appeals go directly to the criminal section but civil appeals first go to the chamber of requests, which forwards those cases with possible grounds for the reversal of the decisions of lower courts. The reversal of a lower court decision means that the case is then sent back for retrial, and the lower court is obligated to utilize the reasoning of the Supreme Court in reinterpreting the case.

In the wake of terrorist activities aimed at impeding President de Gaulle's efforts to settle the Algerian crisis, the government persuaded the legislature to create the Permanent Court of State Security (Cour de Surete de l'Etat). This court is composed of civilian judges and senior military officers and was intended to prevent subversive activities. There is no jury in this court, and its decisions may be appealed to the Supreme Court of Appeal.

There is, finally, a High Court of Justice, which can try the president or other members of the government for high crimes and misdemeanors. In order for this chamber to be convened, however, indictments must be voted by a majority of both the National Assembly and the Senate.

THE PERSONNEL OF THE LAW

The Legal Practitioners

The French legal profession is far more complex than either its British or American counterpart. There are at least five types of practitioners found in France: *avocates*, *avoues*, *agrees*, *notaires*, and *conseil juridiques*. The *avocat* has traditionally corresponded to the British barrister, with a virtual monopoly on pleading in most trial courts. The *avoues* serve functions similar to the British solicitor. While they have usually pleaded cases in minor courts, their major role in the legal system is to do all the writing necessary in litigation as well as to supervise the execution of judgments. Like the solicitor's, the importance of the avoue's work is often overlooked, ''but it is evident to disinterested persons that the smooth functioning of French justice owes much to the part played by avoues in the legal process.''[18] The *agrees* have traditionally performed the same functions as the avoues, but in commercial courts. The *notaires* have been concerned with the preparation of legal documents such as wills, contracts, and property settlements. Finally, the *conseil juridiques* have been one among many in the legal system who are permitted to give legal advice.

A reform act in December 1971 attempted to simplify the profession by fusing the functions of the avocat, avoue, and agree. The act enabled the avocats to fulfill all the legal functions in the lower courts and to practice together in a multimember firm. It also regulated all legal personnel involved in out-of-court settlements. The act, however, did not bring about a complete fusion of the profession, for avoues still continue to practice at the appellate level, primarily because magistrates of those courts prefer to deal with them rather than with avocats.

In 1982 there were slightly more than 31,000 avocats in France.[19] The avocat, along with the magistrate and the law professor, is considered to be the elite of the French legal profession. Each avocat must pass an accreditation examination as well as serve for three to five years as an apprentice. Since 1954 they have been regulated by bar associations (barreaux). The jurisdiction of each bar is usually equated with that of a district court. Each avocat may have one professional domicile and be a member of one bar.

In 1982 there were approximately 55,000 notaires in France.[20] The French notaires are quite distinct from the British and American notary public. They have a virtual monopoly over conveyancing and draft mortgages, wills, and contracts. In addition, they certify documents to be used as evidence in court proceedings and serve as depositories for original copies of legal documents, such as wills (such documents are kept in the notaire's office for 125 years and then turned over to national or district archives). Those law graduates who wish to become notaires must pass a special examination and then wait for a vacancy, for the number of notaires is regulated by law. The notaire often becomes a family's trusted legal advisor and handles many of its legal concerns. In contrast to the avocat, the notaire is thought of as an impartial legal practitioner, advising all parties involved in the legal transactions to which he is a party.

In addition to the notaire, there are a multiplicity of professionals practicing outside of the courts. These include the fiscal and legal counsellor (*conseil fiscal et juridique*), business agent (*agent d'affairs*), C. P. A. (*expert-comptable*), arbitrator (*arbitre rapporteur*), bailiff (*huissier*), receiver in commercial and civil tribunals (*syndic*), and the legal expert attached to agricultural syndicates (*expert judiciare*). Most of these have a rather limited field of expertise and, therefore, do not constitute a threat to the avocat. This, however, is not true of the conseil fiscal et juridique (usually referred to as "conseil juridique") who "fulfills precisely those functions that are commonly perceived as being within the province of the 'modern lawyer,' whose practice is becoming continually more oriented toward legal advice than toward litigation."[21]

While the conseil juridiques have been in existence since the nineteenth century, they have only been regulated since 1971. Since that date the avocats have responded to competition from the conseils by first attempting to eliminate them and then by attempting to become one with them. Neither of these efforts have met with any success. In fact, the conseils have reacted to this pressure by creating their own national organization (with regional chapters), which has very successfully lobbied the government to promote their goals. The existence of such an organization (a similar national organization for avocats has not been formed because of the fear of the power of the Paris bar among the provincial bars) makes the likelihood of eventual fusion somewhat remote.

French legal education is part of a national system of open admission public education guaranteed by the Constitution of the Fifth Republic. Any student wishing to study law at a French university (there are universities in most major cities—over 40 in all offering courses in the law) must first pass the baccalaureate (a series of comprehensive examinations in philosophy, literature, mathematics, natural sciences, and languages).[22] The university course of study is for four years, and the primary method of teaching is the lecture. The student is expected to pass an examination at the end of each year and is granted a general studies degree (D.E.U.G.) after the first two years. At the end of a third year the student receives a licence en droit, the equivalent of a B.A. in law. A maitrise en droit, the equivalent of an M.A. in law (the basic French law degree), is acquired at the end of the fourth year. Some students complete a fifth year of study leading to a national diploma, the Diplome d'Etudes Approfondies (D.E.A.) or a Diplome d'Etudes Supenfures Specialisees (D.E.S.S.). This becomes the prerequisite for the preparation of the doctoral thesis, leading to the Docturat d'Etat.

The present structure of legal education in France is interdisciplinary in nature and represents a sharing of power over curriculum between the national government and the universities. While legal education has been in existence in France since the Middle Ages, it has seen a struggle between those concerned with a practical education and the proponents of a more liberal education. This struggle reflects the larger disagreements within French society over its own goals and values: "The fundamental character of French legal education, which emphasizes the educating of jurists as opposed to the training of lawyers, is the product of a set of factors which are deeply rooted in French history and are part of the basic intellectual assumptions of French culture."[23] The present state of French legal education is seen as representing a reassertion of the view of legal education as an intellectual endeavor rather than one of merely practical training.

The last major statute passed by the National Assembly that dealt with legal education was the *Loi d'orientation de l'enseignement superieur* (*The Law Concerning the Direction of Higher Education*), in the wake of the 1968 student riots. While the statute did not alter the basic pattern of legal education, it did give much greater autonomy to the universities in controlling the course of legal education. By doing so, it made the curricula of legal education the joint responsibility of both the universities and the Ministry of National Education. The government could now set national standards for the conferring of degrees, but the universities were responsible for carrying out these requirements as well as supplementing them with their own requirements.[24]

Legal Scholars

Legal scholars have played a much greater role in the development of the law in France than have their counterparts in the common law systems. This is largely due to the fact that legal scholars in civil law systems were both the draftsmen of the codes and the doctrine of legislative supremacy. Once the codes were in place, it was only natural to turn to the same legal scholars to interpret them. Nagourney writes on the present role of legal scholars:

Much of the energy devoted to the preparation of casebooks by American and English faculty members is instead directed towards the elaboration of doctrinal syntheses by their French counterparts. In addition to this synthetic treatment of a certain topic, faculty members systematically write articles in which they analyze important judicial decisions. While these doctrinal discussion (which may be found in textbooks, reference works such as legal encyclopedias, and law reviews) and *Commentaires d'Arrets* are not, strictly speaking, binding authority, they nevertheless are highly influential.[25]

The impact of legal scholars is also seen in the great prestige afforded law professors. Access to law teaching positions is limited to those few who have both completed their doctoral work and have passed a very rigorous, competitive, national examination. Once appointed to a position, a professor may move to more prestigious universities when openings occur. (The *Gourman Report* lists the top law programs in France as the University of Paris, University Jean Moulin, and the University of Montpellier.)[26] A professor teaches whatever subject an opening at a university affords; this produces a broader approach to the law than that found in the common law countries. Most law professors view the rigors of litigation as a barrier to legal research, and few, as a result, opt for membership in the bar. On the contrary, their legal opinions attempt to be as detached from legal controversy as possible.

It is likely that the position of legal scholars will remain prestigious within the French legal community. There are probably two major reasons for this: (1)

All other actors in the system receive their training from the scholars who transmit to them a comprehensive and highly ordered model of the legal system that to a great extent controls how they organize their knowledge, pose their questions and communicate with each other. This model is not only taught in the universities but constitutes the latent framework of the treaties and articles produced by the professors[27]

and (2) the bar tends to rely upon legal periodicals that discuss new legislation and court opinions. These journals are usually controlled by the professors of law.

The Judiciary

There are major differences between the judiciary in France and that found in the common law countries. First among these is that the French judge is a member of the civil service. This greatly reduces the possibility of political pressure and should, in theory, allow for greater judicial independence. Second, because appointment to the bench comes early in one's career, members of the judiciary tend to have different temperaments and approaches to the study of law than do the legal practitioners. In fact, judges often feel more in common with law professors than with practitioners. Finally, because members of the judiciary are isolated from the bar, they have easily developed a feeling of group solidarity among themselves.

In 1982 there were 4,700 judges in France. While there has been a significant increase in the number of judges, the total today is still less than before World War II. If we compare France with its largest neighbor, Germany, we can see the relative absence of judges in France. Germany, with a population of 60 million (compared to 52 million in France) has four times the number of judges.[28] There are generally three levels of French judges: trial judges, those sitting on appellate courts, and those sitting on the Supreme Court. In addition to the judges (often called magistrates), there is a class of individuals employed by the Public Ministry (attached to the Ministry of Justice) who play a significant role in the legal system. One must choose between a career on the bench or as a pleading or prosecuting magistrate (a member of the Public Ministry). One may move from the bench to a position as a prosecutor and back. While this may enable the judge and prosecutor to gain similar experiences, some complain that this practice may prejudice the views of judges toward the prosecution.

Since 1970 all members of the judiciary must attend the Ecole Nationale de la Magistrature (ENM) in Bordeaux. Students normally enter the school after graduation from a law school and the passing of a very competitive entrance examination. Civil servants in the top two ranks (Levels A and B) who are under the age of thirty-five may also take the same entrance examination. In addition, the following may also petition the Ministry of Justice for appointment to the school: (1) lawyers who have at least three years experience beyond the apprenticeship period and those admitted to practice before the Council of State and Cour de Cassation, and (2) those holding the doctorate of law or those employed as assistant professors in law in a French law school for at least three years.[29] Each candidate for a judgeship (*auditeurs de justice*) undergoes a twenty-eight-month training period—twelve months of formal training at Bordeaux, followed by a series of internships, called "stages." The twelve-month period at Bordeaux is divided into two sections: separate six-week internships at various agencies of criminal justice (police departments, juvenile and adult correction agencies) as well as a similar internship as a law clerk. All of this serves as an introduction to the formal course work—judicial practice and various aspects of the law (taught by senior judges) and social sciences (mostly psychology). Each student must pass a comprehensive examination at the completion of the mandatory course. The student then spends the next sixteen months in an internship center located in an appellate district. Each center is headed by a senior judge, who serves as the supervisor for both the internal and external phases of the internship. The former provide first-hand experiences in the problems and activities of judges, while the latter are assignments outside the judicial system (such as learning management skills by working in a business firm).[30]

Initial appointments to the bench are made by the president of the Republic. Each candidate is given a rank-ordering based upon his/her performance in the course work and internships. The candidate then chooses a position from those listed by the Ministry of Justice. Any student who does not successfully complete the course of study may stay at the school for another year or take a position as a court administrator.[31] While, in theory, there is complete judicial independence, political considerations often do play some role in decisions to promote judges and "a long uphill struggle has been waged in France, and elsewhere, to wrest discretion from the executive, which has an irresistible tendency to reward loyalty and conformism when possibilities for judicial advancement open up."[32] Judges may only be removed for misconduct in office and the inability to discharge their functions due to ill health. The present retirement age for judges is sixty-seven (judges of the Supreme Court may retire at seventy).

French judges tend to come from solidly middle-class backgrounds. There are, however, differences, depending upon the age of the judge. Those appointed to the bench prior to the development of the ENM tend to come from solidly middle-class backgrounds, often with a long judicial history. Those appointed since 1970 still tend to be middle class in origin but one-third are of lower-middle-class or working-class origins.[33] Because of the virtual halt to recruitment in the 1950s, judges tend to be under forty or over fifty-five years of age. In fact, France now possesses the youngest judiciary in Western Europe. Nearly

44 percent of the present judiciary is under the age of thirty-five. In addition, the French judiciary has seen an influx of female judges (twenty-one percent of the present members of the bench are female).[34] The other major changes in the composition of the judiciary are its decolonization (an increasingly large number of judges have been appointed from North Africa and overseas) and its unionization.[35]

There are two unions that represent magistrates in France. The newer of the two is the Syndicat de la Magistrature. This union has a membership of one thousand, most of whom are young and politically radical (some of its members are called ''red judges''). As an indication of the nontraditional orientation of some of its judges, in the late 1970s, one of the members of this union sent a company director to jail who had been accused of being responsible for a fatal accident in his factory. The older of the two unions is the Union Syndicate des Magistrats (USM). This union has two thousand members, is generally seen as more politically conservative, and only shifted from a professional association to a union in response to competition from the more radical Syndicat.[36] Both unions have expressed concern over the need to simplify the language used in the courts, the meager pay for magistrates, and the need to liberalize the penal code and reform the court structure.

The French system is, once again, different from the Anglo-American pattern in that it is characterized by an inquisitorial rather than an accusatorial system. This system places far less emphasis on the rights of the accused and is more concerned with the protection of societal rights. In fact, there is no presumption of the innocence of the accused in France. The judge is asked to decide whether a prima facie case exists against the accused. In making this decision, the judge may call witnesses and look at the record of the accused. The judge is in complete control at the trial and has the ability to interrogate witnesses. Interestingly, the personality of the judge plays virtually no role in the disposition of a case. All cases (except for minor ones) are heard by a panel of judges. Decisions of the judges are always anonymous, and minority opinions are forbidden. Judges can, therefore, gain no fame through the quality of their decisions.

Finally, the general supervision of the judiciary is in the hands of the Council of the Judiciary, presided over by the president and the minister of justice. The Council plays an advisory role on the appointment of judges and additionally acts as a disciplinary council. It is composed of nine members who are appointed by the president for a four year term.

PUBLIC PERCEPTIONS AND THE ROLE OF THE COURTS

In a political system often characterized by alienation, suspicion, and distrust, it is not surprising to find negative feelings toward the judiciary. Charles Hargrove recently wrote: ''French judges are an unloved fraternity. They are accused by the police and a substantial section of the population of being too lenient and left wing; and by the Opposition of being too repressive and beholden to the government. And by everybody of being too slow and inefficient.''[37] Polls have consistently given the judicial system poor ratings. For example, no more than 35 percent of the population gave the judiciary positive ratings (''works very well,'' or ''works rather well'') in four polls conducted for *L'Express* through the 1960s and early 1970s.[38]

The concept of an independent judiciary is not as deeply rooted in France as in the Anglo-American pattern. It should, therefore, not be surprising to find widespread skepticism regarding the independence of the contemporary French judiciary. For example, a poll conducted by IFOP (Institut Français de l'Opinion Publique) found that only 50 percent of the French people perceived the judiciary to be ''wholly'' or ''relatively'' independent of the government, and 48 percent found it independent of the police.[39] Similarly, in 1981, Robert Badinger, a leading legal scholar (and presently minister of justice in the Mitterand government), articulated the French lack of concern regarding an independent judiciary: ''It is thought of as a public service, like the post office or the army. The general feeling is that just because you've passed the examination to become a judge this does not entitle you to more independence than any other civil servant.''[40] Finally, the suspension and ultimate removal of a left-wing judge, Jacques Bidalou, because of twenty-six charges brought against him, many that were related to his political activities, and the fact that more legal actions had been brought against judges in the last few years of the 1970s than in the previous 150 years, had, once again, called the independence of the French judiciary into question.[41] The lowered prestige of the judiciary has made it increasingly difficult to fill vacancies on the bench (full page advertisements have appeared in newspapers and magazines noting such vacancies).[42] In addition, the judiciary's falling prestige is reflected in the miniscule budget for the Ministry of Justice (from which all judicial personnel are paid)—less than 1 percent of the national budget for the past thirty years.[43]

The potential influence of the French judiciary has been further limited by a narrow conception of a judge's proper role. This limited role is clearly a reaction to the negative role that the judiciary was seen to have played in the decades prior to the French Revolution. In prerevolutionary France the parlements, the high royal courts, assumed both legislative and judicial functions. The antiegalitarian attitudes of many of the judges of these courts resulted in unpopular actions and were seen as having prevented reforms by the king. As a reaction to these actions, postrevolutionary France has generally opposed the concept of judicial review. It has proclaimed that only the legislature can make laws and that questions regarding those laws should be dealt with by the legislature. Judicial review (or ''gouvernement des judges,'' as it is disparagingly labelled) still has few adherents in France today:

This attitude had found its conceptualization in Montesquieu's description of the judges as the mere ''mouths of the law,'' ''inanimate beings'' whose only task should be to apply blindly, automatically, and uncreatively the supreme will of the popular legislature.

. . . It has represented a basic tenet of political and constitutional philosophy in France and, through French influence, in the rest of continental Europe, well into our century.[44]

The Constitution of the Fifth Republic differs from its predecessors in that it has attempted to establish roughly coequal legislative and judicial branches of the government. Because the legislature is no longer free to act as it chooses, the Fifth Republic recognizes some form of judicial review. While the main agency for this new role is the Constitutional Council, the Council of State and Cour de Cassation have also been involved in judicial review.

The Constitution of the Fifth Republic specifically limits the areas in which parliament may legislate (Article 34). All other areas are delegated to the president (Article 37). In a 1959 decision the Council of State invalidated an executive decree on the grounds that it violated some of the basic principles of the French "higher law" (among these were the Declaration of the Rights of Man, and the preambles of both the 1946 and 1958 constitutions). While the actions of the Council of State (and the Constitutional Council) are those of administrative judges, actions by the Cour de Cassation are those of more "ordinary" judges, and, therefore, represent, in some ways, an even greater movement toward judicial review. In a complex 1975 decision, this court held that French law could not be applied that was promulgated after and conflicted with the law of the European Economic Community. While it is not clear how far-reaching this decision will ultimately be, one school of thought sees it as a clear example of judicial review.

The most important organization involved in judicial review is the Constitutional Council. The Council is composed of all the ex-presidents of France plus nine other individuals, selected by the president of the Republic and the presidents of the two legislative chambers. The ex-presidents serve for life, and the nine appointed members (most of whom are lawyers who have been active in politics) are elected for staggered nine-year terms. The Council has the power to declare unconstitutional ordinary laws, treaties and protocols, as well as organic laws (i.e., appointment or removal of high officials), and the rules of procedure of both houses of the legislature.

The Council does suffer from four serious limitations in its judicial review function. First, private groups or individuals may not challenge the constitutionality of a statute. Only four individuals—the president of the Republic, the prime minister, and the presidents of the two chambers of the legislature—can bring such challenges. Second, the ability of the Council to challenge the constitutionality of a statute is limited to a very brief time period—that between the parliamentary approval of a bill and its promulgation. Third, only the substance, not the procedural application of a law, may be challenged. Finally, the Council was seen as a watchdog protecting the executive's lawmaking powers rather than a constitutional court:

The Conseil's declared raison d'etre was to assure that Parliament would never legislate outside of the subject matter indicated in article 34, thereby intruding into the legislative jurisdiction, or pouvoir reglementaire, of the executive. In other words, the new Conseil was essentially aimed at preventing the re-emergence of the historical rule that Parliament's legislative jurisdiction is unlimited.[45]

Despite these limitations, the Council has played an active role in the Fifth Republic, by invalidating proposed rules of the National Assembly as well as statutes regarding personal liberty (among these are decisions on automobile searches and the detention of illegal aliens), equality, the right to travel, the right to vote, the right to a criminal trial, and procedural due process.[46]

While it cannot be suggested that the Council plays a role similar to that of the U.S. Supreme Court or even the German Federal Constitutional Court, it has broken new ground in overturning both legislative and executive actions to protect a number of democratic values. In initiating a judicial review function, the Council has not only protected certain rights from executive or legislative abuses, but has also helped to legitimize the actions of the system. This has all been done within the context of the separation of powers demanded by the Constitution of the Fifth Republic:

Building on the techniques of pre–1958 executive separation of powers revue, the Council has identified fundamental values and has required governmental action in derogation of these values to respect the classic tripartite classification of functions. The result has been a tolerably effective system of judicial review that protects substantive values without posing a direct challenge to democratic political theory. Far from imposing its own value choices, the Conseil constitutionnel has insisted only that the branches of government remain within their spheres of activity.[47]

NOTES

1. R. David, *French Law: Its Structure, Sources and Methodology* (Baton Rouge: Louisiana State University, 1972), p. vi.

2. Ibid., p. 3.

3. Ibid., p. 5.

4. F. H. Lawson, A. E. Anton, and L. Neville Brown, *Amos and Walton's Introduction to French Law* (Oxford: The Clarendon Press, 1967), pp. 27–28.

5. David, *French Law*, pp. 6–7.

6. Ibid., pp. 9–10.

7. See, for example, Lawson, *Amos and Walton's*, pp. 32–34 and R. David and P. de Vries, *The French Legal System: An Introduction to Civil Law Systems* (New York: Oceana Publications, 1958), pp. 12–16.

8. Lawson, *Amos and Walton's*, p. 31.

9. David and de Vries, *The French Legal System*, pp. 13–14.

10. David, *French Law*, p. 16.

11. David and de Vries, *The French Legal System*, p. 15.

12. Lawson, *Amos and Walton*, p. 4.

13. W. Safran, *The French Polity* (New York: David McCay Co., 1977), pp. 57–58.

14. Ibid., p. 55.

15. B. Neuborne, "Judicial Review and the Separation of Powers in France and the United States," *New York University Law Review* 57, no. 3 (June 1982), pp. 378–79.

16. S. Riesenfeld, "The French System of Administrative Justice: A Model for American Law?" *Boston University Law Review* 18 (1938), p. 48.

17. H. J. Abraham, *The Judicial Process: An Introductory Analysis of the Courts of the United States, England and France* (New York: Oxford University Press, 1975), p. 269.

18. Lawson, *Amos and Walton's*, p. 23.

19. "Combien Sont-ils?: Combien Pesent-ils Dans L'Economie?" *Le Point* 78 (October 17, 1983), p. 53.

20. Ibid.

21. T. Le, "The French Legal Profession: A Prisoner of Its Glorious Past?" *Cornell International Law Journal* 15 (Winter 1982), p. 87.

22. H. P. Tseng, *The Law Schools of the World* (Buffalo: William S. Hein & Co., 1977), pp. 122–36.

23. T. E. Carbonneau, "The French Legal Studies Curriculum: Its History and Relevance as a Model for Reform," *McGill Law Journal* 25 (1980), p. 446.

24. Loi No. 68–978 du 12 Novembre 1968, D. 1968. p. 317.

25. J. Y. Nagourney, "France," *Comparative Law Yearbook*, vol. 5 (1981), p. 51.

26. Tseng, *The Law Schools*, p. 28.

27. M. Glendon, M. W. Gordon, and C. Osawke, *Comparative Legal Traditions in a Nutshell* (St. Paul: West Publishing Co., 1982), p. 87.

28. H. W. Ehrmann, *Politics in France* (Boston: Little, Brown & Co., 1983), p. 176.

29. J. P. Richert, "Recruiting and Training Judges in France," *Judicature* 57, no. 4 (November 1973), p. 146.

30. Ibid., pp. 147–48.

31. Ibid., p. 149.

32. Ehrmann, *Politics in France*, p. 178.

33. Ibid., p. 177.

34. Ibid.

35. J. Bodiguel, "Qui Sont les Magistrats Francais?: Esquisse D'Une Sociologie," *Pouvoirs* 16 (1981), p. 35.

36. M. Berlins, "Judges Who Have Their Own Union," *The Times of London*, May 14, 1976, p. 18.

37. C. Hargrove, "French Rebel Judges Called Before the Bench Council," *The Times of London*, July 24, 1980, p. 7.

38. *L'Express*, April 26, 1971, p. 68.

39. *Sondages*, No. 1–2 (1971), p. 92.

40. R. Eder, "Judges in France Being Pressed to Take a Harder Line on Crime," *New York Times*, March 31, 1981, p. 11.

41. "French Judges Urged to Strike One Dismissed," *The Times of London*, February 9, 1981, p. 6; Hargrove, *French Rebel Judges*.

42. F. J. Prial, "French Judges Unhappy with the Police and Laws Controlling Them," *New York Times*, December 19, 1980, p. 20.

43. Ehrmann, *Politics in France*, p. 176.

44. M. Cappelletti, "The 'Mighty Problem' of Judicial Review and the Contribution of Comparative Analysis," *Southern California Law Review* 53 (1980), p. 413.

45. Ibid., p. 417.

46. See Neuborne, "Judicial Review," for an excellent analysis of the role of the Conseil constitutionnel.

47. Ibid., p. 410.

BIBLIOGRAPHY

Abraham, H. J. *The Judicial Process: An Introductory Analysis of the Courts of the United States, England and France.* New York: Oxford University Press, 1975.

Aldisert, R. J. "Rambling Through Continental Legal Systems." *University of Pittsburgh Law Review* 43 (Summer 1982), pp. 935–93.

Ardagh, J. *France in the 1980's.* Middlesex, England: Penguin Press, 1982.

Beardsley, J. "Constitutional Review in France." *Supreme Court Review* (1975), pp. 189–259.

Berlins, M. "Judges Who Have Their Own Union." *The Times of London*, May 14, 1976, p. 18.

Bodiguel, J. "Qui Sont les Magistrats Francais?: Esquisse d'Une Sociologie." *Pouvoirs* 16 (1981), pp. 31–42.

Cappelletti, M. "The 'Mighty Problem' of Judicial Review and the Contribution of Comparative Analysis." *Southern California Law Review* 53 (1980), pp. 409–45.

Cappelletti, M., and W. Cohen. *Comparative Constitutional Law: Cases and Materials.* Indianapolis: The Bobbs-Merrill Co., 1979.

Carbonneau, T. E. "The French Legal Studies Curriculum: Its History and Relevance as a Model for Reform." *McGill Law Journal* 25 (1980), pp. 445–77.

"Combien Sont-ils?: Combien Pesent-ils Dans l'Economie?" *Le Point* 78 (October 17, 1983).

David, R. *French Law: Its Structure, Sources and Methodology.* Baton Rouge: Louisiana State University, 1972.

David, R., and P. de Vries. *The French Legal System: An Introduction to Civil Law Systems.* New York: Oceana Publications, 1958.

Ehrmann, H. W. *Politics in France.* Boston: Little, Brown & Co., 1983.

Glendon, M., W. M. Gordon, and C. Osawke. *Comparative Legal Traditions in a Nutshell.* St. Paul: West Publishing Co., 1982.

Hargrove, C. "French Rebel Judges Called before the Bench Council." *The Times of London*, July 24, 1980, p. 7.

Hayward, J. *The One and Indivisible French Republic.* New York: W. W. Norton & Co., Inc., 1973.

Lawson, F. H., A. E. Anton, and L. Neville Brown. *Amos and Walton's Introduction to French Law.* Oxford: The Clarendon Press, 1967.

Le, T. "The French Legal Profession: A Prisoner of Its Glorious Past?" *Cornell International Law Journal* 15 (Winter 1982), pp. 63–104.

Martaguet, P. "Comment Devient-on Magistrat?" *Pouvoirs* 16 (1981), pp. 107–18.

Nagourney, J. Y. "France." *Comparative Law Yearbook*, vol. 5 (1981), pp. 45–68.

Neuborne, B. "Judicial Review and the Separation of Powers in France and the United States." *New York University Law Review* 57, no. 3 (June 1982), pp. 363–442.

Noonan, L. G. *France: The Politics of Continuity in Change.* New York: Holt, Rinehart and Winston, 1970.

Prial, F. J. "French Judges Unhappy with the Police and Laws Controlling Them." *New York Times*, December 19, 1980, p. 20.

Rendel, M. *The Administrative Function of the French Conseil d'Etat*. London: Weidenfeld and Nicolson, 1970.

Richert, J. P. "Judicial Service in the French Manner." *Trial* (January 1976), p. 18ff.

———. "Recruiting and Training Judges in France." *Judicature* 57, no. 4 (November 1973), pp. 145–49.

Ridley, F. F., ed. *Government and Administration in Western Europe*. New York: St. Martin's Press, 1979.

Riesenfeld, S. "The French System of Administrative Justice: A Model for American Law?" *Boston University Law Review* 18 (1938), pp. 48–82.

Safran, W. *The French Polity*. New York: David McCay Co., 1977.

Tallon, "Constitution and the Courts." *American Journal of Comparative Law* 27 (Fall 1979), pp. 567–87.

Tseng, H. P. *The Law Schools of the World*. Buffalo: William S. Hein & Co., 1977.

7

INDIA, PAKISTAN, AND
BANGLADESH

Alan N. Katz

The destinies of the nations of India, Pakistan, and Bangladesh are inextricably linked to each other. Despite the partition of India and Pakistan in 1947 and the creation of Bangladesh out of what had been East Pakistan in 1971, these three areas had been united under the British Raj and still share much together. Equally as important, these three nations have struggled with the problems of poverty, governmental inefficiency, and corruption, which are seemingly endemic in the Third World. All have also tried to develop democracies (often unsuccessfully) where no deeply rooted democratic tradition existed:

> With the exception of twenty-eight years of democratic government, and perhaps some of the more halcyon days of the British Raj, India over the centuries had known little but despotism, at the hands of native Mogul, Portuguese, Dutch, and French rulers. It had no tradition of parliamentary democracy, of general elections, of civil liberties. Even the tradition of ''maintaining law and order'' and the independent judiciary to insure it were not indigenous; before the British Raj was established, in 1858, anarchy and despotism had been pervasive. In fact, the most abiding tradition was that of an authoritarian, arbitrary government.[1]

As we shall shortly see, the law, the legal system, and legal practitioners have played and continue to play a crucial role in these struggles today in the Indian subcontinent.

INDIA

Indian civilization probably began in the Indus Valley in the third century B.C. The initial inhabitants of the subcontinent were most likely the Dravidian-speaking ancestors of those living in the south of India today. An invasion by Sanskrit-speaking Aryans from central Asia around 1500 B.C. had forced the former into southern India. The Aryans were pastoral tribesmen and warriors who brought with them their own hymns and prayers (collectively known as the Vedas) as well as the beginnings of a caste system to distinguish the fair-skinned invaders from the darker-skinned inhabitants. During this period (which lasted until approximately 500 B.C.) Hinduism was developed as a synthesis of the religion of the Aryans and the indigenous people. The head of the Aryan tribe was the king (or Raja), who was served by his nobles. The power of the king was not absolute, for his acts needed the approval of the *sabha* (the popular assembly) composed of all fighting-age males.[2] While the administration of justice was in the hands of *kshatriya* judges and brahmin assessors, decisions at the village level were taken by the village council. Both the king and the village councils were given a good deal of power, with the former being able to promulgate regulations that would be put into archives for future reference and the latter allowed to enact its own by-laws.[3]

The Development of the Legal System

India was then divided into northern and southern areas until the Muslim invasions in the seventh century (in fact, India was really not unified until the British incursions in the seventeenth century). The first great empire in the north, the Mauryan Empire (321–185 B.C.) began with the ousting of Alexander the Great's successor by Chandragupta. Chandragupta's reign saw the establishment of both criminal and civil courts where cases were heard by three judges, advised by individuals well-acquainted with the law (though most civil cases were heard by juries of fellow caste-members of the litigants). Decisions in criminal cases were often harsh, with the death penalty and maiming exacted as punishment for certain crimes and both torture and trial by ordeal utilized to obtain the truth.[4] This empire reached its zenith under Asoka (273–232). Asoka's reign was characterized by toleration, with the relaxation of the harsh laws of his grandfather, the throwing open of the jails on the anniversary of his coronation, as well as an attempt to prevent religious wars.[5] The Mauryan Empire dissolved after Asoka's death, when the area was invaded by Greeks and others from the north. The next great empire, the Gupta Empire (A.D. 320–499), saw a revival of Hinduism and a decline of Buddhism, great political stability, and a great upsurge in trade between India and her neighbors.

The time from the end of the Vedic period (500 B.C.) until the beginning of the Muslim invasions (A.D. 711) saw some significant developments in the administration of justice. Some of these were begun in the early period. For example, the Dharma Sutras, the first manuals of human conduct, and probably the earliest sources of Hindu law, were likely begun between the sixth and second centuries B.C. These were later remodelled in verse form. Among the earliest of the Dharma Sastras ("Instructions in the Sacred Law") is that of Manu, which is concerned with human conduct generally. The Sutras and Sastras, taken together, are known as the Smirti, or "remembered" literature, as distinct from the earlier, Sruti, or "heard" Vedic literature.[6] It was the responsibility of the king to maintain the Dharma. By doing so, he was known as the Dharma incarnate, and the failure to heed his responsibilities would result in his suffering in hell. The responsibility of the king to protect the Dharma was dictated by a view of human nature as evil and corrupt. For example, in the words of Manu: "If the king did not inflict punishment untiringly on evil-doers the stronger would roast the weaker like a fish upon a spit."[7]

Most Indian courts at this time were composed of a bench of magistrates rather than a single judge. Judges were sought who were learned in the law, religious, and impartial. In some kingdoms, the king's legal advisor was responsible for justice and might also act as a judge. The king's own court was usually limited to appeals and serious crimes against the state. This period also saw the introduction of lawyers. This was seen in both the utilization of Brahmins as experts appearing before the court as well as the use of proxies by litigants who would receive a share of the money involved in the case.[8] In addition, there were councils of villages, guilds, and castes who handled minor criminal matters. Basham writes about these tribunals: "They could punish offenders by fines and excommunication, the latter a very serious penalty indeed, and they probably played as important a part in the life of the community as did the king's courts. Unfortunately we have little knowledge of their procedure."[9]

The period from the seventh century until the western incursions in the sixteenth century saw India led by a succession of Muslim rulers. The early Muslim invaders were primarily Turkish soldiers of fortune who were not concerned with imposing new forms of government upon the people. As such, the nobles ruled primarily through local princes, who were given a good deal of local autonomy. As Alan Gledhill points out, through much of this time (but specifically during the Turkish Sultinate of 1206–1526) the government "could do no more than defend its territories, suppress rebellion, punish crime, and enforce contracts."[10] There was little division of power, and the state was primarily concerned with the collection of revenue and maintenance of the strength of the imperial army. While justice might be more humane and fairly administered at certain times (as, for example, during the reign of Akbar), there was no single unifying legal system in India prior to the British. While the Muslim rulers established a general hierarchy of courts with the right of appeal, there existed no consistent supervision of the work of the lower courts. In addition, Hindus were allowed to develop their own tribunals, and when conflict existed in the royal courts, the Hindu law was applied. Further, neither the Muslim law nor its courts extended very far into India's rural villages.[11]

British involvement in India began with the activities of the East India Company in the early seventeenth century. As the British shifted from indirect to direct colonial rule, their goals for the legal system changed. While the British felt no need to impose their own standards of conduct upon the Indians, they increasingly felt the need to develop procedures for defining relations between themselves and the Indians and rules to enable the Indians to operate under their own norms.

The formation of mayor's courts in the presidency towns of Calcutta, Bombay, and Madras in 1726 were the first British actions to impact upon the court system of the subcontinent. These courts were dominated by the executive and weakened by judges (most of whom were not lawyers) who were uneducated about the complexities of English law. In these courts "justice was largely discretionary depending upon the notions of equity and fairplay entertained by the presiding judge."[12] The development of Supreme Courts in each of the presidency towns soon replaced these courts. The Supreme Courts were manned by professionally trained judges who were assisted by the English bar. These courts were independent of the executive and, in some cases, administered justice beyond the boundaries of the presidency towns.

The administration of justice in northern India had been in the hands of courts run by the Moghul emperors. The East India Company ultimately took over responsibility for the administration of justice in the rural areas outside the presidency towns. It established provincial civil courts (*mofussil dewanny adalats*) and criminal courts (*foujdary adalats*) in each district. These courts effectively dealt with the needs of the people, gained greater independence from executive control, and employed a number of Indians.

Therefore, until 1862, and the introduction of the High Courts, there were two court systems in India: the first, the Supreme Courts in the presidency towns, were established as replicas of British courts to primarily cater to the needs of the English residing in those towns; the second, the adalats (known as "mofussil"), in the territories, dealt with a predominantly Indian population. The latter courts were developed when it became clear to administrators such as Warren Hastings that justice could best be administered to those living in rural India by the application of their own laws.

The High Courts Act of 1862 created courts to replace all of the existing courts in India. The High Courts exercised both original and appellate jurisdiction (through different branches of the courts) as well as superintendence over the courts in the mofussil. With their establishment, all of the courts in India were, for the first time, under one unified system. Civil courts were soon established in each of the provinces, and the criminal court system was reorganized. Appeals from the High Courts were heard by the Judicial Committee of the Privy Council in England. This procedure had obvious disadvantages and the Federal Court of India (later changed to the Supreme Court of India) became the final court of appeals for India.

While the British were committed to retaining, rather than changing many of the Indian customs, the colonial law did differ from that before it in a number of important ways: (1) people were to be treated equally under the law rather than have their status influence the outcome of court decisions; (2) the courts made decisions between "right" and "wrong" and those decisions were to be enforced; (3) judges were to be neutral and lawyers zealous advocates for their clients; and (4) there was a search for a definitive precedent to utilize the best custom in the making of decisions.[13] The British legacy with regard to the administration of justice in India was, therefore, twofold: first, it modernized a legal system, affording equality before the law and, for a time, creating a large and well-respected legal profession; and second, it created an extraordinarily litigious society where "People's cynicism about the quality of English justice was only matched by their ambivalent, gambler-like hopes for personal success."[14]

The Organization of the Court System

Despite its federal structure, the Indian court system is a single hierarchical system with the Supreme Court at the apex, high courts in the various states, and lower courts in the districts and localities. The Supreme Court has the power to interpret the Constitution (its decisions are binding on all other courts as well as officeholders) and serves as the final court of appeal in India. The former function is a carry-over from that of the former Federal Court, while the latter is a prior function of the Privy Council.[15] The Court is composed of a chief justice and seventeen other justices and generally does not sit en banc but, instead, hears cases in panels, the composition of which is determined by the chief justice.

The jurisdiction of the Supreme Court may be original, appellate, or advisory. In addition, it has the right to grant a wide range of writs to redress grievances relating to fundamental rights. The Court has original jurisdiction in a dispute between the central government and the states or between two or more states as long as the dispute involves some questions of law that affect the fundamental rights of the litigants and that the dispute is of a civil and not political nature (the court does not have original jurisdiction in cases relating to a treaty or those involving an ambassador or public minister).[16]

The Supreme Court's appellate jurisdiction extends to appeals from the High Courts and other tribunals that involve significant questions of law. Generally, the Court hears appeals when the High Court in question certifies that a question of constitutional interpretation is involved. If the High Court refuses to do so, the Supreme Court may still hear the case by the granting of a special leave. In addition, the Court hears appeals of any decision in the High Court that involves more than 20,000 rupees. Any death penalty demanded by the High Court is automatically appealed to the Supreme Court.

The Supreme Court can function in an advisory capacity as well. It may give an opinion (or refuse to do so) if the president determines that a constitutional question of major import exists and it would be helpful for the Court to comment on that question. While there was some concern that this would involve the Court too often in either the administrative or legislative process, it is now believed that the Court's positive response to presidential requests for advice have averted some governmental crises.[17] In addition, the Supreme Court supervises and controls each of the High Courts.

Each Indian state comes under the jurisdiction of one of the seventeen High Courts. Each court is composed of a chief justice and other justices appointed by the president of the Republic, with the number of justices varying from state to state. Each court exercises both original and appellate jurisdiction, supervises all courts within its state, and can issue writs regarding fundamental rights. The original jurisdiction of these courts extends to ordinary civil matters, admiralty and matrimonial issues, as well as election petitions resulting from the Representation of the People Act. The High Courts hear appeals from all District Courts. In addition, they review those decisions of special courts involving more than 20,000 rupees or where the imposition of four or more years in prison or a death sentence is imposed.[18] These courts are generally the final courts of appeals in most criminal cases (the major exceptions being errors in procedure or the incorrect application of a law).

Each Indian state is divided into districts with each having its own District Court. These courts have both original and appellate jurisdiction. Each district is supervised by a District Court judge who is responsible for the judicial work in the area. Each state is also divided into sessions districts, usually composed of one or more judicial districts. Each of these is headed by a sessions judge (and assistant sessions judges) appointed by the High Court. Decisions of judicial magistrates and sessions judges are all subject to review by the High Court.

The Courts of Small Causes are at the bottom of the civil court system. These courts hear petty civil cases (usually to a maximum of 500 rupees). The District Courts and subordinate courts are responsible for all other civil matters at the district level. Minor criminal cases are heard by a variety of magistrates (executive, first class, second class, and metropolitan), and the seriousness of the case determines which level of magistrate hears the case.

There are also a number of small courts called *panchayats* in many villages in India. Since nearly 75 percent of the population of India lives in small, often remote villages, the role played by the panchayats often has a profound impact upon the lives of more Indians than the regular court system. The panchayats are composed of elected officials (*panches*) who, after the election, select one of their members (the *sarpanch*) to serve as their presiding officer. The panchayats deal with minor civil and criminal matters in a fairly informal fashion (for example, attorneys are not allowed to appear before them), and their work is supervised by the district magistrate, who may override their decision. Like the institution of the justice of the peace found in the United States and the United Kingdom, the village panachayat is an efficient and inexpensive method of dispensing justice at the local level: "There is no doubt that the proceedings before the panchayats are speedy and cheap as compared to the ordinary courts. Being local institutions, it is convenient for the parties and their witnesses to appear before them. They, in a way, bring justice to the door of the villager."[19]

Finally there are a series of special courts and quasi-judicial tribunals established under both state and federal laws. These include accident claims and income tax tribunals as well as industrial and labor courts. The decisions of each of these courts may be appealed to the High Courts.

The Personnel of the Law

Legal Practitioners

There are approximately 150,000 lawyers practicing in India today. The current composition and structure of the Indian bar was greatly affected by the Advocates' Act of 1961. This act created a single class of practitioners, known as "advocates." It also established nationwide qualifications for admission to the bar and created both national and state bar councils to regulate the profession.

To be admitted to practice as an advocate in any state in India today, one must: (1) be a citizen of India; (2) be at least twenty-one years of age; (3) hold a law degree from any university in India (or another institution recognized by the Bar Council) or have been a barrister; (4) complete a specific course of study; and (5) pass an examination established by the Bar Council.[20]

For the century prior to the Advocates' Act, there were as many as six different types of legal practitioners in India. These included advocates (similar to British barristers), attorneys (akin to British solicitors), and *vakils* (usually Indian pleaders who, by 1940, were required to both have an LL.B. degree and pass an examination) at the High Court level. Because of the paucity of law school graduates, three other practitioners, pleaders, *mukhtars*, and revenue agents, were found in the lower courts.[21] The act also created a Bar Council of India and various state bar councils, with each state maintaining its separate roll of advocates. The national Bar Council controls the nature of legal education in India and the state bar councils control the admission of advocates to each state roll.

Legal education in India is a graduate-level course of study. There are over 150 universities offering LL.B. degrees—some also offer LL.M., B.C.L. (Bachelor of Canon Law or Bachelor of Civil Law), and Ph.D. programs in India—and there are over 20,000 students in Indian law schools today.[22] To be admitted to a law school, one must be a university graduate. Legal education is a part-time, three-year (though those not intending to practice law may leave after taking an examination at the end of their second year) course of study. Many law schools are overcrowded, have poor facilities, and have only a part-time teaching staff. They spend little time in other than a cursory review of a variety of subjects and do little to develop the research skills of their students. Most schools utilize part-time faculty with yearly renewable contracts. Most of those appointed tend to be junior practicing lawyers who are supplementing their incomes during the early years of practice. The only university requirements for a law professor (all lecturers are given the title "professor") are five years' standing at the bar with an LL.B. degree and three years' with an LL.M. The quality of the law school faculties have received considerable attention. Anklesaria, for example, contends that the faculty is not likely to improve until the pay scales for university service are considerably upgraded, enabling the law schools to hire many more highly qualified full-time faculty.[23] This has resulted in a decline in the prestige of the profession. This reached its nadir a few years ago when a local newspaper advertised, "Wanted, an advocate with a knowledge of the law."[24]

Judges

Judges of the District Courts and subordinate courts are appointed by the state governor in consultation with the appropriate High Court. An individual may be appointed to the District Court only if he has been an advocate for at least seven years and has been recommended by the High Court. The High Court also administers these courts. This entails making personnel decisions (posting, promotion, transfer, leave) for the judges of the district and subordinate courts. These judges may serve until the age of fifty-eight, after which they are entitled to a pension.

Judges of the High Courts are appointed by the president, after consulting with the chief justice of India, the governor of the appropriate state, and the chief justice of the High Court. Members of this court must be citizens of India, and must have been advocates for at least ten years or have served on a lower court. Judges of this court serve until the age of sixty-two. They may also resign by writing to the president or be removed from office prior to retirement by a resolution passed by a majority of the two houses of Parliament on a charge of either misconduct or incapacity.

Members of the Supreme Court are appointed by the president after consultation with members of that Court and the High Courts (though the president need not consult with such members of the judiciary). Article 124(3) of the Constitution states that one must have the following qualifications in order to be appointed to the Supreme Court: (a) be a citizen of India, and (b) have been a judge of the High Court or two or more courts in succession for at least five years, or served as an advocate in the High Court or two or more courts in succession for at least ten years, or, be, in the opinion of the president, a "distinguished jurist." The partisan or ideological backgrounds of judges tend not to be important. In fact, an effort is often made to select judges who do not hold strongly partisan positions.

There has been an uncharacteristically rapid turnover of those who have served as chief justice of the Supreme Court. For example, thirteen different individuals served as chief justice during the first twenty-three years of the Republic—the highest turnover rate of any constitutional court in the world. During this period, three individuals served for less than a year, another for 105 days, and still another for thirty-five days.[25] This phenomenon is caused by a number of factors: (1) the requirement that all Supreme Court judges retire at sixty-five; (2) the selection of puisne (associate) judges of that Court from among the most senior members of the High Court bench; and (3) the selection of the chief justice solely on the basis of seniority on the bench. While the latter is not a constitutional requirement, all chief justices prior to 1973 (when Mrs. Gandhi's abandonment of this principle in the selection of A. N. Ray to be the fourteenth chief justice precipitated the "supercession" controversy) were selected according to the seniority principle.

There are few studies of Indian judges. One study of the thirty-six men who had served on the Supreme Court through 1967 found them to be a remarkably homogeneous group: Hindus (most often Brahmin); members of socially and economically well-off families; graduates of the better Indian and English universities; practitioners of approximately twenty years before the High Court of their home state; not active in politics both before and after independence; generally appointed to the High Court at the age of forty-seven; appointed to the Supreme Court, at the age of fifty-seven, after ten years of service on the High Court.[26] A second study, published nearly a decade later, showed few changes in the background of those serving on the Supreme Court. It found, for example, nearly 90 percent of those appointed to the Court to have been Hindus (nearly 40 percent Brahmins), 40 percent to have received legal training in England, 85 percent with previous experience (many as chief justices) on the High Courts, and few with any prior political experience.[27]

Perceptions of the Legal System and Its Role within the Political System

While there is little empirical research, a strong impression exists that there has been a general decline in the prestige of the legal system of India. There have been four main reasons offered for this: (1) a decline in the functioning of the system; (2) a general lack of respect for the role of law in society; (3) a lessened status for lawyers; and (4) a general perception that the judiciary has been politicized over the last two decades.

Oliver Mendelsohn has contended that the failings of the legal system are so endemic that they can be seen as a "pathology":

The Indian court system is by all accounts unusual. The proceedings are extraordinarily dilatory and comparatively expensive; a single issue is often fragmented into a multitude of court actions; execution of judgements is haphazard; the lawyers frequently seem both incompetent and unethical; false witness is commonplace; and the probity of judges is habitually suspect. Above all, the courts are often unable to bring about a settlement of the disputes that give rise to litigation.[28]

This "pathology" is exacerbated by and further influences the general decline in respect for the law found in India. Baxi, for example, contends that there is a general lack of respect for the law not just among the population at large but even among those who write and administer the law. He contends that government lawlessness in the form of corruption, abuse of power, and nepotism is so profound that it weakens the perceptions of the legality of the system.[29]

After a period of high prestige during the independence struggle and the first decade of the new government, the prestige of lawyers has now fallen to the depths found in the first years of British rule.[30] This is seen in the decline of lawyers in government and the civil service and in the fact that the profession no longer attracts the best minds to it:

The legal profession no longer offers the most honored and profitable work that can be attained in India. It no longer draws the best students, and it no longer dominates the social and political life of the country. The monopoly it had on the leadership of the country for over a century is gone. In a way the rest of society has caught up with the profession.[31]

Finally, the involvement of judges in the political battles of the 1960s and 1970s has both demystified and politicized the judiciary—both harming the judiciary. Gadbois, for example, writes about the "supercession" controversy in the early 1970s:

For 23 years the seniority convention, and the convention of the chief justice having the preponderant voice in selecting his colleagues, served not only to make the appointments non-controversial, but also contributed to the fact that Indians came to know very little about who their judges were. They entered the Court unobtrusively, served for a few years, then moved unnoticed into retirement. But the supercessions brought them out of the closet, and compelled the public to become better acquainted with them. Not all liked what they saw.[32]

The Supreme Court has had a major impact upon the Indian political system. It has, for example, found more than two hundred central and state acts to be unconstitutional and has been quite willing to find fault with the government's actions.[33] This is somewhat surprising in view of the concerns that many had over the judicial review functions of the Court. Compromises in the Constituent Assembly resulted in a document, which, in its attempt to balance the conflicting aims of legislative supremacy and judicial control, reduced the powers of the Court to that of formal review by excluding many acts from judicial review. These compromises have resulted in significant constitutional (there are provisions of the Constitution that preclude judicial review), intrinsic (political or nonjusticiable cases are precluded from judicial determination), and self-imposed (for example, the Court may only deal with an actual, not hypothetical, controversy) limitations that have narrowed the scope of the Court's activities.[34]

The Court, in the famous *A. K. Goplan v. State of Madras* case, while carefully defining its role, did develop the concept of judicial review. The Court expanded from these rather humble beginnings so that, by the mid–1960s, the government saw Court decisions as creating a confrontation with the socialist policies of Indira Gandhi. Three specific decisions, in the Golknath, Bank Nationalization, and Privy Purses cases led to great unhappiness in government circles. The Golknath decision, by a six to five majority, overruled two earlier cases and stated that Parliament was not supreme and could not, by amendments, abridge any of the fundamental rights found in the Constitution. In the second case the Court, by a ten to one majority, ruled that the Gandhi government could not nationalize the nation's top fourteen commercial banks. The final decision, by a nine to two vote, declared that the government could not abolish Privy Purses and other privileges of the ex-princes. A fourth decision, *Kesavananda Bharati v. State of Keralain*, April 1973, while overturning the Golknath decision, further convinced many in government circles that the Court was creating a confrontation with the government. While this decision upheld the concept that Parliament could, by constitutional amendments, abridge rights explicitly established in the Constitution, it also held that the legislature could not, by the same amending process, change the "basic structure" or "basic features" of the Constitution. The "basic structure" would have to be decided on a case-by-case basis in the future.

A final Court action led to the "emergency" in 1975. This was precipitated by a decision of the Allahabad High Court to set aside Mrs. Gandhi's election to Parliament. The government then went to the Supreme Court and asked it to reverse the decision of the Allahabad Court. The Court refused, and Mrs. Gandhi responded with a series of acts to create an emergency regime.

The Gandhi government responded to these Court decisions in two ways. First, it passed a number of amendments that reduced the scope of the Court's powers vis-à-vis the legislature. These included allowing the legislature to amend any provisions of the Constitution (including fundamental rights) and indicating that no amendment could be called into question by any court. Second, it engaged in two sets of activities that effected the career patterns of Indian judges. The first of these attempted to browbeat judges by transferring High Court judges who had disagreed with governmental decisions. The second created what became known as the "supercession controversy." The Indian convention (though not a constitutional requirement) had been for the senior member of the Supreme Court to be declared as its chief justice. However, in 1973 Mrs. Gandhi selected Ajit Ray, the fourth-ranking judge on the Court to be the new chief justice. This was the first time that the seniority principle had been violated, and the three more senior judges on the Court all resigned their positions. The blatantly political nature of this act is seen both in the fact that the three senior judges voted against the government's position in the Golknath, Bank Nationalization, and Privy Purses cases and in the rationale given this decision by Mr. Kumaramangalam, the minister of steel and mines:

Certainly, we as Government have a duty to take the philosophy and outlook of the judge in coming to the conclusion whether he should or he should not lead the Supreme Court at this time. It is our duty in the Government honestly and fairly to come to the conclusion whether a particular person is fit to be appointed the Chief Justice of the Court because of his outlook, because of his philosophy as expressed in his . . . opinions, whether he is a more suitable or a more competent judge.[35]

Despite loud protests, the government once more superceded a Supreme Court judge, Khanna, upon the retirement of Ray. Once again, it tried to justify its actions by stating that Khanna would have to retire in six months (the new chief justice could stay in office for thirteen months). However, the fact that Khanna had dissented from an important case the previous year led many to question whether this act was motivated by primarily political desires.

The supercession decisions were greeted by widespread opposition, with members of the legal profession and the newspapers attacking the government's decisions and the superceded judges being hailed as heroes. Yet, the supercession decisions, transfer of judges, and constitutional amendments had a chilling effect upon the judiciary, and the courts did not confront Mrs. Gandhi during the emergency:

Like other institutions in society, the judiciary suffered enormous agony during the Emergency period; it yielded in substance to the autocratic rule of Mrs. Gandhi and in the process lost its institutional prestige and cohesiveness. The identification of judges and lawyers either as pro-regime or anti-regime created schisms in the membership of the Bench and Bar, and the courtrooms across the country became sites for partisan clashes rather than for civil discussions.[36]

Mrs. Gandhi's defeat in the 1977 elections established a period of depoliticization for India's judiciary. The new government passed amendments to increase the power of the Supreme Court and returned to the seniority principle in appointing the chief justice of that court.

The fall of the Janata government saw a return to hostility between the government and the judiciary. In one of the first acts of the new government, the law minister promised that it would review the appointment process to make sure that judges would be more committed to the goals of the Constitution (presumably as articulated by the government). Later, despite considerable opposition from Chief Justice Chandrachud, the government attempted to transfer judges from one High Court to another so that it could have one-third of the judges (and the chief justice) of each High Court from outside the state. In a December 1981 decision by a badly divided seven-member constitutional bench of the Supreme Court, it was decided that, as long as certain constitutional procedures had been followed, the government was free to transfer, hire, and fire High Court judges and that the last word in the decisions rested with the president. This decision exposed both the internal divisions within the Court as well as the incredible politicization that had once more occurred within the judiciary. For example, there was considerable discussion within the judiciary over "value-packing" of the judiciary—that is, the selection of judges whose values were consistent with that of the majority. Justice Desai, for example, stated: "The three organs of the government created by the Constitution must march in step. All must be imbued with the same values. Judges must be value-packed."[37]

While the supercession controversy did indicate considerable support in India for an independent judiciary,

The supercession was one of those rare events in a nation's experience which provoked attitudes to burst forth into behavior. Both the judges and the Government learned that the Court enjoyed the strong support of a very vigilant and loud, if not broadly-based, constituency. Important Indian groups had come to place a high value on an independent judiciary, and these groups literally leaped into action in defense of the Court when the Government sought to narrow the chasm that had long separated judges from political interference. Given the size of the bar in India . . . its overwhelming and vociferous condemnation of the supercession is significant. And the supercession provoked former Supreme Court judges, for the first time as a group, to protest publicly against what they perceived to be a threat to the judiciary's independence.[38]

The future role of the Supreme Court and an independent judiciary remains in doubt, for while Rajiv Gandhi has developed a number of new programs to improve the efficiency of the Indian government, it is far too early to assess whether his attitudes toward the judiciary will dramatically differ from those of his mother.

PAKISTAN

Decades of religious strife led to the creation of the separate states of India and Pakistan at the conclusion of World War II. However, the government of Pakistan that was created on August 14, 1947, was burdened with serious internal divisions and economic problems that have hampered both its economic and political development. Many of these problems continue today. Probably the most serious of these difficulties is the lack of consensus among Pakistanis regarding the nation-state:

Four years ago, General Zia, speaking about his people, told this correspondent (and he beat on the arms of his throne-like chair to emphasize the point), "We don't know who we are." Because Pakistan lacks a raison d'etre, the people do not know what it is to feel and to be Pakistanis, so they feel all the more strongly that they are Sindhi or Baluchi and so on.[39]

The Development of the Legal System

The newly created government of Pakistan was faced with extraordinary problems in 1947. It was composed of east and west wings, separated by 1,000 miles of Indian territory, and was at a serious economic disadvantage. West Pakistan produced wheat and cotton, but the majority of the cotton mills were now in

India, and East Pakistan was the world's largest producer of jute, but the mills were once again, in India. In addition, most of the other necessary raw materials were in India, not Pakistan. Pakistan, like India, was racked by massive communal violence. These uprisings in Pakistan were followed by an influx of refugees from India. This placed an additional burden upon a political system that was in a less-developed stage than its Indian neighbor.

Pakistan has attempted to establish a democratic government in spite of these difficulties. However, the severity of these problems and the inability of civilian governments to deal with them, have led to three military takeovers in Pakistan—in 1958, 1969, and 1977. These military regimes have not, however, been any more successful in coping with Pakistan's problems:

All three military regimes registered a number of initial gains—i.e., restoration of law and order, resumption of normal economic activities, some measure of efficiency in administrative routines, and relatively moderate socio-economic reforms. However, when it came to the formulation of a viable participatory framework for political action and the creation of an infrastructure for ensuring socio-economic justice, the performance was no better than its civilian predecessors.[40]

Pakistan's first leader, Jinnah, died in September 1948 and his successor as prime minister (though Jinnah had taken the post of governor-general), Liaquat Ali Khan, was assassinated under mysterious circumstances in Rawalpindi in October 1951. These two deaths had a devastating impact on the new polity:

Pakistan had lost its two most able and experienced leaders in the first four years of existence. The paucity of leadership qualities among the survivors soon became glaringly obvious. Moreover, there was no consensus on political norms to override the ensuring scramble for power, the shufflings of office, or the prolonged deliberations of the Constituent Assembly. Instead, differences of opinion on crucial issues intensified.[41]

A succession of civilian leaders followed Liaquat, but none proved to be more effective than the next. Part of the reason for this state of affairs was the continuing mutual suspicions among politicians and, more importantly, their support for personal and regional or local causes over national ones. In addition, there were serious divisions among the leaders over the role of religion in the new state. Most of the western-trained elite, many of whom were lawyers, represented a liberal movement within Islam and saw the government being built around such institutions as *ijma* (consensus of the community). On the other side stood the more traditional *ulama*, who felt that the bodies of law that grew up around the Quran were the best vehicles for developing proper behavior. While the ulama enjoyed great support among the people, the new elite favored (though they could not ignore the ulama for fear of being denounced as anti-Islamic) British-style institutions.[42]

This state of affairs continued until October 1958, when President Mizra declared martial law, suspended the Constitution, and cancelled the elections scheduled for the following year. Within the month, however, he was forced into exile and replaced by the commander-in-chief of the Pakistani army, General Ayub Khan. Khan was to govern until the next military takeover in 1969. The regime of Ayub left the administration primarily in the hands of the bureaucracy and did bring about some reforms in its decade in power: the promulgation of the Constitution in 1962, land reforms, and more equalized divorce laws and the restriction of polygamy. However, the regime was not able to root out the poverty, inefficiency, corruption, and inequality, both social and regional, that had existed in Pakistan since its inception. The government's inability to solve Pakistan's problems and the endemic political jealousies and fissiparous tendencies, coupled with Ayub's declining health, ultimately led to the abrogation of the 1962 Constitution, the imposition of martial law, and the army commander-in-chief, General Agha Mohammed Yahya Khan, assuming the presidency.

The next few years were similiar to those that preceded the military takeover. There were continual political struggles, ultimately resulting in the accession to power of former Foreign Minister Zulfikar Ali Bhutto; accerbation of the secessionist tendencies, resulting in a war with India and the independence for the former East Bengal, now Bangladesh; some governmental reforms (such as the promulgation of the 1973 Constitution); and continued governmental inefficiency and corruption (the new government, for example, issued a number of White Papers, covering more than 2,000 pages describing government corruption by the Bhutto regime), culminating in another military takeover and imposition of martial law by General Zia-ul-Huq in July 1977.[43]

The Organization of the Court System

The Constitution provides for a separate and independent judiciary for Pakistan. At the apex of the system is a Supreme Court. The Court consists of a chief justice and not more than six other judges (though Parliament may increase these numbers). The chief justice is appointed by the president, who also appoints all other justices of the Court after consultation with the chief justice. The Court has original (it hears disputes between two or more governments), appellate (it hears appeals from decisions of a High Court), and advisory (the president may refer any question of law that he deems of public importance to the Court) jurisdiction.

There are High Courts in each of the four provinces (in the cities of Lahore, Karachi, Peshawar, and Quetta) of Pakistan. Each court consists of a chief justice and as many other judges as determined by law, or until so determined, as fixed by the president. Each judge is appointed by the president after consultation with the chief justice of Pakistan, the governor of the province, and, except in the case of the appointment of a chief justice, with the chief justice of the High Court in question. The High Court hears appeals from the decisions of lower courts when a statute provides for such an appeal or revision of a lower court decision.[44] In addition, the High Courts have administrative responsibility for the subordinate courts.

Below the High Courts are the Courts of Sessions (called District Courts on the civil side and Sessions Courts on the criminal side). These courts have both original (they hear more serious cases) and appellate (they hear appeals from the Civil Courts and Magistrates' Courts) jurisdiction. Judges of the Courts of Sessions also have supervisory responsibility (shared with the deputy commissioner of the district) for the subordinate judges and magistrates within their district. In 1961, conciliation courts were established to bring inexpensive justice to the villages. These courts hear minor criminal and civil matters without the use of formal judicial procedures.

There is, in addition, a Supreme Judicial Council of Pakistan composed of the chief justice of the Supreme Court, the next two most senior judges of that court, and the chief justice of each High Court. It is the function of the Council to issue a code of conduct for judges of the upper courts and to decide, upon direction of the president, if a member of these benches is unable to continue in that capacity or deserves being removed from office because of gross misconduct.

The Personnel of the Law

There is little current data on the number of individuals practicing law in Pakistan. In the mid-1960s there were approximately 18,000 individuals trained in the law in Pakistan. Of these, about 13,000 were practicing advocates in one of the courts. In addition, there were approximately 600 judges and law officers (government prosecutors and registrars among others) and nearly 1,400 individuals who had some judicial functions while serving in the executive departments of the provinces.[45]

Advocates are all recipients of both B.A. and LL.B. degrees. Pakistan has four law colleges (at Lahore, Multan, Karachi, and Peshawar) offering two-year programs leading to the LL.B. degree. Students take introductory law courses and an exam at the end of the first year. This is followed by more advanced courses and an LL.B. exam at the end of the second year. The novice advocate must then pass a qualifying examination established by the Bar Council found in each province. After two years of practice at one of the lower courts, the advocate can then apply to be an advocate of one of the High Courts. After five years of practice before that bench, the individual can then apply to the Pakistan Bar Council for the right to practice before the Supreme Court. Advocates with five years experience before this bench can apply for senior advocate status—the equivalent of the British Queen's Council.[46]

Individuals serving on Pakistan's upper benches are generally held in high esteem. No one may be appointed to the Supreme Court unless he/she is a citizen and has served as an advocate of the High Court for fifteen years or a judge on that court for five years. A judge on the High Courts must be a citizen and have either served as an advocate before the High Court for ten years, held judicial office in one of the subordinate courts for the same period of time, or served as a member of the civil service for ten years and as a district judge for three years. Individuals are appointed to the bench by the president, either from lower courts or directly from the bar.

Public Perceptions and the Role of the Courts

The 1973 Constitution both provides for an independent judiciary and gives that branch considerable powers (for example, both the Supreme Court and High Courts may issue writs that amount to judicial reviews of administrative action). In addition, members of the legal profession have traditionally held positions of power and prestige in Pakistan. For example, 39 percent of the members of the First Constituent Assembly (1947–1954) were lawyers.[47] However, the last decade has seen a decline in both the public perception of the profession and its own participation in the inner circles of the government as successive governments have attempted to limit the power of both the judiciary and lawyers. The profession has, in turn, played the role of the opposition and attempted to both oppose arbitrary governmental actions and maintain its own place in society.

This new role for the legal profession has been in direct response to statements and actions by leaders in Pakistan. For example, in September 1960, President Ayub noted that the legal profession was probably overstaffed and that lawyers played a negative role in the system because they aided ''in the fabrication of false evidence to support the case of their client.''[48] Ayub further attempted to reduce the influence of lawyers by barring them from special tribunals, and President Bhutto was accused of attempting to intimidate and bully members of the judiciary. More recently, the government of President Zia has brought about changes in the 1973 Constitution, leading to a diminution of the power of the judiciary:

The major target of these changes was the higher judiciary, which was slowly stripped of its power of judicial review and writ jurisdiction. In March 1981 a Provisional Constitutional Order replaced what was left of the 1973 Constitution and completely subordinated the judiciary to the martial law authorities to take the oath under the Provisional Constitutional Order. They lost their jobs.[49]

The legal community has, since the late 1960s, engaged in a political struggle with the military leadership. The latest round of difficulties began in 1980 after the government, for the second time, cancelled the holding of elections. Since that time, lawyers have held conventions (an October 1982 convention was attended by more than 2,000 delegates), boycotted the courts, held protest marches, and pressed the government for the restoration of civil liberties and the powers of an independent judiciary. While it is unlikely that the legal community will succeed in its struggle against the military regime without the support of the opposing political parties and the people (the legal community is now linked with the former civilian leaders and seen as an exclusive, expensive elite), some observers have marvelled at the cohesiveness of the legal community in the face of martial law restrictions.[50]

This struggle continues to produce a cycle of factionalism, authoritarianism, and a lack of legitimacy for the regime. President Zia recently attempted to establish some legitimacy by holding his long-promised elections in February 1985. Fifty-three percent of the electorate voted to return Zia to power but defeated six of the nine cabinet members who sought reelection. When Zia was sworn in as civilian president on March 23, 1985, he indicated a desire to lift the martial law that has enveloped Pakistan. However, his sincerity can be questioned because he shortly amended the Constitution to prevent the legislature from overturning any presidential orders issued since 1977 (including that of martial law) unless approved by the president. Zia "was, as one senior official put it, showing parliament who holds the reins."[51] Whatever the next stage brings Pakistan, it is clear that the role of the courts is likely to remain limited, and the transition to a true civilian regime will be difficult:

In view of the wide divergence in the perspectives of the ruling generals and the civilian political elite, the military regime will continue to face a crisis of legitimacy. The prolongation of the present political impasse or the enforcement of any form of diluted democracy will accentuate discontent, alienation, and polarization, and give a fillip to political violence. The festering resentment, especially among those who find themselves at the periphery of the system or completely excluded from the decision-making process, will create frequent challenges for the regime and mount heavy strains on the professional and corporate character of the military; in fact, the very fabric of the polity is undermined, thereby making a graceful transfer of power increasingly difficult.[52]

BANGLADESH

The leaders in Bangladesh have faced many of the same problems as those found in Pakistan. For example, the following is a recent assessment of the political situation in Bangladesh:

Bangladesh politics showed extreme volatility in 1983. The military regime of General Ershad, which took power about two years ago, faced stiff opposition from a large number of political parties and factional groups, students, urban lawyers, and workers. Although the military was in no mood to make concessions to the political parties demanding state power, it felt the necessity to acquire a civilian veneer—to legitimize and sustain its rule.[53]

The preceding could have been written about any year in Bangladesh's history and well reflects the struggle between the military rulers and civilian leaders, among the most important of whom are members of the legal community.

The Development of the Legal System

August 1975 saw a military coup against the government of President Sheikh Mujibar Rahman in which the president and all of his family (with the exception of two daughters) were killed. Countercoups and political struggles followed in the succeeding months, culminating in the accession to power of General Ziaur Rahman (Zia). These events fundamentally changed the nature of politics in Bangladesh, ushering in a period of civilian-military rule which has lasted until today:

During the Zia period the state apparatus in Bangladesh was dominated by civil-military bureaucrats. The Zia regime was fundamentally a resurrection of the "administrative state" under Ayub Khan in Pakistan; . . . And like their forebearers in the administrative state in Pakistan, the civil-military bureaucrats in Bangladesh as an exclusive administrative group have been deeply imbued with a "guardianship" orientation. The broad administrative framework in which they worked did not undergo any fundamental change in Bangladesh.[54]

Zia introduced a number of reforms in an attempt to develop a greater sense of legitimacy in the regime. These included a presidential referendum on a nineteen-point economic program (in which he received over 99 percent of the vote), an election for a president with a five-year term (in which Zia received over 75 percent of the vote), the creation of a new political party (the Bangladesh Nationalist Party), parliamentary elections (in which the BNP won slightly over two-thirds of the seats), and the creation of new village institutions in order to develop grass-roots support for the regime.[55] However, opposition to the government from the leading opposition parties continued despite these reforms. More importantly, serious internal divisions within the BNP weakened Zia's rule. These divisions ultimately culminated in the assassination of Zia in May 1981 and the rise to power of Lieutenant-General Hossain Mohammed Ershad in March 1982.

The Organization of the Court System

The Supreme Court of Bangladesh is composed of a chief justice and other judges deemed necessary by the president. The Court is composed of both appellate and high court divisions. The primary function of the former is to hear appeals from the judgments of the High Court. In addition, it may, at the request of the president, issue nonbinding opinions on questions of law. The High Court has both original and appellate jurisdiction. As a result of a government effort to decentralize the court system, branches of the High Court have been set up in three district towns, Comilla (7 judges), Rangpur (5 judges), and Jessore (5 judges), as well as Dacca (8 judges). There are, in addition, District and Sessions courts at the district level as well as three levels of Magistrates' Courts.

The Personnel Of The Law

There are nearly 12,000 lawyers in Bangladesh, a dramatic increase from 7,182 in 1980.[56] At present there are twenty-four law colleges with 360 faculty members and 13,600 students. There are over 1,200 judges sitting on the various benches in Bangladesh today: five on the Supreme Court, twenty-five on the High Court, 120 on the District Courts, and nearly 1,000 on the lower civil and criminal courts.[57]

Perceptions of the Legal System and Its Role within the Political System

Lawyers have a great deal of prestige in Bangladesh. This is seen in both the power of the organized bar and in the large number of lawyers who find their way to political power. For example, in 1979, lawyers made up 26 percent of the members of Parliament—the second largest occupational grouping in that body.[58]

The years since independence have seen continued attempts by the military leaders to establish some legitimacy. As in Pakistan, this has sometimes led to both a decline in the power of the courts and the bar and some considerable opposition to governmental actions by the legal community. The legal profession, for example, vigorously opposed the government's attempts to decentralize the High Court, arguing that the government should simply appoint more judges to the court rather than create new benches. The profession felt humiliated when the government went ahead with its plan without consultation with the bar association. Similarly, in recent months, lawyers have begun to boycott the courts in an effort to force President Ershad to end military rule and restore power to the civilian leaders of the nation. While Ershad has promised reforms and has called for elections, he has consistently maintained that a stable society can only be achieved in Bangladesh by utilizing the skills best found in the military. In a recent interview, Ershad stated that, given those skills, "it will be logical to use the patriotic armed forces for reorganizing the country as a unified, united and powerful nation."[59] In fact, it has been estimated that the armed forces might be given as much as 30 to 40 percent of the seats in the upper house of Parliament in a newly constituted government. President Ershad has recently postponed elections, banned all political activities, and tightened up on the martial law restrictions. A referendum was held on March 22, 1985, to give him a mandate to rule until new elections were held. Ershad received 95 percent of the vote with a 72 percent voter turnout (these are government estimates—foreign observers estimated the voter turnout to be between 25 to 30 percent).[60]

While certainly not desirable, it can be contended that the military's continuing role in Bangladesh politics is a result of a vacuum created in civilian politics: "The near-universal political apathy that has resulted from a decade of anarchy and misrule by rapacious politicians has provided a highly favourable climate for the men in uniform."[61] Like in Pakistan, this situation calls into serious question the role that both the legal profession and an independent judiciary might play in the politics of contemporary Bangladesh.

NOTES

1. V. Mehta, *The New India* (New York: Penguin Books, 1978), p. 53.

2. H. G. Rawlinson, *India: A Short Cultural History* (New York: Frederick A. Praeger, 1954), p. 24.

3. A. L. Basham, *The Wonder That Was India: A Survey of the Indian Subcontinent before the Coming of the Muslims* (New York: Grove Press, 1959), p. 134.

4. Rawlinson, *India: A Short Cultural History*, p. 70.

5. Ibid., p. 77.

6. Basham, *The Wonder That Was India*, pp. 112–13.

7. Ibid., p. 114.

8. Ibid., pp. 116–17.

9. Ibid., p. 121.

10. A. Gledhill, *Pakistan: The Development of Its Laws and Constitution* (Westport, Conn.: Greenwood Press, 1980), p. 7.

11. M. Galanter, "The Displacement of Traditional Law in Modern India," *Journal of Social Issues* 24, no. 4 (1968), p. 67.

12. M. P. Jain, *Outlines of Indian Legal History* (Bombay: N. M. Tripathi Private, Ltd., 1976), p. 2.

13. R. L. Kidder, "Western Law in India: External Law and Local Response," *Sociological Inquiry* 46 (1977), pp. 159–60.

14. Ibid., p. 160.

15. K. S. Nehra, *The Judicial and Legislative Systems in India* (Washington, D.C.: Library of Congress, 1981), p. 11.

16. Ibid., p. 12.

17. Ibid., p. 15.

18. C. S. Rhyne, *Law and Judicial Systems of Nations*, 3d ed. (Washington, D.C.: The World Peace Through Law Center, 1978), p. 338.

19. Jain, *Outlines of Indian Legal History*, p. 315.

20. Rhyne, *Law and Judicial Systems of Nations*, p. 336.

21. S. Schmitthener, "A Sketch of the Development of the Legal Profession in India," *Law and Society Review* 3 (November 1968-February 1969), p. 358.

22. H. J. Tseng, *The Law Schools of the World* (Boston: William S. Hein & Co., 1972), pp. 156–202; Rhyne, *Law and Judicial Systems of Nations*, p. 336.

23. P. Anklesaria, "India," *Comparative Law Yearbook*, vol. 5 (The Hague: Martinus Nijhoff Publishers, 1982), p. 111.

24. Ibid., p. 103.

25. G. H. Gadbois, Jr., "Devices and Defenders Acting to Sustain the Independence of the Supreme Court of India" (Paper delivered at the Midwest Political Science Association Convention, Chicago, Ill., April 29-May 1, 1982), p. 1.

26. G. H. Gadbois, Jr., "Indian Supreme Court Judges: A Portrait," *Law and Society Review* 3 (November 1968-February 1969), p. 317.

27. R. Dhavan, *The Supreme Court of India: A Socio-Legal Critique of Its Juristic Techniques* (Bombay: N. M. Tripathi Private Ltd., 1977), pp. 22–26.

28. O. Mendelsohn, "The Pathology of the Indian Legal System," *Modern Asian Studies* 15, no. 4 (1981), p. 823.

29. U. Baxi, *The Crisis of the Indian Legal System* (New Delhi: Vikas Publishing House Private, Ltd., 1982), p. 22.

30. Schmitthener, "A Sketch of the Development of the Legal Profession," p. 337.

31. Ibid., p. 382.

32. Gadbois, "Devices and Defenders," pp. 35–36.

33. Ibid., p. 1.

34. See S. N. Ray, *Judicial Review and Fundamental Rights* (Calcutta: Eastern Law House, 1974), pp. 74–87, for a detailed discussion of these limitations.

35. Cited in Gadbois, "Devices and Defenders," p. 19.

36. B. D. Dua, "A Study in Executive-Judicial Conflict," *Asian Survey* 23, no. 4 (April 1983), p. 468.

37. S. Sahay, "A Close Look: You Said Value-Packing MiLord," *Statesman Weekly*, January 23, 1982, cited in Ibid., p. 478.

38. Gadbois, "Devices and Defenders," p. 37.

39. "Pakistanis in Never-Never Land," *The Economist*, September 3, 1983, p. 29.

40. H. Rivzi, "The Paradox of Military Rule in Pakistan," *Asian Survey* 24, no. 5 (May 1984), p. 537.

41. R. F. Nyrop et al., *Pakistan: A Country Study* (Washington, D.C.: U.S. Government Printing Office, 1983), p. 42.

42. Ibid., p. 45.

43. Rivzi, "The Paradox of Military Rule," p. 540.

44. Gledhill, *Pakistan*, p. 121, explains that while Indian courts generally enable such overriding of lower court decisions, in Pakistan this is only allowed where the statute provides for such an appeal.

45. R. Braibanti, *Research on the Bureaucracy of Pakistan* (Durham, N.C.: The Program in Comparative Studies of Southern Asia, Duke Commonwealth-Studies Center, 1966), p. 252.

46. Rhyne, *Law and Judicial Systems of Nations*, pp. 552–53.

47. A. Hussain, *Elite Politics in an Ideological State: The Case of Pakistan* (Folkestone, England: William Dawson & Sons, Ltd., 1979), p. 112.

48. Braibanti, *Research on the Bureaucracy*, p. 255.

49. Rivzi, "The Paradox of Military Rule," pp. 546–47.

50. Braibanti, *Research on the Bureaucracy*, p. 260.

51. "Chance for a Genius in Pakistan," *The Economist*, March 30, 1985, p. 49.

52. Rivzi, "The Paradox of Military Rule," p. 555.

53. M. A. Rahman, "Bangladesh in 1983: A Turning Point for the Military," *Asian Survey* 24, no. 2 (February 1984), p. 240.

54. S. S. Islam, "The State in Bangladesh under Zia (1975–1981)," *Asian Survey* 24, no. 5 (May 1984), pp. 561–62.

55. See ibid., pp. 562–66, for a fuller discussion of these reforms.

56. Letter of May 28, 1985, from Dr. A. K. M. Ghulam Rabbani, Director-General, Statistics Division, Ministry of Finance and Planning, Bangladesh Secretariat.

57. Letter of July 3, 1985, from Milton L. Iossi, Counselor for Public Affairs, American Embassy, and Director, USIS, Dhaka, Bangladesh.

58. Islam, "The State in Bangladesh under Zia," p. 566.

59. N. Chanda, "The March to Democracy," *Far Eastern Economic Review* 121, no. 35 (September 1, 1983), p. 21.

60. "Bangladesh—A Vote Too Much," *The Economist*, March 30, 1985, p. 50.

61. Chanda, "The March to Democracy," p. 22.

BIBLIOGRAPHY

Anklesaria, P. "India." *Comparative Law Yearbook*, vol. 5. The Hague: Martinus Nijhoff Publishers, 1982. Pp. 103–12.

Basham, A. L. *The Wonder that Was India: A Survey of the Indian Subcontinent before the Coming of the Muslims.* New York: Grove Press, 1959.

Basu, D. D. *Shorter Constitution of India.* 8th ed. New Delhi: Prentice-Hall of India, 1981.

Baxi, U. *The Crisis of the Indian Legal System.* New Delhi: Vikas Publishing House Pvt. Ltd., 1982.

Braibanti, R. *Research on the Bureaucracy of Pakistan.* Durham, N.C.: The Program in Comparative Studies on Southern Asia, Duke Commonwealth-Studies Center, 1966.

Chaudhuri, M. A. *Government and Politics in Pakistan.* Dacca: Puthigar Ltd., 1968.

Dhavan, R. *The Supreme Court of India: A Socio-Legal Critique of its Juristic Techniques.* Bombay: N. M. Tripathi Private Ltd., 1977.

Dua, B. D. "A Study in Executive-Judicial Conflict." *Asian Survey* 23, no. 4 (April 1983), pp. 463–84.

Gadbois, G. H., Jr. "Devices and Defenders Acting to Sustain the Independence of the Supreme Court of India." Paper delivered at the Midwest Political Science Association Convention, Chicago, Illinois, April 29-May 1, 1982.

———. "Indian Supreme Court Judges: A Portrait." *Law and Society Review* 3 (November 1968-February 1969), pp. 317–36.

Galanter, M. "The Displacement of Traditional Law in Modern India." *Journal of Social Issues* 24, no. 4 (1968), pp. 65–91.

———. "The Study of the Indian Legal Profession." *Law and Society Review* 3 (November 1968-February 1969), pp. 201–17.

Gledhill, A. *Pakistan: The Development of Its Laws and Constitution.* Westport, Conn.: Greenwood Press, 1980.

———. *The Republic of India: The Development of its Laws and Constitution.* Westport, Conn.: Greenwood Press, 1970.

Gupta, D. C. *Indian Government and Politics.* New Delhi: Vikas Publishing House Private Ltd., 1978.

Hussain, A. *Elite Politics in an Ideological State: The Case of Pakistan.* Folkestone, England: William Dawson & Sons, Ltd., 1979.

Islam, S. S. "The State in Bangladesh under Zia (1975–1981)." *Asian Survey* 24, no. 5 (May 1984), pp. 556–73.

Jain, M. P. *Outlines of Indian Legal History.* Bombay: N. M. Tripathi Private, Ltd., 1976.

Kidder, R. L. "Western Law in India: External Law and Local Response." *Sociological Inquiry* 46 (1977), pp. 155–79.

Kulshreshtha, V. D. "Restructuring Indian Legal Education: Some Suggestions." *Journal of the Bar Council of India* 5 (1976), pp. 305–20.

Mendelsohn, O. "The Pathology of the Indian Legal System." *Modern Asian Studies* 15, no. 4 (1981), pp. 823–63.

Muhith, A. M. A. *Bangladesh: Emergence of a Nation*. Dacca: Bangladesh Books International Ltd., 1978.

Nehra, K. S. *The Judicial and Legislative Systems in India*. Washington, D.C.: Library of Congress, 1981.

Rahman, M. A. "Bangladesh in 1983: A Turning Point for the Military." *Asian Survey* 24, no. 2 (February 1984), pp. 240–49.

Rawlinson, H. G. *India: A Short Cultural History*. New York: Frederick A. Praeger, 1954.

Ray, S. N. *Judicial Review and Fundamental Rights*. Calcutta: Eastern Law House, 1974.

Rhyne, C. S. *Law and Judicial Systems of Nations*. 3d ed. Washington, D.C.: The World Peace Through Law Center, 1978.

Rivzi, H. "The Paradox of Military Rule in Pakistan." *Asian Survey* 24, no. 5 (May 1984), pp. 534–55.

Schmitthener, S. "A Sketch of the Development of the Legal Profession in India." *Law and Society Review* 3 (November 1968-February 1969), pp. 337–82.

Sharan, P. *Government of Pakistan: Development and Working of the Political System*. Meerur, Pakistan: Meenakshi Prakashan, 1975.

Ziring, L. *Pakistan: The Enigma of Political Development*. Boulder, Colo.: Westview Press, 1980.

8

ITALY

Maria Elisabetta de Franciscis

THE DEVELOPMENT OF THE LEGAL SYSTEM

Italy has one of the oldest legal traditions in the world. Its roots can be traced to Roman days. The early form of Roman law was organized in *Leges* and in *Iura*. *Leges* is a broad term that includes *decreta, mandata, rescripta*, and *adnotationes*, which are all forms of itemized legislation. *Iura*, on the other hand, stood for modern-day jurisprudence. Augustus established the system of *ius respondenti*. By such a device and by using his *ex autoritate principis*, the emperor authorized the existence of jurists who could be consulted by judges on the interpretations of legal questions.[1]

In order to create a unified legal system, the Emperor Justinian codified the laws throughout the Empire in the sixth century. The *Novus Justinianus Codex* was published in 529. It did not include the Iura, which appeared the following year in the *Digesta* (also known as the *Pandectae*). The *Digesta* was composed of fifty books and represented a compilation of all the previous legal opinions of the jurisconsults. In addition, Justinian also ordered the promulgation of the *Institutiones*, a four-book manual that was modelled on the *Institutiones of Gaius*.[2] The codex slowly spread as far as the outreaches of the Empire and by the twelfth century influenced the legal systems of all the neighboring countries. It was the leader and the guide for further codification throughout Europe until the scepter was passed on to France and Germany in the sixteenth century.

The fall of the Roman Empire was followed by a period of invasions by barbarians. Yet, as Calisse mentions, the barbarian takeover "was by no means complete; it did not portend the disappearance of ancient civilization. Nor did it reduce Italy in the Middle Ages to a secondary position in the evolution of European institutions."[3] In A.D. 568 the Longobards slowly began to invade Italy. What could have become a totally barbaric takeover developed, instead, into a slow process of acculturation of the Longobards by the Romans. Thus, in 643, a book of laws written in very elementary Latin, known as the *Edict of Rothari*, became the law of the Longobards. King Rothari's successors continued the task of writing down the laws and left us with the *Edictum Regum Longobardorum*. The latter and the *Novus Justinianus Codex* coexisted until the Frankish conquest of Longobard Italy. As of Christmas day 800—coronation day of Charlemagne as Holy Roman Emperor—public law in Italy was Frankish and private law was Longobard.

There were, however, several attempts to unify legislation. The kings of the Regnum ordered the publication of the *Capitula*. A unified compilation of the *Capitula* and the edicts was the *Liber Legis Longobardorum* (known today as the *Liber Papiensis*). The *Liber Papiensis* was completed—including all the glosses—by the second half of the eleventh century. As important as all of these compilations were, only two legal systems survived the proof of time: the canon law and the *Novus Justinianus Codex*. They ultimately became the basis for a number of European legal systems.

Of equal importance was the spread of Christiandom and of the canonic laws. In the year 500 the *Collectio Dionysiana* was published. It represented the most complete of the canonical collections of the day. Of particular interest is the increase in the utilization of Justinian laws in the compilation of the church laws. Very often the church was considered an institution equal or superior to the Empire. The hierarchical structure of the church was a reproduction of that of the Empire but the former had no nationality or class boundaries. In addition, the church ruled over more than just the territories belonging to the Vatican State and its internal structure—priests, pastors, lord-bishops. Most importantly, it ruled over the daily lives of a majority of European people. In particular, the church had the final say on matrimonial and testamentary affairs. "The Roman Church even more truly than the Empire typified the spiritual unity of Christendom; and despite the abuses which in periods of degeneracy it permitted, it was for centuries the asylum of knowledge, from which the unifying elements of European culture were propagated."[4]

The Middle Ages proved to be a trying time for any kind of uniformity of laws. Each city-state, ducato, and principato had its own ruler and set of laws. Despite the efforts of the transcribers, the scholars, and the teachers of the Roman codes (the glossators) feasibility, personal gains, and ruling tendencies prevailed over uniformity. Laws varied as forms of government did. Freedom of interpretation, when the laws happened to be the same, provided for particularism rather than uniformity.

The glossators' efforts proved to be essential for the survival of some uniformity of the Roman codes. They were the most important link between the glorious days of the Empire and the opening of universities in Ravenna, Napoli (Naples), Bologna, and Pavia in the thirteenth century. Unfortunately, this lapse of time was one of generalized cultural decadence. While the glossators pursued their task of transcribing and maintaining the codes, most of the text gradually disappeared because of ignorance or perceived uselessness. Thus, the *Tres Libri* of the *Novus Justinianus Codex*, which dealt with administrative, fiscal, and military matters of the Empire, was simply deleted from the opus.[5] A similar fate awaited the *Digesta*, and only one-fourth of the original codex was preserved in its entirety.

The formation of city-states was an essential cornerstone in the evolution of the legal system. Roman law had succeeded only because the Roman population joined together in the cities and resisted the barbaric innovations. Feudalism provided for economical welfare of the cities. The church enhanced this development by delegating to the citizenry administrative tasks because the load was too heavy to be shouldered by the lord-bishops, on whom the responsibilities of temporal and spiritual powers had fallen. When the relationship between the pope and the emperor became tarnished, the friction between the see (seat) of the Empire and the cities reached a point of no return. In 1158, at the Diet of Roncaglia, the Emperor Frederick Barbarossa reclaimed all those powers that had been usurped. The Diet opened a period of wars in northern Italy, and the *Lega di Legnano* was formed. Several communes joined with Legnano against the emperor and eventually, in 1176, they were victorious. In 1183, the Peace of Constance by which the emperor's rights were saved, if only in appearance, was signed. As a result, the cities were now able to choose their own magistrates. They retained some judicial jurisdiction, and the cases brought in appeal to the imperial vicars had to be decided upon according to the laws of the commune, and the territories occupied during the war were kept.[6]

The roles played by the Church and the universities in the Middle Ages should not be underestimated. To say that both institutions saw to it that legal education and knowledge would not suffer the cultural malaise that was taking over Europe is not exaggerating the truth. Of the oldest Italian universities, Bologna's was the first one to concentrate on jurisprudence. Educational endeavors also continued in Ravenna, regarded as the cultural capital of the Byzantine Empire. While there are no documents proving the existence of a school of law, we are sure that lawyers, judges, and notaries practiced in Ravenna from the fifth through the tenth centuries. Pavia was the cultural capital of the Longobards, and it is there that the first attempts at scholastic studies occurred. Several generations of scholars gathered in Pavia to interpret the laws and make them applicable to individual cases. The kingdom's Supreme Court was in Pavia, as were notaries and judges. All this activity left an abundance of legal treasures, such as the *Exposito Ad Librum Papiensem*, which represents one of the most complete collections of glosses ever to be released in the eleventh century.

Despite the existence of legal studies and practice in Ravenna and Pavia, not until the opening of Bologna's university did the study of jurisprudence become a specialized endeavor. To this time we can date the birth of Italian civil law, which, in turn, was the predecessor of the *Jus Commune*, the European common law.

While Firenze (Florence) became the center of letters and the arts, Rome was the see of the papacy and of the richness of customs and money, Venezia (Venice) and Amalfi were the great trading ports, Bologna "became the center of legal studies, and to it came students from all Italy and, later from all Europe."[7] The work of the glossators represented the bulk of the sources on which both students and scholars of jurisprudence had to base their research and background information. In just two centuries, five large universities were opened and were actively engaged in pursuing knowledge: Bologna circa 1100, Padova 1222, Napoli (Naples) 1224, Perugia 1308, and Pisa 1343.

Although European scholars kept coming to Bologna through the seventeenth century, legal studies did not progress as the reputation of the school would have suggested. Italy had survived the Middle Ages, but it had not been an easy endeavor. While the Italian states succeeded individually in preserving and enhancing the arts, they were not as successful in developing a healthy political and governmental environment. The sovereign was the state; the laws existed insofar as they suited the needs of the chief executive. The church was stripped of most of its temporal powers so as not to rival the sovereign. Calisse superbly describes this painful transition:

Italy, emerging from the Middle Ages, arose still worshipping the greatness of Rome and seeking to imitate her. By grasping and applying the fruit of this ancient knowledge, it succeeded; but not without self-injury, for, clinging to the great illusion and dreaming of a resurrection of the past, it held to the Empire and was diverted by its exalted aim, from the development of the national life which other countries were intent upon. . . . Thus when the rest of Europe had won for itself strong national governments, Italy had not yet even a national sense; patriotism was either confused with loyalty to the new foreign Empire, or was limited by city walls.[8]

France, in fact, had taken the lead in the field of culture, politics, and legal studies. Civil law was still being taught, but it was more according to the *Mos docenti Gallicus* and less and less according to the *Mos Italicus jura docenti*. The difference was in the manner of perceiving the laws. French and German scholars looked upon the *Corpus Juris Civilis* as an ancient text, while Italians considered it a living law.

The period between the sixteenth and the eighteenth centuries was one of increasing interference by the states into the administration and teachings of the universities. This was the time of the Counter-Reformation, a period in which the secular tendencies of the school of natural law would not be accepted in Italy. While it is true that the cradles of knowledge were being painfully subjugated by both the temporal and spiritual authorities, it is also true that with the protection of enlightened patrons the arts and letters were surviving. The contributions of Pietro Muratori and Cesare Beccaria to jurisprudence should not be ignored. Muratori's *Dei Difetti della Giurisprudenza* (1742) pointed out some of the defects of the legal system. He thought legislation lacked clarity and depended heavily on the interpretation of individual lawyers, which enhanced confusion rather than fostered uniformity. Muratori, therefore, supported a thorough codification of the laws. Beccaria's *Dei Delitti e Delle Pene* (1764), on the other hand, concentrated on criminal law. Death penalties and torture were the main subjects for criticism in Beccaria's work. Because of the impact of this book, the death penalty was abolished in the Grand Duchy of Tuscany.[9]

Italy provided a fertile soil for new laws when the French armies took over in 1796. Once the French established themselves, they began exporting their new political ideology. Napoleon became king of Italy in 1805, and the newly acquired territories were incorporated into the administrative branch of the French Empire. By 1806, the French civil code had been translated into Italian and was in effect. The Code of Civil Procedure, the Commercial Code, and the Penal Code followed shortly thereafter. These were the first "new" codes to appear in Europe and did not represent a reelaboration of the old legislations and glosses. In addition, Courts of Conciliation, judges of first instance, Courts of Appeal, Review Courts, and a Supreme Court were established throughout the occupied territories. This period brought to Italy, therefore, many of the principles and institutions that are the foundations of the public law of modern states.[10]

While the French and the Austrians helped Italy to outgrow feudalism and introduced Italy into the modern era, their unenlightened and despotic rule helped develop a sense of nationalism and made poignant the need for unification if the country was to be rid of the foreigners. Until 1831, Italian attempts at revolt kept failing because of betrayals and lack of manpower. However, defeat did not breed acquiescence. Dominated Italians could not openly revolt against their rulers, so they resorted to music, poetry, and novels. Historical novels and poetry were used as a means to protest foreign dominations, to exult heroes, and to complain of political injustices and unfair laws. Beccaria's son-in-law, Alessandro Manzoni (1785–1873), one of the greatest Italian novelists and poets, wrote *I Promessi Sposi*. This novel was a subtle accusation of the repugnance of Austrian domination, the incongruities of the judicial system, the politics of the church, and the indiscriminate autocracy of the squires (Signorotti). While Manzoni was fighting the Austrians, Ugo Foscolo (1778–1827), in *I Sepolcri*, was protesting the use of communal graves to destroy Italian roots and pride in their ancestors and the glories of the past.

Foscolo and Manzoni were but two of those belonging to the Italian intelligenzia who made it possible for the ideas and the movement of the Risorgimento to reach its peak between 1830 and 1848. The small revolutionary groups of the 1820s were not longer alone in their battles. Vittorio Alfieri was essential in changing the role of the intelligenzia from servant of the sovereign to a tool of unification and freedom. Others, such as Cuoco, Foscolo, Mazzini, Gioberti, Balbo, Cattaneo, D'Azeglio, and Cavour, followed his lead.

The Restoration had brought back to power the old kings but it could not or it would not destroy all the products of the Napoleonic Empire. The codes by now were well-embedded and even the most absolute sovereign was not able to ignore them:

The first Italian state to enact a code after the Restoration was the Kingdom of Naples, where, in 1819, the code of the Kingdom of the Two Sicilies, in five parts (Civil, Penal,

Civil Procedure, Criminal Procedure, and Commercial Law), took effect . . . followed by
that of the Duchy of Parma. . . . The French Civil Code was here revised and adopted in
1820. . . . In the Kingdom of Lombardy-Venetia ruled by a king who was also the Emperor
of Austria, the Austrian Civil Code . . . was adopted in 1816, and remained in effect in
the new Italian provinces of Trent and Trieste until after World War I. . . . In the Grant
Duchy of Tuscany the French Code of Commerce was retained as well as the French
laws concerning mortages and rules concerning testimonial evidence.[11]

King Carlo Alberto was the first Italian king to seem to want to give a clear
nationalistic line to his policies. Unfortunately, his nickname was "Il Re Ten-
tenna," the oscillating king. He was not too dependable, and it took him until
March 4, 1848, to grant the *Statuto Albertino*. The Statuto was an attempt to
placate the people. Several constitutions were inaugurated all over Europe, but
they were not able to anticipate the liberal tide that was by now beginning to
sweep the Continent. However, it is important to note that Carlo Alberto's Statuto
and his attempt at unification were the foundation for an Italian state and a
codification of the laws (a Civil Code, followed by a Penal Code, a Military
Penal Code, a Commercial Code, and a Code of Criminal Procedure were all
adopted during this period).

Italy's major struggles for independence began in the year 1848. On March
23, Carlo Alberto led his army in firing the first shots of the first Italian war of
independence. It was an unsuccessful attempt, and Vittorio Emanuele II succeeded his father after the disastrous defeat at Novara. The king was an absolutist
by upbringing, not very well educated, and yet armed with plenty of common
sense. He realized his survival as a sovereign depended on not ignoring the
people and their desires. One more war of independence and slow and patient
work by Camillo Benso, Count of Cavour (1810–1861), resulted in Vittorio
Emanuele II becoming the first king of the Reign of Italy on March 17, 1861.
By 1859 he also had completed his father's project of codification by adding to
the previous codes the Code of Civil Procedures (1854) and a new Penal Code
(1859). The process of unification had been too rapid and, in part, too much
tied-in with the European political situation. The country needed to form a
bureaucracy, an army, a navy, and a united administration. Between 1865 and
1870 more codifications took place. The government issued a Civil Code, a
Code of Commerce, a Code of Civil Procedure, a Navigation Code, and a Code
of Criminal Procedure. In 1866, the third and final war of independence began,
and, in 1870, Rome became the capital of the new kingdom. Complete judicial
unification, however, did not occur until 1923, when Mussolini centralized the
appellate jurisdiction.

After the enactments under Vittorio Emanuele, the codes remained more or
less unchanged until 1913, when the Code of Criminal Procedure of 1865 was
revised. All the codifications and their emendations reflected the new liberal
philosophy that had spurred the unification of Italy. They were unacceptable to
Mussolini, who had the Penal Code and the Code of Criminal Procedure re-

fashioned to more closely mirror the Fascist ideology. These represent the last major changes in the codification of Italian laws.

On January 1, 1948, the new republican Constitution became effective. Under the new Constitution "the judge seeks the intention of the law and becomes its interpreter to ensure its observance and to see that justice is done, being always above the parties."[12] New social needs, a new political regime, and new laws necessarily breed a new approach to jurisprudence. The new doctrine takes into account the ideals of social justice. It establishes judicial review, increases the status of the judiciary, and allows for "theories of interpretation that are more realistic and value-conscious than those of the older model."[13]

Throughout the centuries, Roman law has continually developed and spread throughout Europe. Its influence has been felt both in common and civil law worlds. By keeping the Roman law alive, Italy gave the Western world a solid legal tradition. When Italy was experiencing one of the darkest times in its history, some of the nations that had benefitted from the past Italian splendor helped the country to rise again. There are traces of Roman, French, German, and Swiss influence in today's Italian legal system, and thus "the contemporary Italian legal system is, more than any other, a kind of paradigm of the 'Civil Law System'."[14]

THE ORGANIZATION OF THE ITALIAN COURT SYSTEM

As a consequence of French domination, the influence of the Napoleonic Codes, and of the French Revolution's administrative innovations, the Italian judicial system is modelled after the French. There are four kinds of jurisdiction: ordinary, administrative, accounting, and fiscal. Ordinary courts deal with both civil and criminal matters; administrative with judicial review of the administrative acts; accounting with all state financial matters; and fiscal with matters regarding taxes.

At the bottom of the ordinary court system is the justice of the peace (conciliatore). There is one conciliatore in each municipality and he/she may deal with civil cases of amounts up to one million lira. The conciliatore is an honorary judge, appointed by the Council of State (Consiglio di Stato) on recommendation of the tribunal. There are also approximately nine hundred *preture* (one for each *mandamento*). These courts of original jurisdiction are also serviced by a single judge, called a *pretore*. The jurisdiction of these courts is limited to civil cases of not more than five million lira and criminal cases for which the law does not demand more than three years' imprisonment. A final court of original jurisdiction are 159 law courts (Tribunale) found in each tribunal district. These courts are serviced by three judges, one presiding officer, and two other judges. These courts may hear appeals from the pretura as well as decide civil matters that are above and beyond the competence of the pretori and conciliatori and criminal cases for which the law does not mandate more than seven years' imprisonment. Criminal cases that would imply bigger penalties are brought to the attention of the assize courts (*Corte d'Assise*), a specialized section of the tribunali. There are eighty-nine first degree assize courts and twenty-six assize courts of appeal. Two ordinary judges and six laymen serve on the deliberating board. They all have an equal vote. A majority vote convicts, and a tie acquits. Cases may be appealed to one of the twenty-three courts of appeal (Corte d'Appello), where three judges serve, one as the presiding officer and two as the adjudicating board; or they may be brought to the appellate section of the court of assize. The highest among the ordinary courts is the Court of Cassation (Corte di Cassazione). It has only appellate jurisdiction and may only reverse decisions on matters of law. The court is organized into nine sections, three civil and six criminal. One president and four judges serve on this court unless it is adjudicating in joint sessions. In such an event, the court would be staffed by one president and eight judges. Every decision is reached by a majority vote, and the verdict expresses the opinion of the whole court. Contrary to the Anglo-Saxon system, the dissenting opinion is not made public.

The Administrative Courts (Giurisdizioni Amministrativo), were devised for two main purposes: "to protect the individual against arbitrary and negligent acts by the administration; and to control the use of public funds."[15] Since 1971, each region has had a Regional Administrative Tribunal (Tribunale Amministrativo Regionale), which is staffed with a president and two judges. Until 1984, the prime minister recommended a councillor of state, with at least two years of service, to be appointed president of the tribunal. With the new law (#399, July 30, 1984) it is the Council of the Presidenza del Consiglio di Stato (formed by councillors of state and by councillors of regional tribunals) which recommends a president of a section of the Council of State, with at least two years of service, to be appointed president of the tribunal. There is one tribunal in each region's capital city, although some regions are allowed more than one section. Within sixty days of the tribunal's decision, appeals can be brought before the Council of State (*Consiglio di Stato*), the highest administrative court. It is composed of six sections: three judicial and three "advisory sections which advise ministries and other administrative bodies on the legality of proposed government bills, general regulations, and the codification of legislation (*testi unici*) as well as the legality and merits of proposed contracts, grants of citizenship, etc."[16]

The only court in the accounting jurisdiction is the Court of Accounts (Corte dei Conti). This is an administrative court with jurisdiction over the state's handling of public money. The court has 523 judges throughout the country with ten members serving on each of its sections. Finally, the *ordinamento tributario* deals with taxes and tax returns. It is structured in three fiscal committees: one of first degree, one of second degree, and a central committee. The latter is the ultimate judge on legitimacy.

The Waters' Tribunals (Tribunale delle Acque), is a special section of the Court of Appeal. It adjudicates in first instance on controversies relevant to public waters. The decisions reached by this court may be appealed to the

Superior Tribunal on Public Waters (Tribunale Superiore delle Acque Pubbliche). The Superior Tribunal is chaired by a judge of the ordinary order who has reached the level of first president of an appeal court. He is assisted by eleven members—four councillors of cassation, four councillors of state, and three members of the superior council on public works.

The High Court (Corte Costituzionale), is one of the most recent innovations (it was established in 1956) in the Italian judicial structure. It is the only court to which judges are elected. The court has fifteen "brethren" elected for a term of nine years, and they are not immediately reelectable. One-third must come from the supreme magistrates—the Court of Cassation, the Council of State, and the Court of Accounts; one-third are elected by Parliament; and the final third is appointed by the president of the Republic. The Court elects its own presiding judge for a three-year term. The newly elected president appoints a judge as his substitute in the event he will need one. In case of impeachment of the president of the Republic, the prime minister, or a lesser minister, sixteen people selected by Parliament join the Court. The Constitutional Court was provided for as a check on the legislature. It safeguards constitutionality in the country; its need became obvious throughout the Fascist dictatorship. The primary task of the court is to decide on the constitutionality of the laws.

THE PERSONNEL OF THE LAW

The Legal Practitioners

In Italy there are several legal professions. While legal education for all careers begins at the university level and is basically the same (a doctor of law degree or *dottore in Giurisprudenza* is required), the various legal professions have different apprenticeships, technical training, and guilds.

The Italian notary is quite different from his American namesake. He/she generally has a very lucrative business, and the notary's social status can be very high, especially in the southern part of the country. A notary drafts legal documents and authenticates others, such as applications for competitive national examinations. He/she can draft contracts, wills and testaments, corporate charters, and petitions to be presented in court. A document drafted by a notary is called "a public act" and guarantees that whatever the document deals with, was agreed upon and signed in the notary's presence. The road to a notary's career is long and slow. It begins with four years of law school followed by two years of apprenticeship with an established notary. Having completed the apprenticeship, the applicant can take the competitive national examinations (written and oral), successful completion of which is equal to a license to practice as a notary, but does not guarantee immediate placement. In fact, commissioning occurs upon a vacancy in one of the notarial positions. Priority is given to those who are already in service. The evaluative criteria for the subsequent national competition are seniority, publications, and public service. If a position is still vacant, it will be offered to the most successful examination candidate. Once assigned to a notary business, the newly nominated notary has to confine his/ her practice to the territory appointed to that specific business.

While there are approximately 25,000 individual practicing lawyers in Italy, data on how many notaries and notary businesses there are in Italy is unavailable.[17] There is sufficient data, however, on their caseload. In 1981 a total of 11,890,337 notarial acts were drawn; of these, 928,570 were in reference to sales of real estate and 4,642,453 to sales of motor vehicles. Data relevant to the drafting of wills and testaments, to authentication of signatures, and to all those acts that are not required to be recorded in the notarial archives, unfortunately, was again unobtainable. The available data shows the south trailing the heavily industrialized north by 3,765,237 cases; and yet it is suspected the picture would be a different one, were we able to include the "missing data" in this statistic.[18]

The *avvocati* are the historical heirs of the Roman jurisconsults. They are the professionals who represent clients in court cases. At times, the role of the *procuratore* and that of the avvocato are mistakenly confused. While the avvocato defends a party to the judicial authority, the procuratore represents the party. An avvocato may act without a power of attorney but a procuratore may not. In a dispute, each party must be represented by an avvocato. The law mandates that no one may take the title or practice the profession of lawyer and of procuratore without being registered in the professional list. To be able to register, a person must have honorably practiced as a procuratore for at least six years or have passed the lawyer's qualifying national examinations. Those qualified for the examinations are procuratori who have practiced for at least two years or who have been magistrates (the term magistrates covers a wide range of figures in the Italian judicial system and includes prosecutors as well as judges) in the military and administrative judiciary for four years and university full-professors of jurisprudence and law-related fields who have taught for at least three years. As far as freedom to practice as a professional, the lawyer does not have the territorial limitations that the notary does. The only restriction a lawyer might encounter is the level of jurisdiction. The avvocato may not practice before the Supreme Court of Judicature, the Council of State, and the Court of Accounts unless he/she is qualified to practice before superior jurisdictions. After eight years as a lawyer, he/she may practice before the highest courts. Unless registered in both the law and the procuratori's list, he/she may not practice as both at the same time.[19]

The first Italian universities were the medical school at Salerno and the law school at Bologna in the twelfth century. As did all European countries, Italy restructured its institutions in the last century. A liberal conception of the public education institution was adopted in 1859 through the Casati Law. Although this law had been updated in 1924, 1933, 1935, and 1938, it was not until the laws of 1980 that the University made a serious attempt to answer the needs of an industrial society.

It can be said that actually the Italian University if on the one hand looks to the German model of the nineteenth century, on the other it has opened up towards a mass dimension like the United States' system, without however, the structural diversity of complete self-government, which is the particular characteristic of the latter. In any case, a first step towards a functional readjustment of the system has been recently taken (Law of 21–2–1980, #28; and of 20–8–1980), authorizing the University to experiment new organizing structures—departmental ones.[20]

Since the students' revolt of the fall of 1968 and the parliamentary enactment the following year (Law #910), universities have been open to all citizens who wish to attend. Italy is one of the very few countries in which access to higher education is completely free for all fields of study. The only requirement to enroll in the university is to have passed the *liceo*'s concluding examination, *esame di maturita'*. The examination concludes five years of *liceo* and thirteen years of schooling. Comparing the Italian to the American school system is very difficult; suffice it to say that the liceo's education is equivalent to the American junior college.[21] The overwhelming majority of universities in Italy are state run.[22] It is the Ministry of Education (*Ministero della Pubblica Istruzione*) that decides the very structured curricula. Four years, twenty-eight oral examinations, and a thesis later, the student obtains a Doctor of Law degree. The educational structure provides a means to acquire verbal fluency and analytical skills in discussing concepts and theories at examinations; yet it only allows the student to become familiar with legal research at the time of the thesis.[23]

While the number of courses and their selection are prearranged for the students, there is no maximum time limit on the completion of the program. Thus, there is a discrepancy between the figures given for students enrolled, graduates, and *fuori corso* students. A fuori corso student is one who has fallen behind in the course work and whom it will take longer than the four years optimal time to obtain the law degree. After the 1972–1973 year, the enrollment of students has fluctuated erratically. Law studies show a definite increase from 1972–1973 to 1978–1979, a year in which there were 39,278 students of law, equal to 15.8 percent of all students enrolled in Italy in that year. In the 1980–1981 academic year there were 144,869 jurisprudence students; of which 38,791 were freshmen, 40,593 were fuori corso, and 59,428 were women. Doctor of law degrees were awarded to 7,718 in 1980, 2,690 of which were awarded to women. In the 1981–1982 academic year, 100,112 students were full-time jurisprudence students; of these, 36,676 were freshmen. Over one hundred thousand students enrolled in jurisprudence for the 1984–1985 academic year.[24]

The figures here cited might lead the reader to the conclusion that the legal profession is highly considered. While this is certainly true, one should not lose sight of the fact that a law degree qualifies a person for more professions than the legal ones. In addition to the previously mentioned legal occupations, a law degree qualifies one for teaching positions at all academic levels, banking careers, and for higher entry-level positions in all industries. Nevertheless, a large portion of law students do choose to become legal practitioners. The majority of them come from the south, where a *laurea* (graduate degree) is still looked upon as an achievement and a stepping stone to a better future.

As previously noted, law graduates must undergo a period of practical training and pass a state examination before beginning practice. In addition, those who wish to practice before a number of courts (Constitutional Court, Court of Cassation, and the Council of State, among others) must be admitted to the rolls of the National Law Council. The Council is made up of representatives of each of the twenty-three Court of Appeal districts. The Council is primarily concerned with hearing appeals from the local bar councils regarding regulations of the profession. The local bar councils are found in each Court of Appeal district and are responsible for maintaining the standards of the profession.[25]

The Judiciary

As do other legal careers, a judge's begins with law school. After receiving a law degree, the candidate takes a nationally competitive examination, the examining committee of which is composed of judges and law professors. A judge's career begins as a judicial auditor (*uditore giudiziario*). After twelve months the uditore becomes a functioning judge. After one more year and a review of his/her work by the district and National Council of Judges (Corte Superiore della Magistratura), the judge is made a *tribunal magistrate*. It is at this stage that he/she receives complete tenure. The two most critical stages to a judgeship are the promotion to *magistrato di appello* and to *magistrato di cassazione*—appeal magistrate and cassation magistrate. All of the 7,692 practicing *magistrati* are employed by the government: 6,605 work for the Justice Department (Ministero di Grazia e Giustizia), 1,019 work for the President of the Council (Presidenza del Consiglio), and 68 for the Defense Department.[26]

The judiciary is hierarchically structured and so is the career of a judge. "There is a very specific relation between hierarchy of judicial offices in the sense that holders of higher ranks are assigned to judicial units which are higher on the jurisdictional ladder, or are assigned to lower jurisdictional offices and functions only in a supervisory capacity."[27] In the legal process the lawyer is a partner of the judge in the search for the truth. The judge is expected to apply the law to practical cases that are brought to his attention. He does not take part in the legislative process nor does he make the laws. The laws are not based on customs and traditions. Jurisprudence is the complex of judicial interpretations of a principle of law. It is used as a source of clarification since the latter written law can not foresee all the possible practical cases. Nevertheless, the judge is always free to adjudicate according to his/her knowledge and conscience. His/her opinion will be binding only for the case over which he/she is presiding. As it will be explained later, the judge may also utilize the opinion of university professors.

A different kind of judge is the *pretore*. He can decide both civil and criminal matters. He is considered qualified by jurisdictions and for civil procedures' cases that do not exceed five million lira (Law #399, July 30, 1984). In affairs related to criminal law, he is able to judge crimes for whom the codes have set a penalty of no more than three years in jail.

There are over seven thousand magistrates in Italy.[28] It is said about the magistrate: "The Italian magistrate's powers are enormous. His means, however, are limited. . . . It is not unusual for one instructing magistrate in a big city to handle over 50 cases at once."[29]

In 1933 a royal decree (RDL 10/30/1933 #1611) established two more legal career options within the kingdom: the *procuratore* and the Avvocato dello Stato. The Avvocatura dello Stato is an agency that provides representation and legal advice to state branches and to the state itself. After two years as a *procuratore dello stato*, a person may apply to take a qualifying examination for the position of Avvocato dello Stato. Promotions within the agency occur on recommendation by the prime minister and by a committee composed of high officers in the administration of the Avvocatura, as well as by examination.

There are also several superior courts, and the judges who serve on them are of higher status than those serving on lower courts. Seniority, performance in service, competitive examinations, and elections by fellow magistrates are the ways by which a judge reaches the higher courts. The election system is used only for trade union organizations and for the Superior Council of Justice, which does not practice jurisdictional functions, except when disciplining other judges.

Legal Scholars

The Italian legal system, while exemplifying a true application of the separation of powers theory, also endorses the theory of division of powers. Since the desire to search for the truth in the judicial process allows both the judge and the lawyer to cooperate rather than take antagonistic positions—as they do in common law countries—the task of interpreting the laws falls upon the law professor rather than upon the judiciary. The professors have concentrated their scholarly efforts in building scientific models and abstract systems of laws. They have succeeded in this task by writing monographs, textbooks, and treatises. Italian scholars believe in a "legal science." They look at law as an independent discipline whose purpose is to reach the perfection of knowledge rather than find answers to practical problems.

The Italian's concept of legal history is different from that of Anglo-Americans. The scholar, in fact, studies the different schools of thought rather than the development of legal tradition. This modus operandi is due to several factors: (a) as mentioned earlier, the *corpus juris civilis* has always been considered a validly legal system, not a historical example; (b) the European's *jus commune* has its roots in Roman law; (c) there is no relevant historical legal past for a country that has only reached unity 124 years ago; (d) the Risorgimento brought new ideas to the legal world, and the codes of 1865 are not part of the past but rather of the present; and finally, (e) agnosticism does not allow for a complete picture of the development of a society and culture.[30]

As of the mid-1960s, the field of scholars has multiplied and the study of sociology of law has become a major endeavor. In 1972 Renato Treves wrote that the increasing and widespread interest in the field of legal sociology, which had been evident in the preceding years, was forcing scholars to search for new theoretical bases through the study of cultural movements.[31] The first manifestation of such a trend is to be found in a denial, or at least questioning of, the dogma of certainty of law.

PUBLIC PERCEPTIONS AND THE ROLE OF THE COURTS

To explain the role played by Italian legal practitioners is a difficult undertaking. Italians are a very complex people and thus not easily describable. If the reader wishes to fully understand the influence that both the law and the legal system have played in Italian history and society, further research should be pursued in the fields of anthropology and sociology.

A university degree still represents for many people a large step upward in a class-oriented culture and a doctor of law degree is as prestigious as a medical or an engineering degree. These three professions represent, in fact, the most popular academic attractions in the country. Despite this, as recently as a decade ago, one major work on the Italian political system gave the following negative assessment of the Italian courts and legal profession:

What sort of public image do the courts project? Accusations of venality and corruption are few and far between. It is interesting to note that the alienated Italian public does not view the judiciary as dishonest. But there is a widespread tendency to distrust the judicial process as costly, cumbersome, and unimaginative. The members of the legal profession suffer even more severely in the public eye.[32]

As we shall shortly see, however, changes in the role of the courts and its practitioners has led to a reassessment of this view.

As previously noted, one of the major innovations of post-war Italian government is the Constitutional Court. Zariski has noted, regarding the creation of the Court:

This may well have been a reaction to the ease with which the pre–1922 *Statuto* could be modified by a simple act of Parliament, with no provision for judicial review. Also, it is notable that, after World War II, those nations which had suffered most heavily from the domestic manifestations of Fascist dictatorship—those nations, in other words, which had fallen victim to fascist movements—were in the forefront of the tendency to adopt some form of judicial review. Germany, Italy, and Austria were cases in point.[33]

The fifteen-member Court has broad powers. It can, for example, decide on delegated legislation issued by the executive, resolve conflicts between the national and regional governments as well as different branches of the government, and decide upon the constitutionality of both national and regional laws. Access to the Court is relatively broad. Any individual, group, or regional government can raise the question of the constitutionality of a law. It is then left to a judge of a lower court to raise the issue and bring it before the Constitutional Court. This access is somewhat more limited than in the American system; the Italian judge of the Constitutional Court must wait for lower judges to authorize him to hear a case while the American Supreme Court judges can bring a case before themselves by issuing a writ of certiorari. In addition, the Italian lower court judge can prevent a case from being heard by the Constitutional Court by issuing an interlocutory judgment which notes that the claim of the case is unfounded. It has been argued that the Court has developed a relatively restrained view of its powers because of indifference from the executive branch and the public at large as well as outright hostility from many in the judiciary. Zariski writes:

Because of long-prevalent legal concepts, many Italian judges simply cannot accept the idea of a tribunal with power to hold acts of Parliament unconstitutional or—even worse from their point of view—to declare null and void large segments of the legal codes dating back to the Fascist regime or even to the pre–1922 constitutional monarchy.[34]

Despite these views, the Court has played an important role in the contemporary Italian system, both in protecting civil liberties and more clearly defining the relationships and powers of the national and regional governments. As one indication of its activity, the Court, in the first two decades of its existence, found approximately 20 percent of the laws that it judged to be unconstitutional (a larger proportion than that judged by either the U.S. Supreme Court or the German Constitutional Court).[35]

Many young members of the judiciary have also played an active role in Italian politics. The "tackling pretore" (*pretore d'assalto*) is a reality to which most Italians have grown accustomed. The young pretori no longer separate politics and social issues from the laws but try to make a name for themselves by "attacking" a situation, a problem, an institution, or an individual—all of this activity glamorously treated by the press.

The question of an independent judiciary has been of uppermost importance to magistrates all over the world. The optimum seems to be the British system in which a judge can perform *nec spe nec metu*, without hope (for favors or for a promotion) and without fear (of adjudicating a case contrary to the will of the majority). This has also been an important issue in the Italian legal system. As one indication of the Italian concern about judicial independence, the following remarks were made before a March 25, 1903, meeting of the House of Representatives:

The judiciary is the guardian, the defender and the avenger of all rights and of the rights of all. Life, liberty, honour, personal property, and all the most sacred things to mankind, depend on actions by the judiciary. . . . The dignity and the greatness of the nations are measured on the authority of the judiciary; on people's respect for the magistrates; on faith in them, and on the esteem they command because of their knowledge and character.[36]

In 1961, Alfredo Carlo Moro wrote that a good administration of justice requires adequate means, prepared men, an efficient system, and, most importantly, an independent judiciary.[37]

To this end, two major changes in the judiciary have occurred. In 1959 the Higher Council of the Judiciary (Consiglio Superiore della Magistratura) was created to make sure the judiciary could be as independent as possible from external interferences. Twenty-four members serve on the Council, fourteen elected by magistrates, seven from Parliament, and the last three being the president of the Republic, the president of the Court of Cassation, and the prosecutor general of the Court of Cassation. Among the magistrates elected by their colleagues to the Council are eight who come from the middle and low ranks of the judiciary.[38]

In the decade between 1963 and 1973, Parliament passed several laws aimed at reorganizing the system of promotions. "The cumulative results of the new regulations is that . . . the evaluation of candidates having the seniority requirements to compete for promotion at the different levels of the judicial hierarchy of ranks is no longer based either on written and oral exams, or on the consideration of their written judicial works, but on a 'global' assessment of their judicial performance."[39] As a consequence, judges have been less pressured to perform to satisfy the higher ranks of the judiciary, and have not been as worried about obtaining promotions and recognition within the judiciary.

Although there have been improvements in the judicial structure, there are still several roadblocks to an efficient application of the law. The system is burdened by slowness, which, in turn, promotes high costs and a lack of faith in its operation. A vast literature agrees on the problems, and the solution unanimously called for is a political-social reform focused on the political parties. Justice in Italy is poorly executed because of a lack of personnel, useless formalities, and inadequate procedures, which inhibit the judiciary. Rather than resolving single issues, the judiciary sets aside each issue until a comprehensive reform can be enacted. New legislation should fill the gaps provoked by the High Court's decisions on unconstitutionality.

While the citizenry has manifested dissatisfaction with many institutions, the people have been fairly supportive of the judiciary, especially since the mid-1970s, when the magistrates became targets of the Red Brigade, which attempted to deter the courts from trying terrorists. Its plan did not succeed, and, in fact, might have backfired. Justice survived and sentences were handed down. At the same time, when magistrates went on strike early in 1984, they did not receive total support from the citizenry. The strike was provoked by a government veto on a bill that provided for a 40 million lira (about $20,512 in 1984) payment in arrears wages, and a 500,000 lira (about $256 in 1984) monthly salary increase.

Some citizens felt that magistrates should concentrate on improving the system rather than strike over wages. They claimed members of the judiciary were not working enough and enjoyed muckraking and burying themselves in needless controversies and thus did not deserve a raise. However, the investigation of the Mafia in autumn 1984 and the accomplishments of the magistrates have brought the country to once again support the judiciary and to recognize that the magistrates do represent the "Brave arm of the Law."[40] Politicians, on the other hand, do not like the judiciary primarily because of the role it has played in uncovering many of the political scandals of the last decade.[41] Some magistrates are unhappy with their new, more politicized role, believing "that their newfound influence is a dangerous sign, a symptom of the difficulties Italy's elected institutions are having in dealing with the country's most difficult problems."[42]

To try to remedy some of the built-in deficiencies of the judicial system, especially of the criminal procedures, the cabinet sent to the House of Representatives a list of guidelines for the drafting of a new code of criminal procedures. In July 1984, the House approved the document, albeit with several modifications, by a vote of 338 in favor, 33 against, and 1 abstention. As soon as the proposed guidelines are voted on by the Senate, the cabinet will be able to draft a new bill, which is anticipated to be placed into effect within three years. This newest attempt at codification is expected to provide a more effective exercise of justice. The new code provides for several basic changes. Criminal procedures are envisaged to become more similar to those in the American system. According to the new blueprints, both the prosecutor and the defense lawyer will be equal partners. The office of the inquiring judge (*giudice istruttore*) will disappear; the public prosecutor will not be able to issue arrest warrants; the length of the preliminary investigations will be considerably reduced; and it will not be possible any more to foreclose a case on grounds of "insufficient evidence." The government's initiative in dealing with the problems of the judicial system has been hailed by politicians and citizens alike. How long it will be, however, before the new code will be implemented is yet unclear. The 1983 elections proved the country's loss of patience with rhetoric, intraparty fighting, maladministration, nepotism, and corruption, and a desire for a more active approach to politics by the citizens.[43] Thus it would be fair to state that it is in the politicians' interests to maintain the proposed timetable for the reform of the criminal procedural code.

While it is evident that the Italian judiciary has not been guaranteed warm support from all sectors of the society in the past, it has, however, received such support in recent years. This has been matched by a new vigor on the part of the judiciary as seen in the actions of the "tackling pretore," the Constitutional Court, and the judiciary in general, in dealing with Italy's political crises in recent years. One of the interesting questions for the remainder of this decade, then, is whether the Italian people will continue to support the actions of a more active judiciary. This is not at all clear, given Italy's historic ambivalence toward its judiciary.

NOTES

1. For more on this topic, see M. Cappelletti et al., *The Italian Legal System: An Introduction* (Palo Alto, Calif.: Stanford University Press, 1967), p. 4; A. Berger, *Encyclopedic Dictionary of Roman Law* (Philadelphia: Philosophical Society, 1953); H. W. Ehrmann, *Comparative Legal Cultures* (Englewood Cliffs, N. J.: Prentice-Hall, 1976); F. J. Stimson, *Stimson's Glossary* (Boston: Little, Brown & Co., 1981); A. Englemann et al., *History of Continental Civil Procedure* (New York: Augustus M. Kelley Publishers, 1969).

2. Cappelletti, *The Italian Legal System*, p. 6.

3. C. Calisse, *A History of Italian Law* (New York: Augustus M. Kelley, Publishers), p. liii.

4. Ibid., p. iv.

5. For more on this topic, see Cappelletti, *The Italian Legal System*, p. 11.

6. Calisse, *A History of Italian Law*, pp. 130–31.

7. Cappelletti, *The Italian Legal System*, p. 15.

8. Calisse, *A History of Italian Law*, p. 197.

9. Cappelletti, *The Italian Legal System*, p. 41.

10. Calisse, *A History of Italian Law*, pp. 202–3. See also, Cappelletti, *The Italian Legal System*, pp. 42–43.

11. Cappelletti, *The Italian Legal System*, p. 44 n. 110.

12. Presidency of the Council of Ministers, *Italian Republic, Constitutional: Administration* (Rome: Presidency of the Council of Ministers' Information and Copyright Service, 1976), p. 84.

13. P. A. Allum, *Italy: Republic Without Government?* (New York: W. W. Norton & Company, 1973), p. 181.

14. Cappelletti, *The Italian Legal System*, p. 52, and 52 n. 132.

15. Allum, *Italy: Republic Without Government?*, p. 186.

16. Ibid., p. 188.

17. C. S. Rhyne, *Law and Judicial Systems of Nations* (Washington, D.C.: The World Peace Through Law Center, 1978), p. 369.

18. The data quoted here is derived from Table 110, "Notarial Statistics," in *Annuario Statistico Italiano* (Rome: Istituto Centrale di Statistica, 1982), p. 104.

19. For more on this topic, see A. Favata, *Dizionario dei Termini Giuridici*, 4th ed. (Piacenza: Editrice La Tribuna, 1978), p. 37; and Cappelletti, *The Italian Legal System*, p. 92.

20. D. Fazio, *Universitas*, Anno 1, no. 1, 1980, pp. 37–95.

21. For more, see ibid.; and Cappelletti, *The Italian Legal System*, chapter 3, especially pp. 88–89 and footnote no. 12.

22. Law degrees are given at the following university sites: Bari, Bologna, Cagliari, Camerino, Catania, Catanzaro, Florence, Genova, Macerata, Messina, Milano, Naples, Padova, Palermo, Pavia, Perugia, Pisa, Rome, Salerno, Sassari, Siena, Torino, and Trieste. In addition, there are several private universities at approximately thirty locations offering law degrees.

23. Cappelletti, *The Italian Legal System*, chapter 3, p. 90 ff.

24. This data was taken from *Universitas; Annuario Statistico Italiano*; J. Paxson, ed., *The Statesman's Yearbook, 1983–1984* (London: The Macmillan Press, 1984).

25. Rhyne, *Law and Judicial Systems of Nations*, p. 369.

26. The data was taken from Table 275, "Dipendenti delle Amministrazioni Pubbliche, in *Annuario Statistico Italiano*, p. 260.

27. G. Di Federico, "The Italian Judicial Profession and Its Bureaucratic Setting," *Judicial Review* 21 (1976), p. 43.

28. These figures were taken from *The Statesman's Yearbook, 1983–1984* and *The Economist*, August 18, 1984, p. 43.

29. *The Economist*, August 18, 1984, p. 43.

30. For more on this topic, see Cappelletti, *The Italian Legal System*, pp. 164–97.

31. R. Treves, *Giustizia e Giudici nella Societa' Italiana* (Bari: Editori Laterza, 1972), p. 155.

32. R. Zariski, *Italy: The Politics of Uneven Development* (Hinsdale, Ill.: The Dryden Press, 1972) p. 318.

33. Ibid., p. 307.

34. Ibid., p. 308.

35. Allum, *Italy: Republic Without Government?* p. 195.

36. F. Santosuosso, "Il Consiglio Superiore della Magistratura," in A. C. Moro, ed., *L'Amministrazione della Giustizia in Italia* (Rome: Editrice Studium, 1961), p. 61.

37. Moro, *L'Amministrazione della Giustizia in Italia*, p. 61.

38. For more, see Di Federico, "The Italian Judicial Profession," p. 53; and G. Di Federico, "Le Statut, la carriere et l'independance des magistrats ordinaire en Italie," *Justice et Politique* (Strasbourg: Presses Universitaires d'Alsace, 1974), pp. 39–41.

39. Di Federico, "The Italian Judicial Profession," p. 54.

40. For more on this, read "The Brave Arm of the Law," *The Economist*, August 18, 1984, p. 35; and E. J. Dionne, Jr., "Italy Loves Its Activist Magistrates Even As It Worries," *New York Times*, October 16, 1984, p. 15A

41. *The Economist*, August 18, 1984, p. 35.

42. Dionne, "Italy Loves Its Activist Magistrates."

43. M.E. de Franciscis, "General Elections 1983," *Italian Studies Quarterly* 24, no. 94 (Fall 1983), pp. 65-75.

BIBLIOGRAPHY

Aberbach, J. D. *Bureaucrats and Politicians in Western Democracies*. Cambridge: Harvard University Press, 1981.

Allum, P. A. *Italy: Republic Without Government?* New York: W. W. Norton & Company, 1973.

Almond, G. A., and S. Verba. *The Civic Culture. Political Attitudes and Democracy in Five Nations*. Princeton, N.J.: Little, Brown and Co., 1966.

Balladore-Pallieri, G. *Diritto Internazionale Pubblico*. Varese: Dott. Giuffre' Editore, 1962.

Berger, S. *Organizing Interests in Western Europe*. Cambridge: The University Press, 1981.

Calisse, C. *A History of Italian Law*. New York: Augustus M. Kelley Publishers, 1969.

Cappelletti, M., and J. M. Perillo. *Civil Procedure in Italy*. The Hague: M. Nijhoff, 1965.

Cappelletti, M., J. H. Merryman and J. M. Perillo. *The Italian Legal System*. Palo Alto, Calif.: Stanford University Press, 1967.

Castellano, C., and C. Pace. *L'efficienza della giustizia Italiana*. Bari: Editori Laterza, 1968.

Cuomo, G. *Lezioni di Diritto Costituzionale Italiano e Comparato*. Naples: Liguori Editore, 1977.

de Franciscis, M. E. "General Elections 1983." *Italian Studies Quarterly* 24, no. 94 (Fall 1983), pp. 65–75.

Diambrini-Palazzi, S. *La Giustizia in Italia*. Naples: Cappelli Editore, 1969.

Di Federico, G. *La Giustizia come organizzazione: Il Reclutamento dei Magistrati*. Bari: Editori Laterza, 1968.

———. "The Italian Judicial Profession and Its Bureaucratic Setting." *Judicial Review* 21 (1976).

Di Nanni, L. F., G. Fusco, and G. Vacca. *Giudizio civile innanzi al conciliatore e competenza del pretore nella legge 399/1984*. Naples: Jovene Editore, 1985.

Dogan, M. *The Mandarins of Western Europe. The Political Role of Top Civil Servants*. New York: Sage Publications, 1975.

Ehrmann, H. W. *Comparative Legal Cultures*. Englewood Cliffs, N.J.: Prentice-Hall, 1976.

Engelmann, A., S. Williston, and W. C. Holdsworth. *A History of Continental Civil Procedure*. New York: Augustus M. Kelley Publishers, 1969.

Ferri, E. *Sociologia Criminale*. New York: D. Appleton & Co., 1900.

Kogan, N. *A Political History of Postwar Italy*. New York: Praeger, 1966.

Leone, G. *Elementi di Diritto e Procedura Penale*. Naples: Editore Jovene, 1983.

Milner, G. *La professione dell'avvocato*. Torino: Einaudi Editore, 1981.

Montesquieu, C., Baron de. *L'Esprit des Lois*. Paris: Garnier, 1973.

Morghen, R. *Civilta' Europea: L'eta' Contemporanea*, vol. 3. Palermo: Palumbo Editore, 1974.

Moro, A. C., ed. *L'Amministrazione della Giustizia in Italia*. Rome: Editrice Studium, 1961.

Sawer, G. *Law in Society*. Oxford: Oxford University Press, 1965.

Tesauro, A. *Manuale di Diritto Pubblico*. Naples: Edizioni Scientifiche Italiane, 1973.

Thomas, J. C. *The Decline of Ideology in Western Political Parties: A Study of Changing Policy Orientations*. Beverly Hills, Calif.: Sage Publications, 1975.

Treves, R. *Giustizia e Giudici nella Societa' Italiana*. Bari: Editori Laterza, 1972.

Vanderbilt, A. T. *Judges and Jurors, Their Functions, Qualifications and Selection*. Boston: Boston University Press, 1956.

Zariski, R. *Italy: The Politics of Uneven Development*. Hinsdale, Ill.: The Dryden Press, 1972.

9

JAPAN

Alan N. Katz

Contemporary Japan is a modern, "Westernized," industrial giant. Yet, it is a nation of great contrasts. Nowhere is this more clearly seen than in the relationship between the Japanese and their laws and legal system. For while Japan has a modern legal system, well-trained legal practitioners, and laws modelled after those found in the West, we find a strong aversion to utilize the legal system and a dislike for the law: "To an honourable Japanese the law is something that is undesirable, even detestable, something to keep as far away from as possible. To never use the law, or be involved with the law, is the hope of an honourable people. . . . In a word, Japanese do not like the law."[1] While it might be argued that the above is a bit of an overstatement today, it is clear that the Japanese have, at best, somewhat ambivalent attitudes toward the law. As we shall shortly see, many of these attitudes are the direct result of Japan's long and complex development.

THE DEVELOPMENT OF THE LEGAL SYSTEM

Much of Japan's early history revolves around the desire for autonomy by many of its clans and movements toward unification led by the strongest of the clans. The approximately one hundred clans that existed in Japan were first united by Queen Himiko of the Yamatai state in the third century. During this period Japan was little influenced by foreign civilizations. Instead, religion had a great impact upon the lives of the Japanese people and the rules of law differed little from the rules of religion. Queen Himiko was, therefore, as much a religious figure as a political leader:

Traditional Japanese religion considers ancestors as gods; hence Himiko served the gods and the foundation of her political power was religious. Through prayer she knew the will of the ancestor gods and pronounced oracles which were law. . . . Thus, law was the will of the gods as declared by the person interceding between the gods and the people.[2]

The struggle between the power of the clans and the central government continued over the next few centuries. By the middle of the seventh century a new, more powerful, centralized government emerged. This government was modelled on the Chinese system and utilized legal codes and political institutions similar to those found in China. The codes (the most famous of which was the *Taiho Ritsu-ryo*, promulgated in 710) were built around a legal system called the *ritsu-ryo*, based upon the *ritsu* (a body of penal rules) and the *ryo* (a body of admonitory rules).[3] While the ritsu-ryo was able to concentrate power in the hands of the imperial government, it did not translate well into the culture of Japan and fell into disuse. The succeeding centuries saw the development of a strong military class, and by the twelfth century the Taira clan came to power, soon to be replaced by the Genji clan. Yorimoti, the leader of this clan, set up a military government that ushered in a period of feudalism until the Meji Restoration in 1868. The nearly seven-hundred-year period until the Meji Restoration can be divided into two periods: dual feudalism and unitary feudalism.[4] The former period is known as "dual feudalism" because, while feudalism dominated the economic institution of the great estates, the courtiers of the imperial court operated under the guidelines of the previous political systems. This period was divided into two military periods, with governments established at Kamakura and Muromachi, with a short-lived restoration of the emperor in 1334. There were, in addition, three sources of law during this period: (1) the *kuge-ho*—the customary law that remained from the ritsu-ryo period. This was, however, often replaced by laws passed by the imperial court; (2) *Honjo-ho*—the law that applied to the private manors and varied greatly from region to region; and (3) *Buke-ho*—the series of laws and customs (called *bushido*) that applied to the warrior class.

Power shifted to the rulers of the independent feudal states during the succeeding centuries. This period of decentralization and violence finally came to an end with the founding of the Tokugawa regime in 1603. Noda writes about this period:

The new regime was purely feudal; all of Japan was *bushi*-dominated. The head of the central government, still known as the Bakfu, was just one of the *daiymo*, who was the strongest and greatest of them and had the title of *shogun* (generalissimo). He had the greatest domain, *tenryo* (literally the heavenly domain), which he governed directly, and all the other land was divided into fiefs among the big and small *daiymo* and the direct vassals of the shogun who were not *daiymo*. Even the imperial court was under the shogun's surveillance, but the emperor remained the symbol of national unity.[5]

The Tokugawa period lasted until 1868. It saw limited contact with foreigners (only Dutch and Chinese traders entered Japan), the development of new legal codes, a major role for religion, and the creation of a very stable, unchanging society. The law of this period was the customary law found in each of the territories, legislation drawn up by the central government and the territories, and a variety of codes. The law was greatly influenced by Japan's major religions—Shintoism, Buddhism, and especially Confucianism. The latter held that man must strive to follow the same immutable laws (*dao*) found in nature. Human laws or rites were developed, therefore, to imitate the *dao*. Kim and Lawson write about the Confucian view of law:

This emphasis on the concrete particulars of a human relationship accords with a general emphasis on conduct conforming to a wise intuitive understanding of the particulars of life itself, and not to a set of logical and abstract general rules. In this view, good conduct following the *dao* establishes social harmony; disputes are disturbances of the natural peace of the social order caused by deviating from the *dao*.[6]

Nowhere is the emphasis on human relationships more clearly seen than in the Confucian view that society is built upon "five cardinal relationships" (ruler and subject, father and son, husband and wife, elder and younger, and friend and friend). The very center of this society is the group (especially the family) rather than the individual. This not only proved to be the core of conduct during Tokugawa Japan but is still central today:

Social relationships are modelled on family relationships, even in emotional content; the rules governing the family are regarded as the ideal rules by which other social relationships should be governed. A business firm is still often felt to be analogous to a family, and family ideals therefore colour the field of labour relations. The employment relationship, like family blood relationships, lasts the workers' lifetime.[7]

Commodore Matthew Perry arrived in Japan with his four warships in 1853. His arrival signalled the end of Japan's isolation (treaties were shortly signed with not only the United States but Russia, England, and the Netherlands), created a political struggle over how to respond to the Western incursion, and led to the establishment of constitution and legal codes based on Western models. The Meji Constitution of 1889 was modelled after the Prussian Constitution and created a strong, centralized government while containing a number of democratic provisions. It established divine sovereignty in the emperor, who would be the supreme head of state. At the same time, the Constitution supported some separation of power (for example, judicial power was now exercised by the courts) and guaranteed a number of human rights. The Meji period also saw the adoption of a number of codes—a Criminal Code and a Code of Criminal Instruction in 1880, a Civil Code and a Commercial Code in 1890, and a Code of Civil Procedure in 1891—many based on the French codes. Institutes to train individuals in Western law and the creation of Western-style courts soon followed. While not all of Western law was easily assimilated into Japanese society, the extent of the reforms were such that "by the end of the 1890s, or about thirty years after the Meji Restoration, Japan came to have a fairly sophisticated system of law.''[8]

The next major set of reforms came at the end of World War II. The Allied forces set out to "democratize" the military government of Japan by reorganizing the judiciary and making it independent from other branches, writing a new constitution, and redrafting many of Japan's codes. The new constitution of Japan consists of eleven chapters and one hundred and three articles. The most important articles with regard to the judicial system are Article 76 (which vests judicial power in the courts) and Article 81 (which gives the Supreme Court the power of judicial review). The period after World War II also saw the drafting of a number of new codes: a Criminal Code in 1947 (this was a revision of the Code of 1907, which had replaced the code drafted in 1880), a Code of Criminal Procedure in 1948 (which replaced the 1922 code), and the rewriting of parts of the Civil Code of 1898, the Commercial Code of 1899, and the Code of Civil Procedure of 1890.

Despite the fact that the Japanese have developed a Westernized legal system and code developed upon the Western model, "centuries of tradition are not so easily put to sleep. Western legal shapes and concepts have been filtered through the Japanese mind, and the living law has been bent to an Eastern task.''[9] This is probably best seen in the continued Japanese aversion to the legal process generally (and to litigation more specifically). Kim and Lawson point out a number of reasons for the Japanese reluctance to utilize the judicial process. Among these are: (1) legal solutions represent mechanical responses to problems that often assess "right" and "wrong" while the traditional Japanese view emphasizes the maintenance of harmony and the attempt to work out solutions through conciliation; (2) the traditional Japanese focus upon the group has resulted in the law not being overly concerned with protecting individual rights; and (3) the law is merely seen as a way of keeping society orderly—law is merely an expedient in a society where disputes arose but not a source of societal pride.[10] The Japanese aversion to litigation is seen in the relative paucity of civil cases brought to the courts—estimated at about 5 percent of the per capita number of cases seen in the United States.[11] The Japanese are, however, quite willing to utilize those legal processes that are consistent with their traditions—for example, conciliation and mediation. The goal of conciliation and mediation is to reconcile differences to create harmony, to decide right and wrong in a particular cases—consistent with the traditional Japanese principle of kenka ry-osebai ("both parties are to be blamed").[12] The importance of conciliation is seen by the fact that, in 1981, 73,154 cases were brought to courts of first instance for conciliation procedures (as opposed to 222,791 new actions brought to courts).[13] Kim and Lawson, therefore, conclude about the role of law in Japan today:

it is not quite true that "they don't like the law in Japan," since the law is a respected teacher of morals. There is, however, a widespread antipathy to litigation, and to the attempt to squeeze life into the law's logical compartments. Western students of contemporary Japanese law must appreciate the general features of the traditional Japanese conception of law if they wish to come to understand the living law of Japan.[14]

THE ORGANIZATION OF THE COURT SYSTEM

Japan has a unitary court system where all trials are carried out under an adversary system. The defendant in criminal cases can either hire his/her own lawyer or have one supplied if he/she can not afford one. The percentage of guilty verdicts in Japan is extremely high—99.7 percent since 1948—because the tradition is for public prosecutors to bring indictments only when they are sure of their cases and "lawyers who succeed in obtaining favorable judgements despite these odds win high public esteem."[15] In addition, the state must pay indemnity for the period that the individual is in state custody in those 0.3 percent of the cases where the accused is acquitted. Individuals may represent themselves in civil trials, but most employ attorneys to argue their cases. There are 575 summary courts in Japan.[16] These courts are each manned by a single judge and handle minor civil (their jurisdiction extends to cases that deal with a value of no more than 300,000 yen) and criminal (those in which fines are the main or alternative means of punishment) matters. The summary courts also have exclusive jurisdiction in summary arbitration in which the parties ask the court to record the agreement that has been reached through arbitration.

Family courts are organized in the same manner and have the same rank as district courts. There are a total of fifty family courts in Japan—one for each prefecture; however, Hokkaido has four. In addition, there are seventy-two separate offices throughout Japan where judges adjudicate domestic matters.[17] These courts deal with family problems (such as divorce) and have jurisdiction over cases involving juveniles between the ages of fourteen and nineteen. The importance of conciliation in Japan is once again underscored by the fact that, in 1981, Japanese family courts handled 83,873 conciliation cases.[18]

The district courts have both original and appellate jurisdiction. Any cases that are not, in the first instance, mandated to be heard by other courts, are brought before the district courts. These courts also hear appeals from the summary courts. District courts are composed of both full judges and assistant judges. Simple cases are heard by a single judge, while more complex cases are heard by a panel of three judges, at least two of whom must be full judges.

There are eight High Courts in Japan: in Fukuoka, Hiroshima, Nagoya, Osaka, Sapporo, Sendai, Takamatsu, and Tokyo. These courts are normally intermediate courts of appeal (although they usually act as the final court of appeal in minor civil cases where no constitutional issue is involved). The High Courts also have original jurisdiction in a number of matters, including election disputes and insurrection cases. Each court is headed by a president appointed by the cabinet. The courts act as collegial bodies, with cases normally heard by three judges (insurrection cases must be heard by a panel of five).

The Japanese Supreme Court is located in Tokyo and staffed by fifteen justices, a chief justice and fourteen others. Each of the justices is appointed by the cabinet (the chief justice is designated by the cabinet and appointed by the emperor). The Supreme Court is the final court of appeal in Japan. It is composed of a grand (all 15 members) and three petty (5 members each) benches. A case must be heard by the Grand Bench if:

(i) it involves a constitutional issue for which there is no existing precedent of the Supreme Court, (ii) it concerns a non-constitutional point of law on which a petty bench has found it appropriate to overrule the precedent of the Supreme Court, or (iii) the opinion of the Justices in a petty bench ended up in a tie. In addition, if a petty bench considers that the case under consideration contains an issue of great importance, it will refer the case to a grand bench for decision.[19]

Justices of the Supreme Court must express their views on each case in writing. Because the Court has an enormous workload (for example, in 1981 it handed down judgments on 1,459 civil cases and 2,300 criminal cases), it is staffed by twenty research clerks who do much of the research involved in the hearing of cases.[20] These individuals are recruited from among the best judges of the inferior courts. Their opinions are highly regarded and their comments on important cases are published yearly. A judicial assembly of all fifteen judges is also responsible for the administration of the judiciary in Japan. Other administrative tasks linked to the judiciary are handled by the Ministry of Justice. The minister of justice is a member of the cabinet and is responsible for personnel decisions related to all public procurators. The Ministry is part of the executive branch, but a number of its major bureaus deal with topics (such as prisons, parole, amnesty, commutation of sentences, etc.) linked to the judicial system.

THE PERSONNEL OF THE LAW

The Japanese legal profession is divided into three groups: judges (under the supervision of the Supreme Court), procurators (supervised by the Ministry of Justice), and lawyers (headed by the Nichibenren, the Japanese Federation of Bar Associations). All three of these groups are trained at the Legal Research and Training Institute. After graduation, however, they go their separate ways and follow their own career paths. Individuals usually think of themselves in terms of their own legal functions and not as members of the legal profession. There has been some talk about unifying the profession by allowing for exchanges within it in order to prevent judges and/or procurators from becoming too heavily entrenched in the bureaucracy. This idea has, however, fallen into disuse, and there are now no lawyers who become either public procurators or judges (except for those who are appointed to the Supreme Court). There is an occasional transfer, however, between the bench and the procuracy, and legal scholars are sometimes appointed to the bench.

Lawyers

Attorneys, known originally as *daigennin* (representative) were first authorized to represent clients in civil cases in 1872. No qualifications were established for the profession, and some unscrupulous individuals became attorneys (in fact, the term *daigennin* was one "which sometimes carried a connotation of the shyster or pettifoger").[21] The daigennin were required, in 1876, to pass an examination administered by local authorities and to obtain a license from the Ministry of Justice. The right to counsel in a criminal case, a national examination, and attorneys' associations in each court district were established shortly thereafter. By the 1890s private law schools had been established, and a more rigorous examination was required for lawyers, now called *bengoshi* (attorneys-at-law). The prestige of the profession still remained low, however, and attorneys were supervised by the procuracy. The next major change in the status and roles of attorneys came with the revision of the Attorneys Law in 1933. This both established more rigorous training for attorneys and gave them somewhat more autonomy—both of which increased the status of the profession. Post-war reforms both increased the training for and responsibilities of lawyers and brought that branch of the profession to its present level of fairly high prestige.[22]

There were approximately 12,000 attorneys registered on the Practicing Attorneys Rolls in 1981. In fact, because of the large number of older attorneys (30 percent of those on the rolls in 1970 were over 65 years of age) the actual number of those in practice is even smaller. Of those in practice, 46 percent were in the cities of Tokyo, Osaka, and Nogoya. This produced a serious imbalance and shortage of attorneys in some parts of Japan. For example, while the national average is nearly 1 attorney/10,000 (approximately one-twentieth of the attorney/population ratio found in the United States), only Tokyo, Osaka, and Okinawa have figures of less than 1/10,000, with 15 of the 47 prefectures having more than 30,000 people/attorney and 18 with more than 20,000/attorney. The small increase of 1,300 attorneys over the last decade (largely because of the restrictive admission practices of the Legal Training and Research Institute) gives a clear indication that this problem is not likely to be alleviated in the near future.[23]

Legal education in Japan is similar to that found in many continental European nations. There are 88 undergraduate law faculties (52 with graduate progams) that graduate an excess of 35,000 students each year.[24] This number is somewhat misleading, for the vast proportion of those who graduate from law programs do not enter the legal profession; many prefer government service or to work for corporations, and less than 2 percent pass the National Law Examination. Most students enter the usually four-year program at eighteen to twenty years of age. Students wish to enter the most prestigious universities (Tokyo and Kyoto universities are among the top) both because their chances of passing the national examination and obtaining a better corporate position are enhanced by graduating from these universities.[25] Because the purpose of undergraduate legal education is to train generalists, only the latter half of the students' education focuses on legal training (the first half is dedicated to the study of the humanities). Some students may wish to pursue a *daigakuin*, or graduate course, after completion of the undergraduate exam. This is divided into two cycles: a two-year course of study corresponding to an L.L.M. (Master of Laws) degree and an additional three years leading to the equivalent of a Ph.D. degree in the law. This largely theoretical course of study is most attractive to those who wish to teach in the law faculties (the other avenue for such a career is to become a research assistant).

After graduation from the undergraduate law program, students wishing to pursue a career in law must take the National Law Exam. The exam is given yearly and administered by the Ministry of Justice. Japan's leading judges, lawyers, procurators, and law professors make up the exam, which is composed of three parts: a multiple-choice exam on constitutional, civil, and criminal law; essays on seven subjects (constitutional, criminal, civil, and commercial law are mandated); and an oral exam covering the same seven topics. The number who pass the examination is staggeringly small—for example, in 1980 less than 2 percent (486 of 28,656) passed.[26] This pass rate has remained stable for the past few years and continues a pattern, established over the past three decades, of a continuously declining pass rate.[27] Most students now generally take the exam four times before passing and, consequently, do not enter the Legal Training and Research Institute until the age of twenty-seven. The small number of those who pass is largely dictated by budgetary constraints as well as the limited number of internships available in the courts, procurators' offices, and attorneys' offices as dictated by the institute. While there has been a great deal of discussion about the value of so restricting entrance into the profession, there has been little consensus (and, therefore, there seems little likelihood of change) regarding the examining and training requirements for those wishing to enter the legal profession.[28]

Those who pass the examination receive further training at the Legal Training and Research Institute, an agency of the Supreme Court. The president of the institute is appointed from among the judges of the Supreme Court, and the faculty are appointed by the Federation of Japanese Attorneys' Association from among Japan's most able judges, procurators, and attorneys. All of those studying at the institute are called "judicial apprentices," regardless of which branch of the profession they ultimately plan to enter. The twenty-four-month program is divided into three phases: (1) an initial four months at the institute, where the apprentice further hones his analytical skills and learns how to prepare legal documents; (2) the second, sixteen-month phase involves field work—here the apprentice is assigned to the civil and criminal section of district courts, district procurators' offices, and prefectural lawyers' associations—each for four months; and (3) a final four-month phase at the institute to "consolidate the field experiences, correct discrepancies between apprentices that inevitably result from uneven field experiences, and, more important, administer final educational polishing.''[29] This final phase is followed by a written and oral examination administered by a committee under the direction of the chief justice of the Supreme Court. Very few students fail this examination. After graduation, the individual selects whether to become an attorney, procurator, or judge (the individual wishing an appointment as a procurator or judge applies to the Ministry of Justice). In recent years approximately 16 percent of the graduates opted to become assistant judges, and about 12 percent chose to be public prosecutors—the remainder chose to become practicing attorneys.[30] Shikita writes about these career choices:

The general tendency is that apprentices older than 35, who attach greater value to material affluence, or who wish to stay in a specific locality, become practicing lawyers. Younger apprentices who tend to be more active and policy oriented, quicker in decision making, and more fond of group activity, are more likely to become public prosecutors. And younger apprentices who are more meticulous in legal thinking, more fond of individual activity, or more interested in civil and commercial law, are apt to join the judiciary.[31]

Lawyers are organized into the Nichibenren, a private organization, corresponding to the national bar association. There is one such association in each prefecture in Japan (except for Tokyo and Hokkaido, which have three each), and lawyers must register with the bar association.

There are, in addition to the practicing attorney, four kinds of ''quasi-lawyers'' in Japan today. They are: (1) 14,000 judicial scriveners, who draft documents and help to register various transactions at the registry office but are not allowed to give legal advice or to perform functions normally allotted to the practicing attorney; (2) 25,000 administrative scriveners, who draft papers that are submitted to governmental offices; (3) 2,000 patent attorneys, who deal with patent, trademark, and similar cases; and (4) 30,000 tax agents, who give advice, represent clients, and prepare papers to be filed with the various tax offices in Japan.[32]

Judges

Judges in Japan fall into two groups: the chief justice and other judges of the Supreme Court, and judges of all the other courts. There are over 2,700 judges today in Japan.[33] The number of judges has increased over the decades (there were 1,134 judges in 1920, 1,249 in 1930, and 1,541 in 1940), but the increase has levelled off in recent years (there were 2,261 in 1950 and 2,387 in 1960).[34]

Each Japanese judge is appointed by the cabinet from a list submitted by the Supreme Court. Once appointed, judges remain assistant judges (there are over 700 today) for ten years, and almost all are reappointed as full judges at the end of the ten-year period. During this period the new judges receive additional training from the institute, and, by the end of the ten-year period, they have the same duties as full judges.[35] The only exception to this pattern are the nearly

800 summary court judges, who may be appointed from among nonjurists who have had a good deal of experience with the law, as well as from among former judges, assistant judges with at least three years' experience, public prosecutors, lawyers, and law professors. These judges are appointed by a screening committee composed of Supreme Court judges and other members of the profession.[36]

There are fifteen members of the Japanese Supreme Court. They must be at least forty years of age (though they tend to be appointed in their sixties) and there may be no discrimination according to sex (though through 1981 there have been no women appointed to the Court).[37] The law requires that ten of the appointees be judges, lawyers, prosecutors, or professors of law. The remaining five must be "men of learning and experience." Most of those in the latter category are former bureaucrats, public prosecutors, and legal scholars.

Members of the judiciary constitute an elite. For example, a major study of Japanese High Court judges found them to be middle-aged (the median age was fifty-five), graduates of the most prestigious Japanese universities (72 percent of the High Court and 82 percent of Supreme Court judges graduated from Tokyo and Kyoto universities), and the children of upper-middle-class fathers (11 percent of whom were judges or lawyers and 10 percent of whom were governmental officials).[38] The same pattern appears true for members of the Supreme Court. In addition, there is a clear road to appointment to Japan's highest court:

In regard to the judiciary, the first and crucial rung, at least up to 1966, was graduation from the law faculty of Tokyo University. . . . After graduation . . . the typical steps upward are: assistant judge, district judge (a long stay in Tokyo is helpful), high court judge, president of one of the lesser high courts, president of the Tokyo High Court, and finally the Supreme Court. Assignment to the Supreme Court as research official (cho-sakan) early in a judge's career is helpful, and selection as president of the Legal Training and Research Institute is even better. Sometimes a president of one of the larger high courts, such as Osaka's, has been appointed to the Supreme Court. Although not every president of the Tokyo High Court has gone to the Supreme Court, when there is a vacancy in the court, the Tokyo High Court president is usually the most visible candidate.[39]

After appointment to the bench, a judge generally has lifetime tenure. He may only be removed "for disability, neglect of duty, malfeasance or unbecoming conduct."[40] Japan does, however, have an interesting process, in which appointments to the Supreme Court are reviewed by the Japanese people. Article 79 of the Constitution notes that Supreme Court justices are to be evaluated by the electorate in the first election to the House of Representatives after their appointment. A justice is dismissed if a majority of the voters place an "x" on the ballot, indicating their displeasure with the justice. This process occurs every ten years after the initial evaluation (given that most Supreme Court justices are appointed in their sixties, it usually takes place only one time). As might be expected, no justice has ever been removed by this method.

Public Prosecutors

There are approximately 1,200 public prosecutors in Japan today.[41] District and high prosecutors offices work with the courts at those levels. The public prosecutors are responsible for initiating all criminal actions. They are appointed by the cabinet but can only be dismissed for cause by a special committee made up of six members of the national legislature and five members of the general public.

Juries

Jury trials in courts of first instance were established in 1926. Twelve jurors were to be selected at random from the population at large. Many Japanese refused, however, to utilize jury trials, especially in those cases involving penalties of life imprisonment or death. In addition, the courts were never bound by the juries' decisions and could replace members of the jury. As a result, jury trials were suspended in 1943, and Japan does not utilize juries today.

While there is some concern regarding the relative size of the legal profession in Japan, it is clear that members of that profession are relatively well trained and sensitive to the concerns of the three branches of the profession. This has led to an efficient justice system in Japan. Shikita writes about this:

Because members of each branch are well acquainted with the background information and situations of the other two branches, they really understand the roles of the other parties in legal proceedings. In every district, judges, prosecutors and practicing lawyers have established standing and ad hoc committees to deal with specific problems. . . .

This mutual understanding between judges and prosecutors also facilitates the coordination of governmental agencies at both national and local levels. In addition to holding formal meetings, the judiciary, procuracy, and the police (or any two of them) regularly form study groups to examine possible policy implications, potential complications, and, whenever new policies are adopted, they see that the total system is optimized. In such meetings, the obligations of each organ are discussed frankly and coordinated for optimal effects on the system.[42]

PUBLIC PERCEPTIONS AND THE ROLE OF THE COURTS

The period since the end of World War II has seen a dramatic reversal in the public's perception of the courts and the personnel of the law. Danielski notes four factors resulting in low public awareness of the judiciary and low prestige for judges in the period before the outbreak of World War II: (1) Because of the traditional Japanese antipathy to the law, there was little contact between the common man and members of the judiciary and, "judges lived in a world that was out of sight and usually out of mind, a world associated with criminals, dishonor, and punishment. Judges were viewed in the same manner as procurators; in fact, judge and procurator used to sit on the same bench, and it is not clear which had greater status."[43] (2) Because judges were not perceived as being at the top of the beaucratic hierarchy, the more competent left the judiciary, thus further devaluing public perceptions regarding judges. (3) Many nonjudicial bureaucrats were also trained in the law. More importantly, few of those at the top of their class at Tokyo or Kyoto universities decided to join the judiciary. (4) The behavior of judges tended to be guided by a desire not to meddle in political events and to deal with problems from a technical, legal, and often nonpractical viewpoint—characteristics that would not tend to give the jurist either high visibility or prestige.[44] As but one example of the negative perceptions of the profession, one knowledgeable government officer described the functioning of the courts during the Meji period thusly:

A glance at the courts . . . of today in our country reveals that decisions are not rendered very quickly. They are unable to maintain fair trials. . . . This is probably because the courts are not independent; the judges often do not realize the nature of their position and responsibility, they take into account personal considerations and play politics, they are moved by favoritism and attempt to patch up the mistakes of the police and officials, they do not render judgements in accordance with whether or not a fact exists, and many rely upon the mistaken belief that the way to make one's fame and fortune is to give judgements which will ingratiate oneself with the government . . . procurators, too, do not handle a defendant's case pursuant to their beliefs, but are inclined strongly to pressure judges in compliance with the directions of the police.[45]

A number of public opinion surveys indicate more positive perceptions of judges and procurators today. For example, a 1971 survey asked respondents to rank judges, procurators, lawyers, professors, and politicians with regard to a number of characteristics. Judges were ranked first and procurators second (with 57.0 percent and 39.5 percent, respectively) as a "friend of justice," judges first and procurators third (with 71.9 percent and 62.2 percent) as "trustworthy," judges first and procurators fourth (with 85.9 percent and 78.4 percent) as "intelligent," and judges third and procurators fourth (with 17.1 percent and 11.3 percent) as instilling a "good feeling about them."[46] The low ranking for the last item may be due to the fact that Japanese have indicated that courts are "scary" places.[47] A second survey has ranked judges second (after professors) in terms of occupational prestige.[48]

As previously noted, lawyers have not been highly regarded in Japan. Danielski writes:

Lawyers were not members of the same profession as judges and procurators, and in pre-Occupation Japan could not aspire to those positions the way lawyers in the United States and Great Britain could. Because of the non-litigious character of the society and its emphasis on informal and personal means of dispute resolution, the lawyer's skills were neither especially needed nor valued. Japan's movement in the direction of a contract society in recent years and the Occupation's legal reforms have helped the status of lawyers. Appointment to the bench—even to the Supreme Court—is now a possibility for them. The prestige of the lawyer in Japan seems to be on the rise, but compared with his American counterpart, he still has a long way to go.[49]

The two previously cited polls demonstrate the more positive public perception of lawyers today. The 1971 study found lawyers ranked third (with 38.9 percent) as a "friend of justice," second (with 62.2 percent) as being "trustworthy," fourth (with 78.4 percent) as being "intelligent," and second (with 20.2 percent) as promoting a "good feeling about them."[50] The second study found lawyers to be ranked third in occupational prestige, after professors and judges.[51]

The issue of the independence of the judiciary is one measure both of the perception of the judiciary and the courts as well as the role(s) of the latter. The Japanese Constitution supported both judicial independence and the separation of powers. Article 76 established the independence of the judiciary by stating that "judges are independent in the exercise of their conscience and shall be bound only by the Constitution and the law." Article 78 further states that judges cannot be removed (other than by impeachment) unless they are deemed physically or mentally incompetent to perform their judicial duties. As already noted, the courts are not only protected from executive interference but there is independence within the various branches of the judicial system. The courts, procuracy, and bar are also separate from and independent of each other. There are only two areas where there are any limits in judicial independence: (1) because Supreme Court judges are appointed by the cabinet, there is an indirect political influence in that it is unlikely that anyone unacceptable to the party in power will be appointed; and (2) there is a popular review of Supreme Court judges in the first general election (and every ten years thereafter) after their appointment to the Court—as already noted, however, no Supreme Court justice has been dismissed through this procedure.

The decades since the end of World War II have seen the development of a judicial review function by the final appellate or Supreme Court in a number of countries—for example, France, Germany, and Italy. This has also occurred in Japan. This has been a remarkable development because in prewar Japan "courts had almost nothing to do with the interpretation of the Constitution and it was hardly their responsibility to enforce the Constitution."[52] This changed when Article 81 of the 1947 Constitution gave the Supreme Court the power of judicial review by providing that it "is the court of last resort with power to determine the constitutionality of any law, order, regulation, or official act." The Court did, however, view its power in a very "restrained" manner in the first few decades of its existence. While many criticized the "remarkable reluctance" of the Court to act more aggressively, it has been maintained that this restraint was part of a rational strategy designed to increase the power and legitimacy of the Court.[53]

Many reasons may be offered for the restrained nature of the Japanese Supreme Court. First, the Court has largely been manned by relatively conservative appointees who have been reluctant to overturn governmental decisions. Second, judges of the Court have been members of a fairly homogeneous elite who have shared similar socializing experiences as well as similar political attitudes. Third, courts in federal systems have tended to play a more active role because they are often called upon to define powers of the various governmental units. Japan, as a unitary state, would, therefore, not likely have an activist court. Fourth, there was considerable public sentiment against portions of the new Constitution (for example, sections dealing with individual rights). Given this, it is not surprising to see the Court as unwilling to loosely interpret some of these provisions. Fifth, it is unrealistic to expect the Court to assume an activist stance given the traditional Japanese antipathy to litigation. Sixth, the rapid turnover of the judges on the bench (few serve for more than ten years) would make it difficult for judges to gain the constitutional expertise necessary to make them more willing to assume a more activist pose. Seventh, the large size of the court makes it unwieldy, and the requirement that eight members must vote to strike down a statute (even if there are the constitutionally minimum eleven justices present) makes it difficult for the court to invalidate a law.[54]

One of the areas where the Court has been most widely criticized for its reluctance to invalidate governmental actions has been its interpretation of the famous "Peace clause" (Article 9) of the Constitution in which Japan renounced war as a sovereign right of the nation as well as the use or the threat of the use of force in international disputes. In four specific cases the Court has been widely criticized by the left-wing for its refusal to directly confront the issues in Article 9 as well as to outlaw the maintenance of military forces in Japan or to view the 1950 United States/Japan Security Treaty (or its renewal in 1960) as a violation of that article.[55]

Despite the Court's reluctance to take a more judicially active position, it did declare more acts unconstitutional (five) in the period from 1947 to 1978 than did the United States Supreme Court in the period between 1790 and 1858 (two).[56] Bolz has, in fact, indicated a change in the Court's position:

Though the early United States Court also declared unconstitutional several very significant state laws, it clearly showed "remarkable" restraint vis-à-vis the national legislature. As the Japanese court has gradually acquired experience in exercising judicial review, it has become more willing to challenge the Diet in significant legal areas.[57]

The Court has recently shifted to a more activist mode by overturning three statutes: one involving a portion of the Penal Code that prescribed a more severe penalty for the murder of a relative than for a nonrelation; a second indicating where new pharmacies might be established; and a third much more political decision invalidating the apportionment plan of the lower house of the legislature.[58]

It is unlikely, given the aforementioned restrictions against judicial activism, that the Japanese court will ever assume the same activist role as has the American Supreme Court. However, it can be argued that, by acting with such restraint, it has increased its own legitimacy and, by doing so, likely strengthened the Japanese political system. Bolz writes:

the degree of success that the Court has achieved represents a remarkable break with the past. Testing acts of the Diet in terms of adherence to universal legal principles is a dramatic departure from the traditional idea of unqualified loyalty to the community. The infusion of such universal principles, rather than weakening the state, as had long been feared, may well contribute to the long-run stability and strength of the Japanese polity.[59]

The Court has, unquestionably, become a much more accepted institution in Japan. A recent study, for example, found that 34 percent of those sampled had "very favorable" or "favorable" feelings about the Court as opposed to only 18 percent, who had "unfavorable" or "very unfavorable" feelings.[60] More importantly, there is little doubt that this popular support will likely lead to a more positive role for the Court in the decades to come:

Perhaps as important as the Court's impact thus far has been its popular support, which has developed gradually. In 1947 the Supreme Court came into being largely because the Occupation authorities insisted upon it, and so it was written into the MacArthur Constitution. Its history has been like that of the Constitution. It was accepted politely but not altogether willingly, marked for revision after the Occupation, tolerated, Japanized little by little, and finally established as part of Japanese life. Indeed, the Court is coming to political maturity more quickly than many expected, even more quickly than did its American counterpart after which it was modelled. In its maturity much is expected of it, no less, in the words of a recent editorial, than giving "real life to the Constitution." No court can fully meet that expectation, but the Japanese Supreme Court has a better chance of at least some success than most constitutional courts.[61]

NOTES

1. Y. Noda, *Introduction to Japanese Law*, trans. and ed., A. H. Angelo (Tokyo: University of Tokyo Press, 1976), pp. 159–60.

2. Ibid., p. 21.

3. Ibid., pp. 22–23.

4. See ibid., pp. 26–39 for a discussion of these two periods.

5. Ibid., pp. 31–32.

6. C. Kim and C. M. Lawson, "The Law of Subtle Mind: The Traditional Japanese Conception of Law," *International and Comparative Law Quarterly* 28 (1978), p. 494.

7. Ibid., p. 499.

8. H. Kojo and M. Kojo, "The Legal System of Japan," in K. Redden, ed., *Modern Legal Systems Cyclopedia*, vol. 2 (Buffalo: William S. Hein and Co., 1984), p. 284.

9. Kim and Lawson, "The Law of Subtle Mind," p. 506.

10. Ibid., pp. 501–6.

11. R. C. Christopher, *The Japanese Mind: The Goliath Explained* (New York: Simon and Schuster, 1983), p. 165.

12. Kim and Lawson, "The Law of Subtle Mind," p. 511.

13. Kojo and Kojo, "The Legal System of Japan," p. 313.

14. Kim and Lawson, "The Law of Subtle Mind," p. 511.

15. J. Nomura, *Japan's Judicial System*, "About Japan" Series no. 15 (Tokyo: Kinji Kawamura, Foreign Press Center, 1981), p. 17.

16. Kojo and Kojo, "The Legal System of Japan," p. 303.

17. Ibid., pp. 303, 305.

18. Ibid., p. 306.

19. Ibid., p. 304.

20. Ibid.

21. T. Hattori (assisted by R. W. Rabinowitz), "The Legal Profession in Japan: Its Historical Development and Present State," in A. T. von Mehren, ed., *Law in Japan: The Legal Order in a Changing Society* (Cambridge, Mass: Harvard University Press, 1963), p. 127.

22. Kojo and Kojo, "The Legal System of Japan," pp. 317–18.

23. Ibid., pp. 319–20.

24. Ibid., p. 324

25. Noda, *Introduction to Japanese Law*, p. 141 writes: "A law degree, provided it is from a faculty with a good reputation, opens the door to socially elevated positions in big companies or within the government. In fact, the top personnel of the big companies and of the administration are almost exclusively persons who have law degrees."

26. Nomura, *Japan's Judicial System*, p. 4.

27. For example, H. Tanaka and M. D. H. Smith, *The Japanese Legal System: Introductory Cases and Materials* (Tokyo: University of Tokyo Press, 1976), p. 577, indicate the following pass rates: 1949—10.5 percent, 1950—9.8 percent, 1955—4.2 percent, 1960—4.2 percent, 1965—3.9 percent, 1970—2.5 percent, 1975—1.7 percent.

28. Kojo and Kojo, "The Legal System of Japan," p. 326.

29. M. Shikita, "Law Under the Rising Sun: How Lawyers, Prosecutors and Judges Are Educated and Trained in Japan," *Judges Journal* 20 (Winter 1981), p. 45.

30. Ibid.

31. Ibid.

32. Kojo and Kojo, "The Legal System of Japan," pp. 322–324.

33. Ibid.

34. Hattori, "The Legal Profession in Japan," p. 150.

35. See Shikita, "Law Under the Rising Sun" for an excellent summary of the in-service training of Japanese judges.

36. Nomura, *Japan's Judicial System*, p. 9.

37. Ibid., p. 5.

38. J. A. Dator, "The Life History and Attitudes of Japanese High Court Judges," Part 1, *The Western Political Quarterly* 20, no. 2 (June 1967), pp. 408–39.

39. D. J. Danielski, "The Supreme Court of Japan: An Exploratory Study," in G. Schubert and D. J. Danielski, eds., *Comparative Judicial Behavior* (New York: Oxford University Press, 1969), pp. 128–29.

40. R. Y. Thornton, "Training Lawyers and Judges in New Japan," *Judicature* 58, no. 3 (October 1974), p. 132.

41. Nomura, *Japan's Judicial System*, p. 10.

42. Shikita, "Law Under the Rising Sun," p. 46.

43. D. J. Danielski, "The People and the Court in Japan," in J. Grossman and J.

Tannenhaus, eds., *Frontiers of Judicial Research* (New York: John Wiley and Sons, Inc., 1969), p. 47.

44. Ibid., pp. 47–48.

45. I. H. Ruisan, *Hosei Kankei Shiryo* (Confidential Miscellanea, Materials Pertaining to Legal Matters) 89–90 (Hirobumi Ito, ed., 1934), cited in Hattori, "The Legal Profession in Japan," p. 116.

46. Nihon Bunka Kaigi, *Nihon Jin No Hoishiki* (Japanese Legal Consciousness), 1973, pp. 186–89, cited in D. J. Danielski, "The Political Impact of the Supreme Court," *Notre Dame Lawyer* 49 (June 1974), p. 977.

47. Danielski, "The Political Impact of the Supreme Court," p. 977.

48. Japanese Sociological Association, "Social Stratifications and Mobility in Japan," in International Sociological Association, *Transactions of the Second World Congress of Sociology* (1954), pp. 414–31; and R. W. Rabinowitz, "The Japanese Lawyer—A Study in the Sociology of the Legal Profession" (Ph.D. diss., Harvard University, 1955) cited in D. J. Danielski, "The People and the Court in Japan," p. 52.

49. Danielski, "The Supreme Court of Japan," pp. 124–25.

50. *Nihon Jin No Hoishiki*, cited in Danielski, "The Political Impact of the Supreme Court," p. 977.

51. "Social Stratification and Mobility in Japan" and "The Japanese Lawyer," cited in Danielski, "The People and the Court in Japan," p. 52.

52. Y. Okudaira, "The Japanese Supreme Court and Judicial Review," *Lawasia Law Journal* 3 (1972), p. 69.

53. H. F. Bolz, "Judicial Review in Japan: The Strategy of Restraint," *Hastings International and Comparative Law Review* 4, no. 1 (Fall 1980), pp. 88–142.

54. Ibid., pp. 113–33.

55. *Japan v. Sakata* (1959), *Japan v. Nozaki* (1967), *Japan v. Sakane* (1969), and *Ministry of Agriculture and Forestry v. Ito* (1976). See Bolz, "Judicial Review in Japan," pp. 106–13 for a discussion of these cases.

56. Ibid., p. 134.

57. Ibid.

58. Ibid., pp. 134–37.

59. Ibid., p. 141.

60. Danielski, "The Political Impact of the Supreme Court," p. 972.

61. Ibid., p. 980.

BIBLIOGRAPHY

Abe, H. (assisted by D. F. Cavers and T. S. Williams). "Education of the Legal Profession in Japan." In A. T. von Mehren, ed. *Law in Japan: The Legal Order in a Changing Society.* Cambridge, Mass.: Harvard University Press, 1963. Pp. 153–87.

Beer, L. W. *The Constitutional Case Law of Japan: Selected Supreme Court Decisions, 1961–1970.* Seattle: University of Washington Press, 1977.

Bolz, H. F. "Judicial Review in Japan: The Strategy of Restraint." *Hastings International and Comparative Law Review* 4, no. 1 (Fall 1980), pp. 88–142.

Bunge, F. M., ed. *Japan: A Country Study.* Washington, D.C.: Government Printing Office, Foreign Area Studies, 1983.

Choi, D. "A Study of Japanese Judicial Review System." *Seoul Law Journal* 12 (1978), pp. 68–98.

Christopher, R. C. *The Japanese Mind: The Goliath Explained.* New York: Simon and Schuster, 1983.

Danielski, D. J. "The Supreme Court of Japan; An Exploratory Study." In G. Schubert and D. J. Danielski, eds. *Comparative Judicial Behavior.* New York: Oxford University Press, 1969. Pp. 121–50.

———. "The People and the Court in Japan." In J. Grossman and J. Tannenhaus, eds. *Frontiers of Judicial Research.* New York: John Wiley and Sons, Inc., 1969. Pp. 45–72.

———. "The Political Impact of the Supreme Court." *Notre Dame Lawyer* 49 (June 1974), pp. 955–80.

Dator, J. A. "The Life History and Attitudes of Japanese High Court Judges." Part 1, *The Western Political Quarterly* 20, no. 2 (June 1967), pp. 408–39.

Fujii, S. *The Constitution of Japan: A Historical Survey.* Tokyo: Hokoseido Press, 1965.

Hattori, T. (assisted by R. W. Rabinowitz). "The Legal Profession in Japan: Its Historical Development and Present State." In A.T. von Mehren, ed. *Law in Japan: The Legal Order in a Changing Society.* Cambridge, Mass.: Harvard University Press, 1963. Pp. 111–52.

Henderson, D. F. "Japanese Judicial Review of Legislation: The First Twenty Years." In D. F. Henderson, ed. *The Constitution of Japan: Its First Twenty Years, 1947–1967.* Seattle: University of Washington Press, 1968. Pp. 115–46.

Itoh, H. "How Judges Think in Japan." *American Journal of Comparative Law* 18 (1970), pp. 775–804.

Kim, C., and C. M. Lawson. "The Law of Subtle Mind: The Traditional Japanese Conception of Law." *International and Comparative Law Quarterly* 28 (1978), pp. 491–513.

Kojo, H., and M. Kojo. "The Legal System of Japan." In K. R. Redden, ed. *Modern Legal Systems Cyclopedia*, vol. 2. Buffalo, New York: William S. Hein and Co., 1984. Pp. 275–338.

Maki, J. M., ed. *The Constitutional Case Law of Japan: Selected Supreme Court Decisions, 1961–1970.* Seattle: University of Washington Press, 1977.

McMahon, M. M. "Legal Education in Japan." *American Bar Association Journal* 60 (November 1974), pp. 1376–80.

Noda, Y. *Introduction to Japanese Law.* Translated and edited by A. H. Angelo. Tokyo: University of Tokyo Press, 1976.

Nomura, J. *Japan's Judicial System* "About Japan" Series no. 15. Tokyo: Kinji Kawamura, Foreign Press Center, 1981.

Okudaira, Y. "The Japanese Supreme Court and Judicial Review." *Lawasia Law Journal* 3 (1972), pp. 67–105.

Richardson, B. H., and S. C. Flanagan. *Politics in Japan: A Country Study.* Boston: Little, Brown and Co., 1984.

Shikita, M. "Law Under the Rising Sun: How Lawyers, Prosecutors and Judges Are Educated and Trained in Japan." *Judges Journal* 20 (Winter 1981), pp. 42–47.

Takayanagi, K. (assisted by T. L. Blakemore). "A Century of Innovation: The Development of Japanese Law, 1868–1961." In A. T. von Mehren, ed. *Law in Japan: The Legal Order in a Changing Society.* Cambridge, Mass.: Harvard University Press, 1963. Pp. 5–40.

Tanaka, H., and M. D. H. Smith. *The Japanese Legal System: Introductory Cases and Materials*. Tokyo: University of Tokyo Press, 1976.

Thornton, R. Y. "Training Lawyers and Judges in New Japan." *Judicature* no. 3 (October 1974), pp. 129–33.

Ushiomi, T. "Judges in Japan." *Tokyo University Institute of Social Science Annals* (1974), pp. 1–26.

10

LATIN AMERICA

Scott B. MacDonald

Belonging to the Romano-Germanic family of law and deriving from a common Iberian historical and cultural tradition, the legal systems of Latin American nations have developed along similar lines, although differences exist owing to geographical and political factors. In a geographical sense, Latin America varies tremendously, ranging from Mexico in the north to the relative isolation of Chile in the Andes and Bolivia and Paraguay in the interior. In the same fashion, the role of those involved in the practice of law and the importance of the legal system vary from country to country. The importance and perception of the legal systems of Latin American nations are also dependent on the political climate, be it democratic or authoritarian.

Latin America covers all of South America (except the Guianas—Guyana, Suriname, and French Guiana), Central America (except Belize), and Mexico. Added to these nations are the Caribbean states of the Dominican Republic, Haiti, and Cuba. Those nations excluded from this definition largely derive from British, French, and Dutch colonial traditions and some still not independent.[1] Although Haiti is French-speaking and its population is predominantly of African descent, its history is closely related to the Dominican Republic's and, to a lesser extent, to the rest of Latin America. In further outlining the scope of this study, Latin America includes all the area named in the geographic and cultural definitions, except for Cuba, which has pursued a different path to political and socioeconomic development since 1959, when Fidel Castro came to power. That leaves sixteen nations: Argentina, Bolivia, Brazil, Colombia, Costa Rica, Chile, the Dominican Republic, Ecuador, El Salvador, Guatemala, Honduras, Nicaragua, Paraguay, Panama, Peru, and Uruguay. Considering that a country-by-country review would be exceedingly lengthy, a concentration on six nations with varying political systems offers an opportunity to make comparisons and parallels.

In selecting Argentina, Brazil, El Salvador, Haiti, Mexico, and Venezuela, six different experiences and political systems are observable in their impact on the evolution of the respective legal systems. As the largest country in Latin America, Brazil has moved from being an authoritarian regime to a democratic state. Although the transition is not complete, the legal system has played a significant role in the political reforms. El Salvador is a political ambiguity; the nation is torn by civil strife as it gropes toward democratic government. Seeking, under president Jose Napoleon Duarte, to become fully democratic, the legal system is an important element in the nation's life. Argentina has recently made the transition from military rule to democratic civil rule, an event marked by the renewed significance of the legal system, especially in the realm of civil-military relations. Venezuela is a democracy that, since the 1960s, has followed the rule of law. Mexico, with its close proximity to the United States, has developed its own somewhat unique legal system, shaped by its revolutionary tradition. In sharp contrast to the larger Latin American nations, Haiti's legal system is weak and ineffective, as it is completely overshadowed by the power of the Duvalier family.

There are other reasons for examining these six nations. First and foremost, Argentina, Brazil, Mexico, and Venezuela are four of the most powerful nations in Latin America. Other nations look to them for guidance. Traditionally, they have influenced the affairs of other states. Argentina and Brazil have long sought to gain dominance of the border states of Bolivia, Uruguay, and Paraguay while seeking an alliance with Chile and Peru at different points in history. This tradition of geo-politics has also had an impact on the development of legal systems as reflected by the fact that the Paraguayian system heavily borrowed from the Argentine. In the northern part of Latin America, both Venezuela and Mexico have sought influence in Central America and the Caribbean. Considering the past and acknowledging that these four nations are now very much involved in the future direction of Latin America, a study of their respective legal systems is highly important.

El Salvador and Haiti are examined in this chapter because of the interrelationship between their political and legal systems. Moreover, these two nations, much smaller in size and population, are increasingly part of the North American consciousness. The United States is involved in both for political and economic reasons. Not only is American aid given to the Salvadorean and Haitian governments, but the peoples of those nations are coming to the United States in growing numbers. The crucial concepts of law and order, basic to any society, have taken on different meanings in these nations. In El Salvador, there is a struggle to create a society ruled by law while under attack from the left and the right; in Haiti society is ruled by laws that are dictated and manipulated by a powerful family, the Duvaliers. In many respects, the Haitian case reflects an authoritarian tradition in Latin America now evident only in that nation and in Chile and Paraguay. Haiti further offers a very good example of the manipulation of the legal system by political leaders.

Although these six nations have developed differently in the twentieth century, they share a characteristic common to most Latin American systems. In analyzing the region's "civic culture," Claudio Veliz acknowledged the existence of the "centralist" character of Latin American social and political arrangements, which stemmed from the long period of Spanish and Portuguese colonial rule.[2] To Veliz, the establishment of Iberian empires in Latin America was highly influenced by the Castilian centralization of power and legal authority at the Cortes de Madrigal in 1476. As he noted: "Aged and hardened by centuries of struggle, at the time of the great discoveries Castile had evolved an efficient form of centralized government, a reasonably well-organized bureaucratic establishment, a settled relationship between Church and state, and a system of laws sufficiently developed and complex to be imposed wholesale over a conquered people."[3] Consequently, the Iberian nations created a centralist, civilian, bureaucratic, and legalistic style of politics from which the future Latin American republics have not fully departed.

Concentration of power at the political center and in the person and office of the executive, then the king, was passed on to the New World in the person of the viceroys, who represented imperial authority. This tendency to centralize was strengthened by the absence of (1) the feudal experience from the Latin American tradition; (2) religious nonconformity and the resulting latitudinarian centralism of the dominant religion; (3) any occurrence or circumstance over time that could conceivably be taken as the counterpart of the European Industrial Revolution; and (4) those ideological, social, and political developments associated with the French Revolution which dramatically changed the character of Western European society during the past century and a half.[4]

The rationalizing and centralizing tendencies inherent in Latin America's bureaucratic establishment existed for two centuries before the fall of the Bastille and have retained their preindustrial character. Therefore, five centuries of centralizing tendencies have had a major impact on the behavior of Latin Americans and have also influenced the evolution of the respective legal systems.

The centralist tradition extended its influence beyond the years of the revolutionary movements for independence in the early 1800s and into the first decades of republican experimentation. A "liberal phase" following independence from Spain was a brief interlude from the centralist tradition. An outward-oriented nationalist surge sought to replace the Spanish traditions with the liberal and more attractive cultures in France and Britain. The authoritarian tendencies of the representatives of the Crown, however, were passed on to the military strongmen, called *caudillos*, who came to dominate. For the legal systems of Latin American states, this meant that legal codes, copied from the Napoleonic Codes, had a marginal effect. The president, often times a *caudillo*, concentrated power and authority into his own person, and the legal system was left with little autonomy. In essence, most Latin American countries have political traditions in which elite perceptions and behavior have been (and in some cases continue to be) key in determining the way in which the political and, ultimately, the legal systems function.[5] Constraints exist, but the centralist tradition dominates.

The centralist tradition is one important element in comprehending Latin America's legal systems. Another significant factor, which has evolved in the opposite direction, has been the tendency of strong individualism. Although governed by the Crown and its colonial representatives in an authoritarian manner, that system was limited, as colonial administrators were unable to enforce all their laws in every corner of the empire.[6] As Gary Wynia noted in a report on the Latin American condition made by an imaginary leader:

Even though we considered ourselves loyal to the Crown, we did not hesitate to ignore its more troublesome laws whenever we thought we could get away with it. Our disobedience to colonial law eventually reached the point of political rebellion in the early nineteenth century, when we took advantage of the defeat of the Spanish Crown by Napoleon to declare our independence.[7]

The tradition of strong individualism overlapped into the postcolonial era. As Wynia's imaginary leader further commented: "Although our wars of liberation freed us from the Crown, we have not abandoned our habit of ignoring laws we find unjust or inconvenient."[8] Strong individualism and the centralist tradition combined to create several generations of *caudillos*, who often built democratic facades to help prolong their stay in office.

By the latter decades of the twentieth century, both of these tendencies, influenced by the liberal and conservative currents of the international system, had undergone important transformations. Following World War I, the tide was liberal and democratic; following the Great Depression, it was conservative and authoritarian. In the aftermath of World War II, democracy and the rule of law was on the rise, only to be terminated by a new authoritarian wave, which commenced in Brazil in 1964. Only a few states developed along a more democratic path—Costa Rica, Colombia, Venezuela, and perhaps Mexico. By the 1980s, redemocratization once again became a dominant force as Argentina, Bolivia, Honduras, the Dominican Republic, and El Salvador have struggled to move away from authoritarianism. The correct use of the legal system, rather than the abuse of the system, has been held up as an important element of the return to democracy. Concern for human rights violations, as in Central America and Argentina, have become battlegrounds for those wishing to uphold the law and make it a foundation of a more progressive civil society.

BRAZIL

The Development of the Legal System

Unlike its smaller Spanish-speaking neighbors, Brazil (Portugal's only American colony) peacefully achieved independence from the metropole, first as an empire in the early 1800s, later becoming a republic dominated by competing regional oligarchical elites. The absence of a violent war of liberation guaranteed a high level of continuity for the legal system. Moreover, the military, although an important political force in the background, did not repeatedly intervene in a direct manner in the nation's political life. Despite the corporatist nature of Getulio Vargas's *Estado Novo* (New State), the Brazilian legal system developed into one of the most respected in Latin America due to the relative degree of autonomy vis-à-vis the other branches of the state.

The *Estado Novo*, with the core years of 1937–1945 when the regime was the most authoritarian, mirrored the rise of corporatism in Brazil under the strong political personality of Vargas. Influenced by the Estado Novo of Salazer's Portugal and the rise of European fascism, the Brazilian leader consolidated the power of the central government over that of the states, especially after the suppression of the 1932 rebellion. The federal system's power over the states was embodied in the 1937 constitution and did not change with the movement away from corporatism to democracy in the late 1940s as reflected by the articles of the 1946 constitution.

The autonomy of Brazil's legal system was lost when Brazil's experiment with democracy came to an abrupt end in 1964 when the populist president, "Jango" Goulart, was ousted in a military coup. It was only in the late 1970s that some of that autonomy was recovered. The charter currently in force was enacted by the National Congress on January 14, 1967, and the product of the military government that came to power in 1964. Promulgated by a rubber-stamp congress, the new constitution replaced the one of 1946, which had guided the nation through almost two decades of democracy. It also changed the formal name of the nation from the United States of Brazil to the Federative Republic of Brazil (Republica Federativa do Brasil). Other significant changes were the Institutional Act No. 16, of October 14, 1969, and Institutional Act No. 5, Article 2, part 1, of December 15, 1968. These amendments entrusted the cabinet ministers for the navy, army, and air force with the task of providing an integrated version of the charter. On October 17, 1969, a new constitutional text was enacted. Further amendments were made on May 9, 1972; June 15, 1972; April 23, 1975; and June 25, 1975. The Institutional Act has no apparent legal origin except the self-generating power seized by people or groups under certain circumstances.[9]

The Organization of the Court System

The Brazilian legal system is based on Roman law, with some influence from the Napoleonic Codes. The judicial system consists of federal and state courts. The former is headed by the Supreme Court of Justice (Supremo Federal), which is located in the federal capital of Brasilia. There are eleven judges appointed by the president with the approval of the Senate. Their tenure is for life and is protected under the Constitution. The Supreme Court has appellate and original jurisdiction. Moreover, it has broad powers of judicial review and jurisdiction over disputes between the union and the states. Another federal court located only in the capital is the Federal Court of Appeals (Tribunal Federal de Recursos), which has thirteen judges appointed by the president and approved by the Senate. Lower federal courts are in each state and the federal district and in the territories. There are, in addition, labor tribunals and electoral courts to protect elections.

The highest state court is the Court of Justice (Tribunal de Justicia), which functions as an appellate court with original jurisdiction over the state governor and his ministers. The subordinate state courts are the Courts of the First Instance, presided over by judges of law (Juizes de Dereito); Jury Courts (Tribunales do Juri); and in some states, Mayor's Courts (Tribunales de Alcada).

Outside of the regular courts are the Superior Military Court, the Tribunal of Accounts, labor courts, juvenile courts, and the Maritime Court. Moreover, the penal system has fifty-one correctional institutions, of which twenty-seven are penitentiaries, six houses of custody, twelve penal and agricultural colonies, and six houses of correction.[10]

The Personnel of the Law

The legal profession in Brazil is largely middle class, and there are a number of good law schools (the normal course of study is five years) across the nation. While there are no accurate figures of the total number of lawyers, it is probable that the sum would exceed that of all other Latin American states. The bar association in Brazil (Ordem dos Advogados) is a key institution, as only persons who have a law degree and are registered with it are allowed to practice law. The Brazilian Bar Association was created by law in 1930, and its statutes, approved by law in 1963, included the defense of the judicial order and the Constitution; the promotion of collaboration between the judicial, legislative, and executive branches in the study of problems related to the legal profession; and the promotion of measures aimed at defending the members of the legal profession. The Ordem dos Advogados is an independent and autonomous organization that is not linked to any of the three branches of government.

A lawyer can practice law only within the area of jurisdiction of the section (there are sections in each of the states) in which he or she is registered. A lawyer, however, can register with and practice in more than one section. There are two other groups that practice law besides lawyers: The *advogados provisionados* (provisional lawyers) and the *estagiarios* (trainees). The former do not have a law degree but have passed an examination before the Ordem dos Advogados and can be temporarily licensed to practice in regions where the number of lawyers is fewer than three. The latter are those people who have recently graduated or are matriculated in the last two grades of law school but have not taken their bar exam. They can prepare certain judicial documents and assist in proceedings, although they cannot provide legal counsel or initiate suits.

Public Perceptions and the Role of the Courts

The Brazilian legal tradition is long and well respected. Its members have played an important role in the development of their nation. After the military coup of 1964, lawyers challenged the constitutionality of the act. By the late 1970s the political climate changed. A crucial turning point was reached in 1978 when President-General Ernesto Geisel, acting in accordance with the vocally expressed desires of the Brazilian Bar Association, embarked upon a policy of *abertura* or redemocratization. Despite resistance of hardliners in the military, abertura was strengthened by the revoking of the president's exceptional powers. In effect, this returned certain powers to the Congress. Presidential authority to close Congress was lost, and the right to terminate mandates of elected officials and to suspend the political rights of individuals were relinquished. A new and less severe national security law was promulgated, and the last vestiges of formal censorship were eliminated. Freer programming was allowed, and habeas corpus was restored for political crimes. Moreover, parliamentary immunity was returned, and the judiciary, one of the forces pushing for democratic change, was once again allowed a degree of autonomy.

The democratization process continued in 1979 when amnesty was granted for several thousands, including a pardon and the lifting of banishment orders. In 1980, a constitutional amendment to restore direct elections of state governors and all senators was enacted. In 1982, the elections were held, and opposition candidates were allowed to assume offices in a number of states. Another step forward was taken in 1984 when two civilian candidates, one progovernment and one opposition, squared off for the 1985 presidential elections. The opposition candidate, the seventy-six-year-old Tancredo Neves, ultimately won the contest. Neves, however, was unable to attend his own inauguration due to illness and Jose Sarney, the vice-presidential candidate, was officially sworn in an interim president on March 15, 1985, ushering in the first civilian government since 1964. The death of Neves, shortly after, left Sarney president of Brazil under Article 75 of the Constitution.

Sarney was the constitutional heir to one of Brazil's most popular politicians and his ascendency, though legal, created a political crisis. Although Sarney carried through Neves's program of returning direct elections in May 1985 (including the enfranchisement of an estimated 20 million illiterate adults previously denied the vote), his legitimacy was questioned by calls for new elections in 1986. Moreover, with Sarney as president, there was no vice-president, and hence no legal successor to Sarney. In the temporary absence of Sarney, the president of the Chamber of Deputies would take his place.[11] Next in line would be the president of the Supreme Court and then the president of the Senate. Should the president be incapacitated (resign or die in office), none of the three people would have the right to become president and complete the term—one of them would temporarily be president until elections were called within sixty days.

EL SALVADOR

The role of the legal system has been pivotal in a number of nations in the early 1980s. Among those nations in which the legal system and its members were key elements of change have been Argentina, Brazil, Peru, Ecuador, the Dominican Republic, and Uruguay. However, nowhere has the role of the legal system been more subject to scrutiny, from both within the nation and without, than in El Salvador. Located on the Pacific coast of Central America, it has a population of 4.5 million and is one of the region's smallest states. As El Salvador moved from the authoritarian Romero regime in 1979 to the democratizing government of Christian Democrat Jose Napoleon Duarte, the role of the legal system has been an important area of confrontation between those seeking progressive democratic government, including the protection of human rights, and those opposed to any changes in the status quo that could jeopardize their privileged socioeconomic positions.

The Development of the Legal System

The Salvadorian legal system is based on Roman law and the Napoleonic Codes. The former was passed down from the years of Spanish colonial government, commencing in the 1500s and lasting until the early 1800s, when the latter was introduced by the local government seeking to develop an independent society. Consequently, the Salvadorian legal system is a hybrid of the two types of law and has some similarities with a number of European nations.

The evolution of the constitution of El Salvador, like that of its Central American neighbors, reflects what Thomas P. Anderson called "the confusions arising from the grafting of an alien governmental structure onto a Hispanic legal system."[12] In the colonial period, local government in El Salvador had not been a reflection of the will of the governed. A multitude of often overlapping authorities existed. Roman law, an important component of the Salvadorian (and Spanish) legal system, held that authority came from above. The injection of such concepts as the right to vote and equality during the liberal period following independence created confusion reflected in the several Salvadorian constitutions. Ultimately, these influences left final authority with the chief executive and weakened the judiciary.

The current Constitution was enacted on January 8, 1962. In theory, the charter of the Constitution prevails over all laws, regulations, decrees, orders, and resolutions issued by the executive branch.[13] Laws, decrees, and regulations opposing this charter may formally be declared unconstitutional by the Supreme Court. Moreover, any court of law may decide in the specific cases submitted to their jurisdiction on the inapplicability of executive legislative issuances deemed contrary to the Constitution.

The Organization of the Court System

The Supreme Court, with ten magistrates, is the highest body in the legal system. The Court is divided into three chambers (*salas*), handling civil, criminal, and *amparo* (habeas corpus) cases. Unlike most Latin American states, the

Salvadorian Supreme Court has the right of judicial review and may declare laws and decrees unconstitutional. This power has rarely, if ever, been used.

At the next level there are eight Courts of Second Instance (*camaras de segunda instancia*). Judges of both Supreme Court and the Courts of Second Instance (2 magistrates and 2 substitutes) are elected by the Legislative Assembly for three years and may be reelected. If elected for a third successive term, they can remain on the bench until seventy years of age.

There are forty-four Courts of First Instance (*Juzgado de Primera Instancia*), located in every departmental capital and other cities and towns. Judges are appointed by the Supreme Court. The Courts of First Instance are divided into criminal, civil, and mixed courts. The civil courts are responsible for civil and commercial matters, the value of which exceeds the jurisdictional power of the Justices of the Peace Courts.[14] Outside of San Salvador and Santa Ana, the two largest cities, they also handle landlord-tenant cases, and, where no Labor Tribunals have been established, labor cases. The criminal courts have jurisdiction over criminal matters, cases relating to social defense (*peligrosidad*), and juvenile and traffic cases in areas where no courts have been created to serve these functions. The mixed courts have jurisdiction over all the above matters in the absence of special courts for these subjects.

There are also a number of other specialized trial courts which, in effect, supplement the Courts of First Instance. These include: two general tax courts (Juzgados Generales de Hacienda); two juvenile courts (Tribunales Tutelares de Menores); one landlord-tenant court (Juzgado de Inquilinato); and one military court of first instance (Juzgado de Primera Instancia Militar)—all in San Salvador. Outside of the capital are a number of traffic courts (Tribunales de Transito).

The Personnel of the Law

El Salvador's legal system has largely been the domain of the middle class. It has been regarded as a vehicle for social mobility, although most recognize the political nature of the legal system and its limitations (or dangers). That the study of law does not rank high in prestige is perhaps a comment on the position of the legal profession in the country. In 1977, only 7 percent of those listed as higher education graduates were lawyers compared to 30 percent in engineering and 29 percent in medical science.[15] The course of study lasts from six to seven years for the degree of Doctor in Jurisprudence and Social Sciences and Licence in Juridical Sciences.

Attorneys bear the title of advocate and notary (*abogado y notario*), unless their right to practice as a notary has been suspended. Two other groups of lawyers exist. The first are those lawyers educated outside of El Salvador, but having at least two years of residence and the necessary qualifications to practice as a notary in their own country, and Salvadorians allowed to practice solely as notaries under the law of their country. A special ''examination of sufficiency'' before the Supreme Court is necessary before one can practice as notary in El Salvador.

The second group are those whose functions are limited to representing parties in court. Referred to as *procuradores*, they are allowed to advise clients and file the necessary documents in court proceedings.

Public Perceptions and the Role of the Courts

The judiciary in El Salvador does not have a distinguished history. Judicial posts are not highly regarded and as an observer noted: "they are woefully underpaid."[16] The same observer also made the following statement about all Central American judges: "The temptation is to do as little as possible while holding office."[17] Traditionally, those going into the judiciary were perceived as powerless, although well-meaning. A more cynical view saw them as a corrupt element of the establishment, having a blind eye to progovernmental abusers and a vengeful hand against any antigovernment challengers. Judicial review, a borrowed concept, has been of little value in upholding the law, as those who would be likely to use it could be damaged by its use. As Anderson noted: "In a region [Central American] in which power has often come from naked force, it is a brave Supreme Court indeed that dares defy the executive.[18]

The seeming ineffectiveness of the Salvadorian legal system to meet the demands of creating and maintaining a civil society received crucial support from the Duarte government, which came to power in early 1984. The core legal issue is whether or not the judicial branch of the government and the nation's lawyers can deliver the president's promise to investigate the human rights abuses for an estimated 40,000 deaths in the last five years.[19] In 1982 alone, a Salvadorian academic journal estimated that 4,419 people were victims of political violence and that another 1,045 were captured or disappeared.[20]

The considerable international pressure placed on the government and the security forces to halt the human rights abuses has ended up in the courts. To the Salvadorian judiciary's credit, a number of cases have been reopened that involve military officers implicated in terrorist acts against the population. After considerable pressure from the United States, for example, the five national guardsmen who murdered four American churchwomen in 1980 were tried and found guilty, and each was sentenced to thirty years in prison.

Considering that violence is of such a political nature in El Salvador, there are limits to what the legal system can do. The case of Archbishop Romero, assassinated while saying Mass on March 24, 1980, offers an example of the politicalization of the legal system. In various accounts of what happened, Roberto d'Aubuisson has usually been named as the man most responsible for the murder. D'Aubuisson, the leader of the right-wing Nationalist Republican Alliance (ARENA—Alianza Republicana Nacionalista), was Duarte's major challenger for the presidency. He also had support from officers in the armed forces, many of whom were exclassmates. To arrest d'Aubuisson, in all probability guilty of conspiracy, would risk civil war or a coup from the right. As one Salvadorian judge commented in another case of similar circumstances: "If I got a call right now telling me to go out and order the culprits picked up, I would have to think twice. After all, I have a wife and kids."[21]

There has been a recent movement to stop the long-established habit of ignoring laws perceived to be unjust or inconvenient. The outcome of this movement in El Salvador is, in large part, dependent upon support for the rule of law by the executive. The outcome is, at present, far from certain—as in most Central American states (with the exception of Costa Rica), the rule of force may continue to be dominant over the rule of law in El Salvador.

ARGENTINA

One of the largest and most developed nations in Latin America is Argentina. Located in South America's Southern Cone, it borders Chile in the west and Brazil, Uruguay, Paraguay, and Bolivia in the north. It has a population of 28.2 million and an adult literacy rate of 93 percent, as well as an average life expectancy of seventy-one years.[22] Furthermore, it ranks in the top fifteen most industrialized nations in the world. While Argentina is generally regarded as a modernized society, its political history and the disregard for the rule of law has been amply demonstrated, especially in the twentieth century.

The Development of the Legal System

It took close to seventy years for Argentina to coalesce as a political unit. From the assertion of autonomy in 1810 and the declaration of independence in 1816, through the abortive constitutions of 1819 and 1826, the federal pact between the coastal provinces in 1831, the first and still effective national Constitution in 1853, the first constitutional government of all the provinces in 1862, the identity of Argentina was not complete until the federalization of Buenos Aires in 1880.[23] Even after the long struggle to form a nation, a schism remained between centralists (*unitarios*) and autonomists (*federales*), or between those who favored a strong central government and those who preferred a loose confederation of provinces. Ultimately, Argentina became a federation of provinces with Buenos Aires as the national capital.

The current constitutional text of Argentina was originally enacted in 1853 and, in theory, has heirarchical priority over all other legislative instruments. Amendments can be added. Consequently, it has been subject to a number of changes since its creation. One of the most dramatic of these was the Statute for the Process of National Reorganization (*Estatuto para el proceso de reorganización nacional*), enacted by the military junta in power on March 29, 1976. This statute was predominant over the charter of the Constitution itself and gave the armed forces the authority to dissolve the national congress and dismiss the president of the Supreme Court and a number of high-ranking provincial officials.

The tremendous concentration of power in the executive branch, however, was not a new element in Argentine politics; Juan Peron (in the 1940s and 1950s) had amended the Constitution and impeached members of the Supreme Court. With the return to democracy in 1983 under President Raul Alfonsin, Argentina headed back to the rule of law. The new Radical party government commenced investigations into the abuses of the military governments during the "dirty war" in the 1970s and Alfonsin, a graduate from the law faculty at the National University of Buenos Aires, has used the legal system as his instrument to arrest nine former junta members (all generals) who served between 1976 and 1982.

The Organization of the Court System

Argentina's dual court system is similar to those of Brazil and Mexico, although the actual structure of the judiciary is largely borrowed from the United States. In addition, the system of jurisprudence was taken primarily from France, Spain, and Italy. The Argentine legal system is based on Roman law and the Napoleonic Codes. Of the two, the latter has been important in the practice of law, as many of its codes were adopted for criminal and civil cases. The judiciary is divided between federal and provincial courts. The Supreme Court is the highest federal court. Under the military regimes of the 1970s and early 1980s, the junta had the power to appoint and dismiss the judges on the nation's highest court. Under the Alfonsin government, however, the judiciary has been given greater autonomy and functions once again as it was supposed to under the Constitution.

Below the Supreme Court are the Federal Appellate Courts, each having three judges. These are located in Buenos Aires, Cordoba, La Plata, Parana, Rosario, Bahia Blanca, Mendoze, Tucuman, and Resistencia. Below the Appellate Courts are single-judge district courts located in each province and single-judge territorial courts.

The provincial court structure parallels the federal structure. Each province has a Supreme Court, courts of appeal, and courts of first instance. There are also a number of minor courts for petty offenses, juvenile courts, courts of peace, and *alcaldes* (councils of the mayor). Although the federal and provincial judiciaries are independent of each other, a degree of centralized control is exercised by the secretary of justice in the national Ministry of the Interior.

The Personnel of the Law

There are several law schools in Argentina, with the law faculty at the National University of Buenos Aires having one of the best reputations. Although statistics for the number of law students are not available, it is estimated that there are more than 45,000 law students (about one-half of which will graduate) and close to 36,000 lawyers.[24] Unlike in El Salvador, the Argentine *abogado* is the only category of lawyer in the nation. They may be graduated from the universities as either licentiates or doctors in law, depending upon their plan of study. Besides the abogados, there are *procuradores*, who act as judicial representatives of parties. They are, however, prohibited from pleading cases or performing all the legal functions of an attorney at law. In many aspects, they exist on the periphery of the legal system, as do notaries, both groups taking special courses for their degrees.

The requirements to practice law include a law degree from a "national" university, although degrees from "private" universities have been accepted. A major prerequisite is the registration of the candidate's law degree with the court before he or she is allowed to accept clients or accept fees. Moreover, registration with the highest provincial court of a particular jurisdiction allows one to practice before all inferior courts. Another aspect is that if this certification is registered with the federal Supreme Court, this authorizes practice in all lower federal courts without further recording.[25] Finally, candidates must take an oath before the highest tribunal of the jurisdiction in a formal and solemn proceeding.

Public Perceptions and the Role of the Courts

The Argentine legal profession is relatively well respected, and lawyers and judges have played a significant role in the development of the political system. For the legal system, the 1970s and early 1980s represented a crucial period that witnessed an almost total disregard for the rule of law (especially human rights), as protected under the Constitution. The nation went from unprecedented terrorism in the early 1970s and political and economic disequilibrium under Isabel Peron to the successive military regimes of Generals Videla (1976–1981), Viola (1981), and Galtieri (1981–1982). The leftist terrorist movement was crushed, but at the frightening cost of thousands of missing people who had been carried away in the night and without any trial. This period ended with the defeat of the Argentine military in the Falklands-Malvinas War and the eventual return to democratically elected civilian government in late 1983.

The Supreme Court in Argentina is one of the few in Latin America that has the extra-constitutional function of judicial review. The Supreme Court has, however, rarely made use of this power. Consequently, the development of judicial review in Argentina has lagged well behind the practice in the United States.[26] When an Argentine high tribunal declared a number of decrees proclaimed by the military government in April and May 1945 unconstitutional, a two-year struggle ensued between the judiciary and the executive. The outcome was the impeachment and ouster of the entire Supreme Court. This was a lesson not lost on members of the legal profession in the traumatic 1970s, when the country was locked in an internal struggle against the left-wing guerrillas, the Tupamaros. The return to civilian government in 1983, however, has indicated that the legal system may, once again, have a position of importance in a democratic political system aiming at the rule of law.

VENEZUELA

Venezuela has played an increasingly important role in Latin America and the Caribbean in the late twentieth century. As a democracy armed with substantial oil reserves, it has made its influence felt internationally.

The Development of the Legal System

Venezuela declared its independence in 1811. Since that date it has been governed by twenty-six constitutions—more than any other Latin American republic. Despite the turnover, the constitutions have had a degree of continuity. The long line of caudillos, beginning with the first Venezuelan constitution in 1830, wrote into each constitution considerable powers for the executive. Although power was concentrated in Caracas, the capital, the nation's deep-rooted regionalism was also recognized by the establishment of a federal form of government with some powers for the states.

Venezuela's rule by military strongmen lasted, with few interruptions, until the downfall of the regime of Marcos Perez Jimenez in January 1958. In December of the same year, Romulo Betancourt, the candidate of Accion Democratica (AD), was elected president, hence ushering in Venezuela's as of yet unbroken period of democratic government. In 1968, the AD lost the national elections, and the opposition Copei party won. This was the first time in Venezuelan history that an administration in power turned over the reins of government to an opposition party that had won in a peaceful and orderly election.

The Constitution of 1961, still in force, is a liberal document created with the intention of establishing legitimacy for the new AD government of Betancourt. Like the Mexican Constitution, forged in revolution, the major concerns of the Venezuelan one were the advancement and safeguarding of social welfare, popular government, national self-determination, and socioeconomic development. In its preamble and 252 articles, Venezuela was declared a federal republic in which sovereignty resides with the people. The twenty state governments are largely directed by the governors, who are appointed by and responsible to the president, thus narrowing the states' powers. Although they are given constitutional authority to change state names, to organize local governments, and to perform a number of other functions, the states have less historical basis for participation in a federal system than the Brazilian states or the Argentine provinces. As in most of Latin America, the executive dominates. Since the government of Betancourt, the citizen's rights have been guaranteed. Freedom of the press, speech, and religion are safeguarded, and all have the right of habeas corpus and a prompt trial.

The Venezuelan Constitution may be amended or even rewritten without great difficulty. Amendment requires a simple majority for passage by the Congress. If passed in that legislative body, it requires certification by two-thirds of the states to become part of the Constitution. Moreover, provisions, for reforming or rewriting the Constitution are similar, except that initiation requires a one-third vote by the states or a congressional chamber, passage by a two-thirds vote in the Congress, and approval by a national referendum.

The Organization of the Court System

In contrast to the federal states of Argentina, Brazil and Mexico, the federal state of Venezuela has a unitary court system. As Fitzgibbon and Fernandez noted: ''Since 1945 all courts in Venezuela have been part of the national (that is, federal) system, even though a parallel organization of state courts once existed.''[27]

Venezuela's judicial system is headed by a nine-member Supreme Court, which is divided into three chambers (*salas*), each dealing with distinct types of cases. The jurisdiction of the Supreme Court extends to conflicts in which one party is the Republic, a state, or a municipality, to disputes between the courts, and to cases rising on appeal from the lower courts. With broad and sweeping powers, the Supreme Court even has the function of judicial review. As in the rest of Latin America, however, judicial review is rarely, if ever, used. Judges of the Supreme Court are elected by a joint session of the legislature for nine-year terms. Every three years, one-third of the membership comes up for renewal.

Below the Supreme Court are the Superior Courts. Of these there is at least one in each of the seventeen judicial districts into which Venezuela is divided. They have both original and appellate jurisdiction and admit lawyers to the bar. The lower levels in the judicial system are the courts of instruction, which draw up indictments; municipal courts in every town, with original jurisdiction in cases involving minor sums fixed by law and in civil registry matters; district courts, with both original and appellate jurisdiction in cases involving sums fixed by law; and courts of the first instance, which resemble the federal district courts in the United States. In addition, special courts exist for labor and the military.

The Personnel of the Law

Venezuela has four public and two private universities that offer law degrees. Eleven thousand students were enrolled for legal study during the 1975–1976 academic year.[28] As law is one of the more popular professions, competition for entry is difficult, although, in theory, the only admissions requirement is the successful completion of a secondary education. The course of study is five years and leads to a degree and the right to apply for admission to an Academy of Lawyers.

When the graduate completes the university requirement he or she is made ''Lawyer of the Republic.'' However, actual practice cannot commence until the prospective lawyer petitions to, and is accepted by, the appropriate Academy of Lawyers, which is, in effect, a bar association. Each of the twenty states, two territories, and the Federal District of Caracas has an Academy of Lawyers. Membership is required for the graduate in the Academy of the state or territory in which he/she intends to concentrate their practice. All decisions of the Academy must be made within five days after application, and those denied admission have the right to appeal. A lawyer, once admitted, may practice in any of the nation's federal courts.

In the 1980s, law students have a choice of career, as they do in most countries in Latin America. One avenue is the judiciary, which means becoming judges, public prosecutors, public defenders, clerks of records, or notaries. This track now guarantees tenure and an established promotion system. The other avenues are private practice, university teaching, or work in a public-sector enterprise. As Perez Perdomo noted of the judiciary choice: "A judicial career is less prestigious than private practice, but its importance has increased, and often young law graduates with excellent opportunities in a university career or in private practice opt for the judiciary."[29] With further reforms planned for the judiciary in the late 1980s, this area may have further potential for expansion.

Public Perceptions and the Role of the Courts

Lawyers in Venezuela are confronted by the problems of being too numerous. Simply stated, the universities are creating more lawyers than the legal system can absorb. While there are many lawyers with good reputations, some lawyers are struggling for financial survival, frequently violating the code of ethics or committing blatantly dishonest acts, all of which contribute to the profession's sometime negative public image.[30] This is one of the major problems for the Venezuelan legal system, as competition to find positions in the large private law firms, the judiciary, and state enterprises remain intense.

Lawyers have played an important role in Venezuela's political and economic development. They have played such a vital role largely because the role of law has been central to the political organization of the country since it achieved independence.[31] Lawyers were involved in the Republican side of the War of Independence, helped legitimize the authority of Bolivar's government in 1813, and clarified its territorial limitations. Although the legal system was rarely used in the latter nineteenth century, lawyers remained a respected group, usually linked to commerce.

It was only in the 1950s, when the economy was gradually changing to the exportation of oil, that the legal profession expanded significantly. Venezuelan lawyers were readily used by multinational oil companies seeking concessions. Not only were Venezuelan lawyers able to interpret what was then an underdeveloped system of legal codes, but they also became political contacts for the North American and European oil companies. Furthermore, expansion in commerce and urbanization fostered new demands for legal services, which, in turn, led to reforms in the courts and larger numbers of law students. In the late 1950s, a new generation of law school graduates came to dominate the legal system.

While they provided the impetus for the professionalization of the legal system, they also promoted the specialization of various branches of law, ranging from contracts to nationalization. In the 1960s and 1970s, the nationalization of the petroleum industry was conducted with the aid and supervision, in part, of Venezuelan lawyers.

The legal system has combined with several trends to create a more egalitarian legal and political order. As a nation, Venezuela came into existence only after a long search for the administrative and political design appropriate for its territory. That search was greatly complicated by the contradictions found in the centralist tradition and individualism. The rule of law came only after these Hispanic-American traditions were melded with Anglo-American legalistic and societal concepts. The ultimate product of that melding was the 1961 Constitution, which recognized the need for socioeconomic progress and political order. As John V. Lombardi observed: "The political system was transformed from Hispanic caudillism to North Atlantic populist democracy, and the social system was transformed from a land-based, family-oriented hierarchy to an income-based, technocratic meritocracy."[32] Venezuela's petroleum reserves have, obviously, been a major factor in transforming the nation, but it cannot be denied that the legal system helped provide a foundation and framework for peaceful change since the late 1950s. While the executive, as in the days of the caudillos, may still dominate, Venezuela's future will probably be ruled by law.

MEXICO

The Development of the Legal System

As in the rest of Latin America, the Mexican legal system derives from Roman law and, more directly, from the Spanish codes (though with some influence from the Napoleonic Codes). Moreover, the Mexican legal system, due to its proximity to the United States and complex political history, has a rather unique legal tradition. In Mexico's first half century of independence, there were close to forty forms of government, including federal and centralized organizations, constitutional monarchy, dictatorship, and representative democratic government.[33] Despite this, the nation has had only three constitutions—in 1824, 1857, and 1917. The last, which is the most important, has been in force continuously since its adoption. It has, however, been amended more than one hundred times, reflecting both the influence of the United States Constitution and the Mexican experience of dictatorship and social revolution.[34]

The Constitution of 1917 mirrored the revolutionary government's intentions to regulate the economy and to provide for the basic needs of its citizens in what was then regarded as one of the Western Hemisphere's most radical documents. Written at a time when the government of President Carranza was consolidating its military triumph over remnant rebel elements, the new constitution was based, in part, on the Constitution of 1857, but was more far-reaching. A number of articles emphasized the revolutionary government's nationalism. Article 27 stipulated that aliens may acquire land only if they consider themselves to be Mexican nationals; Article 32 stated that Mexicans are to enjoy preference over aliens for all concessions, government positions, offices, or the nation's armed forces; and Article 33 declares that aliens may be banished from the country without judicial process merely on orders from the president.[35]

Inherent in the Constitution of 1917 were attempts at creating a more equalitarian progressive society in which church and state were stringently separated. Along these lines, Article 3 provides for a free public school education, and private primary schools must impart secular instruction and may be established only subject to official supervision. Moreover, monastic orders are prohibited and the clergy must be Mexican. Article 130 is perhaps one of the most anticlerical in the Constitution, as it prohibits establishment of a state religion; establishes marriage as a civil contract; bans religious oaths; empowers each state's legislature to determine the number of clergy allowed to function within its territory, and prohibits members of the clergy from holding public office, voting, assembling for political purposes, or criticizing the Constitution.

While the clergy's power was officially curtailed in the Constitution, the same document provided land reform for the rural population. Article 27 authorized the federal government to divide large landed estates, to develop small landholdings, and "to establish new centers of rural population with such lands and waters as may be indispensable to them."[36]

Article 123 guarantees the right of workers to organize unions, establishes a normal workday of eight hours, provides for double pay for overtime work, and bars boys under sixteen and all women from late-night work and all unhealthful or dangerous employment. Furthermore, the Constitution prohibits employment of children under twelve years. In one of the most progressive provisions, mothers were given special protection: a three-month vacation with pay before the birth of a child and an additional month of paid vacation after birth.

Added to the nationalism, secularism, anti-clericalism, agrarianism, and social consciousness of the Constitution of 1917, is a certain formula for continuity and stability in government. A number of contradictions exist that have had the positive effect of enabling orderly governmental change: a weak national congress, in which token representation of the opposition is guaranteed; elected state governors, with considerable local autonomy within the limits of loyalty to the chief executive; monopolization of the nation's political life by one party but one that is broadly based; and a very powerful president, who is prohibited from reelection. The Institutional Revolutionary Party (Partido Revolucionario Institucional or PRI), the official government party, has dominated since 1929, when it was formally founded. Created to encompass all sectors of society, the PRI has presided over the nation's political and economic life, in theory, implementing and enforcing the Constitution.

Amendments to the Constitution may only be introduced by the National Congress by a two-thirds vote of the attending membership. As in other countries with a civil law tradition, Mexican law holds that the legislature creates law, which the courts simply apply. Moreover, it is further required that any amendment be approved by the majority of legislatures of the Mexican states.

One of the more important dimensions of the Mexican Constitution is the significance given to the rights of the individual or *garantias individuales*, which limit the powers of the states and municipalities as well as the powers of the federal government. In this context, the *amparo* is a key factor, as it is the legal concept that gives teeth to the bill of rights.[37] In a literal sense, amparo means protection, assistance, or a human refuge and amparo actions, as in other Latin American countries, tend to be mainly habeas corpus writs.[38] Moreover, the Mexican version not only champions the right of physical liberty but safeguards personal equities and property rights as well.

The Organization of the Court System

The leading judicial body in Mexico is a twenty-one-member Supreme Court, supported by a system of federal, state, and local courts. There is also a system of quasi-judicial tribunals referred to as the arbitration and conciliation courts. The president, with the approval of the Senate, has the authority to name the Supreme Court judges, who, in turn, appoint judges for the lower courts. Under the Constitution, impeachment is the only way of removing a federal judge.

There are four general chambers (*salas*) in the Supreme Court. These correspond to civil, criminal, administrative, and labor law. Five justices sit in each of the four chambers, and the position of chief justice is rotated. The chief justice is elected annually by the membership of the court and may be reelected. In the federal court system, the Supreme Court presides over six Circuit Courts and forty-six District Courts. The Circuit Courts are each assigned to one of the Supreme Court justices, while the Supreme Court, as a whole, makes appointments to the lower courts. The Circuit Court is the final court in most amparo cases, and the District Court are courts of first instance for federal law questions.

Modelled after the federal court system, state and local (municipal) courts are provided for in the Mexican Constitution. This court system has a special feature in that complainants in civil and criminal cases can opt to take their disputes to the state or local courts even if a question of federal law is involved.

The Personnel of the Law

The legal profession in Mexico is old and well respected. The legal profession is perceived as middle class and, in the cases of the ''super-lawyers'' and leading judges, is an upper-class profession. The legal profession is also largely staffed by men, although there are growing numbers of women attending law school.

When a law student finishes his or her courses, writes a thesis, and passes an oral examination by five professors of the school of law, he/she takes an oath, hence becoming authorized to practice law. Membership to the bar association is strictly optional. More importantly, the graduate registers his/her diploma with the Department of Education, where he/she is given a *cedula*. Throughout Mexico the cedula proves that the graduate is a full and qualified lawyer, can practice law, and deserves fees. Less than 10 percent of all lawyers in Mexico, whose total now exceeds 30,000, belong to a bar association.[39] Most government lawyers are not members. Those who are usually work in a private practice or for a corporation. For them, the bar associations function in a social security capacity as well as in a political sense, providing a vehicle for group expression.

The major concerns for the Mexican legal system in the 1980s are the need to reduce corruption in the judicial system as well as in the government, the overproduction of lawyers, and how to deal with the problem of international drug trafficking. The latter has created tense relations with the United States, as a drug enforcement officer was killed in Mexico in 1985. His death brought to public attention some of the corruption in the Mexican legal system as well as bringing up the question of North American intervention into a neighbor's affairs.

One of the major dilemmas confronting Mexico's legal system is the growing number of unemployed or underemployed lawyers. As Alberto Mayagoita has noted: "there is not a promising future for the upcoming generations of young attorneys. We have never had a shortage of lawyers, and of late we have far too many."[40] In Mexico the new lawyer can choose a career in government, the universities or established law offices. The prospects for opening up one's own office are not good and many single practitioners need another job in order to survive. Work in one of the older and well-known offices is not always a good path either, as the oversupply of lawyers allows the firms to pick the best and pay wages that are low.

HAITI

The Development of the Legal System

Haiti's legal system is based on the Roman civil law system. While Haiti shares many characteristics with the rest of Latin America, there are a few important differences. First and foremost, Haiti's population is largely of African descent, and its society traditionally has been divided between a lighter-skinned mulatto elite who are culturally more French than they are Latin American and a darker-skinned majority who speak a form of patois. Considering the legacy of plantation agriculture and the influence of the Enlightenment ideas of Rousseau, Voltaire, and Moliere, the French colonial past helped set the eastern part of Hispaniola apart from the surrounding nations. With the French Revolution came the ideas of Liberty, Equality, and Fraternity, part of which were embodied in the August 27, 1789, passage in the French National Assembly of the Declaration of the Rights of Man and of the Citizen. The development of these ideas and their dissemination in Haiti resulted in a tremendous upheaval—the Haitian Revolution.

The revolution of the black slaves in 1793 against French colonial rule ultimately led to the birth of the nation of Haiti in 1804. The first nation to achieve independence from a European nation in Latin America and one of the few successful slave rebellions in history, Haiti's early period was marked by the conquest and occupation of the neighboring Dominican Republic (1822–1844), internal civil wars between the north and south, and isolation in the realm of international affairs. The lack of stability was reflected by the turnover of presidents. From 1843 to the twentieth century most of the fourteen presidents lasted less than two years in office. Those who survived longer, such as Faustin Soulouque and Fabre Geffrard, ruled with a heavy hand. It was not unusual that the Constitution was suspended and the National Assembly dissolved. The rule of law, when possible, was not overly effective and was usually short-lived.

In 1908, economic problems and brutal police measures drove the then president, Nord Alexis, from power. His downfall was followed by the turbulent and short rule of F. Antoine Simon, who was supported by the army. Between his confirmation on December 17, 1908, and 1913, Haiti had four more presidents who rapidly succeeded one another in an accelerated tempo of violence. Two presidents were deposed by revolutions. One was blown up in the presidential palace, and the other was poisoned. The next chief executive, Jean Vilbron Guillaume Sam, died at the hands of an enraged mob on July 26, 1915. It was at this point that the United States, with geo-political considerations, intervened by landing the Marines, who occupied the country to 1934.

While the Americans suppressed a number of insurrections, restructured the Haitian economy, and improved the nation's infrastructure, they also provided Haiti with a new constitution, upon which the later constitutions were partially founded. The Constitution of 1917 reduced the presidential term from seven to four years, provided for the popular election of senators, and required plebiscites on constitutional amendments. Moreover, it guaranteed freedom of assembly and of the press and trial by jury in political as well as criminal cases. A departure in the new constitution enacted during the American occupation was that foreigners were allowed the right to own land. Previously, non-Haitians were prohibited from owning land, a condition that came from the days of the revolution in which the slaves rose against their white masters and the plantation system. In a sense, this constitution removed a law created from the apprehension that white ownership could lead to the re-creation of the plantations.

From 1934 to 1946 Haiti enjoyed relative stability, although the democratic elements of the constitution were circumvented whenever possible. In the late forties and early fifties, instability returned, as the military intervened in politics. In 1950, President Paul Magloire consolidated his power by providing his nation with a new constitution. In the new charter, women were granted the right to vote for the first time; freedom was guaranteed from arbitrary arrest and imprisonment; freedom of speech, of the press and assembly were protected; and social security was provided. The government was divided into legislative and executive branches. The former consisted of a National Assembly comprising a

Senate and a Chamber of Deputies. Workers were also given the right to form unions and to bargain collectively. Moreover, the Catholic religion was to have special privileges based upon the Papal Concordat of 1860. Other religions and cults, such as *vudon*, were recognized. A final stipulation was that the president was to serve for six years and not be immediately reeligible. Added to this was that he was to be elected on the basis of a majority vote of communal electors chosen by direct suffrage and secret ballot.

After Magloire was ousted from power in another coup, power eventually gravitated to Dr. François Duvalier, who ruled in an almost totalitarian style until his death in 1971. "Papa Doc," as he was called, consolidated his position as the nation's undisputed leader, and a new constitution was written in 1964. Incorporating much of the 1950 Constitution, the new one established the supremacy of the charter by creating a law that did not allow any addition to or deletion from the constitutional text. The control of the constitutionality of the laws was entrusted to the Court of Cassation, which decided when the application of law was in question.[41] The Constitution, as amended in 1971, may be amended, provided that a declaration is issued by the legislature stating the need to revise the charter partially and completely. This resulting statement should be made to the president of the Republic and published in the official daily. At that point, the Corps Legislatif (Legislative Chamber) meets as a National Assembly to consider or rule on the proposed revision. Once completed, it is proclaimed in a special session by the National Assembly as the new constitution or as amendments.

The 1964 Constitution was amended in 1971 to help the succession of rule from François Duvalier to his son, Jean-Claude (referred to as "Baby Doc"). The text of the new Constitution has 201 articles divided into fifteen chapters. The reforms concentrated on the form of election of the president for life and the minimum age requirements for public office.[42] When the older Duvalier died in 1971, his son had no problems from the Constitution, the legislature, or the judiciary in assuming the presidency.

There is a crucial difference between what the Constitution says and political reality. In Haiti, the executive totally dominates the rest of the political system. As Rubens Medina and Cecelia Medina-Quiroga noted:

Contradictory to the constitutional precept that the executive, legislature, and judicial powers are independent from one another and may not delegate their assigned functions or trespass each other's limits, each year the Haitian legislature issues a legislative decree suspending a number of constitutional provisions, among these the separation of powers, the legality of administrative acts, restrictions to presidential powers, and procedures for amending the constitution.[43]

The legislature also grants the *président à vie* extraordinary powers to legislate by means of decrees with force of law, a process normally undertaken by the National Assembly.

The Organization of the Court System

The Supreme Court (Cour de Cassation) is the highest court in the land, followed by four Courts of Appeal and the lower courts. Judges are appointed by the president for six years and may not be removed from their positions during their term, except for "special laws setting forth the reasons for which they are to be removed from that post." Employees of the Public Prosecutor's Office and justices of the peace may be appointed and dismissed by the president without restriction.

In theory, the Supreme Court has the power of judicial review. Moreover, under Articles 120 and 121 it can act as an appeals court for all military court decisions. In general, the courts do not enforce governmental administrative orders or decrees unless they are in conformity with the law. Judges of this court must be thirty years of age, must have practiced law for ten years, and must have been either a judge or public attorney for seven years.

The Courts of Appeal hear both civil and criminal cases and are located in Port-au-Prince, Les Cayes, Gonaives, and Cap-Haitien. In the capital, the court has a president and five judges, while the other three courts have a president and three judges. Below these courts are the Courts of the First Instance, known as civil tribunals and criminal tribunals. They are located in thirteen cities and have one judge who hears first instance civil cases. At the lowest level are the Justice of Peace Courts. These are located in each of the nation's 124 communes and hear all cases where the amount involved does not exceed $100 and landlord and tenant cases.

The Personnel of the Law

Members of the legal profession either accept the system as it is, totally dominated by the authority of the president, or they can confront the system, seeking to establish a rule by law. Consequently, many of those who stood against the Duvalier regime in the 1960s and 1970s were arrested, imprisoned, or killed. Law students receive training either at the State University in Port-au-Prince or the private law colleges in Cap-Haitien, Les Cayes, Gonaives, and Jermaine. A small number attend law schools in the United States and France. At times, the democratic ideas encountered outside of Haiti have made the return to Haiti difficult, and many Haitians remain overseas, practicing law elsewhere.

DEVELOPMENT OF THE LATIN AMERICAN LEGAL SYSTEM

One of the major issues in Latin American legal affairs is the interrelationship between law and the development process. As already discussed, those in the legal profession have been involved in the redemocratization movement throughout the region.[44] The linkages between the legal system and economic development have become equally important, especially considering the enormous debt some nations have incurred. The constitutions of Mexico and Venezuela specifically aim at creating egalitarian societies that are ruled by law and guarantee national control over local resources. The legal and bureaucratic networks, dealing with developmental and financial affairs in these two countries, have, in an overall sense, been relatively successful in improving the standard of living for the citizen. Moreover, the rule of law, supplemented by democratic or near-democratic institutions, has provided a stable environment for economic growth.

There has also been a negative side to the legal system and the development process. One of the problems often cited by businessmen, both national and foreign, is the negative impact of legalistic red tape. Peru has a very vibrant market economy that is largely illegal because it is not licensed by the government. Peruvian economist Hernando de Soto has estimated that the underground economy is mainly independent of the formal economy, and it has grown so fast that, in 1983, it produced as much as $11 billion in goods and services—almost none of which is counted in the official $22 billion Peruvian Gross Domestic Product.[45]

While the formal economy is mired in the debt crisis, the informal sector has developed its own manufacturing facilities, retail outlets, and own legal system. The incredible bureaucratic inefficiency (where it can take up to four years to establish a company), has caused the informal sector to grow. Thus comes the need for law. There are questions about ownership of land and contracts. Informal sector lawyers exist who help the process develop. In this system, a person's "word" is crucial. Therefore, contract and property law in Peru's underground economy are well developed.[46]

An example of the development of contract and property law is observable in the situation of Lima's street vendors. With no formal laws to enforce agreements or protect rights, the capital city's 300,000 street vendors, a major sales outlet for much of the informal economy, have developed elaborate "property" rights for the two squares or so of public space each of them occupies for eight hours.[47] The "owner" of a space can sell it for close to $750, and the rights of the new owner will be respected. Underground economy bus drivers, who supply Lima with 85 percent of its public transportation, have also imported buses on contracts secured by "deeds" to property the importers owned in the eyes of the informal economy, although ownership was not recognized by formal Peruvian law.

The problem of overregulation is not restricted to Peru, as most Latin American nations have large underground economies that operate outside of the codes of the formal legal system. Even in Mexico, regarded as one of the more successful nations, legalistic-bureaucratic problems exists that threaten to choke development. As in Peru, many of the new city dwellers in Mexico City attempt to make a living as street vendors or merchants but are stymied by bureaucratic interference. As one Mexican taxi driver commented: "You need a license to sell spit and even for that you must bribe some little bureaucrat."[48]

While some may argue that the dilemma is one of bureaucratic corruption and inefficiency, the fundamental problem is the legal system. In many cases there is a need to reform laws and codes to adjust to modern-day realities and the dictates of the economic system. In a study on legal professions in the Third World, K. L. Abel noted that the practice of law was "underdeveloped," lacking adequate personnel to cover all aspects of operating a functioning and respected system.[49] In many Latin American nations the personnel exists, but, more importantly, the political will for instituting legal reforms usually does not.

CONCLUSION

In examining the legal systems of Latin America, a number of similarities and differences become evident. One of the most obvious similarities is the power of the executive branch vis-à-vis the judiciary. In most cases, including the democracies, the president of the republic exercises considerable power to which the courts usually take a back seat. This is a situation that probably will not change in the near future. Consequently, the legal systems of Latin America will remain, in large part, dependent on the authority of the region's chief executives. At the same time, the trend toward democratic government should be an important factor in strengthening the rule of law.

One off-shoot of the democratic trend has been the development of political battles between the legislature and the president. In Ecuador and Honduras this has been evident to the point that in the latter country the president arrested a congressional appointee to the Supreme Court. In Honduras, there were two Supreme Courts, one appointed by the legislative body and the other appointed by the president. In Ecuador, where the president (Leon Febres Cordero) has a minority in the Congress, the Supreme Court has also become a battleground, while the interpretation of the Constitution has been at the core of a nasty controversy, especially in regard to the right of the Congress to call extraordinary sessions to pass legislation. As the democratic process develops further in Latin America, the continued political battles over exactly what constitutions mean probably will not abate.

The major difference between the legal systems of Latin America is the relationship between the political system and the judiciary. In this, as reflected by the countries reviewed, there are sharp contrasts. In Haiti (as well as Chile and Paraguay) the legal system is totally dominated by the chief executive. Even the constitution is "bent" to his will. The rule of law is, in reality, the rule of the Duvalier family. In the transitory states, Argentina, Brazil, El Salvador, the legal systems—the courts as well as the middle class group of lawyers—have become the battlefield in the push to reach democracy and once there, to strengthen its institutions. The actions of the Alfonsin government in Argentina have been watched by all in Latin America, especially in other transitory states, such as Bolivia and Uruguay, where democratic governments were recently installed in the 1980s.

The legal and political systems of Venezuela and Mexico are far from perfect. At the same time, those nations have been examples that democratic or near-democratic systems can function in Latin America for the benefit of the citizen protected under the charter of the constitution. For the future, even these legal systems are badly in need of reform, especially in the field of criminal law. In many cases, judges, clerks, and lawyers lack modern equipment, are poorly paid, and are swamped by a tremendous work load. Corruption is often a problem. These problems are also found in the Dominican Republic, Colombia, Ecuador, most of Central America, and throughout the Southern Cone countries and Brazil. The problems related to drug trade are also part of the picture. While better salaried and modernized facilities and equipment would help improve the situation, the financial problems of Latin America in the 1980s and possibly continuing into the 1990s make this an unrealistic objective. This gloomy assessment of Latin American legal systems, however, does not provide a complete picture. There are members of the legal profession in every country that adhere to the rules of the system and stand for the rule of law. Although the Venezuelan and Mexican systems have had problems in the past in terms of corruption, their legal systems have played quiet but important roles in safeguarding the constitutional rights of the majority of the people. The actions of Brazil's legal system, its courts, and lawyers indicate that this is the direction being taken in this pivotal nation. Much also depends on the future leadership, in both political and economic spheres, to help create the necessary conditions for the needed reforms to guarantee the nation's population a just rule of law and to meet basic human needs.

NOTES

1. Those states not independent in Latin America and the Caribbean are the Netherlands Antilles, the British Caribbean islands of Anguilla, the Caymans, the Turks and Caicos, Montserrat, the British Virgin Islands, and the French territories of French Guiana, Martinique, and Guadeloupe. To this list could be added Puerto Rico and the American Virgin Islands. The legal systems of each national group are similar to those found in the metropole nation.

2. C. Veliz, *The Centralist Tradition of Latin America* (Princeton: Princeton University Press, 1980).

3. Ibid., p. 10.

4. Ibid., pp. 3–4.

5. D. S. Palmer, *Peru: The Authoritarian Tradition* (New York: Praeger Publishers, 1980), p. 4.

6. G. W. Wynia, *The Politics of Latin American Development* (New York: Cambridge University Press, 1980), p. 11.

7. Ibid.

8. Ibid.

9. R. Medina and C. Medina-Quiroga, *Nomenclature and Heirarchy: Basic Latin American Legal Sources* (Washington, D.C.: Library of Congress, 1979), p. 13.

10. G. T. Kurian, "Brazil," in *Encyclopedia of the Third World*, vol. 1 (New York: Facts-On-File Press, 1982), p. 241.

11. *Latin America Weekly Report*, May 3, 1985, p. 9.

12. T. P. Anderson, *Politics in Central America: Guatemala, El Salvador, Honduras, Nicaragua* (New York: Praeger Publishers, 1983), p. 4.

13. *Constitucion Politica de la Republica de El Salvador 1962* (San Salvador: Presidiencia de la Republica, 1975), Articles 80 and 220.

14. C. S. Rhyne, *Law and Judicial Systems of Nations* (Washington, D.C.: The World Peace Through Law Center, 1978), p. 209.

15. J. W. Wilkie and Stephen Haber, eds., *Statistical Abstract of Latin America*, vol. 22 (Los Angeles: UCLA Latin American Center Publications, 1983), p. 141.

16. Anderson, *Politics in Central America*, p. 5.

17. Ibid.

18. Ibid.

19. L. Chavez, "The Testing of Jose Napoleon Duarte: The First 100 Days of El Salvador's New President," *New York Times Magazine*, September 2, 1984, p. 16.

20. *Estudios Centroamericanos* (ECU), ano 37, no. 410 (December 1982), pp. 1158–59.

21. Chavez, "The Testing of Jose Napoleon Duarte," *New York Times Magazine*, September 2, 1984, p. 16.

22. World Bank, *World Development Report 1983* (New York: Oxford University Press, 1983), p. 149.

23. J. R. Scobie, *Argentina: A City and A Nation* (New York: Oxford University Press, 1977), p. 88.

24. Rhyne, *Law and Judicial Systems of Nations*, p. 22.

25. Ibid., p. 23.

26. R. H. Fitzgibbon and J. Fernandez, *Latin America: Political Culture and Development* (Englewood Cliffs, N.J.: Prentice-Hall, Inc., 1981), p. 309.

27. Ibid., p. 152.

28. Rhyne, *Law and Judicial Systems of Nations*, p. 837.

29. R. Perez Perdomo, "Jurists in Venezuelan History," in C. J. Dias et al., eds., *Lawyers in the Third World: Comparative and Developmental Perspectives* (Uppsala: Scandinavian Institute of African Studies, Sweden, 1981), p. 83.

30. Ibid., p. 85.

31. Ibid., p. 76.

32. J. V. Lombardi, *Venezuela: The Search for Order, The Dream of Progress* (New York: Oxford University Press, 1982), pp. 267–68.

33. J. Kippers Black, H. I. Blutstein, K. T. Johnston, and D.S. McMorris, *Area Handbook for Mexico* (Washington, D.C.: U.S. Government Printing Office, 1975), p. 211. Also see A. Mayagoita, *A Guide to Mexican Law* (Mexico City: Panorama Editorial, S.A., 1981), p. 1.

34. Ibid.

35. L. C. Brown, "Mexico's Constitution of 1917," in James W. Wilkie and Albert L. Michaels, eds., *Revolution in Mexico: Years of Upheaval, 1910–1940* (New York: Alfred A. Knopf, 1969), p. 114.

36. Ibid., p. 115.

37. Black et al., *Area Handbook for Mexico*, pp. 214–15.

38. Ibid., p. 115.

39. This estimate was provided by officials at the Embassy of Mexico in Washington, D.C., in April 1985.

40. Mayagoita, *A Guide to Mexican Law*, p. 123.

41. *The Haitian Constitution* (1964, as amended in 1971) (Washington, D.C.: Organization of American States, 1974), Articles 28 and 121; also printed in *Le Moniteur* (January 20, 1971).

42. *Le Moniteur*, January 20, 1971.

43. Medina and Medina-Quiroga, *Nomenclature and Heirarchy*, p. 65.

44. It should be added that the movement to military governments was often accomplished with the aid of many of the same lawyers and judges who feared the effects of underground terrorist movements.

45. J. L. Rowe, Jr., "Underground Economy in Peru Seen Vibrant, Growing," *Washington Post*, October 30, 1983, p. 9. Also see A. Riding, "Peru's Wall Street: Paltry Profit but No Overhead," *New York Times*, May 4, 1985, p. 2. Riding noted: "Such is the underground economy's importance in sustaining about half of Lima's work force that it has spun off yet another line of business: thanks to support from foundations and universities, it is now fashionable for professors to make a living by studying the phenomenon."

46. Rowe, "Underground Economy in Peru Seen Vibrant, Growing," p. 9.

47. Ibid.

48. D. Asman, "A Mexican Opposition Emerges," *Wall Street Journal*, December 13, 1984, p. 30.

49. K. L. Abel, "Underdevelopment of Legal Professions: A Review Article on Third World Lawyers," *American Bar Research Journal* (Summer 1982), pp. 871–98.

BIBLIOGRAPHY

Abel, K. L. "Underdevelopment of Legal Professions: A Review Article on Third World Lawyers," *American Bar Research Journal* (Summer 1982), pp. 871–98.

Anderson, T. P. *Politics in Central America: Guatemala, El Salvador, Honduras, Nicaragua.* New York: Praeger Publishers, 1983.

Andrade, M. *Codigo de procedimientos civiles para el Distrito y Territorios Federales.* Mexico City: Ediciones Andrade, S.A., 1970.

Black, J. K., H. I. Blutstein, K. T. Johnston, and D. S. McMorris. *Area Handbook for Mexico.* Washington, D.C.: U.S. Government Printing Office, 1975.

Brown, L. C. "Mexico's Constitution of 1917." In J. W. Wilkie and A. L. Michaels, eds., *Revolution in Mexico: Years of Upheaval, 1910–1940.* New York: Alfred A. Knopf, 1969.

Castano, L. *Usted y sus derechos.* Mexico City: Populibros "La Prensa," 1962.

Cespedes, G. *Latin America: The Early Years.* New York: Alfred A. Knopf, 1974.

Chavez, L. "The Testing of Jose Napoleon Duarte: The First 100 Days of El Salvador's New President." *New York Times Magazine*, September 2, 1984, pp. 14–19, 45.

Constitucion Politica de los Estados Unidos Mexicanos. Leyes y Codigos de Mexico Series. Mexico City: Editorial Porrua, S.A., 1974.

Constitucion Politica de la Republica de El Salvador 1962. San Salvador: Presidencia de la Republica, 1975.

Coughlin, G. G. *Dictionary of Law.* New York: Barnes and Noble Books, 1982.

Dias, D. J., R. Luckham, D. O. Lynch, and J. C. N. Paul, eds. *Lawyers in the Third World: Comparative and Developmental Perspectives.* Uppsala, Sweden: Scandinavian Institute of African Studies, 1981.

David, R., and J. E. C. Brierley. *Major Legal Systems in the World Today: An Introduction to the Comparative Study of Law.* London: Stevens and Sons, 1968.

Ehrman, H. W. *Comparative Legal Cultures.* Englewood Cliffs, N.J.: Prentice-Hall, Inc., 1976.

Estudios Centroamericanos (ECU), ano 37, no. 410 (December 1981), pp. 1158–59.

Fitzgibbon, R. H., and J. Fernandez. *Latin America: Political Culture and Development.* Englewood Cliffs, N.J.: Prentice Hall, Inc., 1981.

Flynn, P. *Brazil, A Political Analysis.* Boulder, Colo.: Westview Press, 1978.

Hansen, R. D. *The Politics of Mexican Development.* Baltimore: The Johns Hopkins University Press, 1971.

Imaz, J. L. de. *Los que mandan.* Buenos Aires: Editorial Universitaria de Buenos Aires, 1964.

Kurian, G. T. *Encyclopedia of the Third World*, vol. 1. New York: Facts-On-File, 1982.

Latin American Weekly Report. May 3, 1985.

Logan, R. W. *Haiti and the Dominican Republic.* New York: Oxford University Press, 1968.

Lombardi, J. V. *Venezuela: The Search for Order, The Dream of Progress.* New York: Oxford University Press, 1982.

Lott, B. "Venezuela." In Martin Needler, ed., *Political Systems in Latin America.* New York: Van Norstrand Reinhold Company, 1970.

Loveman, B. *Chile: The Legacy of Hispanic Capitalism.* New York: Oxford University Press, 1979.

Lynch, D. O. "Legal Roles in Colombia: Some Social, Economic, and Political Perspectives." In D. J. Dias et al., eds., *Lawyers in the Third World: Comparative and Developmental Perspectives.* Uppsala, Sweden: Scandinavian Institute of African Studies, 1981.

Mayagoita, A. *A Guide to Mexican Law.* Mexico City: Panorama Editorial, S.A., 1981.

Le Moniteur. Port-au-Prince, Haiti: Government Printing Press, January 20, 1971.

Needler, M., ed. *Political Systems in Latin America.* New York: Van Norstrand Reinhold Company, 1970.

Oduber Quirós, D. *Los problemas socio-politicos de desarrollo en Costa Rica.* San Jose: Ediciones Universidad Estatal a Distancia, 1981.

Oquist, P. *Violence, Conflict, and Politics in Colombia.* New York: Academic Books, 1980.

Organization of American States. *The Haitian Constitution of 1964 as Amended in 1971.* Washington, D.C.: Organization of American States, 1974.

Palmer, D. S. *Peru: The Authoritarian Tradition.* New York: Praeger Publishers, 1980.

Peeler, J. A. *Latin American Democracies: Colombia, Costa Rica, Venezuela.* Chapel Hill: The University of North Carolina Press, 1985.

Pendle, G. *Paraguay: A Riverside Nation.* New York: Oxford University Press, 1967.

Perez Perdomo, R. "Jurists in Venezuelan History." In C. J. Dias et al., eds., *Lawyers in the Third World: Comparative and Developmental Perspectives.* Uppsala, Sweden: Scandinavian Institute of African Studies, 1981.

Rhyne, C. S. *Law and Judicial Systems of Nations.* Washington, D.C.: The World Peace Through Law Center, 1978.

Riding, A. "Peru's Wall Street: Paltry Profit but No Overhead." *New York Times*, May 4, 1985, p. 2.

Rodman, S. *Haiti: The Black Republic, the Complete Story and Guide*. Greenwich, Conn.: The Devin-Adair Company, 1954, 1980.

Roett, R. *Brazil: Politics in a Patrimonial Society*. Boston: Allyn and Bacon, Inc., 1972.

Rowe, James L., Jr. "Underground Economy in Peru Seen Vibrant, Growing." *Washington Post*, October 30, 1983, p. 9.

Scobie, J. R. *Argentina: A City and A Nation*. New York: Oxford University Press, 1977.

Smith, P. H. *Labyrinths of Power: Political Recruitment in Twentieth Century Mexico*. Princeton: Princeton University Press, 1979.

Trueba Urbina, A., and J. Barrera. *Nueva ley federal del trabajo reformada*. Mexico City: Editorial Porrua, S.A., 1974.

Veliz, C. *The Centralist Tradition of Latin America*. Princeton: Princeton University Press, 1980.

Whitley, Andrew. "Sarney Faces Threat After Call for Early Presidential Poll." *Financial Times*, April 26, 1985, p. 5.

Wiarda, H. J. "Law and Political Development in Latin America: Toward a Comparative Framework for Analysis." *The American Journal of Comparative Law*, 19 (1971), pp. 434–63.

Wilkie, J. W., and Stephen Haber, eds. *Statistical Abstract of Latin America*, vol. 22. Los Angeles: UCLA Latin American Center Publications, 1983.

Wilkie, J. W., and Albert L. Michaels, eds. *Revolution in Mexico: Years of Upheaval, 1910–1940*. New York: Alfred A. Knopf, 1969.

World Bank. *World Development Report, 1983*. New York: Oxford University Press, 1983.

Wynia, Gary W. *The Politics of Latin American Development*. New York: Cambridge University Press, 1980.

11

MIDDLE EAST

Lee Epstein, Karen O'Connor, and Diana Grub

In this chapter we examine two legal systems of the Middle East—Egypt and Israel. To some extent, the judicial processes of these nations are representative of those found throughout the region. That is, two basic legal models exist in the Middle East. The first, typified by Israel, contains two sets of courts and law—religious and secular. Such systems, currently existing in Lebanon, Iraq, Iran, Jordan, and Kuwait, among other Middle Eastern states, are prominent throughout the region because they retain religious traditions while succumbing to the needs of a modernizing society.[1] The second model, typified by Egypt (but also operative in Turkey), is that of a secular legal system. In this type of legal structure, there is no separate religious court apparatus nor does religious law play a dominant role.[2] Egypt and Israel were selected for detailed analysis here, then, in part because they represent the basic legal models currently operative within the Middle East.

On the other hand, Israel and Egypt were also chosen because they differ from other Mideast nations. Both now possess modern, streamlined systems, reflecting religious and cultural traditions and emerging needs of modernizing societies. In fact, the legal institutions developed by these countries have become model systems for the region: other states throughout the Middle East have emulated the Egyptian system, in particular, and are now developing legal apparatuses along similar lines. Thus, because of their similarities and differences, Egyptian and Israeli legal structures provide excellent cases for study.

THE DEVELOPMENT OF THE LEGAL SYSTEMS

As many scholars have noted, judicial development is inextricably tied to state growth and transformation. That is, legal systems are heavily influenced by the specifics of their unique pasts. The systems of Egypt and Israel are no exception. Specifically, we have identified four principle historical factors that have influenced the legal traditions of both countries: Ottoman law and legal structures, European authority, indigenous contributions, and religious doctrine.

Egypt

Ottoman Law and Legal Structures

Prior to the Ottoman conquest in 1517, Egypt was ruled by the Mamluks, a Turkish military autocracy. A two-tiered legal system existed within this dynasty. The bottom, or "trial" court level, was run primarily by four chief justices, representing the four rites of *shariah* or religious sacred law. During this period, these justices attempted to apply shariah to all criminal and civil disputes. According to one source, this system was "fairly stable," with each justice working within "well-defined jurisdictions."[3]

Although the shariah judges had some control over judicial administration, they were not completely independent because their decisions could be appealed to the superior court (*mazalim*). This court, which was presided over by members of the military dynasty, did not rely on shariah to decide cases. Rather, the mazalim ruled on the basis of sultanic legislation. And, as one authority noted, through the mazalim "executive officials gradually encroached upon the domain" of the shariah judges.[4]

When the Ottomans gained control of the region, however, the sultan attempted to reorganize judicial administration within the province. One of the first steps taken by the Ottomans was to replace the four chief justices with one, the judge of judges (*qadi askar*). Appointed by the sultan for one-year terms, many chief justices belonged to the *ulema*, a body or family of shariah scholars.

Once the Ottomans reorganized the top of the judicial ladder, they sought to centralize the entire system. They accomplished this by dividing Egypt into twenty-four provinces and then dividing each province into one or more judicial districts (*quadas*), with one court in each. These courts were headed by provincial qadis, who were appointed for two-year terms on the recommendation of the chief justice. Each district was further subdivided into subdistricts (*nahiyyahs*), with a court in each. *Naibs*, who were appointed by qadis, presided over these courts.

Although the "reforms" made by the Ottomans may have led to a more centralized judicial apparatus, there is a great deal of scholarly debate over the actual efficacy and equity of the institutions and law during this period. Some suggest that the shariah judges, described above, and shariah itself, had little influence over Egypt during this period. The following facts tend to substantiate this viewpoint. First, shariah judges eventually "lost whatever jurisdiction they had over criminal and commercial matters" to various members of the executive authority. This decline in power occurred because the Ottoman governors of Egypt sat every Saturday to decide cases of criminal law, without regard to shariah. Thus, in essence, the shariah courts were not the only ones functioning in Egypt. Second, many scholars have questioned the practicality of shariah, even for Ottoman Egypt. According to Islamic doctrine, "the Shariah claims to regulate all actions of men, public and private, social and individual."[5] But because, as some suggest, the law is normative, it has never worked in practice. In fact, even before the advent of the Ottomans, shariah judges were dependent upon the executive to fill gaps in the shariah. "Such a situation," as Ziadeh notes, "could hardly be favorable for the emergence of an independent body capable of maintaining a rule of law."[6]

Others, however, maintain that "given the stereotypes of Islamic despotism, the courts were remarkably free of executive intervention, remarkably even-handed in the administration of justice."[7] In his argument for this viewpoint, Galal El-Nahal makes a number of compelling claims. First, contrary to Ziadeh and others, shariah courts did, in fact, hear criminal cases. In his book on the Ottoman courts in Egypt, El-Nahal devotes an entire chapter to describing the ways in which the shariah courts disposed of criminal cases.[8] He maintains that other scholars may have overlooked court jurisdiction in this area because there were so few criminal, as compared with civil, cases. Second, he refutes the argument that the courts were totally dependent on the executive, claiming that the qadis were charged with safeguarding the state from military oppression. Finally, contrary to others' views of the shariah, El-Nahal believes that it was an "ideal doctrine." He argues that "the shariah provided a solid theoretical foundation for the practical application of law to legal problems. And because the shariah regulated so many areas of men's relations with each other, the courts of Ottoman Egypt were deeply involved in the day-to-day life of everyday Egyptians."[9]

Although some of the criticisms of the Ottoman courts are well grounded, El-Nahal's views seem to be more accurate. Histories of the Ottoman Empire tell us, for example, that any executive decision could be vetoed by the mufti if it was inconsistent with shariah. This seems to imply that shariah and those who administered it, the qadis, were paramount in Islamic society.

European Authority

The judicial system and tradition established by the Ottomans remained intact until July 1798, when Napoleon and his forces occupied Egypt. Although the French kept the shariah courts, they replaced the Ottoman qadi with local judges. They also established a court to adjudicate commercial claims.

Although these changes were few in number, the imprint of the French on the Egyptian legal system was immeasurable. When the French (and British) evacuated Egypt in 1807 and eventually allied with the sultan, the new leader of the province, Muhammad 'Ali, tried to modernize Egypt along French lines. In doing so, 'Ali, who is often called the "Father of Modern Egypt," created a "resurgence of activity in the legal and judicial field."[10]

From the period of 'Ali's reign (1803–1840) through the latter half of the nineteenth century, this "resurgence of activity," in fact, led to several major changes in the Egyptian legal system. First, in 1828, 'Ali sent students to Paris to study law. Upon their return in 1831, they began to translate French textbooks and eventually French codes of civil procedure into Arabic.[11] 'Ali also attempted to revamp the Ottoman judicial system by creating supplementary legal councils and commissions. The first of these, the Judicial Council, was charged with investigating cases, while others dealt with commercial matters. A final reform of this era—the mixed courts of Egypt—well illustrates the strength of foreign influence in the area. One of the major problems faced by 'Ali's councils was their jurisdiction over foreign and Egyptian commercial interests. In short, the situation under the 'Ali regime was chaotic. Foreigners often tried to bring suits to their own consuls rather than to the Egyptian councils and, "If defendants were of different nationalities, suit had to be brought in as many forums as there were defendants."[12]

The demands of foreigners to alleviate this situation led to treaties of capitulation between the Ottomans and the Europeans, which eventually resulted in the creation of the mixed court system in Egypt in 1876. J. Y. Brinton describes the mixed court systems as

the dominating judicial institution of the country. They correspond broadly to the federal judicial system in the United States. All litigation which involves a foreign party or foreign interest . . . comes before them. As the activities of the 150,000 foreigners in Egypt largely control the commercial life . . . there is practically no litigation of any large or general importance which is not attracted to their jurisdiction.[13]

Composed of a court of appeals and three district courts, the mixed court system at one time contained seventy judges, who decided "some 40,000 written opinions" annually. Although the mixed courts were established to represent the complement of European interests, the supremacy of the French should not be overlooked. French was the language used in the courts, and the civil codes of the courts were based mostly on French models.[14] The primary purpose of these was to assuage the demands of foreigners in Egypt. Yet, they also had a major effect on the legal system of Egypt. As Ziadeh notes, "If any one factor were to be singled out as contributing the most to the modernization of Egypt, it would be the establishment of the mixed courts."[15]

Ziadeh's claim is well supported by the historical events following the establishment of the mixed courts. In 1881, the vice-president of the mixed court of appeal argued that "the jurisdiction of the mixed courts be extended to cases between native Egyptians."[16] Although this proposal failed to gain support, the British, who had occupied the country in 1882, sought to establish a system of national courts paralleling the mixed courts. In 1883, this plan was put into effect. A national or native judicial system, with jurisdiction over civil, commercial, and criminal cases, was established. The shariah courts, however, were not abolished—their jurisdiction was simply limited to cases involving "personal status."[17]

Egyptian Contributions

By the time Egypt's independence was established in 1936, its legal system was perhaps "the most highly developed in the Mideast." But further refinements from subsequent Egyptian governments were forthcoming. In 1937, at the Montreux conference, the mixed court system was terminated. Later, in 1948, the noted legal scholar, Abdal-Razzaq al-Sanhouri, drafted an updated civil code. The code, which "was drawn from both Western and Islamic sources, became the model or at least the inspiration for new civil codes throughout most of the Arab world."[18] The Council of State, modelled after a similar institution in France, was also created. Its powers included assessing the legality of governmental activities.

Religious Law

As the above discussion reveals, shariah courts were the basic legal structures of Ottoman Egypt. When the native court system was inaugurated in 1883, however, shariah courts lost much of their jurisdiction, a change from which they would never fully recover.

As the state began the process of modernization, in fact, the situation only worsened. In 1897, for example, the shariah courts were no longer allowed to apply shariah law. Rather, judges were to base their decisions on statute. Years later, after the army revolt of 1952, the courts were finally abolished. As of January 1, 1956, the national courts were and continue to be the "single judicial structure to which all persons and cases were subject."[19]

Although the religious courts were abolished, shariah itself is still applicable to cases involving personal status, such as divorce, marriage, and inheritance. In fact, a constitutional amendment passed in 1980 changed the "identification of shariah" from "a principal source of law" to "the" source.[20] But, as one observer has noted, "the shariah . . . is embraced in the national constitution, but in much of the legal system, its visibility and influence are not substantial."[21]

Israel

Ottoman Law and Legal Institutions

Palestine, like Egypt, was a province of Turkey and thus heavily influenced by the Ottoman and French occupations. While under Ottoman rule, substantial reforms were effectuated, including the "fair and public trial[s] of all accused regardless of religion," the creation of a system of "separate competences, religious and civil," and the validation of testimony on non-Muslims.[22] Specific land codes (1858), civil codes (1869–1876), and a code of civil procedure also were enacted.

The Ottoman reforms that occurred during this period were based heavily on French models. Indicative of the French influence was the adoption of a three-tiered court system. Referred to as Nizamiye, this system was extended to the local magistrate level with the "final promulgation of the Mercelle, a civil code."[23] Specifically, this code was concerned with "law relating to marriage, divorce, alimony, will, and other matters of personal status of Moslems; and the land law adapted to suit the peculiar needs of the Ottoman Empire."[24] The courts used this code as a statutory compilation upon which decisions could be based.

When the religious versus nonreligious controversy arose during this reform period, it was dealt with by formally distinguishing between civil and religious proceedings. One author summarized the change as follows: "In an attempt to unscramble the confused situation with regard to judicial competences, it [an administrative council] laid down that religious matters were to be handled by Religious Courts, and statute matters were to be handled by the Nizamiye Courts without specifying exactly what comprised which."[25] This point concerning the division of case subjects to be heard by either religious or statute courts reveals among other things the rapid growth, change, and reform the Ottoman legal system underwent late in the nineteenth century.

During the transition period between the fall of Turkish Jerusalem on December 7, 1917, and July 1, 1920, Palestine was under British military administration. On June 24, 1918, Proclamation No. 42 was issued by the British reestablishing the "administration of justice" in Palestine. This proclamation reinstated Ottoman laws and judicial organization as the laws in force in the country except for some alterations made by the British officials. A distinction was retained in the jurisdictions of civil and religious courts, and the civil courts were empowered to decide all cases involving foreigners. Therefore, in this interim period, the Mercelle remained in force as the civil code. In regard to other legal matters, "Ottoman law in force on the date of occupation would henceforth be in force in the Courts of Palestine 'with such modifications as may be proper' in the light of private international law and good administration."[26]

European Authority

It was not until the Mandate period that a second major source of the contemporary legal system developed. In the arena of international politics, British legal authority in Palestine rested on the Mandate approved by the United Nations on July 24, 1922. Domestically, though, the Palestine Order-in-Council of 1922 was the ruling authority and base of administration and control. The highest authority was the high commissioner, who could legislate freely so long as the laws were consistent with the provisions of the Mandate. His power was extensive, ranging from legislative to judicial authority. Because Ottoman law was declared as binding, gaps and changes were made by the Mandate administration and its officials, in conformity with the British principles of common law.

These changes, modelled as they were on British jurisprudence, slowly altered the nature of the legal system. Eventually regulations and ordinances "displaced a considerable portion of Ottoman influence" and diluted the Turkish influence in the judiciary. It is not surprising, therefore, that by 1948 Palestine's legal system was based primarily on British law.[27] The logic of these British initiatives is especially understandable when one grasps the ambition, motivation, and goals that drove the British. As expressed by Marver Berstein, the British saw one of their major roles in Palestine as "overhauling . . . the legal system," and "the establishment of an honest and efficient judiciary and magistracy."[28]

In addition to the two major elements in the Israeli judicial fabric discussed above, the effects of British common law and equity on the modern system is one largely of principle and theory. That is, the incorporation of stare decisis (precedent) added a particular flexibility and integrity to the sytem that is still apparent.[29] The British contribution of these principles influenced the philosophical attitudes of jurisprudence, which stressed justice and fairness. Concepts of common law and equity were not rigidly enforced in Palestine, but rather were modified from the English context to suit local situations. Therefore, judges had discretionary power to determine whether a particular British precedent was suitable for Palestine, and if not, in which form it would be suitable.[30] The influence of the British was seen, finally, in the fact that the judicial committee of the Privy Council in London (and not the Palestinian Supreme Court) was the ultimate judicial authority for the area.

Israeli Contributions

On May 14, 1948, the British Mandate over Palestine terminated and the State of Israel was declared independent by the Provisional State Council. At this point, the People's Council was to play the role of legislature temporarily (acting as the Provisional State Council) and the People's Administration would fulfill executive functions (acting as the Provisional Government). After declaring their independence, the new leaders of Israel had to organize a working government rapidly, including as much state apparatus and administration as possible. Among these were the judicial department and all legal functions. Subsequently, the Council made a pragmatic decision, incorporating the existing legal apparatus as the legal system of the states until such changes considered desirable could be made. That is, through a proclamation, the state accepted the original Ottoman structure, with its British revisions, as its own legal system until such time as they were able to rework it. Yet, this ordinance contained some provisions to reduce the dependence on British and Ottoman law. For example, it provided that law could incorporate "modifications resulting from the establishment of the State and its authorities."[31] Because neither the Declaration of Independence nor the Proclamation could technically be considered law, the Provisional State Council reinforced its decision through specific legislation.

With the passage of laws by the Provincial Government and with the passage of time, Israel gradually transformed the existing legal structure into one which was more uniquely Israeli, reflecting the country's values and ideals. This evolving system was composed of various legal traditions and conformed "more closely to the national spirit and needs."[32]

Nonetheless, this gradual evolution of a unique Israeli jurisprudence has not affected a substantial change in the laws and courts. The Israeli judicial system retained a great deal of its initial structure, incorporating the infusion of British influence. But in specific areas, such as civil rights and liberties and appeals to the Supreme Court, Israel has followed the practices of the United States. Subsequently, Israel's legal system is not only a compilation of earlier legal systems, but, through modern legislation, the state has created a judiciary that also parallels contemporary models of justice.

Religious Doctrine

The final element comprising the Israeli legal system is religious law. During British dominance, in the Mandate period, each of the recognized religious communities (Muslims, Jews, and Christians) had a "quasi-autonomous organization with its own judicial system." These religious courts were empowered to decide cases of "personal status," which include such matters as marriage, divorce, and inheritance.[33] For cases involving personal status, these courts had exclusive jurisdiction for members of that community who were not foreigners. But with regard to all other matters, jurisdiction relied on the consent of all parties. If this consent was not obtained, the civil courts exercised jurisdiction. Finally, the authority of these religious courts was significant as seen through the enforcement of their decisions. "Decisions were implemented by officers and processes of the civil courts."[34]

The impact of religious courts in Israel has been extensive. Different courts of jurisdiction applying the particular religious doctrines of their parties is a unique aspect of the Israeli legal structure, which finds its roots in the Ottoman system of justice. And, although the role and authority of the religious courts has fluctuated since the beginning of statehood, the tremendous influence of these courts on the system is unquestionable.

THE ORGANIZATION OF THE COURT SYSTEMS

Egypt

The Egyptian legal system, unlike those of many other nations, is hierarchical and relatively straightforward in design. It is composed essentially of three tiers, beginning with the entry points into the judicial process, the summary tribunals and tribunals of the first instance, and ending with the apex of the system, the Supreme Court.

As of 1978, 209 summary tribunals existed in Egypt. These tribunals are dispersed throughout the country by districts and have jurisdiction over most minor cases. Specifically, the summary tribunals hear cases involving misdemeanors and other minor offenses, minor labor disputes, and commercial or civil cases involving less than 250 Egyptian pounds.

There are twenty-two tribunals of first instance located throughout the major towns of each province. These tribunals have extensive jurisdiction, functioning as courts of first resort and as appellate courts. In the former capacity, the tribunals of first instance have exclusive jurisdiction over all cases involving more than 250 pounds as well as in all major personal status cases that have a statutory right of appeal to the high courts of appeal. In these situations only one justice presides.

The tribunals also act as appellate courts in two situations: (1) they hear appeals from civil or commercial cases involving more than 50 pounds and minor personal status cases—in these cases only one justice presides; and (2) a three-judge chamber of appeals (Chambres des Appels Correctionnels) hears misdemeanor appeals from the summary tribunals.

There are seven high courts of appeal. Each sits in three-judge panels and presides in civil or criminal divisions. The Chamber Civiles hears appeals "in civil, commercial and personal status" cases decided by tribunals of the first instance while the criminal division (the Cours d'Assises), hears cases involving situations in which either the death penalty or "imprisonment with hard labor of 3 to 25 years has been imposed."[35] The high courts of appeals have authority to hear and decide issues of fact and law. A decision of one of these courts is considered final and only issues of law may be appealed to the Supreme Court.

The Supreme Court of Egypt is composed of thirty justices (though five constitute a quorum) selected by the General Assembly. Like the high courts of appeal, the Supreme Court sits in criminal and civil divisions and exercises only appellate jurisdiction with but one exception—it reviews petitions of lower court judges who believe they have been wrongly denied promotion by the Supreme Judicial Council. Appeals on issues of law may be taken by the Supreme Court from: (1) any high court of appeal's judgment, (2) any penal sentence rendered by a Court of Assizes or by a Chambres des Appels Correctionnels, (3) "any contradictory judgments of last resort on the same litigation," and (4) any violations of jurisdictional rules.[36]

If the Supreme Court accepts an appeal, the Court can follow one of two avenues. First, it may settle the legal issues and thereby settle the case. If more information is required, however, the case may be sent to a differently constituted high court of appeals for complete retrial. Decisions of the court are not legally binding on the lower courts, a tradition stemming from the Ottoman court system. Unlike the United States's system of stare decisis, which binds other judges to apply case law as precedent, Egypt utilizes a system of written law. Nevertheless, these decisions generally have strong influence on lower court jurists.

Israel

Israel's judiciary is also hierarchical but more intricate than that of Egypt. Civil, religious, and special jurisdiction courts compose the body of its legal structure. The court system begins with the magistrate courts, proceeds to the district courts, and concludes with the Supreme Court, the highest court in the country.

The magistrate courts were established by order of the minister of justice. These courts exist in most major cities and villages, each with a specific geographic area of jurisdiction that is exclusive, eliminating the possibility of overlapping jurisdiction at this level. Jurisdiction for these courts is restricted to "minor criminal offenses carrying a maximum sentence of three years' imprisonment, and smaller money claims of up to IL 100,000 [Israeli Lira]."[37]

Although the number of judges presiding on a magistrate court may vary (as decided by the Department of Justice), most have three judges. The common practice is for one magistrate to hear a case.[38] Yet, ultimate determination of how many judges will sit for a particular case is decided either by the assigned judge, who may request a larger panel, or by the chief magistrate. In 1983, the total number of magistrates was 135, a large increase over the sixty-two presiding in 1955.[39]

"All judgments of magistrates' are appealable to the district courts," which constitute the next court level in the judicial hierarchy of Israel. These courts are also created, staffed, and located by the authority of the minister of justice. There are five district courts, each corresponding to specific territorial jurisdictions. And, while the distribution of judges is not equally balanced in each district, the total number of district judges in 1982 was eighty-six.[40]

The jurisdiction of these district courts is extensive because they serve a dual function, both as courts of first instance and as appellate courts. In the former capacity, the court hears serious criminal and civil disputes and those cases beyond the jurisdiction of magistrate courts.[41] Further, their jurisdiction also extends to "matters not within the exclusive jurisdiction of any other court or tribunal, [and] over matters within concurrent jurisdiction of any other court or tribunal so long as such court or tribunal does not hear the matter."[42] This broad range of potential jurisdiction emphasizes the significance of this court within the legal system as a whole.

District courts may also hear appeals from magistrate courts and minor courts such as municipal courts or administrative tribunals. When acting as a court of appeal, a three-judge panel presides. This is also the case when "dealing with serious crime as a court of first instance or in hearing other special cases at the request of the President of the Court."[43] Commonly, though, when trying a case as a court of first instance only one judge sits on the bench.

A ruling by the district court trying a case in the first instance is appealable to the Supreme Court. However, this automatic right to appeal does not exist for cases originating at a lower level in the court hierarchy. In fact, these sorts of cases can be appealed to the Supreme Court only if the district court or the president of the Supreme Court (or a member of the Court selected by the president of the Court) or "the Supreme Court itself decides to hear the appeal."[44] The central role of the district courts in the Israeli judicial system is further reflected by their workload. In 1982, the caseload for these courts came to 63,412 cases decided and 56,302 pending.[45] These cases were all of a serious nature, carrying the possibility of nontrivial punishment or sentence. In addition, this level of judicial hierarchy is essential because it has authority both to decide controversies, as well as screen, by means of a hearing, those cases that will eventually arrive at the highest court of arbitration and appeals, the Supreme Court.

The Israeli Supreme Court sits at the pinnacle of the court structure. Creation of this court was authorized through the Courts (Transitional Provisions) Ordinance passed by the Provisional State Council on June 24, 1948. Specifics of the law established a Supreme Court of last resort, whose members would be "appointed by the Provisional Government on the recommendation of the Minister of Justice and subject to approval by the Provisional Government on the recommendation of the Minister of Justice and subject to approval by the Provisional State Council."[46] Although the number has slowly increased, five justices were confirmed soon after the ordinance's passage.

The highest Israeli court serves three functions: (1) as the appellate court for district courts in civil and criminal cases; (2) as a court of last resort in cases involving civil rights and liberties, and (3) as the "regulator" of issues involving "federalism."[47] In addition, when the Supreme Court acts as an appeals court against its own decisions, it decides if a further hearing is necessary and a minimum of five justices rehear the case. The Supreme Court, due to its stature and position, has the authority to intervene into the affairs of another court in the interests of justice. That is, the president or the permanent deputy of the Supreme Court may direct that either the Supreme Court itself or a particular district court retry a case under very specific conditions. For example, a retrial may be held "in a criminal case if it appears to him that any of the incriminating evidence produced in court was based on falsehood or forgery."[48] A retrial may be requested by either the attorney general or the convicted defendant, at which time the court may rule to either acquit or convict. If, in fact, conviction is the outcome of the retrial, the punishment may not exceed the original sentence.

The original practice of staffing the Supreme Court was to nominate district court judges as acting justices, but as this resulted in disrupting the activities of the lower courts, the Supreme Court was consistently enlarged. Presently, the Supreme Court is composed of twelve justices, two of whom hold the titles of president of the Supreme Court and permanent deputy to the president of the Supreme Court. Control over the number of justices that sit on the Supreme Court is retained by the Knesset, as authorized by the Courts Law of 1957. The number of judges required to hold court is normally three, although certain technical decisions can be made by only one justice.

Dual Aspect of the Legal System: Religious Courts

The existence of religious courts is a unique aspect of the Israeli system. Functioning individually, the courts of the various recognized religious communities decide cases by relying on the religious principles and doctrines of their respective faiths. In general, they claim jurisdiction over personal status cases—those involving marriage, divorce, alimony, burial, and wills.[49] Because of the exclusive jurisdiction retained by religious courts on these matters, civil marriage and divorce is illegal for followers of these faiths.

The Rabbinical Courts, for example, have exclusive jurisdiction over the Jewish community (other than foreigners) in the matters mentioned above with the inclusion of cases involving "inheritance and succession when both parties agree to their jurisdiction." In all other matters of personal status of "all members of the Jewish community," even foreigners, the religious courts have concurrent jurisdiction with civil courts if all parties agree.[50] The exception to this authority is that such courts cannot grant a foreigner a divorce or an annulment. There are Rabbinical Courts which serve as courts of first instance, as well as a Rabbinical Court of Appeal. While an appeal may be taken from the Rabbinical Courts to the Rabbinical Court of Appeal, this decision may not be appealed to any civil authority.

The Muslim courts (or shariah courts) are organized along very similar lines. In contrast with the Jewish courts, though, Muslim foreigners, who are "subject by their national law to the jurisdiction of Muslim Religious Courts," also fall under the exclusive jurisdiction of the shariah courts.[51]

Other recognized religious communities in Israel also enjoy distinct religious courts. These include those of the Catholic, Protestant, Greek Orthodox, Melkite, and Maronite communities. These courts function along guidelines similar to those of the previously discussed religious courts. Furthermore, they share several of the other characteristics of religious courts, which add to the effectiveness and cohesion of this branch of the judiciary. First, whenever an action of personal status involves members of different religious communities, the president of the Supreme Court decides which court shall have jurisdiction. If a question arises as to whether or not a matter falls under the category of personal status, the case is preemptorily reviewed by a special tribunal composed of two Supreme Court justices and the president of the highest court of the religious community. Second, the authority of these courts is emphasized by their avenues of enforcement. "The judgments of the Religious Courts are executed by the process and offices of the civil courts."[52] Moreover, the "budgets for these courts are maintained by the state, rather than by each religious community."[53] These aspects, which are common to all the religious courts, reflect the influence of this part of the judiciary within the Israeli system.

THE PERSONNEL OF THE LAW

Egypt

The Legal Practitioners

The profession of law has a long-standing tradition in Egyptian society. Prior to the late 1800s, Egyptians were generally represented by *wukala*, unsavory and untrained lawyers, who "loitered the doorways of the [shariah] courts."[54]

Many rulers of the province tried to abolish or at least discourage wukala; for example, 'Ali ordered qadi to collect fees from wukala who brought frivolous suits. But these and other efforts were unsuccessful—wukala remained on the Egyptian legal scene well into the late nineteenth century.

As is the case with many aspects of the current Egyptian legal system, the example set by the mixed courts led to a professionalization in legal care. European lawyers practicing before the mixed courts were highly trained advocates and not "influence peddlers" as the wukala were often called. These attorneys, in fact, organized their own mixed bar association. Emulating the French system, it eventually established strict standards for membership.[55]

After the establishment of the native court system, the Egyptian government realized that it had to upgrade the quality of its legal care if its practitioners were to be comparable to those of the mixed bar. This was accomplished through several important statutes passed between 1888 and 1912. Perhaps the most effective reform occurred in 1912 with the establishment of the Egyptian National Bar Association. The Bar Association, to which every advocate must belong, maintained high standards, encouraging excellence in practice and in research. It, in fact, became such an important force in Egypt that it later absorbed both the mixed and shariah bar associations.

These reforms helped lay the foundation for the generally high quality legal education and profession found in Egypt today. This is particularly true given the profession's relatively unsavory origins and the short period of time that has elapsed since the reforms were instituted.

Today, Egyptians earn legal degrees (*licencie en droit*) through a four-year course of study similar to a liberal arts education in the United States. Although the quality of education is thought to be high for the region, several problems have plagued the six governmental universities. First, enrollments are high; in Cairo, for example, over 14,000 students are registered, sometimes resulting in classes of over 2,000.[56] These unmanageable numbers have led to a second problem—overcrowding has forced "the law faculty . . . to reduce the process of legal education to rote memorization of rules and principles stated in course outlines prepared by the professor."[57]

Whatever Egyptian attorneys may be losing in the way of legal education, they seem to be gaining in the strict criteria developed by the bar association. Only members of the bar can represent litigants in Egypt, but to become a member of the association, law school graduates must serve a two-year apprenticeship with a practicing attorney. After she/he has finished this training period and has argued at least twenty-five cases, she/he may be admitted to practice before tribunals of the first instance and summary courts. As of December 1976, 4,272 attorneys were admitted to these courts. After three years, advocates can apply for admission to the high courts of appeal, with the ultimate decision made by a special committee. Thus far, 5,755 attorneys have been admitted to these courts. Admission to practice before the Supreme Court can be obtained after seven years of practice before the high courts of appeal. But as Rhyne has noted, "usually no lawyer is admitted to plead before the Supreme Court unless he has a background of at least 20 years inscription to the bar." There are 1,739 attorneys now practicing before the Supreme Court.[58]

Judges

The requirements for appointment to the bench in the Egyptian legal system vary by court level. That is, each type of court maintains its own criteria for ascendency to a judgeship.

Supreme Court judges are chosen by the General Assembly from three eligible populations: (1) distinguished members of a high court of appeal with at least two years seniority, (2) "university professors with at least eight years of teaching and twenty years of legal experience," and (3) attorneys with at least twenty years of legal experience, eight of which they were permitted to practice before the Supreme Court.[59] As is the case for all Egyptian jurists, Supreme Court justices must retire at age sixty.

High courts of appeal judges are selected from another subset of the legal population, which includes presidents of tribunals of the first instance (who are at least thirty-eight years of age), university professors with five years of teaching experience, and attorneys who have been members of the bar for fifteen years. Judges staffing the tribunals of first instance and the summary tribunals are drawn from a similar pool, except that prospective jurists for these courts can be twenty-eight years old and members of the bar for only seven years.

Given the pools from which Egyptian judges are drawn, the quality of those who serve is seemingly quite high for the region. Although the legal profession in Egypt is not quite as prestigious as it is in the United States, Egyptian legal scholars, as Salacuse notes, "dominate legal research of the Arab world."[60] In addition, many of the scholars whose works helped to modernize several of the legal systems of the region went on to serve as Egyptian jurists.

This was not always the case. According to one scholar, during the days of 'Ali, judges were often "lackeys of the executive power."[61] The example set by the first-rate judges brought in by the Europeans to sit on the mixed courts, however, changed this situation. Egypt, with the help of foreign influences, recognized the importance of maintaining a high quality bench.[62] Since that time, it has emulated the European example by creating strict criteria for appointment to the judiciary.

Israel

Legal Practitioners

The process by which lawyers (often called advocates in Israel) are permitted to practice law is fairly straightforward. Uniform rules apply to all laywers in determining rights to begin practicing, continue practicing, and, in general, in maintaining the standards of legal performance. Before 1961, advocates were under the control and supervision of a law council. Membership in the Israeli Bar Association was optional and did not necessarily reflect on the competence of the advocates. On June 13, 1961, however, the Chamber of Advocates Law was passed by the Knesset, reorganizing the requirements and functions of Israeli advocates. The most obvious and significant result of this law was to make membership in the Chamber of Advocates, a controlling body over the legal profession, a requirement. Technically, its function is to

take care of the standards and integrity of the profession, and, for that purpose it is charged with the registration, control, and examination of law apprentices, the authorization of persons to practice as advocates by accepting them as members of the Chamber of Advocates, and the maintenance of disciplinary tribunals for advocates and law apprentices.[63]

There are three requirements for becoming an advocate: completing a legal education, serving a necessary apprenticeship, and passing the examination given by the Chamber of Advocates. To fulfill the educational conditions, an individual must be one of the following: a graduate of one of three Israeli institutions of law (located at Hebrew, Tel Aviv, and Bar-Ilan universities), "a graduate in law of an institution abroad recognized for this purpose by the Hebrew University, Jerusalem, as an institution of higher learning," and an advocate qualified abroad and having practiced abroad for two years or having served a judicial function abroad for two years that requires a legal education.[64] Further, all prospective advocates must complete a two-year apprenticeship, one year of which may be fulfilled simultaneously with the fourth and final year of legal education. Finally, after serving the required apprenticeship with a practicing attorney, examinations must be successfully completed to gain membership in the Chamber. These examinations are conducted by a committee composed of one judge and two advocates.[65]

Along with all the above requirements, restrictions, and qualifications applied to prospective lawyers, there are also some general prerequisites for acceptance into the Chamber of Advocates. Basically, a candidate must be twenty-three years of age, a resident of Israel, and qualified to be an advocate. In addition, foreign advocates especially must prove a "sufficient knowledge" of the Hebrew language before membership into the Chamber can be extended.[66]

Judges

Unlike countries in which various methods are used to select judges, Israeli judges are appointed through a uniform process. The formal appointments are made so that most, if not all, interested parties are involved in the selection procedure. Specifically, all appointments to the civil judiciary are processed as follows. The president of the State appoints a candidate who has been recommended by a nominations committee, chaired by the minister of justice and composed of three justices of the Supreme Court, two Knesset members elected by secret ballot by the sitting members, and two practicing lawyers elected by the Israeli Bar Association.

There are specific qualifications that must be met before consideration for appointment to a bench. As is the case in Egypt, these requirements vary by rank of judicial office. The most stringent requirements pertain to justices of the Supreme Court. To be considered for this position, a candidate must (1) have held office as a judge of a district court for five years, or (2) be "inscribed, or entitled to be inscribed, in the Roll of Advocates in Israel and who, continuously or intermittently, for not less than ten years, including at least five years in [Israel], has been engaged in one or several" of the following: (a) the practice of law, (b) a judicial or legal function approved by the minister of justice, (c) teaching law at a university or law school approved by the minister of justice, or (d) be an "eminent jurist."[67] This last qualification allows for outstanding individuals who have not previously practiced law or held a judicial appointment to become justices. As proof of the emphasis on legal expertise, fifteen of the last twenty-one appointments made to the Supreme Court were individuals who had served as district court judges. More importantly, since 1954, "no private lawyer has been appointed to this bench."[68]

Although not as rigid, the requirements for consideration to a district court judgeship are very similar to the above. These include: (1) holding office as a magistrate judge for four years, or (2) a person inscribed or entitled to be inscribed in the Roll of Advocates for not less than six years, at least three years of which were in Israel, engaged in one of the above occupations.[69]

Finally, for a position as a magistrate court judge, one of the listed professions must have been pursued for three years, at least one in Israel, while being entitled to inscription in the Roll of Advocates, if not so inscribed. Due both to the process of appointment and the above specified qualifications for consideration, "political appointments are rare."[70]

There are other restrictions placed upon judges both before and after gaining a judgeship. One is that judges must be Israeli citizens at the time of appointment. If a candidate for appointment retains dual citizenship with another country, she/he must relinquish this dual nationality. In fact, the nominee "may not be appointed until after he has done all that is necessary on his part in order to free himself" from this additional nationality.[71] Further, once appointed, judges hold office for life, with a retiring age of seventy. A judge's tenure can only be terminated "upon his death, resignation, retirement on pension (upon attaining seventy years), or [removal] from office" by virtue of the Judges Law.[72] This law, which establishes all of the earlier provisions for judges, also created a disciplinary court to monitor the actions of judges, but "so far no judge has been thus disciplined."[73]

PUBLIC PERCEPTIONS AND THE ROLE OF THE COURTS

Egypt

During the Mamluk, Ottoman, French, and British occupations of Egypt, scholars have suggested that the judiciary was anything but independent. Many, in fact, have argued that the qadi were extremely dependent on the executive, as the military imposed its rule at will. Currently, Egypt has taken great care to insure the independence of the judiciary through several mechanisms. First, Chapter 5 of the Egyptian Constitution, which prescribes judicial authority, contains several articles dealing with judicial independence. Article 165, for example, states that "Judges shall be independent, subject to no other authority but the law. No authority may intervene in the cases or in justice affairs." Second, although judges must retire at age sixty, they are "irremovable." Third, Egypt has established an apparatus "to guarantee the independence of the judiciary," the Supreme Judicial Council.[74] Headed by the chief justice and comprised of key jurists and members of the Ministry of Justice, the Council decides "all matters concerning the appointment, promotion, and transfer of judges."[75]

A final way in which Egypt has attempted to insure the independence of its legal system is through judicial review. While the Supreme Court sits at the apex of the Egyptian legal system, Chapter 5 of the 1969 Constitution called for the creation of a Supreme Constitutional Court. According to Article 175, this Court "alone shall undertake the judicial control in respect of the constitutionality of the laws and regulations, and shall undertake the explanation of the legislative texts." Thus, this article gives to the Supreme Constitutional Court the power of judicial review, a power not enjoyed by the Supreme Court. The Constitutional Court alone can nullify laws and regulations passed by the general assembly. Even this court, however, cannot "impede, repeal or nullify an administrative decree."[76] Under the Egyptian Constitution, only the Council of State, composed of university-trained jurists, has the "competence of decisions in administrative disputes." It alone, then, has the power to revoke or declare invalid decrees issued by government officials or ministers.

Israel

The judicial proceedings in Israeli courts are unique in certain respects. Courtroom procedure is generally modelled on British common law. Yet, in Israel there are no juries. Consequently, a judge has complete control over a case, with few competing complications. Thus, although a judge is always accountable to a higher court, all decisions are decided by experienced legal minds rather than by a jury of peers.

In addition, it is within the judge's authority to hold closed trials if it is deemed necessary to "protect national security, protection of morality, or the best interest of a minor.'' When closed hearings are in effect, strict prohibitions exist on publication of proceedings without permission, to safeguard a witness, valuable information, or other concerns that must be kept secret. In addition, it is forbidden to publish anything concerning a pending matter in court that could tarnish the trial.[77] It is due to these powers that judges can retain such great procedural control over cases in their courts.

In sum, authors who have researched the Israeli legal system agree and emphasize the integrity of the courts. The desire to ensure that a judge is "subject to no authority but the law" is fulfilled through the provisions of the Judge's Law and the parameters it has effected. By virtue of the judiciary's disentanglement from politics, especially in the process of the selection of judges, "Israel's Judges in all grades have stoutly maintained their independence."[78] As succinctly stated by Yaacov Zemach:

The Judge's Law secures the judiciary's independence, both in the exercise of judicial power and in matters of appointment and tenure. The law proclaims that "a judge, in judicial matters, is subject to no authority other than that of the law." The statute guarantees judges' independence by minimizing political influence upon appointments and removal, and by prescribing a uniform tenure and retirement system.[79]

To understand the power of the Supreme Court to review governmental acts, it is important that we first describe the jurisdiction of the Supreme Court, which is extensive, encompassing the entire country. The Court may hear cases in which the "grant of relief is deemed necessary in the interest of justice" and those cases not within the jurisdiction of any other court. The specific actions the Court can take in this capacity are numerous. First, the Court can order the release of an unlawfully detained or imprisoned person. It is able to require governmental officials to perform acts required of them by legislative provisions or restrict public officers from exceeding their authority. Furthermore, it is within its authority to curtail actions by public officials unlawfully elected or appointed. Also, the Court can order tribunals or any judicial or quasi-judicial body or official (other than the magistrates' and district courts) to hear or refrain from hearing or continuing to hear a particular case. And, finally, the Court can order religious courts either to hear a case, refrain from hearing, or continuing to hear a case, depending on the courts' jurisdiction over the matter.[80]

Cases can be brought before the Court under four prerogative writs: habeas corpus, mandamus, certiorari, and quo warranto. These writs constitute the authority under which the Supreme Court may hear and decide a case and are defined as follows: a writ of habeas corpus entails the release of a prisoner so that the Court can then decide what legal action is appropriate; a writ of mandamus allows the court to order an individual, corporation, or inferior court to pursue some action required by virtue of the subject's office or duty; a writ of certiorari orders the review of an act taken by an individual, public officer, lower court, or agencies exercising judicial authority; and a writ of quo warranto is the holding of legal proceedings to determine the possession of title to public office or the right to exercise a franchise.[81]

If a case was heard in one of the religious courts, then the Supreme Court only will hear the case if the participants early on raised the question of competence or jurisdiction of this authority.[82] That is, litigants in a case being heard by a religious court cannot appeal to the Supreme Court on the grounds of jurisdictional conflicts after the proceedings are partly complete. This rule curbs attempts to claim conflicting jurisdictions if the decision of the religious court appears to be unfavorable.

The ability of the Supreme Court to review legislative acts and decisions is complex. While the Court does not have the right to review the constitutionality of legislation passed by the Knesset, it is empowered to review the legality of the implementation of laws. Also, the lack of a written constitution creates a situation of nebulous spheres of control for the various governmental bodies. The "delimitation of borderlines" between these agencies, is, therefore, left to the judiciary, specifically the Supreme Court, which decides these cases, using the statutes that have "prescribed the structure of the government, but have not specified their respective substantive functions."[83]

The Supreme Court concerns itself with maintaining the proper division of jurisdiction between national and local legislatures and administrations and also with protecting the rights of the people against illegal behavior or the unlawful usurpation of power by public officials. Thus, the specific types of laws it can review and, if necessary, repeal are those that deal with the particulars of legal applications. The Court can nullify local ordinances, if they infringe on areas of national jurisdiction; administrative regulations promulgated to impose Knesset-approved legislation that violates the property or other fundamental rights of the people; and arbitrary or illegal action or decisions by public officials.[84]

Therefore, many traditions exist regarding what cases the Supreme Court can hear and where its authority is restricted. In general, however, the High Court's judicial power is "couched in discretionary rather than jurisdictional terms." The result of the vague statutes that authorized the creation of the Court is that a decision whether or not to hear and decide a case "remains fundamentally subjective" and depends on "the disposition of the Court to extend or limit the scope of its control."[85] When cases are not heard by Court, it is not due to lack of jurisdiction, but because the Court controls its own jurisdiction through the concept of justiciability. As stated in a major Israeli decision, *Jabotinsky v. Weizman* (1951), "operative limits" on the range of justiciable issues are basically the same in the United States and Israel.[86] Accordingly, Israel accepted the American practice of deciding justiciability on "reasoned and policy grounds."[87] Therefore, the Israeli Supreme Court has refused to "adopt any 'semantic definition' of nonjusticiable questions" so as not to limit and confine the Court's influence.[88] This policy also reinforces the Court's stature as a whole. And while every court will be "guided by a rule laid down by a higher Court," a "rule laid down by the Supreme Court will bind every court except itself."[89]

CONCLUSIONS

At the onset of this chapter, we stated that the legal systems of Egypt and Israel typify the two basic legal models found in Middle East. As our analysis has revealed, it is not surprising that there should be similarities among the legal systems of the region; the Middle East has been under the rule of common regimes who left their imprints on the judicial structures throughout the region.

Although foreign forces played a prominent role in the development of Egypt's and Israel's legal institutions, as they have elsewhere in the region, the two nations have now moved beyond their historical roots. Both now possess modern, streamlined systems, reflecting religious traditions and indigenous needs. As we have also demonstrated, Egypt's and Israel's systems may represent the kinds of modern legal structures that will emerge in other less-developed Middle Eastern states.

NOTES

1. Although these states fit into the religious-secular model, as a result of indigenous legislation, each deviates to some extent from the Israeli system. At least through 1978, the judicial process in Iran, for example, clearly fit the religious-secular model. Two types of courts existed. The Iranian civil code, however, is based upon Roman and Islamic law. The Iraqi legal system also contains both religious and secular courts. The laws enforced by these courts, however, are relatively unstable, as they are based on "working papers" and are constantly reviewed for their compatibility with the ideology of the regime in power. Lebanon, through the 1970s, possessed a relatively straightforward three-tiered religious-secular legal apparatus. Yet, law there is based on French and Islamic teachings. The Jordanian system is similar to the Lebanese, but there are two kinds of religious courts: Muslim and ecclesiastical. The law in Jordan is also comprised of a blend of English, Islamic, and French law. And, although the legal system in Kuwait does not contain religious courts per se, judges are supposed to use religious doctrine to decide civil disputes.

2. Although the Turkish legal system is secular, it deviates from the Egyptian model in at least two ways. First, it is much more complicated in design than the three-tiered Egyptian system. Turkey created specialized lower courts to adjudicate claims involving civil, commercial, and criminal law. Also, its highest appeals court contains fourteen divisions to deal with specific areas of the law. Second, the Turkish civil code was derived primarily from the Swiss system.

3. F. Ziadeh, *Lawyers, the Rule of Law and Liberalism in Modern Egypt* (Stanford, Calif.: Hoover Institute on War, Revolution and Peace, 1968), p. 4.

4. G. H. El-Nahal, *The Judicial Administration of Ottoman Egypt in the Seventeenth Century* (Minneapolis: Bibliotheca Islamica, 1979), pp. 6–7.

5. R. Nolte, *The Modern Middle East* (New York: Atherton Press, 1963), p. 157.

6. Ziadeh, *Lawyers*, p. 4.

7. El-Nahal, *The Judicial Administration*, p. 73.

8. Ibid., pp. 25–35.

9. Ibid., p. 72.

10. Ziadeh, *Lawyers*, p. 10; see J. W. Salacuse, "Back to Contract: Implications of Peace and Openness for Egypt's Legal System," *American Journal of Comparative Law* 28 (1980), pp. 315–33, for further discussion on this.

11. Ibid., pp. 19–21.

12. Ibid., p. 26.

13. J. Y. Brinton, *The Mixed Courts of Egypt* (New Haven, Conn.: Yale University Press, 1968), p. ix.

14. Ibid., p. x.

15. Ziadeh, *Lawyers*, p. 24.

16. Ibid., p. 31.

17. The law applied by the native courts was based on the French codes used in the mixed courts.

18. Salacuse, "Back to Contract," p. 318.

19. Ibid.

20. A. S. Banks and W. Overstreet, eds., *Political Handbook of the World* (New York: McGraw Hill, 1982/1983), p. 139.

21. N. J. Ackerson, "Journal of a Hoosier Lawyer in Cairo," *Res Getae* (June 1983), p. 610.

22. R. H. Eisenman, *Islamic Law in Palestine and Israel* (Leiden, The Netherlands: E. J. Brill, 1978), pp. 12–13.

23. Ibid., p. 14.

24. H. E. Baker, *The Legal System of Israel* (Jerusalem: Israel Universities Press, 1968), p. 61.

25. Eisenman, *Islamic Law*, p. 15.

26. Ibid., p. 18.

27. O. Kraines, *Government and Politics in Israel* (Boston: Houghton Mifflin Co., 1961), p. 138.

28. M. H. Bernstein, *The Politics of Israel* (Princeton, N.J.: Princeton University Press, 1957), p. 16.

29. Kraines, *Government and Politics in Israel*, p. 139.

30. Ibid.

31. Ibid., p. 140.

32. Y. S. Zemach, *Political Questions in the Courts: A Judicial Function in Democracies—Israel and the United States* (Detroit: Wayne State University Press, 1976), p. 22.

33. Kraines, *Government and Politics in Israel*, p. 141.

34. Ibid., p. 142.

35. C. S. Rhyne, ed., *Law and Judicial Systems of Nations*, 3d ed. (Washington, D.C.: The World Peace Through Law Center, 1978), p. 206.

36. Ibid., pp. 204–5.

37. W. Frankel, *Israel Observed: An Anatomy of the State* (published by the author, 1980), p. 121.

38. Kraines, *Government and Politics in Israel*, p. 143.

39. *Statistical Abstract of Israel, 1983–1984* (Jerusalem: Central Bureau of Statistics, 1984), p. 595.

40. Ibid., p. 613.

41. Kraines, *Government and Politics in Israel*, p. 144.

42. Rhyne, *Law and Judicial Systems*, p. 364.

43. Frankel, *Israel Observed*, p. 121.

44. Kraines, *Government and Politics in Israel*, p. 144.

45. *Statistical Abstract of Israel*, p. 616.

46. Kraines, *Government and Politics in Israel*, pp. 145–146.

47. Ibid., p. 146.

48. Ibid., pp. 146–47.

49. See Rhyne, *Law and Judicial Systems*, p. 366; and ibid., pp. 148–49.

50. Kraines, *Government and Politics in Israel*, p. 149.

51. *The Middle East and North Africa, 1983–84* (London: European Publications Limited, 1984), p. 393.

52. Baker, *The Legal System of Israel*, p. 209.

53. Kraines, *Government and Politics in Israel*, p. 150.

54. Ziadeh, *Lawyers*, p. 21.

55. Ibid., pp. 28–30.

56. Ackerson, ''Journal of a Hoosier Lawyer,'' p. 610.

57. Salacuse, ''Back to Contract,'' p. 322.

58. Rhyne, *Law and Judicial Systems*, p. 202.

59. Ibid., p. 205.

60. Salacuse, ''Back to Contract,'' p. 322.

61. Ziadeh, *Lawyers*, p. 27.

62. When the native courts were first established, several foreign judges were assigned to each court level. As Egypt acclimated to the new system, the number was ''reduced gradually.'' See ibid., p. 34.

63. Baker, *The Legal System of Israel*, p. 232.

64. Ibid., p. 236.

65. An immigrant lawyer who has already practiced for two years abroad must only apprentice for six months to one year (see Frankel, *Israel Observed*, p. 134). If a foreign advocate has practiced for less than two years, then the period of apprenticeship is set by the chamber (see Baker, *The Legal System of Israel*, p. 238).

66. Rhyne, *Law and Judicial Systems*, p. 362.

67. Baker, *The Legal System of Israel*, p. 205.

68. M. Edelman, ''The Judicial Elite of Israel: Societal Context'' (Paper delivered at the Interim Conference, Research Committee for Comparative Judicial Studies, IPSA, University of Southern California, 1984), p. 10.

69. Baker, *The Legal System of Israel*, p. 205.

70. Frankel, *Israel Observed*, p. 126.

71. Baker, *The Legal System of Israel*, p. 205.

72. Zemach, *Political Questions in the Courts*, p. 26.

73. Frankel, *Israel Observed*, p. 126.

74. Banks and Overstreet, *Political Handbook*, p. 139.

75. Rhyne, *Law and Judicial Systems*, p. 207.

76. Ibid.

77. Kraines, *Government and Politics in Israel*, p. 155.

78. Frankel, *Israel Observed*, p. 126.

79. Zemach, *Political Questions in the Courts*, p. 26.

80. Kraines, *Government and Politics in Israel*, p. 147.

81. Ibid.

82. Ibid., p. 148.

83. Zemach, *Political Questions in the Courts*, p. 32.
84. Kraines, *Government and Politics in Israel*, p. 148.
85. Zemach, *Political Questions in the Courts*, p. 28.
86. 1 *S.J.* at 86–87, cited in ibid., p. 29.
87. Ibid., p. 176.
88. Ibid., p. 175.
89. Baker, *The Legal System of Israel*, p. 202.

BIBLIOGRAPHY

Ackerson, N. J. "Journal of a Hoosier Lawyer in Cairo." *Res Getae* (June 1983), p. 610.

Baker, H. E. *The Legal System of Israel*. Jerusalem: Israel Universities Press, 1968.

Banks, A. S., and W. Overstreet, eds. *Political Handbook of the World*. New York: McGraw-Hill, 1983.

Bernstein, M. H. *The Politics of Israel*. Princeton, N.J.: Princeton University Press, 1957.

Brinton, J. Y. *The Mixed Courts of Egypt*. New Haven, Conn.: Yale University Press, 1968.

David, R., and J. E. C. Brierley. *Major Legal Systems in the World Today*. London: Stevens & Sons, 1968.

Edelman, M. "The Judicial Elite of Israel: Societal Context." Paper delivered at the Interim Conference, Research Committee for Comparative Judicial Studies, IPSA. University of Southern California, 1984.

Ehrmann, H. W. *Comparative Legal Cultures*. Englewood Cliffs, N.J.: Prentice-Hall, 1976.

Eisenman, R. H. *Islamic Law in Palestine and Israel*. Leiden, The Netherlands: E. J. Brill, 1978.

El-Nahal, G. H. *The Judicial Administration of Ottoman Egypt in the Seventeenth Century*. Minneapolis: Bibliotheca Islamica, 1979.

England, I. *Religious Law in the Israel Legal System*. Jerusalem: Alpha Press, 1975.

Eorsi, G. *Comparative Civil (Private) Law*. Budapest: Akademiai Kiado, 1979.

Fein, L. J. *Politics in Israel*. Boston: Little, Brown and Co., 1967.

Frankel, W. *Israel Observed: An Anatomy of the State*. (published by author), 1980.

Hill, E. "Comparative and Historical Study of Modern Middle Eastern Law." *American Journal of Comparative Law* 26 (1970), pp. 279–304.

Kraines, O. *Government and Politics in Israel*. Boston: Houghton Mifflin Co., 1961.

The Middle East and North Africa, 1983–84. London: European Publications Limited, 1984.

Nolte, R. *The Modern Middle East*. New York: Atherton Press, 1963.

Peretz, D. *The Government and Politics of Israel*. 2d ed. Colorado: Westview Press, 1983.

———. *The Middle East Today*. New York: Holt, Rinehart and Winston, 1978.

Rhyne, C. S., ed. *Law and Judicial Systems of Nations*. 3d ed. Washington, D.C.: The World Peace Through Law Center, 1978.

Rubinstein, A. *Law and Religion in Israel*. In M. Lissak and E. Gutmann, eds. *Political Institutions and Processes in Israel*. Jerusalem: Hebrew University of Jerusalem, 1971. Pp. 569–619.

Salacuse, J. W. "Back to Contract: Implications of Peace and Openness for Egypt's Legal System." *American Journal of Comparative Law* 28 (1980), pp. 315–33.
Shimshoni, D. *Israeli Democracy: The Middle of the Journey*. New York: Macmillan, 1982.
Statistical Abstract of Israel 1983–1984. Jerusalem: Central Bureau of Statistics, 1984.
Zemach, Y. S. *Political Questions in the Courts: A Judicial Function in Democracies—Israel and the United States*. Detroit: Wayne State University Press, 1976.
Ziadeh, F. *Lawyers, the Rule of Law and Liberalism in Modern Egypt*. Stanford, Calif.: Hoover Institute on War, Revolution and Peace, 1968.

12

PEOPLE'S REPUBLIC OF CHINA

Richard C. DeAngelis

The concept of law that developed in the Western legal tradition has its origin in the religions of ancient civilizations. The earliest written law codes of ancient Mesopotamia, such as the Code of Hammurabi, are claimed to have been revealed to mankind by a divine source. This is also true of the expression of the Judaic, Christian, and Islamic law. Formulations of law in the Graeco-Roman tradition adopted a naturalist secularism. Law was that which reason dictated, a force in itself that was regarded as essential to a moral order of human society. Sir William Blackstone, in the Introduction to his *Commentaries* (1765), acknowledged the divine origin of revealed law through inspired Scripture and "sought to make secular law approximate to the dictates of God and of nature."[1]

The positivist school denies a divine basis for law and rejects any moral or ethical consideration. It views law as a creation of the secular state "which the lawyer has to understand in order to gain the greatest advantage in the protection of the interests of his clients."[2] Both naturalist and positivist conceptions elevate law above the conflicts that appeal to it, even above the will of the lawgiver, and hold it to be the guarantor of the social order. The Western constitutional polity is founded upon this impartial and transcendent notion of the law.

The Western conception of law as the supreme arbiter resulted in the elaborate codification of the law to which all men owe obedience. Societies hailed themselves as governments of law and not of men as the power of monarch and state were held in check by the restraining rule of law. China has been one of those nations regarded by the West as an example of the capricious rule of men rather than law. Such a judgment seems precipitous. An examination of how the Chinese define law and the role it plays in ordering their civilization will help us to understand how law is administered in China.

THE DEVELOPMENT OF THE LEGAL SYSTEM

Fa and Li in Chinese Law

Ancient China was composed of diverse groups of people who blended into the relatively homogenous culture of the Yellow River basin during the first millennium B.C. Various religious and philosophical traditions synthesized into a corpus of intellectual beliefs that endured with remarkable continuity into the present century. Often referred to as Confucianism, this intellectual tradition had its origins in a primitive cosmology that antedates Confucius's own era. For the Chinese, the essential principle of nature was a harmony that was reflected in human social relations. Conflict, if left unresolved, it was argued, would result in great discord.

The Chinese term that conveys the positivist idea of law is *fa*. Used to mean "the law" or "laws," fa implies a model of behavior imposed under threat of authority. Fa was applied to those transgressions of the social order that upset the harmony of man and nature, and, as such, may be thought of as penal law. As written law, fa was expressed in codes dating back to the sixth century B.C., when the state of Cheng cast its code in bronze.[3] Yet, the notion of fa predates the written codes. The Duke of Zhou, the twelfth-century ruler whom Confucius held up as a model sage and regarded by tradition to be the author of the *Zhou Li*, rejected law as the proper governing agent of moral behavior.

Duke Zhou advocated *li* over fa as the correct determinant of human behavior. Li may be simply defined as the rules of propriety—a concern for ceremony, ritual, and observance of the proper conduct in all social relationships. As its meaning was refined, li came to epitomize the behavior of the Confucian gentleman. Confucianists stressed that man, as a rational creature, should be guided by virtue rather than fear of punishment. As this passage of the *Analects* indicates:

If the people are to be guided by law, and non-observance of law is to be corrected by punishment, they will learn to avoid punishment but have no sense of shame. If the people are to be guided by virtue, and non-observance of law is to be corrected by *li*, they will have the sense of shame, and, also, they will transform themselves into better persons.[4]

Confucianists versus Legalists

The breakup of the Zhou feudal order resulted in political anarchy. Known as the "Warring States Period," the four centuries preceding the Christian era of the West saw the rise and fall of contending states. The political and social disintegration produced a period of great philosophical activity that spawned a "Hundred Schools of Thought," as the great minds of the period sought answers concerning the fundamental order and harmony in social relations. Two of the schools that vied with each other for influence over political rulers were the Confucianists and Legalists.

The Confucian school took the view that human nature could be cultivated to provide moral leaders who would direct society through their example. This could be achieved through education designed to foster ethical and moral behavior that would bring society into harmony with the cosmos according to the will of heaven. For Confucianists, the proper moral behavior was founded in li rather than fa; the superior man did what was right because it was right, and not because of fearing the consequences of failing to do so.

To the Confucian mind, the enforcement of law by authority was a tacit admission that the cultivation of virtue through education had failed. Confucian gentlemen viewed the application of sanctions as "a regrettable necessity," a last resort for vulgar people only.[5] The educated Chinese dislike of fa is reflected in the common expression of China: "One does not read the codes."

Opposed to the Confucian disdain for fa was the Legalist school. This view, expressed most impressively by Han Fei-tzu in the third century B.C., rejected the optimism of the Confucianists and declared that man was bad and could be held to moral account only through the strict rule of law. Contemptuous of the view that the moral example of Confucian sages could protect society by insuring harmony, Han Fei-tzu insisted that law should be written, clear and easy to understand, applied objectively and universally, and binding on the lawgiver himself.[6] The Legalist prescription sought a rigid code of regulations that would discipline a highly trained bureaucracy to implement imperial rule. Moral behavior would be piloted by a harsh code of punishment and reward rather than depend upon the Confucian concept of li. The contest between these two schools was resolved temporarily in favor of the Legalists when the first emperor of the Qin dynasty unified China by force and adopted legalism as the basis of his political order. Influenced by Legalist disciples, the Qin rulers undertook a harsh persecution of Confucian scholars, which included the destruction of the philosophical writings of the Confucian school. The triumph of the Legalist system was as brief as the reign of the Qin emperors (221–206 B.C.). The succeeding Han dynasty (202 B.C.-A.D. 220) enlisted the administrative skills of Confucian scholars as it sought to establish its political rule throughout the land. The adoption of a bureaucratic structure staffed by the educated Confucian elite carried with it the moral code of this group.

The Han rejected legalism, and the bureaucracy sought to ground the justification of the state on Orthodox Confucian principles. Aspects of the harsh Legalist system persisted: beheading, mutilation, and forced labor were still applied to common offenders, but the universality of law gradually yielded to the Confucian idea of moral suasion, and a hierarchy of penalities were imposed commensurate with the offenders' rank in society.[7] The newly adopted Han Code suspended the draconian prescriptions for officials and members of the aristocracy whose penalties were reduced to exile, dismissal from office, or frequently to fines.[8] Thus began the "Confucianization of law" that subsequently resulted in the complete dominance of the Confucian political philosophy and moral code.

The Han adoption of a legal code and its revision and enlargement by later dynasties preserved the Legalist aspect of statutory law of the earlier Quin. To the Confucianists, the statutory sanctions imposed by the legal code were viewed as a last resort and could be avoided by the proper inculcation of Confucian moral principles. Sima Qian, the Han historian, saw li and fa as serving two distinct purposes: "To impress restraint before the fact, is *li*; to impose restraint after the fact, is law."[9] Thus li, the moral code, operates outside of and independent of the formal statutory code (fa) of government law. As the moral code was preserved by the educated Confucian elite, it remained free from the direct control of dynastic officials while, at the same time, influencing the behavior of those officials, most of whom were recruited from the Confucian elite through the formal examination system that governed entrance into the bureaucracy.

Traditional imperial China was governed by a dual authority, one element of which was the statutory basis of law enforcement through punishments to ensure the government's political will; the other was the Confucian code, a moral source of authority akin to natural law that regulated the behavior of the Confucian scholars themselves, the guardians of this moral system who handed it down to later generations. The long history of Chinese imperial culture serves as testimony to the fact that these dual sources of authority reinforced each other in support of a system that, despite crises, survived the rise and fall of successive dynasties for almost two millennia of Chinese history.[10]

Imperial Governance and the Administration of Justice

Disputes in China have traditionally been resolved through the use of mediation and litigation. Of these two forms, mediation is employed to resolve the vast majority of conflicts. The basic goal of Chinese social philosophy is to attain harmony, and mediation is compatible with this Confucian ideal. Another reason for the use of mediation was that, despite the size and vast population, traditional China's imperial administration down to the district level was accomplished with no more than three or four thousand administrative officers.

The governing structure of imperial China evolved over two thousand years during which time shifts in organization and practice occurred, often intentionally, as a means of restraining a system in which power yielded to centrifugal tendencies inherent in the vast size of China. Acknowledging these shifts and hiatuses of authority, we can speak of a traditional "pattern" of imperial government that endured from the Song dynasty (960–1279) until the collapse of the Qing dynasty in 1912.

The emperor ruled from the capital through half a dozen or so boards and commissions, which were responsible to advise him on matters of administration under their jurisdiction by the preparation of "memorials" suggesting policy. The emperor's comments and signature defined the official policy, which the boards would then implement. Membership on these boards was usually attained after a distinguished career in the imperial bureaucracy involving broad experience and successfully passing the highest levels of the imperial examinations.

Below this elite circle was a hierarchy of Confucian bureaucrats, the mandarins, that spread through a network of territorial divisions. Each of the eighteen provinces was headed by a governor (often two or three provinces came under a governor-general) who directed the activities of the mandarins at the subdivision levels of circuit, prefecture, department, and district. The officers of each of these levels had specialized assistants. Although serious legal offenses would proceed up the hierarchy and the death penalty would be reviewed by the Board of Punishments in the capital, it was the lower echelons, especially the district (*hsien*) level, where most conflicts were resolved.

The District Magistrates and Judicial Administration

Figures for the Ming and Qing periods of Chinese history (1369–1912) report that the number of hsien was between 1,200 and 1,300, each with a population of 200,000 or more.[11] The magistrate's office (*yamen*) was located in one of the larger cities with a population that numbered in the tens of thousands and bore the entire responsibility for local government of the hsien, including the rural villages that ranged in size from a few hundred people to market town communities of several thousands.

Although the local magistrate was the lowest ranking officer in the imperial hierarchy, his position is not analogous to the lowest echelon of Western civil service bureaucracies. The magistrate was not on the bottom rung of a career ladder that normally led to a series of higher positions; more often than not, the office represented the apex of a government career. While local magistrates came to their posts through various avenues and served with varying records of distinction, the recorded cases of exemplary magistrates makes it possible to construct a model of a typical local magistrate.

Candidates for the imperial civil service prepared themselves through a classical Chinese education that placed emphasis on Confucian philosophy and literary and artistic achievement. This education virtually assured that most, though not all, came from comfortable economic backgrounds that could afford the necessary years of tutoring and support for the budding scholar. Passage of the civil service examinations given on several levels was the means of entrance into the service. Normally, passing the second level, the provincial examinations, granted eligibility for the posts of district magistrate. Scholars who attained this degree could sit for the metropolitan exams given every few years at the capital. Success at this higher level admitted one to the Confucian intellectual elite from which the emperor appointed the highest officials.

The education and examination of scholars showed little regard for training in the mundane administrative, economic, or legal skills associated with the post of magistrate. The practice of earlier dynasties that the education of officials show some concern with matters of law and public policy was abandoned in the Ming and Qing era, when the emphasis shifted to Confucian orthodoxy and literary accomplishments. Upon passing the imperial examinations, minimal qualifications for the magistrate's office, a candidate entered a period of waiting for an official appointment. During this time his judgment would mature through valuable experience gained in managing clan or family economic matters and perhaps as a member of the local gentry participating in local affairs. He might even serve on the staff of a district magistrate or train to become a secretary of law, the key position in service to a local magistrate. The long-awaited initial appointment of a magistrate, generally in his thirties or forties, was not expected to lead to a career involving subsequently higher appointments in the administrative hierarchy.

By law, the new magistrate was appointed to a province other than that from which his family came, due to a Confucian system of checks designed to inhibit corruption. The new appointee arrived in a strange district ignorant of the local politics and power groups, adjusting to a staff whose interests did not always coincide with his, and, in many cases, speaking a dialect (often Mandarin, the northern Chinese dialect) different from that of the local populace and necessitating the use of interpreters.

Well versed in poetry and literature, perhaps an accomplished poet and painter, the magistrate often lacked training in his two most important responsibilities: judicial administration and tax collection. The duties of the magistrate were awesome. His trust was to maintain the peace of the hsien, to serve as the highest judicial officer, and to ensure the economic well-being of the community by overseeing public works, flood control, disaster relief, government granaries, and an equitable tax administration.

He was responsible for the preparation of a seemingly endless flow of paperwork: censuses, tax reports, financial statements, judicial records both civil and criminal, reports on the operation of his yamen with special "memorials" to his superiors upon inquiry concerning any subject within his administrative purview. He had the special responsibility to accommodate visiting government delegations passing through the area. As a member of the official Confucian cult, he had ritual and ceremonial duties to perform, all carefully judged by the local Confucian elite with whom he was engaged in constant strategic maneuvering among local powerful interests. As a scholar he had to exemplify the Confucian virtues deemed essential to govern the uneducated masses, and he spent a good deal of his time and personal money in patronage to the educational, religious, and cultural development of the community. Upon the expiration of his tenure in office, normally three to five years (sometimes longer but often cut short by the mourning retirement required upon the death of a parent), he would receive no further appointment but would retire to his home locale as a member of the gentry.

The routine work of the yamen was handled by the magistrate's staff. This included personnel of various grades such as runners and clerks. Runners were local people who performed the functions of messengers and bailiff. Often a rough lot, poorly paid, and illiterate, they engaged in bribery and extortion in the conduct of their work, making them a necessary evil in the magistrate's service. The clerks were government-paid employees whose specific skills were necessary to the operation of the yamen and who usually served a succession of magistrates. Their primary responsibility was record-keeping and processing of enormous numbers of documents exchanged in the routine operation of the magistrate's office. Numbering in the hundreds in a small yamen, the clerks oversaw the daily routine of collecting taxes, public works management, and the administration of justice. As with the yamen runners, the clerks posed a constant threat to the new magistrate of limited experience. That the magistrate was at all able to carry out the responsibilities associated with his office was due to the use of private secretaries.

The private secretaries were experts in the administration of law and taxation. A magistrate would employ several carefully selected secretaries. The secretaries were scholars who held examination degrees and had acquired training and experience in law and taxation. Often they had passed the examination for the office of magistrate and were awaiting appointment. Private secretaries were not government officials but were considered the equal of officials and superior to the clerks. They were paid by the magistrate and given room and board within the yamen, where they maintained close contact with the magistrate.

The most important of the private secretaries was the legal secretary, whose status and salary were greater than the others. Some yamen had more than one secretary of law and several assistant secretaries of law, the number regulated by the ability of the magistrate to pay their salaries. The legal secretary had the enormous responsibility of managing the magistrate's legal work, closely scrutinized by the magistrate's superiors, in a system involving a complex law code and a detailed corpus of administrative regulations. As the code and regulations admitted severe punishments for minor infractions on the part of officials, the legal secretary's work also required that he prevent the magistrate from making serious errors. All cases of homicide and larceny came directly under the secretary of law; lesser offenses involving fighting, fraud, and marriage disputes were dealt with by his office and staff. The legal secretary would review complaints and write a formal rescript for the magistrate's approval. This rescript was important; it determined whether a complaint would be granted a hearing and investigation or would be rejected. The rescripts were posted on a public bulletin board, and a good rescript would discourage a plaintiff from exaggerating his case. The reasons for rejecting a complaint had to be stated clearly to deter a plaintiff from taking his case up the ladder to a higher level.

The secretary of law arranged the dates for hearings. Prior to the hearing he prepared a summary of the case, with documents, so the magistrate would know how to proceed. He also decided who would be summoned to court. The secretary himself did not attend the court sessions but was informed of the disposition of the case by the magistrate afterward. If the secretary raised objections to the disposition of the case, a second hearing might be held. The secretary's absence from the hearing was a safeguard, since he and his staff had prepared the case; it was also an obvious obstacle to the efficient handling of legal matters.

Serious cases involving death, banishment, or penal servitude had to be reported to the magistrate's superiors. The secretary of law carefully prepared these reports. When a proposed decision was rejected by superiors, it was the secretary's responsibility to respond to all points raised, providing fuller information, if necessary, to see a final disposition of the case. Since all levels of officials employed private legal secretaries, the resolution of disputed cases was generally worked out through correspondence between the respective secretaries to the satisfaction of the officials. A competent secretary of law was a necessity for any official and was hard to find. An official awaiting appointment would explore the recommendations of relatives and colleagues in search of a legal secretary. Competent secretaries would serve an official for many years and often were taken with the official when transferred to a new post. Law prohibited a superior official from recommending a secretary to a subordinate, but this was often ignored. Under regulations passed in 1723, a governor could recommend a secretary for official appointment subject to the secretary's examination and review by the Board of Civil Office. An official who recommended an incompetent secretary would be demoted and dismissed from his office.[12]

The district magistrate's duties as judicial officer encompassed two major activities: presiding as a trial judge and serving as the highest-level mediator in the hsien. To one familiar with Western law, these two aspects of the Chinese judicial system may seem paradoxical. To the Chinese, among whom the Confucian ideal of harmony is central to all social relations, the primary aim of conflict-resolution is to restore the harmony of social relations in their daily lives. In cases involving serious criminal activity, harmony would be restored with apprehension and punishment of the criminal; civil complaints were more often resolved through mediation on some level designed to restore the parties in conflict to their previous state of harmony. In such civil matters, litigation would normally be unnecessary and avoided until attempts at mediation had proven fruitless.

Contrary to the image of the Confucian sage mediating disputes and rendering judgments according to some inscrutable Oriental form of Solomon-like wisdom, the district magistrates labored under the burden of a detailed legal code that had evolved continuously since at least the second century B.C. The Chinese code was a legacy of the short-lived victory of the Legalists over the Confucianists during the Qin dynasty. Periodic reorganization of the code from the Tang through the Qing dynasties resulted in an elaborate set of statutes and substatutes, most of which originated with imperial decrees and subsequent administrative rulings (similar to the Western judicial precedents of case law) promulgated to deal with special problems and incidents. Thus, the Chinese codes reflected highly specific responses to particular issues rather than a general formulation for a legal system.[13] Most articles of the code defined specific acts of wrongdoing and their required punishments. In this sense it was a penal code but not limited to solely criminal matters; the codes contained articles dealing with violations of the proper filial relations between family members, destruction of property, embezzlement of the property of another, usury, and false claims or forged documents concerning land boundaries. These civil matters were believed deserving of state punishment, since they violated the Confucian social harmony.

The magistrate was the only official who served as trial judge in his district of several hundred thousand people. Court was held only six or seven months a year due to prescribed recesses and holidays. Criminal cases attracted his immediate attention and, upon the registration of a complaint, were investigated under the auspices of the legal secretary. Regulations governing the time between the complaint and the trial were routinely ignored and the defendant might languish in jail before trial to encourage a speedy settlement, even in civil cases involving violations of specific statutes.

Trials were open to the public in all cases except treason. In criminal cases, the defendant was hauled before the magistrate's elevated seat, often in chains, and forced to kneel. Torture was commonplace both before and during the courtroom procedure; the purpose of the trial was to obtain a written confession from the accused in which he clearly admitted and defined his wrongdoing. No jury was used, nor were there attorneys to act on behalf of the defendant. Any testimony favorable to the accused would have been offered to the yamen runners under the legal secretary during the investigation phase and included in the secretary's summary. In criminal cases clearly covered by the code, the magistrate retired after the trial to prepare, with his legal secretary, a summary statement of the evidence, confession, and proposed disposition of the case. This summary was sent to the magistrate's superiors; in cases subject to the right of appeal, the summary would be reviewed by the superiors pending appeal. The magistrates' recommendations in appellate cases were reviewed by the provincial judge who served as a representative of the Board of Punishments in Peking. All serious cases involving homicide or where the punishment was greater than penal servitude were retried at the provincial court. The findings of the provincial judge were then sent to the Board of Punishments in Peking, which was the final appeals court except for cases involving capital punishment. Capital decisions went eventually to the emperor himself, who, with his advisors, reviewed the cases and often applied a formula for commuting the death sentence.

Litigation, even in civil disputes, was generally avoided due to its high cost (with no assurance of a favorable judgment) and the risk of having an essentially civil matter converted into a penal issue, since the Chinese code had almost two hundred articles prescribing punishment for what Western law would view as strictly civil matters. A land boundary dispute, for example, might result in the magistrate charging that one party had made a false boundary claim. Such a verdict would result in the guilty party being beaten with bamboo, the prescribed punishment.

The pursuit of litigation meant that the plaintiff, usually uneducated and illiterate, had to place his trust in some relatively literate person who earned a living by filing documents for claims. The general level of corruption in the bureaucracy was such that the litigant was expected to pay bribes to the various runners, clerks, and assistants in the process of filing the papers. Beyond this, there were the official litigation fees to be paid and generous gifts to be offered to the legal secretary and even to the magistrate himself, whose salary was less than the cost of administering his office. Once the litigant entered the arena, he could not be sure that the person representing him had the requisite skills to match those of his adversary's, nor could he be assured that the magistrate would not decide in favor of the party presenting the largest gift. Social status was another factor; in hierarchical China, the family of high prestige and position had the advantage. Thus, a tenant who withheld his rent or defaulted for a legitimate reason, might lose to a landlord and be required to pay his rent and be whipped because the code stipulated such punishment for refusing to pay rent. The latitude of options open to the magistrate as judge in resolving civil conflict could turn a minor complaint into a case that could bankrupt a family. Such uncertainty attached to litigation and the limit on the number of cases a magistrate could hear served to direct most civil matters toward another form of conflict resolution widely employed in China—mediation.

The dual tradition of mediation and litigation in the Chinese judicial system represents the coexistence of both the Legalist and Confucian ideas of law enforcement. Legalist ideas incorporated into the system were "Confucianized" in the practice of administering the law. A rigid legal code was adopted and maintained to provide punishments when the essential Confucian moral philosophy of example, education, and mediation failed to maintain social harmony. While litigation might be used in cases of serious criminal behavior, most instances of family and village conflict would be resolved through mediation. As Martin Shapiro notes, "the person of greatest moral virtue is not the one with the more legitimate interests, but the one who is willing to yield more of his legitimate interests in order to restore harmony with his opponent."[14]

To the Confucian mind, men must choose a moral course to achieve social harmony in their daily lives. It is through moral suasion that the uneducated are led to the Confucian virtues. The success of Chinese mediation is dependent upon the cultural notion that the party who sacrifices more to restore harmony does not lose, but, in fact, wins because he gains more in moral stature. Confucian mediation is not a compromise in which the claimant to the greatest loss may be awarded the decision and thus be encouraged to make exaggerated claims. Rather, it is the party who is least assertive and willing to yield, whatever the stakes, who gains the moral advantage and perhaps the benefit for the mediator's decision.

Prior to entering into formal mediation, the disputants would seek out a third party to help resolve the conflict. Family disputes might be brought before the eldest male in his role as head of the family or be referred to trusted outsiders. Village conflicts might be resolved by any member of the village who was held in esteem and reputed to be a good mediator. Often such persons were village elders or authorities, members of the gentry, or clan or guild leaders. Mediation was often required by clan, guild, or village rules before one could finally bring a complaint to a district court. Upon registration of a complaint, mediation had to cease and the matter be left to the court.

Once engaged, the mediators would visit with the disputants and conduct an investigation of the facts. Individuals who made unreasonable demands soon became the subject of subtle but mounting social pressure, including perhaps, pressure from the magistrate himself. During this process the mediators kept informed of public opinion, which served as a strong sanction for their work. When the mediators proposed a solution, it was usually one that represented village consensus and that the magistrate would endorse. A disputant who withdrew from mediation was guilty of a serious breach of decorum and subject to public ostracism. If either party rejected the proposed solution of the mediators and took the matter to court, they might be faced with a dissatisfied magistrate who would impose the mediators' solution or perhaps a harsher settlement. On the other hand, the successful resolution of a conflict was often celebrated by festivities and a banquet to cement the bonds of harmony between the former adversaries.

This survey of traditional China's judicial process yields several points of interest that remain a part of contemporary China: a harsh but flexible statutory code that sometimes blurs the distinction between purely civil and criminal punishments; a preference for mediation that allows the Confucian virtues of example, education, and moral suasion to effect a conversion of the wrongdoer; and a trial procedure, as a last resort, designed to exact confession and acknowledgment of moral shame from the accused.

The Republican Period, 1912–1949

The decline of China's traditional Confucian order began long before the Qing dynasty was overthrown by the Revolution of 1911. The Manchu conquerors of China, who established the Qing dynasty (1644–1912), had been resented before the traumatic impact of Western imperialism that began with the Opium Wars (1839–1842). Disorder led to chaos at the turn of the century as a growing revolutionary movement sought redress for China's plight.[15] Following China's humiliating defeat in the Sino-Japanese War (1894–1895), a brief reform movement in 1898 failed, and the dynasty's reaction was manifested in the Boxer Rebellion of 1900. Enlightened intellectuals became concerned with the need for China to undertake institutional reform in order to deal with the crisis that, in their view, resulted partly from the enormous cultural and technological gap between China and the West.

One issue outstanding between China and the Western nations was China's archaic legal system and brutal penal code. To escape Chinese jurisdiction, Western nations had forced China to concede to a system of extraterritoriality in which foreigners or persons residing in areas under foreign jurisdiction became subject to the legal system of the foreign power enjoying administrative authority over Chinese soil, a de facto violation of China's sovereignty.

Even as Sun Yatsen and other revolutionaries were preparing to topple the ineffective Qing rulers, a series of belated reforms were undertaken. In 1902, the dynasty established a Law Codification Commission to draft modern criminal and civil codes. Later, in 1907, laws were drafted to reorganize China's court system. Unfortunately, these reforms remained on paper and were not implemented. Sun Yatsen's followers succeeded in triggering a revolution on October 10, 1911, while Sun was actually out of the country. On December 2, this group promulgated the Organic Law of the Provisional Constitution, a document that greatly reformed China's political institutions along Western parliamentary lines.

A series of complicated events resulted in Sun's yielding the presidency of China to Yuan Shikai, a former military man who had served the Manchus and, in fact, had been commissioned to crush the Revolution. Yuan took office and on March 11, 1912, promulgated a Provisional Constitution that subsequently underwent six drafts by 1925. Yuan, who had served as a member of the 1902 Codification Commission, held no sympathy for republican institutions. He dressed his regime in constitutional garments through the passage of a series of commercial laws and a law on the administration of the court system, while at the same time making preparations to be installed as the emperor of a new dynasty. When Yuan died suddenly in June of 1916 the centrifugal forces in Chinese politics resulted in the gradual disintegration of the country at the hands of militarist factions. Thus, China entered the chaotic warlord era which lasted until the "unification" of the country in 1928 under the banners of the Kuomintang (KMT), commonly known as the Nationalist party.

This essay will treat the legal reforms of the Nationalist era very briefly for two reasons. First, while the legal system that developed under the KMT was largely the work of men educated in the West and served to bring China's legal system closely in line with Western practice, the period of Nationalist control in China was short-lived (1928–1937), and the new legal reforms never penetrated deeply into Chinese society, especially in the rural areas. The second reason is that the KMT legal system has had little impact (except perhaps, for organizational structure) on the legal system of the present People's Republic of China. In fact, much of it has been repudiated as part of the corrupt national bourgeois culture of feudal China by the Communists.

The Nationalist government established itself in Nanjing in October 1928 under the Organic Law of the Nationalist government and, despite the fact that it had only nominal control over most of China's provinces, began promulgating a series of national reforms. By the end of 1930, a civil code that included commercial and banking reform laws was enacted. A Provisional Constitution setting forth a government composed of five branches, or *yuan*, was promulgated to last for five years during which period the nation would be under the one party tutelage of the KMT. This period would be used for the drafting of a final constitution, which would then be adopted and usher in a democratic republic with competing political parties. The Japanese encroachments in China and the coming of war resulted in the Provisional Constitution being retained until 1947.

The Provisional Constitution contained some surprisingly Western-style articles insuring civil liberties and personal rights. By 1935 a new criminal code and law of criminal procedure were introduced. A court structure composed of a Supreme Court, a High Court for each province, and local (hsien) courts, with special courts for certain administrative areas such as municipalities and subject to the High Courts was established.

The new system was slow to take root due to a nonvigorous policy of implementation (due to the semi-independent status of some of the warlords, who had nominally joined the Nationalist government) and the difficulties of the masses to understand and accept Western legal practices. By 1946, there were only 500 court units established in the 2,000 hsien and municipalities of China, while most hsien were served only by a detachment of a provincial court.[16] Guarantees of due process and human rights were frequently ignored and bandits (often Communists) and robbers were summarily executed on location without reference to trial procedure, a practice of traditional China.

The Draft Constitution of May 5, 1936, met with widespread cirticism due to revisions increasing the authority of the central government and reducing guarantees of civil liberties. The Japanese invasion in July 1937 resulted in a constitutional hiatus, as the government retreated to central China under the press of Japanese military superiority. Following the Japanese defeat and surrender, the KMT promulgated a new, more liberal, constitution on January 1, 1947, and ushered in the long-awaited phase of Sun Yatsen's constitutionalism. Based on Western standards, the legal system of the new constitution stipulated an independent judiciary administered by the Ministry of Justice under the Judicial Yuan, a special branch of government responsible for the interpretation of the constitution.

The Constitution of 1947 established criminal and civil codes and procedural codes that insured the protection of civil and personal rights in a way that most Western jurists would find acceptable. However, the resumption of civil war between Nationalists and Communists in 1947 led to half-hearted implementation and eventual governance under emergency regulations (referred to in the West as martial law), which suspended the absolute protections of the Constitution. This document, amended some, still serves as the Constitution of the Republic of China on the island of Taiwan today.

The defeat of the Nationalists by the forces of Mao Ze-dong in 1949 led to the withdrawal of the KMT to Taiwan, where they continue to maintain the government of the Republic of China as a government-in-exile. Mainland China, under the control of the Chinese Communist Party (CCP), entered a new phase as the CCP sought to consolidate its rule and modernize the nation through the adoption of Marxist political, social, and legal institutions.

The First Decade of the People's Republic of China

The People's Republic, established by the CCP under the direction of Mao Ze-dong, promulgated no codes of substantive or procedural law prior to 1979.

The party ruled the state under a series of revolutionary statutes and directives. During the early years, criminal acts were regarded as political crimes against the state and generally tried under the "Regulations of the People's Republic of China for the Punishment of Counter-Revolutionaries," promulgated in 1951. The "Act for the Punishment of Corruption," issued in 1952, provided for the punishment of economic crimes and violations of CCP-defined discipline. The issuance of the "Arrest and Detention Act" of December 1954 provided a basic procedural law for the prosecution of offenders. Beside these three basic acts, the CCP poured out a steady flow of directives to enforce particular shifts in policy.

Prior to 1952–1953, when the courts were purged of holdovers of the Nationalist era and the party began to have confidence in its judicial reforms, much criminal punishment took place outside the courts. In the spring of 1953, China adopted a Soviet-style legal system and the new Constitution of 1954 contained articles governing the administration of justice. A court system similar to the present one and a national procuracy to serve as the prosecutor's office were established. Russia's de-Stalinization campaign was observed in China with a liberalization of the judicial process. By 1956, there were 800 legal advisory offices staffed by 2,500 full-time and 300 part-time lawyers. The National People's Congress, China's legislative organ, completed drafting a comprehensive criminal code in 1957, which was never promulgated because of the "Hundred Flowers" and the ensuing antirightist campaigns.[17]

In May 1956, Mao had announced "let a hundred flowers bloom, let a hundred schools of thought contend," an invitation to the people to express themselves freely on the development of China since liberation. Finding few takers, Mao reiterated the appeal in a speech concerning his collectivization program in February 1957. Summarized in the press, the speech was hailed as an attack on bureaucratism, which could be rectified through criticism by the people. Given assurances that Mao's speech represented an invitation to criticize the CCP, the intellectuals poured forth a torrent of criticism in May and June of 1957. Neither Mao nor the CCP expected the condemnation of the CCP and its cadres, who were viewed by the critics as having become a new class: elitist, bureaucratic, and unconcerned with the masses. Mao had called for a "hundred flowers" and, instead, discovered a garden overgrown with "poisonous weeds" which the party began to uproot immediately in its counter-attack against rightists.

The antirightist campaign that began in 1957 virtually destroyed China's legal system. Under the Security Administration Punishment Act of October 1957, a person could be fined and detained for fifteen days pending investigation by the public security organs (police), whose decisions were not subject to judicial review.[18] Public trials were virtually suspended except for those cases where the party sought some educational purpose. Defense counsel became obsolete, as they served only to represent the criminals' interest; judges were driven from their benches for decisions that failed to represent the directives of the state. The society was divided into "red elements" (those advancing the cause of socialism and the CCP) and "black elements" (those critics considered counter-revolutionary). The class background and social status of the accused became the determinants of the sanctions imposed in judicial hearings. Intellectuals and lawyers, the "stinking ninth category" of "black elements" were dealt with most harshly.[19]

The campaign halted all efforts at codification. Law schools remained open until 1967 but the curriculum shifted from professional to political education. Under the slogan of "smashing permanent rules," civil and human rights were violated through a process in which complaint, arrest, hearing, sentence, and execution all took place in one afternoon.[20] Finally, in 1959, the Ministry of Justice was abolished and the organized lawyers associations dismantled.

The Cultural Revolution Period, 1960–1976

The two decades that followed the opening of the antirightist campaign saw the continued development of a state ruled without benefit of a legal system but subjected to the shifting policies of party factions in conflict. Underscoring all events was Mao's drive to purge China of its "bourgeois reactionaries" and "counter-revolutionaries" and to instill in the younger generation revolutionary experience and values in order to produce the truly socialist men who would insure the establishment of a Marxist utopia. The "bad years" (1960–1963) witnessed an economic depression in China comparable to the Great Depression of 1929 in the United States.[21] Much of this was due to the dislocations and excesses of the antirightist campaign and the "Great Leap Forward Movement" (1958–1963) that followed.

When a socialist education campaign failed to stir the party and masses to fulfill his hopes for China, Mao called for a cultural revolution to completely transform China into the leading socialist state. This could only be attained through the development of "proletarian thought," a state of selfless dedication to one's comrades without any concern for personal advantage. Finding the party still reluctant to follow, Mao turned to the youth of the nation, who had been organized as Red Guards, and called on them to criticize party bureaucrats, teachers who still held bourgeois attitudes, and even their families. In the summer of 1966 Mao called on these Red Guards to "make revolution" and launched the Great Proletarian Cultural Revolution (GPCR).

The GPCR dealt the death blow to any vestiges of judicial procedure that might have survived the earlier campaigns. Under banners declaring "In Praise of Lawlessness," students from junior high school through university age began criticizing their teachers, school officials, and party bureaucrats; the criticism turned into a violent storm of searches for evidence of bourgeois thought, beatings, and struggle sessions in which the accused was criticized at a mass rally, humiliated, made to confess to alleged "crimes," beaten, and in some cases, executed by the mob on the spot. Millions of Red Guards mounted China's rail network and travelled about "making revolution." By 1971, there were pitched battles between radical and moderate Red Guard factions who had seized weapons from armories—necessitating the use of China's army to subdue them.

Between 1966 and 1970 nearly all the schools and universities in China had been closed, interrupting the education of China's youth for as long as ten years. Libraries were ransacked and Western books often put to the bonfire; admonished not to be "slaves to foreign things," Red Guards particularly sought out the Western classics, which were destroyed along with Western sheet music and musical instruments. China's cultural heritage was not exempted; students destroyed Confucian and Taoist temples and museum pieces and ransacked ancestral graveyards in the name of eradicating "the old."[22]

Radical groups within the CCP seized the opportunity to gain power. Mao's wife and several sycophants, later known as the "gang of four" used the chaos of the times and Mao's declining health to seize leadership. Top-ranking party members were subjected to struggle-sessions and removed from their posts and often sent to labor camps.

The death of Mao in 1976 made possible the return of more moderate forces in the CCP. The eventual rehabilitation of Deng Xiaoping (who had been purged during the GPCR) in 1978 brought in its wake the exoneration and restoration of responsible leaders long opposed to Mao's policies. Those leaders who suffered most from the suspension of the legal process have been earnestly trying to reconstruct a legal system for China during the last five or six years.

The Post-Mao Legal Reforms

Within a month after the death of Mao Ze-dong in September 1976, Hua Guofeng, his "chosen" successor, boldly arrested Mao's wife, Jiang Qing, and the three other members of the "gang of four," who were later expelled from the party and then prosecuted in a trial that was widely broadcast throughout China and the world. Hua then began to rehabilitate several moderate party leaders who had fallen during the GPCR and this group began the task of reconstructing the social, political, and legal order. Deng Xiaoping, one of the early fathers of the CCP, rose rapidly to new heights of power, ironically elbowing Hua out of the spotlight as Mao's designated heir.

The new leadership showed its sincere concern for the condition of China by proceeding rapidly with a series of substantial reforms. In March of 1978 a new constitution was drafted by the National People's Congress and promulgated in December 1982. The new constitution significantly restores some fundamental civil rights to citizens and reinstitutes the courts and the People's Procuratorates under the Ministry of Justice, which was reestablished in 1979.[23]

The National People's Congress (NPC), China's legislative body, assumes the responsibility to oversee all aspects of the legal system. The NPC adopted, in 1979, seven major legal and procedural codes that were promulgated on January 1, 1980. These codes reflect the traditional socialist approach to law, but their framers also studied the legal systems of Western societies. While we are interested here in the legal system and not the law or its codes per se, it is instructive to examine the "rule of law" in China to better understand the role legal practitioners play in the system. Richard Herman draws this distinction between American and Chinese views of law. American law has two principles, that all should obey the law and that the law must be made by the government according to established procedures that control the government's action; law in China is a body of rules imposed by a particular political leadership to direct the citizens to achieve the ends mandated by the party's Marxist-socialist ideology.[24]

This difference in the purpose of the two systems becomes evident upon examination of the Chinese Constitution and codes. China's criminal law system resembles the civil law system of continental Europe; it emphasized substantive matters rather than procedural methods. Cases do not go to trial unless the pretrial investigation shows a degree of guilt. There is no presumption of innocence, and thus there is little need or latitude for courtroom forensics.

The new Criminal Code of 1980, with 192 articles, clearly states that the law is designed to protect the socialist state first and the personal rights of the citizens second.[25] The specific language of some of the articles, which clearly define acts of wrongdoing, is revealing. The code narrowly defines "counter-revolutionary" crimes. It requires that the accused must have committed some overt act with intent; simply harboring (or being believed to harbor) thoughts contrary to the "dictatorship of the proletariat and the socialist system" is no longer a punishable act. Despite these specific assurances of personal rights, both the code and the Constitution are virtually nullified by the declaration of the NPC on November 29, 1979, that most laws and decrees promulgated since 1949 would remain in force.

The new Code of Criminal Procedure of 1980 is a major step toward the rule of law, if scrupulously observed. It declares that all citizens are equal before the law and forbids discrimination based upon one's social background as long as citizens "support socialism." Article 26 provides for the right of defense with the assistance of counsel, requires a warrant for arrest and that the accused be arraigned within two days of the arrest, although there is no habeas corpus. The law requires that the family of the accused be notified within twenty-four hours and limits detention during the investigation period to three months. The code calls for public trials and grants the accused the right to call witnesses and cross-examine them, argue the facts of the case, and the right of appeal. The law bans the use of torture to extract confession and specifically states that a defendant may be convicted without a confession. Article 144 provides for a mandatory review of all death sentences by the People's Supreme Court.[26]

THE ORGANIZATION OF THE COURT SYSTEM

The Constitution of 1982 established a new court system responsible to the National People's Congress through the NPC Standing Committee. A four-tiered court structure, which parallels the geographic administrative subdivisions, is composed of the Supreme People's Court (SPC), High Courts, Intermediate Courts, and Basic (local) Courts. The Supreme People's Court is administered by a president, elected by the NPC for five-year terms (not to exceed two consecutive terms). Judges for the SPC are appointed for the same terms and may be removed without cause by the NPC Standing Committee. The SPC is primarily an appellate court and, while it has no right of judicial review (reserved to the NPC), it has been given the power to offer "explanations on questions concerning specific applications of laws and decrees in judicial procedure".[27] While the rulings of the SPC have not been published or made public, the Court has recently announced that it will do so in the future.[28]

High Courts exist on the provincial leval and in municipalities under the central government and in autonomous regions. Officers of the Court are appointed by the provincial-level people's congress and may be removed without cause by the people's congress or its standing committee. The High Courts are supervised by the SPC. In the lower courts the officers of the court are appointed and subject to recall by the corresponding people's congress and are supervised by the court of the next higher level and, in turn, supervise the court inferior to them.

Intermediate Courts function in provincial cities and districts under the direct authority of the province, while Basic Courts serve the subdivisions of larger cities under provincial authority and the districts and cities under district administration. Large urban areas are subdivided into districts each of which has a Basic Court and is served by a Basic Level People's Procuratorate. Law enforcement in these urban districts is carried out by a Public Security Bureau (China's basic police force), and is subdivided into criminal and traffic divisions. There is a strong secret police network concerned primarily with political crimes about which there is little reliable information. There are, in addition, special courts for the military, railway transport, water transport, and new forestry courts. Court sessions are presided over by a panel of odd-numbered judges; certain appellate sessions may have three or five judges but the routine operation of the courts are handled by a panel of three, consisting of one judge and two "people's assessors." People's assessors are laymen (recently they have been given some rudimentary legal education) who are elected from citizens' lists by the appropriate people's congress for a three-year period. They are subject to the same recall procedure as judges.

China's courts have a "two-trial, one appeal" system in which the convicted party may appeal to the court higher than the court of first instance. The higher court would then reinvestigate the case and, if deemed necessary, retry the case at the higher level. The new Criminal Procedure Code provides that all cases of capital crime be tried in the Intermediate Court in the first instance and appealed to the higher court of the jurisdiction. Whether appealed or not, in cases where the death sentence is imposed by the higher court, that sentence must be ratified by the Supreme People's Court, which may hand down a two-year postponement.

If a death sentence is imposed by an Intermediate Court and granted a two-year reprieve, then only the approval of the higher court of jurisdiction is necessary.[29]

Since being reorganized, the courts of China have been consumed with appellate reviews. According to Jiang Hua, the current president of the SPC, by the end of June 1980 the people's courts had reviewed more than 1.1 million criminal conviction cases of the GPCR era and had rectified 251,000 cases of injustice involving more than 267,000 persons.[30]

A significant change in the new constitution concerning the courts is their removal from the direct supervision of the local governments (which had become dominated by "leftist" factions of the CCP during the GPCR) and making them accountable only to people's congresses. Another important change is the new regime's frequent declaration that all trials will be open to the public except in extreme cases bearing on matters of state secrets.

The Constitution of 1982 reestablished the People's Procuratorates to serve as the prosecution organs of the state. The procuratorates parallel the lower court structure with jurisdiction on the basic provincial, county, and district levels and special branches for autonomous areas and for those cities and districts administered by either the central government or the provincial government. In addition, there are military and special procuratorates. All levels of the procuratorate are under the Supreme People's Procuratorate, which is administered by the procurator-general. The Supreme People's Procuratorate is responsible to the NPC, and the procurator-general is selected by the Standing Committee of the NPC. Lower-level chief-procurators are elected by their respective people's congress under the same provisions as judges.

The Organic Law for the People's Procuratorates declares the procuratorates as the "organs of the state supervising the administration of justice" and states that they "shall exercise their procuratorial authority independently . . . and shall not be subject to interference by other administrative organs, organizations or individuals."[31] The procuratorates share with the Public Security Bureau the responsibility of law enforcement as the state's chief prosecutor. They are given the additional charge of supervising the legality of the courts' proceedings. The Chinese seem to see no inherent conflict in Article 135 of the Constitution, which mandates that the public security organs, the people's courts, and people's procuratorates "shall coordinate their efforts and check each other to insure correct and effective enforcement of law." Article 9 of The Organic Law instructs the procurators to follow the "mass line" and "heed the people's opinions" as they conduct their work.[32]

The Supreme People's Procurate has released some information on its work between January 1979 and June 1980. These figures state that procuratorates at all levels processed more than 10,000 cases dealing with violations of citizens' democratic rights, such as illegal detention, illegal search, and the use of torture to gain confessions. In 8,000 cases there were more than 9,000 persons found guilty of violating the law and/or governmental procedures.[33]

The Criminal Procedural Code divides a trial into four stages: investigation, debate, appraisal by collegiate bench, and judgment. Upon arrest of a suspect by the Public Security Bureau, the procuratorates are called in to review the evidence and the facts of the case. If the facts warrant it, the procurator must file an indictment with the court within thirty days. Should the procurator not indict, the public security organ may appeal that decision to a higher level procuratorate.[34] The president of the Supreme People's Court must not interfere in the pretrial investigation.[35]

At the trial, the prosecutor reads out the charge and presents the evidence. The judge then interrogates the defendant and explains the significance of the crime for the benefit of the public present. At this point, the defending counsel or a spokesman for the accused asks questions and offers explanations of mitigating circumstances. Normally, no witnesses are introduced. There is no jury present. After hearing the evidence and testimony of the defense, the judge and the two "people's assessors" retire. The judicial panel then returns and announces their judgment and sentence. Observers of Chinese trials have been impressed with the simplicity of the proceedings and, despite the rather one-sided nature of such hearings, the judgments rendered are often fair and just.[36]

PERSONNEL OF THE LAW

China's current leadership has expended great effort to reconstitute the legal profession, shattered during the GPCR. Aware that the success of China's modernization and her interaction with the West in fostering commercial relations depends on a stable society, the leadership is sponsoring a rapid increase of trained lawyers and paralegals. Although lawyers in China have never had the influence of their Western counterparts, the state of the profession is dismal by any comparison. China has one lawyer for 50,000 persons while the United States has one lawyer for each 600 citizens.[37] In a 1980 report, Deng Xiaoping referred to the severe shortage of trained legal personnel:

We are at least one million short—I think it is two million—in the number of cadres capable of doing judicial work, including judges, lawyers, judicial officers, procurators and special policemen. There are very few cadres who can act as judges and lawyers, who have studied law and understand it and who can also enforce the law in a fair and impartial way.[38]

To deal with this shortage, the government has expanded legal education on a broad front and reformed the statutes governing the practice of law. The Provisional Regulations for Lawyers was passed by the Standing Committee of the NPC on January 1, 1982. The twenty-one articles of the Regulations define the education, examination, and standards for the practice of law. The qualifications to become a lawyer require that candidates be "citizens who love the People's Republic of China, support the socialist system and have the right to vote and stand for elections and who have passed the required examinations."[39]

The specific prerequisites to sit for the qualifying exams further define candidates as:

1. Those who have graduated from institutions of higher learning after completing their course of law and have engaged in judicial work, teaching, or researching law for more than two years;
2. Those who have been trained in law and have acted as judges in people's courts or procurators in procuratorates;
3. Those who have received higher education and have engaged in economic, cultural and educational, scientific, and technical work for at least three years; who are familiar with their specialities and laws relating to their specialties, have been trained in law, and prove to be suitable for the work of a lawyer;
4. Others who have met the requirements as listed in 1 or 2 above; and who have a college level education and prove to be suitable for the work of a lawyer.[40]

Admission to a legal education program has become a "hot-ticket" to what are seen as good careers in China.[41] The prospective student must be judged to be "academically, morally, physically fit," and one who is "politically clean, loves labor, the Communist Party and the country."[42] All applicants take the National College Entrance Examination, which contains questions on politics, history, Chinese language, mathematics, and geography. Different from American law school admission tests, the Chinese exam contains specific questions on politics and ideology. Typical examples are:

What are the four basic principles we must adhere to in order to achieve the four modernizations?

What is the historical mission of the proletariat?

Refute the erroneous view that "socialism in our country is inferior to capitalism."

What is the basic difference between materialist dialectics and metaphysics? Criticize the "Gang of Four" for spreading the fallacy of metaphysics.[43]

China's legal studies programs began to reopen in 1978, and, by 1979, approximately 2,000 students were enrolled in them. Legal studies are undertaken at two kinds of schools: law departments of universities and institutes of politics and law. Reports indicate that there are now eighteen universities with law departments providing a four-year, full-time, undergraduate curriculum in law leading to the bachelor's degree. There are at least four institutes designed to train people for the Ministry of Justice, the procuratorates, and the public security organs, as well as advocates.[44] Among the various schools, the Beijing University law department and the East China Institute in Beijing are considered the most prestigious. One recent visitor states that even if the present number of 13,000 students currently enrolled in full-time legal studies programs is tripled, China will not meet her need for lawyers and legal officials.[45]

In addition to the university and institute programs, there are eleven schools that provide on-the-job training for judicial cadre; 70,000 have completed this form of preparation in recent years while 11,000 are currently enrolled.[46] In 1981, Li Yanching, first vice-minister of justice, reported that "57,000 outstanding army officers" had been transferred to civilian work and were receiving legal training.[47] An additional one hundred colleges offer part-time correspondence courses in law. These schools train lower-echelon judicial cadres, court clerks and administrators, law clerks, and specialists in other fields who need practical legal education.[48] Education in law has been established in the curricula of middle schools in Shanghai and is being considered elsewhere.[49] There has also been a massive campaign to educate the masses in the importance of the rule of law in the nation's modernization. A "television university" features programs and short courses on law, and there are large billboard displays in public areas, often with photographs, reporting significant cases of economic crime and violations of the new legal order.[50]

A most recent development is the introduction of graduate legal studies; at least five major institutions now offer full-time graduate studies to train law professors and high-calibre legal researchers.[51] A small number of legal professionals are also being sent abroad for study. Those in America are at the finest law schools and serving internships with American law firms.[52]

Western legal specialists have been granted visits to China's law schools only since 1979 and find their contacts limited by officials who consider law "a sensitive area."[53] Recent visitors have been able to learn more about the curriculum and teaching of law, although little is known about the particulars of specific courses. Under Mao, the curriculum followed directives of the state and much of the teaching material was developed by faculty committees. Presently, the law schools are supervised by the Ministries of Justice and Education. The Ministry of Justice has recently approved fifty-four legal textbooks compiled by a group of 300 legal experts working under the ministry's direction since 1980. These books have been edited into fourteen concise texts to be used for secondary schools and special law training courses.[54]

The curriculum of each institution must be approved by the Ministry of Justice. Most schools require some nonlegal general courses, a prescribed core of law courses, and some broad elective courses. One visitor reported that he heard of no courses on administrative law or public administration but was given a description of a course in the theory of jurisprudence that taught Chinese law from a Marxist perspective with emphasis on the role of law in China's modernization.[55]

The primary teaching method is the lecture. Since few cases have been published in the past, there is little or no use of the case method. Problem-solving or simulation techniques, widely used in the United States, are not employed. Full-time, four-year students at the East China Institute also acquire practical experience through an internship program that sends them to court to prosecute cases.[56]

There is, not unexpectedly, a shortage of qualified law professors. During the GPCR the law faculty were dispersed throughout China, engaged either in physical labor to reform their "bourgeois consciousness," or assigned to primary or secondary schools. Because lawyers were classified as among the worst of the "stinking ninth category" of intellectuals, their harsh treatment resulted in many deaths and suicides during those years. Many of the law professors currently teaching are older people who received their education prior to the GPCR or were educated abroad in the United States, England, Japan, and the Soviet Union. Law professors are among the highest paid professionals, earning about 200 yuan a month, or four times the wages of an average industrial worker.[57] It is hoped that the new graduate law programs and students abroad will staff the law faculties for the next generation.

The opening of the law schools and the new position accorded to legal studies has produced some new efforts at legal scholarship. There are several professional journals published by the various law departments and institutes and a weekly newspaper for the profession. Cohen observed that "more material on law is now published in a single day than used to appear in a year."[58] Some of the law reviews have published articles that go beyond reciting the current state of the law in China; one author, for example, boldly called for the separation of powers in the Constitution and urged the adoption of certain Western features of law.[59] Despite the critical need to upgrade both the education and numbers of legal professionals, the state and the party maintain a strong influence on the process. Jiang Nanxiang, the minister of education, stated the official goals of legal education: "It is imperative to educate students with socialist consciousness . . . [this] is the fundamental difference between socialist and capitalist education."[60]

The Provisional Regulations for Lawyers declares that lawyers are "state legal workers" who have the duty to "protect the interests of the state and the collective and the legitimate rights and interests of citizens"; they are to "propagate the socialist legal system," and to "act on the basis of facts and take the law as their criterion."[61] These three principles guide the actions of lawyers and serve as a code of conduct.

Lawyers are supervised by the Ministry of Justice, which oversees their certifications, enforces discipline, and sets compensation. Lawyers are organized into collectives called Legal Advisory Offices, and the fees charged for their services go to the state.[62] There are currently about 12,000 lawyers (approximately 8,600 full-time and 3,500 part-time) organized in some 2,350 Legal Advisory Offices throughout China.[63] In 1982 these advisory offices answered 1.45 million "peoples's inquiries," including 580,000 legal questions, and drafted 135,000 legal papers. *Beijing Review* also states that lawyers handled more than 90,000 criminal cases in 1982.[64] The advisory offices are called upon to provide services for government enterprises, public organizations, and people's communes. The procuracy, moribund in 1978, now employs over 116,000 legal officials, a striking comparison to the numbers available for defense counsel through the legal advisory offices.[65]

Lawyers are assigned by the state to either the procuratorates, legal advisory offices, the special state organizations, the Public Security Bureau, or to China's burgeoning economic enterprises. The rapid pace of economic development and cooperation with foreign companies in joint-venture enterprises has created a need for commercial lawyers.

The work of lawyers as defense advocates gives us a good indication of the role of lawyers in China. The Constitution and the Criminal Procedure Law declare the right of the accused to defense. This does not mean a defense by a trained lawyer, as the courts do not consider a defense lawyer essential at the trial. A person may defend himself or choose a family member, friend, or colleague. With the exception of trial cases involving the deaf or mute or minors, the assignment of a lawyer is discretionary with the court. Therefore, lawyers have no role during the investigatory phase (conducted by the public security organs and procuratorate) and become involved with an accused only a few days prior to trial.[66] The Regulations deal briefly with the rights of the lawyer in the performance of his work. Article 7 grants the right to "meet with and correspond with the accused," and "to research materials relevant to the case," and to "investigate related organizations and persons."

Since only criminal cases in which the public security organ and the procuratorate have clearly established the guilt of the accused actually go to trial, there is no equality between the procurator and the defense attorney; the former represents the state, the latter represents the defendant—a criminal. The defense counsel may call witnesses on behalf of his client and cross-examine the state's witnesses. Friendly witnesses are generally character witnesses. The defense has little to challenge, since there are no rules governing the admission of evidence. He may offer extenuating circumstances and explanations for his client's wrongful act and recommend mitigation or remission of punishment in the interest of the accused.

Lawyers are required "to maintain secrecy when they come into contact with state secrets and shameful personal records in their work." A lawyer may refuse to represent a defendant who he believes is not telling the truth. He is prohibited by criminal statute from sheltering guilty persons from the state's justice: "Any judicial worker who . . . deliberately shields a guilty person from prosecution or stands truth on its head . . . will be sentenced to detention or imprisonment."[67] One advocate in Tianjin told a visiting American lawyer, "I represent the facts and the law, not the client. In our society the lawyer works for the state. In yours he works for the client."[68]

The Regulations provide for professional associations of lawyers for "promoting their work and strengthening their ties with lawyers at home and abroad," and such associations have been revived. In Beijing, the China Law Society (CLS), "a national mass organization," was recently established "to unite judicial workers all over China to conduct research into the Marxist science of law . . . and the practice of China's socialist legal system." Wu Xinyu, vice-chairman of the Commission of Legal Affairs of the NPC Standing Committee was elected president of the new CLS.[69]

PUBLIC PERCEPTIONS AND THE ROLE OF THE COURTS

Given the significant role that the courts and lawyers play in the governing process of Western democracies, the public perception of the integrity of the legal system may be more critical than in a state like China. Nevertheless, the current leaders of China know that the success of the modernization program needs the cooperation and support of her citizenry. We have seen that the Chinese have long believed that a society governed by coercive laws and punishments is inferior to one in which behavior is led to match the philosophical ideal by means of education and the example of moral leadership. To the extent that the leaders of China have been trying to implement the legal reforms through education and the example of punishing transgressors, party members as well as ordinary citizens, they are more likely to be respected for this approach. China's family and group traditions have responded well to the emphasis on mediation, which is still in widespread use in civil matters and cases of minor wrongdoing.

Lawyers were never highly regarded in China; the imperial age saw them as tricksters and the Communists have denounced them as tools of the exploiting class. Now we find China's rulers placing great emphasis on legal professionals to help establish the rule of law. In this, they are motivated by the desire for a stable climate for economic development and fear of a recurrence of the lawlessness of the Cultural Revolution. This fear of such a recurrence places the leaders and the people on common ground; both suffered greatly during that period. But in the minds of the people it was the leadership, the arbitrary power of the CCP, that precipitated those events.

There remains widespread skepticism among the citizenry that the party is now willing to be governed by its own rules. The post-Mao era, since 1976, has been the longest period of stability without any major political movements since the Communist victory in 1949. In conversations with Chinese in 1981 and 1982, virtually all of them expressed the hope, but not the belief, that the peace would be long-lasting.

Individuals were not optimistic that the new Constitution, promulgated in 1982, would guarantee the stated personal freedom and rights. They expressed a sense of helplessness against the public security organs. If accused wrongly, many felt there was "no way out" (*mei-fazi*) of receiving some form of punishment.

Perhaps the most alienated group are the former Red Guards, who were merely teenagers at the time of the Cultural Revolution and believed they were serving their leadership. In conversation, they showed much bitterness; the society largely condemns them and distrusts them for their role in the GPCR. Ironically, some of these former Red Guards were among the first to enter the reopened universities and have become the new lawyers.[70]

Older Chinese express appreciation for the formal sanction now given to mediating minor disputes by the state, and several spoke of good experiences with the new legal advisory offices.[71] One thing is certain: the vast majority of people in China want the legal system to work fairly. The leadership seems to share this desire, but it will take time to break ingrained practices. As one party official who suffered in the past told Jerome A. Cohen, a leading authority on China's legal system, "The Cultural Revolution gave us a better legal education than even Harvard could."[72]

It is obvious from the discussion of the courts, the procuratorates, and lawyers that there is limited judicial independence in China. We have seen that the agencies responsible for the legal system, the NPC and the Ministries of Justice and Education, are dominated by the CCP. Ernest Gellhorn states that the reality of China is that the party remains the first and sole authority.[73] The critical factor here is the degree to which the party will observe its own policy not to interfere in legal proceedings. If the party allows the new system to work in the areas of criminal law, then China will have a measure of judicial independence and a relatively just system. Should the party return to the earlier GPCR belief that all crimes are political acts and thus counter-revolutionary, the system will collapse into the former mockery of law. As long as the role of the state and the party are defined as they now are in China, there can be nothing approaching genuine independence. If the legal system contributes to stability and the modernization program continues to transform China, the party may come to accept real distinction between nonpolitical criminal behavior and counter-revolutionary activity.

There seems little doubt that China's legal system plays an active role in that society today. According to statistics released by the Supreme Peoples' Court, since 1978 courts at all levels have handled 1.65 million civil cases of the first instance and more than 100,000 appeals. Of these cases 830,000 were marriage related and 820,000 were property disputes. Eighty percent of the cases were resolved through mediation.[74] The traditional Chinese preference for mediation involving family, friends, and coworkers contributes greatly to a relatively smooth running civil law process despite the high number of cases.

The new Constitution and the Criminal Procedural Codes of 1980 offer China hope for a just legal system. It is important to note that these recent reforms are not designed to instill Western legal ideals but reflect two concerns of China's present leaders. First, there is a sense of urgency in the belief that an established legal system will protect against a recurrence of the official lawlessness of the GPCR.[75] Second, there is the feeling that these reforms will insure the stability necessary for China to proceed with her modernization program to catch up with the level of industrial and technological development of the other nations of Asia.

The new reforms remain clouded by vestiges of the old order. Jerome Cohen notes that a key test will be the extent to which "rehabilitation through labor" is applied. This practice was revived at the time the new codes were promulgated; it permits the state to circumvent the new criminal process by sending people to labor reform camps for three or more years without a court hearing or right of appeal. This violation of China's own socialist legality is justified by party officials on the ground that no criminal stigma is attached and therefore a court trial is unnecessary.[76] It is this dual system of law that provides the challenge for China's courts and lawyers.

NOTES

1. W. A. Robson, *Civilization and the Growth of Law* (New York: Macmillan Co., 1935), p. 48.

2. F. Michael, "The Role of Law in Traditional, Nationalist, and Communist China," *China Quarterly* 9 (January-March, 1962), p. 125.

3. C. O. Hucker, *China's Imperial Past* (Stanford, Calif.: Stanford University Press, 1975), p. 52.

4. *The Analects* as quoted in K. C. Wu, *The Chinese Heritage* (New York: Crown Publishers, 1982), p. 407.

5. J. A. Cohen, "Chinese Mediation on the Eve of Modernization," *Journal of Asian and African Studies* 2 (January-April 1967), p. 59.

6. Michael, "The Role of Law," p. 129.

7. Ping-Ti Ho, "Salient Aspects of China's Heritage," in Ping-Ti Ho and Tang Tsou, eds., *China in Crisis*, vol. 1 (Chicago: University of Chicago Press, 1968), p. 11.

8. Hucker, *China's Imperial Past*, pp. 164–65.

9. Wu, *The Chinese Heritage*, p. 407.

10. Michael, "The Role of Law," p. 130.

11. T'ang-Tsou Ch'u, *Local Government in China Under the Ch'ing* (Cambridge, Mass.: Harvard University Press, 1962), pp. 1–2.

12. Ibid., pp. 98–109.

13. A scholarly analysis of the Chinese codes is contained in D. Bodde and C. Morris, *Law in Imperial China* (Chicago: University of Chicago Press, 1981), p. 158.

14. M. Shapiro, *Courts: A Comparative and Political Analysis* (Chicago: University of Chicago Press, 1981), p. 158.

15. For a summary treatment of this period see J. K. Fairbank et al., *A History of East Asian Civilization, East Asia: The Modern Transformation*, 2 vols. (Boston: Houghton-Mifflin Co., 1965), 2:80–178.

16. P. M. A. Linebarger et al., *Far Eastern Governments and Politics: China and Japan* (Princeton, N.J.: Van Nostrand Co., Inc., 1956), p. 167.

17. J. A. Cohen, "China's New Lawyers Law," *American Bar Association Journal* 66 (1980), p. 1533.

18. Hungdah Chiu, "China's New Legal System," *Current History* 79 (September 1980), p. 29.

19. For a description of how one family suffered from the antirightist campaign see, L. Heng and J. Shapiro, *Son of the Revolution* (New York: Alfred A. Knopf, 1983), Chapters 1–4.

20. J. A. Cohen, *The Criminal Process in the People's Republic of China, 1949–1963: An Introduction* (Cambridge, Mass.: Harvard University Press, 1968), p. 214.

21. "GNP in 1961 had dropped by at least 15 percent and possibly as much as 25 percent from its peak in 1958. Per capita income was down by 32 percent, industrial production by 40 to 45 percent. Per capita production fell back to the level of 1955, a drop of 19 percent. The average person took in only 1790 calories per day, 19 percent

less than in 1958, and 26 percent less protein. . . . For the first time since the founding of the new government, China imported grain, buying 6.2 million tons in 1961, mostly from Canada and Australia.'' M. Gasster, *China's Struggle to Modernize*, 2d ed. (New York: Alfred A. Knopf, 1983), p. 131.

22. An account by a Red Guard who participated in these events is given in Heng and Shapiro, *Son of the Revolution*, Chapters 5–11.

23. For the text of the new Constitution see *Beijing Review* 26:52 (December 27, 1982), pp. 10–29.

24. R. A. Herman, ''The Education of China's Lawyers,'' *Albany Law Review* 46 (Spring 1982), p. 801.

25. For the text of the Criminal Law of 1980, see *Foreign Broadcast Information Service: Daily Report, Peoples Republic of China*, Supplement (July 27, 1979), pp. 33–62. Hereafter cited as *FBIS*.

26. For a summary of the Procedural Code, see Shao-chuan Leng, ''Criminal Justice in Post-Mao China,'' *China Quarterly* 87 (September 1981), pp. 449ff.

27. Leng, ''Criminal Justice,'' p. 444.

28. D. Bonavia, ''The Liberal Swing,'' *Far Eastern Economic Review* 128 (June 27, 1985), p. 49.

29. Leng, ''Criminal Justice,'' p. 466.

30. ''Report of Jiang Hua to the NPC,'' *FBIS*, Supplement (September 23, 1980), p. 42.

31. For the text of ''The Organic Law of the People's Procurates,'' see *FBIS*, Supplement (July 27, 1979), pp. 27–33.

32. For the cryptic nature of the procurator's instructions see B. G. Baker, ''Chinese Law in the Eighties: the Lawyer and the Criminal Process,'' *Albany Law Review* 46 (Spring 1982), p. 763.

33. Leng, ''Criminal Justice,'' p. 451.

34. Ibid., p. 73.

35. D. Bonavia, *The Chinese* (New York: Penguin Books, 1982), p. 156.

36. For accounts of trials observed by Western lawyers, see B. G. Baker, ''Chinese Law,'' pp. 768–71; and ''The People's Law in China,'' *Juris Doctor* 8, no. 4 (April 1978), p. 11.

37. E. Gellhorn, ''The Developing Role of Law and Lawyers in China,'' *Albany Law Review* 46 (Spring 1981), p. 687.

38. Quoted in Leng, ''Criminal Justice,'' p. 448.

39. Zhang Zhiye, ''How Do China's Lawyers Work?'' *Beijing Review* 26 (June 6, 1983), p. 20.

40. Ibid.

41. J. A. Cohen, ''Rebuilding China's Shattered Legal System,'' *Asia* (November-December 1983), p. 48. 'Hot-ticket' is translated from *re-men* or 'hot-gate' in Chinese.

42. Herman, ''Education,'' p. 793.

43. Ibid., p. 793–94.

44. Leng, ''Criminal Justice,'' p. 443. The rapid increase in the number of legal training programs leads to varying statistics between observers over the last two years. Herman gives the figure of twenty; Baker says there were fifteen; Cohen, ''Rebuilding,'' mentions twenty-six university law departments and three institutes. The figure cited here is from Zhang Zhive, ''Legislative and Judiciary Work in China,'' *Beijing Review* 26 (August 15, 1983), pp. 21–22.

45. Cohen, "Rebuilding," p. 48.
46. *Beijing Review* (August 15, 1983), p. 22.
47. Baker, "Chinese Law," p. 774.
48. Herman, "Education," p. 792.
49. *Beijing Review* (August 15, 1983), p. 22.
50. The author saw one of these displays in Shanghai in 1982 and spoke to pedestrians about the public awareness campaign.
51. Herman, "Education," p. 792.
52. Cohen, "Rebuilding," p. 48.
53. E. Eliasoph and S. Grueneberg, "Law on Display in China," *China Quarterly* 88 (December 1981), pp. 669–70.
54. *Beijing Review* (August 15, 1983), p. 22.
55. Herman, "Education," p. 796.
56. Ibid., p. 797.
57. Ibid., p. 795.
58. Cohen, "Rebuilding," p. 48.
59. Herman, "Education," p. 798.
60. Ibid., p. 803.
61. Baker, "Chinese Law," p. 758.
62. Ibid., p. 758–59.
63. *Beijing Review* (June 6, 1983), p. 19. These figures represent a recent official count. American lawyers visiting China as late as 1981 reported 5,500 full-time and 1,300 part-time lawyers organized into 1,280 collectives.
64. Ibid., p. 20.
65. Cohen, "Rebuilding," p. 48.
66. Baker, "Chinese Law," p. 766.
67. Ibid., p. 760.
68. Ibid., p. 771.
69. "China Law Society Founded," *Beijing Review* 25 (August 10, 1981), p. 6.
70. Informal street conversations with Chinese and former Red Guards during the author's three trips to the PRC in 1981 and 1982.
71. Conversations with Chinese during author's trip to Shanghai, 1982.
72. Cohen, "Rebuilding," p. 49.
73. Gellhorn, "Developing Role," p. 688.
74. "Settling Civil Disputes Through Mediation," *Beijing Review* 25 (August 16, 1982), p. 7.
75. Baker, "Chinese Law," p. 752.
76. Cohen, "Rebuilding," p. 49.

BIBLIOGRAPHY

Baker, B. G. "Chinese Law in the Eighties: the Lawyer and the Criminal Process." *Albany Law Review* 46 (Spring 1982), pp. 751–75.
Bodde, D., and C. Morris. *Law in Imperial China*. Philadelphia: The University of Pennsylvania Press, 1973.
Bonavia, D. *The Chinese*. New York Penguin Books, 1982.
———. "The Liberal Swing." *Far Eastern Economic Review* 128 (June 27, 1985), p. 44.

Cheng, Y. "China's Law of Civil Procedure." *Beijing Review*, August 16, 1982, pp. 20–22.

"China Law Society Founded." *Beijing Review*, August 10, 1982, p. 6.

Chiu, H. "China's New Legal System." *Current History* 79 (September 1980), pp. 29–32.

———. *Criminal Justice in Post-Mao China: Analysis and Documents.* Albany, N.Y.: State University of New York Press, 1985.

Ch'u, T'ang-Tsu. *Local Government in China Under the Ch'ing.* Cambridge, Mass.: Harvard University Press, 1962.

Cohen, J. A. "China's New Lawyer's Law." *American Bar Association Journal* 66 (1980), pp. 1530–37.

———. *The Criminal Process in the People's Republic of China, 1949–1963: An Introduction.* Cambridge, Mass.: Harvard University Press, 1968.

———. "Rebuilding China's Shattered Legal System." *Asia* (November–December 1983), pp. 14–15; 48–49.

Cohen, J. A., R. Edwards, and F. C. Chen, eds., *Essays on China's Legal Tradition.* Princeton, N.J.: Princeton University Press, 1980.

Eliasoph, E., and S. Grueneber. "Law on Display in China." *China Quarterly* 88 (December 1981), pp. 669–685.

Ginsburgs, G., and A. Stahnke. "The People's Procurates in Communist China: The Institution in the Ascendant, 1954–1957," *China Quarterly* 34 (April-June 1968), pp. 82–132.

Heng, L., and J. Shapiro. *Son of the Revolution.* New York: Alfred A. Knopf, 1983.

Hsing, K. "The Revised Constitution of the CCP: An Analysis." *Issues and Studies* 17 (October 1980), pp. 29–37.

Hudspeth, S. M. "The Nature and Protection of Economic Interest in the People's Republic of China." *Albany Law Review* 46 (Spring 1982), pp. 691–739.

Leng, S. "Criminal Justice in Post-Mao China." *China Quarterly* 87 (September 1981), pp. 440–69.

———, and H. Chiu. *Criminal Justice in Post-Mao China: Analysis and Documents.* Albany, N. Y.: State University of New York Press, 1985.

Linebarger, P. M. A., D. Chu, and A. W. Burks. *Far Eastern Governments and Politics: China and Japan.* Princeton, N.J.: Van Nostrand Co., Inc., 1956.

Ma, H. P. H. "American Influence and Chinese Constitutional Law." *Sino-American Relations* 6 (Fall 1980), pp. 21–41.

Ma, H. H. "Communist China and the Role of Law: Theory and Practice in Review." *Issues and Studies* 17, no. 7 (July 1981), pp. 76–93.

Michael, F. "The Role of Law in Traditional, Nationalist, and Communist China." *China Quarterly* 9 (January-March 1962), pp. 124–48.

"The Role of Lawyers." *Beijing Review*, February 15, 1982, p. 9.

Zhang, Z. "How Do China's Lawyers Work?" *Beijing Review*, June 6, 1983, pp. 19–27.

13

SCANDINAVIA

Alan N. Katz

The Scandinavian states of Denmark, Norway, Iceland, Sweden, and Finland are a remarkably homogeneous group often described as a "family of nations."[1] Their populations in the early 1980s ranged from Sweden, the largest (8.3 million), to Iceland, the smallest (230,000), with Norway (4.1 million), Finland (4.8 million), and Denmark (5.1 million) clustered in the middle.[2] The nations of Scandinavia have, however, had somewhat different developmental experiences. This has resulted, to some degree, in the different governmental patterns seen today: constitutional monarchies in Sweden, Denmark, and Norway and republics in Finland and Iceland.

THE DEVELOPMENT OF THE LEGAL SYSTEMS

The nations of Scandinavia have similar legal traditions. Zweigert and Kotz contend that it is somewhat difficult to place the Nordic nations in either the common law or civil law traditions, though they fit more easily into the latter:[3]

It is clear that these Nordic laws cannot be allocated to the Common Law, for only the legal systems which belong to the Common Law are those which are historically traceable to medieval English law, and the history of the Nordic systems has been quite independent of English law. Furthermore, Nordic law has few, if any, of the "stylistic" hallmarks of the Common Law, such as the typical methods of finding law, the strong emphasis on judicial decisions in important areas of private law, and the standing and career of the Anglo-American judge. More difficult is the question of whether the Nordic laws can be attached to the Civil Law, that great family of legal systems such as those of continental Europe which have been more or less imbued with Roman law and which traditionally rely on statutes or indeed comprehensive codes as the primary means of ordering their legal material. There is no denying that Roman law has played a smaller role in the legal development of the Nordic countries than in Germany, and the Nordic states have as yet no codes like the civil codes of France or Germany. Nevertheless we are of the opinion

. . . that it would be right to attribute the Nordic laws to the Civil Law, even though, by reason of their close interrelationship and their common "stylistic" hallmarks, they must undoubtedly be admitted to form a special legal family, alongside the Romanistic and German legal families.[4]

The ties between the nations of Scandinavia are long-lived. In fact, Orfield has noted that "the international relations of the Scandinavian states reveals that their relations have been chiefly with each other."[5] Unquestionably, the period of strongest ties was from 1397 to 1523, when the states of Denmark, Norway, Sweden, and Finland were united under a single king. This Kalmar Union ended in the 1510s, when Sweden broke away from the group. The Nordic Council, established in 1953, was the next (and very different type) union of the states of the region. The council is an advisory body composed of members of the legislatures of each of the five states. It meets for one week each year and makes recommendations to the nations. Its most important role has been to bring about a great deal of cooperation between the states of the area and an almost new sense of geographic citizenship among four of the nations of Scandinavia (because of its geographic isolation, Iceland has not been as affected by the council as have the other four):

In some significant respects, the national boundaries separating the four nations have been erased: passports were abolished in 1952; drivers' licenses of one Scandinavian country are accepted in all the others; customs inspection of non-Scandinavians is limited to the point of entry and is not repeated at the border of the other countries; a free, common labor market—except for certain professions—established in 1954, has meant the abolition of work permits and the opening of jobs to nationals of all the northern nations. The boundaries that divide Scandinavians into separate sovereignties have become formalities in other ways also: a Convention signed in 1956 provided that sickness, accident, old-age, maternity, and other social security benefits be extended, by the country of residence, without reference to citizenship, to Scandinavian nationals; the cost of these benefits are borne by the country of residence and not by the beneficiary's native country.[6]

The common historic links in Scandinavia are far more extensive than that of the Kalmar Union and the Nordic Council. In fact, we can discuss the historical development of the region by dividing it geographically: the east, where Finland remained linked to Sweden from the twelfth century until early in the nineteenth century when Sweden was forced to ceed it to Russia; and the west, where Norway and Iceland, beginning in the fourteenth century, remained linked to Denmark for four centuries.

Denmark, like a number of its neighbors, has a much stronger tradition of customary law than either case law or code law. Its law has been largely influenced by its neighbors, though both German and English law have had some small impact upon the law of Denmark. The earliest of the Danish laws were written down by the Landsthings in the twelfth century. The most important of these, and the earliest civil code, was the Jutland Code, passed in 1240 and remaining in effect until 1683. Orfield notes that this was not like the codes of continental Europe: "The Jutland Code is in the tradition of national legislation. That is to say there is no Imperial Law nor Roman law in it. There is, however, canon law in it."[7] This was ultimately replaced by King Christian V's Danish Law, which was the first of the modern Scandinavian codes. Composed of six books (Courts and Practice; Ecclesiastical Rules; City, Rural, and Family Relations; Maritime Law; a Penal Code; and Obligations and Inheritances), the law was much more a Danish national reaction to events than a code influenced by Roman or German law.[8] To some degree, this code was an attempt by the king to both stem the tide against Denmark and reduce the class struggle within the nation. It did neither. Denmark continued to slip from its preeminent status at the time of the Kalmar Union (a series of military defeats in the seventeenth century were later followed by military disasters linked to the Napoleonic period), and the class structure within Denmark remained unchanged. Denmark's links with both Norway and Iceland were finally severed with the ceding of Norway to Sweden in 1905 and the granting of independence to Iceland in 1918.

Customary law was also the dominant influence upon the laws of Norway. While it has been superceded in many cases by statute law, it is the earliest form of law in Norway and still plays a major role in Norwegian law today:

Customary law has had a great influence on judicial procedure, constitutional law, and private law. It still plays an important part as to torts, transport by land, unincorporated associations, agriculture, and registration of land. In the customary law are to be found the rules of statutory interpretation and the rules as to the application of judicial precendent. It is thus at the basis of the Norwegian legal system.[9]

As in much of the rest of Scandinavia, the first form of government in Norway occurred at the *allthing*, a rural public meeting where yeoman gathered to both settle affairs and pass laws. This was replaced in the tenth century by the *lagthing*. This was a body, with fixed representation from the various parts of the realm, which met periodically. The chamber was led by *lagmann*, who were particularly knowledgeable in the law. While the lagthing could pass laws, much of the law utilized was based on customary law. This system existed until the unification of Norway. This first period in the history of Norwegian law came to a close with the accession to power of King Magnus the Lawmender in the middle of the thirteenth century. Magnus redrafted the regional laws into national laws, many of which were still operative four centuries later. A second period came to an end with the promulgation of King Christian V's Norwegian law in 1688. This period saw the further development of legal personnel (the lagmann were appointed by the king and became virtual judges) as well as a court system (a clear court system was laid down by the beginning of the seventeenth century and developed throughout that century). The third period ended with the separation of Norway from Denmark in 1814. A constitution was written during this period that proclaimed the nation's independence from Denmark. Although Norway was under the control of Sweden for nearly a century, the 1814 Constitution is still in force (though much amended) and May 17, the date of its adoption, is celebrated as National Day.

Despite the fact that Iceland was the first of the nations of Scandinavia to establish a code, much of its early law, like that of its neighbors, was customary law developed by the lawmen and members of the allthing.[10] The Icelandic code was a result of a three-year trip to Norway by Ulfliot, in his day, one of the wisest leaders of Iceland. Iceland remained independent of its neighbors until the middle of the thirteenth century, when it agreed to recognize the Norwegian king. While Iceland became linked to Denmark in the fourteenth century, it continued to trade with England and Germany and did not develop a largely Danish trade until the middle of the sixteenth century. From that time until 1814, Iceland's relations with Denmark became closer, with the Danes not only controlling trade but government as well (the laws were made by the Danish king, and the Danish Supreme Court became the highest court for Iceland as well). Relations between the two countries were severed in 1814 due to the weakening of Denmark caused by the Napoleonic Wars. For the next century discussions were held between Denmark, Norway, the United States (the United States was anxious to buy Iceland after its Civil War), and Iceland over Iceland's status. This ultimately resulted in the Act of Union of 1818 in which Iceland was recognized as a sovereign state (though it remained under the Danish king until the conclusion of World War II).

Swedish law was also influenced by both customary law and the law promulgated by the *landthing*. The lawmen were any individuals learned in the law. These "experts" were elected by the farmers (from a district known as a "land") and presided over the thing, administered justice, and gave legal advice. The early landthings were responsible for legislation, with the king deferring to their wishes. While there was a code by the end of the thirteenth century, there was no real movement toward the centralization of a Swedish legal system until the middle of the following century (during the reign of Magnus Eriksson). This involved the drafting of a code and the modification of the jury system. A series of original and appellate courts were introduced by the early part of the fifteenth century. These courts gradually disappeared, however, because Swedes insisted upon going to the king rather than to the courts for redress of their grievances. This problem was finally solved by King Gustavus Adolphus II, who both organized a final court of appeal and mandated that the judges of the lower courts meet at regular intervals. By the middle of the eighteenth century a nine-part code had been adopted by the legislature and ratified by the king. There were, however, a number of omissions and much of the codes have been replaced by statutes. A new constitution was promulgated by the Riksdag in 1809. This remained in force until it was replaced by a new constitution on January 1, 1975.

Finland was annexed by Sweden after a series of conquests, probably beginning as early as 1155 and concluding by the end of the thirteenth century. Little is known of the Finnish legal system prior to this time. We do know, however, that a Swedish lawman was appointed in Finland, and Finns were given the right to participate in the election of the king by the middle of the fourteenth century. Sweden's laws were established in Finland in the following century, and, by the middle of the seventeenth century, a law faculty and a series of courts had been established. Finland was, however, annexed by Russia after 1809. The relations between the Finns and the Russians were not always amicable and during two periods of oppression (in the 1890s and 1909–1917) the Russians tried to undermine Finland's autonomy.[11] The Russian Revolution did, however, enable the Finns to declare their independence. This was shortly followed by the development of a Supreme Court and a Supreme Administrative Court and the promulgation of a constitution in 1919.

THE ORGANIZATION OF THE COURT SYSTEMS

It is not surprising to find that the organization of the court systems is remarkably similar throughout Scandinavia. All of the systems have courts of first instance (sometimes called "lower courts," "district courts," "town," or "country" courts), intermediate courts of appeals (called "courts of appeals," "provincial courts," or "high courts") and a final court of appeal (called the "Supreme Court" in each) and a variety of "special courts."

There are eighty-four lower court circuits in Denmark (the city of Copenhagen has its own court). These courts of first instance have original jurisdiction over criminal cases (which do not require a jury) as well as less important civil cases. They are manned by a single judge on the civil side and three judges (two lay judges join the proceedings) in most criminal cases. The two High Courts (eastern and western circuits) have both original and appellate jurisdiction. These courts hear appeals from the Lower Courts and have original jurisdiction in more important civil cases as well as those criminal cases requiring a jury trial. Most of the proceedings of these courts are heard before at least three judges. In jury trials, a twelve-member jury determines the guilt or innocence of the accused, and the judges assign the appropriate penalty. The final court of appeal in Denmark is the Supreme Court. This court has only appellate jurisdiction, hearing appeals from the High Courts and the special courts: admiralty and maritime courts; a special court of complaints, which hears special criminal appeals as well as disciplinary actions and criminal cases against judges (this court is made up of three judges—one from the Supreme Court, one from a High Court, and a lower court judge appointed by the king for ten-year terms); and a Court of the Realm, made up of thirty members—fifteen elected by Parliament and fifteen Supreme Court justices. The Court of the Realm tries cases against any minister who has been indicted by either the Parliament or the king of Denmark.

There are approximately one-hundred courts of first instance, called district or city (depending on their jursidiction) courts, in Norway. These courts have original jurisdiction in all minor civil and criminal (crimes which are punishable by less than five years' imprisonment) cases. They are manned by at least one professional judge (larger towns often have a presiding judge and a number of associate judges). These courts handed down decisions in approximately 8,600 cases in 1978.[12] Before a civil case can be brought before either the district or city courts, it must be referred to one of the approximately 450 Conciliation Boards throughout Norway. Each municipality has at least one board composed of three members elected for a four-year term by the municipal council. If the board cannot agree upon a solution to a dispute, it is then referred to one of the courts of first instance. Norway is divided into five appellate court districts with a High Court in each. These courts are usually manned by three professional judges (criminal cases also have a jury of ten and civil cases may see an additional two to four lay judges). They hear both criminal and civil appeals and have original jurisdiction in those criminal cases that exceed five years' imprisonment. The Supreme Court, which sits in Oslo, is the final court of appeal in Norway. It may overturn decisions of lower courts as well as declare laws and royal decrees that violate the Constitution to be unconstitutional. There are, finally, a number of special courts in Norway: fisheries courts; military courts, which have jurisdiction over military matters in wartime (civilian courts retain such juris-diction during peacetime); labor courts; housing courts; courts of public admin-istration of the land, which deal with boundary and joint property disputes; and a Constitutional Court of the Realm, composed of members of the cabinet, national legislature, or Supreme Court for actions in carrying out their duties.

Sweden has approximately one hundred district courts, the courts of first instance. These courts are generally manned by professional judges, assisted by a panel of lay assessors, called ''namnd,'' elected for six-year terms from among eligible citizens by local councils:

The ''namnd'' serves mainly in cases concerning criminal offenses of a more serious nature and in family cases. In these cases the bench consists of a legally trained judge as chairman and five lay assessors. The ''namnd,'' which has medieval traditions in rural courts and has constituted a significant element of democracy in Swedish public life, must not be confused with the Anglo-American and Continental jury. Its members not only are concerned with verdicts but also deliberate with the judge on points of law, such as the sanctions to be imposed in criminal cases. A qualified majority of lay assessors must agree in order to prevail over the contrary opinion of the judge; however, such disagreements seldom occur in practice.[13]

Sweden has six Courts of Appeal. They are generally manned by four professional judges and hear appeals from the courts of first instance. The Supreme Court is the final court of appeal in Sweden. It does not necessarily hear all appeals, for a separate section of the Court determines whether there are grounds for the Court to hear such an appeal. If such a determination is made, a panel of five judges hears the case. Sweden, once again has a series of ''special courts'': land courts, water rights courts, a labor court, rent court, insurance court, and courts martial.

Finland's seventy-one rural district courts and thirty-five city courts serve as courts of first instance for both civil and criminal cases. One of the characteristics of the Finnish court system is that no case is heard by a single judge. Cases in the city courts are heard by a panel of three judges, and those in the district courts are decided by a single professional judge, aided by a panel of lay members (usually seven) that may only overrule the judge if they are in unanimous agreement. This panel is quite different from the Anglo-American jury system:

Two features distinguish the panel of laymen from the Anglo-Saxon jury system: the panel decides also on the substance of the verdict, i.e., the length of prison term within the limits set by law as opposed to the narrower scope of the Anglo-Saxon "guilty-not guilty" verdict; the panel is appointed for a fixed term and is not an ad hoc body summoned for one particular case only.[14]

Finland has six Courts of Appeal that function to hear appeals from the district and city courts. The appeals courts are composed of a number of sections, each manned by four judges (three constitute a quorum on a particular case). The final court of appeal in Finland is the Supreme Court. The appellate function of the court is restricted by law in minor cases. In addition, a case of greater importance may only be appealed to the court with its permission. Finland also has a series of special courts: military courts; water courts; land partition courts; a labor court; insurance court; and a High Court of Impeachment, which has the responsibility for trying members of the government (council of state, chancellor of justice, and members of the Supreme Court and Supreme Administrative Court) for any illegal acts committed in pursuit of their official functions.

Iceland's court system is organized somewhat differently from that of its Scandinavian neighbors. There are forty-one judicial districts, each one served by both a civil and criminal court of first instance. In addition, each district may have other special courts (there are also a number of national special courts as well). Iceland is also the only Scandinavian nation that does not have (since 1920, when the Supreme Court was established) any intermediate appellate courts. The more typical courts in each of the districts are the town courts (for urban districts) and special sessions courts (for rural districts), which are courts of first instance in civil cases, and the criminal courts, which are courts of first instance in the criminal area. In addition, each district has a sheriff's court which, among other duties, manages "execution proceedings for the satisfaction of civil judgements," a probate court, and a court of auction.[15] All of these are manned by a single professional judge who has the power to call two lay assessors to aid him. Each district also has boundary and land courts (there are only thirty-nine of these courts because the city of Reykjavik and the Township of Akureyri do not have such courts), an allotment court (to deal with questions relating to boundaries of allotments and other parcels of land), and a maritime and commercial (there are twenty-one of these courts—one in each urban judicial district) court. The boundary and land courts, allotment courts, and maritime and commercial courts are manned by three judges. There are two other district level courts: fourteen price courts (with two judges each), which adjudicate cases relating to the price laws of Iceland; and forty-one church courts (composed of three judges), which try officials of the Lutheran State Church. All of the decisions of these courts of first instance may be appealed to the Supreme Court (with the exception of the church courts, whose decisions may be appealed to the synodal court). Like Norway, Iceland has a mediation board (here called a Conciliation Board), which generally hears cases before they go to a court of first instance. There are over two hundred such boards, each made up of two lay conciliators appointed for four-year terms. The Supreme Court is the court of last resort in Iceland. In addition, there are a number of national special courts: a shipping court, court of drug offenses, labor court, synodal court, state tax board, and high court of state (which tries impeachment cases against cabinet ministers). The decisions of all of these courts (except the synodal court and High Court of State) may be appealed to the Supreme Court.

THE PERSONNEL OF THE LAW

Denmark has approximately 2,500 lawyers or advocates.[16] There are two law schools in Denmark, one at the University of Copenhagen and one at the University of Aarhus, and approximately 4,000 students were enrolled in legal studies in 1980.[17] The course of study of the law schools lasts approximately four and one-half years, after which the graduate serves as an apprentice to a practicing lawyer for three years. In addition, a committee of the Danish Bar Association offers courses to the recent law graduate as well as refresher courses for the practicing attorney. Each of the Danish judges (fifteen on the Supreme Court, fifty-four on the High Courts, and at least one judge on each of the eighty-four lower courts—although the Copenhagen Lower Court is presided over by a president and twenty-nine judges) are appointed after making application to the Ministry of Justice.[18]

There are approximately 2,000 practicing lawyers (advocates) in Norway. There are, in addition, a large number of law graduates who teach law; work for the government; or are employed by private corporations, trade unions, or employers' associations.[19] There are two law schools in Norway—the University of Bergen and the University of Oslo—with approximately 3,600 students studying law in 1980.[20] The minimum length of study is five years, with the student required to pass examinations at the end of the first, third, and fifth years. Approximately 60 percent of the beginning students ultimately pass all the exams and receive a law degree, though many must take the exams more than once.[21] In order to be licensed as an advocate, a law graduate must serve as an assistant to an advocate, judge, or lecturer or professor in law for two years. In order to be licensed to appear before the Norwegian Supreme Court, an individual must have received a first-class law degree, passed a special examination, and served for at least three years in a legal position (with one year's service as an advocate being required).

There were 264 judges in Norway in 1983.[22] In 1980 there were thirteen women judges (with three serving on the Supreme Court).[23] Any indiviual who wishes to be appointed to the bench must file an application with the Ministry of Justice after an opening has been publically announced. Appointments are made by the king, based upon recommendations from the minister of justice. To be appointed to the bench of the Supreme Court, a candidate must be at least thirty years of age and have graduated from the university with a first-class degree in law. All other judges must be at least twenty-five years of age and have graduated with at least second-class degrees in law (though, in practice, most appointees are graduates with the highest honors).[24] The typical Norwegian judge is, then, a middle-aged (the average age of the first appointment to the bench is fifty) male, with a first-class degree in law. The majority of Norwegian judges have served their two years' apprenticeship as an assistant judge under the supervision of a practicing judge.[25] Therefore, while judicial positions are open to all,

in practice they are usually applied for, and filled by, persons from the central government administration and from the Public Prosecution Authority, and by practicing advocates. Several of the judges of the Supreme Court have previously served as judges of the lower courts. There is otherwise no regular system of promotion from the lower to the higher courts.[26]

There are approximately 1,400 advocates in Sweden. There are three law faculties in Sweden: at the Universities of Stockholm, Uppsala, and Lund. In 1980, there were over 10,000 individuals pursuing degrees in law in Sweden.[27] After the individual has gained the LL.B. (an undergraduate degree which generally takes five to six years to obtain), passed a certifying examination, and practiced law for at least five years (three of which must have been as an advocate), he may be admitted as a member of the Swedish Bar Association. Individuals who are not members of the association may practice law, but the only ones allowed to call themselves "advocates" are members of the association.

There are over eight hundred judges (approximately six hundred in the district courts, two hundred in the courts of appeal, and twenty-four on the Supreme Court) serving on the ordinary Swedish courts.[28] All Swedish judges are appointed by the king. The typical pattern for most of those involved in the judicial system is to serve for two and one-half years as a junior officer in a rural district after graduation from law school. The young lawyer is generally allowed to try simple cases during this period. The future judge then spends six to nine months training in one of the courts of appeal, followed by a rigorous examination. Then,

The successful candidate remains attached to one of the Courts of Appeal, normally serving for a few years as an assistant judge in a rural district court and then as a junior member of the Court of Appeals. The normal career leads to judgeships in the Courts of Appeal or in the courts of first instance. For higher appointments—as a Supreme Court

Justice, a divisional president in the Courts of Appeal, and, in many cases, a president of a rural district court—legislative experience is considered an almost indispensible qualification, and opportunities to gain such experience are regularly offered to capable young men as part of the judicial career. In fact, high judicial posts in Sweden are recruited from among drafters of bills and experts or former secretaries of law revision committees rather than from persons whose experience has been confined to the courts.[29]

There were 9,314 (1,800 women) lawyers in Finland in 1983. Of these, 40.5 percent were involved in state and municipal administration, and 23.5 percent were engaged in commerce or industry.[30] In 1983, there were 4,000 students studying law at the Universities of Helsinki and Turku and the Lapland Institute of Higher Education.[31] The program leading to a Bachelor of Laws generally takes from four to six years and is required for a career as an advocate or judge. After graduation, the individual serves as an apprentice for three years (approximately half of the graduates serve as an apprentice in one of Finland's lower courts).[32] The appointment procedures for members of Finland's judiciary (there are approximately 1,300 judges in Finland—22 on the Supreme Court, an equal number on the Supreme Administrative Court, 462 on city courts and circuit courts, 380 on the Courts of Appeals, and a large number serving on the special courts) are somewhat more complex than in the other Scandinavian nations.[33] The president of the Republic appoints the president of the Supreme Court, the president of the Supreme Administrative Court, and judges of the special courts other than the military, and land and water courts. The president also appoints, upon recommendation of the Supreme Court, members of that court as well as the presidents and members of the courts of appeal and, upon recommendation of the Supreme Administrative Court, members of that court. All circuit judges, assistant circuit judges, chief judges in city courts, court martial judges, judges in water rights courts, and the chairman of land courts are appointed by the Supreme Court; the municipal council is responsible for appointing city court members, members of the housing court, and laymen of the circuit court.[34]

There are three different types of legal practitioners in Iceland: (1) advocates of the Supreme Court, who may plead before all of the courts; (2) advocates of the lower courts, who may only practice before those courts; and (3) lawyers, who, while not allowed to argue before any court, "may act as a deputy for an advocate."[35] There is one law school in Iceland. Approximately 250 students were pursuing a law degree in 1980.[36] It generally takes five years to obtain a law degree. In order to be an advocate of the lower courts, an individual must be a citizen of Iceland, a law graduate of good character, twenty-five years of age, and have satisfactorily pleaded four cases. To be an advocate before the Supreme Court, one must be thirty years of age, have held a law degree for at least three years, and have satisfactorily argued three cases before the Supreme Court. In 1985, there were 700 lawyers in Iceland, 270 of whom were members of the Icelandic Bar Association. Ninety-five of the latter were advocates practicing before the lower or district courts while seventy-five were advocates before the Supreme Court. Approximately one hundred of the members of the bar association were employed by private companies.[37] There are six members of the Icelandic Supreme Court and fifty-two judges of courts of first instance. In addition, there are approximately forty deputy judges, who are professional lawyers serving on the courts of first instance.[38]

PUBLIC PERCEPTIONS AND THE ROLE OF THE COURTS

While the courts in Scandinavia do not play a major role in the political system (for example, there is no strong tradition of judicial review), they are evaluated favorably (though there is a paucity of research in this area), have maintained their independence, and played a very positive role through their links to the ombudsmen, which exist in all of the Scandinavian nations (with the exception of Iceland).

There is no strong tradition of judicial review in Scandinavia. Norway is the only Scandinavian nation with a strong tradition (the 1814 Constitution established the possibility of judicial review and a series of Supreme Court decisions at the end of the nineteenth century further developed this notion) of judicial review.[39] If two or more justices of the Supreme Court decide that a law is at variance with the Constitution, the question is then brought before the Court in plenary session. Despite this, the courts have been reluctant to utilize their power and "have exercised due caution in setting aside statutes and provisional decrees which are alleged to be at variance with the Constitution."[40] Judicial review is even more problematic in Sweden:

If a court, or any other public organ, considers that a statute is in conflict with an enactment of superior legal value or that the enactment procedure prescribed is irregular in an important respect, then such a statute may not be applied. However, if the statute has been enacted by the Riksdag or by the government, the statute may be set aside only if the inaccuracy is obvious and apparent.

This form of judicial review can only be employed in cases that involve "in casu" application of a wrongful statute. Sweden has no constitutional courts that can invalidate the statute "per se," so called "abstract judicial review."[41]

Sweden does have, however, a tradition where the courts may be consulted prior to the drafting of new legislation. Similarly, in Finland the Supreme Court may give advisory opinions regarding legislation.[42] Interestingly, in Finland this has almost resulted in a veto power for the Supreme Court, for Finland's president has not given approval to any law passed by the legislature that was found to be in conflict with the Constitution by the Supreme Court.[43]

While the independence of the judiciary and the positive role that it plays through its relationship with the ombudsman indicates a positive public perception of the courts and legal practitioners, there is very little empirical data on public views of the legal system in Scandinavia. The only exception to this is a survey conducted in 1974 by the Institute for Market Research in Sweden. This study asked Swedes to rank professions in terms of "trustworthiness." Judges were found to rank the highest (with a mean score of 5.9 out of a possible score of 7), followed by physicians (5.8), police officers (5.6), teachers (5.4), attorneys (5.1), cabinet members (4.5), civil servants (4.5), trade union leaders (4.5), tv/radio reporters (4.4), legislators (4.0), and newspaper journalists (3.2). At the same time, however, this study did not find the courts to be perceived as very influential, for they ranked below the cabinet, legislature, tv/radio, business/industry, and trade unions and only above banks, newspapers, police, and teachers.[44]

The concept of an independent judiciary is well established throughout Scandinavia. While there is no notion of separation of powers in Denmark, no judge may be removed from office without proper notice or transferred to another branch unless there is a reorganization of the judiciary.[45] In addition, complaints against Danish judges may only be brought before the court of complaints, composed of three judges.[46] The 1814 Norwegian Constitution did provide for the separation of powers, and the courts have been able to maintain their independence from executive and legislative powers.[47] Judicial independence is also found in Sweden, Iceland (though complete independence does not seem to exist at the bottom of the court system) and Finland (where judges may only be removed from office by decisions of a higher court but are subject to supervision by both the chancellor of justice and the ombudsman.[48]

At first glance, the Scandinavian institution of the ombudsman appears to have little to do with the legal system. There are, however, important links between the two. First the ombudsmen plays an important role in maintaining effective administration within all branches of the government, including the court system. Second, many of the ombudsman are former judges. Finally, the ombudsman plays an important legitimizing role: "It contributes in a high degree to the creation of public confidence in the activities of courts and other authorities."[49]

Denmark has had an ombudsman since 1955. The ombudsman has the power to investigate complaints against local and national officials (including cabinet ministers but not judges) and carry out inspections of state institutions. The ombudsman is required to have had training in the law but need not be a judge. He is elected by Parliament after each election and may be reelected.[50]

The Norwegian ombudsman for administration has existed since 1962 (though there has been an ombudsman for the armed forces since 1952). His powers are very similar to that of the ombudsman in Denmark—investigate complaints against the central government (except for judges, the armed forces and the auditor of public accounts) and local authorities (this power has existed since 1969). As in Denmark, the Norwegian ombudsman for administration is elected after every general election and may be reelected. He must not only be trained in the law, but have the qualifications to be a justice of the Supreme Court (Mr. Andreas Schei, for example, who served as the ombudsman for administration from 1962 to 1974, had been a civil servant and a justice of the Supreme Court prior to his appointment).[51]

The Finnish ombudsman was established by Article 49 of the Constitution Act of 1919. Since 1957, the term of office for the position is four years (though it is not tied to parliamentary elections as in Denmark and Norway). The ombudsmen have had "formal legal education and most have had a long career in the law before they became Ombudsmen."[52] The powers of the Finnish ombudsman are closer to that of the Swedish ombudsman than that found in either Denmark or Norway. The Finnish ombudsman "has jurisdiction over all branches of government, both central and local. He can prosecute all officials, including judges, for breaches of legality. In fact, his jurisdiction is wider than that of the Swedish ombudsman since he can prosecute ministers and local councillors, although he has done so only on rare occasions."[53]

The Swedish ombudsman is the oldest (the Justitieombudsman was established by Parliament in 1809) and most powerful in Scandinavia. Since 1976, Sweden has had four ombudsmen. They have the power to investigate complaints against national and local authorities and nationalized industries; inspect hospitals, courts, prisons, military establishments, and other institutions; and institute disciplinary proceedings against officials. Ombudsmen are appointed by Parliament for a four-year term (they may be reappointed). Most have been judges (they must be trained in the law).[54] Not only are the Swedish Ombudsmen the oldest and most powerful, but they are also indicative of how widely accepted such a position might become: "The letters 'J.O.' are known throughout Sweden and people who want to complain to an Ombudsman merely have to address their envelope to 'J.O. Stockholm' and their complaint will be delivered to the right place."[55]

NOTES

1. N. Elder, A. H. Thomas, and D. Arter, *The Consensual Democracies?: The Government and Politics of the Scandinavian States* (Oxford: Martin Robertson, 1983), p. 1.

2. Nordic Statistical Secretariat, *Yearbook of Nordic Statistics, 1982*, vol. 21 (Stockholm: Nordic Council and Nordic Statistical Secretary, 1983), pp. 22–24.

3. The terms "Nordic" and "Scandinavian" are often used interchangeably.

4. K. Zwigert and H. Kotz, *An Introduction to Comparative Law*, vol. 1 (Amsterdam, New York, and Oxford: North-Holland Publishing Co., 1977), p. 285.

5. L. B. Orfield, *The Growth of Scandinavian Law* (Philadelphia: University of Pennsylvania Press for Temple University Publications, 1953), p. xi.

6. J. H. Wuorinen, *Scandinavia* (Englewood Cliffs, N.J.: Prentice-Hall, Inc., 1965), p. 128.

7. Orfield, *The Growth of Scandinavian Law*, p. 15.

8. Ibid., p. 16.

9. Ibid., p. 170.

10. Ibid., p. 91.

11. J. Uotila, "The Legal System of Finland," in K. R. Redden, ed., *Modern Legal Systems Cyclopedia*, vol. 4 (Buffalo, N.Y.: William S. Hein & Co., 1984), pp. 77–78.

12. S. T. Risa, "The Legal System of Norway," in K. R. Redden, ed., *Modern Legal Systems Cyclopedia*, vol. 4 (Buffalo, N.Y.: William S. Hein & Co., 1984), p. 152.

13. *Fact Sheets on Sweden: Law and Justice in Sweden* (Stockholm: The Swedish Institute, 1981), p. 3.

14. The Union of Finnish Lawyers, *Law and Lawyers in Finland* (Helsinki: The Union of Finnish Lawyers, 1978), p. 9.

15. C. S. Rhyne, ed., *Law and Judicial Systems of Nations*, 3d ed. (Washington, D.C.: The World Peace Through Law Center, 1978), pp. 325–26.

16. Ibid., p. 178.

17. Nordic Statistical Secretariat, *Nordic Statistics*, p. 303.

18. Rhyne, *Law and Judicial Systems*, pp. 178–80.

19. Risa, "The Legal System of Norway," p. 159.

20. Nordic Statistical Secretariat, *Nordic Statistics*, p. 303.

21. Letter of September 15, 1983, from Nils Bugge, Executive Director of the Faculty of Law, University of Oslo.

22. Letter of April 22, 1983, from Nils Bugge, Executive Director of the Faculty of Law, University of Oslo.

23. The Royal Ministry of Justice, ed., *Administration of Justice in Norway: A Brief Summary* (Oslo: The Royal Ministry of Justice, 1980), p. 89.

24. Ibid.

25. Ibid., Letter of September 15, 1983, from Nils Bugge.

26. The Royal Ministry of Justice, *Administration of Justice in Norway*, p. 89.

27. Nordic Statistical Secretariat, *Nordic Statistics*, p. 303.

28. Rhyne, *Law and Judicial Systems*, pp. 707–8.

29. F. Schmidt and S. Strömholm, *Legal Values in Modern Sweden* (Stockholm: The Bedminister Press, 1964), p. 8.

30. The Union of Finnish Lawyers, untitled pamphlet (Helsinki: The Union of Finnish Lawyers, 1983), p. 8.

31. Letter of June 20, 1985, from Rauno Selenius, Lawyer, The Union of Finnish Lawyers.

32. Letter of July 19, 1983, from Olli Tarkka, Secretary to the Finnish Bar Association.

33. Letter of June 20, 1985, from Rauno Selenius, Lawyer, The Union of Finnish Lawyers.

34. The Union of Finnish Lawyers, *Law and Lawyers in Finland*, pp. 14–15.

35. Rhyne, *Law and Judicial Systems*, p. 319.

36. Nordic Statistical Secretariat, *Nordic Statistics*, p. 303.

37. Letter of June 19, 1984, from Hafbor Ingi Jonsson, Icelandic Bar Association.

38. Rhyne, *Law and Judicial Systems*, pp. 322–23.

39. Orfield, *The Growth of Scandinavian Law*, pp. 182–83.

40. The Royal Ministry of Justice, *Administration of Justice in Norway*, p. 88.

41. N. Branstang, "The Legal System of Sweden," in K. R. Redden, ed., *Modern Legal Systems Cyclopedia*, vol. 4 (Buffalo, N.Y.: William S. Hein & Co., 1984), p. 248.

42. J. Nousiainen, "The Role of the Finnish Supreme Court in the Legislative Process," in F. Schmidt, ed., *Scandinavian Studies in Law, 1979*, vol. 23 (Stockholm: Almqvist and Wiskell International, 1979), p. 139.

43. Ibid., p. 143.

44. H. K. Becker and E. O. Hjellemo, *Justice in Modern Sweden*, (Springfield, Ill.: Charles C. Thomas, Publisher, 1976), pp. 63–64.

45. Orfield, *The Growth of Scandinavian Law*, p. 25.

46. I. M. Pedersen, "Denmark's Ombudsman," in D.C. Rowatt, ed., *The Ombudsman: Citizen's Defender* (London: George Allen & Unwin Ltd., 1965), p. 79.

47. The Royal Ministry of Justice, *Administration of Justice in Norway*, p. 86.

48. Orfield, *The Growth of Scandinavian Law*, p. 265; J. C. Griffith, *Modern Iceland* (New York, Washington, D.C., and London: Frederick A. Praeger, Publishers, 1967), p. 117; *The Parliamentary Obmudsman in Finland: Position and Functions* (Helsinki: Government Printing Center, 1976), p. 8.

49. *Fact Sheets on Sweden*, p. 4.

50. See F. Stacey, *Ombudsmen Compared* (Oxford: Clarendon Press, 1978), Chap. 2, for a discussion of the Danish ombudsman.

51. Ibid., p. 36. See Chap. 3 for a discussion of the Norwegian ombudsman.

52. *The Parliamentary Ombudsman in Finland*, p. 5.

53. Stacey, *Ombudsmen Compared*, p. 227.

54. Ibid., Chap. 1 for a discussion of the Swedish ombudsman.

55. Ibid., p. 17.

BIBLIOGRAPHY

Andersson, E. "Distribution of Powers between the Highest State Organs." In F. Schmidt, ed., *Scandinavian Studies in Law, 1972*, vol. 16. Stockholm: Almqvist and Wiskell International, 1972. Pp. 13–36.

Andren, N. *Modern Swedish Government*. Stockholm: Almqvist and Wiskell, 1968.

Becker, H. K., and E. O. Hjellemo. *Justice in Modern Sweden*. Springfield, Ill.: Charles C. Thomas, Publisher, 1976.

Bexelius, A. *The Swedish Institution of the Justitieombudsman*. Stockholm: The Swedish Institute, 1976.

Bogdan, M. "Sweden." *Comparative Law Yearbook*, vol. 5 (1981), pp. 137–44.

Branstang, N. "The Legal System of Sweden." In K. R. Redden, ed., *Modern Legal Systems Cyclopedia*, vol. 4. Buffalo, N.Y.: William S. Hein & Co., 1984. Pp. 221–59.

Elder, N., A. H. Thomas, and D. Arter. *The Consensual Democracies?: The Government and Politics of the Scandinavian States*. Oxford: Martin Robertson, 1983.

Fact Sheet on Sweden: Law and Justice in Sweden. Stockholm: The Swedish Institute, 1981.

Gomard, R. "Civil Law, Common Law and Scandinavian Law." In F. Schmidt, ed., *Scandinavian Studies in Law, 1961*, vol. 5. Goteborg, Stockholm and Uppsala: Almqvist and Wiskell, 1961. Pp. 29–38.

Griffiths, J. C. *Modern Iceland*. New York, Washington, D.C., and London: Frederick A. Praeger, Publishers, 1967.

Mead, M. R., and W. Hall. *Scandinavia*. New York: Walker & Co., 1972.

Nousiainen, J. "The Role of the Finnish Supreme Court in the Legislative Process." In F. Schmidt, ed., *Scandinavian Studies in Law, 1979*, vol. 23. Stockholm: Almqvist and Wiskell International, 1979. Pp. 133–48.

Oakley, S. *A Short History of Sweden*. New York and Washington, D.C.: Frederick A. Praeger, Publishers, 1966.

Orfield, L. B. *The Growth of Scandinavian Law*. Philadelphia: University of Pennsylvania Press for Temple University Publications, 1953.

The Parliamentary Ombudsman in Finland: Position and Functions. Helsinki: Government Printing Center, 1976.

Rhyne, C. S., ed. *Law and Judicial Systems of Nations*. 3rd ed. Washington, D.C.: The World Peace Through Law Center, 1978.

Risa, S. T. "The Legal System of Norway." In K. R. Redden, ed., *Modern Legal Systems Cyclopedia*, vol. 4. Buffalo, N.Y.: William S. Hein & Co., 1984. Pp. 121–78.

Rowat, D. C., ed. *The Ombudsman: Citizen's Defender*. London: George Allen & Unwin Ltd., 1965.

The Royal Ministry of Justice, ed. *Administration of Justice in Norway: A Brief Summary*. Oslo: The Royal Ministry of Justice, 1980.

Schmidt, F., and S. Strömholm. *Legal Values in Modern Sweden*. Stockholm: The Bedminster Press, 1964.

Shaughnessey, E. J. "Legal Lore: The Norwegian Criminal Court." *New York State Bar Journal* 54 (December 1982), pp. 546–52.

Stacey, F. *Ombudsmen Compared*. Oxford: Clarendon Press, 1978.

Strömholm, S. *An Introduction to Swedish Law*, vol. 1. Deventer, The Netherlands: Kluwer, 1981.

The Supreme Administrative Court and the Finnish System of the Application of the Law. Helsinki: The Supreme Administrative Court, 1976.

Tomasson, R. F. *Sweden: Prototype of Modern Society*. New York: Random House, 1970.

The Union of Finnish Lawyers. *Law and Lawyers in Finland*. Helsinki: The Union of Finnish Lawyers, 1978.

Uotila, J., ed. *The Finnish Legal System*. Helsinki: The Union of Finnish Lawyers Publishing Co., 1966.

———. "The Legal System of Finland." In K. R. Redden, ed., *Modern Legal Systems Cyclopedia*, vol. 4, Buffalo, N.Y.: William S. Hein & Co., 1984. Pp. 73–97.

Wuorinen, J. H. *Scandinavia*. Englewood Cliffs, N.J.: Prentice-Hall, Inc., 1965.

Zweigert, K., and H. Kotz. *An Introduction to Comparative Law*, vol. 1. Amsterdam, New York, and Oxford: North-Holland Publishing Co., 1977.

14

SOUTHEAST ASIA

Justus M. van der Kroef

THE DEVELOPMENT OF THE LEGAL SYSTEM

Southeast Asia, comprising ten independent nation states, is characterized by great heterogeneity in cultural traditions, historical evolution, and present political structure. Even so, it is perhaps possible to identify four sets of factors that have shaped the region's legal principles and judicial practices.

First, one notes what generally may be described as customary law, the body of normative indigenous precepts, grounded in and inseparable in practice from local religious beliefs. These beliefs predate the impact both of the great world religions and the period of colonial administration. Second, there is the influence of the world religions, of which Islam, at least in the juridical sense, currently is the most vibrant in Southeast Asia. Third, it is necessary to consider the still-enduring legacy of colonial domination, which only one Southeast Asian country, Thailand, may be said to have escaped. And fourth, there is the incorporation of the previous three sets of factors by the developing codes and jurisprudence of the independent Southeast Asian nations today. Presently three states of the region—the Socialist Republic of Vietnam, the Lao People's Democratic Republic (LPDR), and most of war-torn Cambodia, its government contested by two rival factions—adhere formally to Marxist-Leninist precepts in constitutional and judicial procedures. The other Southeast Asian states fervently reject Marxism-Leninism. This further complicates any comparative analysis of Southeast Asian legal systems.

Customary Law

Though none of the countries of the region is at least without some of its residual effect, applications of customary law may vary widely. In the village sphere, where 80 percent of Southeast Asians still live, recourse to such cus-

290 Justus M. van der Kroef

tomary law, if often on an informal basis, is common, especially when it comes to questions of land tenure and use of village water and other resources. Officials of the national civil administrative and judicial services—like their colonial predecessors—are wise enough to leave well enough alone, unless there are compelling political or judicial reasons to the contrary. Moreover, in some parts of Southeast Asia, especially in sections of Indonesia and Malaysia, local customary law, codified in the colonial era, continues to be applied in judicial decisions.

Through the application of virtually all customary law in Southeast Asia, whether it concerns land use conflicts, family and inheritance questions, or interpersonal disputes, there runs a basic and recurrent theme. That theme is that the members of each local human group, in its formally established villagelike setting, are tied to each other and to the land that sustains them by religious beliefs and rituals that are of normative significance in the life and monsoon cycle. Village officials serve in a magical-religious capacity in adjudicating land needs. Clearing of land belonging to the village reserve, sharing in common obligations in forest clearing or irrigation control and in other forms of mutual assistance, sowing and harvesting—all traditionally are related to animistic or pantheistic beliefs, often syncretically mixed with Hinduistic or Buddhistic notions.[1]

Given its residual but not always officially acknowledged influence, the place of traditional customary law remains an ambivalent one in Southeast Asian legal systems today. Often its role is dictated by the political expediency of national governments in which the need for prudent pragmatism in maintaining public stability among vastly diverse peoples who all happen to live in one young nation state is balanced by the need for advancing legal certainty and judicial uniformity of process.

Nowhere in Southeast Asia today has a distinctive judicial institution exclusively derived from customary law (as distinct from religious law, to be considered presently) survived in or has even been indirectly incorporated by the existing national court systems. For example, neither the Philippine *datu*, nor the Javanese *lurah* (village chief), nor the *zao pong* (tribal leaders) of North Vietnam's Nghe An region has retained its formal judicial authority. This is not to say, however, that outside the national court system such institutions do not survive, or that there is no one prepared to submit a dispute before them. The extent of such voluntary acceptance is not clear, however, and data about it are essentially anecdotal. Moreover, the principles of national legal systems or their judicial rulings on occasion do still reflect the influence of customary law. However residual such influence sometimes may appear, without it, the acceptance of the legitimacy of the national legal system, if not of the national state itself, would be impaired. Southeast Asia national governments, painfully aware of their logistical and political limits in exercising control over the more distant units of their territory, have learned to accommodate in all spheres of public policy, including the legal system.

Religious Law

A more formal acknowledgment in Southeast Asian legal systems today is accorded the influence of the great world religions. The influence of some of these religions, for example, Buddhism in Thailand and Burma, is not expressed through a separate court system. In other cases it is, as, for example, Islam in Indonesia and Malaysia, and less extensively, Roman Catholicism in the Philippines and Indonesia. But Buddhism is deeply interwoven with the cultural life of most Burmese and Thai, including their political and legal values. Even where local customary law and/or the prescriptions of national codes are applied, the sources of ethical conduct and the legitimacy of judicial systems, correctly or not, are perceived as integrated with a transcendent Buddhist value system.

Central to these values is that government and its authoritative claims on the individual cannot be changed; man is responsible for his own conduct and his own good or bad fortunes. Like the cosmic laws, the political system, including its judicial abuses, can neither be appealed nor improved through an expression of the popular will.[2] Hence, the Hinayana Buddhism of both Burma and Thailand confirmed the unquestioned hierarchy of power from village and tribal chiefs through state or provincial governors up to and including the royal center. The political-judicial hierarchy itself blended both with the application of local customary law and such periodic arbitrary deviations from it as human willfulness and passion in an always suffering world might bring. Both of these, in Buddhist precepts, would be borne with equanimity.

The universality of religious experience for all males, including periodic entry into monkhood, linked the Burmese and Thai closer to traditional political organization, since in both countries the power of the kings included regulatory control over the *thathanabaing* (supreme patriarchal abbot) of the Buddhist establishment, who, in turn, at the king's pleasure and that of his own religious council, supervises the local monasteries and their *pongyi* (monks). Over the centuries the collective Buddhist monkhood or religious establishment, usually designated as *sangha*, and the crown and its authority—including the secular magistracy appointed by it—thus came to be inextricably interwoven in the political-legal experience of the common folk.[3] Accusation and trial by the secular arm for whatever transgression of customary law or royal edict thus was not perceived as the occasion for a scholastic exercise in searching for grounds for appeal or mitigating circumstances, but rather tended to be seen popularly as a portal to the application of a cosmically sanctioned and immutable process.

In Burma, the advent of the colonial judicial system and, in Thailand, the constitutional and legal reforms brought in the wake of the Revolution of 1932 modified both the political process and the principles and practice of jurisprudence. Yet, the effect of these traditional ethical norms continue to be felt (except among thoroughly secularized and Westernized individuals). The national court system, the cut and thrust of an adversarial judicial process, the proliferation of codes, the emergence of a distinctive legal profession, the procedural sharpening of rules of evidence, the widening admission of precedent—all these must mingle and compete with the older Buddhist cosmogony.

How sharp, then, appears the contrast between all this and the world of Islamic jurisprudence in Southeast Asia. For here is a world of distinctive courts, judges, and of the categorical legal prescripts derived from the Koran, *Sunnah* (Islamic custom), and *sjariah* (Muslim) law. Here, too, is an immense bibliographic world of scholastic legal and theological interpretation, and of their practitioners, the *ulema* (scholars of the writ) who teach in numerous *pesantrèn* (private Muslim schools), perform the critical life cycle ceremonies, and function as counsel to the *ummat* (community of believers), both in legal and other problems. But here, too, is a world of public policy battlegrounds between those Muslims who urge the formation of a formal Islamic state in their country, in which Muslim law is acknowledged to be dominant, and secularists who see the realization of such a demand as an invitation to serious instability if not civil war. In addition, there is the periodic conflict between local custom law and the sjariah, as in West Sumatra, or in the Negri Semilan state of Peninsular Malaya. Finally, over all of these hovers today the intensifying effect of a worldwide resurgence of Islamic orthodoxy, exemplified and inspired by events in Iran and by the advent of the Ayatollah Ruhollah Khomeini.

An example of these cross-currents is offered by Indonesia, Southeast Asia's largest state, also in terms of the number of its Muslims (about 90 percent of Indonesia's 150 million people). Of this percentage, however, only 30 percent or so should be considered orthodox or fully observant Muslims (usually called *santri*). Most Indonesian Muslims are more eclectic and secularized, mixing Muslim beliefs and life-cycle rituals with animistic practices and/or other religious and ideological values. The term *abangan* customarily is given to the latter group. The distinction between them, also apparent in the rest of Muslim Southeast Asia, deeply affects the role of Islamic jurisprudence.

Application of Islamic law and the appearance of Islamic courts in Indonesia date from precolonial times when, especially in some of the coastal principalities of Sumatra, Kalimantan (Borneo), and Sulawesi (the Celebes), local rulers began promoting the missionary work of Muslim traders and scholars from Gujarat in Southern India, from the Peninsular Malayan sultanates, and from southern Arabia itself. Today, the courts are supervised by Indonesia's Cabinet Department (or Ministry) of Religious Affairs, and, since the judges themselves often reflect the political conflict over the Islamic state issue in Indonesia, virtually every administrative district (*kabupatèn*) in the country now has at least one *pengadilan agama* (Islamic court), composed of a chief judge and from two to eight associate judges, depending on the volume of business, along with clerical staff. There are about a dozen three-man Muslim appellate courts, the largest of which, the Makhamah Islam Tinggi, has jurisdiction over some eighty pengadilan agama on the islands of Java and Madura alone. Other appellate courts used to be found in many of the major provincial capitals. It is generally agreed among Department of Religious Affairs officials, with whom the author talked in June 1983, that of the Muslim appellate courts only the one for Java and Madura is active. Much less is known about the function, if any, of the others located in the outlying provinces. Indeed, the existence of these courts is even doubted by some officials. In those outlying areas the pengadilan agama apparently serve as the only religious courts. In any case, since the inception of the independent Indonesian Republic in 1949, successive governments generally have been careful to make appointments of the judicial and even clerical personnel attached to the courts in conformity with the recommendations of local advisory councils of *ulema*.[4]

The jurisdiction of these religious courts has become increasingly contentious and politicized. The religious courts themselves, backed to a degree by civil statute and by the concurrence of civil (nonreligious) court decisions, consider anyone who claims and is considered by others to be a professing Muslim as falling under its jurisdiction. Religious court decisions must be approved, however, by the *pengadilan negeri* (civil court). This, though often a formality, has produced tensions and de facto appeals by losing parties in a suit. Many Indonesians, particularly *abangan* and ethnic Chinese Indonesians, prefer adjudication by civil judges. The latter, though nominally Muslims themselves, often have been little inclined to acknowledge the jurisdictional claims of religious courts in cases where such claims are disputed in consultation with the Ministry of Justice. The net effect has been that today submission to the pengadilan agama requires, in effect, voluntary recognition of its jurisdiction by all the litigant parties.

This is less of a problem when it comes to such questions as divorce, brideprice payments, and inheritance allocations between male and female heirs. However, cases involving public and criminal law, including offenses such as treason, murder, or theft, though specifically provided for in the sjariah and its interpretations, invariably involve the civil, not the religious, courts in Indonesia.

Governments, as in Indonesia and Malaysia, may seek to promote creedal formulations for national political and legal beliefs that are so broad as to seemingly accommodate almost every segment of the ideological spectrum in these countries. In the Philippines, on the other hand, constitutional and judicial attempts have been made to create a "wall of separation" between the church and state. To resurgent Islamic orthodoxy, however, none of this either provides legitimacy to the state or to the moral and ethical sources of law and jurisprudence. Only when the Koran and sjariah, presumably, have become normative in all phases of public policy can such legitimacy be met, and, as is done in Iran today by the mullahs, in Malaysia and Indonesia it would be the ulema and kiajih who would play the pivotal roles in the daily application of the law.[5]

The development of a national political ideology, to which all are expected to subscribe, presents other difficulties for the more orthodox Muslim in postcolonial Southeast Asia. Malaysia has such national ideological principles, the Rukun Negara (Pillars of the State). They comprise belief in God, loyalty to king and country, support for the Malaysian Constitution, commitment to the rule of law, and "proper conduct and moral behavior." A moderate Malayan Muslim would have no difficulty with it. But Islamic self-consciousness has become particularly strong in recent years in a country like Malaysia, whose 15 million population is divided between ethnic Malays (about 50 percent, who are mostly Muslims), Chinese (about 36 percent), Indians (about 10 percent), and other indigenous minorities like the Dayaks. Ethnic differences over the decades have been sharpened by economic competition, especially as the Chinese element traditionally has dominated most of the country's commerce and financial life. Legally enforced preferments for the benefit of ethnic Malays—in awards of educational scholarships, in obtaining credit for starting new businesses, or in entry to certain government services, for example—have not assuaged a sense of deprivation among young Malays. To these Malays, Islamic puritanism and reform have become a matrix for their demands for fundamental constitutional, political, and legal change, all directed toward creation of an Islamic state. In the 1970s Islamic fundamentalism and revivalism amaong some Malay Muslims known as the *dakwah* or "call to the faith" movement, led to outbursts of violence, including attacks on government offices and police posts, and demands that local governments show greater respect for Islamic precepts in public policy, such as by closing bars and massage parlors.[6]

Falling rice and rubber prices have made it easy for other Muslim fundamentalist organizations, such as the Pertubuhan Angkatan Sabilullah (Organization of Holy Fighters), to stir impoverished Malay small holders and farmers into violent clashes against a government depicted as too compliant to the ways of the *kafir* (infidel). In addition, for more than a decade now, Islamic fundamentalism has been agitating on behalf of secessionist organizations linked with Muslim Thais across the border and committed to the ultimate creation in the region of a separate state founded on Islamic law. That theme today is increasingly heard on a nationwide scale. Parti Islam Sa-Malaysia (Islamic Malaysian Party or Pas), since the early 1980s, began attracting ever larger Malayan crowds at its public gatherings and at mosques and *suraus* (Muslim prayer places) as its leaders hammered on the alleged plight of the *mustadh'affin* (oppressed believers) in Malaysia and on the need to establish a truly Islamic government and state in the country. Pas's chief leader, Mohammed Abdul Rahman, though not a Shiit, is an avowed admirer of the Ayatollah Khomeini's religious fundamentalism, particularly in its social application.[7] Stricter enforcement of dietary laws in public places, recognition for those who wish to observe prayers and other rituals in the work place, increased government support for religious schools, greater recognition and encouragement of the Islamic courts, better government enforcement of the decisions of such courts, the establishment of an Islamic court of appeals for all of Malaysia, a further restriction on Christian missionary activity, especially in the East Malaysia states of Sarawak and Sabah—these are some of the items on the Malay Muslim fundamentalists' agenda today. It is hardly necessary to emphasize that realization of such an agenda would have a deeply disturbing effect on the country's delicate ethnic-political balance and on the perception of non-Muslim Malaysians of the legitimacy of Malaysia's legal system.

In projecting their demands, especially in their struggle to win still more recognition of Islamic law and Islamic court decisions, orthodox Muslims in Southeast Asia do not only collide with the present secular national codes, usually derived through different colonial experiences from Western legal principles and judicial procedures. They also necessarily come into conflict with the residual force of local customary law and with the legal perceptions of Christian Southeast Asians, which seem more in tune with the presently prevailing national codes.

In Indonesia conflict between customary law and its traditional judges and spokesmen, the heads of villages, of extended family units, or indigenous nobility, on the one hand, and Islamic sjariah and *hukum* (doctrine of obligation), on the other, still are common enough, although they are probably less frequent than during the Dutch colonial era, when recognition and protection of Indonesian customary law was considerably greater. Disputes over marriage contracts (for example, the dowry or the groom's practice of paying a bride price), the rights of women in divorce or polygamous marriages, adoption of children, and the manner in which inheritances are divided between male and female heirs have been and still are among the more common conflicts between *adat* and Islamic law in Indonesia.[8] In such cases a local community may experience profound confusion not only over the type of law that exists in its midst but the moral and ethical principles that sustain its own distinctive identity and, finally, the legitimacy of the national secular courts that are called upon to settle what is, in fact, a classic illustration of what the legal profession calls "conflict of laws."

The problem is further complicated when the value systems of two world religions, each modified by its own particular cultural context, begin to clash. In Indonesia, some 4.5 million Christians (about 60 percent of them Roman Catholic), in part because of their more complete and ready adoption of Western life styles, have long played a disproportionately important role in manning the modern state bureaucracy, including the leadership of the politically powerful armed forces establishment. This, in turn, has aroused the ire of Muslim fundamentalism.

In the southern Philippines there is a similar confrontation, but one that also has some significantly different aspects. In parts of Mindanao, where Christian Filipino colonists came to settle in the 1950s on the reserve or unused land belonging by customary law to predominantly Muslim villages, the conflict between them underscored the relative lack of modern cadastral procedures and lack of understanding of modern concepts of land rights and land tenure laws among the Muslim rural folk. The Muslims, in confronting the Christian settlers in their midst, seemed to rely as much on their pre-Islamic communal traditions prohibiting alienation of village land as on their by now heightened Islamic self-consciousness in defending what they perceived to be their rights, and they were prepared to do so by force, if necessary. The contemporary national Philippine court system, emanating from distant Manila and dominated by the overwhelmingly Roman Catholic majority of the Philippine population, has always seemed alien to the Muslim experience. No justice is to be expected from it, and violent resistance to the land claims of Roman Catholic outsiders seems to the Muslim the only culturally appropriate response. As one noted specialist on the Philippine Muslim problem has put it:

Muslims still tend to think of land as belonging to the clan (over which the *datu* presides), whereas Christians think of land as a matter of individual ownership. Muslims still tend to base their claims on unwritten tradition; Christians rely more on legal documents. When conflicts arise Mislims are inclined to extortion or to guerrilla tactics, and Christians to courts of law.[9]

Thus, the persistent separatist movement of the MNLF (Moro National Liberation Front) in the southern Philippines is the result of both a conflict of laws and of differences over methods of conflict resolution. These conflicts are aggravated by the enduring recollection, enshrined as much in Philippine national experience as in local Muslim ethnic lore, of the centuries-long historic conflict between Islam and Christianity. Legal systems in Southeast Asia today, therefore, particularly in Indonesia and the Philippines, still must struggle with the legacy of that conflict.

The Colonial Heritage

In considering the third factor that has shaped these legal systems, it is necessary again to stress the extreme diversity of the region. Colonial legal and administrative institutions and practices could be haphazard and poorly structured, having for that reason even further unsettling effects on an already fragmented transitional society; or, again, a more systematic colonial judicial system could become deeply embedded within the new national polity that emerged eventually from the era of Western domination. French policy in Indochina offers an example of the former, while the Spanish and U.S. systems in the Philippines are more illustrative of the latter. The judicial organization and policy of the Dutch in Indonesia and that of the British in Burma, Malaysia, and Singapore fall somewhere in between these ends of the spectrum.

This is not the place to review the history of the establishment of French power in Indochina or of the other colonial powers in the rest of Southeast Asia. Suffice it to note that the haphazardness of French judicial administration was well reflected in what has been described as the "piecemeal" and uncoordinated process of the French colonial conquest itself. The latter involved nearly three decades, from the middle 1850s to the middle 1880s, and was "punctuated by five campaigns and five treaties, while Paris wavered between expansionist and anticolonial stances."[10]

The heavily Sinicized civilization of the Viet people had established a Confucian-style mandarinate and hierarchical administrative system under the courts and yet left intact the pre-Chinese local judicial powers of the village chief, who administered the customary law, together with a village "council of notables" (a local elite of the prestigious, wealthiest, and learned). Provincial governors, acting as tribunals of appeal of the village chief's or notables' decisions, deferred to a royal council at the Annamite court, which took jurisdiction of the most severe cases. The council reportedly had a reputation for scrupulous observance of evidentiary rules. A sense of obligation to parents and extended family, along with paramount recognition of the need for order, of social status differentials, and of the traditional proprieties of conduct, was the moral basis of the popular sense of law.

In this system the French intervened in almost random, ad hoc, and deeply unsettling ways. The precolonial magistracy and bureaucracy were assimilated as far as possible into a new, poorly coordinated French colonial administrative system, but one with greatly reduced and even demeaning spheres of responsibility for the traditional mandarinate, a development that humiliated and bewildered the Viet population. New judicial codes were promulgated by the French which severely undermined traditional parental authority, loosened social hierarchy, and deeply affronted Vietnamese custom. The new penal code promulgated for Tonkin by the French in 1917, for example, freed Vietnamese children at the age of twenty-one from all obligation to their parents and other family members, while a new French naturalization law of 1913 virtually destroyed traditional paternal authority over children.[11]

French colonial authority also all but shattered the authority of the village council of notables, the body that traditionally had compiled the local census and the tax rolls. Census-taking and the roll drafting and collecting of taxes became direct responsibilities of French provincial governors and their tax supervisors. When village notables and chiefs, now left without obligations to their communities, resisted or began seizing communal land for themselves, the French all but eliminated the village council's remaining authority and altered the basis of the village chiefs' appointment. In precolonial days the chief had been a kind of primus inter pares of the council, arriving through personal prestige and/or traditional status to his office. Now the French made his office an elected one. This might seem democratic, but it soon became evident that the village's welfare depended on the chief's compliance with French colonial authority. The practical result, in time, was that one who had been a member of a natural elite— traditionally also invested according to custom law with judicial authority at this, the first, level of conflict resolution—now became someone wholly dependent on the whims of his French superiors, the governor, executives of provincial administration and of the service departments.[12]

On the one hand, French cultural assimilation policies, for example, in education, religious missionary work, and promotion of more Western life styles, encouraged the creation of a new Vietnamese elite. This new elite entered the French colonial administrative services or the developing commercial and estate economy, but it did not really identify with the French colonial government, even though its members might become formally naturalized French citizens. On the other, an extensive dualism developed between a French colonial service superstructure that functioned in juxtaposition to a native provincial and local administration, with its hierarchies ranging from the precolonial courts (as in Annam and Cambodia), and their respective mandarinates of ministers and governors, to the heads of *huyen* (a grouping of several villages), and the communal chiefs and notables, and *quan-an* (judge), acting as appellate tribunals at the provincial governor's residence.

The two segments of this dyad interacted poorly.[13] The newly assimilated, Frenchified, Vietnamese elite remained largely removed from the indigenous, precolonial mandarinate and the village spheres, including their judicial practices. Modern law, based on the contemporary French codes, applied to the assimiles (indigenous inhabitants who submitted to the colonial legal code) and formally naturalized Vietnamese in the towns, with recourse to the courts in metropolitan France itself. Such naturalization followed quite readily upon completion of a modern education, religious conversion, entry into the French colonial service, and/or residence for some time in France itself. For most rural inhabitants of Indochina, however, the judicial system became a bewildering patchwork, with some authority having been left to village and huyen chiefs in their application of custom law and with appeals possible to the governor's quan-an, and, in rarer cases still, even to the royal courts. But elsewhere in Indochina, as in Tonkin and Cochin China, criminal cases usually were brought before French tribunals, with the mandarinate still acting in an advisory capacity on matters of custom. Both in Annam and Cambodia, the Chinese, in matters of civil law, were tried before their own mandarin magistrates. In Cambodia and Laos, where French influence was less direct, indigenous tribunals appointed by the royal courts, but functioning under the supervision of French "residents" (commissioners), handled cases going beyond the jurisdiction of the village chiefs. The "rule of law" in the pre-World War II heyday of French Indochina was, then, very much a matter of one's degree of modern education and "assimilation," type of residence or geographic location, occupation, and even of one's ethnic or racial affiliation.

In sharp contrast with this judicial melange has been the evolution of the Philippines' colonial legal system. After Spain consolidated its power over most of the Philippines by the end of the sixteenth century, the country remained for nearly two and a half centuries a dependency of Mexico. Mexico's viceroy exercised executive authority through a governor general in Manila, who was checked by the Royal Audiencia (Supreme Court). Both acted in conformity with a massive body of laws and royal decrees, among them the Leyes de Indias (Laws of the Indies), as well as specific codes dealing with criminal offensives, inheritance, and other property questions. In the provinces the *alcalde mayor* (governor), combined executive and judicial authority, and on their holdings the *encomenderos* (estate owners) in feudal fashion dispensed justice. In the villages, barangays, or barrios not under encomendero authority, the *cabeza* (chief) applied customary law. From here appeals usually could be addressed to the *capitan* (community chief magistrate) or *gobernadorcillos* (petty governors) of the nearby pueblo or town.[14]

Intense and systematic missionizing by the friars, combined with the uniformity of the Spanish administrative and judicial system and the existence of a common body of colonial law, led to a far greater degree of assimilation of the population, sense of governmental centralization, and consistency in jurisprudence in the Philippines than marked the French colonial era in Indochina, although the latter, admittedly, was far shorter in duration. Even so, it is well to stress that in the barangays and in the Islamic areas of the southern Philippine islands around the Sulu Sea, precolonial custom and/or religious law retained much of its strength. Moreover, despite the deepening Hispanization process, nativistic and proto-nationalistic uprisings throughout the Philippine islands were common. These were expressive also of the fact that important indigenous Filipino cultural traits, for example, those involving land rights and the judicial powers of traditional datus and barangay cabezas, remained very much alive in the Filipino sense of legal propriety.[15]

With the establishment on July 4, 1901, of U.S. civil government, following the American conquest of the islands in the 1898 Spanish-American War, a new chapter began in Philippine legal history.[16] Under the American military government (1898–1901), the Spanish colonial judicial system already had been thoroughly reorganized. A new Supreme Court, composed of six Filipinos and three U.S. Army officers, was established, and, in 1900, a new uniform system of lower courts of first instance in cities and provinces began functioning, along with the implementation of a new Code of Criminal Procedure reflecting the U.S. federal code. In the following six years further administrative and judicial reforms were introduced by the Philippine Commission. Among these was a new Code of Civil Procedure and a Judiciary Act that further systematized prosecutorial procedures and the structure of the local (including municipal court) system. With the adoption of the 1935 Commonwealth of the Philippines Constitution, began the final drive for complete Filipinization of the personnel of the judiciary, from the municipal courts to the seven-person Supreme Court. Two new courts, patterned after similar U.S. tribunals—a fifteen-person Court of Appeals and a Court of Industrial Relations, were established (the Philippines had previously been divided into nine judicial districts, with corresponding prosecutorial offices).

Yet, even on the eve of World War II, voluntary submission to Islamic courts in the Muslim areas of the southern Philippines continued to be respected. The same would be true for the judicial decisions of barangay chiefs, some of whom eventually acted as justices of the peace in the formal hierarchy of new national courts but rendered their judgment in conformity with customary law.

Both the Dutch and British authorities, though accommodating for those who wished for a process of assimilation with the colonial power's own European legal values, essentially believed the greater wisdom in statecraft to lie in various indirect forms of rule. Until the end, the rule of ethnically similar groups by those of the same group, particularly if they were sanctioned in doing so by their own traditional laws and political-judicial institutions, remained essentially the lodestar of Dutch colonial policy. Neither the split into two mutually alienated legal spheres that characterized the French administration in Indochina nor the steady integration, if not homogenization, resulting from the Spanish and U.S. legal and judicial policies in the Philippines typified the Dutch and English systems.

For two centuries, since the early 1600s, the Dutch East India Company attempted to make its trade both with Europe and within Asia itself the pivot of all its policies; such territorial control and political power as it eventually acquired over the years, including the necessity of governing an indigenous population, came as often unwanted by-products of its commercial policies. Except for its few Dutch, Eurasian, Chinese, or some Indonesian personnel, who resided within the walls of its *factorijen* (forts and trading places) and in a few cities like Batavia (now Djakarta), which the company established or controlled, the Indonesian population was left to its own customary laws and decision of village chiefs, feudal aristocracy, or courts.

Even after 1800, when the East India Company had ceased to exist and its East Indian possessions eventually had passed under the control of the new Netherlands Kingdom, adat or customary law prevailed for most Indonesians, particularly in the large part of the archipelago, where the Dutch exercised little authority. Where that authority was more direct (in most of Java and Sumatra), adat was administered under the supervision of Dutch colonial officials by Indonesian heads of communities or districts (the so-called Regents) who themselves had been incorporated into the Dutch colonial administrative structure. Throughout most of the century and a half of rule by the Netherlands Kingdom over Indonesia (1815–1949), there was continuous Dutch academic and field research into the adat, as well as the application of it in the colonial judicial administration. However, over time, the Dutch (or "European") population in Indonesia, as well as the group of "Foreign Orientals" (mostly ethnic Chinese), steadily grew in numbers, and their distinctive legal needs emerged with the development of a modernizing colony. Hence, since the middle of the nineteenth century, there has come into being separate public legal classifications for "Europeans," "Foreign Orientals," and "Natives" (i.e., Indonesians). Separate codes and court procedures were usually applied to these three categories. Yet, at the same time, there also was frequent overlapping, as, for example, Christianized Indonesians placed themselves in the "European" legal status and had the Dutch family law applied to them. Indonesians could also opt for a wholly adat-based native jurisprudence, particularly beyond Java, or, alternatively, could submit themselves to the so-called government jurisprudence for natives, in which case "European" substantive criminal law was applied. By 1925 virtually all Chinese had come under "European" law, though they, like other resident Asiatics, were aided by advisors to the court, usually adjudicated by their own legal traditions in family and inheritance disputes.[17]

Dutch colonial rule on the island of Java was much more direct and of longer duration than elsewhere in the Indonesian islands. Accordingly, in those non-Javanese areas, the Dutch practice of indirect rule was to leave in place much longer the judicial and executive authority of traditional communal and tribal leaders, of the indigenous aristocracy, and even of the indigenous courts. Even so, by 1914 there were tendencies toward a homogenization in the judicial system, when the so-called *landgerechten* (country courts) were established in Java. These courts of first instance dealt with minor infractions committed by members of any population group. During the last few decades before the outbreak of World War II, the same criminal law code eventually came to be applied to all population groups in Indonesia, except those for whom adat provisions under the so-called native jurisprudence still prevailed. In questions of substantive private law, there remained differences between the way Indonesians were treated on the one hand, and the manner in which Europeans and Foreign Orientals were treated on the other. Other important differences existed in the areas of administrative and constitutional law. These differences, including Dutch respect for adat, were perceived as particularly denigrating in Indonesian nationalist circles, where a homogenized and egalitarian legal system tended to be viewed as inseparable from the vision of an independent Indonesian state.

India had always been considered by the British to be the heart of their Asian colonial presence. To be sure, the British had stiffly competed with the Dutch for the Indonesian spice trade in the early years of the seventeeth century. But it was not until the closing years of the eighteenth century that England's Indian and other Asian commercial interests—the need for a naval station on the more protected shore of the Bay of Bengal and for a transit port to refit British vessels in the booming China trade—refocused London's attention on the Peninsular Malayan principalities.[18]

The British East India Company's hesitant settlement of Penang in 1786 soon acquired added significance in the context of the Anglo-Dutch conflict and ar- chipelagic rivalries during and following the Napoleonic Wars. These rivalries prompted the English occupation of Malacca in 1795 and ultimately led in 1819 to the founding of Singapore. From these three British "Straits Settlements," Britain, though still preoccupied mainly with Indian affairs (the three Malayan colonies were administratively considered to be but a "residency" under the Governor of Bengal), increasingly found itself drawn into traditional Malayan-Siamese territorial disputes and into dynastic squabbles and civil wars among the sultanates of Kedah, Perak, and Johore, and other Peninsular Malayan states. In 1867, London's Colonial Office finally assumed direct control over the "Straits Settlements." With the development of tin mining and rubber production on the Peninsula, the influx of British capital and Chinese coolie labor, the growing importance of Singapore in Pacific naval strategy and in the Asian entrepot trade, and the apparent inability of the old feudal bureaucratic mechanism of the Malay Sultanates to deal with the upheavals brought by the transformation of their economies, Britain in 1874 intervened in force. The effect of this intervention was the establishment of a system of indirect rule through "residents" (British commissioners in certain key Malay states). The "residents" were charged with persuading the native rulers to follow British policy wishes. To bring about greater coordination and the granting of concessionary rights, a scheme of organizational unity, called the "Federated Malay States," came into being in 1896 among the four states of Perak, Selangor, Negri Sembilan, and Pahang.[19]

Peninsular Malaya, like Indonesia under the Dutch authority at this time, seemed politically unfinished. The administrative "edifice" that had been built, in the words of one historian, "looked decidedly odd."[20] Along with the Federated States, there still were the "Straits Settlements," all British crown colonies, governed from Singapore and with a defined local bureaucratic and legal structure that generally followed Britain's. The Johore Sultanate, meanwhile, was outside the Federation, enjoyed near autonomy, and had its own diplomatic arrangement with Whitehall. Such states as Trengganu and Kelantan at this time nominally acknowledged the sovereignty of Thailand's throne. But a hazy de facto British "influence" in economic and political affairs prevailed. Not until a 1909 Thai-British treaty did Bangkok abandon its formal claims, and the northern frontier of "British Malaya" could at least be fixed. At the courts of the "Unfederated States" (Kedah, Perlis, Trengganu, Kelantan, and Johore), British "advisors," functioning under the supervision of the High Commission in Singapore, were virually the only formal channel of Britain's policy impact in these parts of Malaya. It could be argued that the advisors served essentially a diplomatic purpose, but in a symbolic way they also served notice to other powers that these areas were under British influence.

Under the aegis of these forms of indirect rule, legal systems in both the Federated and Unfederated Malay States retained, therefore, much of their pre-Western character during the nineteenth and even early twentieth centuries. Significant in both types of states is that recognition was given to (1) local customary law, (2) precolonial digests of laws compiled at the behest of the Malay Royal courts (these included, for example, important maritime law provisions), and (3) the Islamic codes and Islamic judicial decisions. Yet, over time, the British presence, especially in the Federated Malay States, brought modifications in the application and perceived legitimacy of all of these three. For example, application of property law in Negri Sembilan retained its traditional matriarchal quality, with inheritances passing through the maternal line. But British criminal law had come to prevail in Negri Sembilan since the 1880s, just as it had earlier in the Straits Settlements. Application of the precolonial, heavily Islamized digests of laws at the courts, for example, in Pahang, initially was condoned by the British Resident. But, eventually, British administrators had success in offering the Westernized penal codes and evidentiary procedures in use in British India as useful and acceptable alternatives to frequent conflicts between the Malay customary law and the Muslim sjariah.[21]

To briefly gauge the long-term effects on the legal system of indirect rule, it may be useful to summarize here the official enumeration of legal sources in

1962 in Peninsular Malaya, then called the "Federation of Malaya," an independent nation since 1957.[22] In 1963, this Federation would join with the Borneo states of Sarawak and Sabah and with Singapore—the latter was to secede again in order to become an independent republic in 1965—to form the now existing state of Malaysia. But in 1962, before the last major constitutional change, the following sources of law were officially listed for this Peninsular Malayan Federation:

1. English acts of Parliament served as the model for Malayan mercantile and maritime law, as well as in such areas of private law as divorce and adoption.
2. The Penal Code, law of evidence, and Criminal Procedure Code in the Federation were described as adapted from such British codes as had been in use in British Colonial India.
3. The Federation of Malaya Civil Procedure Code originally also mirrored the Indian Code of Civil Procedure but in 1958 it was largely replaced by decisions of the Malayan Supreme Court following "very closely the Rules of the Supreme Court in England."
4. Indian Contract Law was in use in the Federation of Malaya, except in Penang and Malacca, two of the original Straits of Settlements, where predominantly English contract law had long been used.
5. In Negri Sembilan and in Malacca, local Malay customary law had been given formal legitimacy by acts of local legislatures, except for cases covered by British criminal law, as already indicated, and every state of the Malayan Federation had passed legislation legitimizing various applications of Muslim religious law and obligation for those seeking redress under such law.
6. Land use laws, meanwhile, had particularly varied origins. Existing law throughout the Federation providing for compulsory acquisition of land for public purposes reportedly was "largely borrowed from India." However, in the original Straits Settlements of Penang and Malacca, where British legal practice prevailed, land ownership and transfer rights were governed not by the primacy of village communal land rights (as in most of Southeast Asia) but by the principle that "the ultimate property in all land vests in the ruler of the state."
7. Finally, throughout the federation, the meticulous cadastral surveying and title registration process, derived from the "Torrens system" used first in Australia, had been taken as model.

In Sarawak, which after World War II had reverted to direct British authority under the rule of the Brooke family, there existed, in 1962, a four-tiered court system, capped by a High Court and Court of Appeal. The codes in use largely reflected those in the Federation of Malaya, and in questions affecting the criminal law, in particular, British principles and practices prevailed. In Sabah (North Borneo), as in Sarawak, there was (and is today) also a three-tiered native court system. This system applies the customary law of the *Iban* ("Sea Dayak") of the Kayan, ethnic Malay (including the Melanau and Kedayan), and of other autochthonous groups, primarily at the level of the "Headman's Court's" (the village or extended family chief), with appeals possible to the courts of higher chiefs or to the District and Resident Commissioner's Native Court.[23] Both the practice of the British colonial system, as well as that of the independent Malaysian government today, has been to let the voluntary submission by the disputing parties to local customary or Islamic law govern the adjudication of most civil (but not criminal) cases. In Singapore, however, because of that city's particular background as one of the original and most cosmopolitan of the Straits Settlements, the legal system from the beginning has been more closely patterned upon British substantive law and procedures.

Thus, the British system of indirect rule, like that of the Dutch during most of their administration in Indonesia, was compelled, from the beginning, to perform a balancing of native custom, including religious law, with Western precepts of justice. The formula found to be the most practical in performing this balancing act and one least likely to get the colonial civil servant involved in difficulty either with his superiors or—if they got wind of it—with the public in the metropolitan mother country, was to let disputes perceived by Western law as essentially criminal law matters be adjudicated as much as possible in conformance with Western principles and procedures, but allowing family and property questions to be settled on the basis of local customary or religious laws.

No Dutch or British magistrate, especially in the nineteenth century, escaped the problems of such a balancing act. The first British civil officer and magistrate after England's military subjugation of the region was appointed to the Tenasserim region of Burma in September 1825. He was instructed by his superiors in Bengal to "govern according to local laws and customs," but, at the same time, "to introduce a system in accordance with Liberal ideas." The officer in question discharged this mandate by promising local Burmese that he would apply their own "established laws," be fair and equitable, and protect them from their enemies, but that, at the same time, he would establish and promote a system of the "most free and unrestricted internal and external commerce."[24]

The legal implications of opening Burma—then a dependency of British India—to the "unrestricted" inroads of trade, were apparently as little appreciated at the time as the problem of dealing, in effect, with two different sets of judicial principles. The latter applied as much to the British as to the Dutch, French, Spanish, or American colonial legal experiences. On the one hand, there was the British (or Western) legal approach of first determining the exact facts, thence deriving conclusions, and finally applying the appropriate code of adjudicatory legal provisions. On the other hand, there was the Burmese (or Javanese, or Iban, or Moro) principle that the purpose of a legal procedure—except in obvious cases of major capital offenses—is to arrive at a mutually satisfactory and face-saving agreement between the parties, not a zero-sum type of judgment.[25]

Substituting the certainty of the rule of codified law proved as difficult as relying on the British-style jury system, which was also introduced in Tenasserim in the 1830s. Tenasserim, in fact, set the model for the rest of the nineteenth-century British colonial court structure in Burma. The judiciary consisted of the governor, three chief tax officials, and six British civil officers of lower rank, all with their clerical retinue. Judgment rarely was rendered en banc. Rather, one or two members of the court handled individual cases with the aid of a Burmese adviser on customary law. Understanding the latter required a close study of the *Dhammathat* (a Pali variant of the Hindu-Indian Laws of Manu) as well as various ancient edicts of Burmese kings. All these, however, Burmese judges traditionally had viewed as philosophical legal guides, not as exact prescripts in specific cases brought before them. With the steady opening of the country to both British and Indian commercial and financial interests, a far greater systematization of court procedures became necessary. In 1872 a judicial commissioner was appointed to overhaul and oversee the Burmese legal system. British civil officials began a yeoman's job in drafting and refining a uniform civil code, which was reverential of but not necessarily in strict conformance with the Dhammathat or local customary law. As in India, there emerged a locally trained Burmese legal profession, skilled in applying British judicial procedures as well as in the Indian and the developing Burmese codes. It was not until the first decade of the present century, however, that there came into existence a new, essentially three-tiered, hierarchy of formal courts, topped by a Chief Court with a separate judicial service.[26]

The vast majority of Burmese, however, preferred adjudication of civil disputes by their village and tribal leaders, sometimes with the aid of the Buddhist clergy. This is where the law was alive for most indigenous inhabitants of the country. In criminal matters, however, things were different. Here the British imposed a justice system suffused with Indian and Burmese lawyers and various legal counselors, often with dubious credentials. The system grew rapidly in size and work load and rural unrest grew apace. The increasing population made for mounting pressure on limited resources of arable land, and many seemed to turn to brigandage and violent gangsterism in the closing decades of British rule.[27] An uncomprehending British governor in Burma in 1931 might attribute all this to the ''incredulity'' of ''misguided'' peasants and a corrupted ''younger generation'' of Burmese easily exploited by few revolutionaries.[28] But such assertions did little to explain the widening scope of economic dislocation and social alienation brought by the British colonial administration and even less in illuminating the contradictions and weaknesses of Burma's disjointed colonial legal system.

The Burmese and Vietnamese cases in particular relate the frailties of colonial legal systems to the developing turmoil in parts of Southeast Asia on the eve of World War II. In the Burmese and Vietnamese cases, systems of government, with their respective assimilated or modern educated native bureaucratic or legally trained elites, seemed often far removed from the problems and legal needs of the rural mass. Where legal systems either had been purposely homogenized as much as possible from the beginnings of colonial rule (the Philippines under Spanish and U.S. suzerainty), or where, year by year, the number of those of different ethnic backgrounds and of originally various legal needs gradually were brought more and more under the same legal codes and juridical procedures (Indonesia under the Dutch), the emerging nationalist sentiment and desire for independence might not be any the less, to be sure. But the sense of shared political and legal principles among diverse population groups clearly was a good deal greater—one essential element, undoubtedly, in the forming of a new future national polity.

The problem would turn out to be that neither in the Philippines nor in Indonesia such a shared commonality of principles was to show itself capable of neutralizing an eventual resurgence of Islamic orthodoxy. The difficulty of building a common legal ethos proved equally formidable, but in a different way, in Malaya. Indirect rule in Malaya and the patchwork quilt of legal systems throughout that Peninsula in the Straits Settlements, Sarawak, and North Borneo (Sabah) contributed to the difficulty in finding a consensus on which such a polity might be based. This explains, at least in part, why Malaya was the last Southeast Asian state to achieve national independence (1957) and why the present Malaysian Federation was not formed until 1963.

THE ORGANIZATION OF THE COURT SYSTEM

World War II and the Japanese occupation spelled the end of the old colonial system in most of Southeast Asia. The Japanese Supreme Commander of Southern Areas, headquartered in Tokyo and through him local Japanese commanders-in-chief became the supreme executive, legislative, as well as judicial authority.[29] They allowed only a shadow of the established legal systems to continue. However, they also gave some encouragement to nationalist participation in local administration, and the Japanese, particularly in Indonesia and parts of Malaya, also gave the appearance of formally fostering the place of Islam and of the religious courts.[30] After the turbulence of postwar, revolutionary, nationalist independence struggles, as occurred in Indonesia and Indochina, or more peaceful but equally decisive constitutional changes, as occurred in the Philippines and Malaysia, there eventually emerged new legal systems in the now independent nation states of Southeast Asia. Some of these experienced further structural reforms, as in the case of the dissolution of the federal Indonesian state structure and establishment of a unitary Republic (1950), or as a result of the Communist victory throughout the Indochina states (1975).

Today, the reshaped Southeast Asian legal systems, though in many cases still drawing from their respective colonial antecedents and still having to come to terms in different degrees with the traditions of customary and religious laws, can be divided between those that are based at least formally on the Marxist-Leninist ideology and those that are not. In the first category belong: (a) the Socialist Republic of Vietnam (SRV), formally created when on July 2, 1976, the Vietnamese National Assembly, nearly thirteen months after the Communist occupation of Saigon (now named Ho Chi Minh City), approved the unification of North and South Vietnam, (b) the Lao People's Democratic Republic (LPDR), established formally on December 2, 1975, and the successor to the abolished

Royal Lao Government, and (c) the Hanoi-backed People's Republic of Kampuchea (PRK), formed on January 10, 1979, and now controlling most of Cambodian territory but locked in civil war with its Communist predecessor, the Beijing-supported government of "Democratic Kampuchea" and its non-Communist allies. The SRV, LPDR, and PRK form what Hanoi's media since the early 1980s like to call a "unity bloc." They are reciprocally linked by treaties and agreements of cooperation, making them a de facto political federation whose close integration is reflected also in the similarities of their current legal systems.

The basis of the SRV's present legal system is found in Chapter 10 of the country's present 1979 Constitution.[31] The court system comprises a People's Supreme Court, which is "the highest judicial organ" of the SRV, and is charged with supervising the local People's Courts and the military courts; the Supreme Court president and other members (currently seven in all) are elected by and responsible to the SRV's National Assembly, the "highest state authority." Like assembly members, those of the Supreme Court serve a five-year renewable term. The SRV judicial system closely reflects that in use in the USSR. In the SRV the People's Courts are composed both of judges and *hooij thaamr nhaan daan* ("people's assessors"). The latter usually outnumber the judges on the courts, except at the Supreme Court level. SRV People's Courts function in the chief administrative subdivisions (provinces, districts, and municipalities). Subunits of districts and municipalities (for example, villages and wards) sometimes also may have their People's Courts. The appellate process is not clearly defined; appeals can be heard by People's Courts at higher administrative levels, depending on the prominence that party leaders wish to give the case or the importance of the defendant.

So-called People's Committees, which formally function as executive arms of local People's Councils, also are an important part of the SRV legal system. "Elected by the local people" at various administrative levels for periods ranging from two to four years, the committees are responsible to unspecified "higher level" organs of "state authority." Committees and councils both are charged, under Article 112 of the SRV Constitution, with "insuring observance and execution of law in their respective localities," maintaining "political security," preserving "socialist property," and generally (Article 111) assisting in the "gradual improvement of the living conditions" of the populace. In practice, the People's Committees, especially at the village, city, ward, and municipality levels, serve as watchdogs and coercing organs for maintaining an individual's compliance with Communist party-approved behavior in all phases of public life.

As the party leads and, by its Constitution, supervises the ideological education and transformation of society (the focus here particularly is on troublesome South Vietnam), the de facto, quasi-judicial, and enforcing roles of the People's Committees are vital to regime stability. The return to the community and rehabilitation of those convicted by People's Courts and returnees from the "re-education" camps (in which, shortly after the fall of Saigon, some two to three hundred thousand South Vietnamese officials and their associates found themselves) also fall to a large degree to the local People's Committees.[32]

As in the USSR, there is a centralized SRV Procurate, with local prosecuting staffs, which operate at different administrative levels. Appeal procedure to higher courts is heavily dependent on the Procurate, is clouded by corruption, and appears to be heavily influenced by political influence of friends and families of those convicted. As a result, even People's Courts at the village and municipality level influenced by the Procurate have meted out death sentences and had these sentences almost instantly implemented, in accordance with prosecutorial direction. A contributing factor is that party policy wishes to set an example in cases of black marketeering, speculation, and—especially in South Vietnam— subversion, including occasional armed resistance.

On November 8, 1984, the new penal code of the SRV was published in the Hanoi media. In introducing the new code, SRV Justice Minister Phan Hien noted "the multifaceted war of sabotage" being conducted against the country from abroad, as well as the "schemes" of "toppled class enemies" within. The code identifies a category of so-called counterrevolutionary crimes, including sabotage, espionage, treason, and subversion, all of which carry the death penalty. Other newly specified crimes include "forcing other people to flee the country," dealing in counterfeit money, and hijacking of ships and aircraft. "Illegal acquisition of socialist property" covers any number of offenses ranging from embezzlement to "intentional destruction," and these crimes may be punished by death or life imprisonment. Phan Hien declared that in the face of the continuing "temptations of the bourgeois life style," to which cadres and other state employees were said to have succumbed, effective application of the penal laws was very important, not the least because the nation was engaged in the task of "socialist transformation."[33]

The original judicial system of the French-protected Lao Kingdom was based largely on French codes. At the apex was a Court of Cassation. Intermediate appellate courts heard cases from provincial courts having jurisdiction in both criminal and civil matters. Justice of the peace courts functioned at the lowest administrative levels. Village headmen, assisted by village elders, applied customary law in local communities, a procedure legitimized by most French administrators in the colonial period.[34]

Today, with the Supreme People's Assembly as its highest governing body and the Lao People's Revolutionary Party (LPRP) as its political and ideological vanguard, the LPDR is divided into thirteen provinces. These are further subdivided into districts and subdistricts, at each level of which there function People's Courts as well as organs of a central Procurate General's Office. Major municipalities, acquiring more autonomy, also have People's Courts. The *mvong* (district) is the basic political, economic, and judicial unit of the LPDR, and as there also now are elected People's Assemblies at most administrative levels, a relatively greater degree of decentralized and local autonomy has come to prevail than was the case in royal times.[35]

The historically pervasive influence of Buddhism on Laotian ethical values has been restructured through the creation of tight, new political organizational controls.[36] As in the SRV, tens of thousands of political prisoners—there is no authoritative estimate of the total number—remain in detention. Resident Vietnamese cadres and officials are assisting in supervising development of a People's Committee system, monitoring behavior and coercing compliance with public policy in the same quasi-judicial fashion as is the case in Vietnam. The slowness with which a new Lao Constitution and civil and criminal codes are being implemented or drafted leaves the mass of Laotians in a legal limbo, as courts, including military tribunals, continue to perform their function more on the basis of political and ideological exigency, especially in land reform disputes, than on the basis of defined statutory process.

Even greater uncertainty prevails today in the legal system of Cambodia. On April 17, 1975, victorious Communist Khmer Rouge forces capture Phnom Penh. Within two weeks a special "National Congress" had met to begin work on the restructuring of the new state of "Democratic Kampuchea" (DK), whose Constitution was announced on the following January 5, 1976. For more than three years, however, a drastic and bloody revolution ravaged Cambodian society. Tens of thousands perished in mass executions or as a result of disease and malnutrition aggravated by prolonged forced labor in agricultural projects. There nominally was, according to the new Constitution, a DK "People's Court" system. But summary arrest, imprisonment, and/or execution, with procedures based on a hazy but highly puritanical Communist revolutionary vision of a new society that had to get rid of the "old dandruff" (the common, contemptuous Khmer Rouge term for the pre-DK regime, its institutions and adherents), virtually negated even a semblance of due process or the rule of law. It appears that DK courts—if they were resorted to at all—most commonly consisted of tribunals convened on the spot by elements of the DK Army, or of special party officials vested by DK Premier Pol Pot with investigatory and judicial powers.[37]

In January 1979, after years of periodic border clashes and steadily worsening diplomatic relations, an invading SRV Army installed a new "People's Republic of Kampuchea" (PRK). The DK military and leadership remnant, now driven to an underground government existence in western Cambodia, soon mobilized its own de facto political control in rural regions along the Thai border. Meanwhile, with Vietnamese bureaucratic help and massive international relief assistance, the PRK, by early 1982, had managed to restore a measure of order in its legal system. However, although the courts reportedly closely follow the SRV system, little is known about the actual functioning of the PRK courts.

The China- and Thai-supplied DK insurgents and their non-Communist allies on June 21, 1982, formed a United Nations-recognized rival "Coalition Government," whose collective fighting strength is at least 70,000 men. Armed

clashes are spreading steadily over a wider area of PRK territory. The ensuing
serious dislocation of all phases of public life in the PRK has rendered any return
to a normally functioning legal system ever more problematical. The result has
been judicial fragmentation. In southeastern Cambodia in particular, for example,
local village chiefs, loosely supervised by visiting PRK officials, settle disputes
through a ''Communized'' application of customary law. In the larger cities,
however, a more formal, single People's Court system and a nominally centralized Procurate General's Office deal with both civil and criminal cases. In
the current reorganization of Cambodian society under the so-called *krom samaki*
(solidarity group) system, peasant families and workers unite in party-supervised
production teams.[38] The leadership of these teams, at the same time, functions
as a kind of smaller-scale version of the supervisory People's Committees that
are encountered in the SRV and LPDR.

While the pattern of judicial organization is similar in the Communist states
of the region, non-Communist Southeast Asia shows sharp diversity in its postcolonial legal systems. The position of Thailand, often designated as non-Communist Southeast Asia's ''front-line'' state because of its continuing clashes with
its Indochinese neighbors, is perhaps especially unique. Thailand never experienced a period of Western colonial domination and long was governed by a
royal autocracy and a highly centralized, tradition-oriented, judicial, and bureaucratic system. It was not until a 1932 coup, largely led by ''Young Turk''
Army officers, that the kingdom entered a rocky era of modern parliamentary
constitutionalism interspersed with military rule.

During much of Thailand's history a royally dependent judiciary had applied
traditional Siamese laws based on the Hindu Code of Manu and amplified by a
bewildering plethora of royal decrees. Not until the second half of the nineteenth
century, when corruption, excessive delay, and cruelty in the criminal justice
system aroused strong opposition of the resident Western community, were
significant changes in court procedure undertaken. In 1892, King Chulalongkorn
established the first Ministry of Justice to supervise legal reform. During the
next three decades, a new systematized court system began functioning with
defined appeal procedures, guaranteed rights for the accused, and stricter prosecutorial procedures. These, along with new laws of evidence, were introduced
mainly with the aid of French and Belgian legal advisers. The 1908 Penal Code
was changed and brought up to date after the 1932 Revolution by means of a
new Criminal and Civil Procedures Code (1935) and with promulgation of a yet
further reformed Criminal Code (1956), which still prevails. Today, to be sure,
there is enlarged Supreme Court-sanctioned authority for the military under
various antisubversive measures and the application of martial law in certain
insurgent-infested areas. Prosecutorial authority, however, rests primarily in a
centralized civilian department operating under the Interior Ministry. The Ministry of Justice, meanwhile, has general administrative supervision over the
function of the courts.[39]

In addition to the *Dika* (or Supreme Court), there is the *Uthom* (Appeals

Court), and several Courts of First Instance.[40] Minor disputes, including criminal cases, are heard in the *Kwaeng* (Magistrates' Courts) in some districts of the provinces as well as in Bangkok. More serious cases, both civil and criminal, are brought before one of the eighty-five *Changwad* (Provincial Courts). In Bangkok and Dhonburi, however, there are separate criminal and civil courts of first instance. These have jurisdiction not only over offenses committed within these municipalities, but they also can be designated by the Supreme Court president as the venue for trial of more serious cases coming from the provinces. Neither court jurisdiction nor use of precedent is firmly established in Thai jurisprudence, although the legal system is moving in that direction. The obtrusion of military authority and martial law, however, particularly in the more distant districts, impedes judicial certainty.

In its substantive and procedural laws, the Thai legal system today is thoroughly Westernized, having borrowed from French, Belgian, Italian, and English sources. Nevertheless, some distinctive Thai features remain. The relative homogeneity of Thai culture, supported by the pervasive influence of the *sangha* (Buddhist monkhood), and the public veneration for and widespread and unquestioned public sense of close identification of the Thai royal house with the national culture make for an unusually high degree of common consensus in national civil values. This, by implication, has been carried over in public acceptance of the legal system. Insults against the royal family are virtually considered tantamount to treason and technically punishable as such. Publicly voiced disparagement of the Buddhist religion or its establishment is not protected by constitutional interpretations of the right to free speech. On the other hand, while the jury trial system does not exist, the force of public opinion, especially since the turbulent political and constitutional changes of the 1960s, can give a crusading lawyer fighting for the underdog a new aura of respectability in a society where the legal profession traditionally was viewed as but an arm of autocratic royal authority.

There is a low incidence of "conflict of laws" in Thailand, unlike almost anywhere else in Southeast Asia. Only among the Muslim minorities of such southern Thai provinces as Pattani and Yala is there voluntary submission in civil cases to sjariah and relatively little-known Islamic courts. Appeal is possible to the government courts, but this rarely occurs. In the Meo hill tribe country of the northern provinces, experienced Thai magistrates and administrators occasionally still allow the application of customary law in family disputes. However, extensive hill tribe resettlement and educational programs are integrating many Meos with Thai public life, including the Thai legal system.

The enforced supremacy of a comprehensive uniform ideology and the imposition of a single court system stand today in sharp contrast to the segmented, poorly coordinated legal system in this region during the French colonial period. The process of assimilation of modern legal values and the public acceptance of new codes and procedures of law and of a standardized court system have been facilitated by the absence of a disruptive colonial experience and the relatively historic homogeneity of the Thai people and of their national culture and national institutions.

With the creation of the Malaysian Federation in 1963, a single Federal Court was established as the highest judicial organ of the land, subject only in limited cases to appeal to Malaysia's King and London's Privy Council. Below the Federal Court are two High Courts. One of these is for the Peninsular Malayan States, the other for the Borneo states of Malaysia. High Courts today consist of a single justice assisted by from two to four assessors. Jury trials are required when capital offenses are tried. The High Courts may refer cases to the Federal Court, if necesesary, but criminal appeals ordinarily do not go beyond the level of the High Court. The Federal Court is composed of a "lord president," the two High Court presiding justices, and four other federal justices. The Federal Court interprets the Constitution and adjudicates conflicts between states and high government agencies. It also functions as an appeals court, particularly in civil cases, for all of Malaysia.[41]

There is an elaborate subordinate court system, different for Western (Peninsular) and Eastern (Borneo) Malaysia. In Western Malaysia, Magistrate and Sessions Courts, each presided over by a single judge, adjudicate both civil and criminal offenses requiring punishment of up to ten years imprisonment and/or a $10,000 fine. In Malaysia's Borneo states there are three categories of magistrate courts, as well as separate Native Courts. The latter apply customary law under the district officer's sanction. Both Eastern and Western Malaysia Muslim courts, with both civil and criminal law jurisdiction, concern themselves with Muslims charged with violations of Islamic law. Jurisdiction of these courts is circumscribed, however, by the Malaysian constitutional limits and usually the voluntary compliance of the disputing parties. In Peninsular Malaysia one still encounters the courts of the *penghulu* (headman), who are appointed in a *markim* (a particular subunit of administration). They have jurisdiction over minor offenses (fines of up to $25), but defendants usually elect to be heard in one of the magistrates' courts.[42]

While the decisions of High and Federal Courts prevail throughout Malaysia, the constitutional act establishing the Malaysian Federation specifically preserved the lower court system in the individual Malaysian states, particularly the Muslim and customary law courts, as well as the powers of pardon of the royal heads of the Peninsular Malayan States. In addition, there are many quasi-judicial agencies, for example, Lands Tribunals or a cabinet minister, adjudicating cases involving deprivation of citizenship or detention without trial under current emergency legislation.[43] In issues falling within criminal law, the existing codes and court procedures are much more sharply defined than cases falling within the jurisdiction of customary law and religious courts or within the judicial prerogatives of the rulers. Overlapping jurisdictions, high and seemingly mounting executive powers preempting due process in the face of alleged political extremism, "conflict of laws" among an ethnically and culturally varied population—

all these seem to leave Malaysia's legal system in a prolonged period of uncertain transition.

Singapore today, though retaining a formal sjariah for its Muslim Malay residents, seems almost a model of systematized legal procedure. This is in contrast even with its own colonial past, when its legal life was characterized by a confusing overlay of judicial organizational measures ranging from an 1826 Charter of Justice establishing a "Supreme Court of Judicature," to the application of the judicial provisions of various India acts during the 1840s, to new courts and procedural ordinances, promulgated in 1878 and, earlier, the "Letters Patent" of 1867 governing the legislative and judicial aspects of Straits Settlements government. The present court structure, at its base, provides for District and Magistrates Courts, with original criminal and civil jurisdiction. Appeals go to a High Court and then either to a Court of Appeal for civil matters or a Court of Criminal Appeal. The last three courts comprise the Singapore Supreme Court, whose functions were specified under judicature and procedural codes adopted during 1969–1970.[44] Appeal to the British Privy Council's Judicial Committee remains open but is used much less frequently than in Malaysia.

British legal influence, however, both procedurally and substantively, is paramount with one important exception—in the interests of national security far wider discretionary powers of arrest and incarceration without trial have been provided to the government by various Singapore legislative acts. What is striking, then, about Singapore's legal system among Southeast Asian states is the consonance between legal theory and practice. A streamlined Confucianist legalism pervades public life and, in the opinion of critics, also stultifies cultural and social relationships in the interests of political stability and needed economic growth.

The contrast with Burma could hardly be sharper. This is so even though the Burmese government, since achieving independence in 1948 outside the British Commonwealth and operating in military rather than civilian fashion, eventually was to adopt much the same authoritarian style of executive power as has prevailed in Singapore.

In theory, throughout the states and other administrative units of the Union of Burma today a three-tiered court system prevails. It ranges from magistrate courts, which deal with lesser offenses, through Courts of Sessions found in major urban centers, to the Chief Court in Rangoon. Major felonies are directly referred by the attorney general's office for prosecution to the sessions courts. Little legal reform has been undertaken since the early 1950s, however, though constitutional crises, ethnic discontent, growing problems of land tenure, severe social dislocations, and rising crime cry out for the law's redress. The ten primary volumes of the nearly one-century-old "Burma Code," with its half a dozen or so additional supplements, cover virtually all applicable, partially applicable, and (in the opinion of critics) some long since inapplicable statutes, ordinances, executive regulations, and legal procedures that together make up the Union's criminal law. The basis of the "Burma Code" itself was the long since modified and/or abandoned Indian Penal Code of 1860 and Indian Criminal Procedure Code of 1898.[45]

The main problem is that the Union government's authority and that of its courts does not function very effectively in large parts of the country such as much of Shan State, Kachin State, the Naga Hill country, or the Special Division of the Chins, some of which can be best described as having a nearly autonomous government structure. Here the reach of Rangoon's Chief Court is uncertain, and Courts of Sessions (if any) must function in a delicate balance between the wishes of local Burmese military commanders and those of civil administrators, whose decisions have to remain acceptable to traditional ethnic group leaderships. Much else is adjudicated in local magistrates' courts with an eye to customary law, not necessarily to the "Burma Code" alone. Secessionist movements in parts of Burma remain strong, controlling areas of indefinite size of their own. To add to the uncertainties of the legal system, the constitutional authority of the military, the real locus of power in the Burmese state, remains poorly defined.[46]

The contrast between a seemingly well-defined court structure on the one hand and on the other a much more fluid, uncertain administration of justice based on codes modified by the hazy emergency authority of the executive branch and its military correlates also characterize the Indonesian and Philippine legal systems today. The Indonesian case is perhaps the most complicated because there are four types of courts, sometimes with overlapping authority. For example, military courts have tried civilians on charges of subversion, and decisions of the Islamic courts require concurrence of secular district courts. In addition, the application of customary law remains extensive in the rural areas. Here village headmen or traditional leaderships of extended family units act as judges/arbitrators. In addition to the military and religious (Islamic) courts, there also is a growing number of administrative tribunals. These, often appearing as government regulatory boards or commissions, adjudicate issues ranging from tax to industrial or labor disputes.[47]

Most of the Indonesian legal system today comprises what may be called the "secular," national, or general courts. These—about two hundred in number— hear both civil and criminal cases in the first instance and are found at the local government level of the district and the *propinsi* (province). These courts are topped by four appellate courts in the chief judicial zones and by a National Supreme Court. A single Penal Code now is applicable to all inhabitants, including foreign residents. But the previously noted Dutch colonial tradition of tripartite public law status (involving "Natives," i.e., Indonesians; "Foreign Orientals," i.e., Chinese; and "Europeans") is still alive in commercial cases, contractual disputes, and many other torts. Here the colonial European law code still prevails, unless there are compelling reasons for the district or provincial judiciary to apply the customary law.[48]

Indonesia's legal system today is riven by many unsettled conflicts that go to the very heart of both its efficacy and public acceptance. The limited number of appellate courts makes for intolerably long delays. There is also continuous political controversy over the place of Islam (and therefore of the whole sjariah) in Indonesian national public life. The inability of the Supreme Court to review and/or to set aside acts of the government party-dominated national legislature or of the decisions of the military tribunals is seen by many as robbing the court of its major necessary function. There also remain unsolved disputes over the new 1981 Code of Criminal Procedure, which in the opinion of the government, obstructs the investigatory and interrogatory process, particularly in national security cases. Not the least of these is the lingering problem of the legal status of former political prisoners and the increasingly sharp criticism both in the Indonesian legal community and abroad of the Suharto government's alleged violations of human rights.[49]

Not all is darkness, and slowly, inexorably, there is some public sense of an advance toward legal stability. The standardized prosecutorial system operating through the Attorney General's Office at all levels of local government and of the national court system, as well as implementation of a fundamental law of judicial powers in 1970 that guarantees the independence of the judiciary are seen as important foundation stones. There also have been repeated drives, sometimes even led by local military commanders, to rid the court system of corruption and incompetence. Though attempts continue to be made to continue the scope of power of military tribunals and private legal aid attorneys seek to protect individual rights, martial law and emergency executive decrees make the exercise of constitutional rights uncertain. Meanwhile, in many areas of the civil law, the legal system is still in *statu nascendi*, with the exact scope nationwide of "European" (Dutch-originated), adat and sjariah provisions remaining unclear.

The Philippine legal system today, like Indonesia's, shows marked contrasts between a certain and a defined court structure, and the uncertainty and fluidity of the courts' functions and of the law's application. Below a Supreme Court there is a pyramid of lower courts, in descending order comprised of a Court of Appeal, courts of first instance, and circuit criminal courts (the latter only in some provinces), and finally the municipal and city courts. The latter deal with only minor civil and criminal matters, and more serious felonies and civil cases are tried in the first instance and circuit courts. Additionally, there are special tax appeals—industrial relations, agrarian, and land reform, and other essentially administrative courts and judicial boards. Prosecutorial functions, prior to 1972, were considerably decentralized and were performed by the provincial or municipal fiscal's office and its assistants under the supervision of the solicitor general of the Philippines.[50]

Originally Spanish in character, the criminal and civil law codes and their application were extensively revised during the 1930s and further modified by modern constitutional guarantees and new court procedural rules enacted in 1964. In keeping with U.S. practice, the Supreme Court has powers of judicial review and has exercised them even during martial law. As a result of the 1972 Martial Law proclamation and of the implementation of the 1973 Constitution, a large number of Philippine Army and constabulary (national police) courts were created. All are supervised by the Office of the Judge Advocate General of the Armed Forces of the Philippines. Under martial law, in fact, any case pending before the regular court system could be brought before the military courts. By 1974 over 6,000 cases had been thus transferred. Military sources in Manila informed this author in July 1984 that "at least six hundred" such cases were still before the military courts at that time. Long delay in adjudication and alleged incompetence and corruption in the regular courts were given as reasons for the creation of these military tribunals. Special courts called *Sandiganbayan* were also established under martial law. These, also often presided over by the military, dealt exclusively with more serious allegations of corrupt conduct among government officials, including the judiciary.[51]

The repeal of martial law has left intact the president's emergency powers— powers repeatedly contested but as regularly upheld by the Philippine courts, incuding the Supreme Court. As in Indonesia, the danger allegedly coming from Communist subversion has been among the principal official reasons given for the imposition of martial law and retention of the executive's emergency powers. With the 1981 repeal of martial law, the number of cases before the military courts has begun to diminish. Still, despite the nominal restoration of habeas corpus, instances of prolonged detention and disappearance of political opponents (euphemistically called "salvaging") continue to be alleged against the supporters of the Marcos regime. Today, deep public uncertainty over the extent to which the Philippine Armed Forces are prepared to go in order to keep the Marcos government in power has adversely affected still further an already longstanding cynical perception of the independence and fairness of the Filipino judiciary. When martial law was proclaimed, Marcos obtained a signed but undated letter of resignation from each member of a bench above that of the level of the minor municipal courts. And unless relatively unpolitical criminal or civil cases are involved, Philippine judges—themselves frequently related to ruling establishment families—have rarely issued judgments contrary to the known public policies desired by the Marcos circle.

And yet, despite its obvious and, to some, its fatal weaknesses resulting from the martial law period, the Philippine legal system, compared to that of neighboring countries, still has significant assets. Among these are (1) a high degree of religious-cultural homogeneity and a broadly accepted, single, national court structure; (2) a developed legal profession in which aggressive, indeed crusading, advocacy is still not only possible but publicly admired; and (3) a far more extensive, definite, and up-to-date codification of both civil and criminal law than is the case in Burma or Indonesia.

THE PERSONNEL OF THE LAW, PUBLIC PERCEPTIONS, AND THE ROLE OF THE COURTS

Generalizations about Southeast Asia are always hazardous. Still, based on the foregoing, it is possible, perhaps, to identify briefly some common characteristics of the region's current legal systems. First, and in varying degrees of intensity, there are patterns of "conflict of laws" throughout the area. Second, since the present era of national independence, the political process has been far more interested in insuring the codification and standardized application of criminal law than of any other area of law. This preoccupation is directly related to policy problems of regime stability, threat perception, and the exigencies of "nation building" generally. Third, while formal court structures and organization today are well defined, the courts' function is heavily politicized in much of Southeast Asia, though perhaps the least in Malaysia, Singapore, and, for the moment, in Thailand. This politicization results from either or both of the following: (a) the assumption of extraordinary emergency or martial law powers by the executive branch of government, working in tandem with the military; or (b) ideological and party organizational rigidity in government. Either way, the independence of the judiciary and of its decisions are compromised. Fourth, and not least, as a consequence of the politicization, public attitudes toward the law and the courts are ambivalent, with chronic undertones of cynicism about court decisions. This admittedly is an impressionistic observation; the present writer is not familiar with any objective survey of public attitudes in any Southeast Asian country toward the prevailing legal system. But the present opinion is based on this writer's decades-long close familiarity with the region. The fact is that there is little confidence in the legal system as an effective problem-solving tool. This is so not least because the legal system in most Southeast Asian countries, with the exception of Singapore or Brunei, only rarely has been able to address the staggering problems of economic development, for example land reform or industrial growth, or perceived social and political injustices, especially the nearly pervasive problem of human rights violations.

Application today of (1) customary law; (2) the sjariah (amplified in this, the Khomeini era, by the demands of a politically resurgent Islamic community throughout Asia); (3) the civil and criminal codes/statutory compilations and procedures, most of them rooted in the provisions of the colonial Spanish, Anglo-Indian, French, Dutch, and U.S. laws and regulations; and (4) new national codes and constitutional substantive and procedural rights still has not reached a balance in most of Southeast Asia (with the exception of Singapore). In the village world, where most Southeast Asians still live, customary law, however much buffeted by contemporary public and legal policy, more fully satisfies many perceived legal needs than anything else—whether in matters of land and water use, participation in common village construction projects, payment or cancellation of a bride price or dowry, or other family matters.

But there are other paradoxes. It has already been ten years since then Indonesian Minister for Justice Mochtar Kusumaatmadja noted that it was "peculiar" that, decades after the country had won its independence, the Indonesian legal system still had not fully incorporated the adat into the national law, and that the legal profession, instead, was utilizing positive law regulations dating from the Dutch colonial era. Mochtar urged that Indonesian judges, in developing the country's positive law, strengthen the application of the adat through their own decisions. Mochtar, mark well, spoke at a nationally sponsored seminar on the role of customary law. The seminar concluded that adat not only should be considered an "important element" in the development of Indonesian national law but was seen as vital "in the building up of family law and in the national law of inheritance" in particular.[52]

Today, adat continues to be applied on the basis of existing evidentially verifiable custom; but it is still derived also from written sources first compiled in the Dutch colonial period, and there are very few Indonesian legal scholars who are seeking to develop adat further in the direction of a national family law. As a result, adat threatens to become a kind of legalistic icon, waved about by the Indonesian legal profession and utilized to sanctify judgments or to legitimize felt legal judicial needs. But it is not a growing or methodically directed body of legal precept and practice. This same observation applies to the application of customary law in other parts of Southeast Asia in those judicial decisions made above the level of village headmen.

Far more aggressive in their quest for a national legal evolution are the proponents of sjariah. By its permitted application in Southeast Asia today under the supervision of the regular or secular courts, it is also sjariah that collides frequently and precisely in those same areas where adat also is strongest, for example, family and inheritance law. The promulgation of Indonesia's new secular marriage law of 1974, for example, gave rise to the most bitter controversy, particularly as the law undermines traditional Muslim precepts in such areas as divorce, the custody of children, the division of inheritances, and the rights of widows. Adat traditions on these points also can be in conflict with sjariah. Given this controversy and the bitterness of the opposition that arose to the law from various secular-modernist, Muslim, and adat quarters and from within and outside of the Indonesian parliament, one can only agree with the conclusion of two students of the measure that "the principal reason" why the Suharto government in Indonesia expended so much political capital in getting the law passed at all "was to give impetus to the government's policy of unifying the country through the unification of law."[53]

Nationalist idealism (sometimes accentuated, as in Vietnam and Indonesia, by an intense anticolonial revolutionary experience), as much as the exigencies of sovereignty in the international community, require the independent states of Southeast Asia today to promote such unification of their laws. The road to success is likely to be rocky. Neither appeals to the "creative application of Marxism-Leninism," as in the preamble to Vietnam's Constitution, nor endlessly reiterated pronouncements of the *Pantjasila* (the Five Pillars of the state: belief in God, nationalism, democracy, social justice, and humanitarianism), as Indonesia's one and only official ideology, necessarily provide a readily accepted base for the development of uniform national codes in the countries concerned. Political circumspection is required here. The Indonesian Lawyers Association, unlike its counterparts in Malaysia and Thailand, has been little inclined to pressure the government on behalf of legal certainty and uniformity. This is so probably not least because most law graduates in Indonesia see themselves preferably ensconced in a government service berth rather than in private practice.

There are other obstacles. The legal profession, particularly the judiciary, has only begun to play a role in this process of unification of the law, and, in the systematic resolution of "conflict of laws" generally. For one thing, legal training is still uneven in quality and frequently dependent on the vagaries of regime preference. Burma, with a population of 36 million, has only one officially recognized law school, the University of Rangoon. However, many Burmese lawyers still prefer training in the United Kingdom, and there are only an estimated 2,000 barristers in private practice in the country. Though there is a lawyers' organization, admission to the bar in Burma is little more than a formality for those with the requisite U.K. or Rangoon University credentials and proper political connections. In Indonesia the shortage of legal counsel is even sharper. In a country of 160 million, there were, in 1985, only 1,500 trial lawyers. Yet, there also are some forty law schools in Indonesia today, mostly associated with small, less prestigious universities (state-owned, as well as Muslim, Catholic, and Protestant).[54] Many Indonesian law students do not graduate or else do not seek licenses to practice, preferring appointments, instead, in the business community, government services, or education.

On the other hand, the Philippines, with nearly 54 million inhabitants, has more than fifty private law schools (some of dubious quality), along with the premier College of Law of the University of the Philippines, the only legal training institution run by the government. There were, in 1985, at least 28,000 members of the bar of the Philippines, though only about 22,000 of these are believed to be in actual practice. Nearly a third of all Philippine attorneys work in the greater Manila area. There is a standardized bar admissions procedure, including a formal bar examination, from which only certain U.S. legal practitioners are officially exempt.[55] The quality of legal services in the Philippines and public confidence in them remain controversial, however.

Attempts to upgrade the legal profession are apparent throughout Southeast Asia. In 1984 there were about 2,800 attorneys registered with the Bar Association of Thailand. Most had obtained their four-year legal education, combined with general "foundation courses" in the humanities, at Thammasat, Chulalongkorn, or Ramkhamhaeng Universities; a few were educated at the Thai Bar Association's Institute of Legal Education. The latter institute acts as a strict gatekeeper to the practice of law in Thailand. It sets the bar examination and, in effect, requires all future legal practitioners to take a one-year course after academic graduation in order to become proficient in judicial practice. Entry into the ranks of public prosecutors or "judge trainees" requires still further examinations. Though the Thai Lawyers Association has moved forward rapidly to improve the quality of legal education, there is a shortage of trained, full-time law professors. Since the decade of the 1970s, there has been a virtual explosion of law school enrollment; for example, at Ramkhamhaeng University alone the number of law students grew from 3,233 in 1972 to 27,448 in 1976.[56]

Considerations of national security and other political factors deeply obtrude in admission to the bar in some Southeast Asian countries. Thus, admission in Singapore and Indonesia reportedly involves a deep background check that in its way rivals that of appointees to the procuratorships or of the handful of lawyers in private practice in Vietnam. With a population of 2.6 million, Singapore has some 600 attorneys today, most of them graduates of the island republic's only recognized law school, the Singapore National University. Unlike Thailand and the Philippines, law is not a favorite career objective of Singapore students, in part because of the political atmosphere that spells too many risks to an attorney. In Singapore, a government-controlled Board of Legal Education, headed by the attorney general, supervises qualifications. Before admission to the bar, a six-month "pupillage" experience generally is required in an established lawyer's chambers.[57]

In no instance does formal academic legal training require less than a four-year course beyond suitable secondary school preparation. There are variations, however. In Burma's Rangoon University Law Faculty, the law degree requires two years beyond the B.A., while in Malaysia the three-year course for the Bachelor in Islamic Studies at the National University of Malaysia ranks as legal training and prepares one for appointment to the Muslim religious courts.[58] Some legal training curricula still are steeped in European sources, for example, Dutch colonial law (in Indonesia) or British jurisprudence (in Malaysia and Singapore). On the other hand, the standard Thai university-based legal preparation has only little to say about the French, Belgian, and other European sources that are so evident in Thai codes and procedures. Vietnamese legal training, still centered mainly on the University of Hanoi, though now also available at the university in Ho Chi Minh City (Saigon), derides French juridical practices of the colonial era. Yet, some of the French penal provisions for lesser felonies are still applied.

It is, then, regime pressure or articulation of a particularly partisan political point of view that is the dynamic factor in law code standardization, not a concerted commitment to that end of the country's legal profession. On the other hand, given a particular regime's priority of concern for standardized application of criminal law codes compared to any other area of the law, the legal profession in Southeast Asia today almost uniformly makes its greatest contribution by insuring certainty and impartiality in the procedural aspect of the legal system, not in bringing reform or further development to substantive law. In making this kind of contribution, dramatic confrontations may occur between the regime and a regime-dominated national legislature on the one hand, and the legal profession, backed by various segments of public opinion, on the other. Malaysia offers illustrations. In recent decades, various Malaysian governments, backed by parliaments dominated by their own Alliance government party, have succeeded in pushing through amendments to the 1960s Internal Security Act. The force of the act had been amplified by the never-repealed 1969 "state of emergency" proclamation, which followed in the wake of racial fighting between ethnic Malay and Chinese inhabitants of Peninsular Malaya. Entry of domiciles and search and seizure without warrant, detention without trial, or trial by special courts functioning outside the regular court system (in which the accused, in the interests of national security, is denied the right to confront accusers or cross-examine), and even denial of a specific bill of particulars charging the defendant—all these and more are provided for and have been applied under present Malaysian security laws. In 1983 alone, eighteen persons convicted under the internal security provisions were executed (the death penalty is mandatory upon conviction in such cases, according to law), and in that year "as many as 30 Internal Security Act (ISA) prisoners were awaiting execution."[59]

There is little question, however, that adverse pressure from Malaysian legal, academic, and professional circles and from various foreign human rights groups is bringing about a mitigation in the harshness of the security policies of the Malaysian government. Thus, the Malaysian government has modified the highly restrictive amendments (adopted by the Alliance government party-dominated Malaysian Parliament in 1981) to the so-called Societies Act. This measure renders unlawful the function of any organized group that has not first obtained a license from the Ministry of Home Affairs. The new amendments placed additional burdens of scrutiny on groups seeking to approach or lobby government officials for political purposes. By 1983, again, modification had occurred so as to permit groups refused licensure to seek redress in the courts—a remedy that at first had not been available. Toward the close of 1984, the Malaysian Parliament, under pressure from the Malaysian legal profession and various consumer groups, had begun to modify yet another measure, the 1984 Civil Law Amendment Act. This measure, in the opinion of its critics, including members of the judiciary, had, in effect, improperly closed off redress to the courts in certain cases involving demands for compensation resulting from personal injury.[60]

Sources of conflict remain, however. Tan Boom Kean, a Malaysian journalist, in a prize-winning essay for the Tokyo Foreign Correspondents Club, recently complained that as far as the Malaysian press was concerned it was not just that "the Malaysian government is authoritarian, undemocratic, and seemingly unaccountable to the people," but that, worse, "most of the Malaysian press will tamely accept its fate."[61] Yet, Tan's essay, no less than the above-cited instances of the Malaysian government's retreat from some of its recent authoritarian posture, suggests that the political climate in which the legal profession must work in Southeast Asia is changing. In Malaysia the ISA courts increasingly are under open attack. So are the earlier-mentioned martial law sanctioned military tribunals and the Sandiganbayan in the Philippines, also operating outside the regular court system; and the bloody "salvaging" of Philippine political prisoners. And so is the wave of several thousand summary executions by secret police and military death squads during 1982–1984 of ex-convicts, criminals, and suspected criminal recidivists in Indonesia.

The more assertive stance by the legal profession and the judiciary in parts of Southeast Asia today can only help its hithertofore less-than-attractive image. Studies of the public perception in Southeast Asia of the prestige and status of the legal profession still are as rare as studies of the social or other characteristics of its members. One Indonesian study has shown that though there are dozens of generally well attended and accredited law schools in the country and although 19 percent of Indonesian secondary school graduates show a preference for the study of law, the occupation of lawyer, including that of attorney in government service, ranks at the bottom of twelve major job classifications in the esteem of the students themselves. The fields of medicine, religious service, and private industry, in that order, ranked highest. A likely explanation of this anomaly, confirmed by the present writer's experience in other areas of Southeast Asia, especially in the Philippines and Thailand, is that training in law is seen primarily as a stepping stone to other careers, particularly in private business.[62]

But this emphasis on the essentially preparatory nature of legal training also tends to point up the fact that while law school attendance, like other higher educational courses, increasingly is available to all strata, the social antecedents of those of the legal profession in Southeast Asia are still essentially those of the middle or upper classes—in short, the elites of the country. For it is the members of these "networking" elites who not only can best afford the cost of university legal training, but who also are apt to benefit most from it through more rapid advancement via the requisite connections in the higher managerial strata of the business world and government.

Perhaps the only noteworthy exception to these processes is in the Socialist Republic of Vietnam. But here a different kind of elitist factor influences the entry into and the enjoyment of "pay off" benefits of legal training. Youthful, ideological enthusiasm and party-approved affiliations, as well as "worker" or "peasant" family background (often interpreted flexibly by higher party functionaries), most readily open doors to higher training, including in law. The same applies to appointments to magistracies in the People's Courts, or in the Procuratorships. This has made for the entry of members of nontraditional (non-Mandarinate) elites into legal work. In turn, perhaps because of the broadened social base of professional recruitment, the current national legal reform process in the Communist Indochina states is attempting to resolve both the age-old problem of "conflict of laws," so common in the Southeast Asian region, and of the building of new national SRV law codes in a different way.

The traditional basis of a closely knit rural community reflected in customary law evident throughout Southeast Asia was noted at the beginning of this chapter. Today that same basis is being used as a vital component of public policy in national development by the Vietnam Communist Party. This is particularly true for the party's efforts to accelerate the collectivization process in the rural society. That process has not gone without its serious productivity and management tribulations. A marriage today is being attempted of customary law sanctioned traditional village communalism with modern Marxist-Leninist based agricultural collectivism, even as Hanoi's theoreticians describe in rhapsodic terms the close harmony of the traditional village world where "everyone knew everyone else."[63]

The reality is that enforced collectivization schemes in Vietnam are, as yet, clearly blocking hoped-for food production increases. In that regard, the SRV economic experiment eventually may well parallel the stagnant Soviet and Communist Chinese agrarian collectivization policies over the years. Yet, this experiment remains one distinctive direction in which a concept of national law is being built in Southeast Asia. In other respects, however, the SRV national law-building policies seem only to have managed to aggravate the legal uncertainty and disjointed functioning of the French system. Vietnamese Communists and other critics rail at the evils of the colonial era in Indochina or the authoritarian arbitrariness of the Malaysian, Filipino, or Indonesian legal system today. But despite all its segmented disharmony, there was more certainty of the rule of law in French-dominated Indochina than there is in that same region today. There was no Pol Pot-style holocaust in Cambodia under the French. And, despite the appearance of a carefully constructed People's Court system in Vietnam, complete with lay assessors, there were not, in the French period of control, a score of "re-education" concentration camps.

These camps now hold some 16,000 inmates according to Hanoi's own estimate. The inmates are not just former South Vietnamese officials, but "writers, artists, priests and members of the former neutralist 'third force.' " Indefinite detention without trial and servitude, usually for years and under harsh and debilitating conditions, is the rule. Yet, confining prisoners this way for an indefinite period appears to be in contravention even of the SRV's own penal code (Decree no. 02/SL/76), which provides for a maximum of only one year of pre-trial detention. Nor did the French colonial period witness hundreds of thousands of Vietnamese, Cambodian, and Laotian refugees, whether "boat people" or "border jumpers," who, together, are as eloquent a testimony as any to the quality of life in Indochina today, including its legal system.[64]

The ultimate "conflict of laws" in the Southeast Asian region seems to lie just here: in the problem of a political adjustment between two evolving sets of concepts and structures of law. Both sets strive for an integration within new national unities of their own legal legacies, for example, historically and culturally differing and yet sometimes congruent (as in the role of customary and religious laws) notions and practices of justice. Under the best of conditions and times, such a process of national legal integration would be difficult. In the contemporary world of Southeast Asia, however, riven between mutually confrontational Communist and non-Communist states, the additional problem of regional political adjustment obtrudes. Hence, the temptation to politicize the building of a new, integrated national legal system in the individual countries of the region becomes all the greater, and the search for a new legal consensus within the countries concerned, therefore, is likely to be all the more difficult.

NOTES

1. See H. E. Kauffman, "Some Social and Religious Institutions of the Law (N. W. Thailand)," *Journal of the Siam Society* (January 1972), p. 260; B. Grijpstra, "Social and Economic Structure of the Bidayuh," *The Sarawak Gazette* (Kuching), May 31, 1972, p. 90; and J. C. Stewart, "The Cotabato Conflict: Impressions of An Outsider," *Solidarity* (Manila), April 1972, p. 39.

2. J. Silverstein, *Burma: Military Rule and the Politics of Stagnation* (Ithaca and London: Cornell University Press, 1977), p. 9.

3. J. S. Furnivall, *Colonial Policy and Practice: A Comparative Study of Burma and Netherlands India* (Cambridge: Cambridge University Press, 1948), p. 13; D. E. Smith, *Religion and Politics in Burma* (Princeton, N.J.: Princeton University Press, 1965), Chapter 2; and Silverstein, *Burma*, pp. 8–9.

4. In this and the following paragraph I have relied on D. S. Lev, *Islamic Courts in Indonesia: A Study in the Political Bases of Legal Institutions* (Berkeley and London: University of California Press, 1972), and on interviews with officials of the *Kementerian Agama* (Department of Religious Affairs) in Djakarta, June 1983.

5. See J. M. van der Kroef, *Indonesia After Sukarno* (Vancouver, Canada: University of British Columbia Press, 1971), and "Southeast Asia's Restless Muslims," *Strategic Studies* (Spring 1981), pp. 23–44.

6. See the Agence France Presse despatch, Kuala Lumpur, Foreign Broadcast Information Service (hereafter cited as FBIS) (October 16, 1980; and J. Nagata, "The New Fundamentalism: Islam in Contemporary Malaysia," *Asian Thought and Society* (September 1980), esp. p. 136.

7. "Malaysia-Fundamentalism: A Storm in the North," *Asiaweek* (Hong Kong), August 24, 1984, pp. 23–31.

8. J. Prins, *Adat en Islamietische Plichtenleer in Indonesie* (The Hague and Bandung: Vitgeverij W. van Hoeve, 1950).

9. P. G. Gowing, *Mosque and Moro: A Study of Muslims in the Philippines* (Manila: Philippine Federation of Christian Churches, 1964). See also P. G. Gowing and P. D. McAmis, *The Filipine Muslims: Their History, Society and Contemporary Problems* (Manila: Solidaridad Publishing House, 1976).

10. C. A. Bain, *Vietnam: The Roots of Conflict* (Englewood Cliffs, N.J.: Prentice Hall, 1967), p. 89.

11. T. E. Ennis, *French Policy and Developments in Indochina* (Chicago: University of Chicago Press, 1936), pp. 57–58, 65–67. See also V. Thompson, *French Indochina* (London: George Allen and Unwin, 1937).

12. F. Fitzgerald, *Fire in the Lake: The Vietnamese and the Americans in Vietnam* (New York: Random House, 1972), pp. 72–73.

13. See J. T. McAlister, Jr., *Vietnam: The Origins of Revolution* (New York: Doubleday Anchor Books, 1971), esp. pp. 44–47.

14. G. F. Zaide, *History of the Filipino People*, 3d ed. (Manila: The Modern Book Company, 1964), pp. 44–47; and O. D. Corpuz, *The Philippines* (Englewood Cliffs, N.J.: Prentice Hall, 1965), esp. pp. 24–44.

15. J. L. Phelan, *The Hispanization of the Philippines* (Madison: University of Wisconsin Press, 1959).

16. Data in this and the following paragraph are drawn from G. F. Zaide, *Government*

of the Filipino People (Manila: The Modern Book Company, 1964), esp. pp. 47, 81-82;
J. R. Hayden, *The Philippines: A Study in National Development* (New York: Macmillan
Company, 1945); J. M. Arvego, *The Framing of the Philippine Constitution* (Manila:
University Publishing Company, 1937).

17. Data in this and the following paragraph are drawn from A. Vandenbosch, *The
Dutch East Indies: Its Government, Problems, and Politics* (Berkeley and Los Angeles:
University of California Press, 1944), pp. 189-97.

18. N. J. Ryan, *The Making of Modern Malaya* (Kuala Lumpur: Oxford University
Press, 1963), esp. pp. 77–78.

19. Ibid., pp. 92–130. See also C. D. Cowan, *Nineteenth Century Malaya: The Origins
of British Control* (Kuala Lumpur: Oxford University Press, 1962).

20. K. G. Tregonning, *Malaysia* (Vancouver: University of British Columbia Press,
1965), p. 18.

21. R. Winstedt, *The Malays: A Cultural History* (New York: Philosophical Library,
1950), pp. 91–119.

22. Federation of Malaya, *Official Year Book, 1962* (Kuala Lumpur: Government
Press, 1962), vol. 2, pp. 118-19.

23. Government of Sarawak, *Sarawak Annual Report, 1962* (Kuching: Government
Printing Office, 1962), pp. 192–94.

24. Furnivall, *Colonial Policy and Practice*, p. 30.

25. Ibid., p. 31.

26. Ibid., pp. 131-35. See also J. F. Cady, *A History of Modern Burma* (Ithaca, N.Y.:
Cornell University Press, 1958).

27. Furnivall, *Colonial Policy and Practice*, pp. 136–41.

28. See the remarks of Burma's governor, Sir Charles Innes, "An Official View of
Rebellion in Burma," in H. J. Benda and J. A. Larkin, eds., *The World of Southeast
Asia: Selected Historical Readings* (New York and London: Harper and Row Publishers,
1967), pp. 141–44.

29. W. W. Elsbree, *Japan's Role in Southeast Asian Nationalist Movements, 1940–
1945* (Cambridge, Mass.: Harvard University Press, 1953), p. 77.

30. See H. J. Benda, *The Crescent and the Rising Sun* (The Hague and Bandung: W.
van Hoeve, 1958).

31. The text of the SRV Constitution appears in *FBIS*, September 21, 1979 (Supplement).

32. On the "re-education" camps, see D. Rees, *Vietnam Since "Liberation": Hanoi's
Revolutionary Strategy*, Conflict Studies no. 89 (London: Institute for the Study of Conflict, 1977), p. 9.

33. On the new SRV Penal Code see VNA (Vietnam News Agency) dispatch, Hanoi,
FBIS, November 9, 1984.

34. D. P. Whitaker et al., *Area Handbook for Laos*, (Washington, D.C.: U.S. Government Printing Office, 1972), pp. 155–56.

35. G. C. Gunn, "Theravadins and Commissars: The State and National Identity in
Laos," in M. Stuart-Fox, ed., *Contemporary Laos: Studies in the Politics and Society
of the Lao People's Democratic Republic* (St. Lucia, London: University of Queensland
Press, 1982), pp. 86–87.

36. J. J. Zasloff, and M. Brown, "Laos: Coping With Confinement," in *Southeast
Asian Affairs, 1982* (Singapore: Institute of Southeast Asian Studies, 1982), pp. 217–18.

37. For various assessments of the DK Regime, see F. Ponchaud, *Cambodia: Year*

Zero (London: Penguin, 1978); and B. Kiernan, and C. Boua, eds., *Peasants and Politics in Kampuchea, 1942–1981* (New York: Sharpe Publishers, 1982).

38. C. Boua, "Observations of the Heng Samrin Government 1980–1982," in D. P. Chandler, and B. Kiernan, eds., *Revolution and Its Aftermath in Kampuchea* (New Haven: Yale University Southeast Asia Studies, 1983), p. 261.

39. F. M. Bunge et al., *Thailand: A Country Study* (Washington, D.C.: Foreign Area Studies, 1981), pp. 264–68.

40. The following discussion derives from C. S. Rhyne, ed., *Law and Judicial Systems of Nations*, 3d ed. (Washington, D.C.: World Peace Through Law Center, 1978), pp. 732–35.

41. H. E. Groves, *The Constitution of Malaysia* (Singapore: Malaysia Publications, 1964), pp. 99–109; R. S. Milne, *Government and Politics in Malaysia* (Boston: Houghton Mifflin Company, 1967), pp. 175–77; and Rhyne, *Law and Judicial Systems*, pp. 452–63.

42. Rhyne, *Law and Judicial Systems*, pp. 452–63.

43. Groves, *The Constitution of Malaysia*, pp. 107–9.

44. Ministry of Culture, Singapore, *Singapore 1971* (Singapore: Government Printing Office, 1971), pp. 87–91.

45. J. W. Henderson et al., *Area Handbook for Burma* (Washington, D.C.: U.S. Government Printing Office, 1971), pp. 290–91.

46. J. Silverstein, *Burma*.

47. F. M. Bunge, ed., *Indonesia: A Country Study* (Washington, D.C.: Foreign Area Studies, The American University, U.S. Government Printing Office, 1983), pp. 184–87, 266–69. I have relied heavily on this source for a description of the Indonesian legal system in the following two paragraphs.

48. Ibid.

49. J. M. van der Kroef, "Dilemmas of Regime Stability: Indonesia's Human Rights Problem," *Journal of Asian-Pacific and World Perspectives* (Winter 1982–1983), pp. 15–22.

50. G. F. Zaide, *Government of the Filipino People*, pp. 141–51; N. Vreeland et al., *Area Handbook for the Philippines* (Washington, D.C.: Foreign Area Studies, American University, U.S. Government Printing Office, 1976), pp. 388–89.

51. Ibid.

52. *Sinar Harapan* (Djakarta), January 17 and 22, 1975, p. 1, cols. 1–2 and 8–9, respectively.

53. J. S. Katz and R. S. Katz, "The New Indonesian Marriage Law: A Mirror of Indonesia's Political, Cultural and Legal Systems," *The American Journal of Comparative Law* 23, no. 4 (1975), p. 681.

54. H. P. Tseng, ed., *The Law Schools of the World* (Buffalo, N.Y.: William S. Hein Co., 1977), pp. 202–12.

55. See Rhyne, *Law and Judicial Systems*, pp. 581–83. The 1985 estimate of the total number of Philippine attorneys was provided by the Embassy of the Philippines, Washington, D.C.

56. Ibid., pp. 727–32; and P. Kasemsup, "Legal Education and Development in Thailand," *Jernal Undang Undang* (1977), pp. 95–110. The 1984 estimate of the number of Thai lawyers was provided the author by the secretariat of the Thai Bar Association, Bangkok.

57. Rhyne, *Law and Judicial Systems*, pp. 646–48.

58. Tseng, *The Law Schools of the World*, pp. 253–54.

59. *Country Report on Human Rights Practices for 1983*. Report Submitted to the Committee on Foreign Affairs, U.S. House of Representatives and the Committee on Foreign Relations, U.S. Senate by the Department of State (Washington, D.C.: U.S. Government Printing Office, 1984, p. 837.

60. *Asiaweek* (Hong Kong), September 7, 1984, p. 14.

61. Tan Boon Kean, "Orwell's Year in the Malaysian Press," *Far Eastern Economic Review* (Hong Kong) (September 20, 1984), p. 40.

62. T. M. Smith and H. F. Carpenter, "Indonesia University Students and their Career Aspirations," *Asian Survey* (September 1974), pp. 816–17.

63. N. K. Vien, *Tradition and Revolution in Vietnam* (Berkeley, Calif.: Indochina Resource Center, 1974), p. 165.

64. Data and citation in this paragraph from *Amnesty International Report 1983* (London: Amnesty International Publications, 1983), pp. 238–41.

BIBLIOGRAPHY

Amnesty International Report 1983. Amnesty International Publication, London, 1983. Especially sections on Burma (pp. 190–91; Indonesia (pp. 199–202); Kampuchea (pp. 190–91); Laos (pp. 211–13); Malaysia (pp. 214–16); Philippines (pp. 223–27); Singapore (pp. 228–30); Thailand (p. 237); and Vietnam (pp. 238–41).

Aung, H. "The Burmese Concept of Law." *Journal of the Burma Research Society* 52 (1969), pp. 27–41.

Ball, J. *Indonesian Legal History: 1602–1848*. Sidney: Oughtershaw Press, 1982.

Barraclough, S. "Political Participation and Its Regulation in Malaysia: Opposition to the Societies (Amendment) Act 1981." *Pacific Affairs* 57 (1984), pp. 450–61.

Carney, T. *Communist Party Power in Kampuchea (Cambodia): Documents and Discussion*. Ithaca, N.Y.: Cornell University Southeast Asia Program, 1977.

Chandler, D. P., and B. Kiernan, eds. *Revolution and Its Aftermath in Kampuchea: Eight Essays*. Yale University Southeast Asia Studies, New Haven, 1983. Esp. "Democratic Kampuchea: A Highly Centralized Dictatorship," by A. Barnett (pp. 212–29); and "Observations of the Heng Samrin Government," by C. Boua (pp. 259–90).

The Constitution of the Socialist Republic of the Union of Burma. Rangoon: Printing and Publishing Company, 1974.

Country Reports on Human Rights Practices for 1983. Washington, D.C.; U.S. Government Printing Office, 1984. Sections on Burma (pp. 729–39); Indonesia (pp. 775–88); Kampuchea (pp. 795–803); Laos (pp. 825–34); Malaysia (pp. 835–42); Philippines (pp. 856–71); Singapore (pp. 872–89); Thailand (pp. 883–92); and Vietnam (pp. 897–909).

Groves, H. E. *The Constitution of Malaysia*. Singapore: Malaysia Publications, Ltd., 1964.

Gungwu, W., ed. *Malaysia: A Survey*. New York: Praeger Publishers, 1964.

Hooker, B. M. *Adat Laws in Modern Malaya: Land Tenure, Traditional Government, and Religion*. Kuala Lumpur: Oxford University Press, 1972.

Kasemsup, P. "Legal Education and Development in Thailand." *Jernal Undang Undang* 4 (1977), pp. 95–110.

Lahiri, S. C. *Principles of Modern Burmese Buddhist Law*. 6th ed., Calcutta: Eastern Law House, 1974.

Leigh, M. B. *The Rising Moon: Political Change in Sarawak*. Sydney: Sydney University Press, 1974.

Lev, D. S. *Islamic Courts in Indonesia: A Study in the Political Bases of Legal Institutions*. Berkeley and London: University of California Press, 1972.

————. "Judicial Institutions and Legal Culture in Indonesia." In C. Holt, ed., *Culture and Politics in Indonesia*. Ithaca, N.Y.: Cornell University Press, 1972. Pp. 246–318.

Mercado, L. N. "An Intellectual History of Filipino Legal Philosophy." *Solidarity* (Manila) 99 (1984) pp. 3–10.

Milne, R. S., and K. J. Ratnam. *Malaysia: New States in a New Nation—Political Development of Sarawak and Sabah in Malaysia*. London: Frank Cass Publishers, 1974.

Osborne, M. *The French Presence in Cochinchina and Cambodia: Rule and Response*. Ithaca, N.Y.: Cornell University Press, 1969.

Padilla, A. *Criminal Law: Revised Penal Code Annotated*. 12th ed., Manila: Padilla Publications, Manila, 1980.

Rees, D. *Vietnam Since "Liberation": Hanoi's Revolutionary Strategy*. London: Institute for the Study of Conflict, 1977.

Republic of Indonesia, Department of Information. *Law Book on the Code of Criminal Procedure*. Act no. 8/1981. Djakarta: Department of Information, 1981.

Revised Rules of Court in the Philippines. Manila: Rex Publishers, 1972.

Rhyne, C. S. *Law and Judicial Systems of Nations*. 3d ed. Washington, D.C.: The World Peace Through Law Center, 1978.

Rosenberg, D. A., ed. *Marcos and Martial Law in the Philippines*. Ithaca and London: Cornell University Press, 1979.

Royal Thai Government. *Constitution of the Kingdom of Thailand* (Translated by the Royal Thai Judicial Council). *Government Gazette* (Bangkok) (special issue) 95, part 146 (1978).

————. *The Criminal Code of Thailand*. Bangkok: International Translation Publishers, 1978.

Saketapy, J. E. "Indonesian Criminal Law in a Nutshell." *Indonesian Quarterly* 9 (1981), pp. 45–52.

Santos, V. A. "The Conduct of Justice Under the New Society." In B. G. Belmonte, ed., *Fookien Times Yearbook 1974*. Manila: Fookien Times Publishing Co., 1974. Pp. 280–83, 293.

"Socialist Republic of Vietnam, Draft Constitution." Complete text, Radio Hanoi, August 15–24, 1979, in *Foreign Broadcast Information Service Reports*, vol. 4, no. 185, Supplement 027, September 21, 1979, pp. 1–24.

Stuart-Fox, M., ed. *Contemporary Laos: Studies in the Politics and Society of the Lao People's Democratic Republic*. St. Lucia: University of Queensland Press, 1982.

Subramanian, N. A. "Some Aspects of Burmese Constitutional Law." *Indian Yearbook of International Affairs 1956*. Madras: University of Madras, 1957. Pp. 123–55.

Suffian bin Hashim, M. *An Introduction to the Constitution of Malaysia* 2d ed. Kuala Lumpur: Di-Chetak Di-Jabatan Chetak Kerajaan, 1978.

————, et al. *The Constitution of Malaysia: Its Development from 1957 to 1977*. Kuala Lumpur and New York: Oxford University Press, 1978.

Suksamaran, S. *Political Buddhism in Southeast Asia: The Role of the Sangha in the Modernization of Thailand.* New York: St. Martin's Press, 1976.

Summers, L. "Democratic Kampuchea." In B. Szajkowski, ed., *Marxist Governments: A World Survey.* London: Macmillan, 1980.

Tadiar, A. F. "Administration of Criminal Justice in the Philippines." *Philippine Law Journal* 47 (1972), pp. 547–602.

Tanada, L. M., and E. M. Fernando. *Constitution of the Philippines.* Manila: R. P. Garcia, 1947.

Tate, C. N. "Political Development and the Philippine Judiciary." *Asian Forum* (January-March 1974), pp. 32–44.

Ter Haar, B. *Adat Law in Indonesia.* New York: Institute of Pacific Relations, 1948.

Tseng, H. P., ed. *The Law Schools of the World.* Buffalo, N.Y.: William S. Hein, 1977.

Vickery, M. *Cambodia 1975–1982.* Boston: Southend Press, Boston, 1984.

Villegas, A. J. "Criminality, Government and Citizenry." In J. V. Abuera and R. P. de Guzman, eds., *Foundations and Dynamics of Filipino Government and Politics.* Manila: Bookmark, 1969. Pp. 87–90.

15

SOVIET UNION

Albert J. Schmidt

Although the Soviet legal system is classified as "socialist," it exists within the family of civil law systems. Despite their initial efforts to break with Russia's legal past—the court system and the bar were both immediately abolished in 1917—the victorious Bolsheviks did return to traditional legal forms and practices in the early 1920s. That Soviet law which evolved is presently codified like that of other Roman civil law systems; however, Soviet law uniquely wears the rhetorical garb of Marxism-Leninism. Marxist-Leninist rhetoric, supplemented by patriotic verbiage, prevails in the preambles of the Constitution (1977) and the various All-Union Fundamental Principles. These inclusions reflect the very considerable exposure that jurists have to Marxist-Leninist doctrine both in their workplace and in higher legal education.

THE DEVELOPMENT OF THE LEGAL SYSTEM

Perceiving economic relations as preeminent, proponents of Marxism-Leninism have depicted a societal evolution from primitive communities to sophisticated capitalism. In this process the class struggle destroys each previous societal form, or better stated, synthesizes a higher level of development. Thus, slavery in antiquity, serfdom in the Middle Ages, and capitalism in modern times have each, in turn, generated class conflict and subsequent societal change. Classical Marxists loathe the law, for, like the state, it is a capitalist instrument of exploitation and a part of society's needless superstructure. Above all, law protects private property, the chief vehicle of capitalist aggrandizement. In the real world of economic relations, modes of production constitute the base of material life. Social classes, state, and law—a part of the superstructure—are all destined for oblivion when communism, a classless society, is realized.

The prospects for the extirpation of capitalism and its creatures appeared good in 1917. In managing the transition to socialism, Lenin allowed the party to supersede the state and law, both of which were destined to "wither away" in any case. "Dictatorship of the proletariat," which he had extracted from Marx and Engels, received star billing during the Civil War epoch of War Communism, 1918–1921. The old court system and bar were eliminated, as workers, peasants, and the military replaced professional jurists in the dispensing of justice. Indeed, summary justice by the military tribunals became the instrument of the Red Terror in dealing with counter revolutionaries. Such legal nihilism did not last for long. The prospect of Bolshevik Russia's social and economic collapse forced Lenin to draw back. His New Economic Policy (NEP), a compromise with petit bourgeois capitalism, hastened reinstatement of the defunct legal system. The circle was now complete. During the NEP years of the 1920s there appeared new civil and criminal codes, based on those drawn up before the Revolution. Classical Marxists, who denounced the very concept of a socialist law, could not but be outraged with this development.

The Soviet debt to the Imperial Russian legal system makes no sense unless placed in a larger historical context. The origin of Russia's legal tradition may be traced to the era of Kiev, which produced the Russkaia Pravda nearly a millennium ago. Not surprisingly, some of this inspiration in law was traceable to Graeco-Roman Byzantium through Orthodox Christianity. During the Mongol interregnum, beginning in the thirteenth century, Russia preserved the spirit of the Russkaia Pravda in the judicial charters of Novgorod and Pskov, cities that escaped Tatar domination. Muscovite Russia, particularly after liberation from the Tartars late in the fifteenth century, issued several law codes immeasurably more sophisticated that the Russkaia Pravda. The third of these, the Ulozhenie of 1649, remained, despite attempts at reform and systematization during the eighteenth century, Russia's legal code for nearly 200 years. Finally in 1833, Mikhail Speranskii, a tsarist minister-reformer, facilitated the codification of Russian law, the Svod Zakonov. Yet Speranskii unsuccessfully coped with Russia's legal malaise, described by one historian as follows:

The Russian judicial system of the mid-nineteenth century lives up to the worst possible expectations. It was organized on a class basis, with separate courts and different punishments for the nobility, the clergy, the urban population, and the remnants of the free peasantry. The intellectual and moral level of judges was notoriously low; bribery was almost universal. The courts were in the control of the centrally appointed provincial governors. Procedure was still entirely written, the evidence being presented in the form of documents prepared by the police. Trial was secret, with the judges appearing in public only to pass sentence or to hand down a judgment. There was a confusion of jurisdictions and instances, with unlimited delays. In 1831, for example, for the province of Petersburg there were discovered in investigation to be 120,000 undecided cases in the courts. There was no professional bar. Legal education was poor.[1]

The emergence of a Russian intelligentsia in the 1830s spawned a group of jurists educated largely outside Russia. Aware of developments in France, Germany, and Britain, they actively engaged in Alexander II's Great Reforms of the 1860s. The reorganization of the court system in 1864 along Western liberal lines and the establishment of a professional bar were undoubtedly the most important of these. Although these reforms encountered difficulty during the political reaction of the 1880s, many survived. Counter-reaction after 1905 produced new reforms, especially exemplified by the earlier (1903) criminal code and draft civil code (1910–1913), both of which were prototypes for NEP codes of the 1920s.

Imperial Russia's appropriation of the civil law reflected a special debt to Germany. Russian scholars looked to the German Pandektenrecht School, which had distilled the basic principles of Justinian's Roman law from the medieval Italian jurists. As one writer has noted:

It was characteristic of the German Pandektistik that the Roman Law was adopted as a general system of jurisprudence. In Russia, too, courses in Roman law were taught as a "general introduction" to the theory of civil law. In defending the study of Roman law, [the Russian jurist I. A.] Pokrovskii argued that there was no thought of replacing the national legal system; rather, Russian law was to be improved by theoretical study of jurisprudence from Roman sources—which he identified as the *corpus iuris*. . . . The Russian legal system was increasingly infused with European law; Russian students had to learn the Latin maxims and the complicated but precise terminology of the *Pandektenrecht*.[2]

This Roman impact via Germany was most evident in the draft civil code of 1910–1913.

By the late 1920s some Soviet legal scholars, who assumed that NEP prosperity would hasten the withering away of both state and law, came to oppose the reemergent law codes. Among these the most creative was Evgenii Bronislavovich Pashukanis. Because law, as he construed it, promoted private enterprise in commodities, it was simply a bourgeois tool. Implicit in this so-called commodity exchange theory was the law's destruction. When the state withered away, inevitably, so would the law. Such legal nihilism was expressed most succinctly by P. E. Stuchka: "Communism means not the victory of socialist law, but the victory of socialism over law, since with the abolition of classes with their antagonistic interests, law will die out altogether."[3]

When Stalin inaugurated the first Five Year Plan in 1928, he appeared to endorse legal nihilism, but by the mid–1930s he reversed this course. The Constitution of 1936 and subsequent developments indicated that "socialist legality," or conventional legal principles and organization, had official sanction. Pashukanis, in turn, was villified and eventually shot. The late 1930s, paradoxically a period of both law and terror, was personified by Andrei Ia. Vyshinskii, whose theory of permanent socialist law eventually became disassociated with the horrors of its origins. Legal reform, long promised by Stalin, became a reality only after his death.

The Party Congresses in 1959 and 1961 were crucial in this respect. Coming in the aftermath of Khrushchev's de-Stalinization performance at the Twentieth

Party Congress in 1956, they substituted "all-people's state" for "dictatorship of the proletariat" and, by so doing, lessened coercion as an instrument of the state. By the time of Khrushchev's ouster in 1964, a very substantial amount of codification, much of which reflected these new concerns about legality, was completed. Under Brezhnev, many of these codes were modified and new ones, along with the Constitution of 1977, promulgated. Whatever the shortcoming of Soviet constitutions, this last one assumes some importance because it

codifies major social and political changes which extend beyond the scope of Brezhnev's leadership alone. In the most general sense, this is demonstrated by the fact that Soviet authorities describe it as the constitution of an advanced industrial society, one which, in Soviet parlance, has reached the state of "developed socialism." . . . More specifically, the Constitution takes full account of the great volume of post-Stalin legislation that has affected nearly every branch and area of Soviet law. In fact, there are few points in the Constitution which have not been raised or institutionalized already in code law, statutory legislation, or the scholarly judicial commentary explicating the extensive post-Stalin legal reforms.[4]

The development of the Soviet legal system provides an insight into both law and politics since 1917. After the Civil War (1918–1921) had left Soviet Russia economically exhausted, Lenin accommodated his ideology to reality by initiating the NEP. Other compromises had occurred. The high ideals of egalitarian justice—citizen participation, simplicity, and flexibility—were discarded or diminished for professionalism, law codes, a constitution, and a formal court structure. While lawyer revolutionaries like Evgenii Pashukanis had hoped that law and its system would wither away, Stalin eventually dispelled the legal nihilists of such notions. After the dislocations caused by industrial planning and forced collectivization, Stalin opted for the appearances of legality.

Although law during the Stalin era became a facade for unprecedented villanies, the legal system endured, awaiting a more propitious moment under Nikita Khrushchev. Despite a preference for populist tinkering with the law as evidenced by comrades' courts and people's patrols and a notable persistence of some illegalities, he gave impetus to the emergence of an incipient legal culture through the legal reforms of the late 1950s and early 1960s. While Pashukanis was posthumously rehabilitated, his ideas remained dormant.

Under Brezhnev "socialist legality" became a code word for stability in a "developed socialist society." The Constitution of 1977, essentially a policy statement, rather obscured the corruption and malaise that characterized the later Brezhnev era. Dissidents, experiencing the rigors of the KGB, quickly discerned the limits of socialist legality. Andropov's reign, though brief, possessed both the aura of reform and severity. His emphasis on labor discipline and anticorruption evidently won respect from a Soviet citizenry longing for firm leadership. Succession of the infirm Chernenko was perceived by many as a return to the indolence of the late Brezhnev period. In this context, Soviet law and the legal system buttressed the aged and embattled leadership rather than mobilized the masses for reform of the system. Gripped by a multitude of internal problems and fearful of unleashing uncontrollable forces in trying to resolve them, the party leadership has turned increasingly to lawyers to assist them in managing change for them. Professor Hazard has noted that

It is in the sphere of managing change that the Soviet jurist is coming to the fore. Although traditionally the jurist has been a technician often ignored by those who make policy, as evidenced by the early years of reliance upon social consciousness rather than law to guide those whose task was to build for the future, respect for jurists is increasing. They are seen now to be men and women of skills, not only technical but political. They are being brought to the fore as members of local soviets and as legal advisers to generalists; and finally one has been seated on the Politburo of the Communist Party. . . . Law has become more than a means of eliminating enemies. It is an instrument to be used to structure a new society.[5]

Today no less than in Lenin's time, law and politics are closely related. It remains to be seen how effectively the party and lawyer Mikhail S. Gorbachev will manage the Soviet future and use law and lawyers to do so.

THE ORGANIZATION OF THE COURT SYSTEM

The present two-tiered Soviet judicial structure, federal and union republics, dates from the adoption of the Fundamentals of Legislation of the USSR and Union Republics on Court Organization in the USSR of December 25, 1958.[6] On the highest, or federal, level are the Supreme Court of the USSR and Military Tribunals supervised by the USSR Supreme Court. On the next level are supreme courts of the Union and Autonomous Republics and the territorial, regional, city, and peoples' courts, and the military tribunals in the USSR Armed Forces. The Supreme Court of the USSR, like any other Soviet court, consists of a judge and two people's assessors when it exercises original jurisdiction. When acting in an appellate role, it has a three-judge panel. The Supreme Court's power resides in its Plenum (plenary session), which has extensive supervisory and even quasi-legislative authority. The latter, principally that of issuing guidelines to lower courts, is discussed in greater detail below. The Court has a chairman, deputy chairman, justices, and people's assessors—all of whom are elected by the Supreme Soviet—and is organized into civil, criminal, and military divisions. The Judicial Division for Civil Cases handles important civil cases and has appellate jurisdiction over civil decisions rendered on the republic and autonomous republic level and arising from protests from the chairman of the Supreme Court of the USSR or the procurator general. The Division for Criminal Cases performs similarly for criminal matters. The Military Division has both original and appellate jurisdiction over military cases. Its appellate role may result from protests of the chairman of the Supreme Court of the USSR, the procurator-general of the USSR, or the chief military procurator.

Military Tribunals, an integral part of the federal court system, try espionage and criminal cases involving military personnel and members of the organs for state security. If the other courts are not functioning, the Military Tribunals may hear both civil and criminal cases. Military Tribunals are supervised by the Supreme Court of the USSR, the Military Division of which is jointly responsible with the minister of defense for its organization and personnel.

On the union republic level there are essentially three groups of courts: the supreme courts of the union and autonomous republics, the so-called intermediate courts, and county and people's courts. The union republic and autonomous republic supreme courts are structured like the Supreme Court of the USSR, having a chairman, deputy chairman, justices, and people's assessors. Their function is that of supervising their respective republic's judicial organs. These republic level supreme courts also have civil and criminal divisions and occasionally sit in plenary session. Most of these courts have a presidium. Although they may exercise original jurisdiction, the union and autonomous republic supreme courts attend mainly to appeals and protests resulting from intermediate court decisions.

Intermediate courts do not exist in every union republic; where they do not, appeals flow directly from the local courts to the union republic supreme court. This lack of uniformity of intermediate courts has largely to do with the size of the union republic. The Russian Soviet Federative Socialist Republic has a rather complex court system corresponding to its division into city districts, territories, provinces, autonomous regions, national areas, and/or republics. Usually, these courts exercise original jurisdiction over important cases and hear cases on appeal from the local courts. Generally, intermediate courts are organized into civil and criminal divisions, have a presidium, and consist of the usual organization of chairman, deputy chairman, justices, and people's assessors.

Most of the action occurs in the local courts, the county and the city people's courts, which function with a judge and two people's assessors. The people's courts hear less important criminal cases and virtually all civil ones. Decisions are by majority vote.

For most Westerners, the components of a legal system inevitably are limited to the courts and the bar. The Soviet system does not lend itself to such strictures, for there are those elements, engaged primarily in control and supervision, that contribute to "the strengthening of socialist legality."

This "supervisory function" has a long history in both the Russian and Soviet past. What Merle Fainsod said years ago of the Soviet bureaucracy in the 1960s still holds true:

The Soviet bureaucracy is . . . characterized by a formidable proliferation of control agencies without parallel in the West. The typical Soviet administrator functions in an environment in which every major decision is subject to the possibility of check, recheck, and counter-check. It is not too far-fetched to describe this complex network of controls as a system of power founded on the institutionalization of mutual suspicion.[7]

A Soviet legal institution that falls most obviously into the pattern of control and supervision is the Procuracy, which dates from the time of Peter the Great. Initially abolished by the Bolsheviks, it was reinstated in 1923 by Lenin to assure uniform application of the law. The task of the Procuracy is one of supervising all administrative, judicial, and law enforcement agencies and supervising the observance of laws where detained persons are incarcerated. The Procuracy is expected to strengthen "socialist legality and legal order in every possible way." That it combines this overseeing of justice with the prosecutorial role would appear to create confusion and even conflict of interest. George Ginsburgs has noted, too, that the misdeeds of the Stalin era were in no way diminished by the Procuracy's determination to maintain legality in Soviet society: "In fact, of all Soviet institutions the Procuracy has been the most stable, the least subject to purges, the most unanimously praised by all and every Soviet ruling clique, and, in return, the Procuracy has served all of them equally faithfully and efficiently.[8]

Although the Procuracy was reinstated early in the NEP period, its centralization did not occur until 1936. In 1955 the Statute on Procuracy Supervision in the USSR constituted the first detailed legislation on procuracy power. The most recent legislation is the Law on the Procuracy of the USSR (1979 and amended 1982). As with the court system, procuracies exist on each administrative-territorial strata as well as for the military and transport. Of all the components in the Soviet legal system, the Procuracy is the most prestigious. Kaminskaya has noted that the best of Soviet law students opt for it; moreover, it has the highest party membership, averaging 83 percent.[9] Of the 17,000 procurators few are women. To a greater degree than elsewhere in the Soviet legal system, continuity prevails in the local procuracies and in the Office of Procurator General. In 1973 more than half had accumulated in excess of ten years service.[10]

The State Notariat is yet another legal agency having much to do with strengthening socialist legality. The Law on the State Notariat (1973 and 1979) enumerates State Notariat tasks as "protection of socialist ownership, of the rights and legal interests of citizens, state institutions, enterprises, and organizations, collective farms, other cooperative, and other social organizations." Its principle responsibility is the "prevention of illegalities by certifying contracts and other transactions properly and in a timely manner, the formalization of inheritance rights, and the endorsement of documents of execution and other notarial activities."[11] During the Revolution the dissolved Imperial Notariat appeared destined to have no successor; instead, this agency was merely decentralized, the authority left with local soviets to open their own notariats. By 1926 a State Notariat was reestablished.

Although neither State Arbitration nor departmental arbitrations, which resolve disputes between economic enterprises, are a part of the regular court system, they do, like components of the judicial system, function on all levels from all-union republics to the city. In resolving disputes, State Arbitration resembles a court, although its chairman may not be a jurist and may decide a case without lay assessors. In 1981 State Arbitration was involved in more than 700,000 cases.[12]

Related to the Soviet legal system are several establishments that are best described as quasi-legal and populist. Apart from legal functions, they mobilize and educate the populace in the cause of socialist legality while imposing a measure of control as well. These include the people's control commissions, the comrades' courts, and the people's patrols. People's Control, according to 1979 legislation, is expected to "carry on a systematic verification of the fulfillment of the directives of the Party, Soviet laws, and decisions of the Government, to resolutely oppose all that harms the interests of the state, and to further the development in citizens of a feeling of responsibility for the affairs of society as a whole."[13] The people's control groups have increased in the two decades after 1962 from two million to more than ten million. Similarly, comrades' courts mobilize the people in the process of settling disputes. Comrades' courts are "elective social agencies called upon actively to promote the nurturing of citizens in the spirit of a communist attitude toward labor, an attitude of care toward socialist ownership, [and] observance of the rules of socialist community life."[14] Established most often in places of work, collective farms, housing projects, and the like, comrades' courts resolve minor disputes. While making no claim to professionalism (their presiding officers rarely possess even intermediate legal education), they do educate Soviet citizens in a forceful way about socialist legality. The comrades' courts had increased from 45,000 in 1938 to some 300,000 in the early 1970s.[15]

Citizen police units existed from an early date in the Soviet Union, but the people's patrols were a Khrushchev creation in 1959–60. This citizen corps is expected to help maintain public order, assist the regular militia as required, engage in educational work in labor collectives, facilitate traffic safety, assist victims of accidents, assist the border guard, and oppose "hooliganism, drunkenness, home-brewing, stealing of state and social property, and also the personal property of citizens, violations of trade rules, speculation, and other violations of law.[16] Finally, in addition to the already noted formal, supervisory and quasi-legal organs, there are a number of secret tribunals. Just what role(s) these bodies perform has recently given rise to an intensive debate.[17]

THE PERSONNEL OF THE LAW

The Legal Practitioners

The Soviet bar does not enjoy the status of its counterpart in the United States; however, it does constitute, as Berman has suggested, a cohesive group consisting of advocates, jurisconsults, judges, procurators, legal scholars, and notaries.[18]

In the mid–1960s approximately 101,000 Soviet citizens with intermediate or higher legal education worked in some judicial capacity and another 45,000–

50,000 were law students.[19] Nearly two decades later there were about 20,000 advocates, 100,000 jurisconsults, 13,500 judges, perhaps 17,000 procurators, more than 3,000 notaries, and 738,751 people's assessors, some of whom had rudimentary legal education.[20]

The College of Advocates, or Advokatura, is the Soviet approximation of the American bar. Because the college is a collective, the advocate is limited in what he or she can and cannot do. The advocate may not accept or reject a case; doing so is the prerogative of the manager of the college. There are guidelines for the advocate's handling the cases assigned to him, and his fees are determined by the collective. The structure of the post-World War II College of Advocates was determined by the decree "Concerning the Advokatura" (1939), superseded in 1979 by the "Law on the Advokatura in the USSR."

Advocates do not have particularly high status within the profession. Dina Kaminskaya has noted that before she joined the Advokatura more than three decades ago "most of the newer members were former investigators of the NKVD (now KGB) or judges who had been dismissed from the bench and by order of the Party were fixed up with jobs in advocacy." Although they had been demoted for one reason or other, generally they were party members, and it was from their ranks that the law office managers were recruited. Although Kaminskaya maintains that mobility from the Advokatura to branches of the judiciary rarely occurred, Barry and Berman believe that jurists frequently move from it.[21]

The Soviet lawyer is compensated from fees paid by the client to the college cashier as determined by a scale of rates for the legal services performed. The fee earned by the advocate is credited to him. At the end of the month these earnings are tallied with taxes and office expenses deducted. Usually, the advocate receives between 70 and 80 percent of what has been credited to him in fees.

Kaminskaya explains that the advocate compensates for this low salary by concentrating on minor cases lasting a few days each, thereby exceeding the stipends of the average engineer, teacher, and doctor and earning more, too, than the jurisconsult in an industrial enterprise, the people's court judge, and the district procurial investigator. The problem arises when the best advocates are assigned to the longer, complicated cases which, for a month's work, result in only 170 or 180 rubles less the usual deductions. For the same period a university professor earns 400 rubles.[22]

The matter of compensation also impinges on professional standards. Most advocates supplement their stipend with a *mixt*, a fee that is not registered. In Kaminskaya's opinion, virtually all lawyers do take or have taken a mixt, for only by doing so do lawyers acquire a reasonably good standard of living. For this reason, when one is transferred downward to the advocacy, the financial rewards at least compensate for unrealized political ambitions or diminished social prestige. Mixt, according the Kaminskaya, is not the principal reason for the greater popularity that the Advokatura enjoys today among professionals. Its standards are higher now, a law degree being the minimum requirement; moreover, there is an independence from the state that attracts recruits even from the judiciary and procuracy. The Advokatura's improved image has resulted from its membership's increasingly frequent election to local soviets, participation in important conferences, and inclusion in delegations of lawyers sent abroad.[23]

The legal profession is also linked to economics, especially in the planning process, through the jurisconsults. The most numerous among members of the legal profession in the USSR and most rapid in recent growth, they act as a kind of house counsel for ministries, departments, enterprises, organizations, and institutions. These lawyers, who have not organized themselves collegially as have advocates, generally are responsible for facilitating legality, whether in planning or in labor relations. Because the jurisconsult has become invaluable, demand presently exceeds supply. Even so, jurisconsults' stipends remain among the lowest in the profession, despite a rise in their level of education.

Another legal practitioner is the notary who functions in the State Notariat. A kind of public servant in the USSR, the notary now does much that a lawyer or solicitor does in Western countries. As of 1975 there were 3,225 notaries, 80 percent of whom were women. Butler notes that 70 percent of their time focused on certification of the accuracy of documents; the remainder was divided between the certification of such legal transactions as wills and contracts and inheritance.[24]

The Plan, the central element in Soviet economic life, has resulted in unparalleled demand for trained legal personnel. An unknown number of lawyers serve State Arbitration and other arbitration, which attempt to resolve disputes over contracts, property, planning discipline, or the like among enterprises, institutions, and organizations.

As the stress on socialist legality has accelerated the training of new lawyers, so has it affected the quality and quantity of legal education in the USSR. At present, forty-six universities, four institutes, and fifteen schools in the Ministry of Internal Affairs (MVD) purvey higher legal education. All fifteen union republic universities, located in the republic capitals, have law faculties, as do additional universities in large noncapital cities. The law institutes are in Moscow, Saratov, Sverdlovsk, and Khar'kov. Moscow's is the All-Union Law Institute Teaching by Correspondence, which plays a major role in the training of lawyers.

Besides these, the Ministry of Internal Affairs established at least six new programs during the 1960s: the Academy of the MVD SSR (Ministry of Internal Affairs Soviet Socialist Republic) and five advanced institutions in Moscow, Gor'kii, Kiev, Tashkent, and Karaganda, each with a legal specialization. The military also has its own establishment for legal education, the so-called Military-Law Faculty of the Military Institute of the Soviet Army, which provides legal education for about 70 percent of the Soviet military. The International Law Faculty of the Institute of International Relations of the MVS SSR graduates each year an unspecified number.[25] Specialized courses in law are also taught in the Diplomatic Academy, the Academy of Foreign Trade, the Institute for the Management of the National Economy, and a variety of other institutes. Senior party members study law in the Higher Party School. Third World students do so at Patrice Lumumba University in Moscow.[26] There is also an increasing emphasis on secondary legal education. "People's universities for legal knowledge," schools with two-year paralegal programs for secondary school graduates, have been established to train paralegals, lay assessors, people's guards, members of the comrades' courts, and the like.[27]

Recent statistics show that there are nearly 90,000 law students of whom approximately 30,000 are full-time. Even with large graduating classes—in 1980 there were 15,800 graduates—Soviet legal needs are not being met. This is especially true among jurisconsults and in remote locations where perhaps 30 to 40 percent of the judges have only secondary legal training.[28]

Despite its problems, legal education in the USSR today is immeasurably better than it was in the recent past. It reached its nadir in the mid–1930s before Stalin abandoned Pashukanis. There were only eight law institutes—those in Moscow, Leningrad, Saratov, Kazan', Sverdlovsk, Minsk, Khar'kov, and Tashkent and the law faculties of the Universities of Baku, Tbilisi, and Erevan.[29] With the war, enrollment dropped from 5,900 in 1940 to 2,732 the next year, and 960 in 1942; in 1945 the numbers rose to 6,550.[30] By the 1950s the number of students enrolled in twenty-five university law departments and four law institutes was about half, some 45,000, of the present total. These included day, evening, and correspondence students. Those graduating, while showing a steady increase, numbered only 2,000 in 1947 and 8,100 in 1955.[31]

The curriculum in Soviet law schools has been greatly affected by ideological shifts. When the law faculties of universities were abolished in 1919 and replaced by the so-called Faculties of Public Sciences, the curriculum was dominated by the social sciences rather than by civil and criminal law. Although law returned to the curriculum during NEP, civil law was deleted in the early 1930s, when Pashukanis "reigned." The triumph of "legality" in the late 1930s occasioned a return to a conventional curriculum.

At present, the curriculum contains an ideological core required of all university students and strictly legal requirements such as history of the Soviet state and law; political doctrines; Roman, socialist, and bourgeois law; and law of former colonial countries. Typical law courses include administrative law, financial law, public international law, family law, economic law, civil law and procedure, criminal law and procedure, correctional labor law, procuracy supervision, labor law, collective farm law, conservation law, law of medicine and psychiatry, and law of social security.

A practicum during the third year entails visits to legal institutions (five weeks), and "production practice" (twelve weeks) in the last two years exposes a student to the workings of a particular legal institution. A student specializes during his/her last two years as confirmed by courses, practicum, and thesis topic. This curriculum is stretched over five years, or ten terms, of university study; in the law institutes, where the practicum is emphasized, the course work is reduced

to eight terms, or four years of study. Those opting for night school or correspondence courses enter what is a six-year program. Teaching is generally by
lecture, approximating thirty hours per week for the first year or averaging twenty
hours per week for the five years with occasional seminars. Principal examinations are oral, and a diploma thesis must be defended in the fifth year.

The two postgraduate law degrees are those of candidate of legal sciences and
doctor of legal sciences. The latter, roughly equivalent to the Ph.D. in the United
States, is more prestigious. To enter a graduate program, one must pass a
competitive examination, have at least two years work experience, and be no
older than thirty-five if a full-time student or forty-five if part-time. Legal research
and a thesis or doctoral dissertation are the foci of postgraduate work, but
examinations in ideological subjects must be taken and passed as on the undergraduate level.

Since lawyers acquire their education at state expense, they are initially placed
according to the needs of the state plan. A university or institute committee
coordinates the specialties of its graduates with the requests submitted by various
state ministries, agencies, or organizations. After a two-year stint, the lawyer
may elect his employment or pursue postgraduate work. The ratio of juridical
personnel to population in the USSR has risen consistently. In 1939 it was 32
to 100,000; in 1959, 38 to 100,000; and in 1970, 45 to 100,000. Presumably
this ratio has continued to rise over the last decade and a half, alhtough some
larger cities appear no longer to have a shortage of legal personnel while communities in remote locations have not always correctly assessed their needs.
Although most prestige positions have been claimed by graduates with higher
legal education, many from "people's universities," where the quality of education is lower, have secured a surprising number of middle-level positions.[32]

In the USSR the legal profession neither exercises control over nor sets standards for those about to enter the profession. There is no bar association to
accredit the law schools and institutes or set minimal curricular requirements.
Indeed, since it is the state through the Supreme Attestation Commission that
approves the awarding of graduate degrees and the Communist Party of the
Soviet Union (CPSU) Central Committee or its plenum that makes decisions
pertaining to legal education, it is evident that the party, not the profession,
determines policy for legal education.

Members of the Soviet legal profession have generally not been held in the
same high esteem as their colleagues in the West.[33] Two decades ago, the best
and brightest among Soviet law students apparently opted for a career in the
Procuracy, where both salary and prestige were greatest. Advocates, rather a
suspect group, lingered, low both in prestige and socioeconomic standing. Over
the years, resourceful ones managed quite well financially, and the group has
apparently improved its professional image as well. Judges have also been poorly
regarded and rewarded. One might expect better treatment for the much-utilized
jurisconsults, who perform valuable service for the Plan, but they receive neither
large stipends nor have the opportunities, available to advocates, for supple-

menting their salaries. That many women populate various branches of the legal system is indicative, too, of the relatively low socioeconomic as well as professional status of lawyering in the USSR.

Although failing to match their American counterparts in achieving success in politics and business and suffering setbacks in law reform, Soviet lawyers have, nonetheless, made themselves heard through forums commonly utilized by lawyers: their academic or professional establishments, scholarly publications, and professional gatherings. In addition, they engage in the kinds of activities common to lawyers everywhere and by doing so, buttress their status as a professional group.

The Judiciary

The bench in the Soviet Union has also increased both in numbers and quality in the last two or three decades. In 1965 there were approximately 9,000 Soviet judges, of whom more than 7,500 presided over 3,502 people's courts.[34] In the early 1980s the number of judges increased to approximately 13,500, of whom 10,304 were people's court judges. The remainder held positions in the union republic supreme and inferior courts above the people's court level. That the June 1982 balloting led to the election of 10,304 suggests that there has been nearly a 40 percent increase in people's court judges and a 50 percent increase in judges altogether in less than two decades. In the 1982 elections, 63.5 percent of those elected were males. In the 1982 elections, 738,751 people's assessors were elected for two-and-a-half-year terms. Each is expected to serve no more than two weeks each year.[35] They generally are paid by their employer for time in court. Judges and assessors may be recalled by the electorate, but they seldom are.

Judges in the USSR, as in Civil Law countries, do not constitute an elite, especially the vast majority who are judges in people's courts. That for many years no legal education requirement existed for judges was indicative of their low professional status. In the mid–1930s only 6.4 percent had any higher legal education compared to a majority of those elected in 1982.[36]

This lowly status has been reflected socioeconomically as well. A former Czech judge probably describes conditions similar to those in the USSR when he states that "the salary scale of judges was only slightly above the national average. A miner, a laborer in a foundry, a bus driver and other skilled workers enjoyed higher incomes." In the USSR a provincial judge earns only 90–100 rubles ($125) per month; in Moscow the stipend is a bit more, 100–110 rubles. Indeed, these low salaries have been a factor in judicial corruption, principally bribe-taking, in the USSR.[37]

That many women are people's court judges is, alas, also an indicator of the relative low socioeconomic status of judgeships. Statistics released in the mid–1970s place the percentage of women employed in the system of justice in the USSR at 47.9 percent. Women (2,829) constituted 32.5 percent of the people's judges and 50.7 percent (329,188) of the people's assessors. In the Latvian and Estonian republics more than 50 percent of the judges were women. In superior courts, those of union and autonomous republics and of regional, territorial and area courts, women held 34.2 percent of the judgeships.[38] While undoubtedly the status and prestige of the judge has improved over the last generation, salaries remain low and independence is restricted.

Constitutional guarantees notwithstanding, Soviet judges lack independence. Kaminskaya, in remarking that she had never seen a truly independent judge, one who did not bow to party and governmental pressures, blames the selection process:

In practice . . . every judge knows that the approval of his candidacy for reelection, and consequently his continuance in the profession, depends on the Party's assessment of his record. Every judge also realizes that he can count on reelection only if he has strictly followed both the general Party directives and the specific instructions of the Party directives and the specific instructions of the Party committee to which he is immediately subordinate. Any show of independence and genuine impartiality is bound to evoke the dissatisfaction of the Party authorities, and in consequence, the loss of judicial office.[39]

Kaminskaya concludes that party control of the judiciary is effected through a party-appointed official "who watches and directs the performance of the local court and procuracy in the name of the Party." That *all* Soviet judges are party members in itself subordinates them to the wishes of the party. Periodically, local party committees hold briefings for the judges, appraising and criticizing their performance. The insecurity of judges is further heightened by their dependence on superior courts, from whom they often received weekly instructions.

One would assume that careers based on election would be precarious, but that is not the case. Barry and Berman have noted that:

The paradox of an elected civil service is resolved by the Soviet system of nominations: the candidacy for each judgeship is limited to a single person, usually chosen on the basis of his professional and political qualifications. However, the tenure of Soviet judges is short—five years—and in fact there is always a considerable turnover at elections of People's Judges, for reasons which we do not know.[40]

Butler similarly states that while senior judicial positions are filled from the ranks of lower court judges, there is no career pattern data.[41]

Perhaps the most effective argument made for the fact that the legal profession in the Soviet Union does not represent an elite group is the limited access that it has had to policymaking. Only Lenin and now Gorbachev have been Politburo members; moreover, very few of the Central Committee of the party have been lawyers. Barry and Berman in the 1960s noted that Procurator General Rudenko and Supreme Court President Gorkin "were the only jurists in the USSR Supreme Soviet out of over 1,500 deputies, and they were the only jurists appointed in 1966 to the 97 member commission to draft a new Soviet Constitution!"[42] Several years ago, when this author queried a Soviet jurist about the dearth of lawyers in high political places, the response was nebulous: "There are many lawyers in the higher judiciary." The most important role performed by jurists since Stalin's death has been their drafting of legislation and supporting legal reform. Debates among jurists in the late 1950s and early 1960s were a crucial factor in the numerous Fundamental Principles. Jurists appear most active at the union republic level. Only in the executive committees of local soviets are jurists represented in governmental agencies in substantial numbers; moreover, they have participated frequently as "staff advisors, consultants, or members of subordinate divisions appointed to assist" higher legislative and administrative agencies.[43]

PUBLIC PERCEPTIONS AND THE ROLE OF THE COURTS

Several factors have influenced the Soviet peoples' perceptions of their legal systems. Among these are the primacy of statutory legislation as inherited from the civil law tradition, historical and popular notions of the Russians concerning law and their legal system, and the functioning of the legal system in the USSR today.

In addition to Soviet law's debt to Marxist, old Russian, and civil law antecedents, the paramount role of statutory law distinguishes it from the common law systems. Judicial precedent, as in the Civil Law systems, has no role. Adhering to the doctrine of popular sovereignty, the Soviets insist that the legislation enacted by the popularly elected Supreme Soviet should not in any way be delimited by "judge-made law." At the apex of the statutory pyramid is the Constitution, followed by the All-Union Fundamental Principles, the Union Republic law codes (which have been issued in great number since the late 1950s), and the statutes (*zakony*), in that order. The republican codes are based on the Fundamental Principles, as approved by the Supreme Soviet. The statute, or *zakon*, represents Supreme Soviet legislation of a narrower sort. Because the Supreme Soviet convenes only briefly during each year, it often enacts legislation based on edicts (*ukazy*) promulgated by its presidium during the course of the year. Other normative legislation are decrees (*postanovlenii*), which issue from the USSR Council of Ministers. More numerous than either zakony or ukazy, these postanovlenii constitute "the main vehicle for determining the direction of the economic and cultural development of the country and are, therefore, the major device used by the Soviet leadership to exert its will in the form of legal norms."[44]

Despite a presumption of citizens' knowledge of the law, many enactments are unpublished and, consequently, unknown to the populace. Publication is required of all zakony but only of ukazy that are of "general importance" or of "normative" character. While it is a fact that many ukazy are published, the same cannot be said for postanovlenii, of which perhaps only 20 percent are published.[45] In the USSR as in other civil law countries decisions play only a minor role and are, therefore, published selectively. Whether they reflect judicial thinking is impossible to conclude. In addition to these higher sources of the law, there are many unpublished lesser ones such as subordinate legislation, orders, instructions, and pronouncements issuing from the Supreme Soviet, the Council of Ministers, various ministries and state committees, trade unions, All-Union Congress of Collective Farmers, the Central Union of Consumer Cooperative, the Communist Party of the Soviet Union (CPSU) in conjunction with some of the above, State Arbitrazh, and the military commands. The limitation on languages used for publishing the laws also impinge on presumption of knowledge of the law. While union republic legislation appears in both Russian and the official language of the union republic, the *Vedomosti SSR* on All-Union normative legislation is published only in Russian.

In any enumeration of the sources of Soviet law, Article 6 of the 1977 Constitution should be noted: "The Communist Party of the Soviet Union shall be the guiding and directing force of Soviet society and the nucleus of its political system and state and social organizations. The CPSU shall exist for the people and shall serve the people." Inclusion of this reference to the CPSU in the Constitution is but a thinly veiled acknowledgment that the true source of Soviet law is the party.

Because of the dominant role of the party and the primacy of statutory law, the USSR, like Civil Law countries, has no tradition of judicial review. An activist court was as much an anathema to the Bolsheviks as to French Jacobins, both of whom stood uncompromisingly for popular sovereignty. While the Supreme Soviet in its legislative capacity supposedly fulfills this commitment, there are, as we have seen, many means to enact normative legislation. What of the courts? While Soviet lawyers do not study casebooks, and decisions are rarely publicized, the authorities presently are less adamant than they once were in rejecting "judge-made law." Indicative of the old posture was a 1940 statement that "court practice cannot and must not create new norms of law, new legislation; it must correspond with precision to existing norms, it must bulwark existing statutes."[46] Despite this, a debate developed as to how court decisions could be used creatively in the application of statutory law. The Supreme Court of the USSR and State Arbitration facilitate this process through their "guiding instructions," which, arguably, are a source of law, although such will never be admitted. Probably the matter has best been laid to rest by Donald Barry's conclusion: "That 'judicial precedent is not a source of law' in the Soviet Union is not disputed among Soviet jurists. On the other hand, most would agree that 'judicial practice' (*sudebnaia praktika*) has been important in the development of the law. But there has been more controversy over whether judicial practice therefore constitutes a 'source of law.' "[47]

That justice is uncertain is by no means a new phenomenon for Russians.[48] Aphorisms about old Russian justice revealed popular doubts, and, of course, the venality of old Russian officialdom was a recurring theme in Russian literature. The corrupt jurist was perhaps best portrayed in the person of Amos

Fedorovich Lyapkin-Tyapkin in Gogol's *The Inspector General*. This judge, "a man who has read five or six books and is hence somewhat inclined to free-thinking," is among those officials quaking at the thought of being investigated.[49] Amos Fedorovich and his kind stereotyped the pre–1864 provincial judiciary only with respect to corruption. In *The Overcoat* Gogol depicted another dimension of injustice—brutality and lack of compassion. Akakii Akakiievich, his warm new overcoat stolen, appears before the justice of the peace, who demeans rather than assists the victim of the crime. Chekhov's *The Culprit* reveals the intellectual and cultural gulf that separated judge and peasant, thus precluding any prospect of justice as perceived by either. These three literary references—corruption, brutality, and ignorance of the law—reflect the history and mythology that the Soviets have had to counter as they attempt to promote "socialist legality." But does a tradition of bureaucratic sloth, corruption, and brutality continue to influence attitudes? Is the peasant mentality in the USSR today still quite as suspicious of a professional judiciary as it was a century ago, or did the judicial reforms in the 1860s change, once and for all, attitudes toward the courts and bar?[50]

While old notions persist, occasional corruption in the present judicial system may have had a more damaging impact on public confidence. Louise Shelley has recently scored the manner in which party members have abused their privileged status by interfering in the courts, actions that inevitably undermine confidence in the system.[51]

Judicial corruption peaked during World War II and immediate postwar years. Kaminskaya describes the 1950s situation in Moscow where

practically the entire body of investigators and prosecutors of Moscow Province, many judges of the Moscow Provincial Court, officials of the Kalininksy district procuracy headed by the district procurator himself, and several people's court judges of the same district were arrested and tried for bribery and corruption.[52]

Those accused of economic crimes during the 1950s were often the very rich, who had the means to bribe. Such bribery still persists, although not to such a degree. Even as recently as 1975–1976 the Russian Soviet Federated Socialist Republic (RSFSR) Supreme Court "convicted a group of investigators of the Ministry of Internal Affairs, who had taken bribes in exchange for dropping cases under investigation or for not bringing charges against people under preliminary observation."[53] Just as Shelley has noted the personal abuse of justice on the party of individual party members, so Peter Solomon has chronicled the 1920s and 1930s, when judicial interference by members of the local Soviets left the courts barely able to function.[54]

The reforms in the law and legal system after Stalin's death accentuated "socialist legality" and by so doing probably enhanced public confidence in the system. These reforms constituted more than merely the promulgation of new Fundamental Principles and Union Republic codes of law. They terminated

Stalinist terror, gave new meaning to procedure and normative law, reorganized the legal system, and invited citizen participation in the judicial process.[55] In part, this improvement resulted from a new perception of the law and the legal system. The status of courts has risen because they are expected to facilitate development of the New Soviet Person as well as dispense justice. Harold Berman has written that

> the Soviet court is not only interested in applying those rules and procedures to the case before it, but it also is consciously concerned to influence—by its conduct of the case— the attitudes of people with respect to those rules. Moreover, many of the rules themselves are intended to influence attitudes, and not merely to regulate conduct.[56]

The post-Stalinist reforms that converted the courts into agents for social change essentially defines socialist legality. The question here is whether this emphasis on "the strict and unflinching observation and fulfillment of Soviet laws by all organs of the Soviet state, by all institutions and social organizations, by all officials and citizens" has really altered perceptions and enhanced public confidence in the court system.[57] One means for publicizing socialist legality among Soviet citizens is the Ministry of Justice's journal, *Citizen and Law* (Chelovek i zakon). Having begun publication in 1971 with a circulation of 700,000, this periodical's circulation by 1984 rocketed to 8,607,000, down slightly from what it had been in 1983.[58] May we assume that rising circulation means socialist legality is catching on and that confidence in the system is rising as a consequence?

Because crimes against socialist property, economic crimes, and official crimes often garner the headlines, it may be fair to assume that successful prosecution of those charged affect attitudes toward the system. We know of application of the death penalty to those guilty of gross theft of socialist property; however, there are other reverberations. Local procuracies have been criticized for showing a reluctance to make charges even when they have necessary facts; investigations, often superficial, avoid implicating those in the higher positions of responsibility, and, finally, indictments often are careless and suffer when brought under incorrect articles of the code. Consequently, court credibility has become an issue. The judiciary has been criticized for not facing up to its large responsibilities of educating the public: "In appropriate cases the courts are expected to issue so-called Special Rulings, commenting on the causes of the crime, the behavior of the individuals and agencies involved in a particular case, and pointing out action that would be taken to remedy defects that have been discovered by the court."[59] Related to this poor institutional performance are charges that law enforcement is impeded by political pressures. The indictment of a "nomenclatured" manager reflects on the party apparatus responsible for the appointment. In such circumstances judges have been reluctant to incur the displeasure of the local party officials by proceeding vigorously in the case.[60]

Although justice, as we understand it, is precluded in political cases, it often falters in nonpolitical cases as well, when the prestige or reputation of party officials is put to the test. In such instances, professionalism may count for very little. Lawrence Friedman and Zigurs Zile have cogently observed:

In a totalitarian society, the need for professionalism arises out of precisely the opposite phenomenon [from that of a democracy where state control is weak]. Here state control is so unlimited and (at least potentially) so unrestrained that the lawyer is gravely tempted to neglect the interests of his clients in order to advance the interests of society (that is, of the state, since totalitarian states define the social interest as identical with state interests). Particularly since lawyers are not directly compensated by their clients, since they are in some sense employees of the state, since advancement and success depend on satisfying the state rather than particular clients—during the darkest days, even personal freedom or life itself depended on satisfying the state—the lawyer needs professionalization as a bulwark against interference with what he considers proper application of his skills in a professional manner. Freedom to act as a lawyer means, in such a society, freedom from excessive dependence on the state; in a democratic society, freedom to act as a lawyer means freedom from excessive dependence on the client.[61]

The penalties incurred by advocates for excessive zeal in defending their clients is illustrative of the encroachments upon professionalism that occur in a totalitarian system. While in most instances such invasions of professionalism occur in political cases, that they do at all cannot but lessen confidence in the system.[62]

What Friedman and Zile have said about the defense attorney applies equally to the judge or procurator. George Ginsburgs perceives the procurator less an instrument of justice than an agent of the party.[63] After such observations one wonders who would defend the Soviet system of justice. The veteran advocate Dina Kaminskaya appears to do just that: "In spite of all I have said, the judicial system in the Soviet does work, and not only convictions but verdicts of acquittal have been given—less often than true justice required, but given they were."[64]

In a closed society it is difficult to assess the willingness of the people to use the legal system for problem-solving. Undoubtedly, that which exists today is far different from that grudgingly established during the NEP period or Stalin's, which functioned along side of but was often superseded by terroristic extra-judicial bodies.

Today's socialist legality, incessantly proclaimed as the means of modelling society and educating its citizenry, facilitates improvements in the legal system, legal profession, and legal education. There is, of course, no longer talk of the "withering away of the law." Rather, the present Soviet regime relies on law to legitimize and stabilize a very unrevolutionary, even conservative, regime. It is not surprising that Soviet citizens do utilize their legal institutions to resolve their problems. Even such populist elements as people's control, people's assessors, comrades' courts, citizens' patrols, and people's accusers and defenders are incorporated into the legal structure. Fundamental Principles and union republic law codes of the late 1950s and 1960s and subsequent modifications, and, finally, the Brezhnev Constitution—all of these marked the triumph of at least a formalistic legality that is probably acceptable to the great majority of Soviet citizens, political dissidents notwithstanding. Economic enterprises, or so-called production associations, operate in accordance with the laws of property, contract, and tort—incorporating such non-Marxist terminology as "juridical personality," "contract," "operative administration," "accountability," and "jurisconsult" in their workaday functions.

That there have been abuses within the Soviet system—influence peddling, political pressures, corruption—goes without saying; moreover, sentences are often severe.[65] During the "reform" era of the late 1950s, the bar made a strong plea for a more just system. These reformist lawyers, it is usually conceded, won more than they had but less than they had hoped for. Although the "rule of law" does not have deep roots in Russian history, the stress on socialist legality over the last two decades has helped to create a legal culture unimagined by the Bolsheviks in 1917 and a degree of justice unanticipated since the brutalities of the Stalin era.

Apart from dissidents, most Soviet citizens confronted with the tiers of courts and procuracies, an expanded and more qualified legal profession and judiciary, diverse civil and criminal codes and other normative legislation, and a barrage of legal propaganda probably regard the system and its laws as authoritative and an improvement over what they had in the past. This conclusion seems a fair one despite a warranted Western perception that the Soviet legal system still harbors many injustices.

NOTES

1. H. J. Berman, *Justice in the U.S.S.R.: An Interpretation of Soviet Law*, rev. ed. (Cambridge, Mass.: Harvard University Press, 1963), pp. 211–12.

2. D. P. Hammer, "Russia and Roman Law," *The American Slavic and East European Review* 16 (1957), pp. 8–9. See also Olympiad S. Ioffe, "Soviet Law and Roman Law," *Boston University Law Review* 62, pt. 1 (1982), pp. 701–28.

3. Berman, *Justice in the U.S.S.R.*, p. 26.

4. R. Sharlet, *The New Soviet Constitution of 1977: Analysis and Text* (Brunswick, Ohio: King's Court Communications, 1978), pp. 6–7.

5. J. N. Hazard, *Managing Change in the USSR: The Politico-Legal Role of the Soviet Jurist* (Cambridge, England: Cambridge University Press, 1983), pp. 1–5, 170–71.

6. C. S. Rhyne, *Law and Judicial Systems of Nations* (Washington, D.C.: World Peace Through Law Center, 1978) proved helpful in the composition of this section.

7. M. Fainsod, *How Russia is Ruled*, rev. ed. (Cambridge, Mass.: Harvard University Press, 1963), p. 388.

8. G. Ginsburgs, "The Soviet Procuracy and Forty Years of Socialist Legality," *The American Slavic and East European Review* 18 (1959), p. 61.

9. W. Butler, *Soviet Law*, (London: Butterworths, 1983), p. 103. In 1975 only 2.3 percent of 4,008 local procurators were women. Butler also notes that 98 percent of all procurators have higher legal education.

10. Ibid.

11. W. Butler, ed., *Basic Documents on the Soviet Legal System* (New York: Oceana Publications, 1983), p. 191.

12. For arbitration statistics, see G. van den Berg, *The Soviet System of Justice: Figures and Policy* (Dordrect/Boston: Martinius Nijhoff, 1985), pp. 169–72.

13. Butler, ed., *Basic Documents*, p. 126.

14. Ibid., p. 238.

15. Butler, *Soviet Law*, p. 128, and A. Boiter in F.J.M. Feldbrugge, ed., *Encyclopedia of Soviet Law*, 1st ed., vol. 1 (Leyden: Sijhoff, 1972), p. 145. A new edition appeared in 1985. The increase in various categories of jurists must be considered in the context of Soviet demographic trends. The total population in 1970 was 241,640,000; in 1979, 262,085,000; the projection for the year 2000 is approximately 308,050,000.

16. Butler, ed., *Basic Documents*, p. 247–48.

17. Special courts have been discussed by G. P. van den Berg, "Special Courts in the USSR: Their Nature and Activities," *Review of Socialist Law* 8 (1982), pp. 237–50; and Y. I. Luryi, "Special Courts in the USSR: A Comment," *Review of Socialist Law* 10 (1984), pp. 251–57; I. Zeldes, "On Special Courts in the USSR," *Review of Socialist Law* 10 (1984), pp. 57–62; and G. P. van den Berg," Special Courts: Lessons from History," *Review of Socialist Law* 10 (1984). Van den Berg discusses this topic in *The Soviet System of Justice*, pp. 22–26.

18. Berman, *Justice in the USSR*, p. 80. D. D. Barry and H. J. Berman, "The Soviet Legal Profession," *Harvard Law Review* 82 (1968), pp. 1–7.

19. Barry and Berman, "The Soviet Legal Profession," pp. 7, 9.

20. Butler, *Soviet Law*, pp. 78, 87, 95, 103, 110. See also van den Berg's forthcoming work on judicial statistics. For 1982 G. van den Berg has tallied 10,312 people's judges of whom 6,150 were in the RSFSR, 1,665 in the Ukranian Federated Socialist Republic, and 340 in the Belorussian FSR. In all he has listed about 12,900 judges. For another numerical estimate of advocates see Z. Zile, "Soviet Advokatura Twenty-five Years after Stalin," in D. Barry et al., eds., *Soviet Law after Stalin*, vol. 3 (Leyden: Sijhoff, 1979), pp. 208–11. In 1984 there were 12,550 lawyers in the RSFSR; in 1983 they "carried out 6,345,000 assignments for citizens—12.7 percent more than two years before. "Improve the Work of Bar Association Presidiums" *Soviet Law and Government* 23, no. 4 (Spring 1985), p. 71. Van den Berg estimates 738,800 lay assessors in the USSR in his judicial statistics.

21. D. Kaminskaya, *Final Judgment: My Life as a Soviet Defense Attorney* (New York: Simon and Schuster, 1983), p. 28; and Barry and Berman, "The Soviet Legal Profession," p. 28.

22. Kaminskaya, *Final Judgment*, p. 28–29. Cf. Butler, *Soviet Law*, p. 80, on fees.

23. Kaminskaya, *Final Judgment*, pp. 29–30.

24. Butler, *Soviet Law*, pp. 110–11.

25. Z. Zile, "Soviet Legal Education in the Age of the Scientific-Technical Revolution," in G. B. Smith et al., eds., *Soviet and East European Law and the Scientific-Technical Revolution* (New York: Pergamon Press, 1981), pp. 172–73.

26. See Butler, *Soviet Law*, p. 71.

27. Ibid. Butler notes that 4,300 "people's universities" had been established by 1980 and had more than 1,200,000 enrollees. See Zile, "Soviet Legal Education," p. 173.

28. Butler, *Soviet Law*, p. 65. Zile, quoting Soviet sources, gives the following statistics for law school enrollment: 1961–1962: 43,317 total with 7,227 day (16.6 percent), 6,387 evening (14.7 percent), and 29,703 correspondence school (68.7 percent); 1974:

78,900 total with 16,900 day (21.4 percent); 1975–76: total 90,000 of whom 24,000 were day (27 percent). Zile, "Soviet Legal Education," pp. 171–74. In 1979 the All-Union Correspondence Institute awarded 60,000 diplomas. Butler, *Soviet Law*, p. 71.

29. S. Kucherov, "Legal Education," in F.J.M. Feldbrugge, ed., *Encyclopedia of Soviet Law*, 1st ed., vol. 2 (Leyden: Sijhoff, 1972), p. 391.

30. Ibid., pp. 391–92.

31. Barry and Berman, "The Soviet Legal Profession," pp. 9, 171. Zile records that graduates in the early 1950s numbered between 6,000–8,000 annually. There were 7,066 in 1952, 40 percent of whom were day students.

32. Zile, "Legal Education," pp. 174–76.

33. For the low perception of law as a career, see M. Yanowitch and N. T. Dodge, "The Social Evaluation of Occupation in the Soviet Union," *Slavic Review* 18 (1969), pp. 619–43. Law is not even mentioned on the "attractiveness" rating list.

34. Barry and Berman, "The Soviet Legal Profession," p. 21.

35. Butler, *Soviet Law*, p. 95. Of those elected lay assessors, 46.5 percent were workers, 8.3 percent were collective farmers, 46.4 percent were candidate members of the Communist party, and 9.5 percent were members of the Communist Youth League. Of the total, 45 percent were men, and 20.7 percent were under thirty years of age.

36. Ibid.

37. O. Ulc, *The Judge in a Communist State: A View from Within* (Athens: The University of Ohio Press, 1972), p. 57. Kaminskaya, *Final Judgment*, pp. 59–60; and K. Simis, *USSR—The Corrupt Society: The Secret World of Soviet Capitalism* (New York: Simon and Schuster, 1982), pp. 96–125.

38. "Female Lawyers (Statistical Data)," *Soviet Law and Government* (Fall 1977), pp. 88–89, 90. In the higher judicial organs, that is, in the supreme courts of union and autonomous republics, and of regional, territorial, and area courts, women numbered 985 or 34.2 percent of the total. Women members of supreme courts of union republics totaled 108, or 24.5 percent of the total. The same statistics are recorded in J. G. Collignon, *Les juristes en Union soviétique* (Paris: Editions du C.N.R.S., 1977), pp. 521–24.

39. Kaminskaya, *Final Judgment*, pp. 56–57.

40. Barry and Berman, "The Soviet Legal Profession," pp. 20–21.

41. "In 1982, 25 percent of the people's court judges were elected for the first time, suggesting that some 2,500 judges had either moved into a superior court or found employment in the legal profession or national economy." Butler, *Soviet Law*, p. 95.

42. Barry and Berman, "The Soviet Legal Profession," p. 32. D. D. Barry, "Leaders of the Soviet Legal Profession: An Analysis of Biographical Data and Career Patterns," *Canadian American Slavic Studies* 6, no. 1 (1972), pp. 73–92.

43. Barry and Berman, "The Soviet Legal Profession," p. 34.

44. D. D. Barry and C. Barner-Barry, *Contemporary Soviet Politics: An Introduction*, 2d ed. (Englewood Cliffs, N.J.: Prentice-Hall, 1982), p. 166.

45. Ibid.

42. As quoted by J. N. Hazard, "The Soviet Court as a Source of Law," *Washington Law Review* 24 (1949), p. 81.

47. D. D. Barry and C. Barner-Barry, "The USSR Supreme Court and the System-ization of Soviet Criminal Law," in D.D. Barry et al., eds., *Codification in the Communist World* (Leyden: Sijhoff, 1975).

48. Cf. Berman, *Justice in the USSR*, pp. 268–73, 379–89. The following old Russian adages on courts are mentioned in Collignon, *Les juristes en Union soviétique*: "In courts

we are all equal, all guilty." "From the courts, as from a pond, nobody leaves without being wet." "Innocent in reality, but guilty on paper." "Don't go to court unless you are brought there." "The court has rendered justice; you have now become poor." And about the venality of lawyers: "A bribe is not God, but as with God a bribe forgives." "Money does not talk, but it produces miracles." "What matters to lawyers is what goes in their pockets." "Recognize merchants by their lies and lawyers by their purses." "To the rich to plead costs a trifle; to the poor it costs life." "Don't fight the strong; don't plead against the rich." "This is our misfortune: you go to justice, but you do not find justice." (pp. 5–6)

49. B. G. Guerney, ed., *A Treasury of Russian Literature* (New York: Vanguard Press, 1943), p. 161.

50. For peasant suspicions see R. Beerman, "The Rule of Law and Legality in the Soviet Union," *Review of Socialist Law* 1 (1975), pp. 97–111; and "Pre-Revolutionary Russian Peasant Laws," in W. E. Butler, ed., *Russian Law: Historical and Political Perspectives* (Leyden: Sijhoff, 1977), pp. 184–85. For a highly positive appraisal of the effects of the 1964 reforms, see S. Kucherov, "The Legal Profession in Pre- and Post-Revolutionary Russia," *The American Journal of Comparative Law* 5 (1956), pp. 443–70.

51. "Party Members and the Courts-Exploitation of Privilege" presented at symposium on *Ruling Communist Parties and Their Status Under Laws*, University of Kiel, June 14–16, 1984 (to be published). See also R. Sharlet, "The Communist Party and the Administration of Justice in the USSR" in D.D. Barry et al., eds., *Soviet Law after Stalin*, vol. 3 (Leyden: Sijhoff, 1979), pp. 321–92.

52. D. Kaminskaya, *Final Judgment*, p. 56.

53. Ibid., p. 62. For more on judicial corruption, see Simis, *USSR—The Corrupt Society*, pp. 96–125.

54 "Local Political Power and Soviet Criminal Justice 1922–1941." Paper presented at the symposium on *Ruling Communist Parties and their Status under Law* at the University of Kiel, June 14–16, 1984 (to be published).

55. H. J. Berman, "The Dilemma of Soviet Law Reform," *Harvard Law Review* 76 (1963), p. 932. See also Berman, *Justice in the U.S.S.R.*, pp. 66–96.

56. H. J. Berman, "The Educational Role of the Soviet Court," *International and Comparative Law Review Quarterly* 21 (1972), p. 91. Examples of this "parental role" of the law appear in G. Feifer, *Justice in Moscow* (New York: Delta Publishing Co., 1965), pp. 29–79.

57. F.J.M. Feldbrugge, ed., *Enyclopedia of Soviet Law*, 1st ed., p. 619.

58. The number of issues printed is noted in each issue. A pessimistic Soviet view is recorded in "Why the Public is Ignorant of the Law," *Current Digest of the Soviet Press* 37, no. 3 (February 13, 1985), pp. 15–16.

59. N. Lampert, "Law and Order in the USSR: The Case of Economic and Official Crime," *Soviet Studies* 36 (1984), p. 375.

60. Ibid., pp. 380–81. See also J. Lowenhardt, "Nomenklatura and the Soviet Constitution," *Review of Soviet Law* 10 (1984), pp. 35–55.

61. L. M. Friedman and Z. L. Zile, "Soviet Legal Profession: Recent Developments in Law and Practice," *Wisconsin Law Review* (1964), p. 36. For the Soviet lawyer, see G. D. Cameron III, *The Soviet Lawyer and His System* (Ann Arbor: Division of Research, Graduate School of Business Administration, University of Michigan, 1978), which contains a good bibliography of available English language sources.

62. Cf. "The Case of the Two Boys," in Kaminskaya, *Final Judgment*, pp. 65–157.
63. Ginsburgs, "The Soviet Procuracy," pp. 34–62.
64. Kaminskaya, *Final Judgment*, p. 62.
65. See G. van den Berg, "The Soviet Union and the Death Penalty," *Soviet Studies* 35 (1983), pp. 154–74. Van den Berg has discussed Soviet sentencing policy in *The Soviet System of Justice*, pp. 59–108.

BIBLIOGRAPHY

The present bibliography is a selective one of accessible English-language works published, with some notable exceptions, in the last few years. For a more extensive bibliography on the Soviet legal system to 1978, the author recommends George Dana Cameron III, *The Soviet Lawyer and His System* (Ann Arbor: Division of Research, Graduate School of Business Administration, University of Michigan, 1978).

Adams, J. S. *Citizen Inspectors in the Soviet Union: The People's Control Committee.* New York: Praeger Publishers, 1977.

Barry, D. D. "Leaders of the Soviet Legal Profession: An Analysis of Biographical Data and Career Patterns." *Canadian American Slavic Studies* 6, no. 1 (1972), pp. 73–92.

———, and C. Barner-Barry. *Contemporary Soviet Politics: An Interpretation.* 2d ed. Englewood Cliffs, N.J.: Prentice-Hall, 1982.

———. "The USSR Supreme Court and the Systemization of Soviet Criminal Law." In D. D. Barry, F.J.M. Feldbrugge, and D. Lasok, eds., *Codification in the Communist World.* Leyden: Sijhoff, 1975.

Barry, D. D., and H. J. Berman. "The Soviet Legal Profession." *Harvard Law Review* 82 (1968), pp. 1–41.

Barry, D. D., G. Ginsburgs, and P. B. Maggs, *Soviet Law after Stalin.* 3 vols. Leyden: Sijhoff, 1977–79.

Beerman, R. "Pre-Revolutionary Russian Peasant Laws." In W. E. Butler, ed., *Russian Law: Historical and Political Perspectives.* Leyden: Sijhoff, 1977.

———. "The Rule of Law and Legality in the Soviet Union." *Review of Socialist Law* 1 (1975), pp. 97–111.

Beirne, P., and R. Sharlet, eds., *Pashukanis: Selected Writings on Marxism and Law.* New York: Academic Press, 1980.

Berg, G. P. van den. *The Soviet System of Justice: Figures and Policy.* Dordrecht/Boston: Martinius Nijhoff, 1985.

———. "The Soviet Union and the Death Penalty." *Soviet Studies* 35 (1983), pp. 154–74.

———. "Special Courts: Lessons from History." *Review of Socialist Law* 10 (1984), pp. 263–76.

———. "Special Courts in the USSR: Their Nature and Activities." *Review of Socialist Law* 8 (1982), pp. 237–50.

———. "The Stalinist System of Justice and Terror and Some Implications for the Present Day." A paper delivered at the Third World Congress for Soviet and East European Studies. Washington, D.C., October 30-November 4, 1985.

Berman, H. J. "The Dilemma of Soviet Law Reform." *Harvard Law Review* 76 (1963), pp. 929–51.

————. "The Educational Role of the Soviet Court." *International and Comparative Law Review Quarterly* 21 (1972), pp. 81–94.

————. *Justice in the U.S.S.R.: An Interpretation of Soviet Law.* Cambridge, Mass.: Harvard University Press, 1963.

————. *Soviet Criminal Law and Procedure: The RSFSR Codes.* 2d ed. Cambridge, Mass: Harvard University Press, 1972.

Berman, H. J., and J. Quigley. "Comment on the Presumption of Innocence under Soviet Law." *UCLA Law Review* 15 (1968), pp. 1230–39.

Berman, H. J., and J. Spindler. "Soviet Comrades' Courts." *Washington Law Review* 38 (1963), pp. 842–910.

Butler, W. *Soviet Law.* London: Butterworths, 1983.

————, ed. *Basic Documents on the Soviet Legal System.* New York: Oceana Publications, 1983.

Christian, D. "The Supervisory Function in Russian and Soviet History." *Slavic Review* 41 (1982), pp. 73–90.

Collignon, J. G. *Les juristes en Union soviétique.* Paris: Editions du C.N.R.S., 1977.

Fainsod, M. *How Russia is Ruled.* rev. ed. Cambridge, Mass.: Harvard University Press, 1963.

Feifer, G. *Justice in Moscow.* New York: Delta Publishing Co., 1965.

Feldbrugge, F.J.M., ed. *Encyclopedia of Soviet Law.* 2 vols., 1st ed. Leyden: Sijhoff, 1972, revised in 1985.

————. *Perspectives on Soviet Law for the 1980s.* The Hague: M. Nijhoff, 1982.

Fletcher, G. "The Presumption of Innocence in the Soviet Union." *UCLA Law Review* 15 (1968), pp. 1203–25.

Friedman, L. M., and Z. L. Zile. "Soviet Legal Profession: Recent Developments in Law and Practice." *Wisconsin Law Review* (1964), pp. 32–77.

Giddings, J. "The Jurisconsult in the USSR." *Review of Socialist Law* 1 (1975), pp. 171–211.

Ginsburgs, G. "The Political Undercurrents of the Legal Dialogue." *UCLA Law Review* 15 (1968), pp. 1226–29.

————. "The Soviet Procuracy and Forty Years of Socialist Legality." *The American Slavic and East European Review* 18 (1959), pp. 34–62.

Gorgone, J. "Soviet Jurists in the Legislative Arena: The Reform of Criminal Procedure, 1956–58." *Soviet Union* 3 (1976), pp. 1–35.

Gray, W. "Legal Education in the Soviet Union and Eastern Europe." *International Lawyer* 5 (1971), pp. 738–49.

Hammer, D. P. "Russia and Roman Law." *The American and East European Review* 16 (1957), pp. 1–13.

Hazard, J. N. *Managing Change in the USSR: The Politico-Legal Role of the Soviet Jurist.* Cambridge, England: Cambridge University Press, 1983.

————. *Settling Disputes in Soviet Society.* New York: Octagon Books, 1978.

————. "The Soviet Court as a Source of Law." *Washington Law Review* 24 (1949), pp. 80–90.

Hazard, J. N., W. Butler, and P. Maggs. *The Soviet Legal System: The Law in the 1980s.* New York: Oceana Publication, 1984.

Hellie, R. "Early Modern Russian Law: The Ulozhenie of 1649" [Distributed at NEH-sponsored symposium on Russian and Soviet law at Rutgers Law School (Camden), May 25-June 1, 1984].

Huskey, E. *Russian Lawyers and the Soviet State: The Origins and Development of the Soviet Bar, 1917–1939*. Princeton, N.J.: Princeton University Press, 1986.

———. "Vyshinsky, Krylenko, and the Struggle for Mastery over Soviet Legal Affairs, 1932–36." A paper delivered at the Third World Congress for Soviet and East European Studies. Washington, D.C., October 30-November 4, 1985.

"Improve the Work of Bar Association Presidiums." *Soviet Law and Government* 23, no. 4 (Spring 1985), pp. 71–78.

Ioffe, O. S. "Soviet Law and Roman Law." *Boston University Law Review* 62 (1982), pp. 701–28.

———. *Soviet Law and Socialist Reality*. Dordrecht/Boston: Martinius Nijhoff, 1985.

Ioffe, O. S., and P. Maggs. *Soviet Law in Theory and Practice*. London and Boston: Oceana Publications, 1983.

Juviler, P. *Revolutionary Law and Order: Politics and Social Change in the USSR*. New York: The Free Press, 1976.

Kaiser, D. *The Growth of the Law in Medieval Russia*. Princeton, N.J.: Princeton University Press, 1980.

Kaminskaya, D. *Final Judgment: My Life as a Soviet Defense Attorney*. New York: Simon and Schuster, 1982.

Kroll, R. "From Russia with Law." *Student Lawyer* (February 1984).

Kucherov, S. *Courts, Lawyers, and Trials under the Last Three Tsars*. New York: F.A. Praeger, 1953.

———. "The Legal Profession in Pre- and Post-Revolutionary Russia." *The American Journal of Comparative Law* 5 (1956), pp. 443–70.

Lampert, N. "Law and Order in the USSR: The Case of Economic and Official Crime." *Soviet Studies* 36 (1984), pp. 366–85.

———. *Whistleblowing in the Soviet Union: Complaints and Abuses under State Socialism*. New York: Shocken Books, 1985.

Lowenhardt, J. "Nomenklatura and the Soviet Constitution." *Review of Soviet Law* 10 (1984), pp. 35–55.

Luryi, Y. I. "Jurisconsults in the Soviet Economy." In D. D. Barry, ed., *Soviet Law Since Stalin*, vol. 3. Leyden: Sijhoff, 1979. Pp. 168–206.

———. "Special Courts in the USSR: A Comment." *Review of Socialist Law* 8 (1982), pp. 251–57.

Maggs, P.B., G. Smith, and G. Ginsburgs. *Law and Economic Development in the Soviet Union*. Boulder, Colo.: Westview Press, 1982.

McCain, M. "Soviet Jurists Divided: Conservatives and Liberals." A paper presented to the Central States Slavic Conference in November 1979.

———. "Soviet Lawyers in the Reform Debate: Cohesion and Efficacy." A paper presented at the American Association for the Advancement of Slavic Studies, October 1979.

Malone, A. "The Soviet Bar." *Cornell Law Quarterly* 46 (1961), pp. 258–89.

Oda, H. "Criminal Law Reform in the 1930s." A paper delivered at the Third World Congress for Soviet and East European Studies. Washington, D.C., October 30-November 4, 1985.

Razi, G. M. "Legal Education and the Role of Law in the Soviet Union and the Countries of Eastern Europe." *California Law Review* 48 (1960), pp. 776–804.

Remington, T. "Institution Building in Bolshevik Russia: The Case of 'State Kontrol'."
    Slavic Review 41 (1982), pp. 91–103.
Rhyne, C. S., ed., *Law and Judicial Systems of Nations*. Washington: World Peace
    Through Law Center, 1978.
Sharlet, R. "The Communist Party and the Administration of Justice in the USSR." In
    D. D. Barry, G. Ginsburgs, and P. B. Maggs, eds., *Soviet Law after Stalin*. Vol.
    3. Leyden: Sijhoff, 1979. Pp. 321–92.
———. *The New Soviet Constitution of 1977. Analysis and Text*. Brunswick, Ohio:
    King's Court Communications, 1978.
———. "Pashukanis and the Rise of Soviet Marxist Jurisprudence, 1924–30." *Soviet
    Union* 1, no. 2 (1974), pp. 103–21.
Shelley, L. *Lawyers in Soviet Work Life*. New Brunswick, N.J.: Rutgers University Press,
    1984.
———. "Party members and the Courts—Exploitation of Privilege." Paper presented
    at symposium on *Ruling Communist Parties and their Status under Law*, University
    of Kiel, June 14–16, 1984 (to be published by Documentation Office for East
    European Law, Leiden).
Simis, K. *USSR—The Corrupt Society: The Secret World of Soviet Capitalism*. New
    York: Simon and Schuster, 1982.
Solomon, P. "The Great Purge and the Administration of Criminal Justice." A paper
    delivered at the Third World Congress for Soviet and East European Studies.
    Washington, D.C., October 30-November 4, 1985.
———. "Local Political Power and Soviet Criminal Justice 1922–1941." Paper presented
    at the symposium on *Ruling Communist Parties and their Status under Law* at
    the University of Kiel, June 14–16, 1984 (to be published).
Szawlowski, R. "The Supreme Control Organs in the USSR—Past and Present." *Review
    of Socialist Law* 5 (1979), pp. 17–46.
Ulc, O. *The Judge in a Communist State: A View from Within*. Athens: The University
    of Ohio Press, 1972.
Voslensky, M. *Nomenklatura: The Soviet Ruling Elite*. Translated by E. Mosbacher.
    New York: Doubleday & Co., 1984.
Wortman, R. *The Development of Russian Legal Consciousness*. Chicago: The University
    of Chicago Press, 1976.
Yaney, G. "Bureaucracy as Culture: A Comment." *Slavic Review* 41 (1982), pp. 104–
    11.
Zeldes, I. "On Special Courts in the USSR." *Review of Socialist Law* 10 (1984), pp. 57–
    62.
Zile, Z. "Soviet Legal Education in the Age of the Scientific-Technical Revolution." In
    G. B. Smith, P. B. Maggs, and G. Ginsburgs, eds., *Soviet and East European
    Law and the Scientific-Technical Revolution*. New York: Pergamon Press, 1981.
    Pp. 170–212.

16

SPAIN

Thomas D. Lancaster and Micheal W. Giles

Liberalization and political reform of authoritarian regimes institutionally and procedurally alter many aspects of a political system. As an integral part of both authoritarian and liberal democratic political systems, democratic reform undoubtedly affects the judiciary's conduct and operations in many ways. Spain's recent transition from Franco's authoritarian regime to the present constitutional monarchy with a parliamentary form of government is no exception. Franco's death in November 1975 ushered in the beginning of the end of nearly four decades of traditional military dictatorship in Spain. This authoritarian rule followed Spain's previous attempt at liberal democracy during the Second Republic of 1931–1939 and its violent end with Franco's Nationalist victory in the Spanish Civil War of 1936–1939. Following Franco's demise and the restoration of the monarchy, King Juan Carlos I initially guided and then oversaw the dismantling of many Francoist political and governmental institutions and the creation, under the leadership of Adolfo Suárez and others, of a new system for liberal democratic behavior. The major events of Spain's peaceful transition to democracy such as the Referendum on Political Reform in 1976, the general elections of 1977, 1979, and 1982, the Socialist victory in this last election, and the process of devolution for Spain's many regions have all received a great deal of attention.[1] However, the impact of these democratic reforms on the country's judicial system has largely been neglected. This chapter seeks to address this shortcoming through consideration of contemporary Spain's judicial structures and processes.

THE DEVELOPMENT OF THE LEGAL SYSTEM

The Spanish legal system, like most European legal systems, bears the essential traits and history of a civil law system. While owing a small debt to pre-Roman customary law, Muslim law, and Germanic law, Roman law is the predominant element in the Spanish legal tradition. Between 200 B.C. and A.D. 400, Spain was part of the Roman Empire and completely within its legal system. Even after the decline of Rome, the Roman legal tradition found expression in Spain through its incorporation in local codes. For example, Alphonsus X of Castile (1252–1282) had drafted a code of laws known as the *Siete Partidas*, which, while incorporating local law and custom, borrowed heavily from Roman law.[2] Ironically, the existence of major compilations like the Siete Partidas actually slowed the advance of the "rediscovered" Roman law during the Renaissance. While, in some areas of Europe, no body of systematic law existed to compete with the Roman law being taught in the Italian universities, this was not true in Spain. The modern period of Spanish law dates from Napoleon's invasion in 1808. Under the French influence, a codification of Spanish law was undertaken that, as the century progressed, saw the introduction of penal and civil codes and codes of commerce and procedure.

While the Spanish legal system falls in the mainstream of the civil tradition, it has two characteristics that somewhat differentiate it from other countries within that tradition. The first is the strong influence of the Catholic church. Perhaps no European country other than Italy has been as openly Catholic as Spain. The Catholic nature of Spain had been recognized in the Papal Concordat of 1753 and 1851 and reestablished with the Concordat of 1953. Spain has been a "confessional" state, with canon law, the law of the Roman Catholic church, being accepted as an area of public law. This influence is most apparent in family law, where the Spanish codes closely parallel the canon law. One example of this influence was the absence of divorce in Spain during the Franco period. The Spanish marriage was exclusive and indissoluble.[3] This influence could also be seen in the existence of "private crimes" such as adultery.[4] The reintroduction of democracy to Spain has altered the position of the Catholic church. First, the democratic Constitution of 1978 is religiously neutral. This has resulted in opposition to its passage by some more conservative elements of the Catholic hierarchy. Second, the Concordat of 1953 was replaced in 1979 by a new set of agreements, which, while recognizing the Roman Catholic church and the inviolability of its places of worship, phases out direct subsidies for the church and makes religious instruction in the schools noncompulsory.[5] In an earlier agreement, King Juan Carlos I gave up his traditional right to appoint bishops, and the Vatican agreed to allow priests and nuns to be tried in civil courts without the requirement of authorization from their superiors. While these changes reduce the formal role of the church, Catholic moralism remains an important force on both the Spanish legal and political systems.

A second differentiating characteristic of the Spanish legal tradition is the impact of regionalism and Spain's strong regional diversity. Several regions of Spain not only have a political history and presence but also distinct legal traditions. The laws unique to these regions are referred to as "foral laws." The existence of foral laws delayed the adoption of a national civil code throughout most of the nineteenth century. A code was only accepted after it made specific provision for the inclusion of appendices of the foral laws of each of the regions.

There was little initial movement toward the compilation of these laws. By 1926, only the Foral Appendix for Aragon had been completed. The creation of the Commission General de Codificación brought renewed activity in the 1960s. In 1959, the compilation for Vizcaya and Alava was enacted followed by that for Catalunya in 1960, the Baleares Islands in 1961, Galicia in 1963, and a revision of the appendix for Aragon in 1967.[6] The foral laws provide a symbol of regional culture and heritage and an element of diversity not common to highly centralized civil law systems.

THE ORGANIZATION OF THE COURT SYSTEM

The Ordinary Courts

While the governmental structure of Spain has shifted since 1800 between monarchy, dictatorship, republicanism, and a parliamentary monarchy, the structure of the "ordinary" courts has remained relatively unchanged. By "ordinary" we refer to courts of general civil and criminal jurisdiction. At the pinnacle of the national court structure is the Supreme Court. The Supreme Court was created in its present form in 1812. The Supreme Court sits in Madrid and has appellate jurisdiction throughout the country. The Court is divided into chambers (Salas de Justicia) each of which specializes in an area of litigation. The first chamber hears civil appeals, the second criminal appeals; the third, fourth, and fifth appeals from special administrative tribunals; and the sixth appeals from the labor courts— Magistraturas de Trabajo.

In civil law countries, the courts generally have eschewed the role of creating law. Legal creativity is attributed to the legislature and its code-making power. While Spain follows this tradition, there is also a clear recognition that the Spanish Supreme Court is a source of law. The Spanish Civil Code specifically recognizes "general principles of law" as a suitable subsidiary source of law in the absence of specific provisions of the code.[7] Moreover, judicial practices that are based on several decisions of the Supreme Court assume the character of legal doctrine (doctrina legal) or, more recently, jurisprudencia. The failure of a lower court to follow these "doctrines" is the basis for appeal to the Supreme Court.[8] Quite expectedly, two-thirds of the lower court judges indicate that they give decisive value to previous decisions of the Spanish Supreme Court when deciding similar cases.[9] The Spanish Supreme Court's decisions thus have a value in some ways like "precedent" in the American and British systems.

The Supreme Court resolves the cases it hears on appeal in one of two ways. If the appeal is based on the contention that a lower court has misapplied a precedent of the Supreme Court, then upon finding for the appellant, the Court may resentence the case. However, if the appeal rests on a procedural or formal matter, the Court will "quash" the decision and return the case to the lower court for resentencing.[10]

The Supreme Court may also meet as a combined court or Plenary Tribunal.

In this configuration, it serves as a court of first instance to try persons of high rank such as politicians, judges, and civil servants. It has rarely performed this function.

The Supreme Court receives cases on appeal from Territorial and Provincial Audiencias. Territorial Audiencias serve geographic areas that correspond to the original kingdoms of Spain. They serve one or more provinces and are headed by a president. The Provincial Audiencias serve subdivisions of the original kingdoms structured to maintain population balance among the courts. A National Audiencia was created in 1977. The audiencias are collegial courts with cases heard by three judge panels. Both Territorial and Provincial Audiencias serve as appellate courts in civil matters for cases previously heard in municipal and regional courts and Courts of First Instance and as trial courts in serious criminal cases. Spain's Constitution of 1978 provides for a jury trial in audiencia courts. Territorial Audiencias also have administrative courts that hear charges raised against local governmental authorities and nonministerial national officials.

Each province is divided into smaller areas served by trial courts—Juez de Partido. These are referred to as Courts of First Instance and Instruction. In civil matters, they are presided over by a single judge. Because Spanish civil procedure is essentially adversarial, the burden of activity rests with the parties while the judge plays a relatively passive role. The procedure differs from that of an American court in two principal ways. First, jury trials are not available in civil cases. Second, although there is an opportunity for an oral hearing, proceedings tend to be more written than oral.[11] Appeal of the judge's decision in civil cases lies with the Provincial or Territorial Audiencia. Table 1 reflects the increasing use of Spain's civil court system, particularly following the end of authoritarian rule.

Spanish criminal procedure is more in the Continental accusatorial than the Anglo-American adversarial mode. In criminal cases, the judge of the Court of First Instance and Instruction acts as an examining magistrate or a court of inquiry. In this capacity, the judge directs the police investigation, takes depositions of witnesses, orders tests, and makes decisions about pretrial detention of the defendant. Upon a finding of sufficient evidence to do so, the judge forwards the case and the written record or "Sumario" to the Provincial Audiencia for trial and sentencing.[12]

The Special Courts

In addition to the national courts, the municipal areas are served by district courts and justices of the peace. These courts hear cases involving minor criminal and civil matters. They have a centralized structure so that a judge may advance ultimately to the position of a judge of a municipal court in one of the large cities.

In addition to the ordinary courts, the Spanish legal system has special tribunals with jurisdiction over limited subject areas. The Franco regime heavily used

Table 1
Contested Civil Law Cases in Spain

Year	District Courts & of the Peace	Courts of First Instance		Territorial Audiencias		Supreme Court First Sala
		Entered	Resolved	Entered	Resolved	Sentences
1970	150,184	78,448	72,220	6412	6402	726
1971	156,035	84,960	82,499	7342	7099	707
1972	144,624	78,660	78,342	7469	7336	628
1973	135,092	75,984	74,171	7260	7309	624
1974	140,925	93,510	87,030	7308	7017	659
1975	139,265	107,786	99,602	7910	7220	580
1976	146,350	114,328	108,143	9055	7602	580
1977	148,572	128,530	117,440	10,132	8362	506
1978	149,661	145,933	133,907	11,616	8802	538
1979	141,859	150,290	137,022	10,837	9171	512

Source: Estadisticas Judiciales de Espana, 1979.
Madrid: Instituto Nacional de Estadistica, 1983,
pages 19,20,21.

such courts, and, while many have been eliminated since the transition to democracy, others still operate. For example, special tribunals such as the labor courts—magistraturas de trabajo—which hear disputes between employees and management, have become increasingly important, as seen in Tables 2 and 3, following Spain's transition and the greater role played by trade unions and other labor organizations. Other special tribunals in Spain include the Tribunal for the Defense of Commercial Competition, which hears complaints concerning antitrust and monopolistic practices, and the self-descriptive Tribunals for Currency Crimes and Tribunal for Customs and Tariffs Infractions. Of most interest are the special courts to hear administrative complaints and the past use of military and other special tribunals for political purposes. The Constitutional Court, which may be considered a "special court," is of sufficient importance to be discussed separately.

In the United States, complaints against the rules, procedures, or actions of administrative agencies, with some exceptions and restrictions, are within the jurisdiction of ordinary courts either at the trial court or the appellate levels. In civil law countries, special administrative tribunals exist to hear such disputes. In some systems, these administrative tribunals are staffed by civil servants and are subject to the appellate supervision of an administrative body. In France,

Table 2
Labor Court Caseloads in Spain

Year	Provincial Magistrates		Central Court of Labour		Supreme Court 6th Sala	
	Matters presented	Matters decided	Appeals entered	Appeals resolved	Infraction of law	Form of lawbreaking
1971	135,074	129,511	5,036	5,199	745	658
1972	131,518	137,672	6,773	5,853	863	914
1973	126,250	129,538	6,493	6,007	699	1,492
1974	171,250	154,870	6,188	6,133	799	1,336
1975	192,838	183,488	6,643	6,493	653	983
1976	259,306	236,077	8,554	6,720	751	1,306
1977	291,909	256,630	11,104	7,197	876	705
1978	385,219	378,117	0,935	7,857	986	1,947
1979	428,913	419,783	12,604	8,145	999	3,600

Source: Estadisticas Judiciales de Espana, 1979. Madrid: INE, 1983, pages 95, 96.

Table 3
Labor Justice in Spain, Decisions by Provincial Magistrates of Labor

Year	Favorable to to the Worker	Partially Favorable to the Worker	Disfavorable to the Worker
1971	31,311	6,012	19,245
1972	33,712	5,530	24,789
1973	32,792	5,482	22,348
1974	38,802	6,693	22,361
1975	45,796	6,798	25,918
1976	64,115	11,636	35,264
1977	74,996	4,722	38,106
1978	97,261	7,029	43,886
1979	105,469	39,167	10,566

Source: Estadisticas Judiciales de Espana, 1979. Madrid: INE, 1983, page 95.

for example, appeals in the administrative court system lie ultimately with the Council of State. The French administrative tribunals are staffed by civil servants and graduates of the Ecole Nationale d'Administration (ENA). The members of the Council of State are drawn similarly from the elite of the civil service and from the ENA. In Spain, on the other hand, since 1956 the administrative courts have been incorporated as a special chamber of the audiencias with appeals to the Supreme Court. Table 4 shows the increasing work of these administrative courts in Spain. Judges of the courts are career jurists recruited in the same manner as the judges of the ordinary courts, but they specialize in administrative law. Thus, unlike most of its neighbors, Spain's administrative tribunals are integrated with and under the supervision of the ordinary courts.[13]

The military courts constitute a set of special tribunals which have been the focus of controversy in the past. The jurisdiction of military courts is traditionally limited to members of the military. Even under conditions of civil war, the United States Supreme Court refused to extend the jurisdiction of military courts to include civilians, so long as the ordinary courts were open and operative.[14] However, this has not been the history of Spanish military courts. Even prior to the rise of Franco, the jurisdiction of Spanish military courts was extended to offenses such as insulting the military in print, support of separatist ideas, and armed robberies, regardless of whether committed by a member of the military or a civilian. Military jurisdiction was restricted under the short-lived Second Republic but expanded again under Franco.[15] Thus, historically the Spanish military courts have been a tool for oppression of potential civilian political opposition. As might be expected, Spain's democratic Constitution of 1978 limits "the exercise of military jurisdiction strictly within military limits."[16]

In 1963, the Franco government created the Court of Public Order. It was staffed with judges drawn from the ordinary courts and had jurisdiction over cases involving subversion defined broadly, for example, rebellion and illegal propaganda. In its first decade, the court heard an estimated 1,000 cases. It was created with the support of the military, which sought to reduce the highly controversial use of military courts to try civilians. The creation of the Court of Public Order appears to have achieved that effect. Between 1955 and 1958, 40 percent of the defendants in military trials were civilians, but between 1963 and 1966 this figure was only 22 percent. The Court of Public Order, as a patently political court, was a focal point of protest. In 1970, the Spanish bar took the unprecedented step of unanimously approving a statement calling for its dissolution.[17] The Court of Public Order was eliminated with the adoption of Spain's 1978 Constitution.

Constitutional Court

The major judicial innovation of the post-Franco Constitution is the creation of the Constitutional Court. Ordinary civil law courts have always been concerned primarily with private law disputes between private parties and not with issues

Table 4

Administrative Justice in Spain: Classification of Decisions of the Territorial Audiencias

Year	Totally favorable to Administration	Partially favorable to Administration	Disfavorable to the Administration
1970	1698 46.7%	511 14.1%	1428 39.3%
1971	1911 50.8%	505 13.4%	1345 35.8%
1972	2080 54.7%	599 15.7%	1127 29.6%
1973	1795 44.3%	669 16.5%	1592 39.3%
1974	3046 48.6%	790 12.6%	2435 38.8%
1975	2314 47.8%	604 12.5%	1928 39.8%
1976	3857 50.5%	820 10.7%	2966 38.8%
1977	4121 52.0%	1030 13.0%	2775 35.0%
1978	4115 55.5%	1020 13.7%	2288 30.8%
1979	4172 53.2%	1026 13.1%	2650 33.8%
Total	29,109 50.9%	7,574 13.2%	20,534 35.9%

Source: Adapted from Estadisticas Judiciales de Espana, 1979. Madrid : INE, 1983, page 76.

of public law. The constitutionality of a state or federal statute in the United States may be the subject of a case before an ordinary court, while civil law systems' ordinary courts traditionally have not performed this function. Since World War II, several European countries have attempted to deal with the issue of the constitutionality of government statutes and actions by the creation of special "constitutional" courts with the power of some form of judicial review. The creation of the Spanish Constitutional Court follows this trend.

The Constitutional Court has twelve members with each judge serving a nine-year term. This even number of judges makes it more difficult to reach a decision, reflecting the Constituent Cortes' conservative orientation and desire to force judicial "votes of quality." The Court's nomination and selection process provides a broad institutional base. The Spanish Cortes (parliament) proposes eight judges, four each from the Congress of Deputies and the Senate. The government proposes two members and the General Council of the Judiciary the other two. Nominations in both parliamentary houses require a three-fifths majority. This selection requirement mandates extensive political or ideological agreement since a three-fifths majority generally requires looking beyond the governmental majority and into the opposition. To be eligible for the Court, an individual must be a jurist of known competence with at least fifteen years of experience. Thus, the nomination process assures the legitimacy and independence of the Constitutional Court by assuring the selection of respected jurists while placing the selection of its members in the hands of politically oriented institutions. The latter slowly adjusts the Court, and its interpretation of the Constitution, to prevalent political and ideological orientations.

The Constitutional Court is an autonomous institution that finances itself through its own budget and administers its own expenditures. The Court also establishes its own internal organization and operations.[18] The president is the Court's highest representative and is elected for a three-year term. The Court hears some appeals of constitutionality and questions of prior control of constitutionality as a twelve judge tribunal or plenum. For cases involving *amparo* appeals, the Court divides into two *salas* with six judges each. The president of the Constitutional Court chairs one sala and the vice-president the other. The Court further divides itself into sections, each with three judges. The sections study the admissibility of appeals and handle the normal office work. The plenum can claim for itself any matter before the Court and not relegate it to one of the smaller, internal subdivisions.

The Constitutional Court hears three types of cases. First, and perhaps most importantly, are cases involving the constitutionality of the statutes, organic laws, and general laws of the General Cortes, the laws of the Autonomous Communities, and executive acts with legal force such as decree-laws. Legislative decrees and the rules of legislative assemblies are also subject to the review of the Court on the issue of constitutionality. The question of constitutionality can reach the Court through three mechanisms. The first mechanism is the *unconstitutionality appeal*. This is a direct petition to the Court to annul a law by declaring it to be contrary to the Constitution. Those able to petition the Court in this manner are the president of the government, the public defender, fifty members of the Congress of Deputies, fifty senators, the executives of the Autonomous Communities, and, when applicable, their assemblies. The unconstitutionality appeal must be made within three months after the law's publication, unlike France where action must be taken prior to promulgation. An unconstitutionality appeal generally does not suspend implementation of a law. The national government, however, may suspend resolutions and laws passed by the Autonomous Communities.[19] The national government in this manner may counter or oppose the Autonomous Communities, legally binding dispositions and resolutions. In such a situation, the Constitutional Court must either ratify or lift the suspension within five months. This judicial procedure permits greater central governmental control and facilitates legal and political uniformity among the Autonomous Communities. This central government prerogative grants political controls comparable to Italian law concerning its regional government.

A second mechanism through which cases of unconstitutionality reach the Constitutional Court is that of *prior control of constitutionality*. When considering a law or treaty under this procedure, the Constitutional Court performs a function similar to that of the "advisory opinions" offered by some state supreme courts in the United States and the highest courts of countries such as Canada but not by the United States Supreme Court. While an appeal of unconstitutionality is made after a law is promulgated, prior control of constitutionality enables the Constitutional Court to intervene and consider the conformity of an act to the Constitution prior to its enactment. The Constitutional Court exercises prior control over international treaties and organic laws such as the autonomy statutes and other disputes over the state's territorial structure. The Court has precedent over other official bodies through prior control even though an issue or conflict has not been submitted to it for consent. Such prior control fixes responsibility for international treaties with the Court even though the government or either parliamentary house has already fully considered the treaty's text. With regard to organic laws, prior control of unconstitutionality strives to avoid disruption of the Spanish judiciary's regular and consistent application of the law through the introduction of norms that will assuredly produce unconstitutional consequences. Prior control in this area, for example, seeks to avoid a situation of having to declare unconstitutional an autonomy statute already approved in a referendum or an organic law already in force regulating the electoral system.

The third mechanism through which the issue of constitutionality can be brought before the Constitutional Court is by the request of a lower court judge. This is a process analogous to the *certification of questions* in the United States, where a federal court of appeal, when confronted with a particularly difficult constitutional question, can send or certify the question to the U. S. Supreme Court for resolution while retaining the case. In Spain, either party involved in the case may solicit the judge or the judge may decide on his own to forward a question of constitutionality pertinent to a case to the Constitutional Court for resolution. When this occurs, the trial recesses until the higher court rules on the question. This procedure is similar to that employed in Italy, although in the latter country the lower court serves as an institutional "screen" for the higher court, determining if the case contains enough prima facie evidence of unconstitutionality to merit access to the Constitutional Court.[20]

The second type of case that is heard by the Constitutional Court involves appeals in the form of *recurso de amparo*. Hispanic public law generally incorporates the amparo appeal. Spain's Republican Constitution of 1931 and the contemporary Constitution of 1978 contain this judicial procedure. It is also available in Latin American countries such as Venezuela and Mexico, which drew upon Hispanic legal traditions.[21] The amparo appeal provides the means for securing relief against an abuse of power or a violation of guaranteed rights. The appeal alleges the argument that an "act or decree authorizing the abuse was contrary to the constitution."[22] The amparo appeal is key to the system of guarantees of constitutionality that established fundamental individual rights and liberties, seeking to protect against the violation of rights recognized in Articles 14 through 29 of the 1978 Constitution and objections of conscience.[23]

The recurso de amparo would appear to be a vehicle for private parties to challenge the constitutionality of a statute. This, however, is not the case. The amparo appeal is "a protection against the application of law, not an action against the law itself."[24] The Court may find that the application of a law is unconstitutional, but its finding is only applicable to the instant case and is not generalizable to other cases. The issue of the constitutionality of a law can only be addressed when raised as an appeal of unconstitutionality by an appropriate government official or body.[25]

The third type of case which is heard by the Constitutional Court involves conflicts of power between the different state institutions and bodies. These include conflicts between the state and one of the Autonomous Communities, between the various Autonomous Communities, and between the institutions of the central state, for example, the government, Congress, Senate, and General Council of the Judiciary. In these cases, the Constitutional Court serves to delimit the scope of the powers of the state and of the Autonomous Communities.[26] This type of case is comparable to the "original jurisdiction" of the United States Supreme Court, which extends inter alia to cases between the states and between the states and the federal government. Like the founding fathers of the United States, the authors of the 1978 Spanish Constitution saw the need for a judicial arbiter for the conflicts that inevitably arise in constitutional systems with multiple components.

THE PERSONNEL OF THE LAW

Legal Practitioners

The legal profession of Spain is divided into three components. One component is the notaries. These have nothing in common but their name with the notary public found in the United States. Notaries are required to possess a university law degree. Virtually all transactions that require forms, for example, contracts and property sales, must be executed by a notary. The notaries are, however, not involved in litigation or case preparation. The second component of the legal profession is the lawyer who is comparable to the solicitor in the British system or an American office lawyer. They perform most tasks attributed to lawyers including case preparation but do not file court cases or plead them. This role is confined to the third component of the profession, the procurator (*procuradores*). Legal practitioners in Spain, both lawyers and procurators, must hold a Bachelor of Laws degree. Such degrees may be earned at any of the university law schools in Spain. Legal curricula are uniform throughout the country, with the exception of such special subjects as the foral laws. The five-year program includes required courses like constitutional, civil, commercial, procedural, criminal, administrative, labor, and international law as well as subjects such as the philosophy and history of law and Roman law.[27] In 1972–1973, the number of students in law schools was 26,744 or 12.7 percent of all university students.[28] Spanish attorneys must also be members of a local Colegio de Abogados. Such a Bar Association exists in every Spanish city with either a Territorial or Provincial Audiencia. The bars assign their members cases and advances their professional interests and concerns.

Judges

Since the 1800s, the Spanish judiciary has formed a largely self-regulating corps of nonpolitical civil servants. Beginning in 1869, the government's discretion to appoint judges was limited by the introduction of competitive examinations (*oposiciones*) to determie eligibility to serve in the judiciary. The examination is open to all students with a bachelor's degree in law from a Spanish university. Students receiving acceptable scores are admitted to a special Judicial School for training. Upon graduation, they are appointed judges and assigned to Courts of First Instance and Instruction. Those scoring the highest on their exams receive first choice of assignment, which may mean placement in a large city rather than a small town. After the initial assignment, promotion to the position of magistrate and to a higher court is based largely on seniority. Transfers to more desirable locations, such as major cities, are also determined by the seniority of those applying for the position. Principal positions such as president of the Supreme Court and its salas are filled by the General Council of the Judiciary. The Spanish judiciary is thus essentially an independent professional civil service with protections and career patterns similar to those of other civil servants. This is stressed by their official title of *funcionario de la carrera judicial* or official of the judicial career.[29]

While sharing many characteristics with civil servants, judges consider themselves as a separate group. Spanish judges see themselves as having higher prestige, doing more important work, and having better preparation for their role than is the case for top civil servants and the legal profession generally. Surveys of members of the Spanish civil service, however, suggest that the high esteem with which the judges hold themselves is not shared by nonlegal social groups.[30] Moreover, when asked about the prominence of several local officials, respondents to a survey in Andalusia gave the least prominence and visibility to judges. The judiciary fell behind the mayor, president of the local farmers union, and the local priest in involvement and prominence.[31] Thus, while a self-conceived elite within the members of the legal community, the Spanish judiciary is far closer to civil servants or bureaucrats than to the socially prestigious and prominent position attributed to judges in Britain and the United States.

The Public Prosecutor

The Constitution grants the government the power to name the state's public prosecutors following consultation with the General Council of the Judiciary. Prosecutors are selected from among the graduates of the Judicial School. Judges and prosecutors share a common educational background but separate careers. The public prosecutor's organization in the judiciary is hierarchical and dependent on the judiciary.[32] The prosecutor has responsibility to promote "judicial action in the defense of the rule of law, of citizens' rights and of the public interest as safeguarded by law . . . as well as that of protecting the independence of the Courts and securing through them the satisfaction of social interest."[33] The prosecutor's most routine and visible role is in criminal cases. The public prosecutor enters this process at the trial before the Audiencia. Since the evidence is contained in the examining judge's *sumario* and the magistrates of the Audiencia question the witness and control the conduct of the trial, the role of the prosecutor is essentially argument (*calificación*) for the government's case.

Defender of the People

The Constitution of 1978 created for the first time in Spain an ombudsmanlike position.[34] The Defender's raison d'être is the protection of the fundamental rights and liberties guaranteed to the people under the new constitution. He protects such rights against intrusions by both administrative and legislative activities, including laws of the Cortes. In its capacity as watchdog of administrative activity, the Defender has open access to public administrative offices at all levels for purposes of obtaining data and other documentation and conducting interviews, with restrictions only in the area of national defense.

The Office of the Defender of the People is a high commission of the Spanish Parliament. The Defender is ultimately accountable to the Cortes in the sense that it selects him and can remove him for failure to fulfill his job. In initiating investigative action, the Defender must act through a parliamentarian, but the Organic Law on the Defender of the People left open the possibility of access to the Defender through interest groups.[35] In other aspects, his position is autonomous. The Defender's office must annually submit a report of its activities to the Cortes.

The Defender possesses several important powers and has several instruments at his disposal. He can recommend changes to administrative authorities and bureaucrats upon completion of his office's investigation. If the administrative authorities ignore such recommendations, the Public Defender can call this to the attention of the appropriate ministry and, if necessary, can ultimately make it known to the General Cortes. In another area, the Defender of the People may place amparo appeals and appeals of unconstitutionality before the Constitutional Court. This power of appeals permits the Defender to respond to the concern of individual citizens, defusing in part criticisms over limitations on individual initiative. In the initial years of this office's existence, the power of appeal has not been heavily utilized. The major question in the development of the Defender of the People, therefore, is one of access.

PUBLIC PERCEPTIONS AND THE ROLE OF THE COURTS

"Judicial independence" refers to the degree to which judges make decisions based on their own judgments and interpretations of the law, unfettered by the wishes or desires of other political and legal actors.[36] When courts have "decisional" independence, they are free to decide cases in ways contrary to the interest of the government without fear of retribution to themselves or to the court system. Related to decisional independence is "structural" independence. Courts are structurally independent to the degree that judges' salaries, promotions, and assignments and court powers and budgets are not subject to control by nonjudicial, that is, political, actors. For example, judges who serve at the pleasure of the government have less structural independence than judges who enjoy life-time appointments. It is presumed that structural independence facilitates decisional independence. That is, judges who are structurally insulated from the control of others are expected to be less influenced by nonjudicial considerations in reaching their decisions.

The presence of judicial independence would appear to be particularly troublesome to an authoritarian regime. However, under Franco, the ordinary courts enjoyed a large measure of both structural and decisional independence. As indicated above, the selection, training, placement, promotion, and discipline of Spanish judges is largely based on professional, nonpolitical criteria. This structural insulation of the ordinary courts from politics predated Franco and was continued during his regime. Only for the post of magistrate of the Supreme Court and presidents of Chambers of the Supreme Court and of Audiencias did the Ministry of Justice under Franco exercise discretionary power in selection. But even in these cases, the procedure was to base the decision on information and recommendations provided by the Judicial Council. The latter was composed of senior members of the judiciary.[37]

Determining whether courts exercise decisional independence is more difficult than determining if they are structurally independent. Two possible indicators of the presence of decisional independence are the presence of a widespread perception that the courts are independent and the willingness of the courts to decide cases against the government.[38] In terms of both indicators, perceptions and action, there is evidence to support the decisional independence of the ordinary courts under Franco. Zaragoza, in a survey of Madrid lawyers during the Franco period, found that over 60 percent consider judges to enjoy "much" or "considerable" independence. Only 16 percent thought that judges had no independence. It is noteworthy that this vision of a largely independent judiciary was held by lawyers of virtually all political persuasions.[39] In a survey of judges conducted in 1973, Toharia found that one-third mentioned an interest in protecting the rights and freedoms of citizens as a desirable characteristic of the ideal judge.[40] Toharia also found a great deal of attitudinal diversity concerning social and political issues such as the death penalty, the application of foral laws, and the use of languages other than Castillian in court. Thus, under Franco the Spanish judiciary was perceived to be independent by relevant actors and, in fact, was an attitudinally diverse body that did not mirror the regime's conservative views. The ordinary courts also did not appear to be particularly sympathetic to the central administration. Between 1960 and 1968, an average of 84 percent of appealed sentences in civil cases were confirmed by the Supreme Court, but only about 43 percent of the decisions taken by the central administration during this period were upheld by the Court. And, as previously seen in Table 4, Spain's administrative courts ruled against the central government 35.9 percent of the time in the 1970s. Thus, under Franco one could take the government to court with the expectation of winning.

How was judicial independence maintained within an authoritarian regime? The answer to this apparent anomaly lies in the restricted jurisdiction of the ordinary courts. Civil law courts deal mainly with disputes between private parties and are not involved in public law disputes that may threaten the power and maintenance of a political regime. Moreover, politically sensitive issues were placed within the jurisdiction of specialized courts whose judges did not enjoy structural independence. As previously indicated, the most volative and threatening cases to the regime were tried by military courts or the Court of Public Order not the ordinary courts. As one Spanish magistrate stated at the time, "they [the courts] are independent *because* they are powerless."[41]

The elimination under the democratic Constitution of 1978 of the civilian jurisdiction of the military courts and the Court of Public Order has resulted in the ordinary courts receiving jurisdiction over politically sensitive cases. Moreover, the new constitution, by authorizing a habeus corpus procedure, has positioned the ordinary courts as a restraint on the arbitrary exercise of police power. Through this procedure, the police can be forced to convince a magistrate of the lawfulness of an arrest or to release the prisoner. The increased power of the ordinary courts under the 1978 Constitution has brought increased concern to insure the structural independence and, hopefully, the decisional independence of the Spanish judiciary. If the courts were independent under Franco because they were powerless, there is concern that an increase in judicial power not necessitate a loss of independence in democratic Spain.

The issue of judicial independence produced a polemical debate during the writing of the Constitution in the Constituent Cortes.[42] In the Congressional Committee's deliberations, for example, the major parties basically agreed on the desire for a relatively independent judiciary. Specification of that desire, however, bred difficulties. The right-of-center parties, the Democratic Center Union (Unión de Centra Democrático—UCD) and the Popular Alliance (Alianza Popular—AP), pushed, on the one hand, for a complete division between the judiciary and politics. They argued, among other things, that judges should be required to sever all association with political parties and trade unions and should be ineligible to hold another public office. The political left-of-center, the Socialist Party (Partido Socialista Obrero Españala—PSOE) and the Communist party (Partido Communista de España—PCE), and some regional parties argued, on the other hand, that no one is above politics and that all individuals, including judges, should possess the right to associate freely. The political left-of-center couched this argument in the public's right to know a judge's political and ideological orientation. Given their numerical weakness in the Constituent Cortes, the Left lost this political debate.

The principle of judicial independence is reiterated specifically in Article 117 of the 1978 Constitution, stating that judicial members "shall be independent and irremovable during their term in office."[43] Moreover, the Constitution states that members of the judiciary are ineligible to serve as deputies or senators in any elected legislative assembly or deliberative political body, or in "a management role in a political party or trade union."[44] The major alteration in the Constitution designed to enhance judicial independence, however, has been the creation of the General Council of the Judiciary. The General Council is the Spanish judiciary's self-administrative body. The Council has assumed the tasks previously performed by the Judicial Council, the Supreme Court sitting in Sala de Govierno, and by the Ministry of Justice. It manages all matters of selection, education, nomination, promotion, administration, and discipline of the judges, magistrates, and judicial secretaries.[45] The General Council has no precedent in Spain, and its creation appears to have been inspired by Italy's Superior Council of Magistrates and, less so, the French Constitution of 1958. It remains in many aspects, however, similar to Britain's ancient Inns of Court, which admit, organize, discipline, and educate bar members and jealously guard the tradition and independence of the British legal and judicial professions.[46]

The General Council consists of the president of the Supreme Court and twenty appointed members. All serve five-year terms. The president of the Supreme Court serves as president of the Council. He is elected by a majority vote of the plenum of the Council for a five-year term, to which he may be reelected once. The president represents the General Council in the Supreme Court and coordinates the Council's activities. The twenty members formally appointed by the king constitute the plenum of the Council. Twelve come from a national electoral college comprised of all active judges and magistrates from all legal categories. The Congress of Deputies and the Senate each propose four of the remaining eight members from renowned lawyers and judges with more than fifteen years legal experience. The General Council is a fully protected constitutional body and is not subordinate to other bodies. The Council's acts, when signed by the king and the minister of justice, possess the power of a Royal Pronouncement.

The Council participates in several functions central to the judiciary. First, it participates in the selection process for other judicial bodies. For example, it nominates the president of the Supreme Court and the presidents of the various salas of the Supreme Court. It also nominates two judges of the Constitutional

Court and is consulted in the nomination of the state's Public Prosecutor.[47] Second, it has the last word in choosing other judicial personnel, being responsible for supplying judges, their nominations, promotions, and discipline.[48] Third, the Council generally determines the qualifications for judicial office. Fourth, the Council has authority over the establishment and modification of the judicial staff of judges, magistrates, secretaries, and other personnel, their salary system, and the initiation of laws affecting the functioning of judicial bodies concerned with personnel and services. Fifth, the Council must annually submit to the Cortes and the government a "State of the Judiciary" report concerning the affairs and activities of judicial administration in Spain. Finally, as previously indicated, the General Council may raise questions in the Constitutional Court over conflicts of power between the government and either house of Parliament.[49]

Courts and the Future of Democracy in Spain

The Spanish courts have, in the past, played a minor role in elaborating the law within the interstices of the code. In contrast, the new Constitution relies heavily on the courts to protect individual rights from government oppression and to assure the integrity of the document itself. In these innovations, Spain follows a trend in other European civil law countries to provide mechanisms to protect individual rights and to restrain government. The creation of institutions, however, does not assure the performance of expected functions. In most civil law countries where ordinary courts are given a power comparable to judicial review in the United States, they rarely employ it. This role is simply alien to the bureaucratic nature of the civil law judge. Even where special "constitutional" courts are created, performance varies widely. For example, both Germany and Italy created such courts as they emerged from authoritarianism at the end of World War II. The German Federal Constitutional Court (*bundesverfassungsgericht*) has proven to be an active and assertive court, averaging 1,500 cases a year. Most of the statutes nullified have been minor, but on one occasion the Court has taken a controversial position. For example, in 1975 the Court struck down as unconstitutional a federal law permitting abortions on request during the first three months of pregnancy holding that the law violated the constitutional provision to "the right to life."[50] The Italian Constitutional Court (*Corte Costituzionale*) presents a considerable contrast. The caseload of that court has averaged less than two hundred per year and, while asserting itself on occasion, the Constitutional Court has not been a major force in Italian political life. Its orders have met with spotty compliance and the Court has preferred to exhort rather than to give orders.[51]

What role will the Spanish courts take in the exercise of their newly granted powers? Will they take an assertive role similar to that of the West German courts or will the weight of tradition restrain the exercise of judicial powers as in Italy? It is too early to answer definitively this question, but initial indications are that the courts will be willing to play their role in assuring the role of law in the new political system.

The Constitutional Court clearly reveals the Spanish court system's independence and its emerging activism. Three examples that have affected public policy merit mention. First, the Constitutional Court ruled in late 1983 with a tie vote that was decided with a vote by the president, that the Socialist government's law appropriating the enormous holding company RUMASA was constitutional. This decision, followed by several others concerning questions of unconstitutionality placed before it by judges of First Instance, helped delineate state appropriation of private companies as a legal economic policy instrument in Spain. Second, on August 10, 1983, the Constitutional Court invalidated, in full or in part, fourteen of the thirty-eight articles of the highly controversial 1982 Organic Law on the Harmonization of the Autonomy Process (LOAPA). The Constitutional Court ruled that certain provisions of LOAPA violated the Constitution, including those which stated that the state's legal norms have automatic precedence over the autonomous regions' and that regional public administrative officials should be nominated by Madrid rather than regionally recruited. Such legal decisions place the Court in the middle of the delicate and difficult devolution process in Spain with its center-peripheral political battles. Third, the Constitutional Court's declaration of the PSOE (Partido Socialista Obrero España) government's "Partial Depenalization of Abortion" law as unconstitutional in April 1985 demonstrated that it is quite willing to rule against the national government no matter which party is in power and that it will directly tackle controversial social policies in addition to economic and political issues.[52]

Several examples also highlight other courts' definition of their role in democratic Spain. First, in a direct break with practices of authoritarian Spain, the 1978 Constitution's Article 17 mandates a habeas corpus procedure and other preventions against unlawful detention. On February 23, 1984, the Parliament's Congress of Deputies passed an Organic Law regulating habeas corpus procedures. The fact that on December 5, 1984, Madrid authorities were forced to release a prisoner under a writ of habeas corpus for illegal detention bodes well for an active use of such guarantees.[53] Second, the reform of the Code of Military Justice in 1980 made possible the Supreme Court's review of sentences of the military officers convicted in the February 23, 1981, coup attempt. After hearing the government's appeal concerning the light sentences, the Supreme Court extended the time to be served in twenty-one of twenty-three of the cases and upheld the thirty-year sentences of the coup's two key leaders. The high court also imposed prison sentences on eight Civil Guard lieutenants who had previously been "acquitted on the grounds of due obedience to superior orders."[54] Such decisions not only signify increased civil control over the military in democratic Spain, but also exemplifies the court system's increasing importance and legitimacy as an adjudicator of system-threatening conflicts and challenges. A third example of the Spanish courts emerging role as protector of democracy concerns the operation of political parties. Herri Batasuna is a radical leftist party closely linked with a Basque terrorist group that seeks independence from Spain. Despite the party's antisystem stance, Courts of First Instance have twice rejected requests to declare Herri Batasuna illegal.[55] Thus, while it is too early to make a definitive judgment, the Spanish judicial system, at many different levels, appears to be willing to assert its new powers to protect the norms of individual freedoms and liberal democracy.

NOTES

The University Research Committee of Emory University provided Thomas D. Lancaster with research support through a 1984 Summer Fellowship. The authors wish to thank Professor Xavier Arbos for his helpful comments on this chapter.

1. The literature documenting Spain's transition to democracy is quite extensive and growing. See, for example, J. Maravall, *The Transition to Democracy in Spain* (London: Croom Helm, 1982); T. D. Lancaster and G. Prevost, eds., *Politics and Change in Spain* (New York: Praeger Publishers, 1985); R. Carr and J. P. Fusi, *Spain: Dictatorship to Democracy*, 2d ed., (London: George Allen & Unwin, 1981); J. F. Coverdale, *The Political Transformation of Spain after Franco* (New York: Praeger Publishers, 1979); M. Caciagli, "Spain: Parties and the Party System in the Transition," *West European Politics* 7 (1984), pp. 84–98; J. de Esteban, and L. L. Guerra, *Los partidos políticos en la España actual* (Barcelona: Planeta, 1982); G. Shabad, "Party Strategies and Mass Cleavages in the 1979 Spanish Parliamentary Elections," *World Affairs* 143 (1980), pp. 163–216; P. McDonough, A. Lopez Pina, and S. H. Barnes, "The Spanish Public in Political Transition," *British Journal of Political Science* 11 (1981), pp. 49–79; J. Marcus, "The Triumph of Spanish Socialism: The 1982 Election," *West European Politics* 6 (1983), pp. 281–286; K. N. Medhurst, "Spain's Evolutionary Pathway from Dictatorship to Democracy," *West European Politics* 7 (1984), pp. 30–49; B. Pollack, "The 1982 Spanish General Elections and Beyond," *Parliamentary Affairs* 36 (1983), pp. 201–17; and M. Roskin, "Spain Tries Democracy Again," *Political Science Quarterly* 93 (1978), pp. 629–46. For a commentary on the Constitution of 1978, see J. Belmonte, *La Constitución: texto y contexto* (Madrid: Prensa Española, 1979); L. Sánchez Agesta, *El sistema político de la Constitución Española de 1978*, 3d ed. (Madrid: Editoria Nacional, 1984); and E. Sánchez Goyanes, *El sistema constitucional Español* (Madrid: Parafino, 1981), and *Constitución Española Comentada*, 2d ed. (Madrid: Paranfino, 1984).

2. R. David and J. E. C. Brierley, *Major Legal Systems in the World Today* 2d ed. (New York: Free Press, 1978), pp. 52–53.

3. M. Fraga Iribarne, *General Introduction to Spanish Law* (Madrid: Publicaciones Españoles, 1967), p. 46; and J. J. Toharia, "The Spanish Judiciary: A Sociological Study" (Ph.D. Diss., Yale University, 1974), pp. 245–52.

4. Toharia, "The Spanish Judiciary," p. 505.

5. See L. Boetsch, "The Church in Spanish Politics," in T. D. Lancaster and G. Prevost, eds., *Politics and Change in Spain* (New York: Praeger, 1985).

6. Toharia, "The Spanish Judiciary," pp. 252–61.

7. Fraga, "General Introduction to Spanish Law," p. 17; and David and Brierley, *Major Legal Systems*, p. 141.

8. David and Brierley, *Major Legal Systems*, p. 132; and Fraga, *General Introduction to Spanish Law*, p. 40.

9. Toharia, "The Spanish Judiciary," p. 37.

10. Ibid., pp. 186–88.

11. Fraga, *General Introduction to Spanish Law*, p. 40.

12. Toharia, "The Spanish Judiciary," p. 181.

13. David and Brierley, *Major Legal Systems*, p. 125.

14. *Ex Parte Milligan* 4 Wall. 2 (1866) and *Duncan v. Kahanamoko* 327 U.S. 304 (1946).

15. Toharia, "The Spanish Judiciary," pp. 400–402.

16. Title 6, Article 117:3.

17. Toharia, "The Spanish Judiciary," pp. 400–404.

18. Agreement of January 15, 1981, published in the *Boletin del Estado* of November 2, 1981.

19. Article 161:2.

20. P. A. Allum, *Italy: Republic Without Government?* (New York: W. W. Norton, 1973), p. 192.

21. T. L. Becker, *Comparative Judicial Politics* (Chicago: Rand McNally, 1970), pp. 207, 210.

22. W. W. Pierson and F. G. Gill, *Governments of Latin America* (New York: McGraw-Hill, 1957), p. 291.

23. See J. L. Garcia Ruiz, *El recurso de amparo en el Derecho español* (Madrid: Editora Nacional, 1980); and V. Gimeno Sendra, "Naturaleza juridica y objeto procesal del recurso de amparo," *Revista Española de Derecho Constitucional* 6 (1982).

24. Pierson and Gill, *Governments of Latin America*, p. 291.

25. A. de Blas, *Introductión al Sistema Político Español* (Barcelona: Teide, 1983), p. 221.

26. Article 59, L.O.T.C. (Ley Orgánico Tribunal Constitucional). See, also, H. Fix-Zamudio, "Problemas Jurisdicos de la administración de justicia federal y regional en Mexico y en España," *Revista de Estudios Políticos* 28 (1982), pp. 7–43.

27. C. S. Rhyne, *Law and Judicial Systems of Nations* (Washington, D. C.: The World Peace Through Law Center, 1978), pp. 667–68.

28. Data obtained from *Anuario Estadístico de España* (Madrid: Instituto Nacional de Estadística, 1975), p. 341.

29. Toharia, "The Spanish Judiciary," p. 32.

30. Ibid., pp. 126–28.

31. Ibid., p. 267.

32. Article 124.2 of the Spanish Constitution of 1978.

33. Article 124.

34. Article 54 creates the institution and outlines its function. Article 70 establishes his incompatibility with either being a senator or a deputy. Article 162 gives him legitimacy to place appeals of unconstitutionality and amparo appeals before the Constitutional Court.

35. Organic Law 3/81 of April 6, 1981, passed by the Chamber of Deputies on April 6, 1983.

36. Becker, *Comparative Judicial Politics*, p. 144.

37. Toharia, "The Spanish Judiciary," pp. 32, 381.

38. Becker, *Comparative Judicial Politics*, pp. 145–50.

39. Cited in Toharia, "The Spanish Judiciary," pp. 411–12.

40. Ibid., p. 58.

41. Ibid., p. 486.

42. The following is discussed in A. Bonime, "The Spanish State Structure: Constitution-making and the Creation of the New State," in T. D. Lancaster and G. Prevost, eds., *Politics and Change in Spain* (New York: Praeger Publishers, 1985), pp. 17–18.

43. Article 159.5.

44. Article 159.4 and also 70.1. The Constitution is referring here specifically to members of the Constitutional Court, but it is generally extrapolated to mean all judiciary members.

45. See Constitution Article 122.2 and Article 2 of the Organic Law. See also, M. Alba Navarro, "Las facultades de iniciativa propuesta e informe en materia legislativa del Consejo General del Poder Judicial," *Revista de Administración Pública* 97 (1982).

46. G. C. Moodie, *The Government of Great Britain* (New York: Thomas Y. Crowell, 1971), pp. 172–73.

47. Article 159.1 of the Constitution.

48. L.O.C.G.P.J. (Ley Organico Consejo General del Poder Judicial) Articles 2 and 3–6.

49. Conforming with Article 73 and Organic Law of Constitutional Court.

50. H. J. Abraham, *The Judicial Process* (New York: Oxford University Press, 1980), p. 318.

51. Ibid., p. 320; and H. W. Ehrmann, *Comparative Legal Cultures* (Englewood Cliffs, N. J.: Prentice-Hall, 1976), p. 144.

52. *El Pais* (Madrid), April 18 and 19, 1985.

53. *El Pais* (Madrid), December 7, 1984.

54. C. P. Boyd and J. M. Boyden, "The Armed Forces and the Transition to Democracy in Spain," in T. D. Lancaster and G. Prevost, eds., *Politics and Change in Spain* (New York: Praeger, 1985) p. 117.

55. *El Pais* (Madrid), October 4, 1984.

BIBLIOGRAPHY

Abraham, H. J. *The Judicial Process.* New York: Oxford University Press, 1980.

Alba Navarro, M. "Las facultades de iniciativa, propuesta e informe en materia legislativa del Consejo General del Poder Judicial." *Revista de Administración Pública* 97 (1982).

Becker, T. L. *Comparative Judicial Politics.* Chicago: Rand McNally, 1970.

Belmonte, J. *La Constitución: texto y contexto.* Madrid: Prensa Española, 1979.

Boetsch, L. "The Church in Spanish Politics." In T. D. Lancaster and G. Prevost, eds., *Politics and Change in Spain.* New York: Praeger, 1985.

Bonime, A. "The Spanish State Structure: Constitution-making and the Creation of the New State." In T. D. Lancaster and G. Prevost, eds., *Politics and Change in Spain.* New York: Praeger, 1985.

Boyd, C. P., and J. M. Boyden. "The Armed Forces and the Transition to Democracy in Spain." In T. D. Lancaster and G. Prevost, eds., *Politics and Change in Spain.* New York: Praeger, 1985.

Caciagli, M. "Spain: Parties and the Party System in the Transition." *West European Politics* 7 (1984), pp. 84–98.

Carr, R., and J. P. Fusi. *Spain: Dictatorship to Democracy.* 2d ed. London: George Allen & Unwin, 1981.

Coverdale, J. F. *The Political Transformation of Spain after Franco.* New York: Praeger, 1979.

David, R., and J. E. C. Brierley. *Major Legal Systems in the World Today.* 2d ed. New York: Free Press, 1978.

de Blas, A. *Introdución al Sistema Político Español.* Barcelona: Teide, 1983.

de Esteban, J., and L. L. Guerra. *Los partidos políticos en la España actual.* Barcelona: Planeta, 1982.

Ehrmann, H. W. *Comparative Legal Cultures.* Englewood Cliffs, N. J.: Prentice-Hall, 1976.

Fix-Zamudio, H. "Problemas Juridicos de la administración de justicia federal y regional en Mexico y en España." *Revista de Estudios Políticos* 28 (1982), pp. 7–43.

Fraga Iribarne, M. *General Introduction to Spanish Law.* Madrid: Publicaciones Españolas, 1967.

Garcia Ruiz, J. L. *El recurso de amparo en el Derecho español.* Madrid: Editora Nacional, 1980.

Gimeno Sendra, V. "Naturaleza juridica y objeto procesal del recurso de amparo." *Revista Española de Derecho Constitucional* 6 (1982).

Gunter, R., G. Sani, and G. Shabad. "Party Strategies and Mass Cleavages in the 1979 Spanish Parliamentary Elections." *World Affairs* 143 (1980), pp. 163–216.

Lancaster, T. D., and G. Prevost, eds. *Politics and Change in Spain.* New York: Praeger, 1985.

McDonough, P., A. Lopez Pina, and S. H. Barnes. "The Spanish Public in Political Transition." *British Journal of Political Science* 11 (1981), pp. 49–79.

Maravall, J. *The Transition to Democracy in Spain.* London: Croom Helm, 1982.

Marcus, J. "The Triumph of Spanish Socialism: The 1982 Election." *West European Politics* 6 (1983), pp. 281–86.

Medhurst, K. N. "Spain's Evolutionary Pathway from Dictatorship to Democracy." *West European Politics* 7 (1984), pp. 30–49.

Pollack, B. "The 1982 Spanish General Election and Beyond." *Parliamentary Affairs* 36 (1983), pp. 201–17.

Prieto Castro, L., J. Almagro Nosete, and N. Gonzalez Deleito. *Tribunales españoles. Organización y funcionamiento.* Madrid: Technos, 1983.

Prieto Sanchis, L. "Dos años de jurisprudencia del Tribunal Supremo sobre cuestiones constitucionales: I, II, III." *Revista Española de Derecho Constitucional* 3 (1981).

Rhyne, C. S. *Law and Judicial Systems of Nations.* Washington, D. C.: World Peace Through Law Center, 1978.

Roskin, M. "Spain Tries Democracy Again." *Political Science Quarterly* 93 (1978), pp. 629–46.

Sánchez Agesta, L. *El sistema político de la Constitución Española de 1978.* 3d ed. Madrid: Editora Nacional, 1984.

Sánchez Goyanes, E.. *Constitución Española Comentada.* 12th ed. Madrid: Paraninfo, 1984.

———. *El sistema constitucional Español.* Madrid: Paranfino, 1981.

Toharia, J. J. "Judicial Independence in an Authoritarian Regime: The Case of Contemporary Spain." *Law & Society Review* 9, no. 3 (1975), pp. 479–96.

———. "The Spanish Judiciary: A Sociological Study." Ph.D. Diss.: Yale University, 1974.

Tomás y Valiente, F. *Manual de historia del derecho español.* Madrid: Tecnos, 1979.

17

UNITED KINGDOM

Alan N. Katz

English law, as distinct from the Romano-Germanic legal systems commonly found in Western Europe and South America, is the basis of the Anglo-American or common law group of legal systems. The common law family includes all of the English-speaking nations (with the exception of Scotland, the Union of South Africa, and the state of Louisiana), and its influence remains great today in almost all of the nations politically linked with England. English law is technically limited to England and Wales, for while the United Kingdom is a unitary state, there is not a single body of law that is universally applied to all of the countries within its limits. Despite the fact that a single parliament has existed in England, Wales, and Scotland since 1707, the Scottish legal system is considerably different in legal procedure and practice as well as its law. Northern Ireland, on the other hand, despite similar legal practices and structures, has considerable differences in the enacted law from that found in England and Wales.

ENGLAND AND WALES

The Development of the Legal System

The common law system evolved in England as a result of the attempts of the Norman conquerors to bring a single, centralized administration to that formerly divided land. The Norman conquest helped to ultimately produce a homogeneous society, free from foreign invasion, and geographically isolated from the European continent. This enabled the English to develop their own legal institutions, insulated from the Continent's reliance on Roman law and later codification of the law.

The nine-hundred-year history of English law can be divided into four periods: (1) the period before the Norman conquest; (2) the period from 1066 to the accession of the Tudors in 1485—in which the common law was formed and the new legal system replaced local custom; (3) the period until 1832, which saw the fulfillment of the common law system despite the development of rival systems; and (4) the modern period, when the common law has had to further adapt itself to legislation and a society increasingly directed by governmental activity.

The Pre-Norman Period

The Roman occupation lasted more than four centuries from the Emperor Claudius (A.D. 41–54) to the beginning of the fifth century. While the Romans brought elements of their culture to Britain—their language, road system, and central heating—their legal system did not cross the English Channel, for "Britain had not been developed, it had been occupied," and Roman law only governed relations between Romans.[1]

The most important characteristic of the pre-Norman period was the existence of local customs. Kiralfy, in fact, writes: "In an illiterate group such as this, custom ruled and men behaved according to their elders. Change was abhorrent, because its results could not be forseen and turmoil might result."[2] The law evolved during this period from the ninety sentences transcribed during the reign of Aethelbert, king of Kent, in A.D. 600 to the much more developed law under the Danes four centuries later. While this is generally seen as one indication of the movement from the tribal period to that of feudalism, no common law existed for the whole of England until 1066.

From the Normans to the Tudors: Development of the Common Law System

When the Norman Duke William (1028–1087) conquered England, he maintained the Anglo-Saxon law. Keeton writes: "The laws of his feudal tenants were a superstructure which left the pre-existing fabric largely unaltered. Both by temperament and policy, William was no innovator. What he sought to do, in legal matters, was to establish certainty and precision where, in Saxon times, these qualities had been rare."[3] William's reign was characterized by centralization of the legal system and greater governmental efficiency. This was nowhere better seen than in the creation of the *Doonesday Book*, which inventoried 15,000 estates and 200,000 homes.

There were two significant legal developments during the Norman period. The first of these was the introduction of the *eyre*. The eyres, or justices, were appointed from the king's central court and saw to it that the shires were governed correctly, the laws obeyed, and that officials carried out their functions. These judges were administrators and not lawyers, for there were, as yet, no professional advocates in the British Isles. Ultimately, as the business of the eyres grew, there arose some division of labor and some specialization but "the eyre constituted essentially an administrative solution to an administrative problem. It brilliantly resolved the crucial problem of all conquest-based empires, how to bring central political authority to bear on the countryside cheaply and without creating local centers of power capable of resisting central authority."[4] The second legal development was the creation of the first book of English law, *Glanvil* or *deligibus Angliae*, during the reign of Henry II (1154–1189). These two developments are generally considered the first steps toward the development of the common law for they "struck at the very root of feudal administration, and also destroyed the chance that any surviving communal courts might further develop their local customary law, as a serious rival.[5]

During early Norman times, there was no separation of powers, with the king acting with his advisors in the Curia Regis, a council exercising executive, legislative, and judicial powers. The council was a place where the king dispensed justice for the most important citizens of the realm. Three royal courts (the Court of the Exchequer, Court of Common Pleas, and Court of King's Bench) ultimately split off from the Curia, no longer proceeding about the country with the king, but residing at Westminster and assuming judicial powers separate from that of the king. These courts played a major role in the creation of the common law, for their judges often placed great reliance on previous judgments in similar cases, giving rise to the doctrine of "judicial precedence" upon which all law, other than legislation, in England is based.

A writ system was soon developed to give citizens the right to appeal before the Crown. The writs enabled the citizen to deliver a writ to the Crown, through the chancellor, who asked for a royal solution to a particular problem. These forms ultimately became standardized and the petitioner submitted the appropriate form to the chancellor. As the standard forms developed, the writs became part of the common law. By the fourteenth century, new writs began to be utilized by the king in Parliament rather than the chancellor, and the common law courts began to initiate new forms of legal action by extending or relaxing the existing writs to cover new situations. This enabled the legal system to respond to increasingly complex situations and, by doing so, to create stronger feelings of loyalty to the central government.

The law as administered by the royal courts relied very heavily on forms of action and procedural techniques. David and Brierley write: "These procedures, from many points of view archaic and typically English, forced a process of 'anglicization' to take place when substantive elements were borrowed from Roman or canon law. The complexity and technical nature of these procedures were also such that they could only be learned through practice."[6] This emphasis on procedure had two consequences: (1) it made the system resistant to Roman law as used on the Continent; and (2) it made the training of judges and practitioners more a function of the legal profession itself than of the universities.

1485–1832: Fulfillment of the Common Law System

The formalist procedures of the common law, however, hampered it during the succeeding decades because such procedures and the prevailing legal conservatism of the time made the common law too rigid to effectively deal with some of the needs of a changing society. As a result, equity developed as a rival that threatened to supplant the common law.

Individuals unhappy with the decisions of the royal courts could now appeal directly to the king. Such requests were normally sent first to the chancellor and then to the monarch. However, at the time of the War of the Roses (1453–1485), it was difficult for the king to sit as judge at his own council. As a response to this difficulty, the chancellor, acting on the king's behalf, began to play a more active role in adjudicating cases: "His decisions, in the beginning made on the basis of 'the equity of the case,' became increasingly systematized and the application of 'equitable' doctrines soon amounted to additions or correctives to the 'legal' principles applied by the royal courts."[7]

The next two centuries saw the continued development of equity, a reconciliation with the common law, and an almost continual struggle between the monarch and Parliament in which the judiciary played no small part. The period also saw the continued expansion of the power of the chancellor, who, acting as judge, increasingly examined petitions using principles of Roman law and canon law rather than the common law. The new powers of the chancellor were approved by the authoritarian Tudors because the actions of the Chancery were more often than not secret, written and inquisitorial rather than oral and public, and because the chancellor's actions replaced the use of the jury in the common law procedures.

The end of the Tudor period did see the strengthening of Parliament as a chamber separate from the king and his council. This was backed by the proponents of the common law as well as those concerned with possible abuse of royal prerogatives. By the end of this period, Parliament was seen as the supreme law-making body in England.

The struggle between the monarch and the legislature intensified during the Stuart period. Those opposed to the Stuarts initially attacked individual judges as having been corrupt and then moved to attack the courts as "having invaded the lawmaking powers of Parliament, or having become cat's paws of the king's financial policies, or having become hopelessly oppressive, corrupt, and inefficient."[8] Charles I convened and dismissed Parliament depending upon its loyalty to the crown and ultimately ruled for eleven years (1629–1640) without Parliament. When Parliament returned, it dismissed the Star Chamber and made government ministers accountable not only to the king but to it as well. In the ensuing civil war, the common lawyers, for the most part, sided with Parliament, while the serving judges were Royalists. The war resulted in the execution of Charles, followed by rule by Parliament and a protector, the restoration of the monarchy in 1660, and a bloodless revolution in 1688. The latter resulted in the promulgation of the Bill of Rights of 1689, which provided for the free election of Parliament, regular parliamentary sessions, and parliamentary approval of the suspension or levying of taxes. Eleven years later, the Act of Settlement created an independent judiciary whose members could be removed only by an act of Parliament.

The seventeenth century established the House of Lords as the ultimate appeals court for cases arising in England and meant that the courts were the servant of the legislature and not the sovereign. Despite this, the power of the judges and courts remained great, primarily due to the need for judicial specialization because of the complexity of the common law:

That bundle of (1) complex common law, (2) guild of common lawyers, and (3) common law judges, which we have earlier seen was at the core of what commentators choose to call judicial independence, reached its tightest and most resistant condition in the eighteenth century. No one could understand the law except the lawyers, who constituted a closed guild that co-opted new membership by apprenticeship. The judges were chosen from and led the guild. The growing theory of parliamentary sovereignty meant little in the face of this reality. The judges were independent because they operated a system of law that was essential to the well-being of the nation but which no one but the lawyers could understand.[9]

The Modern Period

Two nineteenth-century movements weakened much of the autonomy that the English courts previously enjoyed. The first was an attack by the legal philosopher Jeremy Bentham upon the common law as being illogical and overly complex. While the demand for law reform had been present since the sixteenth century, the Benthamite movement succeeded in the nineteenth century. Foremost among the new reforms was a series of statutes, culminating in the Judicature Act of 1873, which both reorganized the court system and simplified its procedures. The Appellate Jurisdiction Act of 1876 restored the House of Lord's appellate function and professionalized its membership by no longer permitting lay members of the House to sit on legal appeals. The second movement, best exemplified by the Reform Act of 1832, broadened suffrage and reaffirmed the electoral system so that Parliament better represented the English people.

While these reforms recognized the importance of equity, they did not diminish the significance of the common law or its lawyers. The reforms in both substantive and procedural law took the form of editing rather than replacing the common law. More importantly, these reforms allowed the common law lawyers to seize control of the top of the appellate hierarchy for both the law lords and the Judicial Committee of the Privy Council were staffed exclusively by lawyers and new judges. The basic organization of the courts found during this period remained unchanged throughout the twentieth century (with the only major change coming about with the Courts Act of 1971, which created the Crown Courts to deal with criminal matters).

The common law system has, therefore, been inextricably linked to the development of the English nation. The creation of the eyres, the writing of the first books of the law, the formation of the royal courts, and the conception and expansion of the royal writs—all during the Norman period—helped to develop feelings of loyalty to the system, which aided in the development of the profound sense of national identification so characteristic of the British. The common law (and the system generally) was later challenged by the need to respond to changing societal conditions. These challenges ultimately resulted in both equity and legislation becoming other important sources of the law, while much of the character of the common law system was retained. Finally, the judicial system became immersed in the struggles between the king and Parliament during much of the Tudor and Stuart periods. The result of these struggles was the supremacy of Parliament. Yet, as we shall see in a later section of this chapter, another outcome of this period was a clear consensus regarding a somewhat limited yet quite significant role for the legal system within England's political system.

The Organization of the Court System

The present legal system in England and Wales depends primarily on legislation passed during the past one hundred years (with the Judicature Acts of 1873–1875 and the Courts Act of 1971 as the landmark acts). Courts are now only created by Parliament and can be divided into "superior" and "inferior" courts. Superior courts are not subject to the control of any other court (except for an appeal), while both courts have much wider jurisdiction. The courts can also be divided into criminal and civil divisions, below the appellate level, though the division is somewhat arbitrary, since the same judges often sit on both courts.

At the apex of the court system is the House of Lords. It hears appeals from the Court of Appeals and the High Court and serves as the final court of appeals for Scotland and Northern Ireland. The appellate judicial work of the House of Lords is carried out by the lord chancellor and eleven law lords (the lords of appeal in ordinary), the latter having been promoted from the English, Scottish, or Northern Irish judiciary. The normal quorum for a case is five, with the lord chancellor sometimes sitting on cases. The judicial proceedings of the House are part of its normal business, but lay members do not attend the reading of appeals. The House of Lords can overrule decisions of all the courts below it and, since 1966, can revise its own decisions. The House does, however, generally hear few appeals. For example, there were only eighty-six appeals entered in 1983, an increase of fifteen over the previous year.[10]

The Judicial Committee of the Privy Council is a parallel body to the House of Lords. It is composed of the same individuals and hears appeals from colonial courts and certain independent regulatory bodies. It technically only makes recommendations to the monarch, but they are always accepted. In 1983 there were fifty-eight appeals entered before the Privy Council—a decrease of four over the previous year.[11]

The Court of Appeals is composed of the master of the rolls, the lord chief justice, and the fourteen lords justices. Justices of the High Court may also occasionally sit on the Court of Appeals. The court hears civil appeals from the High Court, county courts, and a few specialized administrative panels. In 1983, it heard 1,452 appeals, a decrease from the 1,627 appeals heard the previous year.[12] By American standards, however, the work load of this court is not great. For example, in 1969, the federal Court of Appeals heard approximately 3,700 civil cases.[13] The lord chief justice presides over the criminal division, which hears appeals from the Crown Courts and Magistrates' Courts. In 1983 there were 7,299 criminal appeals brought before the court, an increase from the 6,674 brought before it the previous year.[14] By contrast, in 1967–1968, the intermediate court of appeals in the state of California heard 2,000 criminal appeals, not including habeus corpus cases.[15]

The High Court is the trial court with general jurisdiction (there is no limit to the amount of damages it is able to award) in civil matters. It is composed of a maximum of seventy-five judges, all appointed by the monarch, on recommendation of the lord chancellor. The Court is composed of three separate, independent branches, each having its own judges, presiding officers, and specialized attorneys appearing before it. These are: (1) the Queen's Bench Division, which is presided over by the lord chief justice and is concerned with contract and tort claims; (2) the Chancery Division, which is led by the vice-chancellor and deals primarily with business and property law; and (3) the Family Division, which is presided over by the president and hears family relations cases, including divorce, noncontentious probate, and guardianship. In 1983, there were 1,619 appeals entered with the High Court—seventy-seven with Chancery, 1,160 with Queen's Bench, and 382 with the Family Division.[16]

There were 293 county courts in England and Wales in 1983.[17] They sit on a daily basis in busier centers but meet weekly, monthly, or even less frequently in less populous areas. The lord chancellor appoints all county court judges. The county courts have an enormous impact, despite their limited jurisdiction. This is because they deal with "ordinary" transactions such as repossession of automobiles, debt collection, and tenants' rights. In 1983, there were 2,117,383 cases begun in these courts—a dramatic increase over the 1,508,620 initiated a decade earlier.[18]

The Crown Court was created in 1972 to replace the Assizes, Quarter Sessions, and the Central Criminal Court, sometimes known as "Old Bailey." The court has approximately ninety centers, each generally within a day's travel for the entire population. It is responsible for criminal trials, the sentencing of offenders committed for sentencing from Magstrates' Courts, and appeals from those courts. Three different kinds of judges sit on the Crown Courts: (1) justices of the High Court, who preside over more serious (or "upper band") offenses; (2) county court judges, in this setting called "circuit court judges," who preside over "middle band" and "lower band" offenses; and (3) part-time judges, known as "recorders," who spend at least one month per year in judicial service. These volunteers tend to be senior barristers who are often ultimately appointed to a permanent position on the bench. In 1983, the Crown Courts received 73,472 committals for trials, 11,222 committals for sentencing, and 18,869 appeals against decisions of the Magistrates' Courts.[19]

There are approximately nine hundred Magistrates' Courts in England and

Wales. Most criminal cases begin at this level. More serious cases go through their preliminary stages in these courts and less serious cases begin and end here. Each of these courts is staffed by three unpaid magistrates, advised by a clerk to the justices, who is usually legally qualified and is in charge of administering the court. Some large urban areas also have professional, legally qualified, full-time, "stipendiary magistrates" who sit on the bench alone. The lay justices (justices of the peace) on the Magistrates' Courts receive a short period of training after their initial appointment by the lord chancellor. They hear all criminal cases involving less than six months imprisonment as well as enforce marital separation agreements, certain adoption proceedings, and the licensing of pubs and gambling establishments. Appeals from these courts go either to the local Crown Court or to a three-judge panel of the High Court, depending upon the issues involved.

There are, in addition, a variety of special courts in England and Wales. These include: (1) juvenile courts, which deal with the care of criminal proceedings regarding individuals under seventeen years of age; (2) Coroners' Courts, which handle investigations into violent, unnatural, or sudden deaths, where the cause is unknown; (3) Courts Martials, which have jurisdiction over members of the military but do not have the power to deal with major crimes alleged to have been committed by members of the military; (4) a Restrictive Practices Court, which handles matters relating to restrictive trade practices, resale price maintenance, and monopolies; (5) Administrative Tribunals, which exercise judicial or quasi-judicial functions outside the ordinary hierarchy of the courts; and (6) Ecclesiastical Courts.

The Personnel of the Law

Barristers and Solicitors

The English legal profession is divided into two branches, the barristers, known collectively as the "bar" and individually as "counsel" and the solicitors' branch, formerly known as "attorneys." There are presently 3,700 barristers (275 are women) and 36,000 practicing solicitors (2,000 are women) in England and Wales.[20] The former conduct cases in court and give legal advice to solicitors. The barrister is generally thought of as a specialist in legal advocacy for, in the British system, oral evidence and presentation play a much greater role than in other societies. In addition, the barristers also draft pleadings and other legal documents. On the other hand, the barrister is usually dependent for his/her work on the solicitor, since a client generally first goes to see the solicitor. Solicitors undertake "ordinary" legal business (such as the preliminary conduct of litigation, drawing up of wills, conveyancing of land, and the giving of legal advice) for their clients and may appear in Magistrates' Courts, County Courts and, occasionally, in the High Court.

There are a number of steps in gaining admission to the legal profession. First, the individual usually attends a university or a polytechnic. One need not be a university graduate to be either a solicitor or a barrister. In fact, until 1970 fewer than half of those becoming solicitors and one-fifth of the new barristers were university graduates. However, growing governmental and professional pressures have changed this so that by 1974, 69.1 percent of the incoming solicitors and 86.1 percent of the new barristers were university graduates. Second, each student must pass a two-part certifying examination (though some may receive exemptions from the first exam). Third, each individual desiring to become a barrister must attend one of the Inns of the Court for one year as well as engage in the "eating of dinners" at one of the Inns (this requirement is often completed prior to graduation from the university). Finally, each student must enter a period of apprenticeship—a two-year "obligatory period" for solicitors and a one-year period for barristers.[21]

There are presently thirty-two universities and twenty-two polytechnic and other local-authority programs with law programs in the United Kingdom. Twenty-three of the universities offering such programs are in England, three in Wales, five in Scotland, and one in Northern Ireland. In addition, a number of universities offer a "mixed" degree program, where the student may major or "read" in a subject other than law but take the necessary six courses (Contracts, Torts, Criminal Law, Land Law, Constitutional and Administrative Law, and Equity and Trusts) in order to gain exemption from Part I of the professional examination.

Every student desiring to become a barrister must join one of the four Inns of the Court—Lincoln's Inn, Inner Temple, Middle Temple, and Gray's Inn. Each of the Inns is governed by masters of the Bench, usually called "benchers." The Senate of the Inns of the Court (composed of six representatives of each Inn, six representatives of the Bar Council, treasurers of the Inns, chairmen of the Bar Council, and the attorney general) has the general responsibility for the admission of students and their call to the bar, legal education, student welfare, and disciplinary authority over individual barristers. Since 1967, the general policy for legal education has been enunciated by the Senate, but the examination of students is in the hands of the Council of Legal Education, a body set up by the Inns, approved by the Law Society, the governing body of that branch of the profession. The society is governed by a council of sixty-five members who are elected for a five-year term. The society, with the approval of the lord chancellor, the lord chief justice, and the master of the rolls, controls admission and handles disciplining members of that branch of the profession.

All students must also undergo a period of vocational training under the direction of a member of their branch of the profession. The period of training for the barristers is one year. How much one benefits from the training (called "pupillage") depends upon the rapport developed between the pupil and the master, how busy the latter is, and how seriously he takes his responsibilities. In addition, the pupillage will largely determine the extent of any specialized training the new barrister receives. The aspiring solicitor must also engage in similiar vocational training (called "articles of clerkship") with a practicing solicitor of no less than five years' experience for a period of from two to four years, depending upon his/her educational experience. The value of this vocational training will be influenced by factors similiar to those effecting the young barrister's pupillage. Interestingly, despite the complaints of some young solicitors that they have been "exploited" in their work, many master solicitors complain that the apprentices often take up too much valuable time and space and are, therefore, unwilling to employ them.

Each prospective barrister must also eat three dinners in each of twelve terms (there are four terms per year) at one of the Inns of the Court. This is normally completed while the student is at the university but may be satisfied while studying for the bar exam.

The eating of dinners, apprenticeship period, and set curriculum for the certifying examinations are clear examples of the extraordinary control that the professional organizations exert over the training of their members. While such control might normally be applauded, it does have some negative consequences for the profession. (1) It has minimized the role that the universities have exerted over the training of members of the profession. As an example of the peripheral role of the universities in professional training, regular law courses were not offered at the University of London until 1826, and as late as 1900 there were only a few students regularly matriculating in the law. The low esteem in which university education for the law was held is seen in the fact that the present exemptions for part of the certifying examination for law graduates was not instituted until 1922 for solicitors and 1934 for barristers. Abel-Smith and Stevens have described the minor contributions of the universities to legal education in the United Kingdom in the following manner: "historically the leading law schools have created the legal profession in the United States. On the whole, the reverse has been true in England."[22] (2) The requirement that a student eat dinners and, more importantly, serve a period of apprenticeship makes it difficult for the working-class student to gain entrance into the profession. For example, no student is guaranteed finding the necessary pupillage or articles and the Oxford University Appointments Board commented that "the choice of the right father has more to do with obtaining solicitors' articles than any other factor."[23] In addition, the low wages that one can expect during the apprenticeship period, as well as during the early years of one's professional life, places a heavy burden on the poorer student. (3) The profession has been extraordinarily resistant to change. There have, for example, been numerous suggestions for a "fusion" of the profession, arguing that the present separation is costly, inefficient, and does not provide the best legal services. These criticisms and proposed reforms have, for the most part, been met with resistance, especially from the barristers. A second example of this phenomenon has been the profession's reaction to a report (*1971 Ormrod Committee Report to Parliament on Legal Education*), which called for an exemption from Part I of the certifying examination for those students who possess a university degree in the law (agreed to by the profession) and called for a much greater role in the vocational training of lawyers by the universities (opposed by the profession).

Judges

There were approximately 450 judges in England and Wales in 1983, with 345 sitting on the newly created Crown Courts.[24] In addition, in 1984, 931 barristers and solicitors served as recorders and assistant recorders, and part-time judges, who sit on the bench for at least twenty days per year.[25] All judges are appointed by the Crown, acting on the advice of ministers. Most members of the judiciary (all High Court and circuit court judges) are recommended by the lord chancellor. The most important criteria for selection to the bench are professional competence (judges and barristers are usually consulted prior to appointment) and "moral uprightness" (for example, at one point there were no divorced men on the bench). On the other hand, political considerations appear to play little role in the appointment process, though it has been noted that extreme political views will prevent an individual from being appointed to the bench.[26]

A distinction is made between those judges of the first tier (those on the High Court, Court of Appeals, and law lords) and those of the second tier (those serving on the Crown Courts). This is seen both in the qualification needed for appointment as well as the appointment and removal processes. While there are stringent time requirements for appointment to the bench on the first tier (a barrister for ten years but the average is closer to thirty to be appointed to the High Court, a member of that bench or service as a barrister for fifteen years to become a judge on the Court of Appeals, and service in "high judicial office" for two years to be appointed a law lord) the time requirements (ten years as a barrister or five years as a recorder) are far less demanding for appointment as a circuit judge. In addition, since 1971, any solicitor with ten years' standing or five years' service as a solicitor may become a circuit judge. There are also significant differences in the manner in which members of the bar apply (or do not apply) for vacancies on the bench. Aspirants for positions on the first tier are not only expected not to apply for such openings but, according to Lord Goddard "if anyone wished to ensure that he would never be offered a High Court judgeship, his surest course would be to ask for one."[27] On the other hand, any individual who wishes to be appointed a circuit judge or recorder must apply for that position and submit three letters from judges or leading barristers in support of that nomination. Finally, the tenure conditions of the judges on different benches vary significantly. While judges of the first tier may only be removed by the monarch on approval of both houses of Parliament, judges of the Crown Court may be removed by the lord chancellor on grounds of incapacity or misbehavior.

A number of studies have contended that the members of the judiciary constitute a fairly homogeneous elite.[28] They concluded that British judges tend to come from the upper-middle class, to have seen military service in the two world wars, to have some political experience, and to have attended both the British "public" schools and either Oxford or Cambridge. In addition, a scanning of the law list indicates that the bench is a bastion of male supremacy. For example, in 1979 there were seven females on the bench—one on the High Court and six on the Crown Court.[29] Two recent studies, however, have found somewhat less homogeneity within the judiciary. The first of these found those who sat on the High Court from 1867 to 1972 to be far less likely to have had "high family status, family political activity, a high prestige 'Oxbridge' education, holding administrative or elective office, early achievement of Queen's (King's) Counsellor and Bencher statuses, early knighthood, and being initially appointed to the judiciary at or above the High Court level" than those who sat on the Court of Appeals or House of Lords during the same time period.[30] The second study compared all members of the British judiciary in 1979 and found significant differences between those who sat on the first and second tier benches. Those who served as circuit court judges were found to be younger, less likely to have been educated at one of "Clarendon" secondary schools (these included Charterhouse, Eton, Harrow, Marchant Taylors, Rugby, St. Pauls, Shrewsbury, Westminster, and Winchester), as well as at either Oxford or Cambridge, and had received fewer honors from the profession (Queen's or King's Counsel, "Bencher," member of the Bar Council, or member of the Senate of the Inns of the Court).[31]

It has long been held that once one was appointed to a particular bench, one would remain there. Recent studies, however, have found numerous examples of judicial promotions.[32] In fact, 9 percent of those sitting on the bench in 1979 had been promoted from lower courts.

Justices of the Peace

Many observers have noted that the British system is more dependent than most upon a strong "amateur" element—unpaid, volunteer laymen—for the smooth functioning of the system. Nowhere is this more evident than in the legal system, where 25,600 lay magistrates (or justices of the peace) handle over 97 percent of all criminal cases, dealing with more than 2 million defendants.[33] Justices of the Peace (JPs) are expected to sit on the bench for at least twenty-six days each year and receive travel and subsistence allowance as well as financial loss allowance (for actual loss in salary when sitting on the bench) but no salary for their work. The novice JP receives approximately forty hours of instruction on the law and sentencing before assuming his duties. All criminal cases begin before JPs, who decide whether more serious cases warrant prosecution before a higher court. There is a six-month limit and a specified maximum fine that magistrates may impose upon a defendant. Yet, the impact of the JP is enormous, for they yearly send approximately 20,000 people to prison for up to six months. Decisions of the JP may be appealed to the Crown Court or, in appeals dealing with points of law or misuse of power, to the Queens Bench Division of the High Court.

The justice of the peace probably originated in 1195. In that year the Archbishop of Canterbury issued a proclamation calling for four knights out of every one hundred to take an oath from all men over fifteen years of age to aid in the keeping of peace. Whatever the exact date of its origin, there is little doubt that the justice of the peace played a crucial role in the development of the English political system. Charles Beard, for example, has written:

In every shire they (the sovereigns) had their justice chosen from the strongest and most stable elements of the gentry . . . scattered as permanent residents throughout every county, they possessed that intimate knowledge of local persons and conditions which facilitate efficient administration; but . . . they never secured enough corporate independence to endanger the cohesion of the national system. No continental state possessed such a combination of local independence and central control, and it is surely warranted in saying that England's early national unity and internal administrative unity were in large measure due to the institution of the justice of the peace.[34]

The JP is aided and complemented by two "professional" figures: the stipendiary magistrate and the "justices' clerk." In some of the busiest urban courts, the JPs are supplemented by fifty-five paid, legally qualified stipendiary magistrates. These full-time justices are appointed to the bench by the lord chancellor (as is the JP, though local organizations play a significant role in recommending candidates to the lord chancellor) and sit on the bench alone rather than in panels of three. Each Magistrates' Court also has one "justices' clerk" (some also have a number of assistants). The clerk is usually a solicitor or barrister and serves as the legal advisor to the JP. They are appointed by the Magistrates' Court Committee and paid by the local authority. While they answer legal questions of the magistrates, and, in fact, hand down decisions on points of law, the fiction is maintained that the decisions are rendered by the magistrate, not the clerk.

Some critics of the justices of the peace have described them as being amateurish, patronizing, insensitive to the problems of those appearing before them (aside from the fact that 40 percent of the JPs are female, there is little difference in the social background of the JPs and judges of the other English benches— they are middle-aged, middle class, and politically conservative), and tending to believe police witnesses rather than the defendants. Yet, in a system that spent nearly a half a billion pounds in 1982–1983 on the administration of justice and where there are constant comments that the quality of those on the bench is declining, much positive can be said about the JP.[35]

But the English system of criminal justice would collapse without lay magistrates, and on the whole they give satisfaction. The justice they dispense may be crude, but it is cheap and effective. They give good value for little money. In any event, it would be impossible to replace them by professional magistrates, even if it were thought to be desirable. There are just not enough competent and legally qualified people to man the courts without unpaid volunteers.[36]

Juries

While the jury system has been an integral part of the judicial system in England since the twelfth century, jury trials are rarely utilized today. They are now most often used in serious criminal cases (never having been utilized in Magistrates' Courts and rarely in County Courts). Juries are most often composed of twelve members. They have the sole responsibility for deciding the guilt or innocence of the accused in a criminal trial. The decisions of the jury need not be unanimous and, in certain circumstances, majority verdicts of ten to two are accepted. The judge has the responsibility for presiding over the court, guiding the jury by rulings on questions of procedure and evidence, and for discharging or passing sentence on the defendant, according to the verdict of the jury. In civil cases, the jury is not only responsible for deciding questions of fact, but also for fixing the amount of damages to be awarded to the injured party. A unanimous verdict is required in civil cases.

Judicial Administration

The major responsibility for the administration of justice in England and Wales is divided among several government ministers. Among these are the lord chancellor, the home secretary, and the law officers of the Crown. The lord chancellor is the minister responsible for the operation of the courts and appoints, or recommends for appointment, all magistrates and all but the most senior judges. He is, ex-officio, speaker of the House of Lords and spends three to four afternoons each week, when the House is in session, presiding over its debates. He also plays an active role in those debates and is responsible for the legislation passed by that House. The nature of the lord chancellor's office qualifies him for two special types of duties within the cabinet: he is chief legal advisor to the cabinet, and because his administrative department is small and rarely in conflict with others, he often serves as an impartial member of committees dealing with conflicts between different departments.

The lord chancellor fulfills at least two kinds of roles—political (as political executive and legislative leader) and adjudicative (as judge as a judicial administrator). Because of his extensive administrative duties, the lord chancellor has little time to sit in on cases and is generally not expected to spend much time functioning as judge until after he has retired from his political duties. In seeking someone who can balance these difficult roles, the prime minister looks for: (1) political experience—only four of those who have served as lord chancellor this century have not previously seen service in the House of Commons; (2) a qualified barrister; and (3) someone who would be willing to accept peerage, and with it, almost certain disqualification from ever becoming prime minister.

The home secretary is the senior cabinet minister who is concerned with criminal law. He is responsible for the prevention of crime, the apprehension of offenders, and for administering the penal system. The government's principal legal officers are the attorney general and the solicitor general (known as the

"Law Officers of the Crown for England and Wales"). They are senior barristers who have been elected to the House of Commons and hold ministerial posts. The solicitor general has similar rights and duties as the attorney general but is subject to the latter's authority. The attorney general is the chief legal advisor for the government. Because the lord chancellor has no minister in the House of Commons, the attorney general serves as his spokesman on matters affecting the administration of justice in that body. In the civil area, the attorney general may appear before judicial tribunals of inquiry and has the responsibility for instituting proceedings in the High Court for the enforcement of public rights. He has the ultimate responsibility for the enforcement of law in the criminal area, and his consent is required for the institution of certain kinds of proceedings.

Public Perceptions and the Role of the Courts

Public attitudes in England are often characterized by trust, deference, and civility. While recent studies indicate a decline in the traditionally positive perceptions of the political system, there is still widespread allegiance to political authority.[37] Richard Rose, for example, writes: "The readiness of English people to comply voluntarily with basic political laws confirms the legitimacy of government. The very idea of a political crime (in eastern European countries, 'a crime against the state') is unknown in England."[38]

While there has been some recent criticism of the legal system (for example, a 1983 series by *The Economist* pointed out some unhappiness with the slowness and costs of the system and the perceived remoteness of many judges), public perceptions of the judicial system remain generally positive. For example, an April 1974 poll indicated that voters had more confidence in the law courts than all but two (police and medicine) public institutions.[39] Similarly, a 1973 poll found members of the legal profession to be well regarded by the voters. The study asked "Which two of these people do you feel are the most trustworthy? And which do you feel are the least trustworthy?" Judges were ranked second and lawyers third (after doctors) of eleven professions (the others were civil servants, cabinet ministers, union leaders, councillors, MPs, journalists, city financers, and businessmen) as the "most trustworthy" and cited the least often (again, after doctors) as the "least trustworthy." Interestingly, the same study indicated that the public did not see the courts as being very powerful. Only 6 percent of the sample stated that the courts had the "greatest effect" on "how the country is run" and 23 percent the "least effect" (the two institutions seen as having the greatest effect were the trade unions and the prime minister, and the two with the least effect were the Queen and the electorate, with the latter receiving the same 23 percent as the law courts).[40]

There is a general agreement among judges, lawyers, and political leaders on a fairly narrow definition of the proper role for the courts. This consensus has tended to limit the impact that the judiciary has had upon the political system. This less active role for the judiciary was probably best articulated by Lord

Simonds (lord chancellor from 1951 to 1954) in *Midlands Silicones, Ltd. v. Scruttons, Ltd.*:

Nor will I easily be led by an undiscerning zeal for some abstract king of justice to ignore our first duty, which is to administer justice according to law, the law which is established for us by an Act of Parliament or the binding authority of precedent. The Law is developed by the application of old principles to new circumstances. Therein lies its genius. Its reform by the abrogation of these principles is the task not of the courts of law but of Parliament.[41]

Courts and judges can (and do) routinely play a significant role within the British political system despite the absence of a tradition of judicial review. Budge and McCay note a number of areas where the English courts play an important role in the political process: (1) courts can overrule by-laws of local authorities where such regulations are inconsistent with the parliamentary legislation that authorized them; (2) while acts of Parliament often provide wide latitude for ministerial discretion for implementation, ministerial actions are subject to judicial control; (3) while no one asks judges to invalidate acts of Parliament, they routinely do ask them to interpret the meaning of the law; and (4) the courts do have much to say about criminal law and civil law because much of it comes not from acts of Parliament but from the ''common law'' made by judges.[42] They conclude:

All these powers go together to suggest that courts and judges in England are very important indeed; if the judges can create rules that we have to obey, or can alter rules created by Parliament, or can control the exercise of powers given to ministers and authorities *by* [their emphasis] parliamentary Acts, are they not actually governing us? And is not governing precisely what makes an institution ''political''?[43]

Finally, the nonpolitical role of the judiciary has often increased its power. Judges have, because of their assumed neutrality, been asked to preside over Tribunals of Inquiry, which are called upon to investigate allegations against the government. These tribunals are created by resolutions from both houses of Parliament and report their findings and leave it to others to determine the consequences of their facts—similiar to the Warren Commission in the United States. Judges have also played a major role on Royal Commissions. These bodies are often created to investigate particular problems and make recommendations for future courses of action—similar to American congressional committees set up to investigate the creation of a new national policy.

In addition, while most judges subscribe to Lord Simond's more passive view of the role of judges, there have been outspoken members of the judiciary who have favored a more active role. The best known of these is Lord Denning who retired in 1982 after twenty years as master of the rolls. Denning's views on the ''proper'' role for the courts are seen in the following:

The truth is that the law is uncertain. It does not cover all the situations that may arise. Time and again practicioners are faced with new situations, where the decisions may go either way. No one can tell what the law is until the courts decide it. The judges do every day make law, though it is almost heresy to say so. If the truth is recognized then we may hope to escape from the dead hand of the past and consciously mould new principles to meet the needs of the present.[44]

How, then, can we evaluate the role that courts play in England and Wales? Budge and McCay succinctly state that "first, the courts in England do have enormous political power, but secondly, they do their utmost not to use it."[45] This is probably nowhere more true than in the House of Lords, where the judges often defer to other institutions, often frustrating those who have more activist perceptions. This has resulted in the resignation of two of the most strong-willed members of that body—Lords Denning and Devlin—the former to head the lower-ranking Court of Appeals, where he felt he could influence the process by his dissenting opinions, and the latter to write and lecture. Morrison agrees that the more passive view held by most judges has resulted in a more limited role for the courts: "English courts are clearly not unimportant, but in relation to their political surroundings they do not reach the stature of American courts. Their self-perception of judicial role has restricted the perimeter of their vision; their restricted vision has limited their impact."[46]

The political role of the courts has not only been limited by the views of British jurists. More importantly, there has been a clear vision of the role of the political system (and of the courts) in dealing with societal problems. Richard Rose, for example, has written that "Today as in the past, the chief constraints upon the British government are cultural norms of what government should and should not do."[47] Given the nature of the historic development and the extent of consensus regarding cultural and political norms, therefore, it is not surprising to find the courts in England and Wales playing a less active role than their American counterparts.

NORTHERN IRELAND

The Development of the Legal System

The legal system in Northern Ireland is similar to that found in England and Wales. While the original Celtic laws in the area were quite different from those found in either England or on the Continent, the English influence began to grow in Ireland in the twelfth century and was firmly established by the fourteenth century. However, it was not until the seventeenth century that the English model was universally applied throughout Ireland.

Ireland joined the United Kingdom in 1801. The Government of Ireland Act of 1920 separated the twenty-six counties of the south from the six counties of the north—with the former being granted home rule (the Republic of Ireland was finally established in 1949) and the latter remaining part of the United Kingdom. The act created a constitution for Northern Ireland with a legislature and executive subordinate to the supreme authority of the Parliament of the United Kingdom in London. The legislature of Northern Ireland was given the power to enact legislation in the domestic area, and, as a result, contemporary legislation in Northern Ireland differs from the remainder of the United Kingdom both in the source of the law as well as its substance.

This pattern of government remained fairly stable until the early 1970s, when, in response to increasing civil violence, a period of direct rule from England was introduced. This period saw the dissolution of the Parliament in Northern Ireland and responsibility for governing the area turned over to the Parliament in London. Continued violence and opposition to direct rule during the next decade has led to a number of different forms of government—with none receiving the whole-hearted support of all sectors of the population of Northern Ireland. The Northern Ireland Act of 1974 dissolved the Northern Ireland Assembly and reestablished direct rule in the area. The act gave the responsibility for law and order, constitutional matters, and overall planning to the secretary of state, appointed by the British government. The secretary of state is a cabinet minister responsible for Ulster and accountable to the British Parliament. He works out of the Northern Ireland Office, which has eleven divisions in Belfast and four in London. There are seven departments (Civil Service, Agriculture, Economic Development, Education, Environment, Finance and Personnel, and Health and Civil Service) within a separate Northern Ireland Department. The secretary of state is, however, responsible for the direction of the various departments.[48] The latest attempt to break the cycle of violence has been the establishment of a unicameral Northern Ireland Assembly created by the Northern Ireland Act of 1982. The Assembly has the responsibility for making recommendations to the secretary of state regarding the devolution of governmental powers. At least 70 percent of the total membership of the Assembly must approve any recommendations before the secretary of state will send those recommendations to the Parliament (though the secretary, can, in the absence of 70 percent approval, send the recommendations on if he believes that both sides of the community will accept the recommendations).[49] Pending such consensus, however, it appears likely that some form of direct rule will continue in Northern Ireland.

The Organization of the Court System

There are three levels to the court system in Northern Ireland: the Supreme Court of Judicature of Northern Ireland, County Courts, and Magistrates' Courts. The Supreme Court is composed of the Crown Court, High Court and Court of Appeal. The lord chief justice, three lord justices of appeal, and four judges of the High Court preside over the Supreme Court. The Crown Court, established in 1978, hears criminal proceedings anywhere in Northern Ireland. Cases may be heard by the lord chief justice (who is president of the Court) or any High Court, Court of Appeals, or County Court judge. Decisions of the Court may be appealed to the Court of Appeals. The High Court has both original and appellate jurisdiction. It is the superior civil court of first instance and has appellate jurisdiction over County Court cases. The Court is presided over by the lord chief justice and not more than six other judges. The Court is divided into Queen's Bench, Chancery, and Family Divisions, with essentially the same responsibilities as those courts in England and Wales. The Court of Appeals is made up of the lord chief justice and three lord justices of appeal. The Court hears criminal appeals from the Crown Court and civil appeals from the High Court. It may also hear appeals from the County Courts and Magistrates' Courts.

There are eight County Court divisions, presided over by eleven County Court judges (the judges are called "recorders" in Belfast and Londonderry). These courts hear criminal appeals from the Magistrates' Courts and have wide jurisdiction in civil cases (they may generally hear cases in which the amount of the claim is not in excess of 5,000 pounds).[50] At the bottom of the court system are the Magistrates' Courts in the twenty-five sessions districts in Northern Ireland. These courts are presided over by seventeen resident and nine deputy resident magistrates. These courts handle minor civil and criminal matters and their decisions may be appealed to the County Courts.[51]

The Personnel of the Law

The Legal Practitioners

The legal profession in Northern Ireland is made up of barristers and solicitors. The former, known collectively as "the bar," have the right of audience in all courts and, as in England and Wales, serve as advisors on legal problems brought them by the solicitors. In 1981 there were 222 practicing barristers in Northern Ireland—twenty-two senior counsel and two hundred junior counsel.[52] The Inn of the Court of Northern Ireland regulates both admission to the bar and the professional conduct of barristers. There are approximately 1,000 practicing solicitors in Northern Ireland today. Most of them are in private practice, though some are employed by the government.[53] Solicitors, as in England and Wales, are general legal practitioners. They may appear before both County and Magistrates' Courts. The Law Society of Northern Ireland both regulates admission and conducts any disciplinary proceedings for solicitors.

Individuals who wish to become either solicitors or barristers generally study at the Queen's University Faculty of Law (nonlaw graduates may also enter the profession after a two-year academic and one-year vocational course) for four years. Law graduates generally attend the Institute for Professional Legal Studies for one year. The Institute is located within the Queens' University and is governed by members of both branches of the profession. After the passing of a final examination, students spend a year of vocational training (with a senior member of the appropriate branch of the profession) before applying for admission to the profession.

Judges, Juries, and the Administration of Justice

Judges are selected from among the practicing barristers and solicitors. They are appointed by the queen on advice of the lord chancellor and may only be removed from office for proven misconduct or incapacity (though superior court judges can only be removed by the queen). Juries are composed of twelve ordinary citizens in criminal trials and seven in civil trials. The director of public prosecutions for Northern Ireland is responsible for prosecuting all criminal acts. He is responsible to the attorney general. Finally, the lord chancellor is responsible for the administration of the court system in Northern Ireland.

Public Perceptions and the Role of the Courts

There is no available research on public perceptions regarding the legal system of Northern Ireland. Given the depth of feelings and duration of the "troubles," one would expect to find feelings ranging from apathy to alienation regarding Northern Ireland's political system. Richard Rose, for example, found a lack of "competence" with regard to politics (60 percent indicated that they could not understand the national and international issues facing Northern Ireland) and very low levels of "political efficacy" (70 percent indicated that they had "little" or "no" influence over the government) in a study of 1,200 Catholics and Protestants in Northern Ireland.[54]

Northern Ireland does have a jury system independent of the judiciary and an independent judiciary: "The executive cannot delay or disturb the judicial process; the decisions of the courts are inviolate subject only to the right of appeal to a higher court, and to the exercise of the Royal Prerogative of Mercy."[55] The role of the courts within the political system of Northern Ireland is likely to remain a relatively unimportant one as long as direct rule from London continues. In the same way, public perceptions regarding the government of Northern Ireland are not likely to dramatically change until some consensus emerges regarding the goverance procedures for that beleaguered land. Richard Rose states the problem well:

Northern Ireland is neither a nation nor a state. In law, it is a subordinate part of the United Kingdom, ruled by the authority of the British Parliament at Westminster. In fact, Northern Ireland is an insubordinate part of the United Kingdom—governed without consensus when it is governed at all. That is the Northern Ireland problem.[56]

SCOTLAND

The Development of the Legal System

There are significant differences between the Scottish legal system and those of the remainder of the United Kingdom. These are reflected in a different administration of the law and can be seen in two ways: (1) the actual law is applied differently by the Scottish courts; and (2) the sources and general theory of the law are different. Scottish law reflects both common law and civil law traditions for the main sources of the law are the "common law," legislation (acts of Parliament and "subordinate legislation"—orders in council and regulations and orders developed by government ministers), and European Community law.

Little is known about Scottish legal institutions prior to A.D. 100. The Normans first entered Scotland in the late eleventh century, though they had less of an immediate influence there than in England. The "Anglo-Normanization" of Scotland was accelerated, however, during the reign of David I (1124–1153), when the pattern of feudal institutions prevailing in England was extended northward. This involved the granting of land to Anglo-Norman, Celtic, and indigenous chiefs in return for military and other services. The grants of land also entitled the bearer to dispense justice in local courts.

The king was the source of all secular justice (church courts had exclusive jurisdiction over matters such as family relations) and his administrators supervised the work of the local courts. The king's court heard appeals from the local courts. In time, the king's counsellors, meeting in session, evolved into the Curia Regis, consisting of all tenants-in-chief and chief ecclesiastical figures.

The local courts comprised the burgh courts, barony courts, and sheriff's courts. Burghs were market-centers (often adjacent to a royal castle), which developed courts to enforce their regulations and settle disputes. The barony court was composed of the lord and his vassals and heard cases involving feudal obligations between vassals or between the lord and his vassals. The sheriff was the king's local representative, appointed from among the local barons. He served as the king's chief administrative, judicial, financial, and military officer and oversaw the administration of justice in the inferior courts within the sheriffdom. In addition, his court served as the court of appeals for decisions coming from the barony courts within his sheriffdom.

By the end of the thirteenth century a jury system and a writ system, called a "breive," had been introduced into Scotland. The breive was issued by the Royal Chancery to the local courts to convene a jury. While the breive system was much simpler than the writ system found in England, it did play a major role in the development of a uniform system of law throughout the country. Few judicial records have survived this period. However, it appears that *Regiam Majestem*, a commentary on judicial procedures dating from the thirteenth or early fourteenth century, was probably the most important source of medieval Scottish law.

The Scottish Parliament seems to have originated in the thirteenth century, emerging from the meetings of the King's Council. Parliament produced the supreme law of the land and had exclusive jurisdiction in cases of treason and appellate jurisdiction on cases from lower courts. From the beginning, it was clearly a meeting of the Estates (clergy, tenants-in-chief, and burgesses), which exercised judicial functions. By the end of the century it held regular meetings and had become both a court of first instance as well as an appeals court in both civil and criminal matters.

After the Wars of Independence, Scotland's external ties tended to be with France and the Low Countries rather than with England. The period from 1329 to 1460 saw a significant expansion of the alliance with France. Scottish students were increasingly educated on the Continent and influenced by Roman law. Not unexpectedly, the fifteenth century saw the introduction of Roman law into Scotland.

By the sixteenth century, the Lords of Council in Session (previously known as the King's Privy Council) were reorganized as a College of Justice. The judges of the Session now became senators of the College of Justice and sat as a court of fifteen judges, half whom were ecclesiastics (by 1688 all judges were laymen). The Faculty of Advocates and Society of Writers also evolved during this century and their members both became members of the College and gained the exclusive right to be advocates and solicitors.

The reports of the Court of Session's decisions began to be circulated in the seventeenth century. While they gave an outline of the court's decisions, they did not aid in providing a framework for the development of the law. This did not begin until the publication of *Institutions of the Law of Scotland* by Lord Stair, lord president of the Court of Session, in 1681. This work drew from Scottish decisions and laws (as well as Roman law) and set out the law as a series of commonsense principles. While it was later supplemented by Erskine's *Institute* (1773) and Bell's *Commentaries* (1800) in the civil area and Baron Hume's *Commentaries* in the field, its publication is seen as marking the "birth of modern Scots law."[57]

The two most significant factors in the development of Scottish law since 1800 have been the tendency to modify the common law through statutes and the greater reliance on English rather than Roman law. The greater role for statutes has reflected both changes in public opinion as well as the different social, economic, and philosophical changes brought about by Scottish historical development.[58] The termination of the practice of studying abroad by the end of the Napoleonic Wars, the common industrial experiences of the United Kingdom for which English law had discovered some solutions, and the common language and cultures of England and Scotland are reasons offered for the decision to borrow more from the English and not Roman law.[59]

Since the Union in 1707, the Parliament of the United Kingdom has replaced the English and Scottish Parliaments. Its decisions have become binding on all courts and take precedence over all other sources of law. This sometimes produces difficulties for, "Legislation produced by Parliament is often drafted with only a cursory glance of Scottish legal principles and consequently has severely impinged on the symmetry of Scots law."[60] The House of Lords is also the final court of appeals in the civil (but not criminal) area. Scottish concern over the possible domination by the English was somewhat alleviated by certain safeguards for Scottish law and courts provided by the Acts of Union. Article XVIII, for example, states that while: "the laws which concern public and civil government may be made the same throughout the whole United Kingdom . . . no alteration be made in the laws which concern private right except for the evident utility of the subjects within Scotland."[61] In addition, Article XIX states that neither the Court of Session nor the High Court of Justiciary should be subject to the jurisdiction of the English courts.

The strength of Scottish nationalism is also evidenced in the continued calls for greater self-government (last seen in an inconclusive referendum on devolution in 1979). It is clear that many in Scotland see the Acts of Union as being quite different from other acts of Parliament:

In the Scottish mind, emphasis is placed on the origin of the United Kingdom Parliament in a freely negotiated Union between two equals, the sovereign legislatures of England and Scotland. Notwithstanding the numerical preponderance of English members in the Parliament of Great Britain, it was not created by the admission to the English Parliament of Scottish members, but the establishment of a new legislature for Britain as a whole.[62]

The present status of Scottish law (and its relationship to its southern neighbor) can be succinctly evaluated thusly:

Scots law then has moved very far towards that of England. Nevertheless, even now Scots law still maintains her independence and refuses to be totally submerged by English doctrine: "the anchors of the common law have not yet dragged." Scots lawyers will require considerable intellectual toughness to keep things this way.[63]

The Organization of the Court System

The structure of the contemporary Scottish judicial system dates from the Act of Union in 1707. In Scotland, as in England, we may distinguish between "superior" and "inferior" courts. The former are those that have jurisdiction over the entire nation and include the House of Lords, the Court of Session, and the High Court of Justiciary; the latter have jurisdiction over districts and include the sheriffs courts and district courts.

At the apex of the Civil Court structure is the House of Lords. Appeals are only heard by those legally qualified members of the House—the lord chancellor, lords of appeals in the ordinary, and those peers who have held high judicial office. The quorum is three but most cases are usually heard by five (and more important ones by seven) judges. Decisions are rendered by a majority of those judges sitting. There has been a modern custom for at least two of the law lords to be of Scottish origin, but there is no rule that a Scottish law lord must be present to hear a Scottish appeal. The House hears appeals on both questions of law and fact though the latter appeals are rare. While the House of Lords has played a valuable role in hearing appeals from both superior and inferior courts in Scotland, there is some criticism of it. Walker, for example, writes:

By a legal fiction the House of Lords, as the final Court of Appeal from England, Scotland, and Northern Ireland, has judicial knowledge of all the legal systems involved. . . . That is, however, the sheerest fiction, to ascribe to members of the English Bar and Bench, on their promotion to be Lords of Appeal, a sufficient knowledge of Scots law to correct the judges of the Court of Session. . . . The House of Lords has been responsible for some of the worst misunderstandings and confused law in the Scottish books; over and over again English doctrines have been forced into Scots law by English Law Lords who did not realize the fundamental differences of principle and reason which frequently underlie apparent similarities of result, as where remedies are granted in circumstances similar to those justifying the corresponding remedy in English law.[64]

The Court of Sessions has both original and appellate jurisdiction in the civil area. It has exclusive jurisdiction in divorces, actions to declare or nullify marriages, and questions of legitimacy. While it handles cases in a wide variety of civil actions, the bulk of litigation before it concerns divorce and petitions for personal damages. The court was divided into two divisions, presided over respectively by the lord president and the lord justice-clerk, and in 1825 each of the divisions were reduced to four judges, with the remaining seven serving as permanent lords ordinary, sitting only in the Outer House. The Inner House is mainly concerned with appeals from the Outer as well as from the Inferior Courts. There are four judges in each division of the Inner House (with three constituting a quorum). Decisions are by a majority vote, and if there is a tie vote, there is a rehearing, usually before a larger court. Judges may be called up from the Outer Court to constitute a quorum, and in difficult and/or important cases the two divisions may sit together, comprising seven or eight judges. The Outer House serves exclusively as a court of first instance. It often deals with uncontested divorces, administrative petitions, and commercial issues.

At the bottom of the civil court system are the Sheriff Courts. Scotland is divided into six sheriffdoms, each composed of fifty sheriff court districts with each district having its own court. The Sheriff Courts are presided over by a legally qualified judge, the sheriff, and deal with the majority of civil litigation. There are generally a number of sheriffs residing in the principal towns of each sheriffdom. They usually hold court in only one place but may meet in more than one town in the sheriffdom. The courts have wide jurisdiction, and there is no upper limit to the value of cases that they may hear. They function as a court of first instance, and appeals may be brought to the sheriff-principal (the senior judge in each sheriffdom) and then to the Inner House of the Court of Session or directly to the latter.

The High Court of the Justiciary was established in 1672 and since the Criminal Procedure (Scotland) Act of 1887 has consisted of the lord justice-general, the lord justice-clerk, and the other eighteen lords of the Court of Session. The Court is both a court of first instance and an appeals court in the criminal area. As a court of first instance it sits in Edinburgh as well as towns within the other three circuits of Scotland. These are: (1) West-Glasgow, Stirling, and Oban; (2) North-Inverness, Aberdeen, Dundee, and Perth; and (3) South-Dumfries, Jedburgh, and Ayr. When the Court sits as a trial court, only one of the judges hears the case. When it sits as an appellate court, three judges hear the case. The Court has exclusive jurisdiction over the most serious crimes, including murder, treason, and rape, and concurrent jurisdiction with the sheriff courts over most other crimes.

The Sheriff Courts may also hear criminal cases in both summary (the judge alone deciding questions of fact and law) procedure and solemn (the jury of fifteen laymen determining questions of fact while the judge deals with questions of law) procedure. The Sheriff Courts in the criminal area are only trial courts and can impose sentences according to the offense laid down by the statute. Decisions of the Sheriff Courts may, again, be appealed to the High Court. The lowest courts in the criminal court system are the district courts. There is one District Court in each of the fifty-six districts in Scotland. These courts are manned by either stipendiary magistrates or justices of the peace and handle minor criminal matters. The decisions of the District Courts may be appealed to the High Court.

The Personnel of the Law

The Legal Practitioners

A distinction can be made in Scotland, as it often is in England, between the legal specialist or consultant and the general advisor. The advocate tends to perform the former role, specializing in advice on complicated issues of law and framing pleadings, both oral and written, before courts and tribunals. The solicitor, on the other hand, tends to be the general legal practitioner, who alone comes into contact with the client and concerns himself with advice, business negotiations, wills, tax questions, as well as pleadings before inferior courts.

The advocate is a member of the Faculty of Advocates. In 1982 there were 396 (179 practicing) members of the Faculty. The nonpracticing members tended to be members of the judiciary, academics, or legal advisors to the business community.[65] The Faculty comprises the Scottish Bar, and its members have a status similar to barristers in England, Wales, and Northern Ireland. Advocates gain entrance to the Faculty by petitioning the court, paying fees, and proving to the Faculty Examiners that they possess the requisite academic qualifications. The Faculty is led by a dean, and he and the senior members of the organization exercise control over the professional conduct of their members, with the ability to censure or even disbar a member for a serious breach of professional conduct.

While advocates have the exclusive right of appearance before the Court of Sessions and the High Court, they are briefed before their appearances by the solicitors. Unlike the solicitor, the advocate may not form partnerships. As in England, the senior barrister may be appointed as Queen's Counsel (this is often called "taking silk" because the Queen's Counsel wears a silk gown in court) by the queen on the recommendation of the lord justice-general. Again, as in England and Wales, "QCs" must be accompanied in court by a junior counsel and it is from the ranks of the Queen's Counsel that most of the appointments to the Superior Court Judiciary are made. In 1982 there were forty-four Queen's Counsels in Scotland.[66]

In 1980 there were 5,687 solicitors on the roll of solicitors in Scotland— nearly a 50 percent increase in the number of solicitors in a decade.[67] Many solicitors are single practitioners or practice in partnership. Others, however, are employed by large corporations or public or local authorities. While they may not appear in the superior courts of Scotland, they tend to do the vast majority of the litigation in Sheriff Courts. In addition, they have a monopoly over the right to act for their clients in the conveyancing of lands as well as to discharge the vast bulk of business negotiations conducted in Scotland. All solicitors are members of the Law Society of Scotland. The Society serves as the governing body for the solicitors and regulates their fees, enforces standards of professional conduct, and makes recommendations for law reform, among other functions.

Admission to study at one of the five faculties of law in Scotland (Glasgow, Edinburgh, Aberdeen, Strathclide, and Dundee) is very selective. In the late 1970s there were nearly 1,900 students reading law at these five centers.[68] Since 1980, the four-year course of study at the universities has been supplemented by a one-year program leading to a Diploma in Legal Practice. This is a program in the more practical areas of the law (which has enabled the undergraduate training to focus a bit more on the philosophical underpinnings of the law) offered at the five universities.[69] This is followed by a period of vocational training: two years as a "trainee" with a solicitor for those wishing to enter that branch of the profession and a short period with a solicitor, followed by a nine-month "pupillage" with a junior counsel for those wishing to become advocates.

Judges

There are two essential characteristics of the Scottish judiciary: (1) there is far greater use made of full-time, legally qualified judges than in England, where the justice of the peace plays a far more active role; and (2) as in the remainder of the United Kingdom, judges in Scotland are selected from among practicing legal practitioners, rather than from those who are trained to be judges from the beginning of their legal careers.[70] Because most of the members of the Scottish judiciary are Queen's Counsels (this is especially true in the superior courts), the Scottish judiciary is open to the same criticism found in the remainder of the United Kingdom, namely, that the judiciary tends to disproportionately come from the upper classes and to have rather narrow experiences prior to elevation to the bench.

Scottish members of the House of Lords are appointed by the queen on recommendation of the prime minister. They must have been practicing members of the Scottish Bar for at least fifteen years or have held judicial office for at least two years. Most vacancies are filled from the Court of Sessions, but individuals may be appointed directly from the Bar. The retirement age for the lords of appeal in the ordinary is seventy-five.

Twenty-one individuals simultaneously sit on both the Court of Sessions (where they are called senator of the college of justice) and High Court of Justiciary (where they are known as lord commissioner of justiciary). Judges are required to have five years' experience at the bar prior to appointment, but most are QCs with considerable experience prior to their elevation to the bench. Appointments are made by the queen on recommendation of the prime minister.[71] Political experience and service within the Faculty of Advocates tend to dramatically improve one's chances of being appointed to the superior courts. For example, since 1800, thirty-nine of the forty-five deans of the Faculty have been appointed to the bench. While women are theoretically eligible to be appointed to the bench (Justice Elizabeth Lane was the first female on the High Court from 1965–1979) no woman has yet to be appointed to the Court of Session.[72] Superior Court judges must retire at seventy-five.

Sheriffs and sheriff-principals are appointed by the queen on recommendation by the secretary of state for Scotland. They must have ten years' experience as either advocates or solicitors. Interestingly, in recent years there has been an increasing tendency to appoint solicitors as sheriffs.[73] Sheriffs and sheriff-principals must retire at seventy-two. Stipendiary magistrates and justices of the peace serve on the District Courts. The former must have five years' experience as either advocates or solicitors and are appointed by the District Councils, on approval of the secretary of state for Scotland. The latter are laymen who are assisted by clerks of the peace. They are appointed by the secretary of state for Scotland, though the District Councils may appoint some ex-officio JPs.

Juries

A jury of fifteen is generally constituted in most criminal trials. A jury of twelve is utilized in civil actions (primarily in personal injury) and cases involving deaths in the Court of Session. Those who are between the ages of eighteen and sixty-five, residents of the U. K. for five years, and registered as electors are eligible to serve as jurors. Women may be exempted on medical grounds, and members of certain professions (such as physicians) may also be exempted from service.

Judicial Administration

The organization and administration of the courts is carried out by the courts and the secretary of state for Scotland, a government minister. He is responsible for the organization and administration of the sheriff courts and, to a much lesser extent, the superior courts. He is aided by a government department, the Scottish Courts Administration.

The two official law officers of the Crown in Scotland are the lord advocate and the solicitor-general. Both may be members of Parliament and are appointed to their posts by the prime minister. The lord advocate is head of the system of public prosecution and he (or the solicitor-general) appears for the Crown in important criminal cases. The lord advocate may appoint assistants to aid him in prosecuting before the High Court. In addition, the lord advocate's department employs a small number of solicitors and advocates to assist the lord advocate and solicitor-general.

Public Perceptions and the Role of the Courts

As already noted, there is some concern in Scotland over the protection of Scottish laws and institutions as well as the feeling that the Acts of Union joined equal partners. While there is little research on public perceptions of legal practitioners or members of the bench, the system is seen as being efficient.[74] Scotland's judiciary maintains the same independence found in the remainder of the United Kingdom. The power of judicial review is generally not found in the United Kingdom. However, it has been argued in Scotland that where "Scottish social and political structure are under threat from Parliamentary legislation, the Courts should adopt an activist approach and declare it invalid."[75] Interestingly, in two recent cases, the Court of Session reserved its opinion on its power of judicial review:

While asserting the power in neither case, it retained the option to choose to do so in appropriate circumstances sometime in the future. . . . For the court of Session is likely to overturn legislation only in an atmosphere of political and social revolution forecasting the breakup of the union. Even to those of a nationalist pervasion [sic], such a scenario is unlikely to ever occur. Nevertheless, the area is of considerable jurisprudential interest and illustrates the intellectual independence of Scots law.[76]

The Scottish courts have played a significant role in ensuring that public authorities have acted within the limits of their powers. Any individual whose rights have been threatened by the action (or inaction) of a public authority may bring an action in the courts to obtain a remedy. The courts have also played an important role in the administrative field. For example, both the Court of Session and the sheriff courts have administrative functions—supervising bankruptcies, managing the affairs of children and others unable to manage their estates, and confirming the executors of the estates of deceased individuals.

Finally, there are a large number of administrative tribunals in Scotland that perform judicial rather than administrative functions.

NOTES

1. M. Glendon, M. W. Gordon, and C. Osawke, *Comparative Legal Traditions in a Nutshell* (St.Paul, Minn.: West Publishing Co., 1982), p. 143.

2. A. K. R. Kiralfy, *Potter's Historical Introduction to English Law and Its Institutions* (London: Sweet & Maxwell Ltd., 1958), p. 15.

3. G. W. Keeton, *English Law: The Judicial Contribution* (Newton Abbot, England: David & Charles, 1974) p. 53.

4. M. Shapiro, *Courts: A Comparative and Political Analysis* (Chicago and London: The University of Chicago Press, 1981), p. 73.

5. Kiralfy, *Potter's Historical Introduction*, p. 19.

6. R. David and J. E. C. Brierley, *Major Legal Systems in the World Today: An Introduction to the Comparative Study of Law* (London: The Free Press, 1978), p. 300.

7. Ibid., p. 302.

8. Shapiro, *Courts: A Comparative and Political Analysis*, p. 98.

9. Ibid., p. 102.

10. Lord Chancellor's Department, *Judicial Statistics, England and Wales for the Year 1983* (London: Her Majesty's Stationery Office, 1984), p. 5.

11. Ibid.

12. Ibid.

13. F. L. Morrison, *Courts and the Political Process in England* (Beverly Hills and London: Sage Publications, 1973), p. 41.

14. Lord Chancellor's Department, *Judicial Statistics*, p. 5.

15. Morrison, *Courts and the Political Process*, p. 42.

16. Lord Chancellor's Department, *Judicial Statistics*, p. 5.

17. Ibid.

18. Ibid., p. 88.

19. Ibid., p. 59.

20. Central Office of Information for British Information Services, *The Legal System of England* (London: Her Majesty's Stationery Office, 1976), pp. 30–31.

21. A. W. Green, "Legal Education in England," *Journal of Legal Education* 28 (1976), pp. 137–38.

22. B. Abel-Smith and R. Stevens, *In Search of Justice: Society and the Legal System* (London: Penguin Press, 1968), p. 345.

23. Ibid., p. 131.

24. "The People on the Bench," *The Economist*, August 13, 1983, p. 50.

25. "The Judiciary: Don't Bother with the Facts," *The Economist*, September 15, 1984, p. 68.

26. S. Shetreet, *Judges on Trial: A Study of the Appointment and Accountability of the English Judiciary* (Amsterdam, Oxford, and New York: North-Holland Publishing Co., 1976), p. 76.

27. Lord Goddard, "Politics and the British Bench," *Journal of American Judicial Society* 43 (1959), p. 124.

28. See, for example, J. A. G. Griffith, *The Politics of the Judiciary* (Glasgow: Wil-

liam Collins & Sons, Co., 1977); H. Cecil, *The English Judge* (London: Stevens & Sons, 1970); and A. A. Patterson, "Judges: A Political Elite?" *Journal of Law and Society* 1, no. 2 (Winter 1974), pp. 118–135.

29. Stevens Editorial Staff, eds., *The Bar List of the United Kingdom, 1979* (London: Stevens & Sons, Ltd., 1979).

30. L. N. Tate, "Paths to the Bench in Britain: A Quasi-Experimental Study of the Recruitment of a Judicial Elite," *The Western Political Quarterly* 30 (1975), p. 120.

31. A. N. Katz, "Patterns of Judicial Recruitment of the English Judiciary: The Limits of Reform" (Paper delivered to the British Politics Group, American Political Science Association Convention, New York, N. Y., September 1981).

32. See, for example, Shetreet, *Judges on Trial*; Tate, "Paths to the Bench in Britain"; and Katz, "Patterns of Judicial Recruitment."

33. "The People on the Bench," *The Economist*, p. 51.

34. C. Beard, *The Office of the Justice of the Peace in England*, p. 71, cited in F. Milton, *The English Magistracy* (London, New York, and Toronto: Oxford University Press, 1967), p. 7.

35. "A Legal System Under Stress," *The Economist*, July 30, 1983, p. 55.

36. "The People on the Bench," *The Economist*, p. 51.

37. See, for example, Dennis Kavanaugh, "Political Culture in Great Britain: The Decline of the Civic Culture," in G. Almond and S. Verba, eds., *The Civic Culture Revisited* (Boston: Little, Brown & Co., 1980), pp. 124–76.

38. R. Rose, *Politics in England* (Boston: Little, Brown & Co., 1980), p. 115.

39. "Public Losing Confidence in Most of the Leading British Institutions," *Times* (London), April 30, 1974, p. 3.

40. G. Young, "MPs, the Unknown Men Who Don't Run Britain," *Sunday Times* (London), July 15, 1973, p. 3.

41. Cited in M. Zander, *The Law-Making Process* (London: Weidenfeld and Nicolson, 1980), p. 211.

42. I. Budge, D. McCay, et al., *The New British Political System: Gopvernment and Society in the 1980s* (London and New York: Longman, 1983), pp. 164–65.

43. Ibid., p. 165.

44. Cited in Zander, *The Law-Making Process*, p. 212.

45. Budge and McCay, *The New British Political System*, p. 177.

46. Morrison, *Courts and the Political Process*, p. 224.

47. Rose, *Politics in England*, p. 97.

48. L. Furey, "The Legal System of Northern Ireland," in K. Redden, ed., *Modern Legal Systems Cyclopedia*, vol. 3 (Buffalo: William S. Hein & Co., 1984), pp. 489–90.

49. Ibid., pp. 488–90.

50. Ibid., p. 494.

51. Ibid., pp. 495–96.

52. Ibid., p. 500.

53. Ibid., p. 499.

54. R. Rose, *Governing Without Consensus: An Irish Perspective* (Boston: Beacon Press, 1971), p. 488.

55. Furey, "The Legal System of Northern Ireland," pp. 497–98.

56. R. Rose, *Northern Ireland: Time of Choice* (Washington, D. C.: American Enterprise Institute for Public Policy Research, 1976), p. 9.

57. "The Legal System of Scotland," in K. Redden, ed., *Modern Legal Systems Cyclopedia*, vol. 3 (Buffalo: William S. Hein & Co., 1984), p. 441.

58. D. M. Walker, *The Scottish Legal System: An Introduction to the Study of Scots Law* (Edinburgh: W. Green & Son, Ltd., 1981), p. 149.

59. Central Office of Information, *The Legal System of England*, pp. 42–43.

60. "The Legal System of Scotland," p. 442.

61. Central Office of Information, *The Legal System of England*, p. 44.

62. From the Royal Commission on the Constitution, cited in ibid.

63. "The Legal System of Scotland," pp. 442

64. Walker, *The Scottish Legal System*, p. 258.

65. "The Legal System of Scotland," p. 468.

66. Ibid.

67. Ibid., p. 467.

68. Ibid., p. 464.

69. Ibid., p. 465.

70. Her Majesty's Stationery Office, *The Legal System of Scotland* (Edinburgh: Her Majesty's Stationery Office, 1977), p. 31.

71. "The Legal System of Scotland," p. 453.

72. Walker, *The Scottish Legal System*, p. 310.

73. "The Legal System of Scotland," p. 454.

74. Central Office of Information, *The Legal System of England*, p. 61.

75. "The Legal System of Scotland," p. 452.

76. Ibid.

BIBLIOGRAPHY

Abel-Smith, B., and R. Stevens. *In Search of Justice: Society and the Legal System.* London: The Penguin Press, 1968.

Ablard, C. "Observations on the English System of Legal Education: Does it Point the Way to Changes in the United States?" *Journal of Legal Education* 29 (1978), pp. 148–69.

Balekjian, W. H. "Scotland." *Comparative Law Yearbook* 5 (1981), pp. 123–35.

Blom-Cooper, L., and G. Drewry. *Final Appeal: A Study of the House of Lords in Its Judicial Capacity.* Oxford: Clarendon Press, 1972.

Budge, I., D. McCay, D. Marsh, E. Page, R. Rhodes, D. Robertson, M. Slater, and G. Wilson. *The New British Political System: Government and Society in the 1980s.* London and New York: Longman, 1983.

Burnley, E. *J. P.: Magistrate, Court and Community.* London: Hutchinson & Co., Ltd., 1979.

Cecil, H. *The English Judge.* London: Stevens & Sons, 1970.

Central Office of Information for British Information Services. *The Legal Systems of Britain.* London: Her Majesty's Stationery Office, 1976.

David, R., and J. E. C. Brierley. *Major Legal Systems in the World Today: An Introduction to the Comparative Study of Law.* London: The Free Press, 1978.

Folsom, R., and N. Roberts. "The Warwick Story: Being Led Down the Contextual Path of the Law." *Journal of Legal Education* 30 (1979), pp. 166–83.

Freeman, M. D. A. "Standards of Adjudication, Judicial Law-Making and Prospective Overruling." *Current Legal Problems* 26 (1973), pp. 166, 200–207.

Furey, L. "The Legal System of Northern Ireland." In K. Redden, ed., *Modern Legal Systems Cyclopedia*, vol. 3. Buffalo, N. Y.: William S. Hein & Co., 1984. Pp. 485–514.

Glendon, M., M. W. Gordon, and C. Osawke. *Comparative Legal Traditions in a Nutshell*. St. Paul, Minn.: West Publishing Co., 1982.

Green, A. W. "Legal Education in England." *Journal of Legal Education* 28 (1976), pp. 137–80.

Griffith, J. A. G. "The Political Constitution." *The Modern Law Review* 42, no. 1 (January 1979), pp. 18–19.

———. *The Politics of the Judiciary*. Glasgow: William Collins & Sons, Co., 1977.

Hazell, R., ed. *The Bar on Trial*. London, Melbourne and New York: Quartet Books, 1978.

Her Majesty's Stationery Office. *The Legal System of Scotland*. Edinburgh: Her Majesty's Stationery Office, 1977.

Jackson, R. M. *The Machinery of Justice in England*. Cambridge: Cambridge University Press, 1977.

Katz, A. N. "Patterns of Judicial Recruitment of the English Judiciary: The Limits of Reform." Paper delivered to the British Politics Group, American Political Science Convention, New York, N. Y., September 1981.

Kavanaugh, D. "Political Culture in Great Britain: The Decline of the Civic Culture." In G. Almond and S. Verba, eds., *The Civic Culture Revisited*. Boston: Little, Brown & Co., 1980. Pp. 127–76.

Kiralfy, A. K. R. *Potter's Historical Introduction to English Law and Its Institutions*. London: Sweet & Maxwell Ltd., 1958.

"The Legal System of Scotland." In K. Redden, ed., *Modern Legal Systems Cyclopedia*, vol. 3. Buffalo, N. Y.: William S. Hein & Co., 1984. Pp. 429–77.

Lord Chancellor's Department. *Judicial Statistics, England and Wales for the Year 1983*. London: Her Majesty's Stationery Office, 1984.

Milton, F. *The English Magistracy*. London, New York and Toronto: Oxford University Press, 1967.

Morrision, F. L. *Courts and the Political Process in England*. Beverly Hills and London: Sage Publications, 1973.

Pannick, D. "The Law Lords and the Needs of Contemporary Society." *Political Quarterly* 53 (July-September 1982), pp. 318–28.

Report of the Committee on Legal Education. Cmnd. 4959, London: Her Majesty's Printing Office, 1971.

Rose, R. *Governing Without Consensus: An Irish Perspective*. Boston: Beacon Press, 1971.

———. *Northern Ireland: Time of Choice*. Washington, D. C.: American Enterprise Institute for Public Policy Research, 1976.

———. *Politics in England*. Boston: Little, Brown & Co., 1980.

Shapiro, M. *Courts: A Comparative and Political Analysis*. Chicago and London: The University of Chicago Press, 1981.

Shetreet, S. *Judges on Trial: A Study of the Appointment and Accountability of the English Judiciary*. Amsterdam, Oxford, and New York: North-Holland Publishing Co., 1976.

Skyrme, T. *The Changing Image of the Magistracy*. London and Bisingstoke: The Macmillan Press Ltd., 1979.

Stevens, R. *Law and Politics: The House of Lords as a Judicial Body, 1800–1976.* London: Weidenfield and Nicolson, 1979.

Tate, C. N. "Paths to the Bench in Britain: A Quasi-Experimental Study of the Recruitment of a Judicial Elite." *The Western Political Quarterly* 30 (1975). Pp. 108–29.

Thomas, P., and G. M. Mungham. "English Legal Education: A Commentary on the Ormrod Report." *Valparaiso University Law Review* 7, no. 1 (February 1972), pp. 87–131.

Ulster Yearbook: The Official Handbook of Northern Ireland, 1983. Belfast: Northern Ireland Information Services, 1983.

Walker, D. *The Scottish Legal System: An Interpretation to the Study of Scots Law.* Edinburgh: W. Green & Son, Ltd., 1981.

Walker, R. J. *The English Legal System.* London: Butterworths, 1976.

Wilson, J. F. "A Survey of Legal Education in the United Kingdom." *The Journal of the Society of Public Teachers of Law* 19 (June 1966), pp. 1–144.

Wilson, J. F., and S. B. Marsh. "A Second Survey of Legal Education in the United Kingdom." *The Journal of the Society of Public Teachers of Law* 13 (July 1975), pp. 239–331.

———. *Second Survey of Legal Education in the United Kingdom, Supplement No. 1.* London: Institute of Advanced Legal Studies, University of London, 1978.

Zander, M. *The Law-Making Process.* London: Weidenfeld and Nicolson, 1980.

18

UNITED STATES

Donald W. Greenberg

THE DEVELOPMENT OF THE LEGAL SYSTEM

The American legal system is based primarily on English common law but has also been significantly influenced in its development by Roman law (civil law) as well as individual legal peculiarities unique to the various states and federal system. For example, in 1812 the United States Supreme Court ruled that no individual could be convicted of a federal crime without an applicable statute.[1] This is a repudiation of a common law principle and an acceptance of a Roman or civil law ideal and is a bedrock for American federal law.

Gilmore has argued that American law began to develop about 1800.[2] Prior to that, the legal system was based on English law, but much legal activity in the colonies was attempts to evade English law, and, as such, obfuscated rather than clarified the law. The law in America floundered for a period before a truly American legal system began to develop. The American legal system, according to Karl Llewellyn, went through two early periods before reaching its present stage. The first period from 1800 to 1860 might be called the "Golden Age" of American law. The law was open-ended and flexible, and attempts were made to clearly make the law compatible with justice. It was in this period that the courts began to assume jurisdiction over issues that in some countries would be considered beyond the courts (Alexis de Tocqueville, for example, observed that sooner or later all matters in America wind up in court). The second period in the development of American law dates from the Civil War to around 1920. It was in this period that the law was used to protect vested interests (primarily economic) and was when the law was restrictive and narrowly interpreted. The third present stage has been an attempt to reach a balance between the two earlier stages.[3]

Regardless of the direction American law has taken, it rests most fundamentally on English common law. Common law has two distinct but related meanings:

a philosophical principle upon which a model of law is built and a term that describes the procedures of a given legal system. It is the inherent law of all the people, and, as it is needed, it is discovered by judges who apply the correct part of common law to a particular case. Common law can be compared, for example, to Newton's laws of nature. They always existed, and Newton did nothing more than discover and label them. Once he did that, others could apply them in a variety of ways, but they would have existed just as absolutely if Newton had not been sitting under that fateful tree. Common law similarly argues that the laws that govern the relations of human beings to each other grow out of the nature of human relations and are always with us. One commentator described common law as "custom so ancient, man's memory runneth not to the contrary."[4] In the eighteenth century, the English jurist William Blackstone wrote extensively on the matter of common law and did a great deal to popularize and legitimize it as the dominant legal philosophy in the United States. Blackstone saw common law as "a priori set of 'external' immutable rules from which the proper resolution of all disputes could be deducted."[5]

Operationally, common law rests on two factors: procedure and stare decisis (precedent). Procedure refers to the rules and regulations governing all aspects of the legal process but, most importantly, those that have to do with the operation of the courts. Common law is a set of arcane and extremely technical procedures that are clearly the purview of experts. An example of the technical nature of common law procedure is complaint. A complaint is when you inform the court of the issue to be litigated. Under common law, failure to follow the exact guidelines for filing the complaint prevents the case from being accepted regardless of the merits of the case.

In order to fully understand the foundations of American law, one must examine not only the procedural nature of common law but also equity law, or as it was known in England, Chancery. The Chancery Court grew in England for a number of reasons, but the two most important were that it increased the power of the king and it offered a means of legal relief to individuals who had been thwarted in common law court, usually because of procedural errors. Chancery Court was established in the fifteenth century.[6] The Chancery Court that developed equity law was a mechanism whereby an individual could petition the king to overturn a decision of the regular court or to hear a case in which he was denied access to court because the dispute was not covered under a common law writ. Chancery was an attempt to bring equity to law, "to grant the relief prayed for as an act of grace, when the common law gave no or inadequate remedy".[7] Equity law was accepted by the colonies, and while at the federal level there has never been a specific chancery court, several states did develop equity or chancery courts.

Stare decisis (precedent) is the other major component of common law important to the development of the American legal system. Precedent is the idea that once a court has made a ruling based on the common law in a particular case, that ruling covers all similar cases that follow. Once a particular law has been discovered, it becomes the immutable guiding principle for all similarly situated issues. To Blackstone, the idea of strict adherence to precedent was a firm principle of common law and could not be breached. The essential component of precedent is that it is judge-made law rather than a fixed body of definite rules such as modern civil law codes. It is important in American law, but its application has been tailored to meet the needs of the American legal system. The law that develops for the society and binds the entire society are the specific rulings made by judges in given cases. These rulings, then, become general principles that apply to other cases or disputes since no two disputes are exactly alike. In fact, judges are called upon to make constant modifications and interpretations of original precedents, which themselves become precedents for later disputes. So the law, while ostensibly fixed in tradition, is, in reality, constantly changing as judges apply precedents to specific disputes.

The roots of the American legal system are clearly found in the English system, but the plant that has grown is peculiarly American. In 1774, the First Continental Congress passed the resolution that Americans were entitled to the common law as well as to English statutes existing at the time of colonization. Similar resolutions were adopted by eleven of the thirteen original states. The separation of American law from its English roots came primarily in four ways: the interpretation of common law by American judges; statutes passed by state legislatures; the growth of equity law; and the use of a written constitution as a guide to what constituted correct law. Concerning the rapid growth and changes of American law, one commentator has stated, "By 1820 the legal landscape in America bore only the faintest resemblance to what existed forty years earlier. Law was no longer conceived of as an internal set of principles expressed in custom and derived from natural law. . . . Judges came to think of common law as equally responsible with legislation for governing society and promoting socially desirable conduct."[8] American law, then, grew in the nineteenth century both horizontally, developing its own legal system and individual interpretations of common law and vertically, with the whole idea of law attempting to reach new heights of purpose.

The development of American law has also been profoundly affected by our written Constitution and the interpretation of the Constitution by the federal courts, most importantly, the United States Supreme Court. In *Marbury v. Madison* (1803), the Supreme Court established judicial review, the practice of using judicial judgment to determine the constitutionality of a legislative act, and in *Swift v. Tyson* (1842) the court ruled federal decisions can be made on their own merits and state precedent need not be considered. Thus, the historical development of the American legal system is marked by the founding influence of English law, the indirect influence of civil or Roman law, the peculiar development of state law, and the separate but important growth of federal law. This has created a system that is fragmented and yet unified.

418 Donald W. Greenberg

THE ORGANIZATION OF THE COURT SYSTEM

It is difficult to discuss the American court system because the various states and the federal government have each developed their own distinctive system of courts. There are some general applicable guidelines but the distinctions between state and federal and between states are substantial. For example, some states still have separate equity courts and Louisiana still operates under the Napoleonic Codes.

The federal court system draws its existence from Article III, Section I, of the Constitution. Article III vests the judicial power of the United States in a Supreme Court and further authorizes the Congress to establish such inferior courts as it deems necessary. The size, jurisdiction, and compensation of judges of all federal courts is left to the discretion of Congress, excepting the Supreme Court where Article III, Section II, outlines partial Supreme Court jurisdiction. The Constitution mandates Supreme Court jurisdiction in "all cases affecting Ambassadors, other public ministers and consuls, and those in which a state shall be a Party." In all other matters, the Court shall have appellate jurisdiction both as to law and fact with such exceptions and under such regulations as the Congress shall make. Original jurisdiction has made up a very small percentage of the Court's docket (it has heard only 148 cases since 1789 under original jurisdiction).[9]

The appellate jurisdiction of the Supreme Court has evolved from precedent decisions and from legislative acts. The controlling legislative act with respect to court jurisdiction is the Judges Bill of 1925. This gave the Court complete discretion on writs of certiorari and established guidelines for writs of appeal. Under a writ of certiorari, four judges of the Supreme Court must vote to hear a case. The Court issues no explanation for refusing the case. The Court will hear an appeal if a substantial constitutional question exists in the minds of four justices. In practical terms, the Court is concerned with these three issues: (1) has a significant procedural error occurred, preventing a defendant from receiving their due process rights under the Constitution? (2) has there been an erroneous interpretation of a valid statute by a lower court? and (3) is the statute or regulation inherently unconstitutional? If any of these three conditions exist and the issue raised is significant, it is probable the Court will hear the case.

When the Supreme Court or any other federal appeals court hears a case, it deals with a frozen record. It does not hear new testimony or deal with the facts of the case per se. Its interest is solely in whether there was a constitutional violation, not whether the defendant was guilty or whether the individual was liable in a civil action. A finding for the original defendant in a criminal action will not result in his exoneration but simply will call for a new trial with the absence of the serious procedural error that caused the basis for the appeal. The facts of the case are, therefore, determined by trial courts and appeals courts do not reopen this aspect of the case.

The structure of federal courts has been established by acts of Congress. There are three levels of federal courts: district courts, appeals and special courts, and the Supreme Court. The district courts are the lowest, and they are trial courts. There were ninety-seven district courts in 1982. They hear all cases involving federal questions, both criminal and civil in nature. Above the district or trial courts are eleven courts of appeal—one for each of the ten regions the country has been divided into and an eleventh that maintains jurisdiction over Washington, D. C. The special courts are also divided, with branches in key cities across the country. Each of the appeals courts has from three to fifteen judges who hear cases and no federal appeal can reach the Supreme Court without first going through one of the appeals courts. Like the Supreme Court, the appeals courts deal with a frozen record and rule only on the constitutional issue involved in the case; they have no interest in the facts of the dispute. The special courts are trial courts. They take direct controversies within their jurisdiction and rule on the matter as a function of the evidence and the law. For example, a patent dispute between an inventor and a corporation would be heard and decided by the U. S. Court of Customs and Patent Appeals. Special court rulings can be appealed only if the appeal raises a constitutional issue. Of all the specialized courts, the one which is probably the most important is the court of claims because it adjudicates citizens' suits for damages against the government of the United States. As such, it provides a legal protection for the individual against the potential abuses of government agencies.

Although each state establishes its own distinct court system, it is possible to provide a reasonably accurate description of state courts. Most states developed court systems that reflect a desire to resolve issues locally. In addition, many state courts have overlapping jurisdiction. An example of the local nature of state courts is the justice of the peace. The justice of the peace is a local, part-time magistrate who is authorized to hear minor legal matters and render a judgment. He/she can usually issue money damages in small amounts and try only minor criminal matters. If a ruling of a justice of the peace is appealed, an entire new trial must be held in the next highest court. The lower courts in the states have limited jurisdiction and include such courts as probate, justice of the peace, municipal, and small claims. These courts exercise specific jurisdiction over matters such as inheritance, municipal violations, traffic laws, zoning, and tort and contract disputes which amount to small sums of money (usually under $500). Parallel to these courts are the common pleas and the superior and appellate courts. The first two are trial courts, which have jurisdiction over important civil and criminal matters, and the latter is the lower level of state appeals court. The highest court in each state is the state supreme court, and it exercises final appeal as well as judicial review with respect to the state constitution. There is no direct connection between federal and state courts save that a matter once fully litigated in state court can be appealed directly to the federal Supreme Court if a substantial federal question is at issue. State courts are bound by the state constitutions, state statutes, and federal guidelines that have been incorporated into state action through the Fourteenth Amendment.[10] The general operation of federal courts in the United States is overseen by the Supreme Court, and the rules and regulations established to operate the federal courts generally serve as a guide to the state courts.

The United States Supreme Court, as the court of last resort, is the most important court in the United States. The Constitution establishes that there must be a supreme court, but it is Congress that determines its size, salary, and, to some extent, jurisdiction. After some experimentation, the number of justices was fixed in the 1870s at its present nine. The Court meets from early October through the end of June. There is one chief justice and eight associate justices. The Court receives about 5,000 petitions for hearing each year and accepts about 125 for argument. Any case refused by the Court is controlled by the decision of the last court to have decided the case. Once a case is accepted, it is argued before the Court, which decides the case, and then a justice is assigned to write a majority opinion. Any other justice can also write a concurring or dissenting opinion, but only the majority opinion is considered holding (law). Once the opinion is written and agreed to by at least five justices, it is announced in open Court. All Supreme Court holdings become, of course, binding on all lower courts.

In order to more clearly understand the courts in the United States, it is necessary to examine the major components of the judicial systems: complaints, juries, evidence, the rule of the judge, and sentencing. Historically speaking, the most difficult aspect of common law was the complaint stage, where a grievance was issued and the complainant asked for a remedy from the court. The complaint under common law was the most critical stage of the entire judicial procedure. In England and the United States equity law and chancery courts were developed to ameliorate some of the excesses of the strict common law procedures. The combination of common law and equity law proved increasingly unwieldy and through the nineteenth century into the twentieth century there were strong reform movements that culminated in the adoption of the federal codes of 1938, which eliminated most of the problems with pleading by demanding a short, plain, simple statement of the issue and what a plaintiff wished from the court. The revision of pleading makes it much less likely that a dispute will be dismissed on the procedural grounds of inadequate statement of issue. The reform, however, has created a new set of problems in that the simple pleading procedure frequently leaves the issue unclarified. A complaint should accomplish three purposes: (1) give the court some idea of what the case is about; (2) enable the opposing party to meet the charge and get ready for the trial; and (3) give the jury a clear issue to decide.[11] In order to ensure the necessary clarity, the American legal system now engages in a process known as "discovery." During the discovery stage, the opposing lawyers question plaintiffs and witnesses and take depositions. Depositions are sworn statements that attorneys can use to prepare their case. The discovery process is a useful tool for helping to clarify issues and bring the dispute into focus for both the litigants and the court. The end process of discovery is the pretrial conference between the involved attorneys and the judge, and many cases are decided at this point. The main disadvantages to discovery are the time it takes and the exercise of the operation. The long discovery sessions in which attorneys can range far afield can be enormously difficult on witnesses as well as very expensive, and much of the information may prove to be unusable in court.

The equivalent complaint in criminal matters is the indictment. An indictment is a presentation to a court, accusing a defendant of a breach of statute. Historically, in the United States, drawing on the English tradition, indictments are made by grand juries. The grand jury is a body of citizens who operate in secret, without lawyers and judges. Their primary function is to weigh requests from the government and, if they agree that a prima facie case exists, authorize an indictment. The Fifth Amendment guarantees a grand jury for federal cases, but the Supreme Court has ruled that grand juries are not required by states in noncapital cases. As of 1979, only twenty states still used grand juries to establish indictments; most others use an investigative procedure known as device of information. The grand juries are, of course, a protection for the individual because it takes the ability to indict out of the hands of the district attorney, who has investigated the crime and will eventually prosecute the accused. It places, at a very critical juncture in the criminal process, an independent body of citizens who are disinterested in the issue. The erosion of grand jury use is seen by many civil libertarians as a blow to individual rights in the United States. Grand juries serve one other function—they can carry out independent, self-generated investigations. Under such a proceeding, a grand jury does not issue an indictment but rather a ''presentment,'' which is an accusation, in essence a recommendation for indictment. While waning, especially at the state level, grand juries still play an important role in the legal process.

The jury is a key element of the American legal system. The Constitution guarantees a jury in the sixth and seventh amendments. Traditionally, juries were absolute both to fact and law, but by the nineteenth century that changed and now juries deal with questions of facts while judges deal with questions of law. Judges may set aside jury judgments if they run contrary to law and, in fact, a judge even can set aside a jury conviction if the judge does not believe the facts warrant a conviction. Juries, like grand juries, come from the ranks of citizens and are chosen by a formula. Traditionally, most states use the ''key man'' system where upstanding citizens submit the names of prospective jurors and then the juries are drawn from these lists. This system was considered biased against minorities and lower income groups and has been abandoned in most states in favor of a system of drawing juries by lot from voter registration. The ''lot'' has been mandated in federal court since 1968.

Once the potential list of jurors is compiled, actual jury selection takes place in court. Each prospective juror is questioned by the attorneys and only those acceptable to both sides are seated. Jury selection is an important step in the trial process, and many attorneys consider cases won or lost at selection time. The procedure can, however, get out of hand; for example, the 1971 Connecticut murder trial of Bobby Seale took four months to impanel a jury. There were 1,525 prospective jurors called and 1,035 actually questioned. Lawyers can refuse or challenge a juror with either a peremptory challenge or for cause. A peremptory challenge is one without cause and usually each side is limited to the number of peremptory challenges they can exercise. There is, however, no limit to challenge for cause, but for each of these the judge must agree that the reason for the challenge is valid. Clearly, jury selection takes a great deal of court time, especially when one realizes that there are two million jurors hearing 200,000 cases per year in the United States.[12] The size of a jury and the need for it to be unanimous to convict have undergone dramatic changes since the mid–1960s. The Supreme Court has ruled that states can have fewer than twelve people on a jury and they need not be unanimous to convict in a noncapital case.[13] Federal juries are still required to have twelve members and to reach a unanimous decision.

Evidence is another major issue that faces the courts. The role of evidence is not in question, but rather what is admissible as evidence and how it should be elicited. The general rule is that evidence must be material (relevant) and competent (reliable). After that, it is up to the jury to weigh the evidence to determine its significance. There are no rules and can be none to guide a juror on whether a witness is to be believed other than the evidentiary and human judgment each individual juror makes. Evidence cannot be generally admitted unless it is direct; that is, the witness has direct knowledge of what he speaks and can be cross-examined concerning it. Hearsay evidence is not admissible except to help establish a collateral point. Documents are evidence only of themselves and not to other documents alluded to, and common knowledge is accepted without formal admission of evidence. It is enough to say on these points that these apparently simple rules have caused no end of difficulty for courts.

The final step in the court process is awards in civil cases and sentencing in criminal cases. Juries can set the range of award but the judge makes the final award in civil suits. The scope and size of the award is subject to appeal, and ultimately awards are almost always modified by the appeals court. In criminal cases, both federal and state courts employ range-sentencing with minimum and maximum times to be served. A sentence will be, for example, no less than five nor more than fifteen years. This type of sentence, in effect, reduces the power of the trial judge particularly, and the courts generally, by giving other actors the ultimate determination of sentence. The judge, in accordance with controlling statutes, and after taking into consideration extenuating circumstances, establishes the range or parameters of the sentence, but a parole board, which has nothing to do with the court, determines the actual length of the sentence. There has been great criticism of the range sentence, but as Richard Neeley, former chief justice of the West Virginia State Courts, has argued, it does dilute the power of the court and allows the political process (appointed parole board members) a significant say in the length of time an individual serves.[14] Fixed sentences, while eliminating potential excesses and abuses of judges and parole boards, has the major defect of ignoring the many extenuating circumstances, which demand that not all individuals be treated precisely the same.

In reality, it is not the indeterminate sentence that has been most criticized, but the practice known as "plea bargaining." Plea bargaining is a device where a defendant, in exchange for a guilty plea, may have the charges reduced. Part of the process of bargaining is negotiation over sentence. An individual who stands charged with, for example, armed robbery—carrying a sentence of ten to fifteen years—might plead guilty to simple robbery and have the sentence reduced to three to five years. The overwhelming rationale for plea bargaining is that without it, the American court system would collapse under its own weight. Well over 90 percent of criminal cases in the United States are disposed of through guilty pleas. In almost all of these cases, there has been a plea bargain. The United States simply does not possess the resources or the staff to try even half the criminal indictments that come before it.

The major objection to the use of plea bargaining is that criminals "get off easy." In fact, Neeley points out that American penalties are significantly stiffer than virtually all Western democracies and that there is a great deal of "fat" in our prison terms.[15] The bargaining process is an attempt, therefore, to achieve a realistic sentence for the crime. Even with the extensive plea bargaining in the American system, American prison terms are longer than any Western nation (except South Africa). It is likely that plea bargaining is the only rational way that the court system can function so that many of the guilty are punished, and those who merit a trial have the opportunity for their day in court.

The state of American courts is and has always been the subject of a great deal of controversy. In a 1906 speech before the American Bar Association, the great American jurist Roscoe Pound identified three major problems with the American courts: a multiplicity of courts; persevering concurrent jurisdictions; and the waste of judicial power.[16] Pound argued that the courts could not continue to operate in the twentieth century with nineteenth century methods. When Chief Justice Warren Burger addressed the same ABA in 1970, he opened his remarks by reaffirming the remarks of Justice Pound. He argued that the same problems that Pound noted in 1906 continued to plague the courts in 1970. Justice Burger identified the following major contemporary problems: the machinery of courts are still outdated; the increase in population has created a great increase in volume; and new cases have been added to court dockets because of social and economic changes.[17]

Two major problems in the American courts revolve around the slowness of the system and the attendant perception that the courts accomplish very little. To some extent, the slowness of American courts is inevitable due to the judicial philosophy of "innocent until proven guilty," combined with the procedural and appeal safeguards built into the American system. Some of the delay is also caused, however, by the essentially autonomous nature of American courts (judges and courts in the American system are virtually autonomous in operation). The formal rules for control and discipline of the courts are completely inadequate to deal with any but the most extreme problems. Each individual court in the various states operates under loose guidelines on schedules that fit the particular needs and circumstances of a court at any given point in time. There are no guidelines for length of trials or costs, so it is possible for a trial on an accident case or manufacturer liability to take a great deal of court time while keeping the docket jammed with a myriad of other equally or more pressing cases. This creates backlogs that encourage courts to allow plea-bargains and other devices to speed up the court calendar. Neeley has argued that the independence of judges, the autonomy of the courts, and the reluctance of the political system to initiate reform keeps the courts in a state of perpetual crisis.[18]

THE PERSONNEL OF THE LAW

Legal Practitioners

There is no special class of persons who become lawyers in the United States. There is certainly no active recruitment by existing attorneys or their associations, and there is no apprenticeship necessary to qualify for the bar. There is a strong tradition in the United States that anyone who wishes to can become an attorney. Well into the nineteenth century there were no formal qualifications necessary to be a lawyer. Any person who was twenty-one years old and a citizen could practice law, and it was without any formal schooling that Abraham Lincoln became a lawyer. Since the early twentieth century, however, one must graduate from one of the 172 American Bar Association-approved law schools and then pass the bar exam in the state in which he/she wishes to practice in order to become a lawyer. Lawyers are not licensed to practice by the federal government but in the particular state where they take the bar exam. Generally speaking, once one has passed the bar in a particular state and practiced for several years (generally five years) one can apply and receive a license to practice in another state. This is known as "reciprocity" and exists between most states in the United States.

Admission to law school in the United States is open to any college graduate and is a highly competitive process. Some of the most selective law schools accept about only 15 percent of their applicants, although 70 percent of applicants are accepted at some law schools.[19] In choosing students, the law schools use college records, references, and generally rely heavily on the standardized law school admissions test administered by the Educational Testing Service. For example, in one year, the University of California Law School at Berkeley, one of the most competitive in the United States, accepted only five out of eight applicants who scored less than in the eightieth percentile on the LSAT, even though they had cumulative college grade points of above 3.75 out of a possible 4.0.[20]

White males dominated American law schools for many years. This has changed a great deal during the last decade. In 1981 there were 127,531 persons enrolled

in American law schools, and 44,986 or 35 percent were female. This compares
to 1965, when out of 59,744 enrolled in law school only 2,537 or 4 percent
were women.[21] Minority enrollments have also shown a marked increase in law
schools. In 1969 there were 2,933 minorities enrolled in law school and by 1981
there were 11,130.[22] Many law schools have committed to accepting freshman
classes which are 50 percent female, but minorities still make up only about 4
to 6 percent of first-year classes.

Law school in the United States is three years, and upon completion the
graduate is eligible to take the bar exam. In most states you are not, however,
allowed to practice law until you have passed the bar exam. Instruction in
American law schools is by the case method. This is somewhat peculiar when
you consider that in American law statutes are supreme, and law schools pay
very little attention to the statutes or laws that will control the lawyers' work.
The case method was developed in the United States. Early legal training in the
United States was by apprenticeship, but by 1780 formal law schools were
established. These early law schools had no particular method of instruction,
and law training differed widely from school to school. In 1870 a revolution in
legal training took place when Christopher Columbus Langdell, Dean of Harvard
Law School, decided the common law could be reduced to principles found in
opinions of appellate courts, in other words, case law.[23] Dean Langdell recruited
full-time faculty, abandoned lectures about law, and instituted the case method.
The system proved workable and popular and, by the turn of the century, had
been adopted by virtually all American law schools. The rationale for the case
method (as opposed to a statutory approach to the study of law) is: (1) it is not
practical or feasible to teach the great body of statutory law; (2) the real purpose
of legal training is to teach legal reasoning, the method by which lawyers and
courts reach conclusions; and (3) the case method is well-suited to helping one
learn the underlying principles upon which the law in the United States rests.

The United States has more lawyers per capita than any country in the world.
In 1982 there were about five hundred thousand lawyers in the United States
and the number is expected to grow to one million by the year 2000. There is
approximately one lawyer for every four hundred Americans. Every year ABA-
approved law schools graduate an additional thirty-five thousand lawyers. Once
graduated from law school, an individual need take and pass the bar exam and
a character examination. If one is found to be of good character, the individual
is admitted to the bar. Admission to the bar in every state rests on an English
statute of 1402: Admit only those found to be good and virtuous, and of good
fame, learned and sworn to do their duty.[24] While it is very difficult to be
admitted to the more competitive law schools, many college graduates can find
a place in an ABA-approved law school. The relative ease of what one has to
do to become a lawyer in the United States undoubtedly contributes to the great
number of lawyers.

It is beyond argument that the United States is a legalistic and litigious society,
and, as such, has a great demand for lawyers. Tocqueville saw the legalistic

nature of American society as a function of the legal profession and its desire to control. He noted "the legal profession constitutes an aristocracy forming the most powerful, if not the only counterpoise to the democratic element."[25] Others have taken a sharply different view. Professor Rembar, in his important work on the history of the American legal system, argues that it protects democracy and that litigation is modern day trial by battle in which advocates for each side engage in a contest of right.[26] A number of other observers of the American legal system have argued that the ability to go to court protects the weak against the powerful and is ultimately the mechanism that keeps the system in balance in both the public and private sphere. As with most complex situations, you can find data to support both sides of this dispute. While there are no hard data on the number of qualified lawyers who practice law, rough estimates are that about 20 to 30 percent of American lawyers do not practice. About 50,000 lawyers work for the government, including about 10,000 judges. It is generally conceded that legal training is valuable for developing analytical skills, research techniques, problem-solving skills, and intellectual discipline. As a result, many employers actively seek law school graduates to fill a variety of jobs. There is little doubt, however, regardless of the number of lawyers who gravitate to alternative careers, that the number who practice law and the amount of litigation will continue to grow in the United States.

As with all professions, lawyers have strict ethical standards and a professional association, the American Bar Association, to oversee the profession. The original Canons of Professional Ethics adopted by the ABA in 1908 were changed in 1969 to the Model Code of Professional Responsibility and, in 1983, became a set of model rules. The ABA rules have no legal force, and each state must establish, by statute, a code for lawyers. The most important ethical principle is to be an advocate for your client. The American legal system is built on an adversary principle, and the lawyer must do all in his power to protect the client's interest. The idea of lawyer-client privilege is an important part of this principle. Anything said by the client to his attorney is absolutely confidential, and the lawyer may not reveal it to anyone without the client's permission. This is not only an important ethical principle of lawyers but is embodied in the law of every state. In addition to confidentiality and client advocacy, there are a number of other ethical principles that govern the American legal profession. These include such principles as the appearance of propriety, strict standards to avoid conflict of interest, standards of professional conduct, and the fact that lawyers are officers of the court. While there are many gray areas concerning what constitutes ethical conduct and reasonable people might disagree in a particular situation, the American legal profession has a strict and generally scrupulously adhered to code of ethics.

Judges

If there is one single most important office or element in the American legal system, it is the judge. The judge is virtually supreme in the court, and, in most cases, not only makes rulings on law but, to a great extent, sets the tone and direction of the court. There are, as a matter of course, a number of discretionary areas which fall to the judge, including such important questions as admissibility of evidence, line and relevance of testimony, appropriateness of examination and cross examination, all rulings on matters of law, conduct of witness, charge to the jury, and frequently awards in civil cases and the range of sentence in criminal cases. In addition to established rules for the general conduct of the court, judges have at their disposal two very powerful weapons to influence behavior: injunctions and contempt citations. Injunctions are commands from the court directed to named individuals, forbidding them to perform certain specified acts, and contempt citations allow judges to punish individuals (through fines or incarceration) for disobeying the court's orders. The contempt citation is defended on the grounds that judges need this power to protect the dignity of the court. The ability of judges to jail an individual for contempt comes as close to anything in the American political or legal system to naked arbitrary power. One can be jailed for contempt and have no recourse to legal help, appeal, or remedy other than complying with the judicial order. The privilege of contempt underscores the importance Americans attach to the courts in general and to judicial authority specifically.

The dignity and importance of the judge has long been debated in the American society, especially in light of the notion that the legal establishment is anti-democratic. As far back as 1790, Jefferson and Hamilton argued over proper dress for judges. Jefferson argued for no robes or special dress and Hamilton for the English model of both robes and wigs. The Jeffersonian model prevailed for some time, but by the late nineteenth century, judicial robes had become commonplace in all state courts. The choosing of judges in the United States reflects the ambivalence between holding the courts in great esteem and the belief that the legal establishment represents an elite that is inherently antidemocratic. All federal judges are appointed by the president and subject to confirmation by the Senate. Once confirmed, they serve as independent entities free from executive or congressional scrutiny or review. There is no mandatory retirement age for federal judges, and the only effective weapon the Congress has is impeachment, but this is so rarely invoked as to be a virtual vestigial structure. States have a variety of schemes for choosing judges, which combine election and appointment with popular election the most prevalent. In 1970, 82 percent of state and local judges ran for election.[27] In states where judges are strictly elected, candidates run for judicial office just as any other office-seeker. The terms vary but generally are six years or longer. In states where judges are appointed, usually the governor appoints and the legislature confirms. The ABA and attorney groups in general do not favor these plans because they argue that unqualified people can, for political reasons, be elected or appointed to the bench. Professional attorney groups favor plans where they may screen candidates and present an approved list to the governor from which he must choose. This is, of course, seen by some as a manifestation of the elitism of the legal profession.

California developed a compromise plan in 1934 that, by 1979, had been adopted by sixteen states. In the California plan, the governor appoints the judges, a professional commission must approve the appointment, and then the electorate can vote the appointee up or down. If the electorate vote approves, the judge serves for a specified time period.

Whatever the method of choosing judges in the United States, political considerations are important. There are no special qualifications for becoming a judge in the United States save that one be a lawyer. Professor Schmidhauser's research indicates that people appointed to the Supreme Court come from economically well off, socially advantaged, upper-class Protestant backgrounds.[28] There is no evidence that this social profile holds true for state or other federal judges. Rather, the evidence is overwhelming that partisan politics is the chief criteria for determining who becomes a judge in the United States. Research indicates that presidential appointment of judges is overwhelmingly political and partisan ranging from a low in Taft's administration of 82 percent of the appointments being politically motivated to a high in Wilson's of 98 percent.[29] Professor Berle has commented, "either elected or appointed, the results are the same, judges are chosen by the chieftains of the political parties involved."[30] Once in office, judges are monitored and disciplined by their own professional associations. The federal courts are administered by the Judicial Conference of the United States and by the administrative office of the United States Courts. The Conference is headed by the chief justice of the United States Supreme Court, and membership includes the chiefs of each of the eleven appeals courts, one district court judge of each circuit court, and the chief judge of the U. S. Court of Claims and Customs. They meet several times a year and make legislative recommendations. The administrative office consists of a director and a deputy appointed by the chief justice, and this office actually administers the courts. At the state level, each state adopts its own scheme for supervising the courts and judges, but Judge Neeley has argued that none of the schemes are any more than minimally effective. Judges are virtually immune from supervision and in only the rarest cases subject to disciplinary sanction. The anomoly exists regarding judges that their elevation to the bench is done in a fashion consistent with democracy and representative government, but once on the bench, their supervision and discipline is in the hands of a body of fellow members of the profession that is highly elitist in nature.

PUBLIC PERCEPTIONS AND THE ROLE OF THE COURTS

Considering the great number of lawyers in the United States, the litigious nature of American society, and the strongly held belief that America is a nation of laws, one would think the populace would hold the legal system in high esteem. The data, however, indicates that this is not the case. Americans are distrustful of the legal system in general and of most of its component parts in particular. A 1982 Gallup Poll asked respondents if they had faith in their legal system. Only 51 percent of Americans expressed faith in the legal system. This is lower than Japan, Great Britain, West Germany, Ireland, and France.[31] When all political institutions were combined, the confidence figure rose to 60 percent, indicating the relatively poor position of the legal system. Not only does the legal system receive low marks from the public, but so do the courts, law enforcement, and, most especially, lawyers. In 1967, Harris found 56 percent of Americans polled believed the American law enforcement system did not deter people from committing crimes, and, by 1982, this figure had gone up to 79 percent.[32] A 1981 Gallup Poll found 78 percent thought courts were too lenient and that criminals were let off too easily.[33] The poll data seem to indicate a lack of faith in the legal system's ability to prevent crime and adequately punish offenders.

Lawyers as a profession fare relatively poorly in the eyes of Americans. A 1983 Gallup Poll asked respondents to rate the honesty and ethics of various professions. Only 25 percent considered lawyers to be very ethical and honest, and they finished behind twelve other professions including doctors, teachers, policemen, bankers, and reporters.[34] A 1981 Gallup Poll sampling for prestige or status of professions had lawyers fifth behind doctors, judges, clergy, and bankers.[35] Other public opinion polls by Harris tend to confirm the results found in Gallup Polls with one important exception. A 1973 Harris poll found that 80 percent believed that lawyers work for the people they represent, and 89 percent agreed that lawyers are important because they give people the help they need for legal protection under the law.[36] So, while people do not hold lawyers in as high esteem as other professions, nor do they consider them as ethical, there is recognition of their importance to legal protections and their advocacy of their clients.

There are little or no hard data on why Americans hold the attitudes they do about the legal system, but unquestionably the politicized nature of the legal system and the type of media attention the legal system receives are important factors. The criminal justice system and the courts are a continuing major political issue in the United States. Candidates for office at all levels of government make the criminal justice system a constant campaign issue; they are almost always pointing out alleged faults and problems. Little is ever done about the situation, so the public hears an almost continual harangue about the major deficiencies of the criminal justice system. The media, as well, portrays the legal system as one beset with problems. Coverage of the system is almost always critical, and, when specifics are dealt with, they are problems or abuses. With all of this, however, there is no question that the American public has fundamental faith in the legal system, and it remains one of the strongest and most important American institutions.

The linkages between the American legal system and the political system are fundamental, dramatic, and inevitable. The points of interaction between them are numerous and continual. First, all funding for activities of the legal system come from general tax revenue and are, therefore, decided by the elected political system. Second, the fact that the courts exercise judicial review has profound political implications. Supreme Court decisions have repeatedly created enormous political controversy within the body politic. Third, crime and its implications have traditionally been a major political issue in the United States. Finally, the United States is a litigious society where, for a wide variety of reasons, political issues and problems are brought into the legal system for resolution. This alone creates an inextricable set of linkages between the political and the legal systems.

At the most fundamental level, the parameters of the American legal system are determined by the political system. As Professor Fleming has argued, we cannot have a perfect system but must strike a balance.[37] The difficulty is, of course, that reasonable people differ sharply on what the mix of that balance should be. Take, for example, the classic dilemma of the rights of the accused versus the rights of the society. John Adams argued that it is better to let some of the guilty go free rather than ever punish the innocent. In this way we ensure respect for the system because each individual knows that he can never be imprisoned if he obeys the law. In today's world, especially in urban areas, where many feel beleaguered and are in constant fear of crime, the view might be to lean toward making sure the guilty will be punished even if the consequence is an occasional innocent person punished as well. This type of decision is not made by the American judicial system but largely by the actions of political systems.

Costs for the legal system are almost exclusively funded by tax dollars. This creates another major linkage between the political and legal system. In 1981, states spent 2.5 billion dollars on police and an additional 5.0 billion dollars on corrections. This sum is projected to grow at least with the rate of inflation. When tax battles take place, not only is there frequent opposition to spending additional revenue but how the revenue should be spent.

While there is constant criticism of the American legal system, there is remarkably little reform. At the most fundamental level, efforts to change the judicial system fail because the courts have political power. The courts in the United States are inextricably linked to the political system and are a source of power for some and a disadvantage for others. As Judge Neeley has pointed out, "so called court reform bills are introduced all the time; however, they are not usually neutral 'reform' bills but are rather efforts by one interest group or another to achieve a more favorable result in the courts."[38] There is no neutral court or legal system, and, since advantage within the court system is created by the actions of the political system, the link between the two is clearly critical.

An example of the nonneutral reality of the American legal system is fees for attorneys. In the United States each litigant pays his own attorney fees, and this has caused enormous controversy on both sides of the question. It has been argued that if the losing party was responsible for legal fees or that contingency fees were outlawed, it would significantly cut down on the huge number of lawsuits in the country and make the entire legal system function more efficiently and smoothly. The argument further contends that the number of law suits and frequent huge settlements disrupt normal activities and put a great strain on many elements in the society. The prime example cited is the medical profession, which must always operate with an eye toward potential malpractice suits. The other side contends that without contingency fees and equal responsibility, the individual could never hope to get redress in the legal system. The expense of litigation would keep out even valid claims, and only the wealthy and the corporations could litigate. Malpractice, for example, could flourish, and there would be virtually no effective way to hold the physician responsible or accountable. The point is that court reform is clearly not a matter of what is best for the society, but who is disadvantaged and who advantaged under a particular system. This is a political question and is fought out in the United States in the political arena.

Roscoe Pound underscored the linkage of law in the United States to the general social system when he argued that the growth of American law and legal profession began with the rise of trade and commerce in the nineteenth century.[39] The development of the legal system has since reflected that reality combined with the growth and importance of government in the United States. Data indicate that much civil litigation in the United States involves zoning, education, taxation, and employee claims.[40] Suits against the government are difficult because governments are generally immune from them. The Eleventh Amendment specifically makes states immune from suits. The amendment was a direct reaction to a 1793 Supreme Court case in which a state was sued in federal court by a private citizen over the state removal of a charter for land.[41] The Supreme Court upheld the right of the suit and the states reacted by passing the Eleventh Amendment. Over the years, the degree of state liability has increased some by statutes and some by court rulings. Today, governments are generally immune from suits when the action is governmental but not when it is proprietary or when it involves wrongful action by a public official. The federal government waived much of its own immunity from citizen claims against it with the passage of the 1946 Federal Tort Claims Act, which waived government immunity from tort liability.

The entire issue of why and who people sue in the United States is an important one for understanding the legal system generally and its specific relationship to the political system. There are more lawsuits filed in the United States than in any other country in the world. This is by no means a modern phenomenon, and Tocqueville commented in 1830 ''hardly any question arises in the United States that is not resolved sooner or later into a judicial question.''[42] In a very important book, Marlene Adler Marks examines why people sue in the United States.[43] She indicates that beside the conventional reasons—to enforce a contract, recover damages, and redress a legal wrong—people sue for political and social change, vindication of a position or point of view, harassment, revenge, honor, anger or frustration, and, in some cases, because it is the last resort. They can think of nothing else to do to deal with a particular situation. While money is frequently an important consideration in a lawsuit and is, of course, the remedy the courts have in civil suits, it is not always the reason people sue. There are numerous cases where people seek damages of one dollar in order to prove they are right. The use of the lawsuit is, in the United States, an important political and social weapon that frequently proves more effective than the use of the political system.[44] In 1984, for example, retired General William Westmoreland sued the Columbia Broadcasting System for remarks made in a 1971 documentary about the Vietnam War. The documentary alleged Westmoreland falsified estimates of enemy casualties to make it appear that the United States was winning the war. While the suit asked for one hundred and fifty million dollars in damages, the issue was not the money but the political vindication of not only Westmoreland but American military conduct in Vietnam. For other actors involved in the suit, it was an attempt to harass the networks for perceived political views with which these groups disagreed. For still others, the suit was an attempt to curb the perceived growing power of the electronic media. The suit, which ended in an eleventh-hour out-of-court settlement, was seen by many as a practical method to deal with a set of basically political problems. The use of litigation in the United States is, therefore, one of the most significant components in the relationship between the legal and the political system.

Another linkage between the legal system and the political system is the Supreme Court. This is true because of the importance of the Court's decisions to the political system, its use of judicial review, and the political nature of Court appointments and removals.[45] Presidents actively seek individuals who share their political philosophy and usually also choose people of the same political party. Once appointed by a president and confirmed by the Senate, the formal relationship between the president and the justice is usually severed. There is no evidence that sitting presidents attempt to influence their appointees on specific cases, but the general politicized nature of the appointment and ratification process remains. Federal judges sit for life and can be removed only by impeachment. This, too, is a political issue, although forcible removal of judges by impeachment is extremely rare in the American political system.

The practice of using judicial judgment to determine the constitutional validity of a legislative act is known as "judicial review." Judicial review was established by the Supreme Court in 1803 in the case of *Marbury v. Madison.*[46] The court ruled that parts of the Judiciary Act of 1789 were unconstitutional because Congress had overstepped its legislative prerogative. Chief Justice Marshall, writing for the majority, argued forcefully that the Court had the inherent duty to examine legislative acts to determine if they were consistent with the written Constitution. To not have this right, Marshall argued, would make an act of the Congress equivalent to the Constitution and that would render the Constitution meaningless. If the Constitution is to have meaning greater than simply a legislative act, it must stand above the legislative act and there must be a review board independent of the Congress, and in our federal system the only such review mechanisms were the federal courts. While *Marbury* was a controversial decision, its major idea of judicial review was accepted and became a firm principle of the American legal system. Judicial review is a critical component to the American legal system because it thrusts the courts into the middle of a political system, gives to the courts a profoundly political role, and has helped to establish the idea that courts in the United States make law by reviewing legislative acts not only procedurally but substantively. This very powerful function reached its apex in the period between 1875 and 1937, when the court introduced the idea of substantive due process, a device in which the Supreme Court could rule on the constitutionality of a legislative act even if there was not a specific part of the Constitution with which the act conflicted.[47] Judicial review has, therefore, a profound impact on the American legal system because it thrusts the court into the legislative area, and, as such, affects the whole court system. The courts are bound up in the political process, and that reality must affect how the courts function and how they are perceived. The fact that the courts perform an ultimately political function by reviewing the legitimacy of legislative acts has profoundly colored the entire reality of the American legal system.

NOTES

1. *United States v. Hudson and Goodwin* (7 Cranch) 32.

2. For a complete discussion of this, see G. Gilmore, *The Ages of American Law* (New Haven, Conn.: Yale University Press, 1977).

3. Ibid., p. 11.

4. C. Rembar, *The Law of the Land* (New York: Simon and Schuster, 1980), p. 32.

5. Ibid., p. 46. See Rembar for a thorough discussion of Blackstone.

6. H. J. Abraham, *The Judicial Process*, 4th ed. (New York: Oxford University Press, 1980), p. 14.

7. Ibid.

8. M. J. Horowitz, *The Transformation of American Law, 1780–1866* (Cambridge, Mass.: Harvard University Press, 1977), p. 30.

9. Abraham, *The Judicial Process*, p. 180.

10. The Fourteenth Amendment states "No state shall make or enforce any law which shall abridge the privileges or immunities of citizens of the United States; nor shall any state deprive any person of life, liberty, or property without due process of law; nor deny to any person within its jurisdiction the equal protection of the laws." This has come to mean that the first ten amendments of the United States Constitution are applicable to state as well as federal actions.

11. Rembar, *The Law of the Land*, p. 242.

12. Abraham, *The Judicial Process*, p. 117.

13. *Williams v. Florida* 399 U. S. 78 (1970); and *Johnson v. Louisiana* 406 U. S. 356 (1972).

14. For further discussion of this issue, see R. Neeley, *Why Courts Don't Work* (New York: McGraw Hill, 1982).

15. See ibid. for further discussion of this issue.

16. W. F. Murphy and C. H. Pritchett, *Courts, Judges and Politics* (New York: Random House, 1961), p. 69.

17. H. James, *Crisis in the Courts* (New York: David McKay, 1971), p. iii.

18. For a complete discussion of this issue, see R. Neeley, *Why Courts Don't Work.*

19. Law School Admission Council and Association of American Law Schools, *Pre Law Handbook 1983/84* (Washington, D. C.: Law School Admission Council, 1983).

20. Ibid., p. 71.

21. Ibid., p. 14.

22. Ibid., p. 18.

23. Murphy and Pritchett, *Courts, Judges and Politics*, p. 127.

24. Ibid.

25. R. Scigliano, *The Courts: A Reader in Judicial Process* (Boston: Little, Brown and Co., 1962), p. 161.

26. Rembar, *The Law of the Land*, p. 111.

27. Abraham, *The Judicial Process*, p. 35.

28. J. R. Schmidhauser, "The Justices of the Supreme Court: A Collective Portrait," *Midwest Journal of Political Science* 3 (1959), pp. 1–57.

29. Scigliano, *The Courts*, p. 66.

30. Ibid., p. 98.

31. G. Gallop, *Faith in the Legal System, 1982* (Wilmington, Del.: Scholarly Resources Inc., 1983).

32. L. Harris, "Law Enforcement, 1973," in L. Harris, ed., *The Harris Survey Yearbook of Public Opinion, 1973* (New York: Louis Harris and Associates, Inc., 1976).

33. Ibid.

34. Ibid.

35. Ibid.

36. Harris, "Law Enforcement, 1973."

37. For a complete discussion of this issue, see M. Fleming, *The Price of Perfect Justice* (New York: Basic Books, 1974).

38. Neeley, *Why Courts Don't Work*, p. 81.

39. J. Honnalit, *The Life of the Law* (London: The Free Press, 1964), p. 52.

40. K. Dolbeare, *Trial Courts in Urban Politics* (New York: John Wiley & Sons, 1967).

41. *Chisolm v. Georgia* 2 U. S. (2 Dall) 419 (1793).

42. Abraham, *The Judicial Process*, p. 22.

43. M. A. Marks, *The Suing of America* (New York: Seaview Books, 1981).

44. D. Greenberg, "The Use of Litigation to Achieve Political Goals: A Comparison of the United States and Britain" (Paper presented at the Northeastern Political Science Association Convention, Boston, Mass., November 1984).

45. Scigliano, *The Courts*, p. 453.

46. *Marbury v. Madison* 5 U. S. (1 Cranch) 137 (1803).

47. *Lockner v. New York* 198 U. S. 45 (1905).

BIBLIOGRAPHY

Abraham, H. J. *The Judicial Process*. New York: Oxford University Press, 1980.

———. *The Judiciary: The Supreme Court in the Governmental Process*. 3d ed. Boston: Allyn and Bacon, Inc., 1973.

Auerbach, J. S. *Justice Without Law?: Resolving Disputes Without Lawyers*. Oxford: Oxford University Press, 1983.

Ehrlich, T. E., and G. C. Hazard, Jr. *Going to Law School.* Boston: Little, Brown and Co., 1975.

Fleming, M. *The Price of Perfect Justice.* New York: Basic Books, 1974.

Grilliot, J. *Introduction to the Law and the Legal System.* Boston: Houghton Mifflin Books, 1975.

Honnalit, J. *The Life of the Law.* London: The Free Press, 1964.

Horowitz, M. J. *The Transformation of American Law, 1780–1866.* Cambridge, Mass.: Harvard University Press, 1977.

Kunen, J. S. *"How Can You Defend Those People?": The Making of a Criminal Lawyer.* New York: Random House, 1983.

Marks, M. A. *The Suing of America.* New York: Seaview Press, 1981.

Murphy, W. F., and C. H. Pritchett. *Courts, Judges and Politics.* New York: Random House, 1974.

Neeley, R. *Why Courts Don't Work.* New York: McGraw Hill, 1982.

Rembar, C. *The Law of the Land.* New York: Simon and Schuster, 1980.

Rohde, D. W., and H. J. Spaeth. *Supreme Court Decision-Making.* San Francisco, Calif.: W. H. Freeman & Co., 1976.

Tribe, L. *American Constitutional Law.* Mineola, N. Y.: Foundation Press, 1978.

ABOUT THE CONTRIBUTORS

PAUL J. BEST is Professor of Political Science and Coordinator of Soviet and East European Studies at Southern Connecticut State University in New Haven, Connecticut. Professor Best received his doctoral degree from New York University. He has written extensively on contemporary Polish politics in articles in *The Polish Review* and *Connecticut Review* and was the guest editor of the *International Journal of Politics* for an issue devoted to "Contemporary Politics in Poland." He has been managing editor of *The Polish Review* since 1969 and a member of the Executive Board of the New England Slavic Association since 1976. Professor Best is the author, with K. R. Rai and D. F. Walsh, of *Power and Conflict in Three Worlds: An Introduction to Political Science* (1985).

RICHARD C. DEANGELIS is Associate Professor and Chairman of the History Department at Fairfield University, Fairfield, Connecticut. Professor DeAngelis received his doctoral degree from St. John's University. He has delivered a number of papers and written extensively on Chinese history and contemporary politics. A frequent visitor to the People's Republic, Professor DeAngelis has most recently published articles on Chinese politics in the *Bulletin* of the Institute for Modern History, Academia Sinica.

MARIA ELISABETTA DE FRANCISCIS is a Ph.D. candidate in Political Science at the University of Connecticut at Storrs. A native of Italy, Ms. de Franciscis is the recipient of a fellowship for her graduate work from the Italian Ministry of Public Education. In addition to completing the work on her dissertation and the chapter in this volume, Ms. de Franciscis has written an article on the 1983 Italian elections for the *Italian Studies Quarterly*.

LEE EPSTEIN is Assistant Professor of Political Science at Southern Methodist University in Dallas, Texas. She received her doctoral degree from Emory University. She has delivered a large number of papers and written extensively on the relationship between political parties and interest groups and the U. S. Supreme Court. She has had articles published recently (coauthored with Karen O'Connor) in the *Harvard Journal of Law and Public Policy*, *Social Science Quarterly*, *Judicature*, *Journal of Politics* and *Law and Society Review*, among others. Professor Epstein has served as a manuscript reviewer for the *Journal of Politics*, *Social Science Quarterly*, and John Wiley Publishers. She is the author of *Conservatives in Court*, forthcoming, and (with Karen O'Connor) *Public Interest Law Firms—An Institutional Analysis*, to be published by Greenwood Press.

HARVEY M. FEINBERG is Professor of History and co-ordinator of the African Studies Program at Southern Connecticut State University in New Haven, Connecticut. He received his doctoral degree from Boston University. Professor Feinberg has travelled throughout Africa and had done field work in Ghana and South Africa. He has written extensively on a variety of topics in African history, most recently publishing articles in the *Journal of African History*, the *International Journal of African Historical Studies*, *History in Africa*, *Ghana Notes and Queries*, and *African Perspectives* (Leiden).

ALBERT L. GASTMAN is Professor of Political Science at Trinity College in Hartford, Connecticut, where he teaches International Law and International Relations. Born in the Netherlands, he has travelled extensively in Asia, Latin America, and the Caribbean, as well as Europe and North America. He is fluent in English, Spanish, Dutch, and French. Professor Gastman has published a number of articles in international and legal journals and is the author of *The Politics of Surinam and the Netherlands Antilles* and *Historical Dictionary of the French and Netherlands Antilles*.

MICHEAL W. GILES is Chairman and Professor of Political Science at Emory University, Atlanta, Georgia. He received his doctoral degree from the University of Kentucky. Professor Giles has written extensively on a number of topics, including politics and the courts, racial desegregation in the schools, and campaign contributions and legislative elections. He has most recently published articles in the *American Journal of Political Science*, *Social Science Quarterly*, *Journal of Politics* and *American Political Science Review*. Professor Giles is the author (with G. E. Berkeley, N. C. Kassof, and J. Hackett) of *Introduction of Criminal Justice: Police, Courts and Corrections* and (with E. Cataldo and D. Gatlin) of *School Desegregation Policy: Compliance, Avoidance and Metropolitan Remedy*.

DONALD W. GREENBERG is Chairman and Associate Professor of Politics at Fairfield University in Fairfield, Connecticut. He received his doctoral degree from the City University of New York. Professor Greenberg teaches courses on the U.S. Supreme Court and has delivered a number of papers and written articles on interest groups and the courts in both the United States and Great Britain.

DIANA GRUB resides in Atlanta, Georgia. She received her B. A. from Emory University in 1985, graduating *summa cum laude*.

ALAN N. KATZ is Professor of Politics at Fairfield University in Fairfield, Connecticut. He received his doctoral degree from New York University. He teaches courses in comparative politics and has delivered papers and written articles on Indian politics, the political socialization of law students, and comparative legal systems. Professor Katz has been an Affiliated Scholar of the American Bar Foundation since 1974.

THOMAS D. LANCASTER is Assistant Professor of Political Science at Emory University in Atlanta, Georgia. He received his doctoral degree from Washington University. He teaches courses in comparative politics and has delivered a number of papers and written articles on a large number of topics, especially contemporary Spanish politics. He is the coeditor (with G. Prevost) of *Politics and Change in Spain*.

SCOTT B. MACDONALD received his Ph.D. in Political Science from the University of Connecticut. He has travelled extensively in the Caribbean, Latin America, and Europe, and his articles have appeared in the *Caribbean Review, Latin America and Caribbean Contemporary Record, Financial Times, Times of the Americas*, and *Inter-American Economic Affairs*. He is the author of *Trinidad and Tobago: Democracy and Development in the Caribbean*, to be published by Greenwood Press in 1986.

KAREN O'CONNOR is Associate Professor of Political Science at Emory University in Atlanta, Georgia. She received her Ph.D. and J. D. degrees from the State University of New York at Buffalo. Professor O'Connor has written extensively on a number of topics, including interest groups and the American Supreme Court. She has most recently published articles (coauthored with Lee Epstein) in the *Harvard Journal of Law and Public Policy, Social Science Quarterly, Judicature,* and the *Journal of Politics*. Professor O'Connor is a manuscript reviewer for a large number of social science journals and has been quite active in the American Political Science Association, Southern Political Science Association, Midwest Political Science Association, and Women's Caucus for Political Science. She is the author of *Women's Organizations' Use of Courts, Women's Rights* (coauthored with N. E. McGlen), and *Public Interest Law Firms—An Institutional Analysis* (coauthored with Lee Epstein).

ALBERT J. SCHMIDT is Bernhard Professor of History in the College of Arts and Sciences and School of Law at the University of Bridgeport, Bridgeport, Connecticut. He received his doctoral degree at the University of Pennsylvania and has done postdoctoral work at a number of institutions, including Moscow University, Harvard Business School, and New York University School of Law. Professor Schmidt has written on a wide number of topics in *Huntington Library Quarterly, Lincolnshire Historian, The South Carolina Historical Magazine*, and the *Slavic Review*. He has most recently contributed to the *Encyclopedia of Soviet Law*. Professor Schmidt previously served as both the Dean of the College of Arts and Sciences and the Vice President for Academic Affairs at the University of Bridgeport.

JUSTUS M. VAN DER KROEF is Dana Professor and Chairman of the Department of Political Science at the University of Bridgeport, Bridgeport, Connecticut. He received his doctoral degree from Columbia University. Professor van der Kroef has been a Senior Fellow in the Research Institute on Communist Affairs at Columbia University and a Post-Doctoral Fellow at the University of Queensland, Brisbane, Australia. He has held Rockefeller and Mellon Foundation grants for research in contemporary Southeast Asian problems and has served as Visiting Professor of Asian Studies at universities in Singapore, The Philippines and Sri Lanka. He is a member of the editorial boards of *Asian Affairs* and the *World Affairs Quarterly* and has served as Associate Editor for the journal *Asian Thought*. Among his most recent books are *Communism in Southeast Asia* and *Kampuchea—The Endless Tug of War*.

INDEX

Abogado (Latin America), 200–201
Abogado y notario (Latin America), 197
Administrative Tribunals (France), 110
Advocates. *See* Lawyers
Advocates' Act (India), 131
Advogados provisionados (Latin America), 194
Africa: development of legal system of, 9–11; courts of, 11–15; magistrates, 13–15, 18; legal education in, 15–16; lawyers, 16–19; perceptions of legal profession and system, 17; constitutions, 19–21; judicial independence, 21–28
Agrees (France), 45, 112
Alarician Breviary, 106
Albania, development of legal system of, 73
Ali, Muhammad, 221–22
Allthing (Norway), 275
American Bar Association, 424, 426
Amin, Idi, 25, 26
Appellate courts: Netherlands, 41–42; Belgium, 42–43; Luxembourg, 43; Canada, 55; Australia, 56; New Zealand, 57; Eastern Europe, 74; Federal Republic of Germany, 89–90; France, 111; India, 129–30; Pakistan, 139–40; Bangladesh, 143; Italy, 156–57; Japan, 173–74; Brazil, 193–94; El Salvador,

196–97; Argentina, 200; Venezuela, 203; Mexico, 207; Haiti, 211; Egypt, 227; Israel, 228; People's Republic of China, 260–61; Denmark, 277; Norway, 278; Sweden, 278; Finland, 279; Iceland, 279–80; Socialist Republic of Vietnam, 307; Malaysia, 312; Burma, 313; Vietnam, 307; Malaysia, 312; Burma, 313; Indonesia, 314; Philippines, 315; Soviet Union, 335–36; Spain, 361–62; England and Wales, 386–88; Northern Ireland, 398–99; Scotland, 403–5; United States, 418–20
Appellate Jurisdiction Act of 1876 (England and Wales), 385
Argentina: development of legal system of, 199–200; courts, 200; lawyers, 200–201; legal education in, 200–201; perceptions of legal profession and system, 201; judical independence, 201; judicial review, 201
Aryans, 125–26
Asoka, 126
Assessors, 14, 78, 92, 278, 279, 312
Auditeurs de justice (France), 116
Australia: development of legal system of, 53–54; courts, 56–57; lawyers, 58; legal education in, 58; judges, 58–59; perceptions of legal system and profes-